Apple Pro Training Series

macOS Support Essentials 10.12

Kevin M. White and Gordon Davisson

Apple Pro Training Series: macOS Support Essentials 10.12
Kevin M. White and Gordon Davisson
Copyright © 2017 by Peachpit Press

Peachpit Press
www.peachpit.com
To report errors, please email errata@peachpit.com. Peachpit Press is a division of Pearson Education.

Apple Series Editor: Nancy Davis
Development Editor: Victor Gavenda
Production Coordinators: Maureen Forys & Kate Kaminski, Happenstance Type-O-Rama
Technical Editor, Reference Materials: Steve Leebove
Technical Editor, Exercises: Adam Karneboge
Apple Instructional Designer: Susan Najour
Apple Project Manager: Debbie Otterstetter
Copy Editor: Liz Welch
Proofreader: Scout Festa
Compositor: Cody Gates, Happenstance Type-O-Rama
Indexer: Jack Lewis
Cover Illustration: Paul Mavrides
Cover Production: Cody Gates, Happenstance Type-O-Rama

ISBN 13: 978-0-13-471385-4
ISBN 10: 0-13-471385-0
9 8 7 6 5 4 3 2 1
Printed and bound in the United States of America

I could not have made this journey without the support of my family and loving wife, Michelle.

This book is dedicated to my greatest works: Logan, Sawyer, and Emily.

—Kevin White

Much appreciation to my amazing wife, Berit Benson, and her uncanny ability to sense when I needed coffee the most.

—Gordon Davisson

Acknowledgments In addition to the amazing Peachpit staff members who were instrumental in completing this work, we would like to thank the development team for their hard work: Steve Leebove, Adam Karneboge, and Susan Najour. Additional thanks go out to Craig Cohen, Eugene Evon, Arek Dreyer, Schoun Regan, and MacSysAdmin. Also, the accuracy of this guide has been greatly enhanced by feedback from those who reviewed early versions of the guide during the beta class, including Craig Cohen, Samuel Valencia, Christopher Holmes, Kennedy Soo Hong, Andrew Baker, Jeff Walling, Ben Levy, Steve Leebove, Gordon Davisson, Weldon Dodd, Kyle Slater, and Sarah Garwood.

Contents at a Glance

Network Configuration

Network Services

System Management

Table of Contents

File Systems and Storage

Network Services

System Management

About This Guide

The Apple Pro Training Series *macOS Support Essentials 10.12* guide prepares learners for the macOS Support Essentials 10.12 exam. To prepare for the macOS Support Essentials exam, learners can use the guide alone or they can use the guide in the macOS Support Essentials 10.12 course. Either way, if learners pass the macOS Support Essentials 10.12 exam, they're eligible for the Apple Certified Support Professional (ACSP) 10.12 certification.

Read this section to find out more about this guide published by Peachpit Press and the Apple course, exam, and certification.

Audience

Whether you're an experienced system administrator or you just want to dig deeper into macOS, you'll learn the technical information and processes that ACSP IT professionals use to install, configure, maintain, diagnose, and troubleshoot Mac computers that run macOS Sierra.

You should be comfortable using a Mac before you read this guide or take the course. If you're not sure about basic Mac use, visit Mac Basics at http://www.apple.com /support/macbasics.

This guide and the course are aimed at these types of professionals:

▶   Help desk specialists

▶   Technical coordinators

▶   Service technicians

▶   System administrators

▶   Others who support macOS users

How to Use the Guide

This guide gives you an in-depth tour of macOS. It also teaches you how to best support macOS users and troubleshoot their systems. After completing this guide, you should be able to:

▶ Explain how macOS works

▶ Explain best practices for configuring and using macOS

▶ Explain macOS troubleshooting and repair procedures

▶ Demonstrate macOS diagnostic and repair tools

Lessons and Exercises

For example, in Lessons 19 through 21, you'll learn networking concepts; you'll use network configuration and troubleshooting applications like Network preferences and Network Utility; and you'll explore methods for resolving network issues. Each lesson has a reference section, which teaches essential concepts, followed by an exercise section that develops your skills through step-by-step instruction.

NOTE ▶ "Note" resources, like this one, offer important information or help clarify a subject.

TIP "Tip" resources, like this one, provide helpful hints, tricks, or shortcuts.

MORE INFO ▶ The "More Info" resources, like this one, provide ancillary information. These resources are merely for your edification and are not considered essential for the coursework.

For the most part, the exercises in this guide work in the classroom or at home. If you're learning from home, make sure you have the following:

▶ A Mac that meets the requirements to install macOS Sierra

▶ macOS Sierra (Exercise 1.2, "Upgrade to macOS Sierra," includes instructions for downloading macOS Sierra if you do not already own it)

▶ A high-speed Internet connection

▶ Student Materials demonstration files (see Exercise 2.5, "Download the Student Materials Independently" for instructions)

▶ A new or existing Apple ID (no credit card information needed for free applications)

These optional items aren't required but can be helpful to have:

▶ A new or existing iCloud account.

▶ An erasable external USB, FireWire, or Thunderbolt disk with a capacity of at least 1 GB (8 GB for Exercise 3.2, "Create a macOS Install Disk").

▶ An isolated network or subnet with an exercise-specific configuration. You can use a small network Wi-Fi router with multiple Ethernet ports—for example, the Apple AirPort Extreme (www.apple.com/airport-extreme/). Get the setup instructions from your Account page at www.peachpit.com/register.

▶ A Wi-Fi interface in your Mac and access to at least two Wi-Fi networks (with one being visible).

▶ An additional Mac running macOS Sierra. This Mac can have macOS Server 5.2 installed and set up with an exercise-specific configuration. macOS Server 5.2 costs $19.99. Get the setup instructions from your Account page at www.peachpit.com/register.

▶ The required FireWire, Thunderbolt, or USB-C cable to connect two Mac computers in target disk mode.

▶ A magnifying glass. This could help in Exercise 26.2, "Use Single-User Mode."

You can complete the exercises in any order, except for the following:

▶ Lesson 1, "Install macOS Sierra"—If your Mac isn't running macOS Sierra, you must perform the appropriate exercises.

▶ Lesson 2, "Set Up and Configure macOS"—You must perform the appropriate exercises to set up your Mac for later exercises.

▶ Exercise 5.1, "Create a Standard User Account"—You must perform this exercise for later exercises.

▶ Exercise 6.1, "Restore a Deleted User Account"—You must perform this exercise for later exercises.

Some exercises have dependencies on other exercises. These exercises list the dependencies as prerequisites.

NOTE ▶ The exercises may be disruptive to your system. To complete the exercises, please use a Mac that isn't critical to your daily productivity.

NOTE ▶ Unless otherwise specified, references to Apple operating systems in this guide refer to macOS Sierra 10.12. Because macOS Sierra is updated as necessary, some screens, panes, features, and procedures may be slightly different than they are presented in this guide. You can check for updates to this guide at www.peachpit.com /apts.macossierra.

Additional Learning Materials

Apple Support

This guide includes references to the latest free online Apple Support articles. You can find the articles at the Apple Support website (www.apple.com/support/). Please use these articles and the site for macOS support.

Lesson Files

Lesson files and bonus materials are available online when you register your guide at www.peachpit.com/register. The online "Lesson Review Questions & Answers" appendix checks your knowledge regarding each lesson through a series of questions. You're encouraged to use the guide and the Apple Support website to answer the questions. After you attempt to answer the questions on your own, you can refer to the provided answers to confirm your knowledge. The "Additional Resources" appendix contains a list of relevant Apple Support articles and recommended documents as they relate to topics in each lesson.

Web Edition/Content Update Program

This guide is part of the Peachpit Content Update Program. As Apple updates macOS Sierra, this guide may also be updated. Updates are delivered to you via a free Web Edition, which contains the complete guide, including updates. When you purchase this guide from Peachpit (in any format), you automatically get access to its Web Edition.

Accessing the Lesson Files and Web Edition

If you purchased an eBook from peachpit.com, your Web Edition will automatically appear under the Digital Purchases tab on your Account page. Click the Launch link to access the product. Continue reading to learn how to register your product to get access to the lesson files.

If you purchased an eBook from a different vendor or you bought a print book, you must register your purchase on peachpit.com in order to access the online content:

1. Go to www.peachpit.com/register.

2. Sign in or create a new account.

3. Enter ISBN: 9780134713854.

4. Answer the questions as proof of purchase.

   The Web Edition will appear under the Digital Purchases tab on your Account page.

5. Click the Launch link to access the Web Edition.

6. The Lesson files can be accessed through the Registered Products tab on your Account page. Click the Access Bonus Content link below the title of your product to proceed to the download page. Click the lesson file links to download them to your computer.

   MORE INFO ▸ Access to the Web Edition doesn't automatically provide access to your lesson files, or vice versa. Follow the instructions above to claim the full benefits of your guide purchase.

Apple Training and Certification

Course

Students use this guide in the macOS Support Essentials 10.12 course, a three-day, hands-on course that provides in-depth training on macOS Sierra. Apple Certified Trainers teach each course and give presentations and demonstrations. Students practice macOS support with hands-on student exercises. The course prepares you for the macOS Support Essentials 10.12 exam. If you pass the exam, you become eligible for the ACSP 10.12 certification. To find out more about Apple courses, exams, and certifications, visit http://training.apple.com.

Exam

Certification exams are offered through LearnQuest and Apple Authorized Training Providers worldwide.

To prepare for the macOS Support Essentials 10.12 exam, do the following:

► Read the reference sections of this guide.

► Complete the exercises in this guide.

► Complete the macOS Support Essentials 10.12 course.

► Gain experience on a Mac running macOS Sierra.

► Study the macOS Support Essentials 10.12 Exam Prep Guide.

To learn more about Apple certifications and to find the macOS Support Essentials 10.12 Exam Prep Guide, visit http://training.apple.com.

> **NOTE ►** Although the questions in the macOS Support Essentials 10.12 Exam are based on this guide, nothing can substitute for time spent learning the technology. After you read this guide, or take the course, or both, spend some time working with macOS on your own to become more familiar with it and to ensure your success on the certification exam.

Certification

Apple's macOS certifications are for IT professionals who:

► Want to know how to add a Mac to a Windows or other standards-based network

► Support macOS users

► Manage networks of Mac computers running macOS—for example, a teacher or a technology specialist who manages classroom networks or computer labs

► Manage complex, multi-platform networks that include Mac computers running macOS

An ACSP 10.12 certification verifies your understanding of macOS core functionality and your ability to configure key services, perform basic troubleshooting, and support multiple users with essential macOS capabilities. Passing the macOS Support Essentials 10.12 exam makes you eligible for an ACSP 10.12 certification. To learn more about Apple certifications and to find the macOS Support Essentials 10.12 Exam Prep Guide, visit http://training.apple.com.

Installation and
Configuration

Install macOS Sierra

Every new Mac comes with the latest Mac operating system. Mac operating systems are usually updated more often than Mac computers. So, Mac computers will eventually need a Mac operating system upgrade that provides the latest features and updates. Because macOS Sierra is free, anyone with a qualifying Mac can upgrade at no cost.

NOTE ▶ Some exercises in this lesson involve significant changes to your Mac setup. Some of the steps are difficult or impossible to reverse. If you perform the exercises in this lesson, you should do so on a spare Mac or an external disk that doesn't contain critical data.

GOALS

▶ Describe new macOS features

▶ Prepare a Mac for a macOS Sierra upgrade

▶ Prepare a Mac for a new installation of macOS Sierra

▶ Troubleshoot an upgrade or installation

Reference 1.1
About macOS Sierra

macOS Sierra is the latest version of the Apple operating system. Since its introduction in 2001, macOS (formerly known as Mac OS or OS X) has become an increasingly attractive alternative to other operating systems because of its innovative technologies. macOS is the only operating system that combines a powerful open source UNIX foundation with a state-of-the-art user interface. It offers all the ease of use for which Apple is known. Furthermore, Apple provides an exceptional software development platform, as evidenced by the large selection of high-quality third-party software available for macOS.

History of macOS

macOS Sierra 10.12 is the 13th major release of the Mac operating system since its initial non-beta release in 2001. Each release of the Mac operating system has a version number (10.12) and associated name (Sierra).

In this guide older Mac operating system versions are called out with the version name and number. The following table shows the most recent versions of the Mac operating system. These versions are compatible with macOS Sierra.

NOTE ▶ The following table shows only versions of macOS that are supported on Mac computers also capable of running macOS Sierra.

Name and version	Release date	Latest version	Latest date
Mac OS X Snow Leopard 10.6	August 28, 2009	10.6.8 v1.1	July 25, 2011
OS X Lion 10.7	July 20, 2011	10.7.5	October 4, 2012
OS X Mountain Lion 10.8	July 25, 2012	10.8.5	October 3, 2013
OS X Mavericks 10.9	October 22, 2013	10.9.5	September 17, 2014
OS X Yosemite 10.10	October 16, 2014	10.10.5	August 13, 2015
OS X El Capitan 10.11	September 30, 2015	10.11.6	July 18, 2016
macOS Sierra 10.12	September 20, 2016	10.12.1	October 27, 2016

MORE INFO ► You can find a full list of Mac system versions and their numbers in Apple Support article HT201260, "Find the macOS version number on your Mac."

What's New in macOS Sierra

In addition to the features found in previous versions of OS X, macOS Sierra includes hundreds of small improvements and a few significant new features. Many of the new macOS features are borrowed from other Apple operating systems (iOS, tvOS, and watchOS) or improve the user experience between macOS, iOS, tvOS, and watchOS.

Possibly the biggest change in macOS Sierra is the addition of Siri. Advanced search, voice control, and even speech dictation are not new to macOS; however, Siri enables voice queries and responds with results from resources within the Mac and from Internet services.

Another significant change to macOS Sierra is systemwide support for tabbed windows. Tabs enable you to switch between multiple panes of content within a single window, as opposed to the traditional OS X method of having multiple separate application windows. All applications, even third-party applications that aren't updated for macOS Sierra, can take advantage of tabbed windows.

iCloud Drive can now sync the entire contents of a user's Desktop and Documents folders. As more items are safely stored in iCloud, it's no longer necessary to permanently store those items on the Mac computer's local drive. To this end, macOS Sierra also includes Optimized Storage, a suite of storage management techniques that automatically free up space on the local drive.

Several new macOS Sierra features improve integration between Apple devices. You can now:

► Unlock a Mac with an Apple watch

► Use Apple Pay on a Mac

► Copy and paste between Apple devices with Universal Clipboard

Finally, several built-in macOS Sierra applications were updated to provide feature parity with their iOS 10 counterparts. This includes improvements to many applications, such as iTunes, Maps, Messages, Notes, and Photos.

MORE INFO ► A full list of the new macOS Sierra features can be found at www.apple.com/macos/sierra/.

Integration Through Standards

Much of the success of macOS can be attributed to Apple embracing industry-standard formats and open source software. Adoption of common standards saves engineering time and allows for much smoother integration with other platforms. When Apple developers must engineer a technology for a new feature, Apple often releases the specs to the developer community, fostering a new standard. An example of this is Bonjour network discovery, which Apple pioneered and has maintained as an industry-standard protocol commonly known as Multicast DNS (mDNS) for others to develop and use.

Here are some examples of common standards supported by macOS:

▶ Connectivity standards—Universal Serial Bus (USB), IEEE 1394 (FireWire), Thunderbolt, Bluetooth wireless, and the IEEE 802 family of Ethernet and Wi-Fi standards

▶ File-system standards—File Allocation Table (FAT), New Technology File System (NTFS), ISO 9660 optical disc standard, Universal Disk Format (UDF), and the Xsan file system based on the StorNext file system

▶ Network standards—Dynamic Host Configuration Protocol (DHCP), Domain Name System (DNS), Hypertext Transfer Protocol (HTTP), Internet Message Access Protocol (IMAP), Simple Mail Transfer Protocol (SMTP), File Transfer Protocol (FTP), Web Distributed Access and Versioning (WebDAV), and Server Message Block/Common Internet File System (SMB/CIFS) including SMB3

▶ Application and development standards—Single UNIX Specification v3 (SUSv3), Portable Operating System Interface (POSIX), C and C++, Objective C, Ruby, Python, Perl, and Swift

▶ Document standards—ZIP file archives, Rich Text Format (RTF), Portable Document Format (PDF), Tagged Image File Format (TIFF), Joint Photographic Expert Group (JPEG), Portable Network Graphics (PNG), Advanced Audio Coding (AAC), and the Moving Picture Experts Group (MPEG) family of media standards

Reference 1.2
Select an Installation Method

How much of this lesson you'll want to complete depends on the state of your Mac. You can read through the entire lesson, but you probably won't want to attempt all the techniques described here on your working Mac.

TIP ▶ If you don't know what version of macOS your Mac is running, simply choose About This Mac from the Apple menu.

Odds are, your Mac falls into one of the following general categories.

Running macOS Sierra with No Significant Problems

If this is the case, upgrading isn't necessary, and you probably don't want to reinstall the operating system. You may still wish to read through this lesson, but don't perform any of the exercises.

Running macOS Sierra but Has Significant Problems

If this is the case, back up important data, erase the system disk, and perform a "clean" installation. You should have access to Time Machine and macOS Recovery. However, keep in mind that restoring a full system backup may also restore the problematic items, so you may need to manually restore individual items to result in a stable system.

You will be best served by first familiarizing yourself with Lesson 15, "Manage Time Machine," and Lesson 3, "Use macOS Recovery," and then returning to this lesson to learn about reinstallation options. When you're ready for reinstallation, read Reference 1.4, "Prepare the System Disk," and Reference 1.5, "Upgrade and Install macOS." Then perform the steps outlined in Exercise 1.3, "Erase a Mac System and Install macOS Sierra."

Not Running macOS Sierra, but Running OS X Lion 10.7 or Later with No Significant Problems

If this is the case, you can perform a standard upgrade-in-place installation of macOS Sierra.

To perform a standard upgrade installation, read Reference 1.3, "Prepare to Upgrade a Previous System," and Reference 1.5, "Upgrade and Install macOS." Then perform the steps outlined in Exercise 1.1, "Prepare a Mac for Upgrade," and Exercise 1.2, "Upgrade to macOS Sierra."

Not Running macOS Sierra, but Running OS X Lion 10.7 or Later with Significant Problems

If this is the case, back up important data, and then create an external macOS Recovery disk. After starting up the Mac from the macOS Recovery system, you can erase the built-in system disk and perform a "clean" installation. You have access to Time Machine but not the Sierra version of macOS Recovery, so you will be best served by first familiarizing yourself with Lesson 15, "Manage Time Machine." You also need to create an external macOS Recovery disk, as covered in Exercise 3.2, "Create a macOS Install Disk." Once you have access to the Sierra version of macOS Recovery, you can return to this lesson to learn about reinstallation options.

When you're ready to reinstall, read Reference 1.4, "Prepare the System Disk," and Reference 1.5, "Upgrade and Install macOS." Then perform the steps outlined in Exercise 1.3, "Erase a Mac System and Install macOS Sierra."

Running Mac OS X Snow Leopard 10.6

Apple doesn't support upgrading to macOS Sierra from any version prior to OS X Lion 10.7.5. However, if you have a Mac with Mac OS X Snow Leopard 10.6, you can eventually get to macOS Sierra by updating to 10.6.8, then upgrading to OS X El Capitan 10.11, and finally upgrading to macOS Sierra.

First you must perform the necessary system software updates to get the Mac to version 10.6.8. You can either use the built-in Software Update application, or manually download and install the update combo from the Apple Support website: https://support.apple.com/kb/dl1399?locale=en_US.

Once the Mac is updated to 10.6.8, you can then use the Mac App Store to download OS X El Capitan 10.11. You are not able to search for older versions of macOS on the Mac App Store, but you can access it via the process outlined in Apple Support article HT206886, "Upgrade to OS X El Capitan."

Reference 1.3
Prepare to Upgrade a Previous System

Every Mac ships with macOS installed, so the majority of macOS Sierra installations are upgrades. In addition to the existing Mac operating system that the installer will upgrade, the system disk will probably contain important user data.

A macOS upgrade retains nonsystem data, like user accounts and added applications. With every new release, millions of Mac operating systems are successfully upgraded without issues.

However, upgrading an operating system is a complicated process and not entirely risk free. Apple engineers work hard to ensure that the macOS upgrade process is reliable, but other variables could still lead to issues. For instance, hardware failure could prevent a successful operating system upgrade. For these reasons, you should take preparatory steps to prevent installer issues and data loss.

Verify Installation Requirements

Verify that the Mac and Mac operating system that you have meet the requirements for an upgrade to macOS Sierra. If you're not sure of the specifications, use System Profiler or System Information to find out.

System Profiler (for OS X Snow Leopard 10.6) and System Information (for OS X Lion 10.7 and later) are in the /Applications/Utilities folder. In either application, you can verify the Mac computer's specifications by selecting and viewing the various content areas in the Hardware section.

Before installing macOS Sierra, note the Mac computer's memory capacity and serial number. Also, check the SATA/SATA Express or Storage sections for the amount of free space on the system disk, which is often named Macintosh HD.

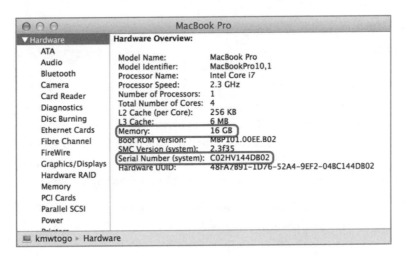

Upgrading to macOS Sierra has the following general requirements:

- ▶ OS X Lion 10.7.5 or later
- ▶ 2 GB of memory
- ▶ 8.8 GB of available storage
- ▶ Apple ID (for some features)
- ▶ Compatible Internet service provider (for some features)

Beyond this, you need to find out whether your Mac is supported. Once you have the Mac computer's serial number, you can check it against the Apple Support Tech Specs website (http://support.apple.com/specs/). Navigate to this website, enter the Mac serial number in the Search Tech Specs field, and click the Search button.

The search should return the model name for the Mac. Note that the preceding screenshot shows a Mac identified as a MacBookPro10,1. Although MacBookPro10,1 is a specific identifier, it's not the name that Apple uses for technical specifications. Entering this Mac computer's serial number in the Apple Support Tech Specs website returns the official model name used for technical specifications: "MacBook Pro (Retina, 15-inch, Mid 2012)."

macOS Sierra supports the following Mac models:

- ▶ MacBook (late 2009 or newer)
- ▶ MacBook Pro (mid 2010 or newer)
- ▶ MacBook Air (late 2010 or newer)
- ▶ Mac mini (mid 2010 or newer)
- ▶ iMac (late 2009 or newer)
- ▶ Mac Pro (mid 2010 or newer)

macOS Sierra Feature Requirements

Some macOS Sierra features have requirements beyond the minimum system requirements. Many of these features depend on other devices or services. For example, to take advantage of Handoff features, like the ability of your Mac to handle the cell phone calls or SMS text messaging of an iPhone, you would need an iPhone that supports Handoff. Another example is that broadband Internet access is required for Siri or Spotlight.

A Mac may need specific hardware to support new features. For example, Continuity (Handoff, Instant Hotspot, and Universal Clipboard) requires Mac computers with low-energy

Bluetooth 4.0. Another new feature, Auto Unlock, needs time-of-flight calculations that are only possible on Mac computers with the latest 802.11ac Wi-Fi.

Learn more about macOS Sierra feature-specific requirements at www.apple.com/macos/how-to-upgrade/.

Newer Mac Requirements

Mac computers ship with a release of the Mac operating system engineered specifically for them. Additional bundled software may also be included for certain Mac computers. This guide assumes that you are using a standard version of macOS Sierra. You may find that some details vary if you are using a future Mac-specific installation of macOS Sierra that was not available at the time of this writing.

Another future consideration is that macOS versions don't support Mac computers that are newer than them. In other words, you could come across a Mac that's newer than the macOS Sierra installer you're trying to use. In this case, the installation may fail to start up the Mac or refuse to install at all. If this happens, use macOS Recovery.

> **MORE INFO** ▶ See Apple Support article HT204319, "OS X versions and builds included with Mac computers," and article HT201686, "Use the version of OS X that came with your Mac, or a compatible newer version."

Prepare for an Upgrade Installation

Although you could start a macOS upgrade without completing some preliminary steps, you reduce your chances of upgrade problems or data loss by first taking four crucial steps:

1. Verify application compatibility.
2. Back up important files and folders.
3. Document critical settings.
4. Check for Apple software and firmware updates.

> **NOTE** ▶ This may seem like a no-brainer, but you don't want to lose power during an upgrade. Plug the Mac into AC power during the upgrade to ensure that the upgrade is successful.

Verify Application Compatibility

When you upgrade to macOS Sierra, your third-party applications may need updates to function properly. You can use System Profiler or System Information to view installed applications.

If you're using System Profiler, verify that View > Full Profile is selected to reveal the Applications section in the Contents list. Selecting Applications from the Contents list prompts the Mac operating system to scan common locations on the local disk for available applications.

You don't have to worry about the applications installed as part of the Mac operating system; those are replaced when you install macOS Sierra. However, you may have to do your own research by visiting vendors' websites to determine whether third-party applications require updates.

macOS also includes a list of known incompatible software. If the macOS Installer application detects incompatible software during an upgrade, it usually moves that software to an Incompatible Software folder. In some cases, the incompatible software isn't moved, but macOS prevents you from opening it and displays a warning dialog stating that the software is incompatible. Find out more about this feature in Apple Support article HT201861, "About incompatible software on your Mac."

Back Up Important Files and Folders

It's always crucial to keep backups of your important files and folders. Having a current backup is even more critical when you make significant changes to a Mac, such as installing a new Mac operating system. If a new installation or upgrade is done improperly, it could result in complete data loss.

If the Mac is already running OS X Leopard 10.5 or later, you can use Time Machine to create a backup before you start your installation. Using Time Machine is covered in **Lesson 15, "Manage Time Machine."**

Document Critical Settings

The macOS installer helps ensure that you don't lose previous settings when you upgrade to macOS Sierra. But some settings are so vital to your Mac that you should document them in case something goes wrong.

Specifically, you should document your network settings before you upgrade. Open System Preferences and click the Network icon to see your current network settings. Avoid missing settings by navigating through all the available network interface and configurations.

> **TIP** You can quickly document your settings by using the screen capture keyboard shortcut Command-Shift-3 to capture each network configuration.

Check for Apple Software Updates

As mentioned previously, to upgrade to macOS Sierra you must have OS X Lion 10.7.5 or later. Apple applications may also have been updated since you installed them. For example, Pages, Numbers, and Keynote undergo updates between Mac operating system version releases. Ensure that your Mac has the latest Apple applications and firmware.

Assuming the Mac is connected to the Internet, choose Software Update or App Store from the Apple menu. Then install all available updates that are not the macOS Sierra installer. If no other updates are found, your Mac is running the latest software, which ensures a smooth upgrade.

More recent versions of macOS use the Mac App Store for accessing software updates. In this case, selecting Software Update will automatically open the Mac App Store, and macOS Sierra will be listed as the first upgrade item. You can certainly start the upgrade process from here, but be sure you have completed all the suggested upgrade preparation steps before selecting the option to perform the free upgrade. Details on the upgrade process are covered later in this lesson.

Check for Apple Firmware Updates

Some Mac computers may require a firmware update to properly access all the macOS Sierra features. Firmware is low-level software that facilitates the startup and management of system hardware. Apple may release firmware updates for some Mac models so that they operate properly with new Apple software, although these updates occur less frequently than normal software updates. Often these updates are caught by the software update mechanism or are installed automatically via the macOS installation process. However, in some cases a Mac may require manual firmware updates. It's always best to check for firmware updates before installing a later version of macOS.

The default view for System Profiler or System Information (again, found in the /Applications/Utilities folder) shows the versions of the two types of firmware on Intel-based Mac computers. The first, listed as Boot ROM Version, is for the Extensible Firmware Interface (EFI), which is responsible for general hardware management and system startup.

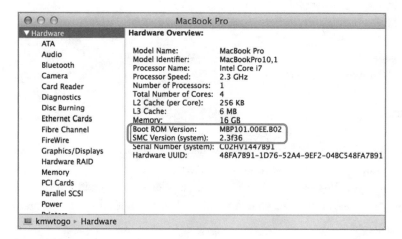

The second, listed as SMC Version, is the System Management Controller (SMC) firmware, which is responsible for managing hardware power and cooling. Once you have located your Mac computer's firmware versions, you can determine whether you have the latest updates by accessing Apple Support article HT201518, "About EFI and SMC firmware updates for Intel-based Mac computers." In this article, Mac models are listed by their model identifier, which can also be located in the same System Information view as the firmware version.

> **NOTE** ▶ The macOS installation process may automatically upgrade the firmware on many late-model Mac computers with a version later than what is listed on the Apple Support website. In other words, you only need to be concerned if your Mac computer's firmware version is older than what's listed on the Apple Support website.

If you determine that your Mac requires a firmware update (if it was not updated by the automatic software updates), you need to find the correct update at the Apple Support Download website, http://support.apple.com/downloads. Like other system software updates, a firmware update requires administrative user authorization and a restart.

However, some older Mac computers have an extra requirement for firmware updates: after the initial installation process, you must shut down and then restart the Mac by holding down the power button until you hear a long tone. This initiates the remainder of the firmware update process. Be sure to carefully read any instructions that come with a firmware updater! Failing to properly update a Mac computer's firmware could lead to hardware failure.

NOTE ▶ If you experience an unsuccessful update on an older Mac, you can restore your Mac computer's firmware with a Firmware Restoration CD. You can find out more about acquiring and using this CD from Apple Support article HT201692, "About the Firmware Restoration CD (Intel-based Macs)."

Keep Up to Date

For the most recent information on the installation and upgrades, your best source is the Apple Support website. A good place to start is the macOS Sierra support page at https://support.apple.com/macos. Anytime you intend to install macOS, visit these resources to catch any recently discovered issues. The Apple Support articles are sprinkled throughout this guide for a reason. They are the best source for official, up-to-date support information.

Reference 1.4
Prepare the System Disk

Whether you need to perform an erase and install for a "clean install" or you are planning on changing the disk structure by repartitioning the existing disk or adding a new disk, you have to prepare the disk before installing macOS. Specifically, macOS installs only on disks that are partitioned via the GUID Partition Map (GPT) scheme and contain at least one Mac OS Extended (Journaled) formatted volume.

NOTE ▶ Any disk containing OS X Lion 10.7 or later is already properly formatted for macOS Sierra. In other words, if you only need to upgrade OS X Lion or later, you don't need to make any system disk changes, and you can simply follow the steps in Exercise 1.2, "Upgrade to macOS Sierra."

New macOS Installation

A new macOS installation (also called a clean install) overwrites all content on the disk. Erasing the disk before a macOS installation may be necessary. Doing this erases any existing data, but sometimes this is required. For example, if you are upgrading the Mac computer's internal disk to a bigger or faster disk, it must be properly formatted for macOS. Or if a Mac operating system has serious issues, erasing it and installing a "clean" copy of macOS may resolve the issues.

Reasons for repartitioning your system disk are a bit more complex, so they are covered in the next section. Nevertheless, the process of repartitioning may require erasing data on the disk, which is thus often done prior to installing macOS. Use Disk Utility for erasing and repartitioning the disk. Disk Utility can be found on any Mac in the /Applications/Utilities folder or (as covered in Lesson 3, "Use macOS Recovery") from macOS Recovery. If you're going to make changes to the system disk before you install macOS, be sure to start up from a system on another, physically different disk.

> **MORE INFO** ▶ This lesson does not include details about erasing or repartitioning disks; these procedures are covered extensively in **Lesson 9, "Manage File Systems and Storage."** Specific steps can be found in Apple Support article HT202796, "How to install OS X on an external drive connected to your Mac."

About Partitioning Options

Before selecting a destination disk, you may want to consider the various disk partition methodologies that are available as installable macOS destinations. Most Mac computers have a single disk, formatted with a single large system volume that defines nearly the entire space on that disk. This is the macOS default partition setup. However, by repartitioning the disk, you can choose to break up that single large volume into separate smaller volumes. This allows you to treat a single physical storage device as multiple separate storage destinations.

Just as installing a new Mac operating system has long-lasting ramifications for how you use your Mac, so does your choice of partitioning. Thus, before you install a new Mac operating system, you should consider your partition philosophy. The following lists present the pros and cons of various partition options. Again, many of these concepts are further discussed in **Lesson 9, "Manage File Systems and Storage."**

Single Partition

▶ Pros—Most macOS systems are formatted with a single large system volume by default, so no disk partitioning changes are necessary. Also, a single system volume is often the most efficient use of space on your disk—having separate partitions can potentially lead to wasted space if not sized correctly.

▶ Cons—Having only a single system volume limits administrative flexibility. For example, some testing and recovery tasks require the use of another storage volume. With only a single local volume, you will have to use an additional physical storage device to accommodate those needs.

Multiple Partitions

▶   Pros—Multiple partitions allow you to have multiple operating systems and multiple storage volumes on a single device. Having multiple operating systems allows you to run different versions of macOS or even other third-party operating systems and software from one disk. Or you can create utility systems that can be used to repair the primary system or test new software. Also, with multiple storage volumes, replacing a damaged operating system can be much easier if all of the user's data resides on another nonsystem volume.

▶   Cons—Most disks need to be repartitioned to accommodate multiple volumes. Although macOS Sierra supports dynamic partitioning without losing data, it can do so only when working within the free space of a disk. Therefore, certain partition configurations may require you to completely erase the disk. Any future partition changes may require you to sacrifice data on the disk as well. Additionally, several technologies in macOS become more complicated to manage when using multiple volumes on a single disk. Finally, multiple volumes can be very space-inefficient if you don't plan carefully—you may end up with some volumes that are underused or others that run out of space too soon.

NOTE ▶ A multiple-partition system can cause the following complications: Boot Camp Assistant cannot add more partitions to a multiple-partition disk; enabling FileVault encrypts only the system volume, leaving other volumes unencrypted; and additional partitions on Fusion Drive volumes cannot take advantage of fast flash storage.

Reference 1.5
Upgrade and Install macOS

Apple is known for designing every operation to be as easy as possible, and the macOS installation process is an example of this ease. However, anyone tasked with supporting macOS computers should be fully familiar with all the procedures needed to ensure a smooth installation.

Acquire the macOS Installer

macOS Sierra is a free upgrade that is available for download only from the Mac App Store. However, once you have downloaded the macOS installer, you can also create your own external macOS Install disk by following the instructions in Exercise 3.2, "Create a macOS Install Disk."

If you are acquiring macOS Sierra for the first time, the process is as simple as purchasing a free application from the Mac App Store. Also, as covered previously, more recent versions of macOS will automatically prompt you to upgrade to macOS Sierra when performing a routine software update.

Using the Mac App Store to download the macOS Sierra installer does have a few prerequisites, though:

▶   You must be running Lion 10.7 or later.

▶   You must be connected to the Internet, ideally at broadband speeds. The macOS Sierra installer is just under 5 GB, so it can take a while to download even on "fast" connections.

▶   To download an item from the Mac App Store, you must sign in with an Apple ID. This is because even items that are free in the Mac App Store, like the macOS Sierra installer, must be purchased using an Apple ID with verified billing information. If you have previously purchased items from an online Apple store, like iTunes or the Mac App Store, your billing information is likely already configured. However, if you have yet to purchase items from an Apple online store, you can set up your billing information within the Mac App Store.

MORE INFO ▶ Details on the Mac App Store are covered in **Lesson 16, "Install Applications."**

Assuming you meet these criteria, simply open the Mac App Store from the Apple menu. macOS Sierra will likely appear as one of the featured items on the store, so it should be easy to find. The Sierra installer may also appear in the software updates list, which appears when you click the Updates button in the Mac App Store toolbar. Again, assuming the default automatic software update settings of OS X El Capitan, the system may have already downloaded the installer for you.

If the macOS Sierra installer hasn't already been downloaded to your Mac, just click the Free Upgrade or Download button. The installer automatically opens once the download is complete, but you can also find it in the Applications folder if necessary.

NOTE ▶ If you already have macOS Sierra installed on your Mac, the Mac App Store will note that it's already installed or downloaded. In this case, the macOS Sierra installer may still be in the Applications folder. If not, you also have access to the installer via the steps covered in Lesson 3, "Use macOS Recovery."

Install macOS Sierra

The installation process involves a few simple choices up front, followed by the actual installation. This means you need to spend only a few moments choosing the installation destination, and then you can leave the Mac unattended while the installation completes. During the normal installation, the Mac will restart on its own at least once, and possibly multiple times.

TIP ▶ If a power loss or disk disconnection occurs, simply restart the installation.

Upgrade versus Install

The installer automatically chooses the appropriate installation type for your selected destination: upgrade or new. Upgrade installations upgrade the existing Mac operating system and upgrade it to a later version. New installations place a new copy of macOS on a disk without an existing Mac operating system.

In either case, the installer never deletes nonsystem data on the selected destination. Specifically, the macOS installer is designed to ensure that third-party applications and user data remain functional after an installation. As far as installation destinations go, the macOS installer can upgrade your current Mac operating system, or you can install it to another disk attached to your Mac.

NOTE ▶ You cannot upgrade macOS if any other users are currently logged in to the Mac via fast user switching. You need to either have those users log out of their sessions or restart the computer to forcibly end the other user sessions.

Perform a Clean or New Installation

As covered previously, if you want to perform an erase and install, also known as a clean install, you must manually erase the destination system disk using Disk Utility before running the macOS installer. If the destination is another system disk, like an external disk, you can erase and install from your currently running Mac. However, if you want to erase the system disk your Mac is currently running from, you need to start up from another system, as covered in Lesson 3, "Use macOS Recovery."

Select the Installation Destination

During installation of macOS Sierra, the only choice you need to make is the installation destination—you are simply selecting the disk volume where macOS will be installed. This can be an internal or external disk, as long as it's properly formatted. The default selection is the current startup disk; you have to click the Show All Disks button to choose an alternate destination.

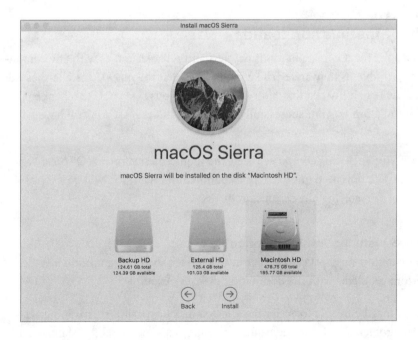

You may notice that the installer does not let you select certain disks or partitions. This is because the installer has determined that your Mac cannot start from that location. Possible reasons include the following:

▶ The disk does not use the proper partition scheme for your Mac. Intel Mac computers use the GPT scheme. You can resolve this issue by repartitioning the disk using Disk Utility.

▶ The specific partition is not formatted properly. macOS requires a partition formatted as a Mac OS Extended (Journaled) volume. You can resolve this issue by erasing the partition using Disk Utility.

▶ The macOS installer does not support installing to a disk containing Time Machine backups. For more information, see Apple Support article HT203322, "If you can't install OS X on a Time Machine backup disk."

Again, the system automatically determines whether the selected destination already has a version of macOS installed. If there is an existing system, the installer upgrades the system to the new version.

Reference 1.6
Troubleshoot Installation Issues

For most systems the macOS installation is painless and reliable. Yet, as with any complicated technology, problems may arise. The good news is that the macOS installer has the ability to "back out" of an installation and restore the previous system. If this happens, obviously the installation was not successfully completed, but at least you still have a functioning Mac.

Thoroughly verifying that your computer meets the requirements for macOS Sierra and completing the installation preparation steps as outlined in this lesson will go a long way toward preventing or resolving any serious problems.

General macOS Installer Troubleshooting

Beyond the preparation steps covered earlier in this lesson, the most common installation failures arise from problems with the destination disk. For example:

▶ The installer may be unable to verify the selected disk or partition. This indicates serious disk problems. Refer to the troubleshooting steps in Lesson 9, "Manage File Systems and Storage," to resolve this issue.

▶ An error message may appear saying that some features of macOS are not supported on the selected disk. This happens if your system disk is a software RAID (Redundant Array of Independent Disks) set or uses nonstandard Boot Camp partitioning. In this case, the installer cannot create a macOS Recovery HD, but you can still install macOS Sierra.

▶ In some cases, even when a disk is partitioned and formatted properly, the installer does not let you select that disk. This error most often occurs when there is also a Boot Camp partition on the disk. The resolution in this case involves slightly decreasing the size of the Mac partition to make room for the macOS Recovery HD.

MORE INFO ▶ See Apple Support article HT203482, "Installer reports 'OS X could not be installed on your computer' or 'This disk cannot be used to start up your computer.'"

About the Installer Log

The granddaddy of all troubleshooting resources for macOS is the log file. Nearly every process writes entries in a log file, and the installer is no exception. The Installer log contains progress and error entries for nearly every step of the installation process, including steps not shown by the standard interface.

During the initial phases of the installation process, you can access the Installer log by simply choosing Installer Log from the Window menu. Information in the Installer log helps you to more precisely pinpoint problems or verify installation.

TIP ▶ You can also use this technique to check on the progress of any general software installation via the Installer application.

After the preliminary installation process, the installer will enter the main installation stage and the screen will be completely locked out from user input. During this time you can only watch the installation progress bar. If the installation is failing at this point, again the system will restart to the previous OS.

After the Mac resumes normal operation, you can access the full Installer log from the /Applications/Utilities/Console application. Once Console is open, select the /var/log folder in the far left column, and then select install.log in the second column. In the Spotlight search filter field, enter the text osinstaller to show only entries created by the system installer.

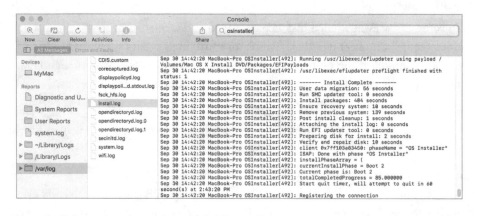

You may find that, even during a successful installation, the OSInstaller process reports many warnings and errors. Many of these reported issues are benign, and you should only concern yourself with them if you are trying to isolate a showstopping problem. When the installation is successfully completed, the summary entries in the Installer log look similar to those in the preceding screenshot.

TIP ▶ There is obviously a wealth of information available via the logs accessed in the Console application. Other lessons in this guide will suggest inspecting specific logs when appropriate.

Exercise 1.1
Prepare a Mac for Upgrade

▶ **Prerequisites**

- ▶ This exercise is necessary only if you are upgrading your computer from an earlier version of OS X to macOS Sierra.

- ▶ Your computer must be running OS X Lion 10.7 or later to perform this exercise. Computers running Mac OS X Snow Leopard 10.6 must upgrade to OS X El Capitan 10.11 before upgrading to macOS Sierra.

In this exercise, you will verify that your computer's hardware and firmware support macOS Sierra, as well as check for old software and record important settings.

Use System Information to Check Hardware, Firmware, and Application Compatibility

1 If necessary, log in to your existing administrator account on your computer.

2 In the Finder, navigate to the /Applications/Utilities folder (you can use the Finder keyboard shortcut Command-Shift-U).

3 Open System Information.

System Information

> **NOTE ▸** If the application is named System Profiler instead of System Information, your computer is running Mac OS X Snow Leopard 10.6 or earlier, and cannot be upgraded directly to macOS Sierra. See Reference 1.2, "Select an Installation Method," for more information. If you want to, you can continue through the rest of this exercise to find out if your Mac meets the minimum hardware requirements to run Sierra.

4 If necessary, select the Hardware category in the sidebar.

5 Verify that the Memory entry is at least 2 GB. If it is less than that, you cannot use Sierra on this computer.

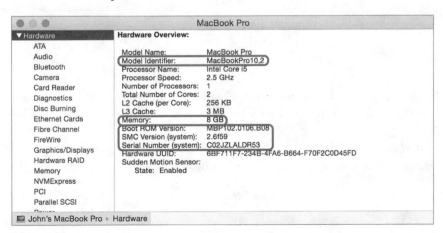

6 Make notes of the Model Identifier, Boot ROM Version, SMC Version, and Serial Number entries:

Model Identifier: _____

Boot ROM Version: _____

SMC Version: _____

Serial Number: _____

7 Select the Storage category in the Hardware section of the sidebar. If there is no Storage entry, select the entry for the bus your computer's startup disk is attached to (for most models, this is the Serial-ATA or SATA/SATA Express bus).

8 If necessary, select your startup disk in the listing at the top right.

9 Find your startup volume in the listing at the right, and verify that it has at least 8.8 GB of available space. Ideally, there should be a lot more than 8.8 GB available, but 8.8 GB is the minimum requirement for installing Sierra.

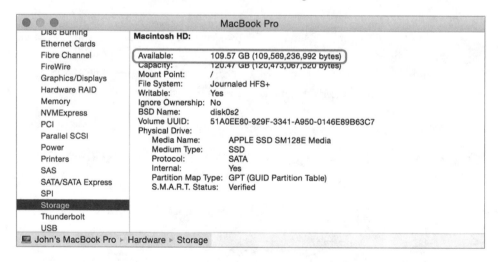

10 In the sidebar, under Software, select Applications, and wait for it to gather information on the applications installed on your computer.

11 Click the heading for the Last Modified column on the right. If the column's triangle is pointing down, click again so that it points up.

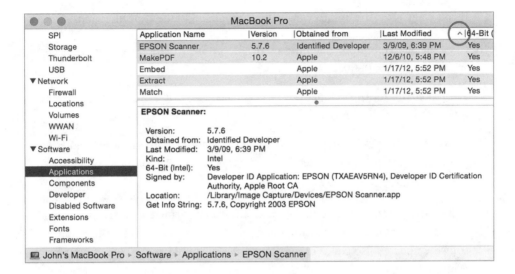

Your applications are listed with the oldest ones at the top. In general, your oldest applications are the most likely to be incompatible with newer versions of macOS. You may want to research the older applications to see whether they are compatible with Sierra or whether updates are available for them. Often, the developer's website has information about compatibility and updates.

12 If there is a Kind column, click the heading for that column, and scroll through the list to see whether you have any PowerPC or Classic applications. These kinds of applications are not supported by Sierra. Some applications may have a blank in this column; this does not indicate a problem.

13 Quit System Information.

14 Open Safari, and navigate to the Apple Tech Specs website (http://support.apple.com/specs/).

15 Click the Browse by Product button.

16 Enter your computer's serial number (recorded in step 6) in the Search Tech Specs field, and press Return.

A link to your computer's technical specs, listed by its model name, appears. Verify that the model name is on the list of supported models in Reference 1.2, "Select an Installation Method."

17 If you want, click the link to view your computer's detailed specifications.

18 Click the Search button (magnifying-glass icon) near the top right of the page, enter HT1237, and press Return.

This takes you to Apple Support article HT1237, "About EFI and SMC firmware updates for Intel-based Macs."

19 Find your model in the list. Note that you can find it by either model name (which you found in step 16) or model identifier (which you also found in step 6).

20 Verify that the Boot ROM and SMC versions you found in step 6 are at least as high as the listing. If they are not, update your computer's firmware before upgrading OS X. The easiest way to do this is with automatic software updates (note that automatic software updates also check other things, so you should run it even if your firmware is up to date).

NOTE ► You can find more information about automatic software updates in **Lesson 4, "Update macOS Software."**

21 From the Apple menu, choose App Store or Software Update; if necessary, click the Updates icon in the toolbar, and wait while your software and firmware are checked for updates.

22 If a message appears informing you that "Your computer is up to date" or there are "No Updates Available," proceed to the "Document Network Settings" section of this exercise.

23 If you are using OS X Lion 10.7 and a dialog appears informing you that updates are available for your computer, click Show Details to view the updates it found.

Look through the available updates, and deselect any that you do not want to perform at this time. Then click Install *x* Items, where *x* is the number of items you have chosen to install, and follow any prompts and instructions to complete the updates. Note that the process for updating firmware can vary from model to model.

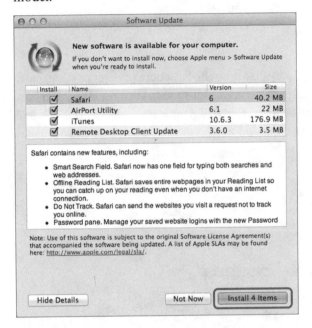

24 If you are using Mountain Lion 10.8 or later and the App Store lists available updates, click the Update buttons for any updates you want to install. Note that you may have a More option available to show a more detailed list of system updates and an Update All button to install all available updates. Follow any prompts and instructions to complete the updates. Note that the process for updating firmware can vary from model to model.

These versions use an update process similar to that of macOS Sierra, so you can refer to **Lesson 4, "Update macOS Software,"** for more information about the update process.

25 After the updates have finished, repeat starting at step 21 to verify that all updates installed successfully and that no more updates have become available.

Document Network Settings

1 From the Apple menu, choose System Preferences.

2   In System Preferences, click Network.

Network

3   Select each of the network services (listed on the left of the preference pane), and record any special settings assigned to them. You need to click the Advanced button for each service to see the full settings. Generally, the easiest way to do this is to take screenshots with the shortcut Command-Shift-3 to give you a "permanent" record to work from.

4   If your computer has more than one location defined, repeat this process for each location.

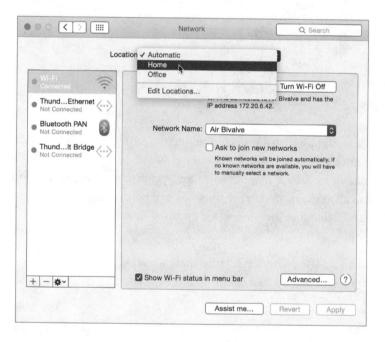

Back Up Your Data

In case anything goes wrong during the system upgrade or any of the exercises in this guide, back up any important data on the computer (including the settings recorded earlier in this exercise). macOS includes a backup utility, Time Machine, which is documented in **Lesson 15, "Manage Time Machine."** There are also many third-party options for backing up Mac computers.

Whichever backup option you choose, make sure your backup is up to date and includes all important data before proceeding. The process depends on your chosen backup solution, but usually the best test is to try restoring critical data from the backup.

Exercise 1.2
Upgrade to macOS Sierra

▶ **Prerequisites**

▶ This exercise is necessary only if you are upgrading your computer from an earlier version to macOS Sierra.

▶ Your computer must be running OS X Lion version 10.7.5 or later to perform this exercise.

▶ Perform Exercise 1.1, "Prepare a Mac for Upgrade," before beginning this exercise.

In this exercise, you will download macOS Sierra from the Mac App Store and install it as an upgrade on your computer.

Use the App Store to Download the Installer

1   Log in to your existing administrator account on your computer.

2   From the Apple menu, choose App Store. If App Store is not one of the choices in the Apple menu, you may be running a version of OS X that is too old to use this method of upgrading to Sierra.

3   In the search field of the App Store window, enter Sierra, and press Return.

4   Find macOS Sierra in the search results, and click the button under its name (it is labeled either "DOWNLOAD" or "GET").

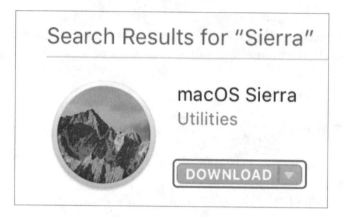

5   If a dialog appears asking you to sign in, you will need to either sign in to an Apple ID account or create a new Apple ID to download Sierra. See **Reference 16.1, "About the Mac App Store,"** and **Exercise 16.1, "Use the Mac App Store,"** for more information about using Apple IDs with the App Store.

6   If the App Store requests any additional information, supply it as requested.

7   Wait for the Install macOS Sierra application to download.

When the download is complete, the application opens automatically.

NOTE ▸ The installation process deletes the Installer application. If you want to upgrade several computers or create a Sierra install disk, quit the installer and make a copy of it before proceeding. You can find the process for creating an install disk in Exercise 3.2, "Create a macOS Install Disk."

Upgrade Your Computer to macOS Sierra

1   If necessary, open the Install macOS Sierra application.

Install macOS
Sierra

2   At the first screen, click Continue.

3   Read the license agreement, and if its terms are acceptable to you, click Agree.

4   In the confirmation dialog that appears, click Agree.

At this point, you can select the install destination.

5   The default selection is the current startup volume; if other volumes are available, click the Show All Disks button to select a different destination.

6   Click Install to start the installation. If you are warned about not being connected to a power source, connect your power adapter before continuing.

7   Enter the password of your administrator account to authorize the installation.

To see the details of the installation process, follow the instructions in Exercise 1.4, "Verify System Installation," as soon as the installation has started.

The installation normally completes automatically without further interaction, although it will restart several times during the process.

The first time you log in to your account after upgrading, you may be prompted to sign in with your Apple ID. You can skip this step by selecting "Don't sign in" because you will explore the Apple ID and iCloud features of Sierra in later exercises.

You may also be prompted to enable Siri. Siri will not be used for these exercises, but you can enable it if you want to.

Now that your computer is running Sierra, follow the instructions in Exercise 2.2, "Configure an Existing macOS System for Exercises," to set up your computer for the rest of the exercises in this guide.

Exercise 1.3
Erase a Mac System and Install macOS Sierra

▶ **Prerequisites**

▶   This exercise is necessary only if your computer needs to be erased before installing macOS Sierra, as covered in Reference 1.2, "Select an Installation Method."

▶   You need a Sierra recovery partition or a Sierra install disk (see Lesson 3, "Use macOS Recovery," for details).

WARNING ▶ This exercise erases all existing data on your computer. If you want to keep any of this data, you must ensure that it is safely backed up to another computer or disk.

If your computer is having trouble, it may be best to erase the existing data and start with a clean installation of macOS Sierra. To do this, you must start up from another disk, erase your computer's internal disk, and then install a new operating system.

Start Up from Recovery or an Install Disk

1   Before proceeding with this exercise, make sure all the files you want to preserve from this computer are safely backed up elsewhere.

2   If your computer is running, shut it down.

3   If you are replacing an existing installation of Sierra (and want to perform the installation from the computer's existing Sierra recovery partition), press the power button on your computer to turn it on, and then immediately press and hold the Command and R keys until you see the Apple icon appear in the middle of the screen. Once you see the Apple icon, release the keys and skip ahead to the next section, "Erase Your Computer's Disk Drive."

4   If you are using an external Sierra install disk, connect the disk to your computer.

5   Press the power button on your computer to turn it on, and then immediately press and hold the Option key until you see a row of icons appear on the screen.

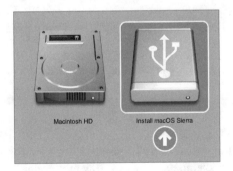

6   Click the install disk's icon (usually labeled "Install macOS Sierra").

7   Click the arrow that appears under the icon.

The computer starts up into the installer/recovery environment. Lesson 3, "Use macOS Recovery," has more information about using these modes.

Erase Your Computer's Disk Drive

1   If a language selection screen appears, select your preferred language, and click the right-arrow button to continue.

2   Open Disk Utility.

▶   If a macOS Utilities window appears, select Disk Utility, and click Continue.

▶   If an installer screen appears instead, choose Utilities menu > Disk Utility from the menu bar.

Disk Utility opens. **Lesson 9, "Manage File Systems and Storage,"** has more information about using Disk Utility.

3   From the sidebar, select the disk or volume you want to install Sierra on.

NOTE ▶ If you started up from an external install disk, you can select the disk (the top entry), which will erase the entire disk and all data on it. If you would prefer to erase only a single partition, you can select the partition's entry under the disk drive in the sidebar. If you choose this option, you must also verify that the disk is formatted with a GUID partition table (GPT). See **Lesson 9, "Manage File Systems and Storage,"** for more details on disk formatting and erasure options.

4   Click the Erase button near the top of the Disk Utility window.

5   Enter a new name for your computer's disk. The rest of this guide assumes that it is named Macintosh HD.

6   From the Format pop-up menu, choose Mac OS Extended (Journaled).

7   If there is a Scheme pop-up menu, choose GUID Partition Map.

8   Click Erase.

9   When the process finishes, click Done.

10   From the menu bar, choose Disk Utility > Quit Disk Utility.

Install macOS Sierra

1   If a macOS Utilities window appears, select Install macOS or Reinstall macOS, and click Continue.

2   In the Install macOS Sierra window, click Continue.

3   If you are notified that your computer's eligibility will be verified with Apple, click Continue.

4   Read the license agreement, and if its terms are acceptable to you, click Agree.

5   In the confirmation dialog that appears, click Agree.

6   Select your computer's disk drive from the list of available volumes, and click Install.

7   If you are prompted to, enter your Apple ID to sign in to the App Store. See Reference 16.1, "About The Mac App Store," and Exercise 16.1, "Use the Mac App Store," for more information about using Apple IDs with the App Store.

To see the details of the installation process, follow the instructions in Exercise 1.4, "Verify System Installation," as soon as the installation begins.

The installation completes automatically without further interaction, although it will restart several times during the process.

Upon restart, you are greeted by the full Setup Assistant experience, as covered in Lesson 2, "Set Up and Configure macOS." Follow the instructions in Exercise 2.1, "Configure a New macOS System for Exercises," to set up your computer for the rest of the exercises in this guide.

Exercise 1.4
Verify System Installation

▶ **Prerequisite**

▶   You must have started installing macOS Sierra using the instructions in
Exercise 1.2, "Upgrade to macOS Sierra," or Exercise 1.3, "Erase a Mac System
and Install macOS Sierra," to perform this exercise.

In this exercise, you will use the Installer log to examine the installation process as it
happens.

Examine the Installer Log

Any time during the installation process, you can bring up the Installer log by following
these steps:

1   If the installer is running in full-screen mode, you can't see the menu bar. Move
your mouse to the top of the screen and leave it there for a few seconds to reveal
the menu bar.

2   From the Window menu, choose Installer Log (or press Command-L).

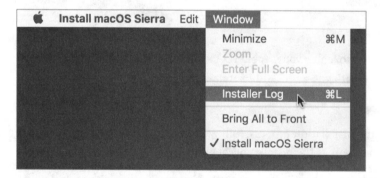

3   Choose Show All Logs from the Detail Level pop-up menu to view the entire contents
of the Installer log.

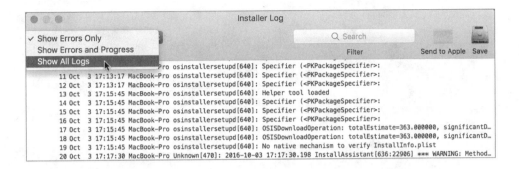

4   Use the Spotlight search field in the toolbar to isolate specific entries in the Installer log.

5   To save the Installer log, click the Save button in the toolbar.

> **NOTE ▸** The installer restarts the computer partway through the installation process. When the computer restarts for the second phase, the log window does not automatically reopen.

Lesson 2

Set Up and Configure macOS

This lesson focuses on both initial setup and ongoing macOS configuration. With a new installation of macOS, you use Setup Assistant for configuration. After that, you almost always use System Preferences and configuration profiles. This lesson also introduces the tools you use to verify system information.

GOALS

▶ Complete an initial configuration of macOS

▶ Adjust common system settings

▶ Identify and install a configuration profile

▶ Verify system information

Reference 2.1
Configure a New System

If you are using a new Mac for the first time or you have just completed an upgrade installation of macOS Sierra, you will see Setup Assistant. For new Mac computers or clean installations of macOS, Setup Assistant guides you through the preliminary configuration required for a new system.

If you have just upgraded an existing Mac with a previous version of an Apple operating system, you will still see Setup Assistant, but you will be presented with fewer configuration steps. Most importantly, you will be prompted to enter your Apple ID and password to complete the iCloud setup. Even if you previously set up iCloud on an existing Mac, when Setup Assistant is running you need to reenter your authentication information to complete the upgrade to macOS Sierra.

TIP ▶ iCloud is optional and free of charge, and as you'll see throughout this guide, many powerful macOS Sierra features require iCloud.

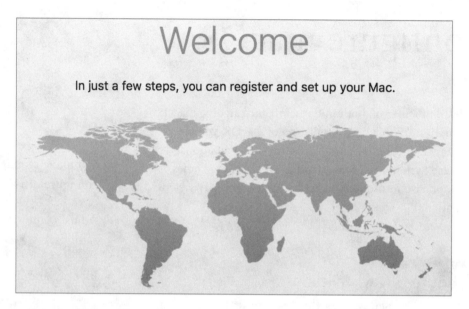

Several Setup Assistant steps are optional, and some steps may not appear depending on the Apple operating system configuration. Even so, a few steps are required to set up macOS Sierra. While you're in Setup Assistant you cannot skip these steps:

▶ Language selection

▶ Country selection

▶ Keyboard setup

▶ Apple terms and conditions acceptance

▶ First account creation

You can easily change the settings you select in Setup Assistant by accessing corresponding settings in System Preferences. Changing settings after completing Setup Assistant is covered later in this lesson.

NOTE ▶ Attempting to use the Command-Q keyboard shortcut in Setup Assistant will prompt you to choose to either shut down or continue.

NOTE ▶ Mac computers managed by a school or business may present different Setup Assistant options than the defaults shown here. In certain managed situations, some of the default screens may be skipped and you may encounter additional organizational configuration screens. These differences are controlled by an administrator via mechanisms outside the Mac. Thus, you may have to contact the organization's primary administrator to properly complete the Setup Assistant process.

Setup Assistant: Language, Country, and Keyboard

The preliminary screens of Setup Assistant are required to configure appropriate user interaction for the system. If a new Mac has never been used before, the first Setup Assistant screen requires that you select the default language to be used by the system and applications.

Next, the Setup Assistant screen requires that you select your country; this information is used to set regional language options, set the appropriate Apple online stores, and complete the registration processes. At this point, you will also have to select the primary keyboard layout. System language and keyboard layout settings can be changed later from Language & Region preferences.

MORE INFO ▶ Alternatively, during the initial stages of Setup Assistant, users who have a visual disability can choose to enable VoiceOver to interact with macOS using only audio cues. You can find out more about assistive technologies from Apple's accessibility website, www.apple.com/accessibility/.

Setup Assistant: Network Settings (Optional)

Setup Assistant will attempt to establish a connection to the Internet by automatically configuring the Mac computer's network settings. It will first attempt to automatically configure via Dynamic Host Configuration Protocol (DHCP) on an Ethernet network or open Wi-Fi network. If a connection is made this way, you won't be prompted to set up networking.

Otherwise, the assistant will try to figure out which type of network connection you need to set up and present you with the appropriate configuration screen. On most Mac computers, this will be the Wi-Fi network setup screen, where you can select a wireless network and authenticate to it. Alternatively, you can postpone setting up networking at this point, and do it later from Network preferences. **Lesson 19, "Manage Basic Network Settings,"** covers this topic in greater detail.

Setup Assistant: Transfer Information (Optional)

Using this optional utility, also known as Migration Assistant, you can transfer computer and user information from another computer or a backup to the new system. Completing the transfer from another system enables you to skip most of the remaining steps of Setup Assistant, as the configuration is gathered from the previous system. **Lesson 6, "Manage User Home Folders,"** covers transferring information via Migration Assistant in greater detail.

If you do not have a previous system to migrate settings and data from, leave the default choice, and click Continue to proceed with the Setup Assistant process.

Setup Assistant: Location Services (Optional)

Enabling Location Services will allow the system and applications to locate your Mac using a Wi-Fi–based geolocation technology. Location Services is required for Find My Mac, which can also be enabled later during Setup Assistant. You can further adjust Location Services in Security & Privacy preferences. **Lesson 7, "Manage Security and Privacy,"** covers Location Services in greater detail.

Setup Assistant: Sign In with Your Apple ID (Optional)

Again, both new systems and systems upgraded to macOS Sierra may prompt you to enter your Apple ID authentication. New systems will present this screen only if the Mac is connected to the Internet. At this screen you can enter an existing Apple ID, recover a lost Apple ID, or create a new Apple ID.

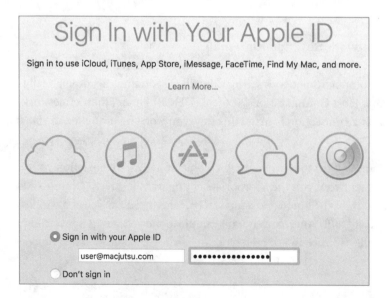

About Apple ID

An Apple ID is free to set up and provides login access for Apple online and store services. If you have ever purchased anything online from Apple, such as from the iTunes Store, you already have an Apple ID.

Once you have entered or created an Apple ID during Setup Assistant, the account is automatically configured for several services, including Messages, FaceTime, Game Center, and iCloud. Additionally, if the Apple ID has been previously used for purchasing, it will be automatically configured in the various online store applications including the Mac App Store, iTunes Store, and iBooks Store. If you use separate Apple IDs for iCloud and store purchases, you also have the option to enter both Apple IDs during the Setup Assistant process. Lastly, in subsequent Setup Assistant steps, this Apple ID will be preentered for optional configuration of computer account setup and system registration.

> **MORE INFO ▸** For more information about Apple ID, see the Apple ID Support website, https://support.apple.com/apple-id.

About Two-Step Verification and Two-Factor Authentication

Your Apple ID grants access to so many Apple services and features that protecting access to your Apple ID is paramount. No longer is using only a name and password considered adequate security. Thus, to significantly improve the security of an Apple ID, you can enable two-step verification or two-factor authentication. Although these two security measures for Apple ID have differences, they are fundamentally similar in that they provide additional authentication mechanisms beyond name and password.

Two-step verification for Apple ID was introduced in 2013 and can be enabled from the Apple ID account page, https://appleid.apple.com/. Because of its age, two-step verification can support older Mac operating systems and iOS versions.

Two-factor authentication uses improved methods to trust devices and deliver verification codes, and offers a more streamlined user experience. However, two-factor authentication is only available to Apple IDs with iCloud enabled and at least one device that's using iOS 9 or OS X El Capitan 10.11 or later. Further, two-factor authentication can be enabled only from a Mac or iOS device meeting these system requirements.

When entering an Apple ID while using the macOS Sierra Setup Assistant, a variety of situations can occur depending on the security configuration of your Apple ID:

▸ If you're entering an Apple ID that already has two-step verification or two-factor authentication enabled, you will be prompted to verify your Apple ID via additional steps. At the time of this writing, if your Apple ID has two-step verification enabled, you are not required to update to two-factor authentication.

▶ If you're creating a new Apple ID, you will be prompted to enter security information, including the option to enable two-factor authentication. Because you're using macOS Sierra, you will not have the option to enable the older two-step verification method.

▶ If you're entering an Apple ID that hasn't been used in a while and doesn't have additional security features enabled, you will be prompted to update your security settings, including optionally enabling two-factor authentication. Again, because you're using macOS Sierra, you will not have the option to enable the older two-step verification method.

MORE INFO ▶ For more information about two-step verification, see Apple Support article HT204152, "Frequently asked questions about two-step verification for Apple ID." For more information about two-factor authentication, see Apple Support article HT204915, "Two-factor authentication for Apple ID," article HT205075, "Availability of two-factor authentication for Apple ID," and article HT207198, "Switch from two-step verification to two-factor authentication."

About iCloud

iCloud is a free cloud-storage and communication service that you can set up on any Apple device. Though not required for completing Setup Assistant, iCloud is the easiest way to share information between macOS, iOS, and even non-Apple devices. As you will see throughout this guide, macOS Sierra features deep integration with iCloud services.

Only Apple IDs that have signed in to iCloud on a Mac or an iOS device have access to iCloud services. If an existing Apple ID has never been used for iCloud, entering this account during Setup Assistant will upgrade the Apple ID to include iCloud services. Further, Setup Assistant will automatically configure your Mac to use iCloud for most services.

The following iCloud services will be enabled by default in most cases: iCloud Drive, Photos, Contacts, Calendars, Reminders, Safari, Notes, and Find My Mac. If the Apple ID you enter belongs to the @mac.com, @me.com, or @icloud.com domain, then Mail is also automatically configured. After you create your local computer account, Setup Assistant will also prompt you to enable iCloud Keychain.

NOTE ▶ If you're entering an Apple ID that belongs to someone under the age of 13 (made possible via Apple School Manager or iCloud Family Sharing), no iCloud services will be enabled by default.

After setup, you can verify and modify iCloud service settings from iCloud preferences. iCloud is covered in this guide where appropriate—specifically, in **Lesson 7, "Manage Security and Privacy," Lesson 17, "Manage Documents," and Lesson 22, "Manage Network Services."**

MORE INFO ▶ For more information about iCloud, see the iCloud Support website, https://support.apple.com/icloud.

Setup Assistant: Terms and Conditions

Accepting the Apple terms and conditions is a requirement to complete Setup Assistant. The content of the Terms and Conditions page will vary depending on whether you entered an Apple ID in the previous step. Accepting the terms and conditions does not send any personal or technical information to Apple. In fact, you can accept them even if your Mac is offline and never accesses the Internet.

MORE INFO ▶ For more information about Apple terms and conditions, visit the Apple Legal website, at www.apple.com/legal/.

Setup Assistant: Create a Computer Account

After the Terms and Conditions step, you arrive at one of the most important steps of the setup process, the "Create a Computer Account" screen. Here you must create the initial administrative user account for the system. At first, this account will be the only administrative user account allowed to modify system settings, including the creation of additional user accounts. Therefore, until you create additional administrative user accounts, you must remember the authentication information for this account.

Apple ID Provided During Setup

If you previously entered an Apple ID, that information will be used to configure services for a new local administrator account. As a default in macOS Sierra, you can also optionally use your Apple ID information to create the new computer user account.

Setup Assistant will automatically populate the full name based on your Apple ID. The account name, used to create the user's home folder, is also prepopulated. For either name you can enter something different than your Apple ID.

You must provide a new password for the local administrator account. Importantly, the password you define for this account does not need to match the Apple ID password.

> **NOTE ►** Your Apple ID and your local computer account are two separate accounts. Even if you set the names and passwords to match, the system does not synchronize the names or password between the accounts. In other words, if you change the names or password for one account, it will not automatically change the other account.

As you can see in the previous screenshot, two methods are provided to help you recover from a lost password. First, you can define a password hint, which is a clue intended to help you if you forget this account's password. Although you can define more than one word for the password hint, you cannot set the password hint to the same text as the password. In this case, a better choice is to allow your Apple ID to reset this account's password. This feature can also be disabled, but it will come in handy later should you forget your account password.

Apple ID Not Provided During Setup

If have not entered an Apple ID during Setup Assistant, the name fields will not be pre-populated and you will not have the option to reset the computer account password with an Apple ID. However, after setup, you can modify local user accounts from the Users & Groups preferences, and adjust iCloud service settings from the iCloud preferences. Additional user account creation and management are detailed in Lesson 5, "Manage User Accounts."

Time Zone

Finally, below the user information, you'll note that macOS is configured to automatically set the time zone based on the computer's location. The system is also configured to automatically set the date and time using the Apple time servers. The automatic configuration of the time requires an Internet connection and that Location Services be enabled.

If you choose not to set the time via Location Services or it isn't enabled, you will be required to manually set a time zone for the system by selecting a city in your time zone. After setup, you can verify and modify these settings from the Date & Time preferences.

Setup: iCloud Keychain (Optional)

After creating the local administrator account, if you previously entered an Apple ID, you will be prompted to optionally enable iCloud Keychain. This feature securely saves your private information, like service usernames and passwords, to your iCloud account. This allows for easy access from multiple devices. If your Apple ID is using two-factor authentication then iCloud Keychain setup is automatic. For Apple IDs without two-factor authentication, enabling iCloud Keychain will prompt you to set up an iCloud Security Code if it hasn't already been set.

If you choose not to set up iCloud Keychain at this point, you can do so later from the iCloud Preferences. Lesson 8, "Manage Password Changes," covers this topic in greater detail.

Setup: iCloud Drive (Optional)

If you previously entered an Apple ID that has not been upgraded to support iCloud Drive, you will be prompted to upgrade your previously stored iCloud documents. This one-time process is required if you intend to access documents stored in iCloud on

OS X Yosemite 10.10 and later or iOS 8 and later devices. However, if you are setting up a new Apple ID with iCloud, or if you have already been using iCloud Drive, your account will not need to be upgraded.

New in macOS Sierra is the ability to save the user's local Desktop and Documents folders to iCloud Drive. Users signed in with an Apple ID that supports iCloud Drive will see the option to move their local Documents and Desktop folders to iCloud Drive.

If you choose not to upgrade to iCloud Drive or move the Documents and Desktop folders to iCloud Drive at this point, you can do so later from the iCloud preferences. **Lesson 17, "Manage Documents,"** covers this topic in greater detail.

Setup: FileVault Disk Encryption (Optional)

FileVault can be used to protect the system volume by encrypting its contents. If you are working through Setup Assistant on a late-model portable Mac that doesn't have FileVault enabled, you may be prompted to enable this feature. This screen will appear on both new systems and systems upgraded to macOS Sierra, but only if the system has a single local user account and that account has also signed in to iCloud.

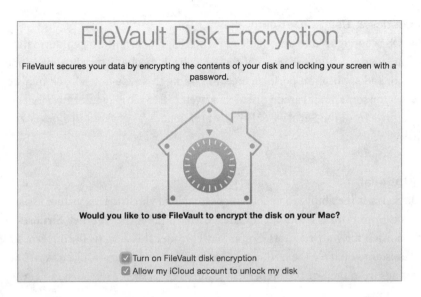

If you select the option to turn on FileVault, you will also be allowed to save a FileVault recovery key to iCloud. If you don't choose the option to allow iCloud to unlock the disk, then you will be presented with another screen showing the FileVault recovery key. In this case, you are responsible for manually saving the recovery key to a safe location.

> **NOTE** ► The macOS interface sometimes uses "iCloud account" instead of "Apple ID." However, because all Apple services, including iCloud, are accessed via Apple ID authentication, this guide uses the term "Apple ID" when discussing Apple service authentication.

After Setup Assistant is complete, the system will begin to encrypt the contents of the system volume. The computer will not have to restart, and the encryption will complete silently in the background. Because this option appears only on systems with a single local user account, only that local account will be allowed to unlock the encrypted system during startup. If the account password is lost, the disk will remain locked unless it is reset using a FileVault recovery key.

If you choose not to enable FileVault at this point, you can do so later from the Security & Privacy preferences. **Lesson 10, "Manage FileVault,"** covers this topic in greater detail.

Setup: Diagnostics & Usage (Optional)

By default, macOS is configured to automatically send diagnostic and usage information to Apple and third-party developers. Both of these feedback mechanisms allow developers to improve system and application performance. Providing this type of feedback may be a privacy concern for some, so it can be disabled as well. After setup, you can verify and modify these settings from the Security & Privacy preferences, as covered in Lesson 7, "Manage System Security."

Setup: Siri (Optional)

New in macOS Sierra is the ability to vocally request actions via Siri. This virtual assistant can perform tasks or find things both locally on the Mac and on the Internet. Siri uses a microphone to listen for your requests. Some may consider this a security concern, so during Setup Assistant you have the option to disable Siri. After setup, you can verify and modify Siri settings from the Siri preferences, as covered in Lesson 7, "Manage Security and Privacy."

> MORE INFO ▶ The latest MacBook computers featuring Touch ID will present additional setup screens. You can find out more about this in Apple Support article HT207054, "Use Touch ID on MacBook Pro."

Reference 2.2
Manage System Settings

Once Setup Assistant has completed the initial configuration, you'll find that there are two primary methods for modifying macOS system and user settings: System Preferences and profile installation.

System Preferences

The System Preferences application is the primary interface for adjusting user and system settings. You will use System Preferences throughout this guide and anytime you are setting up or reconfiguring a Mac system. The quickest access to System Preferences is from the Apple menu, because it's available from any application that shows the menu bar.

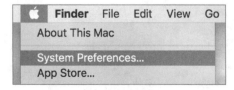

TIP ► The System Preferences application can also be found in the /Applications folder. You can use any shortcut method you like to access the System Preferences application, including clicking its icon in the Dock. With a default installation of macOS, System Preferences appears in the Dock, but it can also be removed like any other icon in the Dock.

When you open System Preferences, you'll notice it is divided into four or five separate categories (rows) of preference icons. The first four categories of preference icons are built into macOS. Although the rows are not labeled in the interface, the first four categories represent personal, hardware, Internet, and system settings. A fifth, and final, category of preference icons will automatically appear if any third-party preferences are installed.

TIP ► While you're in System Preferences, the View menu can give you quick access to all the preferences. You can choose to organize the preferences alphabetically or to hide individual preferences.

 If you are ever confused about where to find a particular setting among the various preferences, use the Spotlight search option in the upper-right corner of the System Preferences window. Entering text in this field will automatically highlight preferences containing your search criteria.

Accessing a set of preferences is as simple as clicking the relevant preference icon. Most System Preferences changes are instantaneous and don't require you to click an Apply or OK button. In the System Preferences toolbar, clicking the Show All button (representing a grid of icons) to the right of the navigation arrows returns you to the view of all preferences.

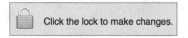

You may notice that some preferences have a lock in the lower-left corner. These can be accessed only by an administrative user account. If a set of preferences you need to access is locked from editing, simply click the lock icon, and then authenticate as an administrative user to unlock it.

Click the lock to make changes.

If you are logged in as a nonadministrative user in macOS, more preferences will be locked than if you are logged in as an administrative user. For example, if you are logged in as an administrative user, Mac App Store preferences will not show the lock icon, whereas if you are logged in as a nonadministrative user, Mac App Store preferences will be locked by default.

The lock icon appears in a variety of places, not just in System Preferences. The lock icon is a general indication that access to the item requires administrative authentication. This is often the case when an item represents a change that affects all users.

Configure via Profile

An alternative method for system setup is to install profiles. Profiles were originally created to provide easy configuration and management for iOS devices, but they are now also used in macOS.

A profile is a document that includes instructions for specific settings. For example, profiles can contain settings for Internet accounts or network preferences. Profile documents can be identified by their icon and the filename extension of .mobileconfig.

Settings.mobileconfig

When a profile is installed, user and system settings are automatically configured based on the profile's content. Thus, an administrator can create a profile that contains a complex variety of settings and then share this profile document with multiple users. The users can then easily install the profile themselves instead of having to manually configure settings. In other words, profiles can save administrators as well as users a lot of time.

Both Apple and third-party developers provide software for creating profiles. Apple alone is responsible for multiple tools that can create profiles, including Xcode, the Apple Configurator application, and the Profile Manager service of macOS Server.

Different general types of profiles are tailored to specific purposes. For example, configuration profiles contain settings that automatically configure certain functions. Trust profiles contain digital certificates, which are used to validate and secure service connections. Enrollment profiles are used to establish a connection to a profile management service, more commonly known as a mobile device management (MDM) service.

Administrators can provide profiles through any means that one would use to share any other document. For example, an administrator could send a profile via email or make it available as a download from a link on a website. Alternatively, administrators can automatically push profiles to a macOS system that is enrolled in an MDM service like that provided by the Profile Manager service of macOS Server. Details regarding the creation of profiles are beyond the scope of this guide, but every Mac administrator should be familiar with how to identify and verify these profiles.

> **MORE INFO** ▶ You can find out more about Profile Manager in macOS Server at www.apple.com/macos/server/.

Profile Installation

If you are presented with a profile that needs to be installed, simply double-click the file to install it. This automatically opens the profile document in the Profiles pane of System Preferences. Profiles preferences appear only when profiles are installed.

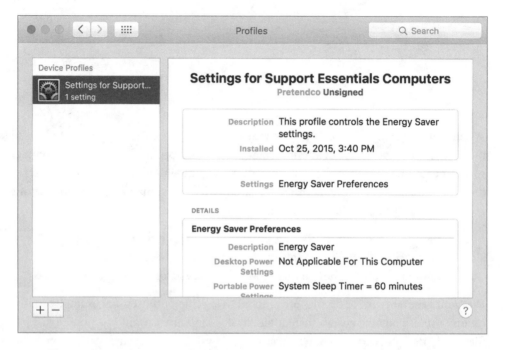

From Profiles preferences, any user with administrative privileges can install, verify, or delete a profile. The previous screenshot shows an installed trust profile that contains a digital certificate. Delivering this type of information via a profile is ideal, because it simplifies a process that would take several more complicated steps using a traditional method.

> **NOTE ▶** The installation of some profiles may require entering additional authentication information. For example, a profile that configures VPN settings will likely require that the user enter a password to authenticate a VPN session.

Verifying the results of an installed profile is a bit more difficult, because the profile could contain multiple settings that affect a variety of services and applications. However, inspecting the details section of an installed profile in Profiles preferences is a good starting point. Again, in the previous example, the Settings section shows that this is a trust profile containing a digital certificate. As covered in **Lesson 8, "Manage Password Changes,"** you can open the Keychain Access application to verify the installation of this certificate.

Reference 2.3
Inspect System Information

Knowledge of your Mac computer's specifications is always important when installing new software, updating installed software, performing maintenance, or troubleshooting a problem. In this section you will learn how to gather essential system information with the About This Mac window, the System Information application, and the Console application.

About This Mac Window

Your first stop in discovering a Mac computer's specifications is the About This Mac window. You can open it from any application by choosing About This Mac from the Apple menu.

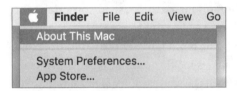

The initial view of the About This Mac window shows you the system software version, Mac model name, processor type and speed, total system memory, graphics card information, and Mac serial number. Clicking the system version number reveals the system build number.

NOTE ▸ Mac computers that have had their logic boards improperly replaced may not display the correct serial number in the About This Mac window.

Of the information in the About This Mac window, a few items are vital to the identification of the macOS system and Mac hardware:

▸ System version number—This number represents the specific system software version currently installed on the computer. The first part, 10, obviously represents the tenth generation of the Mac operating system. The second section, 12, represents the twelfth major release of macOS. The final portion, in this case 2, represents an incremental update to the operating system. Incremental updates generally offer few feature changes but often include a number of security and bug fixes.

▸ System build number—This appears when you click the system version number and is an even more granular representation of the specific system software version installed on the computer. Apple engineers create hundreds of versions of each system software release as they refine the product. The build number is used to track this process. Also, you may find that the computer-specific builds of macOS that come preinstalled on new Mac hardware differ from the standard installation builds. This is an important detail to note if you are creating system images for mass distribution—computer-specific builds of macOS may not work on other types of Mac hardware.

▸ Mac model name—The Mac computer's model name is most often derived from the product marketing name for the Mac, followed by a relative release date. For example, the previous screenshot was taken on a "MacBook Pro Retina, Mid 2012." Because Apple releases very few Mac models each year, this naming convention is specific enough for hardware support identification.

▸ Mac serial number—The hardware serial number is also located somewhere on the Mac case, but sometimes it can be difficult to find. Serving the same purpose here as it does on many other mass-produced products, the serial number is a unique number used to identify that particular Mac for maintenance and service issues.

Clicking the buttons across the About This Mac window's toolbar reveals more details about the computer's hardware and support options. Quite possibly the best feature of this window is the Support and Service buttons, which link directly to specifically useful areas of the Apple Support website. The contents of the links are generated dynamically to show the most up-to-date support information about macOS and your Mac. For example, the Specifications link opens a webpage with the full specifications for your specific Mac.

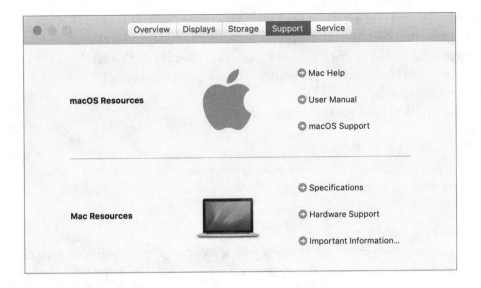

System Information Application

The information in the About This Mac window is only the tip of the iceberg compared with what you can find via the System Information (formerly System Profiler) application. From the About This Mac window, click the System Report button to open System Information. You can also open this application in the Finder by double-clicking /Applications/ Utilities/System Information.app. Opening using either method opens a new System Information window revealing all available reporting options.

You will use System Information to locate critical system details in nearly every lesson of this guide. Additionally, one of the most important uses of System Information is as a documentation tool. Anytime you need to document the current state of a Mac, you can use System Information to create a detailed system report by choosing File > Save from the menu. This creates a System Information–specific file (with the .spx filename extension) that can be opened from other macOS systems.

TIP For quick access to the System Information application, select the Apple menu and then hold down the Option key. The About This Mac menu option changes to System Information while the Option key is pressed.

Console Application

In general, when using macOS, error dialogs will appear only if the issue is something relatively easy for users to resolve on their own, or if the issue presents a significant problem that requires immediate attention. Otherwise, processes and applications that are running will often leave more detailed information in log files found throughout the system. The idea is that log files can contain a lot more information that would be useful for an administrator or developer, but would be too much for a user to understand if presented in an error dialog.

Although these log files are stored in various locations on the system disk, you can easily locate and inspect log files via the /Applications/Utilities/Console.app. Opening Console reveals a list of log files under the Reports column. You'll note some items in the Reports column are actually folders containing additional multiple log files. Simply select an item in the Reports column to reveal its contents.

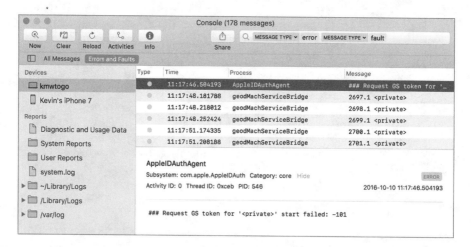

The Console application is all new for macOS Sierra and includes useful new features such as the ability to easily find errors across all log files, and the ability to view the log files from iOS and tvOS devices connected via USB. Additionally, should you need to share a log file with others, you can do so easily by selecting the log file and then clicking the Share button in the toolbar.

You will use Console throughout this guide to uncover detailed information for various applications and processes.

Exercise 2.1
Configure a New macOS System for Exercises

▶ **Prerequisites**

- ▶ This exercise is necessary only if you have not already set up your computer. If you are using a Mac computer with existing accounts, perform Exercise 2.2, "Configure an Existing macOS System for Exercises," instead.

- ▶ Your computer must have a new installation of Sierra and not have been set up yet.

The initial macOS configuration is simple, thanks to Setup Assistant. However, in this lesson you will learn how a few of these initial configuration settings can have fundamental and widespread effects on the system.

In this exercise, you will configure a clean installation of macOS on your class computer. Configuring macOS for this class entails answering a few basic questions and setting up the initial administrator user account. Completing these tasks will acquaint you with the Setup Assistant application.

Configure macOS with Setup Assistant
The following steps walk you through the basic setup of macOS using Setup Assistant:

1   At the Welcome screen, select the appropriate region, and click Continue.

NOTE ▸ If you pause for a few moments at the Setup Assistant Welcome screen, a VoiceOver tutorial begins. This is an optional tutorial that explains how to use the VoiceOver assistance technology designed for those with disabilities.

2   At the Select Your Keyboard screen, select the appropriate keyboard layout, and click Continue.

Setup Assistant evaluates your network environment and tries to determine whether you are connected to the Internet. This can take a few moments.

3   If you are asked to select your Wi-Fi network or how you connect to the Internet, configure it appropriately for your Internet connection. If you are performing this exercise in a class, please ask your instructor how you should configure your computer.

If you are not asked about your Internet connection, your computer's network settings have already been configured via DHCP, and you may move on to step 4.

4 At the "Transfer Information to This Mac" screen, select "Don't transfer any information now," and click Continue.

   If you were replacing a computer, the other options would assist you in migrating user data and system information from the old computer to the new one.

5 If the "Enable Location Services" screen appears, select "Enable Location Services on this Mac," and click Continue.

6 If the "Sign in with Your Apple ID" screen appears, select "Don't sign in," click Continue, and then click Skip in the confirmation dialog that appears.

   You will set up an Apple ID account in a later exercise.

7 At the "Terms and Conditions" screen, read the macOS software license agreement. If there is more than one agreement, you may need to click "more" under each agreement to get the full text. When you have finished reading, click Agree.

8 In the confirmation dialog that appears, click Agree.

9 At the "Create a Computer Account" screen, enter the following information:

   NOTE ▸ It is important that you create this account as specified here. If you do not, future exercises may not work as written. This guide uses this bold blue text to indicate text you should enter exactly as shown.

   Full name: Local Admin

   Account name: ladmin

   Password: If you are performing this exercise in a class, enter ladminpw in the Password and Verify fields. If you are performing this exercise on your own, select a more secure password for the Local Admin account. Be sure to remember the password you have chosen since you will need to reenter it periodically as you use this computer.

   You may provide a password hint and change the other options if you want.

   NOTE ▸ "ladminpw" is too easy to guess to provide any real security, and should never be used for anything other than classroom or demonstration purposes. On "real" computers, you should always use unpredictable passwords.

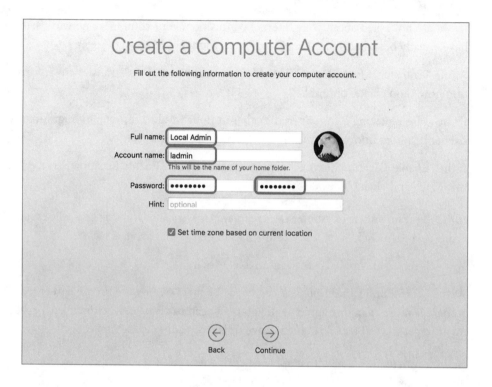

10 Click Continue.

11 If you are prompted to, select your location to set the computer's time zone; then click Continue.

12 If you are prompted to share diagnostics and usage, choose whether you want to share diagnostic information with Apple and application developers, and then click Continue.

13 If you are prompted to enable Siri, deselect "Enable Siri on this Mac," and click Continue.

14 If you are prompted to set up Touch ID, click Continue, then click Set Up Touch ID Later, then click Continue in the confirmation dialog. These exercises do not use Touch ID.

Skip Exercise 2.2, "Configure an Existing macOS System for Exercises," and proceed to Exercise 2.3, "Examine System Preferences," to configure your preference settings.

Exercise 2.2
Configure an Existing macOS System for Exercises

▶ **Prerequisites**

- ▶ Your computer must be running macOS Sierra.

- ▶ Your computer must already have been set up, and you must have an existing administrator account on it. If your computer has not been set up (that is, if the initial administrator account has not been created), perform Exercise 2.1, "Configure a New macOS System for Exercises," instead.

To provide a consistent environment for the rest of the exercises in this guide, you will use System Preferences to create a new administrator account.

Create a New Administrator Account in System Preferences

1   If necessary, log in to your existing administrator account.

2   From the Apple menu, choose System Preferences.

3   In System Preferences, click Users & Groups.

4   In the lower-left corner, click the lock icon.

5   In the dialog that appears, enter the password for your existing administrator account, and click Unlock.

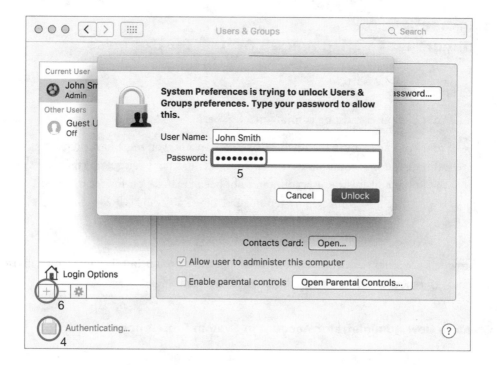

6 Click the Add (+) button below the user list.

7 In the dialog that appears, enter the following information:

NOTE ► It is important that you create this account as specified here. If you do not, future exercises may not work as written. If you already have an account named "Local Admin" or "ladmin," you will have to use a different name here and then remember to use your substitute name throughout the rest of the exercises. This guide uses this bold blue text to indicate text that you should enter exactly as shown.

New Account: choose Administrator

Full Name: Local Admin

Account Name: ladmin

If you are performing this exercise in a class, enter ladminpw in the Password and Verify fields. If you are performing this exercise on your own, select a more secure password for the Local Admin account. Be sure to remember the password you have chosen since you will need to reenter it periodically as you use this computer.

NOTE ► "ladminpw" is too easy to guess to provide any real security, and should never be used for anything other than classroom or demonstration purposes. On "real" computers, you should always use unpredictable passwords.

You may provide a password hint if you want.

New Account:	Administrator
Full Name:	Local Admin
Account Name:	ladmin
	This will be used as the name for your home folder.
Password:	••••••••
Verify:	••••••••
Password hint: (Recommended)	Hint (Recommended)

Cancel   Create User

8   Click Create User.

9   If you are prompted to turn off automatic login, click Turn Off Automatic Login.

10 Quit System Preferences, and log out.

11 At the login screen, select the Local Admin account, and enter its password (ladminpw, or whatever you chose earlier).

12 Press Return.

13 When you are prompted to sign in with your Apple ID, select "Don't sign in," and click Continue.

You will set up an Apple ID account in a later exercise.

14 When a dialog appears asking if you are sure you want to skip signing in, click Skip.

15 If you are prompted to enable Siri, deselect "Enable Siri on this Mac," and click Continue.

16 If you are prompted to set up Touch ID, click Continue, then click Set Up Touch ID Later, then click Continue in the confirmation dialog. These exercises do not use Touch ID.

17 If you are prompted to share diagnostic data with application developers, choose whether you want to do so, and click Continue.

Proceed to Exercise 2.3, "Examine System Preferences," to configure your preference settings.

Exercise 2.3
Examine System Preferences

▶ **Prerequisite**

   ▶ You must have created the Local Admin account in either Exercise 2.1, "Configure a New macOS System for Exercises," or Exercise 2.2, "Configure an Existing macOS System for Exercises."

In this exercise, you will configure some preference settings to make the rest of the exercises easier. This exercise also introduces configuring application and system preferences in macOS.

Adjust Finder Preferences

The default Finder settings make it easy for users to find and work with their own files but are not optimal for system administrators who frequently access files outside their home folder. Since you will be exploring the macOS system more than working with your own files, some customization is in order.

1 If a notification informs you that software updates are available for your computer, click Later, and select Remind Me Tomorrow from the pop-up menu that appears.

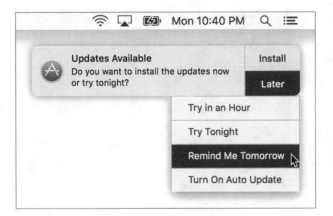

You will install updates during the **Lesson 4, "Update macOS Software,"** exercises.

2 If a notification suggests turning on auto updates, click Not Now.

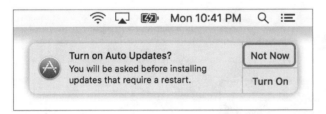

3 If any dialogs open with a "Do you want to use *some volume* to back up with Time Machine?" prompt, click Don't Use in each dialog.

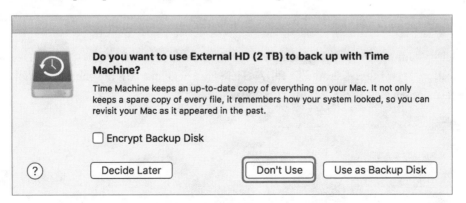

4 From the menu bar, choose Finder > Preferences. If you prefer, you can use the keyboard shortcut Command-Comma instead.

You can configure the Finder preferences in much the same way as any other macOS application.

5 Select the options to show hard disks and connected servers on the desktop.

6 From the "New Finder windows show" pop-up menu, choose your startup volume (typically named Macintosh HD).

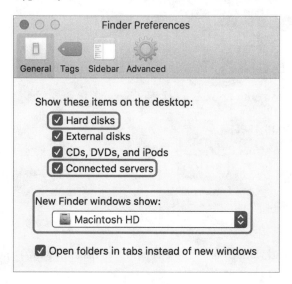

7 At the top of the Finder Preferences window, click the Sidebar button.

8 Select "ladmin" in the Favorites section of the sidebar and "Hard disks" in the Devices section. "Hard disks" should be fully selected (a check mark in the checkbox), not just partially selected (a dash in the checkbox).

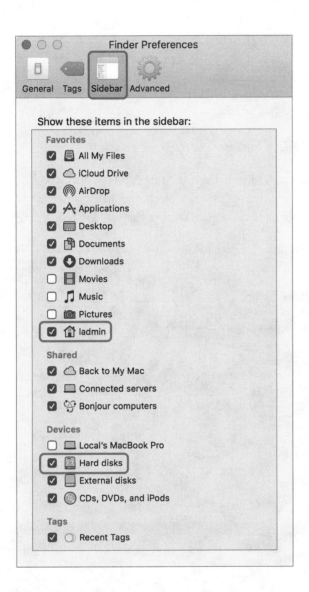

9   Close the Finder Preferences window.

Set the Computer Name

If you are performing these exercises as part of a class, your computer has the same name as all the other students' computers. To avoid confusion, give your computer a unique name.

1   From the Apple menu, choose System Preferences.

2   In System Preferences, click the icon for Sharing preferences.

TIP   If you aren't sure where to find something in System Preferences, you can use the Spotlight search field in the top right of the window. It searches for matching or related settings and highlights the preference panes where they are located.

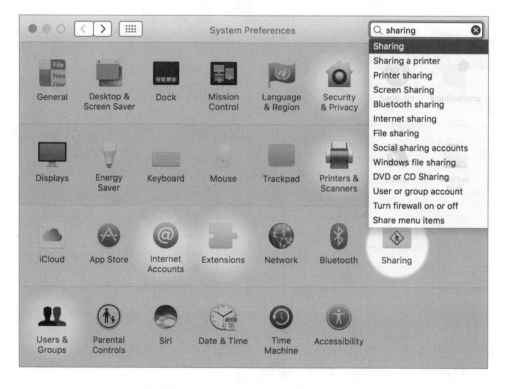

3   Enter a unique name for your computer in the Computer Name field. If you are performing these exercises in a class, your instructor may recommend a naming convention.

4   Press Return.

Notice that your local host name (.local name) that is displayed under your computer name updates to match your new computer name.

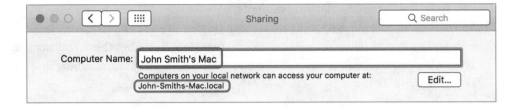

5   Depending on whether you are performing these exercises in a class or on your own, you may or may not need to set up the Remote Management service.

   If you are performing these exercises on your own, skip ahead to "Adjust Your Trackpad/Mouse Preferences."

6   If you are performing these exercises in a class, select the Remote Management checkbox.

   NOTE ▸ In a classroom situation, Remote Management allows your instructor to control the keyboard and mouse, gather information, and update your Mac throughout this course, enabling him or her to assist you with steps if necessary.

   A dialog asks what you want users to be able to do using Remote Management.

7   Hold down the Option key while clicking one of the checkboxes to select all the options in the dialog.

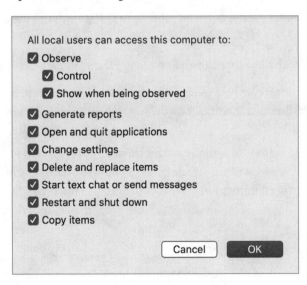

8   Click OK.

Adjust Your Trackpad/Mouse Preferences

In macOS you can customize the user interface to fit your personal preferences. For example, depending on what you are used to, you may want to change the default scrolling behavior. Also, you can control how the system recognizes primary and secondary mouse clicks (analogous to left- and right-clicks in other operating systems).

Note that since Control-click always works as a secondary click, these instructions describe it as Control-click.

1   Click the Show All (grid icon) button in the toolbar.

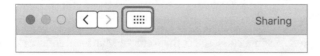

2   If you are using a trackpad, select the Trackpad pane.

▶   Adjust the "Tap to Click" and "Secondary click" options to your liking. (A secondary click opens shortcut menus, normally the right mouse button or Control-click.)

▶   Click "Scroll & Zoom," and use the "Scroll direction: natural" option to adjust which direction it works. The default is that moving two fingers up moves the window contents up.

▶   Check the other options under "Scroll & Zoom" and "More Gestures" and make any appropriate changes.

3   If you are using a mouse, select the Mouse pane.

▶   If your mouse has a scroll wheel (or equivalent), use the "Scroll direction: natural" option to adjust in which direction it works. The default is that pushing the wheel up moves the window contents up.

▶   If your mouse has multiple buttons, use the "Primary mouse button" option to control which button is the primary (used for selecting; usually the left button) and which button is the secondary (used for opening shortcut menus; usually the right button or Control-click).

4   Quit System Preferences.

Proceed to either Exercise 2.4, "Download the Student Materials in a Classroom," or Exercise 2.5, "Download the Student Materials Independently," depending on whether you are performing these exercises in a classroom or independently.

Exercise 2.4
Download the Student Materials in a Classroom

▶ **Prerequisites**

▶ You must have performed Exercise 2.3, "Examine System Preferences."

▶ You must be performing these exercises in a class or have set up your own server configured as in the Mainserver Setup Instructions file. If you are following these exercises on your own and have not set up a server to support the exercises, perform Exercise 2.5, "Download the Student Materials Independently," instead.

NOTE ▶ This exercise is for students performing these exercises in a classroom environment. You can also use this exercise if you have set up another Mac computer as a server to support these exercises. If you want to do this, navigate to www.peachpit.com/register (you'll need to create an account if you don't already have one) and enter this book's ISBN number (9780134713854). Answer the challenge question as proof of purchase; then go to the Registered Products tab on your Account page. Click the Access Bonus Content link below the title of your product to proceed to the download page. Then download the Mainserver Setup Instructions file onto the computer you will use as a server, and follow the enclosed instructions.

If you are following these exercises on your own and have not set up a server to support the exercises, perform Exercise 2.5, "Download the Student Materials Independently," instead.

In this exercise, you will download the student materials required for the rest of the exercises in the guide.

Connect to Mainserver
You need to connect to the file server (called Mainserver) to download the student materials. The details of networking, connecting to, and providing network services will be covered in later lessons.

1 If necessary, open a new Finder window by choosing File menu > New Finder Window or by using the shortcut Command-N.

Look for the server named Mainserver in the Shared section of the sidebar. If Mainserver is not shown, click All to view all the shared items.

2 Select Mainserver. If you had to click All in the previous step, you will have to double-click the Mainserver icon.

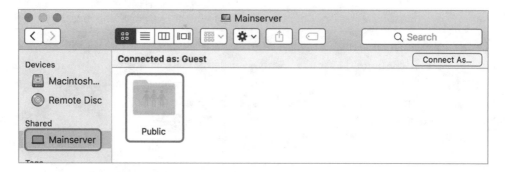

3 Open the Public folder.

Copy the StudentMaterials Folder to Your Computer

1 In the Public folder, select (single-click) the StudentMaterials folder.

2 Copy the folder by choosing Edit menu > Copy "StudentMaterials" from the menu bar, by pressing Command-C, or by Control-clicking the folder and choosing Copy "StudentMaterials" from the shortcut menu.

3 Open the Macintosh HD (either from your desktop or from the Finder window sidebar).

4 Open the Users folder.

5 Open the Shared folder.

6 Paste the StudentMaterials folder into the Shared folder by choosing Edit menu > Paste Item, by pressing Command-V, or by Control-clicking in the Shared folder and choosing Paste Item from the shortcut menu.

This creates a copy of the student materials on your computer. If your instructor has included software updates in the student materials, it may take several minutes to download them. You do not need to wait for it to finish.

7   Drag your copy of the StudentMaterials folder to the right side of the dividing line in the Dock. (The Dock is divided into two sections; the left side holds applications, and the right side holds folders and documents.) Be sure to place it between other entries (so it is added to the Dock) rather than over another entry (which would move it into that folder).

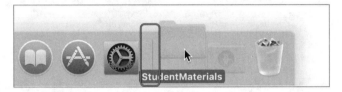

You will be opening the StudentMaterials folder frequently, and this gives you an easy shortcut to it.

8   Optionally, you can drag the StudentMaterials folder to the Finder sidebar in the Favorites section to give yourself another shortcut to access it. As in the Dock, be sure to place it between other entries.

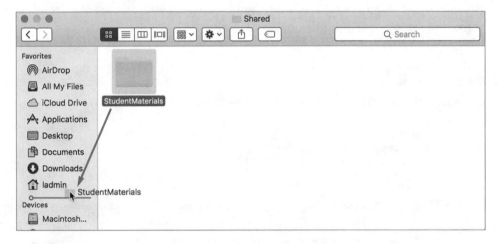

9   Choose Go menu > Applications (or use the shortcut Command-Shift-A).

10 Drag the TextEdit application into the left side of your Dock so that you will always have an easy way to launch it.

11 If it hasn't finished yet, wait for the StudentMaterials folder to finish downloading to your computer.

12 Unmount the Public folder by dragging its icon from the Desktop onto the eject icon at the right side of the Dock. The eject icon replaces the Trash icon when something ejectable is selected.

You should now skip Exercise 2.5, "Download the Student Materials Independently," and proceed to Exercise 2.6, "Install a Configuration Profile."

Exercise 2.5
Download the Student Materials Independently

▶ **Prerequisites**

▶ You must have performed Exercise 2.3, "Examine System Preferences."

▶ Do not perform this exercise if you are in a class or have set up your own server configured as in the Mainserver Setup Instructions file. If you have access to a server configured to support these exercises, perform Exercise 2.4, "Download the Student Materials in a Classroom," instead.

In this exercise, you will download the student materials required for the rest of the exercises in the course.

Download the StudentMaterials Folder from the Web

You need to connect to the Pearson Education web server to download the student materials.

1   Open Safari.

2   Navigate to www.peachpit.com/register.

3   Enter the ISBN number for this book: 9780134713854.

4   If you already have a Peachpit account, sign in to it. If you do not, follow the prompts to create one.

5   Answer the challenge question[s] as proof of purchase.

6   Click the Registered Products tab on your Account page.

7   Click the Access Bonus Content link below the title of your product to proceed to the download page.

   NOTE ▶ If you purchase or redeem a code for the electronic version of this guide directly from Peachpit, the student materials will automatically appear on the Registered Products tab without the need to redeem an additional code.

   NOTE ▶ If you have access to another computer running macOS Sierra and want to configure it as a server to support these exercises, do not download the student materials here. Instead, download the Mainserver Setup file onto the computer you will use as a server, and follow the enclosed Mainserver Setup Instructions.

8   Click the link to download StudentMaterials.zip.

   The student materials for these exercises will be downloaded as a ZIP archive and automatically expanded into the StudentMaterials folder.

9   Click the Downloads (down-arrow icon) button near the top right of the window.

10 Click the view (magnifying-glass icon) button next to StudentMaterials.

Your Downloads folder opens in the Finder, showing the StudentMaterials folder inside it.

11 On your desktop, find the icon for your startup disk (generally Macintosh HD), and double-click it.

This opens a new Finder window showing the contents of the startup disk.

12 Open the Users folder.

13 Open the Shared folder.

14 Drag the StudentMaterials icon from the Downloads folder into the Shared folder.

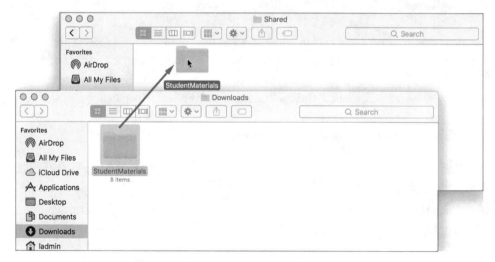

15 Close the Downloads folder.

16 Drag the StudentMaterials icon from the Shared folder to the right side of the dividing line in the Dock. (The Dock is divided into two sections; the left side holds applications, and the right side holds folders and documents.) Be sure to place it between other entries (so it is added to the Dock) rather than over another entry (which would move it into that folder).

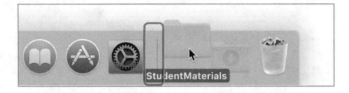

You will be opening the StudentMaterials folder frequently, and this gives you an easy shortcut to it.

17 Optionally, you can also drag the StudentMaterials folder to the Finder sidebar in the Favorites section to give yourself another shortcut to it. As in the Dock, be sure to place it between other entries.

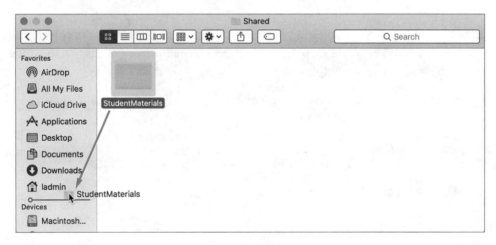

18 Choose Go menu > Applications (or use the shortcut Command-Shift-A).

19 Drag the TextEdit application into the left side of your Dock so that you will always have an easy way to launch it.

Exercise 2.6
Install a Configuration Profile

▶ **Prerequisite**

▶ You must have downloaded the StudentMaterials folder, using the instructions in either Exercise 2.4, "Download the Student Materials in a Classroom," or Exercise 2.5, "Download the Student Materials Independently."

In addition to manually configuring settings on macOS computers, you can control a computer's settings by installing profiles. This capability allows you to easily standardize the configuration across multiple computers.

In this exercise, you will demonstrate this by setting your Energy Saver settings with a configuration profile.

Change Your Energy Saver Settings with a Configuration Profile

1 If necessary, open System Preferences by choosing it from the Apple menu.

2 Select the Energy Saver pane.

3 Note your computer's sleep settings. Depending on the model you are using, they may differ from those shown here.

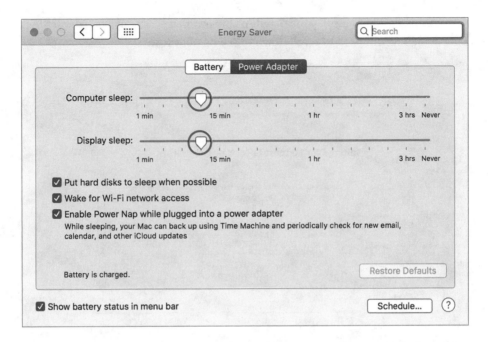

4   Quit System Preferences.

5   Open the StudentMaterials folder. Remember that you put a shortcut to it in your Dock.

6   Open the Lesson2 folder.

7   Open Energy_Saver.mobileconfig.

The profile automatically opens in the Profiles pane of System Preferences.

8   Click Show Profile to display the details of the profile and its payload (the settings it contains). You will need to scroll down to see its full contents.

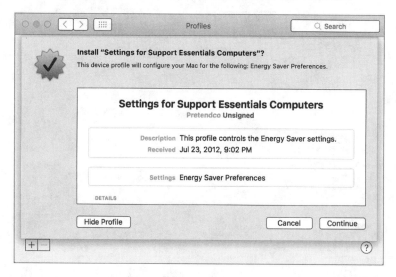

9   Click Continue.

10   Click Install.

11   Enter the Local Admin account's password (ladminpw, or whatever you chose earlier) when prompted.

The Profile pane now lists the configuration profile as installed.

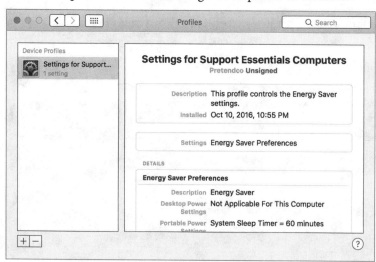

12 Click the Show All (grid) button in the toolbar, and then select the Energy Saver pane.

The Energy Saver settings have changed to match those in the profile.

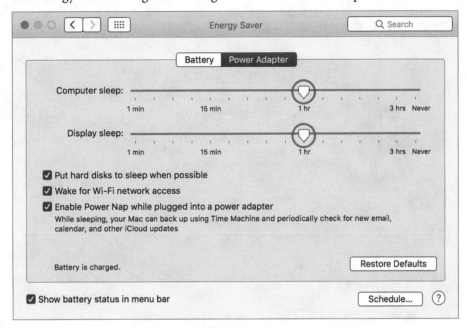

NOTE ▶ Although the new Energy Saver settings take effect immediately, the display in System Preferences does not always update. If you still see the old settings, try logging out and back in to the Local Admin account, and then recheck System Preferences.

13 Quit System Preferences.

Exercise 2.7
Examine System Information

System Information is the primary tool for gathering configuration information in macOS. In this exercise, you will explore its features.

Use About This Mac and System Information

System Information displays information and options for repair and warranty coverage of your computer.

1 From the Apple menu, choose About This Mac.

A dialog appears showing basic information about your computer.

2 Click the macOS version number (below the large "macOS Sierra"). The build number (a more specific identifier for the version of macOS you are using) is displayed.

3 Click through the Displays, Storage, and (if it is shown) Memory tabs in the About This Mac window's toolbar to view more information about your computer hardware configuration.

4 Click the Service tab.

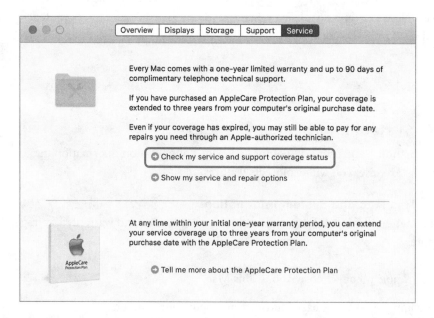

5   Click "Check my service and support coverage status."

6   In the confirmation dialog that appears, click Allow.

Safari opens and displays a coverage check page at apple.com.

7   If the website asks you to enter a code (a CAPTCHA challenge), do so.

The coverage page shows your computer model name and warranty status.

8   Quit Safari.

9   In the About This Mac window, click Overview.

10   Click the System Report button.

System Information opens and displays a more detailed report about your computer hardware, network, and software configuration.

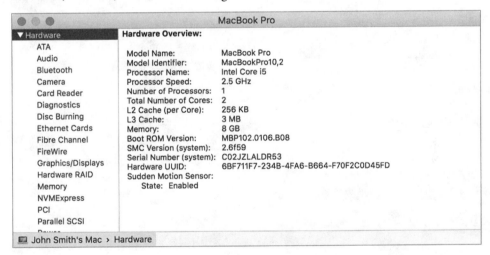

11   Explore the system report by clicking information categories in the report's sidebar. Some categories may take a while to load.

12   From the menu bar, choose File > Save, enter a name for your system's report, and then click Save.

When saving reports like this, it can be helpful to choose a naming convention that includes the computer name (or other identifier) and the date.

System Information finishes gathering information on your computer and saves it in a report that documents your computer's current status.

13 Quit System Information.

> **TIP** ▶ You can also find the System Information application in the /Applications/ Utilities folder or in the Other section of Launchpad. You can use any shortcut method you like to access System Information, including placing it in the Dock.

> **TIP** ▶ You can also directly access System Information from the Apple menu by holding the Option key. This changes the About This Mac menu choice to System Information. When you open System Information directly, you skip the summary About This Mac window and are presented with the full system report.

Lesson 3

Use macOS Recovery

From a troubleshooting viewpoint, one of the most useful macOS features is macOS Recovery. Via macOS Recovery, you can not only reinstall macOS but also access a variety of administration and troubleshooting utilities. macOS Recovery is, by default, located on the primary system disk. This allows easy access to recovery utilities without the need for additional media.

In this lesson, you will learn how to access macOS Recovery both on new Mac computers that came with macOS preinstalled and on computers that have been upgraded to macOS Sierra. You will also briefly explore the utilities available from macOS Recovery. As long as you don't make any permanent changes using the utilities in macOS Recovery, you can safely explore without damaging your primary macOS system. Finally, you will learn how to create an external macOS install disk that can be used in cases where local macOS Recovery isn't available.

Reference 3.1
Start Up from macOS Recovery

Mac computers running macOS Sierra, including both computers that shipped with macOS Sierra and upgraded computers, include a hidden macOS Recovery system on the local system disk. This hidden partition, dubbed Recovery HD, does not appear when a Mac is running macOS. The Recovery HD partition is automatically created during macOS installation from the last 650 MB or so of the system volume.

> **MORE INFO** ▶ You can verify the existence of the Recovery HD partition by examining the internal disk using the System Information application. This is detailed further in **Lesson 9, "Manage File Systems and Storage."**

To start up from macOS Recovery on the local system disk, simply restart the computer while holding down Command-R. In most cases, once macOS Recovery fully starts, the macOS Utilities window appears. From there you can install (or reinstall) macOS and choose from a variety of maintenance applications. If, however, the macOS Installer appears, you can continue with the installation if you need to, or quit the Installer (using the Command-Q keyboard shortcut) to return to the macOS Utilities window.

If for some reason macOS Recovery doesn't start or isn't installed on the local system disk, you have three alternatives for accessing it:

▶ If you have a Mac model released in mid-2010 or later—If your Mac has the latest firmware updates, it can access macOS Internet Recovery. If the local Recovery HD partition is missing, late-model Mac computers should automatically attempt to access macOS Internet Recovery. You can also force a system to start up to macOS Internet Recovery by holding down Command-Option-R. When you do this, your Mac tries to redownload macOS Recovery from Apple servers. If successful, this process re-creates the local Recovery HD partition.

> **MORE INFO** ▶ For more about using macOS Internet Recovery, see Apple Support article HT201314, "About macOS Recovery," and article HT202313, "Computers that can be upgraded to use OS X Internet Recovery."

▶ If you have an external macOS Recovery Disk—Connect the Recovery Disk to your Mac, and restart while holding down the Option key. This opens Startup Manager, where you can use the arrow and Return keys or the mouse or trackpad to select the external macOS Recovery Disk. The default name for an external macOS Recovery Disk created using the methods outlined in this lesson is "Install macOS Sierra." Reference 3.3, "Create a macOS Recovery Disk," and Exercise 3.2, "Create a macOS Install Disk," cover creating this disk in greater detail.

▶ If you have a local Time Machine backup disk—The Time Machine backup service automatically creates a hidden macOS Recovery partition on local backup disks. To access macOS Recovery, connect the Time Machine backup disk to your Mac and restart while holding down the Option key. This opens the Mac computer's Startup Manager, where (as earlier) you can use the arrow and Return keys or the mouse or trackpad to select the Time Machine backup disk. **Lesson 15, "Manage Time Machine,"** covers this topic in greater detail.

NOTE ▶ If the Time Machine backup disk is encrypted, you need to enter the disk encryption password to successfully start up macOS Recovery. This password is unique to the encrypted backup disk and is not associated with or synchronized to any user account passwords. Again, **Lesson 15, "Manage Time Machine,"** covers this topic in greater detail.

Reference 3.2
About macOS Recovery Utilities

When you start up from macOS Recovery, you have access to several system administration and maintenance tools. The recovery system even has a few utilities you cannot find anywhere else in macOS. Again, in most cases, when you first start macOS Recovery you see the macOS Utilities window.

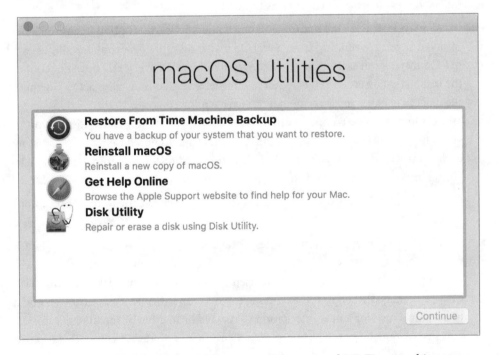

When a Mac is started up from macOS Recovery, Ethernet and Wi-Fi networking are available if the network provides DHCP services. Ethernet is automatically enabled if the Mac is physically connected to the network. If a Wi-Fi network isn't automatically connected, you can select one from the Wi-Fi menu item.

NOTE ► If manual network setup is required during use of macOS Recovery, refer to instructions in Apple Support article HT200168, "Using Lion Recovery when no DHCP service is available."

NOTE ► While running from macOS Recovery, if the Mac computer's system disk is protected by FileVault, any access to this disk first requires that you unlock the disk. In most cases, any local user's password on the system will unlock the system FileVault disk. **Lesson 10, "Manage FileVault,"** covers this topic in greater detail.

From the macOS Utilities window in macOS Recovery, you can access the following functions:

► Restore From Time Machine Backup—Use this option to restore a full Mac Time Machine backup from either a network or a locally connected disk. **Lesson 15, "Manage Time Machine,"** covers this topic in greater detail.

► Install macOS or Reinstall macOS—As the name implies, this option opens the macOS installer. If you are running from a macOS install disk, the disk contains all the macOS installation assets. However, the local hidden Recovery HD does not contain the installation assets and thus requires Internet access to reinstall macOS. Further, the macOS installer must verify that the user is allowed access to the macOS Sierra assets. On older Mac computers that have been upgraded to macOS Sierra, you must verify the installation by providing the Apple ID used to purchase macOS. For Mac computers that shipped with macOS Sierra, this verification is automatic. Lesson 1, "Install macOS Sierra," covers this topic in greater detail.

► Get Help Online—This option opens Safari, taking you directly to the Apple Support website.

► Disk Utility—This application handles storage-related administration and maintenance. It is especially useful when the Mac has started up from macOS Recovery, because Disk Utility can be used to manage a system disk that otherwise can't be managed when in use as the startup disk. Specifically, Disk Utility can be used to prepare a disk for a new installation of macOS or to attempt repairs on a disk that fails installation. **Lesson 9, "Manage File Systems and Storage,"** covers this topic in greater detail.

► Startup Disk (by clicking the close button or quitting)—If you attempt to quit the macOS Utilities window, you will see a prompt to start the Startup Disk utility. From this utility you can select the default system startup disk. The default startup disk can be overridden using any of the alternative startup modes discussed in **Lesson 26, "Troubleshoot Startup and System Issues."**

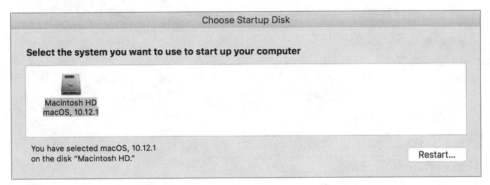

Wait, there's more! macOS Recovery has a few extra features tucked away in the Utilities menu at the top of the screen:

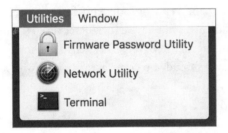

▶ Firmware Password Utility—This utility allows you to secure the Mac computer's startup process by disabling all alternate startup modes without a password. You can disable or enable this feature and define the required password. Learn more about firmware passwords in **Lesson 8, "Manage Password Changes."**

▶ Network Utility—This is the main network and Internet troubleshooting utility in macOS. Its primary use in macOS Recovery is to troubleshoot any network issues that could prevent the download of macOS installation assets. Network Utility is further discussed in **Lesson 21, "Troubleshoot Network Issues."**

▶ Terminal—This is your primary interface to the UNIX command-line environment of macOS. The most useful command you can enter from here is resetpassword followed by pressing the Return key.

▶ Reset Password assistant opened via Terminal—This utility allows you to reset the password of any local user account, including the root user's, on a selected system disk. Obviously, this utility can pose a serious security threat, and consequently it can be run only from macOS Recovery. Further, it's hidden from plain view—you can only open it by entering the resetpassword command in Terminal. You can find out more about the Reset Password assistant in **Lesson 8, "Manage Password Changes."**

NOTE ▶ The utilities available from macOS Recovery can certainly be used to compromise system security. Then again, any system whose default startup disk can be overridden during startup is wide open to compromise. Therefore, in secured environments, it's often necessary to use the Firmware Password Utility to help protect your systems, as covered in Lesson 8, "Manage Password Changes."

Reference 3.3
Create a macOS Recovery Disk

In some cases, a Mac with macOS installed does not have a local Recovery HD. For example, if you just replaced the internal disk with a new disk, nothing will be on the new disk. Also, macOS systems on RAID (Redundant Array of Independent Disks) sets and disks with nonstandard Boot Camp partitioning will not have a local Recovery HD. In these cases, you would need to start up from an external Recovery Disk. Also, having an external Recovery Disk handy can be a real lifesaver should you come across a Mac with a dysfunctional system disk.

NOTE ▶ When creating your own macOS Recovery Disks, be sure to keep track of the specific version of macOS you are using. As covered in Lesson 1, "Install macOS Sierra," newer Mac computers do not support older versions of macOS and may require computer-specific builds of macOS. Thus, you should always keep your macOS Recovery Disk updated to the latest version of macOS available from the Mac App Store.

macOS Sierra includes a do-it-yourself solution to convert a standard disk into a macOS Recovery Disk. This method involves using a special command-line tool, named createinstallmedia, found in the Install macOS Sierra application. This tool copies both a macOS Recovery system and the full macOS installation assets to an external disk. Consequently, this method requires a disk of at least 8 GB, which is a common size for a small USB flash drive. Exercise 3.2, "Create a macOS Install Disk," outlines the steps necessary to create this type of disk.

NOTE ▶ It's not recommended to use the legacy Recovery Disk Assistant method to create external macOS Recovery Disks for macOS Sierra.

Exercise 3.1
Use macOS Recovery

▶ **Prerequisite**

 ▶ Your computer must have a local hidden Recovery HD partition. This partition
   is normally created by the macOS Sierra installation process.

In this exercise, you will start up your computer in macOS Recovery. macOS Recovery
is stored on a hidden partition named Recovery HD that is created automatically when
macOS is installed on the hard disk. You will review the included utilities and how macOS
Recovery can reinstall the system.

NOTE ▶ You will not perform an installation, but you will get an opportunity to look
at the steps leading up to the installation.

Start Up Using macOS Recovery

To access the installer and other utilities in macOS Recovery, you need to start up from
the hidden Recovery HD partition.

1 If your computer is on, shut it down by choosing Shut Down from the Apple menu.

2 Press the power button on your computer, and then hold down Command-R until the
   Apple logo appears on the screen.

   When you hold down Command-R during startup, the computer attempts to start up
   using a recovery partition on the hard disk.

   If no recovery partition is available, Mac computers with newer firmware can start up
   from an Apple server over the Internet and get access to the macOS Recovery utilities.

   If your computer starts up to the login or Welcome screen instead of macOS Recovery, you may not have held Command-R long enough. If this happens, click the Shut
   Down button (at the login screen) or press Command-Q (at the Welcome screen) and
   try again.

3 If a language selection screen appears, select your preferred language and click the
   right-arrow button.

4   After macOS Recovery starts up, you see a "macOS Utilities" window. This window is
    the primary interface for macOS Recovery.

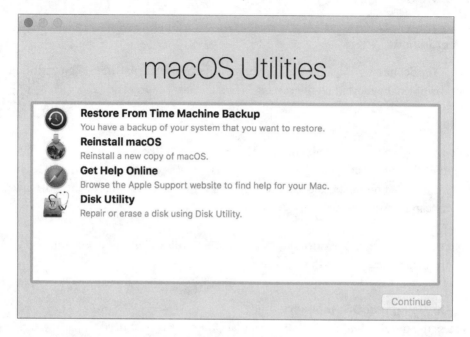

Examine the macOS Recovery Utilities

While using macOS Recovery, you have access to utilities for recovering, repairing, and
reinstalling macOS. In this part of the exercise, you will get to know some of these utilities.

View macOS Recovery Help

You can use Safari to view the built-in instructions of macOS Recovery and to browse the web.

1   Select Get Help Online, and then click Continue.

    Safari opens and displays a document with information about how to use macOS
    Recovery. Take a moment to skim the document.

    This document is stored on the Recovery HD partition, but as long as you have an
    Internet connection available, you can also use Safari to view online documentation
    such as the Apple Support articles.

2   If a dialog indicates that Safari wants to use the "login" keychain, leave the Password
    field blank and click OK.

3   Click in the "Search or enter website name" field, enter apple.com, and press Return.

Safari now displays the Apple website.

4   If Safari displays a message that says "You are not connected to the Internet," you can join a wireless network using the Wi-Fi icon near the right side of the menu bar.

5   Click the Support link near the top right of the page.

You are taken to the Apple Support site. If you were experiencing a problem with your computer, this would be a good place to look for solutions and information. You will use some of the Apple Support resources later in this guide.

6   From the menu bar, choose Safari > Quit Safari (or press Command-Q) to return to the main utilities screen.

Note that closing the Safari window does not quit Safari. This is common among Mac applications, but if you are accustomed to using Microsoft Windows, it may be contrary to your expectations. Generally, the best way to quit a Mac application is to choose Quit *<Application Name>* from the application menu (the menu next to the Apple menu, named for the current application). Or you can use the keyboard short-cut Command-Q.

Examine Disk Utility

Disk Utility lets you repair, image, reformat, or repartition your computer's disk.

NOTE ▶ If the Mac computer's system disk is protected by FileVault, any access to this disk will require the disk to be unlocked first. In most cases, any local user's password on the system should be allowed to unlock the system FileVault drive. **Lesson 10, "Manage FileVault,"** covers this topic in greater detail.

1   Select Disk Utility, and then click Continue.

In the device list on the left, you see your startup disk and a Base System disk image. You may also see several untitled volumes. Note the primary entry for each disk device and an indented list of volumes on each device (this is discussed in more detail in **Lesson 9, "Manage File Systems and Storage"**).

2   Select the lower entry for your startup volume. Typically, it is named Macintosh HD.

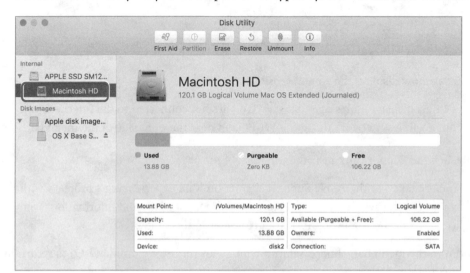

Note the buttons in the Disk Utility toolbar. These buttons represent functions that are discussed in detail in Lesson 9.

With Disk Utility you can verify or repair the startup volume file structure or, if necessary, erase the volume before reinstalling macOS.

3   Select the upper entry that represents your startup disk (just above the startup volume), and note that the partition option is now available.

4   Quit Disk Utility by choosing Disk Utility menu > Quit Disk Utility or by pressing Command-Q.

You are returned to the macOS Utilities window.

Examine Time Machine Restoration

If you backed up your computer with Time Machine, macOS Recovery has the capability to do a full system restoration from that backup. **Reference 15.2, "Configure Time Machine,"** covers setting up Time Machine.

1   Select Restore From Time Machine Backup, and then click Continue.

A "Restore from Time Machine" screen appears, with notes on the restoration process. It is important to realize that this restoration interface erases all current data and replaces it from the backup; **Reference 15.3, "Restore from Time Machine,"** examines other restoration interfaces that let you control which files or folders are restored.

2   Click Continue.

A "Select a Backup Source" screen appears. If you had configured a Time Machine backup target, it would be available here as a source for restoring your system.

3   Click Go Back to return to the "Restore from Time Machine" screen.

4   Click Go Back again to return to the macOS Utilities screen.

Examine the macOS Installer

Now you will examine the reinstallation process, but you will not perform the installation. By going through the following steps, you can experience the configuration of an installation without actually waiting for the macOS software to be copied to your Mac.

1   Select Reinstall macOS, and then click Continue.

The Installer application opens.

2   Click Continue.

A dialog appears indicating that this computer's eligibility will be verified with Apple.

3   Click Continue.

4   At the license agreement, click Agree.

5   In the license confirmation dialog, click Agree again.

The installer displays a list of partitions where you could install or reinstall macOS.

NOTE ▶ Do not click the Install button. If you do, the installer reinstalls macOS.

6   Quit the installer.

Verify Your Startup Disk and Restart

The Startup Disk utility lets you select the volume from which to start up. If you encounter problems during startup from your Mac computer's internal disk, you could connect a second disk, with macOS installed, and use Startup Disk to configure your Mac to start up from the new disk.

1   From the Apple menu, choose Startup Disk.

Startup Disk lists all available startup volumes. The options may include Network Startup or one or more NetBoot images, depending on what Startup Disk finds on your network.

2   Verify that your computer's normal startup volume (typically named Macintosh HD) is selected; if necessary, select it.

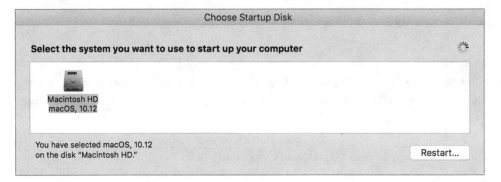

3   Click Restart.

4   In the confirmation dialog, click Restart.

You could also restart without using the Startup Disk utility by choosing Apple menu > Restart.

Exercise 3.2
Create a macOS Install Disk

> **Prerequisites**
>
> ▶ You need an erasable external disk with a capacity of at least 8 GB.
>
> ▶ You must have created the Local Admin account (Exercise 2.1, "Configure a New macOS System for Exercises," or Exercise 2.2, "Configure an Existing macOS System for Exercises").

In this exercise, you will create a macOS install disk, which includes not only the macOS Recovery environment and tools but also a full set of installation assets. With a disk created by this method, you can reinstall macOS without needing to redownload the installer application from the Internet.

NOTE ▶ When you create your own macOS install disk, record the macOS version you're using. Newer Mac computers don't support older macOS versions. (See Exercise 1.3, "Erase a Mac System and Install macOS Sierra.") Always keep your macOS install disks updated to the latest macOS version, which is available from the App Store.

Get a Copy of the Install macOS Sierra Application

If you upgraded to Sierra following the instructions in Exercise 1.2, "Upgrade to macOS Sierra," and saved a copy of the installer application, you may use it and skip this section.

If you are performing these exercises as part of a class, the instructor may have provided a copy in the StudentMaterials/Lesson3 folder. Otherwise, you can redownload the installer with the following procedure:

1   Log in as Local Admin (password: ladminpw, or whatever you chose when you created the account).

2   From the Apple menu, choose App Store. For more about the Mac App Store, see **Lesson 16, "Install Applications."**

3   In the search field of the App Store window, enter Sierra and press Return.

4   Find macOS Sierra in the search results, and click the DOWNLOAD or GET button
    under its name.

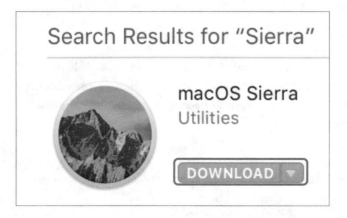

5   If a confirmation dialog appears, click Continue.

6   If a dialog appears asking you to sign in, you will need to either sign in to an Apple
    ID account or create a new Apple ID to download Sierra. See **Lesson 16, "Install
    Applications" (Reference 16.1, "Use the Mac App Store," and Exercise 16.1, "Use the
    Mac App Store"**), for more information about using Apple IDs with the App Store.

    When the installer application finishes downloading, it will open automatically.

7   Quit both Install macOS Sierra and the App Store.

Reformat the External Disk

Most external disks come preformatted with the Master Boot Record (MBR) partition
scheme. To allow a Mac computer to start up from it, you must reformat this disk with
the GUID partition map (GPT) scheme. For more information about disk formats, see
Lesson 9, "Manage File Systems and Storage."

WARNING ▶ This operation erases all information on the external disk. Do not perform this exercise with a disk that contains any files you want to keep.

1   Open Disk Utility. It is located in the Utilities folder, which is in the Applications folder. You can navigate to this folder in Finder by using the Finder shortcut Command-Shift-U, or you can open Launchpad in the Dock and then click the Other icon in Launchpad.

2   Plug the external disk into your computer.

3   If you are prompted for a password to unlock the disk, click Cancel. You don't need to unlock the disk to erase it.

4   Select the external disk device entry in the Disk Utility sidebar. Be sure to select the device entry, not the volume entry indented beneath it.

5   Check the partition map listed at the bottom of the window.

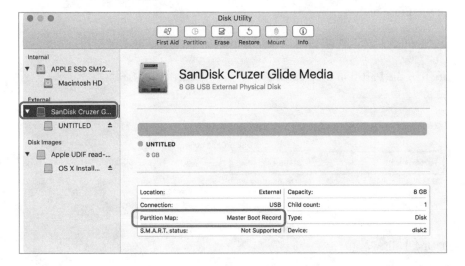

Depending on what this disk was used for most recently, the partition scheme could be anything. To convert the disk to the GPT scheme, you will erase the disk. If it is already using the GPT scheme, this is not strictly necessary, but you should erase it just to be sure.

It is also possible to partition the disk and use only part of it for the installer volume. See **Reference 9.4, "Manage File Systems,"** for more information about the partitioning procedure.

6   Click the Erase button in the toolbar.

7   Give the disk a descriptive name, choose Mac OS Extended (Journaled) from the For-
     mat pop-up menu, and choose GUID Partition Map from the Scheme pop-up menu.

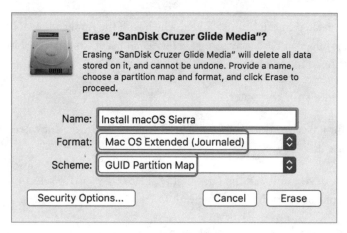

Erase "SanDisk Cruzer Glide Media"?

Erasing "SanDisk Cruzer Glide Media" will delete all data
stored on it, and cannot be undone. Provide a name,
choose a partition map and format, and click Erase to
proceed.

Name: Install macOS Sierra

Format: Mac OS Extended (Journaled)

Scheme: GUID Partition Map

Security Options...   Cancel   Erase

8   Click the Erase button.

9   When the process finishes, click Done to dismiss the erase dialog.

10   Verify that the Partition Map entry is now GUID Partition Map.

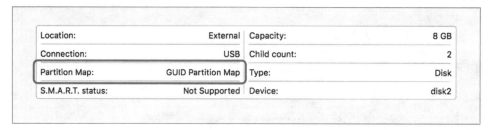

Location:	External	Capacity:	8 GB
Connection:	USB	Child count:	2
Partition Map:	GUID Partition Map	Type:	Disk
S.M.A.R.T. status:	Not Supported	Device:	disk2

11   Quit Disk Utility.

Create a macOS Install Disk

1   Open Terminal from the Utilities folder.

2   Switch to the Finder, and then navigate to where the "Install macOS Sierra" application is:

     ▶   If you are performing this exercise in a class and the instructor provided a copy of
     the installer application, open the Lesson3 folder in StudentMaterials. Remember that
     you created a shortcut to the StudentMaterials folder in your Dock.

▶   If you downloaded the installer application with the App Store, open the Applications folder. You can do this in the Finder by choosing Go menu > Applications or by using the keyboard shortcut Command-Shift-A.

3   Control-click the "Install macOS Sierra" application, and choose Show Package Contents from the shortcut menu that appears.

For more about packages, see **Reference 12.2, "Examine Bundles and Packages."**

4   Inside the installer package, open the Contents folder, and then open the Resources folder inside that.

5   Drag the file named "createinstallmedia" from the Finder window into the Terminal window.

This inserts the full path to createinstallmedia into Terminal.

6   Switch back to Terminal, and press Return.

This executes the createinstallmedia tool as a command-line program. It prints a usage summary, explaining how to use the tool.

7   Begin another command by typing sudo followed by a space, but do not press Return until step 13.

8   Drag createinstallmedia from the Finder window into the Terminal window again.

9   In Terminal, enter --volume (note that there are two dashes at the beginning) followed by a space.

10   Drag the Install macOS Sierra (or whatever you named it) volume icon from the desktop to the Terminal window.

11   In Terminal, enter the text --applicationpath (again, there are two dashes at the beginning) followed by a space.

12   In the Finder, navigate back to the Applications folder, and drag the "Install macOS Sierra" application to the Terminal window.

At this point, the Terminal command should look something like this (although the lines may wrap differently):

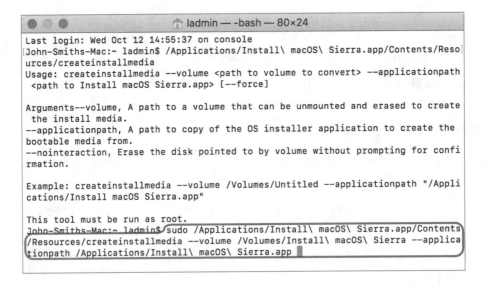

13 Switch to Terminal, and press Return.

This operation requires admin access, so it prompts you for your password.

14 Enter the Local Admin account password (ladminpw, or whatever you chose when you created the account), and press Return. Note that nothing displays as you type.

15 Since this operation will erase the disk, you are prompted to confirm the operation. Verify that the volume name (listed after "/Volumes/") is the one you intend to use; then enter Y and press Return.

16 Wait as the install disk is prepared. This may take several minutes, depending on the type of external drive you are using and its speed.

When the process is complete, it prints "Copy complete." followed by "Done."

17 Quit Terminal.

Test the macOS Sierra Install Disk

If you want, you can now test the installer disk, although you should not actually reinstall macOS.

1 Restart your computer by choosing Apple menu > Restart and then clicking Restart in the confirmation dialog.

2   Press and hold the Option key until you see a row of icons appear on the screen.

3   Click the install disk's icon.

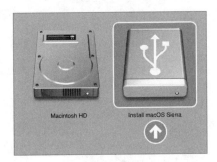

4   Click the arrow that appears under the icon.

The Mac starts up into the installer environment, which is similar to the recovery environment. You can explore it as much as you want, but do not reinstall macOS at this time.

5   When you have finished, choose Apple menu > Restart to restart your computer normally.

Lesson 4

Update macOS

Adding new capabilities is the very reason "software" exists. It's expected that you will add new applications to increase the capabilities of your Mac and, as products are refined, add new software updates as well. In this lesson, you will configure and use the macOS software update technology, which is an automatic method to keep all your Apple-sourced software up to date. You will also explore an alternative to automatic software updates: manually downloading and installing software update packages.

GOALS

▶ Configure automatic software update settings

▶ Automatically update Apple-sourced software

▶ Manually update Apple software

Reference 4.1
About Automatic Software Updates

Keeping current with software updates is an important part of maintaining a healthy computer. For that reason, macOS includes an easy-to-use software update mechanism that automatically checks the Apple servers via the Internet to make sure you're running the latest Apple-sourced software. Automatic software update checking is enabled by default as soon as you start using your Mac.

NOTE ▶ In macOS Sierra, both administrator and standard accounts are allowed to install system software updates via the Mac App Store. If your organization restricts this type of activity for nonadministrator users, you can disable automatic software updates, as covered later in this lesson.

Both automatic and manual software updates require an Internet connection to download update installers. The automatic software update mechanism checks only for updates of currently installed Apple-sourced software, including software bundled with macOS and any software purchased from the Mac App Store.

For most users, Mac App Store software updates require appropriate Apple ID authentication. If you have not previously signed in to the Mac App Store from the computer you're working on, you will be required to authenticate with an Apple ID. If a Mac App Store item was installed with a different Apple ID and you wish to update the item, you must authenticate with the Apple ID used to purchase the original item.

> NOTE ▶ Some software updates require that you also agree to a new Apple Software License Agreement.

> NOTE ▶ Institutions taking advantage of Volume Purchase Program (VPP) Managed Distribution can install Mac App Store items on macOS computers without signing an Apple ID in to the Mac App Store. You can find out more about Apple management technologies at https://support.apple.com/business-education/.

Automatic Software Update Behavior

macOS features automatic software updates for all items you installed from the Mac App Store, including macOS itself and applications created by either Apple or third parties. The Mac App Store provides a single location for updates to all Apple software. The Mac App Store is integrated with Notification Center to let you know as soon as new updates are available.

> MORE INFO ▶ Although it's covered here in terms of its update abilities, using the Mac App Store to install new applications is discussed further in **Lesson 16, "Install Applications."**

By default, important macOS updates (for example, security updates) are automatically downloaded and installed. Other macOS and Mac App Store updates are automatically downloaded in the background but not installed. When updates are ready to be installed, notifications let you know by displaying "Updates Available" in a banner.

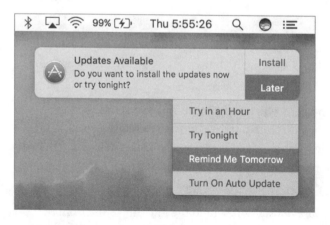

From the banner you can click Install or Later. If you click Install, macOS immediately installs the updates and restarts the Mac if necessary. If you click Later, you can select an option to update the software at a more convenient time. This is useful because some system updates prevent you from using the Mac while the installation completes, and they may require a restart. The last item in the banner menu, "Turn On Auto Update," allows you to enable automatic updates for Mac App Store items. This option is not enabled by default in macOS Sierra.

Again, by default in macOS Sierra, Mac App Store updates don't automatically install. You may receive an additional banner notification to "Turn on Auto Updates?"

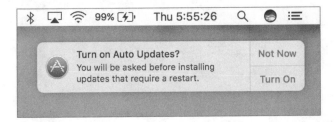

Clicking the Turn On button from this notification enables automatic installation for Mac App Store items. As stated previously, by default, important system and security software are always updated.

After deferring updates, when you are ready to install updates or want to manually check for new updates, you can do so at any time using the following methods:

▶ In the About This Mac window, click the Software Update button.

▶ In the Mac App Store preferences, found in the System Preferences application, click the Check Now button.

▶ In the toolbar of the Mac App Store, click the Updates button.

   TIP When software updates are available, a number badge (indicating the number of available updates) will appear next to the Mac App Store icon, the Mac App Store toolbar Updates button, and the Mac App Store selection in the Apple menu. Also, when you try to restart or shut down the computer, you may be reminded to install available updates.

Mac App Store Update Details

When the Mac App Store opens to show you new updates, each update is listed with information about the software update contents. The information provided includes the update name, the version, and a description. Updates that require a system restart include a notice below the update's name.

The Updates list is split into three sections:

▶ At the very top are macOS software updates. This section contains only updates for macOS itself or updates for Apple software installed outside of the Mac App Store. Thus, updating these system items does not require that the user be signed in to the Mac App Store. (This is similar to the software update mechanism available in earlier versions of macOS.) To simplify the view, multiple software updates in this top section are hidden. You can see all the updates and their descriptions by clicking the More link next to the Update button in the top section.

▶ In the middle are individual Mac App Store updates. Items purchased from the Mac App Store, aside from macOS itself, always appear as separate update items. In this screenshot, both Xcode and Microsoft Remote Desktop require updates. Again, you can see more information about any individual software update by clicking the More link in the description. If the Install macOS Sierra application is still on the system, you may also notice that an update appears for this application within the Mac App Store updates. The purpose is to update any older macOS installer with the latest version.

▶ At the very bottom are previously installed updates. This section lists only updates installed by this user from the Mac App Store within the last 30 days. It does not list updates installed outside of the Mac App Store or by other users. You can view a complete list of installations by using System Information, as covered later in this lesson.

NOTE ▶ If you don't believe the items listed in the Updates view to be accurate, you can refresh available updates by choosing Store > Reload Page from the menu bar or by pressing Command-R.

To install a single update, simply click the corresponding Update button, or click the Update All button to install all available updates. If none of the updates requires a restart for installation, the software automatically installs without any further interaction.

However, if any of the updates requires a restart after the install process, you are given the option to restart or again defer the installation. If the update items have already been downloaded, a notification displays.

If any of the update items haven't been downloaded, a different dialog appears so that you can confirm you want to download the items and then restart.

In either case, when you select a restart option, the system verifies the downloaded updates, logs out the current user, installs the updates, restarts the system, and then automatically logs back in to the user account that initiated the updates. In the case of an update that requires a restart, through much of the update process the computer will be unusable by the user.

NOTE ▶ Some system updates may require that you accept new Apple Terms and Conditions, verify your Apple ID, or both. In these cases, the update will not complete until a user interacts with these dialogs.

You can, of course, choose the Not Now button, but you will eventually have to restart to take advantage of the new software. Alternatively, if updates requiring a restart are already downloaded, you can choose an automatic installation option from the Later pop-up menu in the restart notification (shown previously) or from the pop-up menu to the right of the Update All button in the Mac App Store. As you can see in the following screenshot of the Later pop-up menu in the Mac App Store, you can choose to automatically defer the software installation and system restart to a time when it's more convenient.

About New Mac Bundled Applications

New Mac computers come with iMovie, GarageBand, Pages, Numbers, and Keynote installed along with macOS. Updating these applications requires that the user's Apple ID owns licenses of the applications. To facilitate this on new Mac systems, a user may "adopt" or "accept" the free application licenses that came bundled with the Mac in the Mac App Store with his or her Apple ID. For more information about accepting these applications, see Apple Support article HT203658, "Accept bundled apps using the Mac App Store."

Older Mac computers upgraded to macOS Sierra that also have a previous version of iMovie, GarageBand, and the iWork suite of applications can upgrade, for free, to the latest Mac App Store versions. The software update process automatically detects these updates, but you have to authenticate with an Apple ID to accept the licenses for the new versions. For more information about updating these applications, see Apple Support article HT201064, "Update iMovie, Pages, Numbers, Keynote, and Apple Remote Desktop apps that came with your Mac."

> **TIP** ▶ Once a user's Apple ID owns a license for an application, that user can install the application on any other Mac by signing in to the Mac App Store. In other words, a user can accept the bundled applications from a new Mac and then sign in on an older Mac to install the latest versions of the applications.

Automatic Software Update Preferences

App Store preferences, accessed via the System Preferences application, enable you to control the software update automation. Changes made in App Store preferences apply system-wide, so these settings will affect all users and how they interact with the Mac App Store.

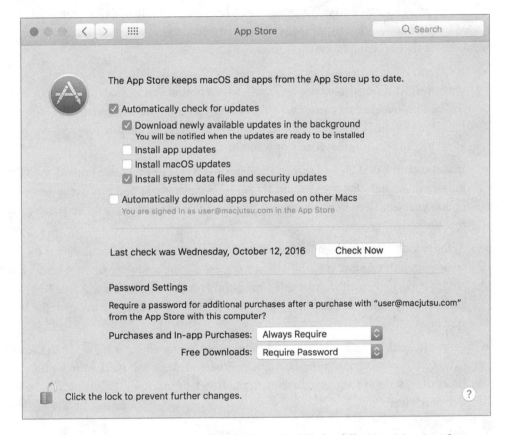

From the App Store preferences, you can enable or disable the following Mac App Store and automatic software update options:

▶ Automatically check for updates—When this option is enabled, the system checks for updates once a day. Note that "check" means that only a small amount of Internet bandwidth is needed to determine whether updates are needed.

▶ Download newly available updates in the background—In this case, the update system may need to use a large amount of bandwidth to download updates. It's not uncommon for macOS system updates to weigh in at over 1 GB. Also, because this option will automatically download updates for applications purchased from the Mac App Store, systems with more applications will likely use more bandwidth.

▶ Install app updates—This option is not enabled by default, but as covered previously, the system prompts you to enable this option via a notification. Once it's enabled, you are notified after new Mac App Store items are automatically updated or if you need to quit the application to apply the update. Importantly, automatic Mac App Store updates do not require a system restart.

▶ Install macOS updates—This option is not enabled by default, but as covered previously, you can also enable this option via a notification. Once it is enabled, you will be notified after new macOS system items are automatically updated, as long as they don't require a restart. Again, any macOS updates that require a system restart allow you to restart immediately or wait until later.

▶ Install system data files and security updates—If Apple deems these updates important enough that they should always be installed, it's a best practice to leave this option enabled. Keep in mind, though, that some system and security updates require that the system be restarted.

▶ Automatically download applications purchased on other Macs—This feature is disabled by default. If this feature is enabled, when you are signed in to the Mac App Store with an Apple ID, new installations made from another Mac using the same Apple ID will automatically install on this Mac as well. This is handy for those who use multiple Mac systems.

▶ Password Settings—These settings likewise apply only if a user is signed in to the Mac App Store with an Apple ID. Adjusting these settings will reduce the number of times users have to authenticate their Apple ID when making multiple purchases and free purchases.

In App Store preferences, you can also click the Check Now/Show Updates button to manually open the Updates section of the Mac App Store.

MORE INFO ▶ Standard users can be individually restricted using parental controls, which include the ability to block access to the Mac App Store. You can find out more about parental controls in Lesson 5, "Manage User Accounts," and more about the Mac App Store in **Lesson 16, "Install Applications."**

Reference 4.2
Manually Install Updates

Before the Mac App Store or automatic software updates, all Mac software was acquired and installed manually. Fortunately, the Mac operating system has always featured relatively simple software installation. In fact, many applications require only that the user copy a single application file to the local Applications folder. On the other hand, more complex software may require multiple resources to be placed in a variety of specific locations on your Mac.

A prime example of a complicated software installation is any system software update. In some cases, it may be more convenient to manually install an update, as opposed to using automatic software update via the Mac App Store. For example, perhaps you need to install a particularly large software update for a system with limited Internet bandwidth. It may be better to manually download the update to a portable flash disk at a location with more bandwidth, and then use the flash disk to apply the update to the Mac that needs it. An experienced macOS support specialist will always have an external disk with the most common large updates handy for just such an occasion.

TIP ▶ You have the option of manually downloading and installing Apple software updates. You can find all Apple updates at http://support.apple.com/downloads/. After you download the updates, use the Installer application to apply them.

Installer Application

The Installer application makes complicated application installations simple. Often, software developers will create an "installer package" with all the instructions and resources necessary for the Installer application to set up the new software on your system.

BrotherPrinterDrivers.pkg

NOTE ▶ Third-party software developers may choose to use a proprietary, non-Apple installer for their product. These installers do not use the PKG or MPKG file type and often behave differently from the Apple Installer.

Double-clicking one of these software installer packages opens the Installer application and begins the installation process. Much like the macOS installation process, the Installer application guides you through the steps necessary to install or update software. This may include agreeing to software licenses, selecting a destination, selecting package options, and authenticating as an administrator user.

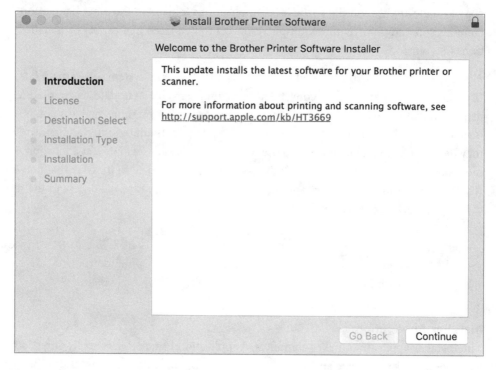

Unlike the Mac App Store, the Installer application requires administrator access to install many items. This security mechanism is in place because anyone is allowed to make and distribute traditional macOS installer packages, including those who may have nefarious goals. Another mechanism in macOS, known as Gatekeeper, also provides an additional level of protection against unknown installation packages and software. You can find out more about application installations and Gatekeeper in **Lesson 16, "Install Applications."**

> **TIP** In an effort to save space, after installation is complete, you will be prompted to delete the original installer package since it's often no longer needed.

Advanced Installer Features

If you're curious about what an installation package is actually doing to your Mac, you have two ways to find out. First, you can view the Installer log at any time while using the Installer application by choosing Window > Installer Log or pressing Command-L. The Installer log is a live view of any progress or errors reported during the installation process.

TIP After installation, you can access the Installer log from the /Applications/ Utilities/Console application. Once Console is open, select the /var/log/ folder in the Reports column and then the install.log item in the log list column.

The second method allows you to inspect the contents of an installer package before installation. After opening an installer package in the Installer application and passing the initial welcome and license screens, you can preview the list of files to be installed by choosing File > Show Files or pressing Command-I.

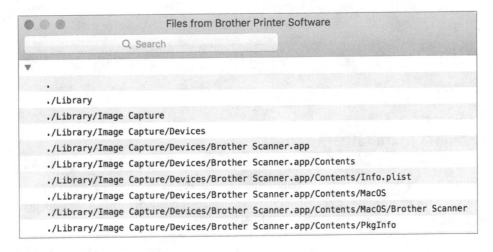

TIP Save time looking for what you need by using the search field in the toolbar when examining the Installer log or file list.

Apple has endeavored to increase the security and reliability of software installation packages by supporting signed packages. These packages contain special code used to validate the authenticity and completeness of the software during installation. This makes it nearly impossible for malicious parties to insert illegitimate files in trusted installation packages. You can recognize a signed installer package by the small lock icon in the far right of the installer window title bar. Clicking this icon displays details about the signed package, including its certificate status.

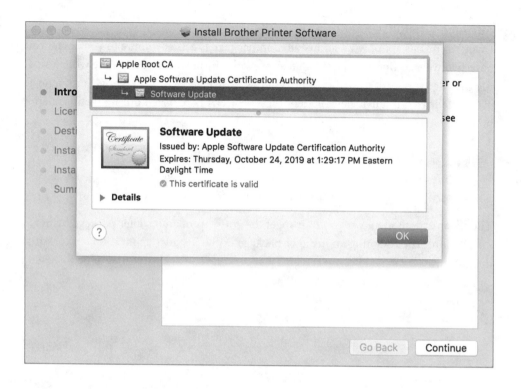

Reference 4.3
Examine Installation History

The automatic software update mechanism in macOS makes it incredibly easy for the average user to maintain an up-to-date system—so much so that the user often isn't even aware of how many updates or installations have been applied. Yet from a support perspective, it's important to know exactly which installations have taken place.

As you may have seen, the update screen in the Mac App Store shows recently installed updates. However, this list of updates doesn't show the complete history of all installations, but only recent installations from the Mac App Store, and only for the currently logged-in user account.

Fortunately, the System Information application features a complete installation history report. To view this history, open /Applications/Utilities/System Information, and then select the Installations item in the left column. This interface shows all software installed via the Mac App Store or the Installer application, including both new and update installations from either Apple or third parties. You can see the name, version, acquisition source, and date installed.

Software Name	Version	Source	Install Date
Gatekeeper Configuration Data	80	Apple	9/9/15, 12:03 AM
Core Suggestions Configuration Data	699	Apple	9/9/15, 12:03 AM
MRT Configuration Data	1.2	Apple	9/9/15, 12:02 AM
OS X		Apple	9/6/15, 12:30 AM
XProtectPlistConfigData	1.0	Apple	9/5/15, 10:22 AM
Evernote	6.1	3rd Party	9/1/15, 10:29 PM
Gatekeeper Configuration Data	78	Apple	9/1/15, 1:43 AM
MRT Configuration Data	1.1	Apple	9/1/15, 1:43 AM
CoreLSKD Configuration Data	8	Apple	9/1/15, 1:42 AM

XProtectPlistConfigData:

Version: 1.0
Source: Apple
Install Date: 9/5/15, 10:22 AM

kmwtogo › Software › Installations › XProtectPlistConfigData

Exercise 4.1
Manually Install Software Updates in a Classroom

▶ **Prerequisites**

▶ This exercise is for students performing these exercises in a classroom environment. If you are following these exercises independently, perform Exercise 4.2, "Manually Install Software Updates Independently," instead.

▶ You must have created the Local Admin account (Exercise 2.1, "Configure a New macOS System for Exercises," or Exercise 2.2, "Configure an Existing macOS System for Exercises").

If your instructor has chosen to download any software updates and distribute them as part of the student materials, you can follow these steps to install them. Your instructor will tell you whether you need to do this.

Install Updates from StudentMaterials

1   In the Finder, open the Lesson4 folder in the StudentMaterials folder. Remember that you created a shortcut to the StudentMaterials folder in your Dock.

2   For each software update in this folder (note: your instructor may additionally specify an order in which they should be installed), do the following:

▶   Open the disk image file. After a short time, a new volume mounts. It contains the update package.

▶   Open the update package. The installer opens and walks you through the installation process.

▶   Continue through the installer prompts, and agree to the license agreement if required.

▶   When prompted, authenticate as Local Admin again (password: ladminpw, or whatever you chose when you created the account). Installing software updates manually requires administrator privileges.

▶   When each update has installed, click Close or Restart as appropriate.

3   Repeat these steps until all the updates have been installed.

4   If you did not restart, eject the disk image or disk images before proceeding. You can do this by Control-clicking in the background of the image's window and choosing Eject from the shortcut menu or by using the Eject button next to the disk image's name in the Finder sidebar.

Exercise 4.2
Manually Install Software Updates Independently

▶ **Prerequisites**

▶   This exercise is for students performing these exercises independently. If you are performing these exercises in a classroom environment, perform Exercise 4.1, "Manually Install Software Updates in a Classroom," instead.

▶   You must have created the Local Admin account (Exercise 2.1, "Configure a New macOS System for Exercises," or Exercise 2.2, "Configure an Existing macOS System for Exercises").

If you want to keep a copy of an update or want to install additional software (such as printer drivers) available for download from the Apple Support site, this exercise shows you how to download and install updates manually.

Download an Update from the Internet

1   Open Safari.

2   Navigate to https://support.apple.com/downloads/.

   This page shows the featured updates Apple has made available for download. If you do not see the update you want, you can either click one of the categories under "Browse Downloads by Product" or use the Search Downloads field to find the update you need.

   The following screenshots use the Savin Printer Drivers package as an example, but you can choose any update for which your computer is eligible.

3   When you find the update you want to install, click its Download button.

4   Wait for the download to complete. Note that a progress indicator in the Safari Downloads button, near the top right of the window, shows the status of the download.

5   Click the Downloads (down-arrow icon) button near the top right of the window.

6   Click the View (magnifying glass icon) button next to the update you downloaded.

   Your Downloads folder opens in the Finder, and the disk image containing the update is selected.

Install the Update

1   Open the disk image file.

The disk image mounts, and you will see the installer package it contains.

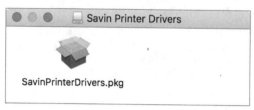

2   Open the installer package.

The installer opens and walks you through the installation process.

3   Continue through the installer prompts, and agree to the license agreement if required.

4   When prompted, authenticate as Local Admin (password: ladminpw, or whatever you chose when you created the account).

Manual software updates usually require administrator privileges to install.

5   After the update installs, click Close or Restart as appropriate.

6   If you are prompted to move the installer to the trash and if you do not want to reuse the package on another Mac, click "Move to trash."

7   If you did not restart, eject the disk image before proceeding. You can do this by Control-clicking in the background of the image's window and choosing Eject from the shortcut menu or by using the Eject button next to the disk image's name in the Finder sidebar.

Exercise 4.3
Use Automatic Software Update

▶ **Prerequisite**

▶ You must have created the Local Admin account (Exercise 2.1, "Configure a New macOS System for Exercises," or Exercise 2.2, "Configure an Existing macOS System for Exercises").

In this exercise, you will use the automatic update feature of the Mac App Store to check for, download, and install updates for macOS. You will also see how to view installed software and updates.

Check Your App Store Preferences

1   From the Apple menu, choose System Preferences.

2   Select the App Store preference pane.

Notice that by default the system automatically downloads new updates in the background and then notifies you when they are ready.

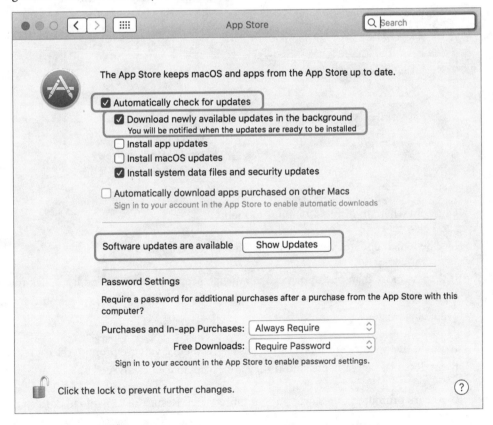

Near the middle of the preference pane, there is a line that either shows the last time updates were checked (and has a Check Now button) or indicates updates are available (and has a Show Updates button).

3 Click the Check Now or Show Updates button.

The App Store application opens, and its Updates tab is selected. Note that you can also open the App Store application directly from the Apple menu.

Update Your Software

1 Wait as the App Store checks for new software.

2 If you see a message that says "No Updates Available," your computer is up to date. Skip the rest of this section and proceed to "Check Installed Updates."

3 Click the small triangle next to the Update All button. A pop-up menu appears, with options to install updates later.

4 Click elsewhere to dismiss the pop-up menu.

5 Decide which updates you want to install on your computer.

6 If there is more than one update, you can click More to see a detailed list. Click the Update buttons for the updates you want to install, or click Update All if you want all available updates.

7 If any of the updates are subject to license agreements, you are prompted to agree to them. Read the agreements, and if they are acceptable, click Agree.

8 If you are prompted to restart your computer, click Restart or Download & Restart.

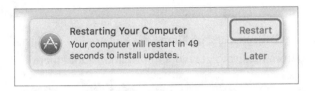

9   If a dialog appears asking if you want to automatically update macOS, click Not Now to keep your current update preference.

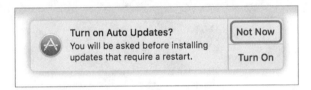

10 If the update restarted your computer, log back in to the Local Admin account. If you are prompted to sign in with your Apple ID, select "Don't sign in," click Continue, and then click Skip in the confirmation dialog.

11 Reopen the App Store application and check for additional updates. Some updates must be installed in sequence, so you may have to repeat the update process several times.

12 When all updates have been installed, quit the App Store and System Preferences.

Check Installed Updates

1   Hold down the Option key while you choose System Information from the Apple menu. Note that the System Information menu item appears in place of About This Mac only when the Option key is held down.

System Information opens and displays its report.

2   In the Software section of the sidebar, select Installations.

A list of installed software and updates appears, including the updates you just installed. You can select specific updates from the list to get more information about them.

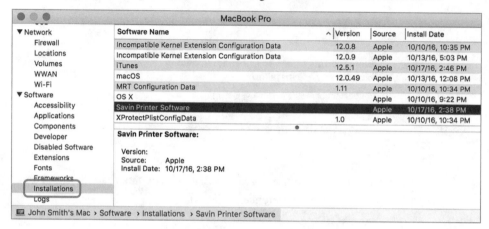

3   Quit System Information.

User Accounts

Lesson 5

Manage User Accounts

One of the hallmarks of a traditional computer operating system is support for multiple user accounts. UNIX operating systems, like macOS, have a long history of providing such services. Apple has made many improvements to the UNIX functionality, such as advanced user-management features and streamlined administration tools, all with traditional Apple ease of use.

In this lesson, you will explore the technologies that allow individuals to log in and use a Mac. You will also learn how to create and manage multiple user accounts in macOS Sierra.

Reference 5.1
About User Accounts

With the exception of macOS Recovery or single-user mode, you must log in with a user account to perform any task on a Mac. Even when the computer has just been started up and is showing the login window and you haven't yet authenticated, the system is still using a handful of system user accounts to maintain background services. Every single file and folder on a Mac computer's hard disk, every item and process, belongs to some type of user account. Consequently, you need a thorough understanding of user accounts to effectively administer and troubleshoot macOS.

> **NOTE** ▶ This lesson focuses on user accounts that are available only to a single local Mac. Network user accounts, however, are available to multiple Mac computers and are hosted from shared directory servers. You can find out more about Apple management technologies at https://support.apple.com/business-education.

User Account Types

The majority of home Mac users are only aware of, and therefore only use, the account created when their computer was initially set up with Setup Assistant. macOS is engineered to mimic a single-user operating system by default. As a security precaution, macOS defaults to requiring a user login even if only a single user account is created for the computer. This behavior is also necessary if the user is to enable FileVault.

macOS also supports multiple simultaneous user accounts. Several types of user accounts are available to facilitate different levels of access. Essentially, you choose a specific account type to grant the defined level of access that best meets the user's requirements.

User accounts are categorized into five types: standard accounts, administrator accounts, the guest account, sharing-only accounts, and the root account. Apple has made these different account types available to provide greater flexibility for managing user access. Because each account type is designed to allow different levels of access, you should also be aware of each account type's potential security risk.

Standard Accounts

Standard accounts strike the best balance between usability and security; they are also commonly used when multiple people share a computer. This account type is very secure, assuming an appropriate password is set. Standard accounts have read access to most items, preferences, and applications. Standard accounts also have full control over their own home folder, which allows them to install applications into their own home folder.

Standard user accounts are allowed to use nearly all the resources and features of the Mac, but they generally can't change anything that might affect other users on the system. The lone exception to this rule is that standard account users can install application and system updates from the Mac App Store. This ability includes applying system updates, which obviously have systemwide effects.

Even though standard accounts are allowed full access to the Mac App Store, they are not allowed to manually modify the /Applications folder or use other installation methods that attempt to modify shared parts of the system. This means that standard account users are not allowed to install many items that are distributed outside the Mac App Store. This may seem unfair for developers who don't distribute via the Mac App Store. However, Apple has instituted tight controls over Mac App Store distribution that provide assurance that the content remains safe for standard account users to install.

If your organization needs to restrict users' ability to install their own applications, install system updates, or install Mac App Store items, then you should create managed accounts.

A managed account is a standard account with parental controls enabled, as covered in Reference 5.3, "Restrict Local User Access."

Administrator Accounts

Administrator accounts aren't much different from standard accounts, with one important distinction: administrator accounts are part of the admin group and are allowed full access to all applications, preferences, and shared resource locations, like /Applications and /Library. Thus, administrator account users are allowed to install and run most software as long as they successfully authenticate when the installer application asks for authorization.

By default, administrator account users do not have access to other users' items outside of shared items like the Public folders. Despite this, administrator account users can bypass these restrictions both in the graphical environment and using Terminal, if needed.

Because an administrator account is the initial account type created when the Mac is configured for the first time using Setup Assistant, many use this as their primary account type. This is advantageous because it lets the user change literally anything on the computer, as is required for system management. The downside is that this user is allowed to make changes or install software that can render the system insecure or unstable.

Additional administrator accounts can be used for daily tasks, but this isn't always the best idea, because, again, all administrator accounts are created equal. In other words, all administrator accounts have the ability to make changes to virtually anything on the system, including deleting or changing the passwords to other administrator user accounts. Administrator users can also change the administrator rights for any other user account, either disabling current administrators or changing standard users into administrators. Further, opening poorly written or intentionally malicious software as an administrator user could cause harm to any user's home folder items or compromise the security of the system.

Most significantly, though, any administrator user can enable the root account or change an existing root account password using the Directory Utility application, located in the /System/Library/CoreServices/Applications folder. For these reasons, you should seriously consider limiting the number of administrator user accounts on your Mac systems. Additional standard accounts can be created for more secure daily use, but managing macOS requires access to at least one administrator account.

> **MORE INFO** ▶ As a default on macOS Sierra, System Integrity Protection (SIP) prevents all user account types from modifying core system files. You can find out more about SIP in **Lesson 13, "Manage System Resources."**

Guest Account

Because enabling the guest account may be considered a security risk, it is disabled by default on macOS. Once enabled, the default guest account is similar to that of a nonadministrator user, but without a password. Anyone with physical access to the computer can use it to log in.

However, when the guest user logs out, the guest account's home folder is deleted, including any home folder items that would normally be saved, like preference files or web browser history. The next time someone logs in as a guest, a brand-new home folder is created for that user.

Even though the guest home folder is deleted every time a guest logs out, the obvious security risk here is that literally anyone has access equivalent to that of a standard user account, including access to the /Users/Shared folder and users' Public folders. Unlike the guest user's home folder, the contents of these other folders remain after the guest logs out. This means a guest user could execute some potentially nasty applications or fill your disk with unwanted files. Guest users can also restart or shut down your Mac, potentially allowing them to compromise the system during startup.

Fortunately, parental controls enable you to restrict the guest account from running unapproved applications or restarting the Mac. Giving the guest account only limited access, as covered in Reference 5.3, "Restrict Local User Access," can provide a safe mechanism for temporary user access. Additionally, you can change the access permissions on shared folders so that the guest account is not allowed to copy any items to your disk. Changing file and folder permissions is covered in **Lesson 11, "Manage Permissions and Sharing."**

> **NOTE ▶** Enabling Find My Mac on a system will also enable the guest account for local login. It's a trap—for the thief! The intent is that a stolen Mac will be locked when found; however, the culprit can choose Guest as a login option upon system startup or wakeup, which allows limited access to the system. Assuming the default settings, the thief would be allowed only to select a Wi-Fi network and use Safari. When the stolen Mac is back online, the owner can use Find My Mac to locate it. You can find out more about this in **Lesson 7, "Manage Security and Privacy."**

Sharing-Only Accounts

macOS allows you to create user accounts that have access only to shared files and folders. Sharing-only accounts have no home folder and cannot log in to the Mac computer user interface or Terminal. Sharing-only user accounts are, by default, allowed file sharing access to users' Public and Drop Box folders, so, like the guest user, these users could potentially fill the disk with unwanted files.

Sharing-only user accounts cannot log in to the Mac otherwise, and can be required to use a password, so designating sharing accounts is generally much safer than using the guest account for file sharing. You can further control sharing-only account users' access to your files by adjusting file and folder permissions

Root Account

The root account, also known as the System Administrator account, is turned off by default on macOS clients, and for good reason: the root account has unlimited access to everything on a Mac. A user with access to the root account can read, write, and delete any nonsystem file; modify any setting; and install any software. Since many system processes run as the root account, it needs to exist on the system; otherwise, macOS wouldn't be able to start up.

The potential for nefarious activity is quite high with root account access. To help prevent abuse of this account, the default macOS configuration does not have a password set for the root account, and therefore you cannot log in with the account.

However, as covered previously, any administrator user can choose to enable the root account or change an existing root account password using the Directory Utility application. Again, because it only takes an administrator account to initially access the root account, strictly limiting administrator usage is the key to safeguarding the root account.

> **NOTE** ▸ Anyone with access to macOS Recovery can reset the password for any local account, including the root account. If security is a concern in your environment, it's highly recommended that you enable FileVault, set a firmware password to restrict macOS Recovery access, or both. Enabling FileVault is covered in **Lesson 10, "Manage FileVault."** Setting a firmware password is covered in Lesson 8, "Manage Password Changes."

Local Group Accounts

Essentially, a group account is nothing more than a list of user accounts. Groups are primarily used to allow greater control over file and folder access. macOS uses several dozen built-in groups to facilitate secure system processes and sharing. For instance, all user accounts are members of the staff group; administrator user accounts are also members of the admin group; and the root account has its own group, known as wheel. Using groups to manage sharing is discussed in **Lesson 11, "Manage Permissions and Sharing."**

NOTE ▶ Standard accounts are always members of the staff group, and administrator accounts are always members of both the staff and admin groups.

Reference 5.2
Configure User Accounts

Once you have a fundamental understanding of macOS user accounts, you're ready to create new users and manage existing users. In this section, you'll examine both simple methods and more complex, yet more flexible, methods for managing local user accounts.

Users & Groups Preferences

In macOS, the Users & Groups preferences window in System Preferences is the primary interface for managing local user accounts, local group accounts, and login settings. From this preference pane, local users can manage basic settings for their own accounts, and any user with administrator privileges can unlock this pane and manage attributes for all local accounts.

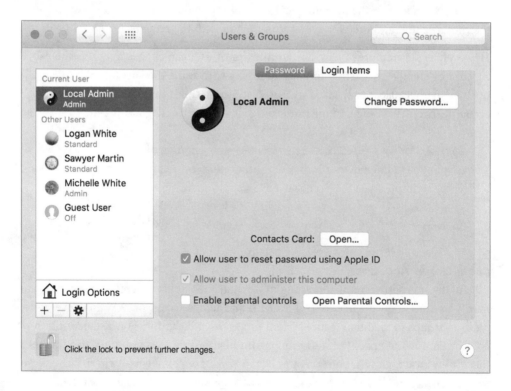

Creating New User Accounts

From the Users & Groups preferences, after authenticating as an administrator, you can manage any account by selecting it from the list and then modifying items to the right. Create a new account by clicking the small plus button at the bottom of the Users & Groups list. A dialog appears where you can define the basic attributes for the new user account.

The pop-up menu at the top of the user creation pane allows you to define the type of local user account being created: Administrator, Standard, Managed with Parental Controls, or Sharing Only. When creating a new local user account, you should enter a full name, an account name, and the initial password for the user. You can also enter an optional Password hint, but the text cannot match the user's password.

> **NOTE ▶** OS X El Capitan allowed you to create local user accounts that use an Apple ID password as the computer login password. macOS Sierra still supports existing accounts with this feature enabled. However, in Sierra you can no longer create new users with this feature enabled. You can find out more about passwords in Lesson 8, "Manage Password Changes."

New User Setup Assistant

The first time new users log in to a Mac, they see the new user Setup Assistant. This is similar to the Setup Assistant process described in Lesson 2, "Set Up and Configure macOS," except abbreviated to the point where the user is asked to enter an Apple ID.

Users can choose not to sign in, but if they do enter their Apple ID and password, the Mac automatically sets up macOS features that require an Apple ID. This includes iCloud services and the Mac App Store. Further, this will set up Find My Mac if it has not been previously enabled for the Mac computer.

> **NOTE ▶** If you're entering an Apple ID that belongs to someone under the age of 13 (made possible via Apple ID for Students, Apple School Manager, or iCloud Family Sharing), no iCloud services are enabled by default.

If two-step verification or two-factor authentication is enabled for the user's Apple ID, the user will also have to provide additional verification. The user may also be asked to enable iCloud Keychain, update to iCloud Drive, and enable iCloud Desktop and Documents, as detailed in **Lesson 17, "Manage Documents."** Finally, the user will be prompted to accept a new Terms and Conditions agreement and enable Siri before the new user Setup Assistant completes.

> **NOTE ▶** Mac computers managed by a school or business may present different Setup Assistant options than the defaults shown here. In certain managed situations, some of the default screens may be skipped and you may encounter additional organizational configuration screens. These differences are controlled by an administrator via mechanisms outside the Mac. Thus, you may have to contact the organization's primary administrator to properly complete the new user Setup Assistant process.

User Account Attributes

Although the login window lets you log in to the Mac environment, it's the Open Directory system that's responsible for maintaining the account information. Open Directory stores local user account information in a series of XML-encoded text files located in the /var/db/dslocal/nodes/Default/users folder. This folder is readable only by the System Administrator (root) account, but if you were to inspect these files, you would discover they are organized into lists of user attributes and their associated values.

Fortunately, most of these attributes can also be easily accessed from Users & Groups preferences. An administrator can access these normally hidden user account attributes by using a secondary (or Control-) click on a user account to display the Advanced Options dialog.

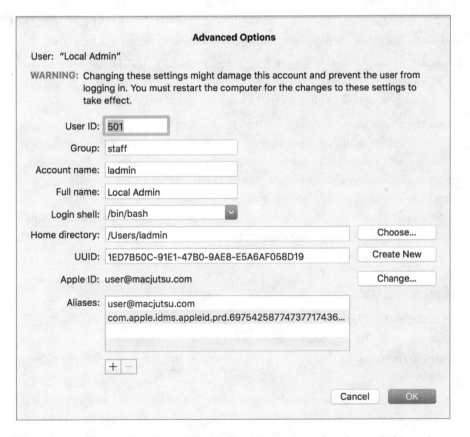

Each user has a variety of attributes that define the account details. And although you can easily edit these attributes to make a desired change or fix a problem, you can just as easily break the account by entering improper information. For example, you can restore access to a user's home folder by correcting the Home Directory information, or you can accidentally prevent a user from accessing his or her home folder by mistyping this information.

User account attributes include the following:

▶ User ID—A numeric attribute used to identify the account with file and folder ownership. This number is almost always unique to each account on a single system, though overlaps are possible. User accounts start at 501, whereas most system accounts are below 100. It's important to note that the user ID is only "unique" from those of other users on the local system. Every other Mac system uses similar ID numbers, so between computers, this uniqueness is lost. For example, every first user created on a Mac computer will have the ID number 501. Further, if you delete a user, that user's ID is now up for grabs, and the system will reuse it for a new user.

▶ Group—The user's primary group. As covered previously, the default primary group for all local users is the staff group. This means that when you create a new file, it belongs to your user account and to the staff group.

▶ Account name—Sometimes also referred to as "short name," this is the name used to uniquely identify the account and by default also to name the user's home folder. A user can use either the full name or the account name, interchangeably, to authenticate. However, no other account on the system can have the same account name, and it cannot contain any special characters or spaces. Special characters not allowed include commas, slashes, colons, semicolons, brackets, quotes, and symbols. Allowed characters include dashes, underscores, and periods.

▶ Full name—The full name of the user. It can be quite long and contain nearly any character. However, no other account on the system can have the same full name. You can easily change the full name later, at any point.

▶ Login shell—This file path defines the default command-line shell used in Terminal by the account. Any user who is allowed to use the command line in Terminal has this set to /bin/bash by default. Both administrator and standard users are given this access by default.

▶ Home directory—This file path defines the location of the user's home folder. All users except for sharing users, who do not have home folders, have this set to /Users/<name>, where <name> is the account name.

▶ Universally Unique ID (UUID)—Sometimes also referred to as Generated UID, or GUID, this alphanumeric attribute is generated by the computer during account creation and is unique across both space and time. Once the attribute is created, no system anywhere will ever create an account with the same UUID. It is used to refer to the user's password and for group membership and file permissions. It's important to note that while UUIDs may be truly unique, one Mac won't be able to identify another's UUID. In other words, UUIDs created on one Mac are not known by another. Thus, locally created UUIDs cannot be used between Mac computers for mutual identification.

▶ Apple ID—Used to associate the local Mac user account with an Apple ID that can be used to reset the local account password. This is configured automatically if the user enters an Apple ID during Setup Assistant or signs in to iCloud. However, setting or changing an Apple ID from the Advanced Options pane in Users & Groups does not affect the user's iCloud service configuration.

▶ Aliases—Used to associate the local Mac user account with other service accounts. For example, a user's Apple ID can be associated with a local account. This attribute is optional for macOS, but it is required for integration with Apple Internet services like iCloud and its Back to My Mac feature.

NOTE ▶ Local user account passwords are stored as an encrypted attribute to enhance security. Password management is covered in detail in Lesson 8, "Manage Password Changes."

Reference 5.3
Restrict Local User Access

macOS includes an extensive collection of managed preferences that let you further restrict what users can and cannot do. Apple labels these managed preferences "parental controls," but they are also applicable in business and institutional settings. Because parental controls are designed to further limit standard user accounts, they cannot be applied to an administrator user.

MORE INFO ▶ Parental controls make up a limited subset of a much more extensive profile management system known as mobile device management (MDM). macOS Server includes an MDM service called Profile Manager. You can find out more about Profile Manager in macOS Server at www.apple.com/macos/server/. You can find out more about Apple management technologies like MDM at https://support.apple.com/business-education/.

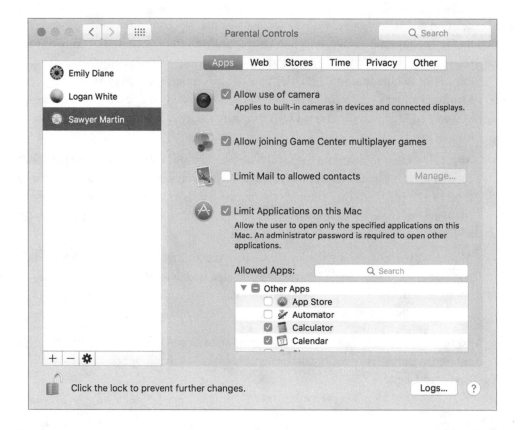

TIP ▶ You can use the Action pop-up menu (gear icon) at the bottom of the Parental Controls user list to copy and paste complex settings from one user to another. From this menu you can also enable the ability for parental controls to be remotely managed from another Mac computer.

Management options available via parental controls are organized into the following functions:

▶ Apps—Disallow use of the camera and Game Center, limit contacts in Mail, and limit the user to only specific applications.

   MORE INFO ▶ Find out more about restricting access to the Mac App Store in **Lesson 16, "Install Applications."**

▶ Web—Enable automatic Safari website content filtering, or manually manage a list of permitted websites or a combination of both automatically and manually permitted websites.

▶ Stores—Disable iTunes and iBooks stores, restrict explicit music, restrict explicit sexual content, and limit age ratings for content.

▶ Time—Set weekday and weekend time-usage limits.

▶ Privacy—Limit changes to privacy settings, thus preventing users from choosing which applications and services can access potentially private user information.

▶ Other—Disable system dictation, limit editing of printers and scanners, prevent burning of optical discs, restrict explicit language in Dictionary, prevent modification of the Dock, and enable Simple Finder for a simplified user interface.

▶ Logs button—Maintain Safari, Messages, and application usage logs. The logs show both allowed and attempted-but-denied access.

NOTE ▶ Most third-party applications don't honor the parental controls content filters or account limit settings. Examples include the Firefox browser and the Outlook email client. You can, however, easily remedy this by using parental controls to restrict access to those applications, as described earlier.

Reference 5.4
Configure Login and Fast User Switching

The login process may seem simple, but because it's the front door to your Mac, you, as an administrator, should become familiar with the security options for managing login behavior. Primarily, these options provide either higher security or greater accessibility. Additionally, macOS allows multiple users to be logged in at the same time via fast user switching. However, this feature is not without issues inherent to having multiple users attempting to access resources simultaneously.

MORE INFO ▶ Login behavior can also be managed remotely via an MDM service like Profile Manager.

Manage User Login Items

Individual users can adjust the items that automatically open during login from the Login Items pane of the Users & Groups preferences. These settings can only be accessed locally when logged in as the user. Even administrator users cannot manage other users' login items unless they log in as the user they wish to manage.

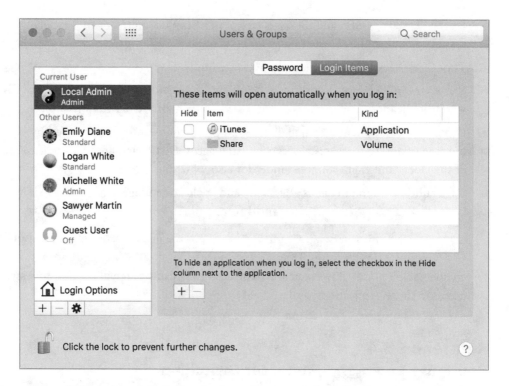

A user can add login items, including both applications and Finder destinations, by dragging them into the Login Items list or by clicking the Add (plus) button and then browsing for the item. Removing items is as simple as selecting an item from the list and clicking the Remove (minus) button. Also note the Hide checkbox, allowing the user to define an application that should open but then hide itself from view. This option is useful for applications that provide a background function that doesn't require you to see the application itself, like a streaming music application.

Manage System Login Window Options

You can adjust systemwide behavior of the login window from the Users & Groups pane by authenticating as an administrator user and then clicking Login Options at the bottom of the user accounts list.

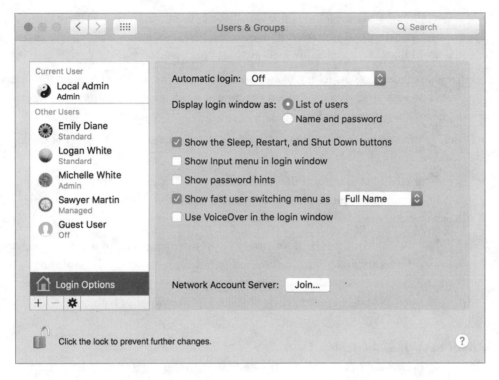

Login window options include the ability to:

▶ Enable or disable automatic login as the Mac starts up. This option is off in macOS by default, unless during the macOS Setup Assistant process the user deselected the option to require a password for login. Obviously, you can define only one account for automatic login.

▶ Choose whether the login window shows a list of available users, the default setting, or blank name and password fields. Choosing to have name and password fields is more secure.

▶ Select the availability of the Restart, Sleep, and Shut Down buttons at the login window. Mac computers in environments that require more stringent security should not have these buttons available at the login window.

▶ Specify whether users can use the input menu. This allows users easy access to non-Roman characters, like Cyrillic or Kanji, at the login window.

▶ Determine whether the login window will show password hints after three failed password attempts. This may seem like an insecure selection, but remember that password hints are optional for each user account.

▶ Disable the fast user switching menu and adjust the look of the menu item. In other words, the fast user switching menu can appear as the user's full name, the account name, or the generic user icon.

▶ Enable users to take advantage of VoiceOver audible assistant technology at the login window.

▶ Configure the Mac to use accounts hosted from a shared network directory. Again, you can find out more about Apple management technologies at https://support.apple.com/business-education.

> **TIP** ▶ You can configure a short three-line message for the login window from Security & Privacy preferences, as covered in Lesson 7, "Manage Security and Privacy." If your organization requires a full login banner, you can configure it via the instructions in Apple Support article HT202277, "About policy banners in OS X."

About Fast User Switching

Often, two users want to use a Mac at the same time. Although it's not possible for two users to use a Mac simultaneously, it is possible for multiple users to remain logged in to a Mac at the same time.

Fast user switching lets a Mac move between user accounts without users having to log out or quit open applications. This allows a user to keep work open in the background while one or more other users are also logged in to the computer. Returning users can later resume tasks instantly, right where they left off.

> **NOTE** ▶ Fast user switching is not recommended for or compatible with network user accounts.

Fast user switching is enabled by default in macOS, but the fast user switching menu doesn't appear until additional local user accounts are created. This menu item appears on the far right, next to the Spotlight search menu. By default, the fast user switching menu appears as your user account full name. If you don't see this menu item, you can turn it on from the Login options pane of Users & Groups preferences. When another user is logged in, you can initiate the switch to another user by simply selecting that user's name from the fast user switching menu and then entering the appropriate password.

TIP ▶ You can move the fast user switching menu item, or any other menu item on the right side of the menu bar, by dragging the item while holding down the Command key.

Fast User Switching Contention Issues

Apple has made fast user switching a reliable feature. Many of the built-in macOS applications are fast user switching savvy. For instance, when you switch between accounts, iTunes automatically mutes or unmutes your music, Messages toggles between available and away chat status, and Mail continues to check for new messages in the background. In some circumstances, resource contention may occur when more than one user attempts to access an item.

Examples of fast user switching resource contention include:

▶ Application contention—Some applications are designed such that only one user at a time can use them. If other users attempt to open these applications, either they encounter an error dialog or the application simply doesn't open. Most of the applications that fall into this category are professional applications, which tend to be resource intensive, so it's better to keep only one instance running at a time.

▶ Document contention—Sometimes one user has a document open and remains logged in with fast user switching, often preventing other users from fully accessing the document. As an example, Microsoft Office applications such as Word and Excel allow other users to open a document as read-only and display an error dialog if the user tries to save changes. Other applications do not allow other users to open the document at all. In the worst-case scenario, an application allows two people to edit the file simultaneously but will save only changes made by the user who saved last. In this case, the application's developers simply didn't account for the possibility that two users might edit the same document at the same time, so you often won't even see an error message.

▶ Peripheral contention—Many peripherals can be accessed by only one user at a time. This becomes a fast user switching issue if a user leaves an application running that has attached itself to a peripheral. The peripheral will not become available to other applications until the original application is quit. Examples of this include video cameras, scanners, and audio equipment.

Fast User Switching Storage Issues

Fast user switching also has interesting ramifications for nonsystem disks. For example, if one user attaches an external storage device, the disk is available to all other users on the system, even if they weren't logged in when the storage was attached. Mounted disk images are handled a bit more securely. Only the user who mounted the disk image has full read/write access to it. However, other users may still have read access to the mounted disk image.

Shared network volumes remain secure in a fast user switching environment. By default, only the user who originally connected to the share can access it. Even if multiple users attempt to access the same network share, the system automatically generates multiple mounts with different access for each user. The exception to this rule is network home folder shares used by network accounts. While one network user can successfully log in, additional network users from the same server will not be able to access their network home folders. For this reason, fast user switching does not support network accounts.

Resolving Fast User Switching Issues

Unfortunately, because each resource and application can act differently, fast user switching issues are not always consistently reported or readily apparent. macOS doesn't have a "fast user switching is causing a problem" dialog. Still, if you are experiencing access errors for files, applications, or peripherals, your first step should be to check whether any other users are still logged in. If so, have them log out and then reattempt access to the previously inaccessible items.

If you cannot log out the other users—perhaps because they are currently unavailable and you don't know their passwords—your options are to force the other users' suspect applications to quit or to force the other users to log out by restarting the Mac. Changing a logged-in user's password isn't an option at this point, because administrators cannot manage user accounts that are currently logged in. These accounts will be dimmed and not available in Users & Groups preferences, as shown by the Michelle account in the following screenshot.

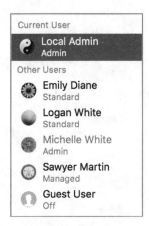

Thus, an administrator will have to either force the other users' applications to quit or restart the Mac to free up any contested items or make any changes to the logged-in users. Neither option is ideal, because forcing an application to quit with open files can result in data loss. If you have no other choice, though, you can force an open application to quit, using techniques covered in **Lesson 18, "Manage and Troubleshoot Applications."**

TIP ▸ If you have already set the master password, you can reset a currently logged-in user's password from the login window using the master password. Setting the master password and resetting a user's password is covered in Lesson 8, "Manage Password Changes."

However, attempting to restart reveals another fast user switching issue: if any other users are still logged in, an administrator will have to force those users' open applications to quit in order to restart. The system makes it easy for an administrator to force these applications to quit via an authenticated restart dialog, but once again, this may cause data loss to any open files.

Exercise 5.1
Create a Standard User Account

▶ **Prerequisites**

   ▶ You must have created the Local Admin account (Exercise 2.1, "Configure a New macOS System for Exercises," or Exercise 2.2, "Configure an Existing macOS System for Exercises").

   ▶ This exercise is required for most of the remaining exercises, so do not skip it.

You already created an administrator account during the initial configuration of your computer. In this exercise, you will create an additional account to gain a better understanding of the user experience. The next user account will be a standard user. It is a best practice to use a standard user account for day-to-day use. You should use the Local Admin account only for system administration tasks such as software installation and system configuration, and you can perform most of these tasks while logged in as a standard user, simply by providing the administrator account's name and password.

You will also have the option to link the new account to an Apple ID to allow access to Apple iCloud services. This is not required but is recommended and will enable you to do other exercises later in this guide that take advantage of iCloud.

Create a Standard User Account

These steps guide you through account creation.

1   If necessary, log in as Local Admin (password: ladminpw, or whatever you chose when you created the account).

2   Open System Preferences, and click the Users & Groups preferences.

3   Unlock the Users & Groups preferences by clicking the Lock button and authenticating as the Local Admin user.

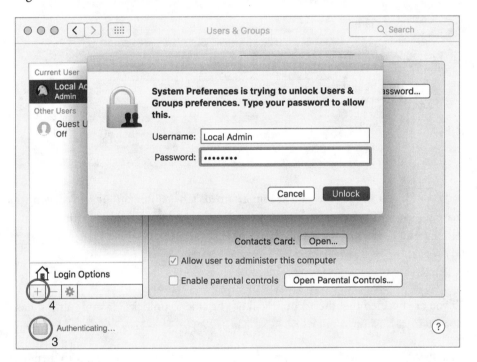

4   Click the New User (+) button beneath the account list, and enter the following information:

New Account: Standard

Full Name: Chris Johnson

Account Name: chris

If you are performing this exercise in a class, enter chris in the Password and Verify fields. If you are performing this exercise on your own, select a more secure password for the Chris Johnson account. Be sure to remember the password you have chosen, as you will need to reenter it periodically as you use this computer. If you want, you can provide a hint to help you remember the password.

NOTE ▸ If you already have an account named "Chris Johnson" or "chris," you will have to use a different name here and then remember to use your substitute name throughout the rest of the exercises.

5   Click Create User.

6   If you are notified that the account will not be able to unlock FileVault until it has logged in at least once, click OK.

7   If a dialog appears with an "Automatic login is turned on. Do you want to turn it off?" prompt, click Turn Off Automatic Login.

Note that because you authenticated as an administrator, you could configure several other account properties here, including changing Chris's user icon, granting Chris admin rights, or using parental controls to limit the account.

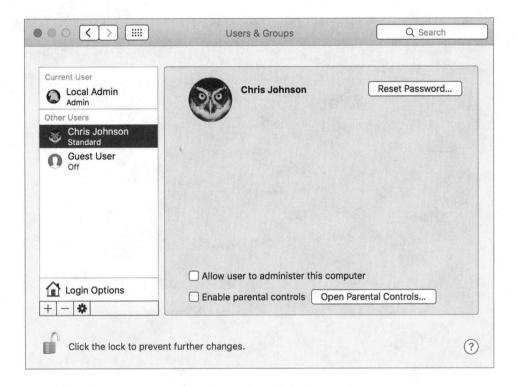

Log In to the New User Account

In these steps you log in to Chris's user account to verify that it was created correctly.

1   From the Apple menu, choose Log Out Local Admin.

2   In the dialog asking if you are sure, click Log Out.

3   At the login screen, select Chris Johnson and enter the password.

You are now logged in as Chris Johnson. Since this account is not yet tied to an Apple ID account, a screen appears to allow you to configure an Apple ID. There are several ways to do this. Choose the appropriate one for your situation:

▶   If you are performing these exercises in a classroom environment, the instructor will provide you with an Apple ID to use with the "Option 1: Link Chris Johnson with an existing Apple ID" instructions that follow.

▶   If you are performing these exercises on your own and have an existing Apple ID that you want to use, you can use your own Apple ID with the "Option 1: Link Chris Johnson with an existing Apple ID" instructions.

▶   If you are performing these exercises on your own and do not have an existing Apple ID or prefer to use a new Apple ID for these exercises, follow the "Option 2: Create a New Apple ID" instructions that follow.

NOTE ▶ If the Sign In screen does not appear, your computer may be having trouble reaching the iCloud servers over the Internet. In this case, you may proceed with the exercise by skipping ahead to the "Adjust Chris Johnson's Preferences" section, but you will need to create an Apple ID in order to perform the iCloud sections in later exercises. After troubleshooting your Internet connection, you can create an account in the iCloud pane in System Preferences.

Option 1: Link Chris Johnson to an Existing Apple ID

If you are performing these exercises in a classroom environment, or wish to use your existing Apple ID for these exercises, follow these instructions to link the Chris Johnson account to the Apple ID.

NOTE ▶ If you are performing these exercises in a classroom environment, you should use an instructor-provided Apple ID rather than your own Apple ID.

1   Enter the Apple ID and password your instructor provided (or for your own Apple ID account), and click Continue.

2   If you used an Apple ID with two-step verification or two-factor authentication, you are prompted to verify your identity via one of your devices. Follow the prompts to finish authenticating.

3   If a Terms and Conditions screen appears, read through the terms, and if they are acceptable, click Agree; then click Agree in the confirmation dialog that appears.

4   If you are prompted to enter the password from one of your other devices, do so.

5   If an iCloud Keychain screen appears, select "Set up later," and click Continue.

6   If an iCloud Drive screen appears, this Apple ID has been used with an older version of OS X or iOS and has documents stored in an older format. See **Reference 17.5, "Use iCloud Drive,"** for more information about iCloud Drive.

▶   If you are performing these exercises in a classroom environment, select "Upgrade to iCloud Drive," click Continue, and then click Continue in the confirmation dialog that appears.

▶   If you are performing these exercises on your own and want to upgrade your iCloud account's document storage to iCloud Drive, select "Upgrade to iCloud Drive," click Continue, and then click Continue in the confirmation dialog that appears.

▶   If you are performing these exercises on your own and do not want to upgrade your iCloud account's document storage at this time, select Not Now, click Continue, and then click Don't Upgrade in the confirmation dialog that appears.

Note that you can always upgrade later in iCloud preferences.

7   If an "All your files in iCloud" screen appears, deselect "Store files from Documents and Desktop in iCloud Drive," and click Continue.

You are welcome to experiment with this feature on your own, but having it turned on for the Chris Johnson account may interfere with subsequent exercises.

8   If an Enable Siri screen appears, deselect "Enable Siri on this Mac," and click Continue.

9   If you are prompted to set up Touch ID, click Continue, then click Set Up Touch ID Later, then click Continue in the confirmation dialog.

Option 2: Create a New iCloud Account

If you are performing these exercises independently and wish to create a new Apple ID to use in these exercises, follow these instructions to link the Chris Johnson account to a new Apple ID.

NOTE ▶ Do not use this option in a classroom environment. Apple limits the number of Apple ID accounts that can be created using this method on a particular computer, so doing this on a classroom computer may interfere with future classes. If you are using your own computer for these exercises and already have an Apple ID, you might also want to use it (with the Option 1 instructions) to avoid affecting your computer's quota.

1   In the "Sign In with Your Apple ID" window, click "Create new Apple ID."

2   If you are notified that you cannot create an Apple ID because "This Mac is no longer eligible to create Apple ID accounts," your computer has reached the number of accounts it is allowed to create. In this case, you have two options:

▶   You may create an Apple ID account on another Mac computer or iOS device, and then click the Back button and follow Option 1 (the preceding section) to use the new account.

▶   If you cannot create an Apple ID account on another device, you can click Continue, and then skip ahead to the "Adjust Chris Johnson's Preferences" section of this exercise. In this case, you will not be able to perform the iCloud sections in later exercises unless you create an Apple ID on another device, and then use the iCloud pane of System Preferences to sign in to iCloud for the Chris Johnson account.

3   In the first "Create an Apple ID" screen, use the pop-up menus to enter your birthday, and then click Continue.

4   Enter your name.

5   Depending on whether you want to create an Apple ID linked to an existing email address or create a new iCloud.com email address, do one of the following:

▶   To use an existing email address, enter the address in the Email address field.

> ▶ To create a new iCloud.com email address, click "Get a free iCloud email address," and then enter the account prefix you would like.

6   Choose a password, and enter it in the "password" and "verify password" fields.

7   Click Continue.

If you see a warning that says your Apple ID couldn't be created because the email address you chose is "no longer available" or "in use by another Apple ID," choose a different name.

8   Choose three security questions, enter their answers, and click Continue.

9   In the Terms and Conditions screen, read through the terms, and if they are acceptable, click Agree; then click Agree in the confirmation dialog that appears.

10   In the iCloud Keychain screen, select "Set up later," and click Continue.

11   If an "All your files in iCloud" screen appears, deselect "Store files from Documents and Desktop in iCloud Drive," and click Continue.

You are welcome to experiment with this feature on your own, but having it turned on for the Chris Johnson account may interfere with subsequent exercises.

12   If an Enable Siri screen appears, deselect "Enable Siri on this Mac," and click Continue.

13   If you are prompted to set up Touch ID, click Continue, then click Set Up Touch ID Later, then click Continue in the confirmation dialog.

14   If you linked your Apple ID to an existing email address, the new account is not fully enabled until you verify ownership of the email address. Check your existing email account for a verification request, and follow the instructions in that message.

Adjust Chris Johnson's Preferences

Just as you did with the Local Admin account, you can adjust Chris Johnson's preferences to allow easy access to system files.

1   In the Finder, choose Finder menu > Preferences.

2   Select the options to show hard disks and connected servers on the desktop.

3   From the "New Finder windows show" pop-up menu, choose your system volume (typically Macintosh HD).

4   Click the Sidebar button at the top of the Finder Preferences window.

5   Select "chris" in the Favorites section of the sidebar and "Hard disks" in the Devices section. Note that "Hard disks" should be fully selected (a checkmark in the checkbox), not just partially selected (a dash in the checkbox).

6   Close the Finder Preferences window.

7   Navigate to the /Applications folder (choose Go menu > Applications or press Command-Shift-A).

8   Just as you did in the Local Admin account, drag the TextEdit application into the left side of Chris's Dock.

9   Navigate to /Users/Shared. Since Chris's Finder preferences are set to show the hard disks on the desktop, you can open Macintosh HD from the desktop, open Users, and then open Shared.

10   Drag the StudentMaterials folder into the right side of Chris's Dock.

11   Open System Preferences, and click the Desktop & Screen Saver preferences.

12   Select a different desktop picture.

13   If you like, adjust the Mouse and Trackpad preferences to your personal taste, just like you did in the Local Admin account.

Examine Chris Johnson's Account

1   In System Preferences, open Users & Groups preferences.

Notice that you have different options than you had when logged in as Local Admin. For instance, you cannot allow yourself to administer the computer or turn on parental controls for yourself. You can, however, configure a Contacts card or add login items (which will open every time you log in). Also, you cannot select any account other than your own.

2   In the lower-left corner, click the Lock button, and authenticate as Local Admin (either the full name Local Admin or the account name ladmin). This unlocks Users & Groups preferences and allows you to make changes to other user and group accounts while remaining logged in as Chris.

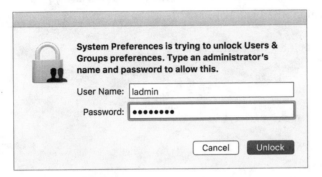

3   Control-click Chris's account in the account list, and choose Advanced Options from the shortcut menu.

The Advanced Options dialog appears and displays the hidden attributes of the Chris Johnson account.

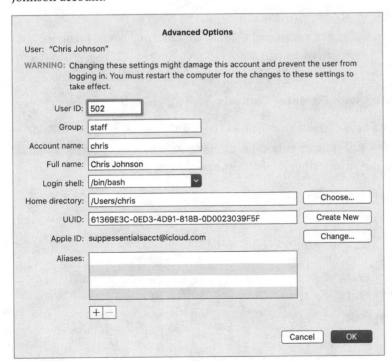

Note that your alias list may have entries relating to your Apple ID. This depends on whether you linked the account to iCloud and exactly how your iCloud account is configured.

4   Click Cancel (or press Command-Period) to dismiss the dialog. It is always a good idea to cancel a settings dialog when you have not made changes to it.

5   Leave System Preferences open for the next exercise.

Exercise 5.2
Create a Managed User Account

▶ **Prerequisites**

> ▶ You must have created the Local Admin (Exercise 2.1, "Configure a New macOS System for Exercises," or Exercise 2.2, "Configure an Existing macOS System for Exercises") and Chris Johnson (Exercise 5.1, "Create a Standard User Account") accounts.

In this exercise, you will create a managed account with parental controls applied and observe the resulting restrictions on that account.

Create an Account with Parental Controls

1   If necessary, log in as Chris Johnson, open Users & Groups preferences in System Preferences, and authenticate as Local Admin (again, remember that you can use the account name ladmin instead of the full name Local Admin).

2   Click the New User (+) button beneath the account list, and enter the following information:

New Account: Managed with Parental Controls

Age: 4+

Full Name: Johnson Junior

Account Name: junior

Password: If you are performing this exercise in a class, enter junior in the Password and Verify fields. If you are performing this exercise on your own, select a more secure password for the Johnson Junior account. Be sure to remember the password you have chosen because you will need to reenter it later.

You may provide a password hint if you want.

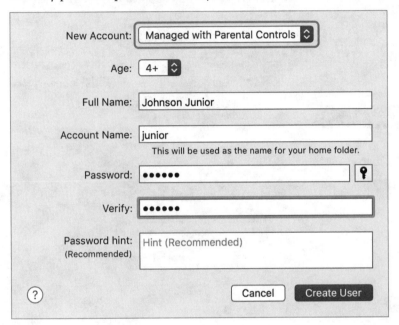

NOTE ▶ If you already have an account named "Johnson Junior" or "junior," you will have to use a different name here and then remember to use your substitute name throughout the rest of the exercises.

3 Click Create User.

4 Verify that Johnson Junior's account is selected in the account list.

Since you created the account as managed, the "Enable parental controls" checkbox is selected.

5 Click Open Parental Controls.

This takes you to Parental Controls, another pane in System Preferences.

6   If you are prompted to authenticate again, enter Local Admin's account name and password.

7   On the Apps tab, make sure that "Limit Applications on this Mac" is selected.

8   Click the Other Apps disclosure triangle to see what applications are allowed by default.

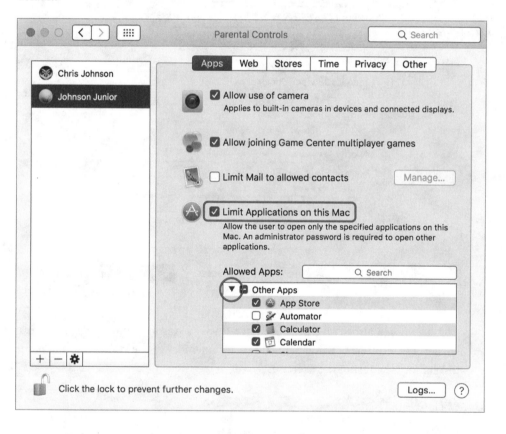

9   Click the Web tab to configure Junior's web restrictions.

10 Make sure the "Allow access to only these websites" option is selected, and leave the default site list.

11 Click through the Stores, Time, Privacy, and Other tabs of Parental Controls to see what other restrictions are available.

12 On the "Other" tab, select Use Simple Finder.

13 Quit System Preferences, and log out of the Chris Johnson account.

Test the Managed User Account

You can now log in to Johnson Junior's user account to see the effects of the parental controls you have configured.

1 At the login screen, select Johnson Junior, enter the password (junior, or whatever you chose), and press Return.

2 If you are prompted to sign in with your Apple ID, select "Don't sign in," click Continue, and then click Skip in the confirmation dialog.

3 If you are prompted to enable Siri, deselect that option, and then click Continue.

Because you restricted Junior's account to the Simple Finder, the interface looks a bit different than normal.

4 If you are prompted to set up Touch ID, click Continue, then click Set Up Touch ID Later, then click Continue in the confirmation dialog.

5 Look at the options available in the Apple, Finder, File, and Help menus. Notice that most of the usual Finder capabilities are missing.

6 In the Dock, click the leftmost of the folder icons (marked with a stylized *A* for Applications).

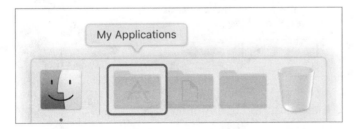

The Simple Finder application launcher opens and shows icons for the applications Junior is allowed to open.

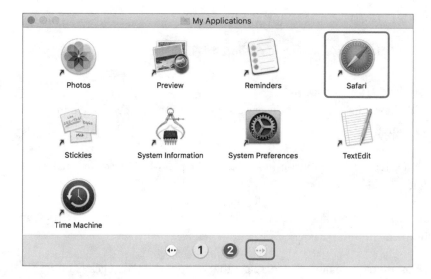

7 Open Safari. If Safari is not shown on the first screen of applications, click the right arrow to show more applications.

Use the Safari address bar to navigate to www.wikipedia.org.

8 Since Wikipedia is not on the list of allowed sites, an error message appears.

9 Click Add Website, and authenticate as Local Admin.

10 If necessary, reload the page by choosing View menu > Reload Page or pressing Command-R.

This time, the Wikipedia front page loads.

11 Quit Safari, and log out as Johnson Junior.

Lesson 6

Manage User Home Folders

Aside from the initial account attributes, such as the account name and password, every other item the user is likely to create or need is stored in that user's home folder. As mentioned earlier, the default location for a locally stored user home folder is /Users/<*name*>, where <*name*> is the user's account name.

Reference 6.1
About User Home Folders

When a new user account is created, the system generates a home folder that contains several default folders. Users can create additional folders to store their items, but it's best practice for them to keep all personal files in their home folder using the default locations. Most applications suggest an appropriate default folder, whereas others don't even ask users and simply use the assigned default folder.

GOALS

▶ Understand user home folder layout and contents

▶ Delete users and archive home folder content

▶ Migrate and restore a user's home folder

All the contents of the default folders inside a user's home folder are viewable only by that user, with the exception of the Public folder. Other users can view the contents of the Public folder, but they cannot add items or make changes, except to put files in the Drop Box folder. Others can add files there, but they cannot see its contents.

It's important to note that, by default, other users are able to view items at the root (or beginning) level of any user's home folder. This is necessary in order to allow other users to navigate into the Public folder. However, this also means that if you store any items at the root of your home folder, other users will be able to see those items. Of course, you can change all these defaults by adjusting file and folder access permissions, as outlined in Lesson 11, "Manage Permissions and Sharing."

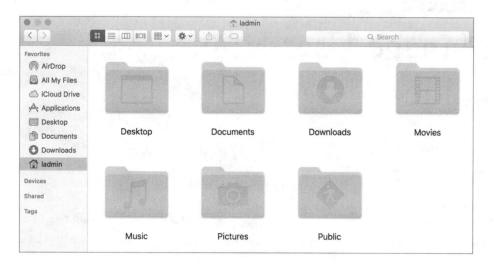

The default items in a macOS user's home folder are:

▶ Desktop—Although many Mac users store files on the desktop, it's not recommended. Along with adding to visual clutter, having an excessive number of items on the desktop may slow system login and Finder actions. More appropriate folders are provided for most user items, as covered here.

▶ Documents—This is the default storage location for any document type that does not have a dedicated folder. For example, Microsoft Office prefers this folder as the default location for all its user documents and Entourage/Outlook profiles. Putting items here is a better alternative than cluttering up the desktop—or is at least a good start.

> **NOTE ▶** With macOS Sierra a user can choose to store their Desktop and Documents folders in iCloud Drive. If this option is enabled, these two folders will appear in the Finder sidebar under iCloud Drive and will not appear in the default home folder location. You can learn more about iCloud Desktop and Documents in **Lesson 17, "Manage Documents."**

▶ Downloads—Internet applications use this folder as the default location for storing downloaded files. Sequestering all Internet downloads to this folder also makes it easier for virus and malware protection utilities to identify potentially harmful files.

▶ Library—Earlier versions of Mac operating systems showed this folder, but since OS X Lion 10.7, it has been hidden from the default Finder view. This folder is a collection point for many user resources. This includes, but is not limited to, user-specific preference files, fonts, contacts, keychains, mailboxes, favorites, screen savers, widgets, and countless other application resources.

TIP ▶ The quickest way to reveal the user's Library folder is to manually go to the folder in the Finder. While holding down the Option key, choose Go > Library to reveal the user's hidden Library folder. You can learn more about hidden items in Lesson 12, "Use Hidden Items, Shortcuts, and File Archives."

▶ Movies—This is the obvious default location for movie files, and it is therefore often preferred by applications such as iMovie.

▶ Music—This is, naturally, the default location for music files, so it's often preferred by applications such as GarageBand, Logic, and iTunes. It is also the default location for synced iOS application resources and backups, which are managed by iTunes. Further, any movies that are part of an iTunes library end up in this folder, as opposed to the default Movies folder.

▶ Pictures—The default location for picture files, which is often preferred by applications such as Photos and Aperture.

▶ Public—The default location for users to share files with other users. Everyone who has access to the Mac, either directly or via remote access, can view the contents of this folder. This folder contains a Drop Box folder, where others can place files that only the owner of the home folder can see.

Optional items commonly found in a Mac user's home folder are:

▶ Applications—This optional folder must be created manually, but the system recognizes it as a special folder. As the name implies, this is the preferred location for users to install their own applications.

▶ Sites—This legacy folder might appear for home folders that have been upgraded or migrated from earlier versions of the Mac operating system. It was the default location for personal websites when Web Sharing was enabled. OS X Mountain Lion 10.8 and later do not support enabling Web Sharing via Sharing preferences; however, other local users can still view the contents of this folder.

Reference 6.2
Delete User Accounts

Deleting a user account in macOS is even easier than creating one. To delete a user account, simply select it from the list of users in the Users & Groups preferences and then click the Delete (–) button at the bottom of the list. An administrator needs to make only one choice when deleting a user account: what to do with the user's home folder contents.

NOTE ▶ If a user has a particularly large home folder, the "delete user account" dialog may take several minutes to appear.

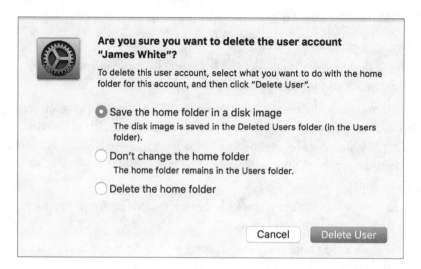

The administrator deleting the user account can choose one of three options:

▶ Save the home folder in a disk image—This option creates an archive of the user's home folder as a disk image file. The disk image file is saved in the /Users/Deleted Users folder, with the account name as the name of the disk image file. Retaining the home folder as a disk image makes it easy to transport it to other systems or to import archived items to another user's home folder.

Keep in mind you must have sufficient free disk space available on the local system disk—essentially, enough to duplicate the original home folder—to create the archive disk image. This process can take quite a bit of time, depending on the size of the folder.

▶ Don't change the home folder—This option leaves the user's folder unchanged, except for its name. It simply appends "(Deleted)" to the home folder's name, letting you know that the user account no longer exists. The deleted user's home folder maintains the same access restrictions as a normal user home folder. Subsequently, however, even though this is a much quicker and more space-efficient method compared to the archival option, an administrator will have to manually adjust file ownership and permissions to access the items. Further, there is the potential that a newly created user account may be granted access to the deleted user's home folder content. Both of these issues can be resolved using methods covered in Lesson 11, "Manage Permissions and Sharing."

▶ Delete the home folder—This option deletes the home folder contents immediately. The items are not stored in a Trash folder before they are deleted, so they cannot easily be recovered if you use this method.

MORE INFO ▶ The method used to delete a user's home folder is equivalent to a quick erase. Thus, the contents are potentially recoverable using third-party data recovery tools if you don't have FileVault enabled. macOS Sierra no longer supports securely erasing a deleted user's home folder. If data security is a concern in your environment, then you should enable FileVault as detailed in Lesson 10, "Manage FileVault."

Reference 6.3
Migrate and Restore Home Folders

Usually, the best way to move or restore a user's account and home folder is with Apple Migration Assistant. But it's not *always* the best solution, and you may have to manually restore a user's account. In this section, you'll explore both Migration Assistant and the manual steps for restoring a home folder.

About Migration Assistant

This handy application is a huge time-saver that enables you to easily transfer all the settings, user accounts, and data from another Mac or Windows computer to your new Mac system.

With Migration Assistant, you can migrate:

▶ From another Mac computer, Time Machine backup, or startup disk—This option scans the local network looking for other Mac computers running Migration Assistant and ready to transfer their information. If you don't have a local network, you can directly connect two running Mac computers via Ethernet, FireWire, or Thunderbolt, and the two of them will create a local network. Alternatively, this option will also scan all locally mounted disks and the local network looking for Time Machine backups. Finally, it will also scan all locally mounted disks for a previous system. This includes any external disks or other Mac computers in target disk mode connected via FireWire or Thunderbolt. Using target disk mode is further detailed in Lesson 9, "Manage File Systems and Storage."

MORE INFO ▶ See Apple Support article HT204350, "Move your content to a new Mac."

▶ From a Windows PC—This option will scan the local network looking for Windows PCs running Migration Assistant and ready to transfer their information. This allows migration from Windows XP SP3 or later, assuming those systems have Windows Migration Assistant installed; it can be downloaded from the Apple Support website.

MORE INFO ▶ See Apple Support article HT204087, "Move your data from a Windows PC to a Mac."

As covered in Lesson 2, "Set Up and Configure macOS," Migration Assistant runs as part of macOS Setup Assistant on new or newly installed Mac systems. However, you can also run this application at any point by opening /Applications/Utilities/Migration Assistant.

NOTE ▶ Before using Migration Assistant, always check for Apple software updates on both the source and destination computers. This process ensures that you are using the latest copy of Migration Assistant on all computers.

NOTE ▶ Migration Assistant can migrate a Legacy FileVault–protected user account to a Mac only during the initial Setup Assistant process.

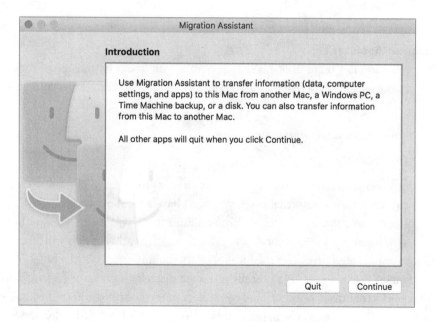

Clicking the Continue button will start the Migration Assistant process; however, you will have to first authenticate a user with administrator rights to start the process. Further, starting the Migration Assistant process will quit all running applications and log out all user accounts.

The Migration Assistant process has three modes: transfer from another Mac source, transfer from a Windows PC source, or transfer to another destination Mac. The first two options assume that you are transferring from another computer source to this Mac as the destination, whereas the last option assumes you are transferring from this Mac as the source to another destination Mac via network. In this case you will need to open Migration Assistant on the destination Mac as well.

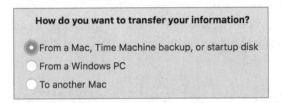

If you choose to transfer from another computer source, Migration Assistant scans all attached disks and the local network for any possible migration sources. Alternatively, you can enter a specific Time Machine server as the source by clicking the Other Server button at the bottom of the Migration Assistant screen.

Once a source is selected, Migration Assistant scans the contents and presents you with a list of items you can migrate. If multiple disks are available on a system, you can choose to migrate that data as well. However, the migration process does not create new partitions on the new system; instead, it creates folders on the new system with the contents of the migrated disks.

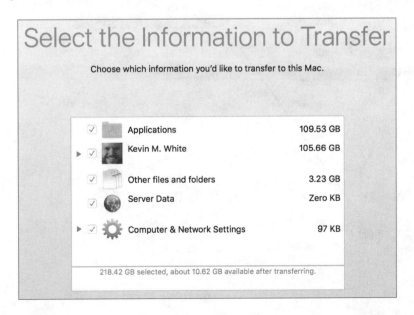

Once you make your selections, you can begin the transfer process. The more data you have selected to transfer, the longer the process will take. Mature systems with lots of data can take several hours to migrate.

Manually Restore a User's Home Folder

In certain situations, you may need to erase and install a new system to repair or update a Mac. Unfortunately, you can't always count on the user having a recent Time Machine backup of the system. Thus, erasing the system disk would also destroy any user accounts on the Mac. In this case, because you're working only with a single Mac, as opposed to moving from one Mac to another, and you don't have a Time Machine backup, Migration Assistant isn't going to work for you.

If you find yourself in a situation like this, where Migration Assistant won't fit your needs, you can manually move the user's home folder data. Although this doesn't require another Mac, it does require that you temporarily copy the user's home folder to another "backup" storage disk. Once you have additional backup storage available, log in to the user's account and, in the Finder, simply drag the home folder to the backup disk. As long as you copy the root of the user's home—the folder with the user's account name—then the Finder copies the entirety of the home folder in one move.

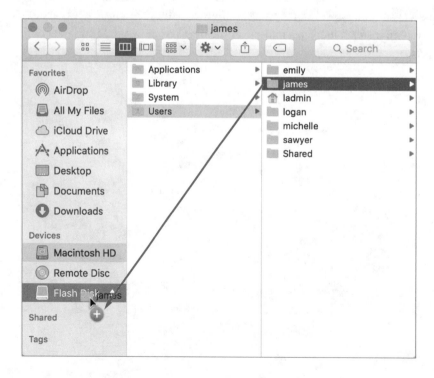

NOTE ▶ If you are creating a copy of another user's home folder contents, you are prompted to authenticate as an administrator user to continue. This is because the default file-system permissions often prevent one user from accessing another user's content. Administrator users are allowed to temporarily override permissions in the Finder if they authenticate.

Once you are sure you have a complete copy of the user's home folder on the backup storage, you can erase the system disk and repair it. With the new system in place and working, first start by creating an administrator account with a different name from the user account to be restored. You must set up this other administrator account because the proper method for manually restoring a user's home folder requires that the user account not yet exist on the system.

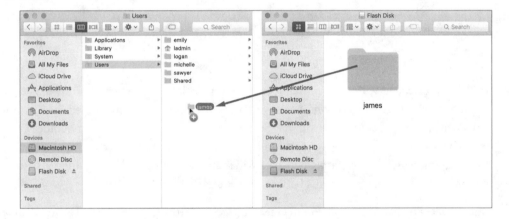

To complete the home folder restore, in the Finder, copy the backup of the user's home folder into the /Users folder, making sure the home folder's name is titled appropriately.

Finally, in the Users & Groups preferences, create the user's account; be sure to use the same account name. Upon creation of the new user account, if the names match, the system will recognize this and prompt you to use the existing folder.

If you click the Use Existing Folder button, the system will associate the manually restored home folder with the newly created user account. This includes setting the proper home folder permissions so that the new user has access to the restored home folder content. If you click the Cancel button, the system will stop the creation of the new user account.

Exercise 6.1
Restore a Deleted User Account

▶ **Prerequisite**

  ▶ You must have created the Local Admin account (Exercise 2.1, "Configure a New macOS System for Exercises," or Exercise 2.2, "Configure an Existing macOS System for Exercises").

In this exercise, you will create a user account and populate the home folder for the user. Then, you will delete the account, preserving the contents of the home folder. Finally, you will create a new account, ensuring that the new user gets the old user's home folder contents. Besides illustrating how to restore a deleted user account, this technique can be used for changing a user's short name. It also provides an alternative to the Migration Assistant method for moving user accounts between computers.

The scenario is that HR asked you to create an account for Marta Mishtuk. Her real name is Mayta Mishtuk, so you'll need to fix the error.

Create Marta Mishtuk's Home Folder

1   If necessary, log in as Local Admin (password: ladminpw, or whatever you chose when you created the account).

2   Open System Preferences, and select the Users & Groups pane.

3   Click the Lock icon, and authenticate as Local Admin.

4   Click the Add (+) button under the user list.

5   Enter the account information for Marta Mishtuk:

New Account: Standard

Full Name: Marta Mishtuk

Account Name: marta

Password: marta

Verify: marta

Do not provide a password hint.

6   Click Create User.

7   Control-click Marta's account, and choose Advanced Options from the shortcut menu.

Now you will take a screenshot of the System Preferences window to record Marta's account attributes for later reference.

8   Press Command-Shift-4, followed by the Space bar.

Your mouse cursor changes into a camera icon, and the region of the screen it is over is highlighted in blue. If you see a crosshair cursor instead, press the Space bar again.

9   Move the camera pointer over the System Preferences window, and then click to record its contents.

This is one of several ways of taking screenshots in macOS. Command-Shift-3 records the entire screen, Command-Shift-4 (without the Space bar) lets you select a rectangular region to record, and Command-Shift-4 with the Space bar lets you select a single window.

The image is saved to your desktop, named "Screen Shot," followed by the date and time it was taken.

10   In the Advanced Options dialog, click Cancel, or press Command-Period, which is a way to select Cancel in most macOS dialogs.

11   Log out as Local Admin.

12   Log in as Marta Mishtuk (password: marta).

13   If you are prompted to sign in with your Apple ID, select "Don't sign in," click Continue, and then click Skip in the confirmation dialog.

14 If you are prompted to enable Siri, deselect "Enable Siri on this Mac," and click Continue.

15 If you are prompted to set up Touch ID, click Continue, then click Set Up Touch ID Later, then click Continue in the confirmation dialog.

16 In the Dock, click the Launchpad icon.

Launchpad gives users an easy way to open applications that aren't in their Dock, without having to navigate to the Applications folder in the Finder.

17 Click the "Other" application group in Launchpad.

18 In the "Other" group, click the TextEdit icon to open TextEdit.

19 In the Untitled document, enter the text This is Mayta's project document. ("Mayta" is not a typo.)

20 Choose File menu > Save (or press Command-S) to save the file.

21 Name the file Project, and save it to Marta's desktop. You can use the shortcut Command-Shift-D to select the desktop.

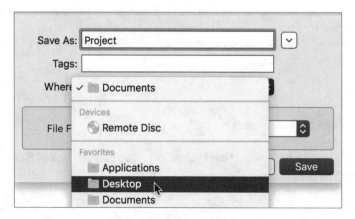

22 Quit TextEdit, and log out of the Marta Mishtuk account.

Delete Marta's Account

You will delete Marta's account, preserving her home folder in a disk image file. A disk image is a file that contains a file system.

1 Log in as Local Admin.

2 Open Users & Groups preferences in System Preferences, if necessary. Unlock the preferences pane.

3 Delete Marta's account by selecting her name and then clicking the Delete (–) button.

4 In the dialog that appears, make sure "Save the home folder in a disk image" is selected.

5 Click Delete User.

While Marta's account is being archived, it is listed in the Users & Groups list as "Deleting Account."

6 Wait for the archive to complete and Marta's account to vanish from the list, and then quit System Preferences.

Restore Marta's Account for Mayta

Marta's files (actually Mayta's) have been preserved in a disk image. Now you need to copy them to Mayta's new home folder so that when the new account is created, she gets her old (the Marta account's) files.

Note that since disk images are portable and easy to store, you could use this technique to re-create the account on another computer, even long after it has been deleted.

1   Navigate to the folder /Users/Deleted Users.

You can reach this folder by opening Macintosh HD from your desktop, opening the Users folder inside that, and then opening Deleted Users inside that.

If you don't have permissions to open the Deleted Users folder, you may be logged in as a standard user. Log out, and log back in as Local Admin.

2   Open marta.dmg.

The disk image opens and displays the contents of the marta account's home folder. However, as Reference 12.1, "Navigate Hidden Items," discusses, an invisible subfolder named Library contains account settings and preferences for the marta account; to fully restore this account, you need to restore the entire home folder, not just its visible contents.

3   Close the "marta" window (but do not eject the disk image). The disk's icon is still visible on your desktop.

4   Select (single-click) the "marta" icon on your desktop.

5   From the Finder's File menu, choose Duplicate (or use the shortcut Command-D).

The Finder copies the contents of the image (including the hidden Library folder) to a folder named "marta" on your desktop.

6   Once the copy finishes, unmount the "marta" volume by clicking the Eject button next to its entry in the Finder sidebar. Note that you may need to scroll to view more of the sidebar to see the icon.

7   Select the new "marta" folder on your desktop, and press Return.

This allows you to edit the folder's name.

8   Change the folder's name to mayta, and press Return.

9   In the remaining Finder window, navigate back to the /Users folder. You can do this by clicking the left arrow in the window's toolbar, by pressing Command-[(left bracket), or by Control-clicking the folder name in the window's title bar and choosing Users from the shortcut menu.

10   Drag the "mayta" folder from your desktop to the /Users folder.

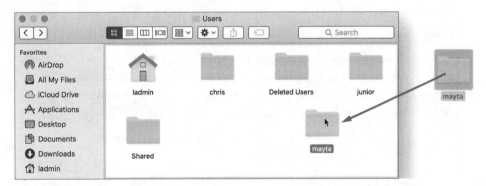

The file permissions on the /Users folder do not allow you to add items to it. The Finder asks you to authenticate as an administrator to override this.

11 Click Authenticate; then enter Local Admin's password, and click OK.

12 Open the "mayta" folder and then the Desktop folder inside that.

You see Mayta's Project document. Since you (Local Admin) created this copy of Mayta's home folder, you own it and have full permission to access it.

Create and Verify Mayta Mishtuk's Account

You will now create the Mayta Mishtuk user account using the restored home folder as the new account's home folder.

1 If necessary, open System Preferences, and select Users & Groups.

2 Click the Lock button, and authenticate as Local Admin.

3 Click the Add (+) button to create another account:

New Account: Standard

Full Name: Mayta Mishtuk

Account Name: mayta

Password: If you are performing this exercise in a class, enter mayta in the Password and Verify fields. If you are performing this exercise on your own, select a more secure password for the Mayta Mishtuk account. Be sure to remember the password you have chosen because you need to reenter it periodically while you use this computer.

You may provide a password hint if you want.

4 Click Create User.

A dialog appears that asks whether you want to use the "mayta" folder for this account.

5   Click Use Existing Folder.

6   Control-click Mayta's account, and choose Advanced Options from the shortcut menu.

7   Open the Screen Shot file on your desktop, and compare the account attributes of Mayta's new account with her original account. The user ID of the old account may have been reused for the new account, but the UUID will be different. Each account is assigned a completely new UUID when it is created.

8   Quit Preview.

9   In the Advanced Options dialog, click Cancel, and then quit System Preferences.

10   Try to reopen the Desktop folder in Mayta's home folder now. If your Finder window is still displaying the Desktop folder, click the back button, and then double-click the Desktop folder. You no longer have permission because the files are now owned by Mayta's new account.

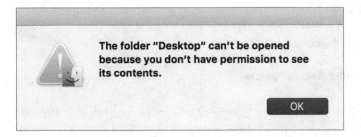

11   Close the Finder window.

Verify Mayta Mishtuk's Home Folder
To make sure Mayta's files are all here, you can explore her restored home folder.

1   Log out as Local Admin, and log in as Mayta.

2   If you are alerted that the system could not unlock Mayta's keychain, click Update Keychain Password, and enter marta (the original password for the Marta Mishtuk account).

For more information about keychains, see Lesson 7, "Manage Security and Privacy," and Reference 8.2, "Reset Lost Passwords."

3   Verify that the Project file is on the desktop.

4   In the Finder, open Mayta's home folder by choosing Go menu > Home (or by pressing Command-Shift-H).

5   Make sure all the usual subfolders are there: Desktop, Documents, Downloads, Movies, Music, Pictures, and Public.

6   Open the Desktop folder, and verify that you see the Project document.

7   Navigate back to the home folder, and then open the Public folder, where you see a Drop Box folder. For more information about these folders, see Lesson 11, "Manage Permissions and Sharing."

In addition to the visible folders inside Mayta's home folder, it should contain an invisible Library folder.

8   Hold down the Option key, and choose Go menu > Library. Note that the Library choice is hidden except when you are holding the Option key.

Mayta's Library folder contains a large number of subfolders. For more information about this folder and its contents, see Reference 12.1, "Examine Hidden Items," and **Lesson 13, "Manage System Resources."**

9   Close the Library folder, and log out as Mayta Mishtuk.

Lesson 7

Manage Security and Privacy

The primary purpose of a multiple-user operating system is to provide all users with a secure work environment. macOS offers a relatively secure out-of-the-box experience for most situations. Yet some situations call for greater security than the defaults afford. This lesson focuses on the built-in advanced security features of macOS and how best to manage and troubleshoot these features.

GOALS

▶ Understand password types and their usage

▶ Manage secrets saved in Keychain

▶ Enable and manage iCloud Keychain

▶ Manage system security and user privacy

Reference 7.1
About Password Security

Most computer systems and services rely on passwords as the primary method for verifying a user's authenticity. There are other, more elaborate systems for proving a user's identity, such as biometric sensors and two-factor random key authentication, but these approaches require additional hardware. It's a pretty safe bet that every computing device is attached to an alphanumeric input device such as a keyboard, so passwords are still the most relevant security authentication method.

About Passwords Used by macOS

If you look closely at the security system used by macOS, you discover that it uses a variety of passwords at different levels to secure the computer. Most users are familiar only with their account password, but the Mac can also have a firmware password, a master password, many resource passwords, and several keychain passwords.

Individual users may use several types of passwords, each with a specific purpose:

▶ Local account password—Each local user account has a variety of attributes that define the account. The local account password is the attribute used to authenticate users so that they can log in to macOS. For security reasons, a user's local account password is stored as encrypted data in the account record.

▶ Apple ID and password—This is a user name and password combination that can be used to authorize many Apple services, including iCloud and various online stores. The creation and use of an Apple ID requires an Internet connection. In addition to providing secure access to Apple services, a user's Apple ID can reset a lost local account password, as covered in Lesson 8, "Manage Password Changes."

   NOTE ▶ OS X El Capitan allowed you to create local user accounts that use their Apple ID password as their computer login. macOS Sierra still supports existing accounts with this feature enabled. However, in Sierra you can no longer create new users with this feature enabled.

▶ Legacy FileVault password—Versions of Mac operating systems prior to OS X Lion 10.7 supported home folder–based encryption. If an earlier system is upgraded or migrated with Legacy FileVault user accounts, the home folders remain encrypted. The password for a Legacy FileVault user account can be reset only by using a known master password. Resetting and disabling Legacy FileVault user accounts is covered in Lesson 8, "Manage Password Changes."

▶ Keychain password—With the exception of the user's account password, macOS protects all other important authentication assets in encrypted keychain files. Each keychain file is encrypted with a keychain password. The system attempts to keep keychain passwords synchronized with the user's local account password. However, you can maintain unique keychain passwords separate from an account password as well. Maintaining synchronization between a user's keychain password and account password is covered in Lesson 8, "Manage Password Changes."

▶ Resource password—This is a generic term that describes a password used by nearly any service that requires you to authenticate. Resource passwords include email, website, file server, application, and encrypted disk image passwords. Many resource passwords are automatically saved for the user by the keychain system. Details on keychain features are covered later in this lesson.

There are also system passwords, which are not associated with an individual user. Again, each has a specific purpose:

▶ Master password—The master password is used to reset standard, administrator, and Legacy FileVault user accounts when users forget their account password. Use of the master password is covered in Lesson 8, "Manage Password Changes."

▶ Firmware password—The firmware password protects the Mac during startup. By default, anyone can subvert system security settings simply by using one of the commonly known startup-interrupt keyboard shortcuts. For example, anyone can hold down the Option key during startup to select an alternate operating system, thus bypassing your secure system. Setting the firmware password prevents unauthorized users from using any startup-interrupt keyboard shortcuts. Setting a firmware password is covered in Lesson 8, "Manage Password Changes."

About Keychain

Much as service workers might keep a keychain containing all the keys needed during their workday, macOS keeps all your resource passwords, certificates, keys, website forms, and even secure notes in encrypted storage. Every time you allow macOS to remember a password or any other potentially sensitive item, it saves it to the keychain system. Only your account password remains separate from all the other items saved to your keychains.

Because so many important items are saved via the keychain architecture, the keychain files themselves are encrypted with a very strong algorithm. They are impenetrable unless you know the keychain's password. In fact, if you forget a keychain's password, its contents are lost forever. Not even the software engineers at Apple can help you—the keychain system is that secure. Yet probably the single best feature of the keychain architecture is that it's entirely automatic using the default settings. Most users never know just how secure their saved passwords are, because the system is so transparent.

The primary tool you use to manage keychains is the Keychain Access application, found in the /Applications/Utilities folder. With this application you can view and modify nearly any keychain item, including saved resource passwords, certificates, keys, website forms, and secure notes. You can also create and delete keychain files, as well as change keychain settings and passwords. Additionally, you can manage web-specific keychain items from the Safari preferences.

About Local Keychain Files

Keychain files are stored throughout the system for different users and resources. Here are a few of note:

▶ /Users/<*username*>/Library/Keychains/login.keychain—This keychain appears with the name "login" when using the Keychain Access application. Every standard or administrator user is created with a single login keychain. As a default, the password for this keychain matches the user's account password, so this keychain is automatically unlocked and available when the user logs in. If the user's account password does not match the keychain's password, it does not automatically unlock during login.

> **TIP** Users can create additional keychains if they want to segregate their authentication assets. For example, you can keep your default login keychain for trivial items and then create a more secure keychain that does not automatically unlock for more important items.

▶ /Users/<*username*>/Library/Keychains/<UUID>—This keychain folder is also created for every user account. This folder contains the keychain database used by the iCloud Keychain service. Use of iCloud Keychain is detailed later in this lesson. Even if the iCloud Keychain service has not been turned on, this local keychain database is still created. When the iCloud Keychain service is not enabled, this keychain appears with the name Local Items in the Keychain Access application. Alternatively, if the iCloud Keychain service is enabled, this keychain appears with the name iCloud in the Keychain Access application. The chosen UUID (universally unique identifier) name of the folder does not match the user's local account UUID, but this item is associated with the user due to its location in the user's home folder.

▶ /Library/Keychains/System.keychain—This keychain appears with the name System in the Keychain Access application. This keychain maintains authentication assets that are not user specific. Examples of items stored here include Wi-Fi wireless network passwords, 802.1X network passwords, and local Kerberos support items. Although all users benefit from this keychain, only administrator users can make changes to it. You'll also find additional keychains in this folder for use by Legacy FileVault and the Apple Push service.

▶ /Library/Keychains/FileVaultMaster.keychain—This keychain doesn't appear in the Keychain Access application by default, but it is created when the system master password is set, so it can be unlocked only with that password. This keychain, as the name implies, is used by the Legacy FileVault and FileVault system disk encryption mechanisms. Managing and troubleshooting Legacy FileVault and the master password are covered in Lesson 8, "Manage Password Changes."

▶ /System/Library/Keychains/—Most of the items in this folder do not appear in Keychain Access application by default. The one item you will see in Keychain Access from this folder is System Roots. This keychain stores root certificates that are used to identify trusted network services. Once again, all users benefit from these items, but as a default in macOS, these items cannot be modified.

NOTE ▶ Both Apple and third-party developers create keychains for securely storing a variety of data. Thus, keychain files with seemingly random names can be found throughout the system. It's best to leave these files alone unless you are specifically instructed by a trusted source to take action to resolve an issue.

Reference 7.2
Manage Secrets in Keychain

To manage all keychain items, including saved passwords, start by opening /Applications/ Utilities/Keychain Access. The default selection shows the contents of the user's login keychain, but you can select another keychain from the list to view its items.

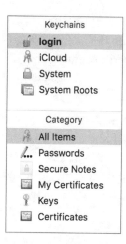

Simply double-click a keychain item to view its attributes. If the item is a password, you can reveal the saved password by selecting the "Show password" checkbox. You'll find that this and other changes often prompt you for the keychain's password. This is a safety measure to ensure that only the keychain's owner can make changes. Once you have authenticated, you can change any attribute in the keychain item dialog, including any saved passwords. You can also click the Access Control tab to adjust application access for the selected item.

NOTE ▶ The iCloud authentication mechanisms create many keychain items that you may not recognize. Many of these are in the form of certificates or keys, the contents of which should not be tampered with. In short, refrain from "cleaning out" keychain secrets that seem unfamiliar.

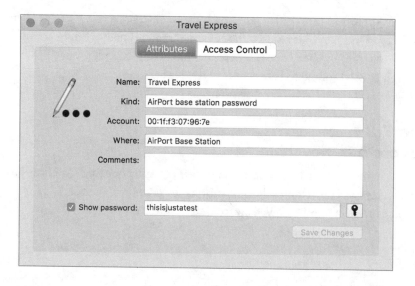

TIP ▶ To easily search through keychain items in Keychain Access, you can filter the list by selecting a keychain Category view on the left, or you can search for a specific item via the Spotlight search in the upper-right corner of the toolbar.

TIP ▶ The safest place to store secure text on your Mac is in keychains. In Keychain Access, you can create a new secure note by choosing File > New Secure Note Item.

Manage Safari Keychain Items

The built-in macOS web browser Safari is a great example of where a user would interact with the keychain system on a daily basis. By default, the AutoFill system in Safari automatically prompts the user to start saving web-form information and site passwords. Further, the latest version of Safari includes new AutoFill features such as the ability to suggest secure website passwords and store credit card purchasing information.

NOTE ▶ Despite the dialog's text, Safari AutoFill doesn't require the iCloud Keychain service. If the iCloud Keychain service isn't enabled, Safari will save secret information to the Local Items keychain.

When the user revisits a site or navigates to a new site with similar form information, Safari AutoFill automatically fills in information for the user, as long as the keychain file is unlocked. Safari also pulls information from the user's contact information, if allowed.

You can find the Safari AutoFill settings by choosing Safari > Preferences from the menu and then selecting the AutoFill tab. These settings give you fine-grained control over what items are automatically saved and filled. Further, Edit buttons allow you to inspect and manage individual items such as website passwords and saved credit cards.

With the exception of the user's contact information, which is stored in the Contacts application, all Safari AutoFill data is securely stored in the keychain system. Thus, you can also view and manage the AutoFill items from the Keychain Access application. The easiest way to find these items in Keychain Access is to enter Safari in the Spotlight search field. Again, double-clicking any item in Keychain Access allows you to inspect that item. However, you can actually see more information about AutoFill items in the Safari preferences.

NOTE ▶ Some websites remember your authentication inside a web cookie, so you might not see an entry in a keychain file for every website that automatically remembers your account. Website cookies can be viewed and deleted from the Security tab of Safari Preferences.

Reference 7.3
Use iCloud Keychain

Previous Mac system versions featured Keychain synchronization through the Apple MobileMe service. Although otherwise functional, this service lacked a very important feature: iOS compatibility. Many of the same secrets are used across the two platforms, so having your secrets shared automatically between devices is hugely convenient. It's even handier given the limited screen size and absence of a physical keyboard on iOS devices, which make managing secrets even more difficult.

Enter iCloud Keychain, supported on Mac computers with OS X Mavericks 10.9 and later and iOS devices with iOS 7.0.3 and later. This service automatically shares your commonly used secrets between devices via iCloud.

> **MORE INFO** ▸ iCloud services are designed with strong personal security in mind, as detailed in Apple Support article HT202303, "iCloud security and privacy overview."

About iCloud Keychain

As covered previously in this lesson, the system automatically maintains two keychains for each local user account: the legacy login keychain and the Local Items/iCloud keychain. Again, the Local Items keychain is renamed iCloud if the iCloud Keychain service is enabled. Note that the previous Keychain Access screenshots in this lesson show the iCloud keychain, as it is the default for users signed in to iCloud via an Apple ID with two-factor authentication.

As the name implies, contents in the iCloud keychain are also stored on the Apple iCloud servers and then automatically pushed to other configured Apple devices. Thus, this service not only provides a secure mechanism for accessing your secrets from any Apple device connected to the Internet, but also acts as a secure backup for your important secrets.

> **NOTE** ▸ Only standard or administrator user account types can take advantage of iCloud Keychain.

At this point, you may notice differences in content between the user's login keychain and the user's Local Items/iCloud keychain. The differences between these two user keychains are caused by technical differences in the keychain storage system. Items in the user's login keychain are stored using an older method that is compatible only with legacy Mac applications. Items in the user's Local Items/iCloud keychain are stored using a newer method compatible only with newer Mac applications and with iOS.

For users upgrading from older versions of the Mac operating system, a background process automatically migrates items from any legacy keychains to the iCloud keychain. Obviously, only the items in the iCloud keychain are saved to iCloud and subsequently pushed to other appropriately configured devices. As new secrets are saved or created on behalf of the user, the keychain system automatically saves compatible items to the iCloud keychain and legacy items to the user's login keychain.

NOTE ▸ Although macOS supports multiple local user keychains, only items saved in iCloud Keychain will be available to other iCloud Keychain–enabled devices.

Importantly, items in the iCloud keychain will never migrate back to the local keychain files. This step would be unnecessary anyway, because as long as your devices can see the iCloud keychain, they can access its content without copying items to a legacy local keychain. Again, if the user chooses to disable the iCloud Keychain service, the iCloud keychain will be renamed Local Items, and the user can choose to keep the secret items intact locally.

Lastly, the user's Local Items/iCloud keychain is accessed using the same password as the user's login keychain. In other words, the password used to unlock and manage the user's login keychain is also used to unlock and manage the Local Items/iCloud keychain. Thus, changes to the login keychain password are automatically applied to the Local Items/iCloud keychain. For this reason, the Keychain Access application does not allow you to change the Local Items/iCloud keychain password.

Create an iCloud Security Code

Keeping the contents of your iCloud keychain safe is of paramount importance. After all, once it's enabled, your secrets are stored in a manner that makes them accessible to anyone on the Internet who knows your credentials. In short, no matter how strong your Apple ID password is, single-factor authentication is still not good enough for the iCloud Keychain service. This is why the iCloud Keychain service is only enabled by default when you use an Apple ID that has two-factor authentication turned on. Alternatively, when you first enable the iCloud Keychain service using an Apple ID without two-factor authentication, the system prompts you to choose an iCloud Security Code that is used to further protect your valuable secrets.

NOTE ▸ It's important to recognize that the iCloud Security Code is a separate security mechanism from two-step verification or two-factor authentication for Apple ID. Again, only Apple IDs lacking two-factor authentication are prompted to set up an iCloud Security Code." For more information about two-factor authentication see Apple Support article HT204915, "Two-factor authentication for Apple ID," article HT205075; "Availability of two-factor authentication for Apple ID;" and HT207198, "Switch from two-step verification to two-factor authentication."

Enabling the iCloud Keychain service using an Apple ID lacking two-factor authentication prompts you to select one of the following security code options:

▶ Code plus verification—The default iCloud Security Code mechanism is a simple code paired with SMS text message verification. This requires that you select a six-digit numeric code and provide a phone number that can receive SMS text messages for further verification.

▶ An advanced option to manually set a complex iCloud Security Code. You can create a code up to 32 characters long, but it's your responsibility to keep track of this code in a safe place.

▶ An advanced option to have a random complex iCloud Security Code generated and then paired with an SMS text message verification. The system first randomly generates a 32-character code, but again, it's your responsibility to keep track of this code in a safe place. Then you provide a phone number that can receive SMS text messages for further verification.

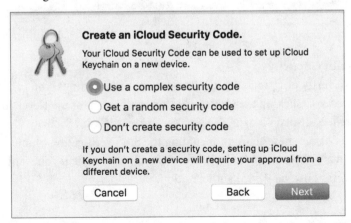

As the preceding dialog states, you do not have to use an iCloud Security Code for initial setup of the iCloud Keychain service. If you choose not to, enabling the iCloud Keychain service on any additional devices requires physical access to another device that has already been configured for the service.

After you have made your choice for the iCloud Security Code, the iCloud Keychain service is enabled for your first device. As described earlier, the iCloud keychain appears in Keychain Access and is made available to all compatible applications and services.

Authorize Device for iCloud Keychain

Again, if you sign into another device using an Apple ID with two-factor authentication, the iCloud Keychain service is automatically enabled. For Apple IDs without two-factor authentication you can grant access for additional devices via a simple device authorization mechanism. The idea is that any device currently configured with the iCloud Keychain service is a trusted device. Thus, any trusted device can be used to verify additional devices for the iCloud Keychain service.

For example, after setup of the iCloud Keychain service on a Mac, when you attempt to enable this service on an iPad, you have to approve this action from the original Mac. Alternatively, if you set up an iCloud Security Code, you can use the code as additional verification instead of device-based authorization.

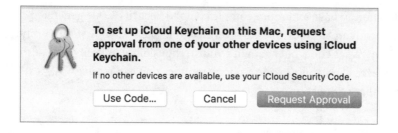

Manage iCloud Keychain Security

If at any point you want to verify or change the iCloud Security Code settings, you can do so from the iCloud preferences. Clicking the Options button to the right of the Keychain item in the iCloud preferences displays a pane showing the current iCloud Security Code settings and allows you to change these settings, including the SMS verification phone number. Note that you can also choose to disable the use of a security code if you want to allow iCloud Keychain access only via device authorization.

NOTE ► If you have an Apple ID with two-factor authentication, there is no Options button next to the Keychain item in the iCloud preferences.

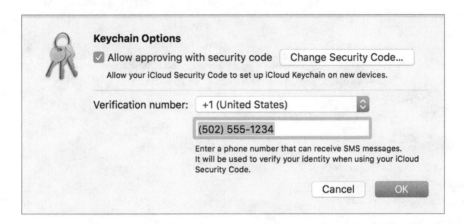

Reference 7.4
Manage System Security

In addition to account passwords and keychain items, there are systemwide security preferences that affect all users on the Mac. Several of these options are disabled by default because the average Mac user would probably consider them inconveniences. However, if your environment requires greater security, these additional security features are indispensable.

Security & Privacy: General Settings

The Security & Privacy preferences pane is a combination of both system settings and personal settings that allow you to tailor the security features of macOS. As with all other system settings, administrator authentication is required to make changes to any items that may affect the system or other users. When using Security & Privacy preferences, note that system settings are dimmed when the lock is present, but personal settings are always available.

The General settings pane provides another location, besides the Users & Groups preferences, for users to change their password.

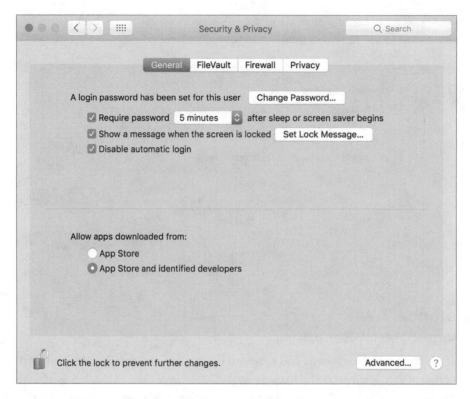

You can also choose to require a password to wake the computer from sleep or screen saver mode and to define a delay before this requirement sets in. Both standard and administrator users can set this for their account, but an administrator cannot set this for every account from Security & Privacy preferences. The exception is that systems with FileVault system disk encryption always require a password on wake. Such systems do not show the option to disable that requirement.

Administrators can also configure a custom message to show at the login window or when the screen is locked. When setting the message, you can press Option-Return to force a new line. However, the system allows for only three lines of text.

The final login option is the ability to disable automatic login for all accounts. This system setting is also always required on systems with FileVault system disk encryption. Those systems do not show the choice to disable automatic login.

Finally, at the bottom of the General pane, you'll find settings for a significant security feature of macOS, dubbed Gatekeeper. This allows administrators to restrict applications downloaded from the Internet based on the trustworthiness of the source. **Lesson 16, "Install Applications,"** covers this topic in greater detail.

Security & Privacy: Advanced Settings

Additional security settings are available to an administrator who unlocks Security & Privacy preferences and then clicks the Advanced button in the lower-right corner.

Administrators can choose to require that users automatically log out of accounts after a certain amount of inactivity and that all system preferences with locking access require an administrator password every time. For example, the default setting allows an administrator user to change Date & Time preferences without actually authenticating. Enabling this option requires an administrator to enter his or her password to use Date & Time preferences.

Security & Privacy: FileVault Settings and Legacy FileVault Settings

This pane is where you enable and configure FileVault system disk encryption (also known as FileVault 2). If a Mac has been upgraded from a system prior to OS X Lion 10.7, you may also see Legacy FileVault settings in the Security & Privacy preferences. This is technology used prior to the current FileVault to encrypt individual users' home folders. Lesson 10, "Manage FileVault," covers both of these topics in greater detail.

Security & Privacy: Firewall Settings

This pane is where you enable and configure the personal network firewall settings. Lesson 23, "Manage Host Sharing and Personal Firewall," covers this topic in greater detail.

Use Find My Mac

From a security standpoint, one of the most significant features of iCloud is Find My Mac. This service helps you locate a lost Mac by allowing you to remotely access the computer's Location Services service. In addition to locating a lost Mac, the service allows you to remotely lock, erase, and display a message on the Mac.

> **TIP** iCloud can also be used to locate a lost iPhone, iPod touch, or iPad. This service is collectively known as Find My iPhone, which is also the name of a free iOS app that can be used to find both Mac computers and iOS devices.

Several prerequisites must be met to use Find My Mac:

▶ The Mac system must have Wi-Fi enabled and have an active Internet connection. If Wi-Fi is disabled, the Mac computer's location cannot be resolved.

▶ The Mac system must have Location Services enabled. If this service hasn't already been enabled during Setup Assistant or from the Security & Privacy preferences, you will be prompted to enable it when you turn on Find My Mac.

▶ The Mac system must have a local Recovery HD partition.

▶ The Mac system must be configured for iCloud with Find My Mac enabled. As covered in Lesson 2, "Set Up and Configure macOS," the initial system setup includes prompts to enable Find My Mac. You can also configure or disable Find My Mac at any time from iCloud preferences. Although multiple users can sign in to most iCloud services on a single Mac, only one iCloud account per device can be enabled for Find My Mac.

Once you configure Find My Mac, you search for a lost device from another computer by accessing the iCloud website: www.icloud.com. Log in with the appropriate iCloud account, and then select Find iPhone on the iCloud homepage. As you can tell from the name, the "Find" services use the same Location Services technology for both iOS and Mac devices, but an iPhone is more vulnerable to loss than a Mac.

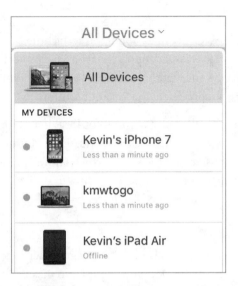

If Find My iPhone is successful, the web interface displays a map with the relative location of all the devices configured for this iCloud account. Selecting a located device on the map allows you to play a sound, send a message, or lock or wipe a device. You can even see the power status in the upper-right corner of the device's view. For example, the following screenshot shows that the portable Mac is almost fully discharged.

TIP ▶ OS X El Capitan 10.11 and later support iCloud Family Sharing, which allows a group of iCloud accounts to access each other's devices when using Find My Mac. This allows you to easily locate a device from another user's device or iCloud account as long as they are part of your iCloud Family Sharing group. However, to prevent unintended actions, the lock and erase commands require additional authentication by the iCloud account that enabled Find My Mac on the device. You can find out more about iCloud Family Sharing at www.apple.com/icloud/family-sharing/.

Both the remote lock and erase functions immediately restart the selected Mac system. The remote lock lets you set a new four-digit PIN for the Mac, and upon restart the Mac prompts you for the new number. If a remote erase is issued, upon restart a Mac protected by FileVault system disk encryption will delete the encryption keys necessary to decrypt the system disk, whereas other Mac computers simply delete the system partition.

Enabling Find My Mac on a system will also enable the guest account for local login. It's a trap for thieves. The intent is that a stolen Mac will be locked when found. The culprit can choose Guest User as a login option upon system startup or wakeup, which allows limited access to the system. Assuming the default settings, the thief would be allowed only to select a Wi-Fi network and use Safari. This enables the stolen Mac to get back online so that the owner can use Find My Mac to locate it.

> **NOTE** ▸ Disabling the Find My Mac feature does not also disable the guest account. Thus, if you intend to permanently disable Find My Mac, you should also disable the Guest User account in the Users & Groups preferences if you'll have no need for it.

Reference 7.5
Manage User Privacy

A primary tenet of Apple design is to create devices and services that protect the user's information. As such, macOS includes a variety of privacy measures that are enabled as a default for every user. However, these measures may prevent functionality that the user would benefit from. In this case, the user may choose to allow access to private information by adjusting settings in a variety of locations covered here.

> **MORE INFO** ▸ You can find out more about Apple's deep commitment to personal privacy at www.apple.com/privacy/.

> **MORE INFO** ▸ Managing privacy for Siri and Spotlight are detailed in **Lesson 14, "Use Metadata and Search Technologies."**

Security & Privacy: Privacy Settings

This pane gives both administrators and standard users the ability to adjust various services' access to personal information. However, in cases where an administrator has specified a privacy selection (enabled or disabled), this choice will override the standard user's ability to make that selection. For example, if an administrator has disabled the ability for Google Chrome to access Contacts information, it will remain disabled for all standard users as well.

When a new application requests information that is considered personal, the system automatically asks you for permission. For example, the Maps application asks you to allow Location Services so that the Mac system can be located for the default map view. Any Mac with Wi-Fi capabilities can use Location Services to identify its location. Thus, Wi-Fi must be enabled to use Location Services.

> **TIP** Anytime an application takes advantage of Location Services, the Location Services status menu appears near the upper-right corner of the screen. The menu item appears as a northeast compass arrow, similar to that seen in the Privacy pane of the Security & Privacy preferences.

From the Privacy pane, a user can view all the applications that have asked for this information and choose to allow or disallow further attempts to collect information. Examples of the types of services an application may request include Location Services, Contacts, Calendars, Reminders, and Twitter, LinkedIn, and Facebook information.

NOTE ▸ The list of items in the Privacy pane varies based on configured services. For example, the Twitter service appears only after the user has configured Twitter in Internet Accounts preferences.

Enabling access for assistive applications in previous versions of macOS was found in the separate Accessibility or Universal Access preferences. In macOS Sierra, you'll find the Accessibility settings listed in the Privacy pane of the Security & Privacy settings.

In macOS you must manually enable access for assistive applications by application. This is because, through the Accessibility mechanism, these assistive applications will be granted access to control computer input and modify the interface behavior. In other words, a malicious or poorly written assistive application has the potential to cause all kinds of trouble throughout the system. Thus, an administrator user must individually allow assistive applications to control the system.

The final privacy setting in the list, Diagnostics & Usage, allows administrators to disable the reporting of diagnostic information to Apple. The primary source of information sent with this option is application hangs or crashes. This information helps Apple resolve recurring issues faster.

About Dictation Privacy

The macOS Dictation feature is enabled and managed via the Dictation pane of the Keyboard preferences. This feature supports a variety of languages, including multiple regional dialects of widespread languages like English and Spanish. When the system is set to one of these languages or dialects in Language & Region preferences, it helps this feature automatically enter the correct text. Further, the Dictation function supports basic text-related spoken commands for formatting and punctuation.

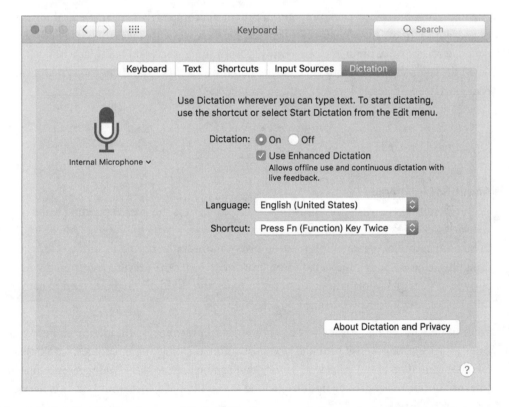

The default behavior for the macOS dictation feature actually sends the spoken audio to Apple servers across the Internet. This may seem like an excessively complex solution, but it's the only way to create a dictation system that contains a huge library of words and doesn't require any user training or excessive local storage. Because of this round-trip between the Mac and Apple servers, the transcription response could be a few seconds.

Also, from a security perspective, this server-based dictation method isn't ideal, because you are literally sending your words directly to Apple's servers. Further, the server-based dictation in macOS also sends other user information, like your Address Book contacts, to provide more accurate transcription. Apple never uses this information for any purpose beyond improving the server-based dictation service, but this may still be unacceptable for those requiring greater privacy.

Alternatively, macOS offers the Enhanced Dictation option, which relies on locally stored assets to perform the transcription. Selecting the Use Enhanced Dictation checkbox downloads the dictation assets, which require roughly 760 MB. In this case, all transcription is completed by the local Mac, and nothing is ever transmitted to the Apple servers.

Obviously, the Enhanced Dictation option provides a completely private method for taking advantage of the macOS dictation feature. Further, when this feature is enabled, user data and recent voice input data are removed from Apple servers. Finally, as a bonus, when the transcription is completed entirely on the local Mac, the dictation system can provide more immediate text feedback as you dictate.

> **MORE INFO ▶** You can find out more about the macOS Dictation feature from Apple Support article HT202584, "Use your voice to enter text on your Mac."

About Safari Privacy

With regard to privacy, another growing area of concern is the ever-expanding reach of website tracking systems. As more user services blossom across the Internet, those looking to take advantage of personal information invent more sophisticated techniques for gathering this data. Although the default web browser, Safari, can't prevent you from giving away your personal information, it can try to block the "hidden" methods used to gather information about your web usage.

You can find additional privacy settings in the Safari preferences window. From here you can manage existing website cookies or adjust automatic blocking of cookies. Cookies are bits of information about your web history that can be used to track your presence on the Internet. Other Safari privacy options include the ability to further limit Location Services and website tracking.

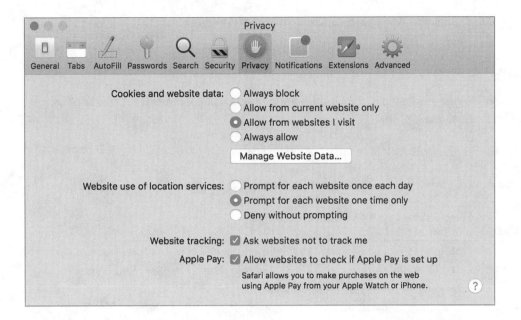

Exercise 7.1
Manage Keychains

▶ **Prerequisite**

▸ You must have created the Chris Johnson account (Exercise 5.1, "Create a Standard User Account").

By default, when users log in to their account, their keychain is automatically unlocked and remains unlocked until they log out. However, in environments where more security is desired, it's possible to configure the keychain to lock after a period of inactivity or when the computer goes to sleep.

In this exercise, you will explore various keychain management techniques.

Configure the Keychain to Lock Automatically

1   Log in as Chris Johnson (password: chris, or whatever you chose when you created the account).

2   In the Finder, open the Utilities folder by choosing Go menu > Utilities or by pressing Command-Shift-U.

3   In the Utilities folder, open Keychain Access.

4   Choose Keychain Access menu > Preferences (or press Command-Comma).

5   Select "Show keychain status in menu bar."

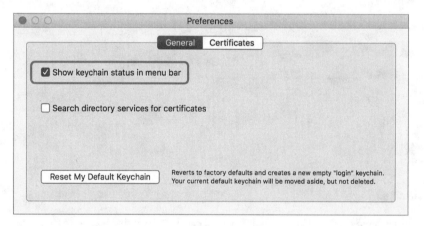

This places a Lock icon in the menu bar, making it more convenient to perform various security-related functions.

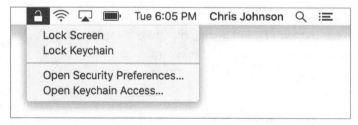

6   Close the Preferences window.

7   Choose Edit menu > Change Settings for Keychain "login."

8   Select both "Lock after 5 minutes of inactivity" and "Lock when sleeping."

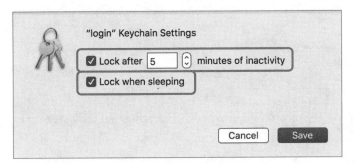

9   Click Save.

10 Open System Preferences, and select the Security & Privacy pane.

11 If necessary, deselect the "Require password" option.

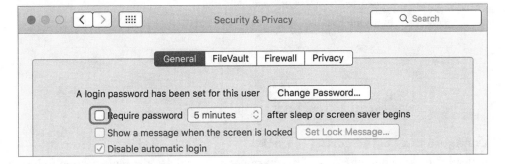

12 If you are prompted to enter Chris Johnson's password (chris, or whatever you chose when you created the account), do so and click OK.

    This is a per-user preference setting, so administrator authorization is not required.

13 If a confirmation dialog appears, click Turn Off Screen Lock.

14 Choose Apple menu > Sleep.

15 Wake the computer by pressing any key.

16 Click the keychain status (lock icon) menu bar item.

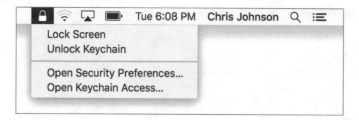

Notice that the lock icon appears locked, not open, indicating that the keychain is now locked.

17 Under the keychain status menu bar item, choose Unlock Keychain.

18 Enter Chris's password and click OK.

The lock icon opens and your keychain unlocks.

Configure the Login Session to Lock

Instead of locking only the keychain, you can configure the entire login session to lock on sleep or after a period of inactivity.

1 If necessary, open System Preferences, and select the Security & Privacy pane.

2 Select "Require password," and choose "immediately" from the pop-up menu.

3   Choose Apple menu > sleep.

> **NOTE ▸** There are many other ways to activate this lock. Among other options, you could use the Desktop & Screen Saver preferences to configure a hot corner to activate the screen saver, or if your keyboard has a media eject key or power button, press Control-Shift-(media eject or power) to put your display to sleep.

4   Wake the computer by pressing any key.

You see an unlock screen similar to the login screen, but with only Chris's account shown.

5   Enter Chris's password and press Return.

Your session unlocks. Note that when you entered the password, the keychain unlocked along with the login session.

To simplify the rest of the exercises, you can now relax these security measures.

6   If you want, you can either deselect the "Require password" option or change the lock period in the Security & Privacy preferences. If necessary, click Turn Off Screen Lock in the confirmation dialog.

7   Quit System Preferences.

8   In Keychain Access, choose Edit menu > Change Settings for Keychain "login."

9   If you are prompted to, enter Chris's password to unlock the keychain.

10 Deselect both "Lock after 5 minutes of inactivity" and "Lock when sleeping."

11 Click Save.

Store a Password in a Keychain

Your keychain already has a number of automatically created entries. In this section, you will create an entry manually.

1   Open the StudentMaterials/Lesson7 folder. Remember that you created a shortcut to StudentMaterials in your Dock.

2   Open the file named "Chris's private files.dmg."

This disk image is encrypted, so the system prompts you for the password to open it.

3   Select "Remember password in my keychain."

4   Enter the password private.

5   Click OK.

6   If you are prompted to enter the keychain password, enter Chris's account password (chris, or whatever you chose when you created the account), and click OK.

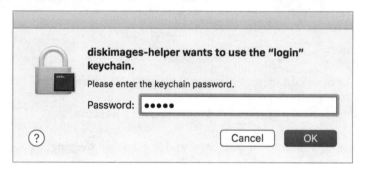

7   Select the disk image on your desktop, and press Command-E to eject it.

8   Open the disk image again.

Since the password is now stored in your keychain and the keychain is unlocked, the image opens without asking you for the password.

9   Eject the disk image again.

Retrieve a Password in a Keychain

Even though passwords are stored to make them conveniently available for applications, there may be times when a user needs to retrieve a stored password. For example, a user who wants to use webmail on a different computer may want to retrieve her email password in order to do so. In this section, you will use the keychain to retrieve a forgotten password.

1 If necessary, open Keychain Access from the Utilities folder. Remember that you can reach this folder in the Finder by choosing Go menu > Utilities or pressing Command-Shift-U.

2 Double-click the password entry named "Chris's private files.dmg." Use the search filter at the upper-right corner of Keychain Access if you need to.

A window opens, displaying information about this password entry.

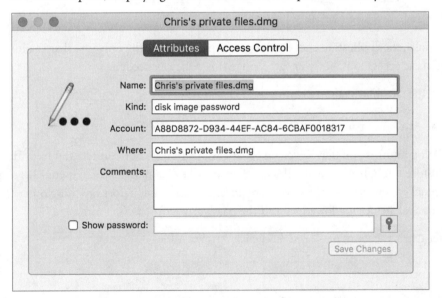

3 Click the Access Control tab.

The Access Control pane displays information about what applications or system components are allowed access to the keychain entry. In this case, the diskimages-helper application can automatically access the password, but if any other application requests access, the system asks the user for confirmation first.

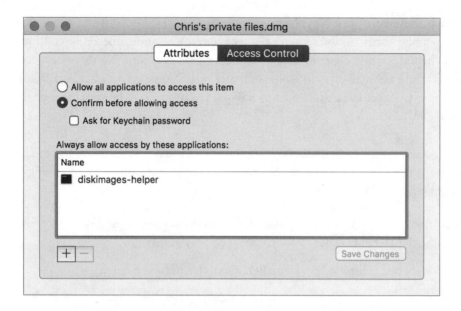

Normally, the application that created a keychain entry is the only one that is allowed automatic access to it, but you can change this policy as needed.

4   Click the Attributes tab.

5   In the Attributes pane, select Show Password.

A dialog informs you that Keychain Access wants to use your confidential information stored in "Chris's private files.dmg" in your keychain. Even though your keychain is unlocked, this item's access policy requires confirmation before anything other than diskimages-helper is allowed to read the password.

6   Enter Chris's account password, and click Always Allow.

The disk image password becomes visible.

7   Click the Access Control tab.

Keychain Access has now been added to the "Always allow access" list for this item. If you had clicked Allow instead, Keychain Access would have been allowed access to the password but would not have been added to this access control list. Since it has been added to the list, Keychain Access can now display the password without asking for confirmation.

8   Close the "Chris's private files.dmg" window.

Move a Password to the System Keychain

Normally, resource passwords are stored in a user's own keychain and are only accessible by that user. However, it is possible to move them to the System keychain, making them accessible to all users.

1   Find the "Chris's private files.dmg." keychain item again, and drag it to the System keychain in the Keychains section of the sidebar.

2   Authenticate as Local Admin (password: ladminpw, or whatever you chose when you created the account) to allow the change to the System keychain.

3   When prompted to allow kcproxy to use the confidential information in "Chris's private files.dmg," click Allow. kcproxy is a tool that Keychain Access uses to move entries into the System keychain.

"Chris's private files.dmg" disappears from your login keychain.

4   Click the System keychain.

"Chris's private files.dmg" is now listed here, along with several automatically created items, and any Wi-Fi passwords stored on your Mac.

5   Quit Keychain Access and log out of the Chris Johnson account.

6   Log in as Mayta Mishtuk (password: mayta, or whatever you chose when you created the account).

7   Open the file /Users/Shared/StudentMaterials/Lesson7/Chris's private files.dmg.

Mayta's Finder preferences have not been customized to allow easy access outside her home folder; however, you can reach this file by choosing Go menu > Computer (Command-Shift-C) and then opening the Macintosh HD > Users > Shared > StudentMaterials > Lesson7 folder.

The disk image opens. Because the keychain item's access controls allow diskimages-helper full access to the item, you are not prompted to authenticate or allow access.

8   Eject the disk image and log out of the Mayta Mishtuk account.

Lesson 8

Manage Password Changes

As covered in the previous lesson, passwords are the most common method to prove the identity of a user, thus allowing access to resources. This lesson focuses on methods to modify passwords and the ramifications of those modifications.

A password change is different from a password reset. A known password can be changed, but an unknown password needs to be reset by some other authorization mechanism. Both methods result in a new password, but resetting a password should only be attempted if the user doesn't know the password. As you'll see in this lesson, changing a password is simple and often trouble-free, but resetting passwords may lead to security issues and possibly even data loss.

Reference 8.1
Change Known Passwords

If you already know your local computer account password but want to change it, you can do so at any time from the General pane of Security & Privacy or by selecting your user account in the Users & Groups preferences. In either case, you can click the Change Password button, which will reveal a series of dialogs allowing you to change the password to your local computer account.

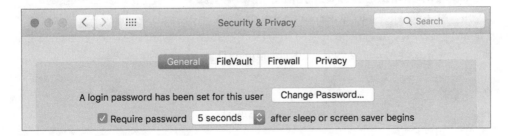

The change password dialogs vary depending on whether your local account is using an associated Apple ID password or a separate local account password. As covered in Lesson 7, "Manage Security and Privacy," although macOS Sierra doesn't allow you to add new local accounts that use an Apple ID password, it will still allow you to use this type of account password.

> **NOTE ▶** The macOS interface sometimes uses "iCloud password" instead of "Apple ID password." Because all Apple services, including iCloud, are accessed via Apple ID authentication, this guide uses the term Apple ID when discussing Apple service authentication.

In most cases, users change their local account password independently from an Apple ID. Assuming this is the case for your account, you will do so via the default local account password change dialog. In the local account password change dialog, you must enter your old password once, followed by the new password twice. You enter the new password twice to avoid typos. Because you are using a local account password, the new password doesn't have to conform to any Apple-mandated password requirements.

Change Password: Local Account Using an Associated Apple ID Password

If you wish to change a local account password, which has an associated Apple ID (or iCloud) password, you are prompted to select whether you want to switch to using separate passwords or to change your current Apple ID password.

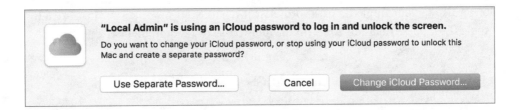

NOTE ► Changes to Apple ID passwords can be made only if the Mac has Internet access. Specifically, the Mac must be able to communicate with Apple's authentication services.

If you want to change your Apple ID password, you will need to enter the password and any additional codes if two-step verification or two-factor authentication is enabled. After the account is verified, you can change the Apple ID password. Again, whenever a password is changed, macOS presents a dialog requiring that the new password be entered twice to avoid typos. Also, because this is an Apple ID password, there are specific password requirements to ensure a strong password.

Change Password

Your password must be at least eight characters and include a number, an uppercase letter, and a lowercase letter.

Old Password: ●●●●●●●●●●●●

New Password: ●●●●●●●●●●●●

Verify: ●●●●●●●●●●●●

Cancel   Change

TIP ► Changes to Apple ID passwords can also be made from another Apple device that is signed in to the Apple ID or via any web browser from the Apple ID website: https://appleid.apple.com. If you change an Apple ID password using another device or web browser, the local user account on the Mac won't take the new password until you log out and back in using the new Apple ID password.

If you choose to switch to using a separate local password, you will be presented with a different dialog. In this case, you must enter the Apple ID password along with a new local account password. Once you complete this dialog, your local account password is no longer tied to your Apple ID password. Also, because your new password isn't tied to your Apple ID, it doesn't have to conform to Apple password requirements.

Create separate password for "Local Admin".

You will no longer be able to log in or unlock your screen with your iCloud password, and you will need to remember both passwords separately.

iCloud password: ••••••••••••

New password: ••••••••••••

Verify: ••••••••••••

Password hint: Not even.
(Recommended)

Cancel   Use Separate Password

NOTE ▶ As of this writing, macOS Sierra won't allow you to change back to using an Apple ID password for login.

Use Password Assistant

Regardless of how sophisticated a security system is, the protection it affords is only as strong as the password you choose. For this reason, new Apple ID passwords must meet minimum password complexity requirements. As you've seen in this lesson, local account passwords don't have to meet any password complexity requirements by default.

TIP ▶ Administrators can enforce local password complexity rules via a configuration profile. You can find out more about configuration profiles in Lesson 2, "Set Up and Configure macOS."

To help you pick a strong password, macOS Sierra includes a handy utility, called Password Assistant, that gauges the strength of your passwords or automatically creates strong passwords for you. Anytime you are creating or modifying a local password that grants access to a substantial resource, like an account or keychain password, you can use Password Assistant. It is available whenever you see the small key icon next to a password field, as you can see in the previous screenshot of the local account password change dialog.

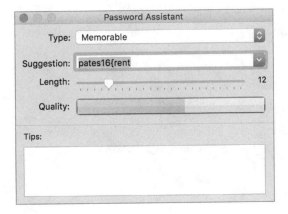

About Master Passwords

The master password can be used to reset regular account passwords and is required to reset Legacy FileVault user account passwords. The master password isn't tied to any local user account, so it's an effective way to provide a password reset mechanism that does not require the creation of an additional administrator account. If you are maintaining a large deployment of Mac computers that are using local accounts, setting a uniform master password is an easy method for ensuring you always have a back door in without having your own local administrator account.

New installations of macOS Sierra do not normally have the master password set. However, there are two cases in which the master password may already be set. The first is if you have upgraded a computer from a previous version of the Mac operating system where the master password was set. The second is if you used Migration Assistant to transfer a Legacy FileVault user account to the Mac, in which case the master password is transferred as well.

If you think you know the current master password and you would like to set a new master password, you can do so in the Users & Groups preferences. Once you have opened Users & Groups preferences and authenticated as an administrator, click the Action pop-up menu (the small gear icon) at the bottom of the users list. A menu with the option Change Master Password appears (if you have not set a master password, then the menu offers the Set Master Password option). As you'd expect, changing the master password requires that you know the current master password.

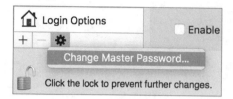

TIP ▶ If you are logged in to a Legacy FileVault account, you can also change the master password from the Legacy FileVault pane of the Security & Privacy preferences.

Reference 8.2
Reset Lost Passwords

Users mistyping or forgetting their passwords is the primary cause of login and access issues on any platform. The second most common issue, specific to macOS, is when a user's login keychain password becomes out of sync with that user's account password. Fortunately, macOS Sierra provides several ways to easily resolve these types of password issues.

About Password Reset Methods

There are multiple methods for resetting a local user account password in macOS Sierra:

▶   Administrator account in Users & Groups—If you have access to an administrator account on the system, you can easily reset other user account passwords from Users & Groups preferences. Authenticate as an administrator, select another user account, and click Reset Password. If the selected user account is configured for Legacy FileVault, you must enter the master password to reset the account password. However, in all other cases, by virtue of previously authenticating as an administrator, you can enter a new password for the user. If the selected user account is using an Apple ID password, during the reset you can change it to a separate local account password.

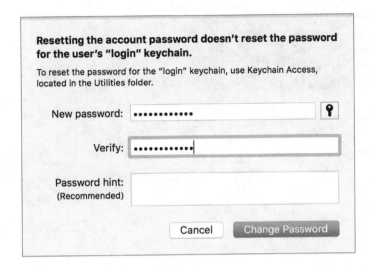

NOTE ▶ You cannot reset the password for another user who is still logged on to the computer via Fast User Switching. You must first restart the system, thus forcing the user to be logged out of their account, as covered in Lesson 5, "Manage User Accounts."

▶ Apple ID website—If the user account is tied to an Apple ID password, the user can try to reset the Apple ID password from any web browser via the Apple ID website: https://iforgot.apple.com. If the Apple ID has two-step verification or two-factor authentication enabled, the user will need to enter additional codes. Alternatively, for Apple IDs without this feature enabled, the user will have to successfully answer the recovery questions and respond to an email sent to the Apple ID. If the user is unable to reset the Apple ID password online, you can still reset the local user account password using the previous method as an administrator or by using the Reset Password assistant, as covered later in this section.

MORE INFO ▶ Resetting an Apple ID may require multiple security verification steps. For more info see Apple Support article HT201487, "If you forgot your Apple ID password."

▶ Master password at login—When the master password is set, users who enter an incorrect password three times at the login window are prompted to reset their account password. Authenticating with the current master password allows you to enter a new password for a local user account. Note that this method does not work for local user accounts with Apple ID passwords. On the other hand, this is the only method for resetting a Legacy FileVault user account at login. If you don't know the master password, it won't help you now, but eventually you can reset the master password, as covered later in this section

▶ Apple ID at login—Two conditions must be met for users to be able to reset their local account password at login using an Apple ID. First, they must not be using Legacy FileVault (most users won't be). Second, the user account must have previously signed in to the iCloud service but still be using a separate local account password. As you can see in the previous screenshot, after three failed attempts at login, local users can enter their Apple ID to reset the password for a local user account. Details on setting up the iCloud service are covered in Lesson 2, "Set Up and Configure macOS."

NOTE ▶ User accounts on Mac systems protected by FileVault system disk encryption cannot have their local passwords reset at the login window using the master password or an Apple ID.

▶ FileVault Recovery Key at Startup—On a Mac with FileVault system disk encryption enabled, users who enter an incorrect password three times at startup are prompted to reset the password using a Recovery Key. Lesson 10, "Manage FileVault," covers this topic in greater detail.

▶ Reset Password assistant via macOS Recovery—Anyone with access to macOS Recovery can use the Reset Password assistant to reset local account passwords. While this last-resort option is useful, it's also a significant security risk, as, by default, it requires no knowledge of any other passwords. Enabling FileVault system disk encryption or a firmware password can mitigate this risk by requiring authentication to access the system disk from macOS Recovery. Use of the Reset Password assistant and firmware passwords is covered later in this lesson

Reset Legacy FileVault Passwords

Legacy FileVault user accounts are unique because the user's home folder is saved inside an encrypted disk image protected by that user's account password. Consequently, it is extremely important for an administrator to be able to reset a Legacy FileVault user's account password so that the user can access home folder files again.

A normal administrator user account is not enough to reset a lost Legacy FileVault user's password. After all, Legacy FileVault wouldn't be very secure if just any old administrator user could come along and break in. Therefore, if a Legacy FileVault user has forgotten the account password, the master password is required to reset the account.

As covered previously, if you know the master password, macOS provides two methods for easily resetting Legacy FileVault user passwords. The first method allows you to reset a Legacy FileVault user at the login window, and the second method involves resetting a Legacy FileVault account password in the Users & Groups preferences.

If the master password, as well as the user's Legacy FileVault password, is lost, you are completely out of luck. You must have at least one of these two passwords to recover a Legacy FileVault user account. Otherwise, you are never, ever going to be able to recover the user's data. Not even Apple can help you. Apple designed Legacy FileVault to be as secure as possible, and thus created only one way to reset a Legacy FileVault user account: the master password. For this reason alone, you should abandon using Legacy FileVault user accounts in favor of FileVault 2 full-system volume encryption.

> **MORE INFO ▸** Turning off Legacy FileVault and using FileVault system disk encryption technology is covered in Lesson 10, "Manage FileVault."

Reset the Master Password

If Legacy FileVault user accounts are still active, it's vital that the master password be properly configured and known by an administrator. If the master password is lost, an administrator user should reset it immediately just to be able to reset normal user passwords. Resetting the master password involves deleting the /Library/Keychains /FileVaultMaster.cer and /Library/Keychains/FileVaultMaster.keychain files.

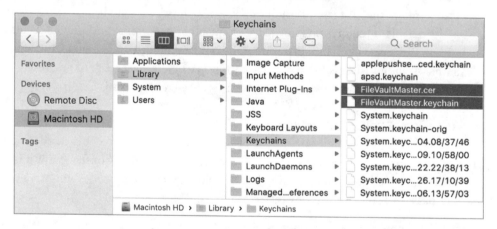

Once these files are deleted, an administrator user can return to the Users & Groups preferences and set a new master password using the techniques covered previously in this lesson. However, just because you can set a new master password for your Mac doesn't mean you can recover a Legacy FileVault user account that was created with the old master password. Only the master password created when the Legacy FileVault user account was enabled can unlock an inaccessible account.

Even if a new master password is set, it cannot reset existing Legacy FileVault user account passwords. This is because macOS does not support reencrypting Legacy FileVault user accounts, which is a necessary step for lost master password resets. Thus, if you lost the master password used to create a Legacy FileVault user account, there is no recovery method if users also lose their password. This is yet another reason to abandon the use of Legacy FileVault user accounts in favor of FileVault 2 system disk encryption.

Reset Password Assistant via macOS Recovery

Many Mac computers intended for personal use have only the single primary administrator user account that was created when the Mac was initially configured with Setup Assistant. Even if more than one person uses this Mac, quite often its owner is not very concerned about security. Thankfully, macOS now defaults to requiring the user to enter a password at login.

However, if the computer was upgraded to macOS, it's common for the primary user account to automatically log in during startup and for a master password not to be set. This can result in Mac owners forgetting their primary administrator account password and not having any way to reset it because they never enabled the master password or created another administrator account. Fortunately, Apple has prepared for these occasions by including the Reset Password assistant in macOS Recovery.

The Reset Password assistant is available only from macOS Recovery system, as covered in Lesson 3, "Use macOS Recovery." Once the Mac is running from macOS Recovery, open the Terminal application (via the Utilities menu), type resetpassword, and then press Return. The Reset Password assistant will open and provide several methods to rest the local user's account.

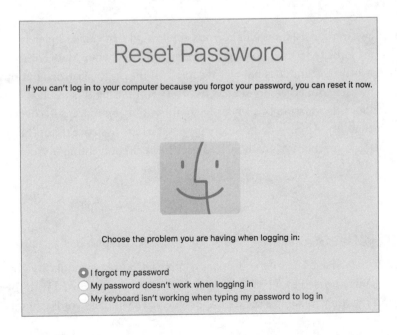

The Reset Password assistant presents several screens that vary based on the system's storage and password configuration:

▶ Storage volume selection—If the system has more than one attached storage volume, you will need to select the system volume containing the account password that you wish to reset.

▶ FileVault enabled volume—If the selected volume is protected with FileVault system volume encryption, you will have to either have the password for a local account on the system that has permission to log in to FileVault or enter the password for the Apple ID that was used to save the FileVault recovery key. Again, Lesson 10, "Manage FileVault," covers this topic in greater detail.

▶ Local user selection—If there is more than one local account user on the selected system volume, you will have to select the specific account you wish to reset the password for.

▶ Local user with associated Apple ID—If the selected local account is associated with an Apple ID, then you may be able to reset the local account password by entering the password for the associated Apple ID. However, this method requires that the system have Internet access when running from the macOS Recovery system.

▶ Local user without an associated Apple ID—If the selected local account is not associated with an Apple ID, then you can simply enter a new password for the local account.

Obviously, the Reset Password assistant is a dangerous application that can completely bypass the user account security settings you've configured to protect your Mac. For this reason, the Reset Password assistant does not run if copied off the original media, but this still doesn't prevent any user with access to macOS Recovery from using this utility. Once again, Apple prepared for this situation by providing another utility on macOS Recovery: the Firmware Password utility. As covered in Reference 8.4, "Secure System Startup," setting a firmware password prevents any unauthorized user from circumventing normal system startup.

Reference 8.3
Reset User Keychains

As detailed in Lesson 7, "Manage Security and Privacy," all macOS user accounts are given local encrypted keychains accessed by a password that is normally synchronized with their account password. So that they remain as secure as possible, keychain passwords cannot be changed by any outside password-resetting process. Apple did not design the keychain system with a back door, because doing so would render the system less secure.

Consequently, whenever a user's account password is reset (as opposed to changed), the user's login and Local Items/iCloud keychain passwords remain unchanged and will not automatically open when the user logs in to the account. As such, when users with a recently reset password log in, they will be prompted with a dialog to update or reset the keychain password.

The default selection, Update Keychain Password, works only if the user knows the previous keychain password, which is probably not the case if you just had to reset the password. In that case, the user should click the Create New Keychain button to create a new login keychain. The system renames the old login keychain and leaves it in the user's Keychains folder in case the user ever remembers the old password. Finally, though it's not recommended, the user can choose to ignore the warning by clicking Continue Log In.

> **NOTE ▶** Creating a new login keychain effectively erases all saved authentication secrets. This means the system will have lost saved authentication for any services, such as those configured via the Internet Accounts preferences and iCloud preferences, including access to additional secrets saved in the Local Items/iCloud keychain.

If the automatic keychain update dialog does not appear, you can still reset the user's login and Local Items/iCloud keychain passwords from the Keychain Access application, assuming the previous password is known. As you'd expect, if you do not know the user's previous keychain password, the contents of that keychain are lost forever.

Manage Keychain Files

At any point while the user is logged in to the system, you can manage keychain files, including resetting a keychain's password, from the /Applications/Utilities/Keychain Access application. As covered in Lesson 7, "Manage Security and Privacy," Keychain Access allows you to manage secrets saved inside the keychain files once they are unlocked. In this lesson you will learn how to manage the keychain files themselves.

Creating a new local keychain is as simple as choosing File > New Keychain and then entering a password, six characters or longer, for the keychain. The default location for new keychains is the Keychains folder inside your home folder.

> **NOTE ▶** The user's Local Items/iCloud keychain is accessed using the same password as the user's login keychain. In other words, the password used to unlock and manage the user's login keychain is also used to unlock and manage the Local Items/iCloud keychain. Thus, changes to the login keychain password are automatically applied to the Local Items/iCloud keychain. For this reason, the Keychain Access application does not allow you to change the Local Items/iCloud keychain password.

You can further adjust a keychain's settings by selecting it from the list and then choosing Edit > Change Settings for Keychain. A dialog appears where you can change automatic keychain locking settings for the selected keychain file.

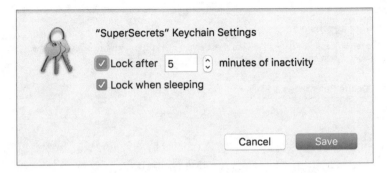

To change a keychain's password, first select it from the list and then choose Edit > Change Password for Keychain. You have to enter the keychain's current password first, followed by a new password and verification.

Finally, to delete a keychain, select it from the list and choose File > Delete Keychain. When the Delete Keychain dialog appears, click Delete References to simply ignore the keychain, or click Delete References & Files to completely erase the keychain file.

It's best to avoid deleting the original keychain file manually in the Finder, because this will confuse the keychain system. Also, it's obviously not a good idea to delete the Login keychain unless another keychain is there to take its place. A user should always have access to at least one local keychain.

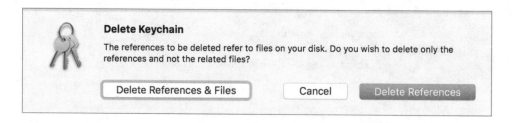

TIP You can move keychain items between keychains by dragging and dropping an item from one keychain to another. The exception to this is the Local Items/iCloud keychain, for which the system automatically manages the addition and removal of items.

TIP For quick access to your keychains and other security features, you can enable the Keychain menu item by choosing Keychain Access > Preferences. Then select the "Show keychain status in menu bar" checkbox to display the Keychain menu item, as indicated by a small key icon.

Manually Reset Keychain Files

If the system is unable to open a keychain file or retrieve secrets from it, the keychain file may have become corrupted. If so, the user's keychain files will need to be replaced or simply reset. As covered previously, the user's keychain files reside in /Users/<*username*>/Library/Keychains.

Ideally users have maintained a backup of their home folder using a backup technology like Time Machine, as covered in **Lesson 15, "Manage Time Machine."** In this case you can manually replace the user's entire Keychains folder with earlier versions of the files. After replacing the keychain files, you should restart the computer and re-log-in as the user. Opening the Keychain Access application will verify the recovered keychain files.

Unfortunately, if the user's keychain files are corrupted and the user doesn't have a backup, the keychain items will need to be reset. In this case, delete the contents of the user's Keychains folder and then restart the computer. Re-log-in as the user, and the system will create new empty keychain items for the user.

Resetting iCloud Keychain

Not only does the iCloud Security Code give you an additional way to add new devices, it also provides a last resort should the iCloud Keychain service become unavailable to all your devices. In other words, if you lose access to all your devices, a new device can be authorized via the iCloud Security Code. However, if you don't create an iCloud Security Code and somehow all your devices are lost or have disabled the iCloud Keychain service, then your iCloud Keychain contents are no longer accessible and must be reset.

> **NOTE ▶** If you lose both your iCloud Security Code and access to authorized devices, the iCloud Keychain service must be reset to regain access to the service. However, if you lose access only to the SMS text message phone number, you can contact Apple Support to help resolve this issue.

> **NOTE ▶** Resetting the iCloud Keychain service destroys all previously saved items in the iCloud Keychain. After a reset, enabling this service will again prompt you to set up an iCloud Security Code.

Also covered previously, as the local login keychain goes, so does the iCloud keychain. If the login keychain is locked, the iCloud keychain is also locked.

Further, if the login keychain password is lost, so is the user's access to the local instance of the iCloud keychain. If a new login keychain is created, as is recommended by the keychain update dialog, the local iCloud keychain is also automatically reset. This results in a new empty Local Items keychain for the user, but the contents of the iCloud Keychain service remain "in the cloud." You can then gain access to your secrets by reenabling the iCloud Keychain service; however, doing so will treat the device as if it were a new device. Thus, you will again be prompted to authenticate with an Apple ID and to use either the iCloud Security Code or device authorization to regain access to the iCloud Keychain service.

> **MORE INFO ▶** You can find out more about iCloud Keychain from Apple Support article HT204085, "Frequently asked questions about iCloud Keychain."

Reference 8.4
Secure System Startup

As covered earlier, setting the firmware password prevents unauthorized users from using any startup-interrupt keyboard shortcuts. This protects your system from someone trying to circumvent an otherwise secure installation of macOS. A firmware password is not in any way tied to a user account. Instead, the password is saved to the Mac computer's firmware chip so it remains separate from the installed software.

> **TIP** ▶ Even without setting a firmware password, enabling macOS FileVault system disk encryption prevents unauthorized access to the encrypted system disk.

With a firmware password set, all startup keyboard shortcuts are disabled except for shortcuts that allow you to choose a different startup system. Further, you must provide authentication to gain access to another startup system. For example, on a Mac with a firmware password enabled, if you start up while holding down the Option key, an authentication window appears, prompting you to enter the firmware password. If you enter the correct firmware password, you can select a different startup disk from the Startup Manager. This gives the administrator the flexibility to start up from another system should the need arise, but otherwise prevents users from affecting the standard macOS startup process.

> **MORE INFO** ▶ All the available startup keyboard shortcuts are covered in **Lesson 26, "Troubleshoot Startup and System Issues."**

If you require the highest level of security for your Mac, you must set the firmware password. This is because any user with access to macOS Recovery can set the password if it hasn't already been set. You can set the firmware password using the Firmware Password utility, available when the Mac is started up from macOS Recovery, as covered in Lesson 3, "Use macOS Recovery."

Once the Mac is started in macOS Recovery, the Firmware Password utility is available in the Utilities menu. If the firmware password isn't currently set, click Turn On Firmware Password and enter the desired password.

If a firmware password is already set for the system, you can change it or turn it off using the corresponding button. However, you must know the current firmware password to change or disable it.

If for some reason the computer's firmware password is lost, it can be reset. For many Mac models made before 2010, you can reset the firmware password by first removing some of the system memory from the Mac. This "proves" that you have access to the internals of the Mac. Then, when you restart the Mac, hold down Command-Option-P-R. Continue holding until you hear the Mac restart; then you can release the keys. At this point, the firmware password has been cleared.

To provide enhanced security, most Mac models from 2010 or later don't support this method of resetting the firmware password. If you are in the position of needing the firmware password cleared on a later Mac, you need to visit an Apple Authorized Service Provider.

> **MORE INFO** ▶ You can find out more about firmware passwords from Apple Support article HT204455, "Use a firmware password on your Mac."

Exercise 8.1
Reset Account Passwords in macOS Recovery

▶ **Prerequisites**

- ▶ You must have created the Local Admin (Exercise 2.1, "Configure a New macOS System for Exercises," or Exercise 2.2, "Configure an Existing macOS System for Exercises") and Chris Johnson (Exercise 5.1, "Create a Standard User Account") accounts.

- ▶ Your computer must have a local hidden Recovery HD partition. This partition is normally created by the macOS installation process.

- ▶ You must not have turned on FileVault encryption on your Mac.

macOS provides a number of ways to reset lost account passwords. In this exercise, you will use macOS Recovery mode to reset Chris Johnson's password.

Reset a User Password in macOS Recovery

1 Restart your computer, and hold down Command-R until the Apple logo appears on the screen.

2 If a language selection screen appears, select your preferred language, and click the right-arrow button to continue.

3 From the menu bar, choose Utilities > Terminal.

Terminal provides access to a command-line (text-based) interface in macOS. This guide doesn't cover the command-line interface, but using it is necessary to reach the Reset Password utility in macOS Recovery.

4 Type the command resetpassword, and press Return.

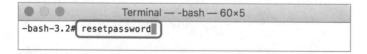

The Reset Password utility opens.

5   If you are asked to select a volume to recover, select your system volume (usually Macintosh HD), and then click Next.

6   Select the Chris Johnson user account, and click Next.

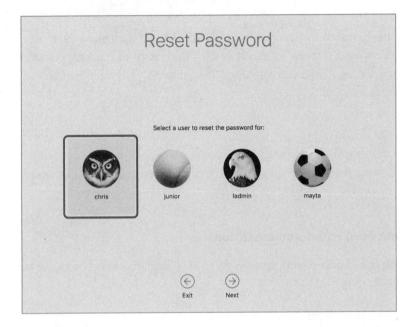

7   Enter the password for the Apple ID account that you linked Chris Johnson to, and then click Next. If you did not link Chris Johnson to an Apple ID, this step will be skipped.

8   If you used an Apple ID with two-step verification or two-factor authentication, follow the prompts to finish authenticating.

9   Enter password1 in both password fields. Leave the hint field blank.

10 Click Next.

11 When you are notified that your user account password has been reset, click Restart.

   NOTE ▸ Chris Johnson's login keychain is no longer synchronized with his login password. You may perform Exercise 8.2, "Reset Account Passwords," next, followed by Exercise 8.3, "Create a New Keychain," or you may skip directly to Exercise 8.3. In any case, reset Chris's keychain by performing Exercise 8.3 before going on to any other lesson.

Exercise 8.2
Reset Account Passwords

▶ **Prerequisite**

    ▶ You must have created the Local Admin (Exercise 2.1, "Configure a New macOS System for Exercises," or Exercise 2.2, "Configure an Existing macOS System for Exercises") and Chris Johnson (Exercise 5.1, "Create a Standard User Account") accounts.

macOS provides a number of ways to reset lost account passwords. In this exercise, you will reset Chris Johnson's password as an administrator and then again using a master password.

Reset a User Password as an Administrator

1   If necessary, log in as Local Admin (password: ladminpw, or whatever you chose when you created the account).

2   Open System Preferences, and select Users & Groups.

3   Click the Lock icon, and authenticate as Local Admin.

4   Select the Chris Johnson account.

5   Click Reset Password.

6   In the dialog that appears, enter password2 in the "New password" field.

7   Click the small key icon next to the "New password" field.

Password Assistant opens to help you choose a better password. It rates the quality of this proposed password (red, to indicate it's bad), suggests a better password (in the Suggestion field), and lists tips on how to avoid such bad passwords.

8   Click the triangle next to the Suggestion field to show more suggested passwords.

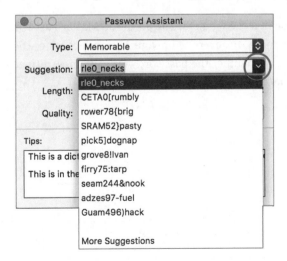

9   Click one of the suggested passwords. The selected password is copied into the "New password," Verify, and Suggestion fields, and the Quality bar expands and turns green to indicate this is a much better option.

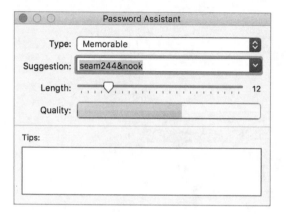

You do not need to memorize or record this password because you will not need it later.

10 Close Password Assistant.

11 Click Change Password.

12 Click the Action (gear icon) menu under the user list, and choose Set Master Password from the pop-up menu that appears.

13 If you are performing this exercise in a class, enter masterpw in the Master Password and Verify fields. If you are performing this exercise on your own, select a more secure master password. Be sure to remember the password you have chosen since you will need to reenter it in the next section.

A master password must be created for this computer to provide a safety net for accounts using encryption.

An administrator of this computer can use the master password to reset the password of any user. If you forget your password, you can reset it to gain access to your home folder even if it is protected with encryption. This provides protection for users who forget their login password.

Master password: ••••••••

Verify: ••••••••

Hint:

Choose a password that is difficult to guess, yet based on something important to you so that you never forget it. Click the Help button for more information about choosing a good password.

Cancel   OK

14 Click OK.

15 Quit System Preferences, and log out as Local Admin.

Reset a Password with the Master Password

1 At the login screen, select Chris Johnson.

2 Enter the wrong password for Chris, and press Return three times.

You'll see options for resetting Chris's password.

Chris Johnson

If you forgot your password, you can...

...reset it using your Master Password

3   Click the arrow next to "reset it using your Master Password."

4   Enter the master password (masterpw, or whatever you chose earlier in the exercise); then enter password2 in the "New password" and "Verify password" fields.

Do not enter a password hint.

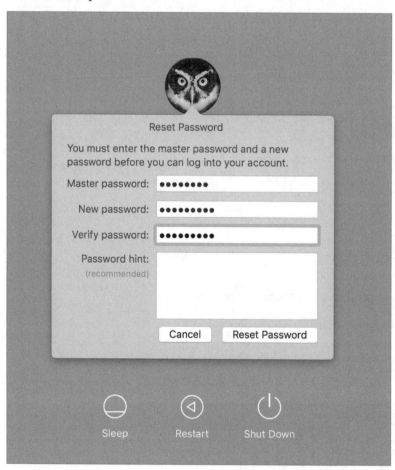

5   Click Reset Password.

A dialog warns that the system was unable to unlock your login keychain. Leave this dialog open for the next exercise.

NOTE ▶ Chris Johnson's login keychain is no longer synchronized with his login password. You need to reset his keychain by performing Exercise 8.3, "Create a New Keychain," before going on to any other exercise.

Exercise 8.3
Create a New Keychain

▶ **Prerequisites**

- ▶ You must have created the Local Admin (Exercise 2.1, "Configure a New macOS System for Exercises," or Exercise 2.2, "Configure an Existing macOS System for Exercises") and Chris Johnson (Exercise 5.1, "Create a Standard User Account") accounts.

- ▶ You must perform Exercise 8.1, "Reset Account Passwords in macOS Recovery," or Exercise 8.2, "Reset Account Passwords," before this exercise.

After Chris's (or anyone's) account password has been reset, his keychain will still be encrypted with his old account password. If Chris remembers the old password, he can update the keychain to match the new account password. But if his password was reset because he forgot it, he will not be able to recover the contents of the old keychain, and he must create a new one using his new account password.

In this exercise, you can assume that Chris's account password was reset because he forgot the old password, and so he needs to abandon the old keychain and create a new one.

Create a New Login Keychain

WARNING ▶ Creating a new keychain makes the old keychain contents inaccessible. If this were a real user's account and there was anything important in the keychain, it would be worth trying to remember the old password before replacing it with a new (blank) keychain.

1   If you aren't already logged in (or logging in) as Chris Johnson, log in now (after the previous exercises, his password is either password1 or password2).

Because Chris's account password no longer matches his keychain password, the system cannot use this password to unlock his keychain, and you receive a warning to this effect.

The system was unable to unlock your login keychain.

If you remember your old password you can update the keychain password. If you do not remember your old password, you can create a new login keychain or choose to leave the login keychain using a different password.

Would you like to update the password, create a new keychain, or continue the login?

Continue Log In   Create New Keychain   Update Keychain Password

2   Click Create New Keychain.

The login session proceeds as usual, and Chris's desktop appears.

3   If a dialog appears indicating that your Mac can't connect to iCloud, click iCloud Preferences.

This Mac can't connect to iCloud because of a problem with "suppessentialsacct@icloud.com".

Open iCloud preferences to fix this problem.

Later   iCloud Preferences...

Since Chris's keychain has been reset, his iCloud credentials have been lost and will need to be reentered.

4   Enter the password for the Apple ID Chris's account is linked to, and click Sign In.

5   If the Apple ID has two-step verification or two-factor authentication, follow the prompts to finish authenticating.

6   Quit System Preferences.

Verify the Synchronization

1   Open Keychain Access from the Utilities folder.

Keychain Access displays the status and contents of your login keychain. Note that the keychain appears as unlocked, which means that the correct password has been supplied and its contents are available.

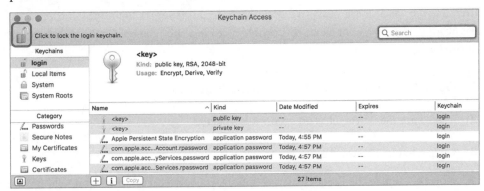

The new keychain normally contains a number of entries, but it consists only of items that are automatically created in a new keychain plus those items relating to the Apple ID Chris's account is linked to. The items that were in the old keychain are no longer available.

2   Click the padlock icon in the upper-left corner of the window to lock the keychain.

3   Click the padlock again to unlock it.

You are prompted for the keychain password.

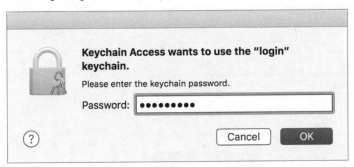

4 Enter Chris's current account password (password1 or password2), and then click OK.

Since this is the new keychain's password, it unlocks.

5 Quit Keychain Access.

Change Chris's Password

Resetting Chris's account password desynchronized it from his login password. A normal password change does not cause this problem. To test this, change Chris's password the normal way.

1 Open the Users & Groups pane in System Preferences.

2 Make sure the Chris Johnson account is selected.

3 Click Change Password.

Note that unlike the Reset Password options you used earlier, this has a field for the old password. It uses this old password to decrypt the login keychain and then reencrypt it with the new password.

4 Enter the following:

Old password: password1 or password2

"New password" and Verify: chris (or whatever you chose when you originally created his account)

You may enter a password hint if you want.

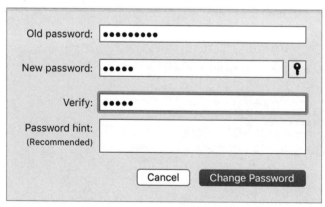

5 Click Change Password.

6 Quit System Preferences.

Reverify the Synchronization

1 Reopen the Keychain Access utility.

2 As you did before, click the padlock twice to lock and unlock the keychain.

3 Enter Chris's current account password (chris, or whatever you chose when you created his account) in the Password field, and click OK.

As before, the account password unlocks the keychain.

4 Quit Keychain Access.

5 Log out as Chris Johnson.

Exercise 8.4
Use a Firmware Password

▶ **Prerequisite**

> ▶ You should perform this exercise only on a Mac computer that you own and for which you can provide proof of ownership.

In this exercise, you will set a firmware password to control the startup process of your computer.

WARNING ▶ If you forget the firmware password, you might have to take your computer to an Apple Authorized Service Provider and provide proof that you own the computer to unlock it. If you do not want to risk this, please skip ahead to the next lesson.

Set a Firmware Password

1   Restart your computer, and hold down Command-R until the Apple logo appears on the screen.

2   If a language selection screen appears, select your preferred language, and click the right-arrow button.

3   From the menu bar, choose Utilities > Firmware Password Utility.

4   Click Turn On Firmware Password.

5   Enter the password apple in both the "New password" and Verify fields.

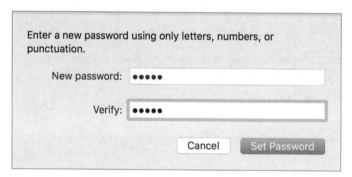

6   Click Set Password.

The utility indicates that password protection is enabled.

Test the Firmware Password

1   From the Apple menu, choose Restart.

Your computer restarts normally. The firmware password does not interfere with a normal startup.

2   At the login screen, click Restart, and then hold down Command-R until a Lock icon appears onscreen.

Alternative boot modes, including macOS Recovery, are not available without entering the firmware password.

3   Enter the password (apple), and press Return.

Remove the Firmware Password

If you are performing these exercises on your own and want to leave the firmware password enabled, restart your computer normally, and skip this section.

If you are performing these exercises in a classroom or you do not want to leave the firmware password set on your own computer, follow these steps to remove the password:

1   Choose Utilities menu > Firmware Password Utility.

2   Click Turn Off Firmware Password.

3   When prompted, enter the firmware password (apple), and click Turn Off Password.

Enter your old password to turn the firmware password off.

Old password: •••••

Cancel   Turn Off Password

WARNING ► There is no simple way to remove or reset a forgotten firmware password. You might have to take your computer to an Apple Authorized Service Provider to unlock it.

The Firmware Password utility shows that password protection is disabled.

4   From the Apple menu, choose Restart.

Your computer restarts normally.

File Systems and Storage

Lesson 9

Manage File Systems and Storage

Although personal computer processor speed has increased around a thousandfold since the first Mac was introduced in 1984, storage capacity has easily increased a million times over. Compare 1984's 400 KB floppy to today's average desktop disk at 1 TB, which is roughly equivalent to 1,000,000,000 KB, or 2.5 million 400 KB floppies. Users have responded by moving thousands of pictures and hundreds of hours of music and video, historically stored in analog form, to digital storage. Even though the Internet has recently changed our perception of what a computer is used for, it's clear that the computer's primary role continues to be as a tool to organize, access, and store our stuff.

In this lesson, you examine the storage technology used by macOS. Storage hardware, such as flash disks, is covered alongside logical storage concepts like partitions and volumes. Naturally, you will learn how to properly manage and troubleshoot these storage assets as well. Lastly, this lesson will show you how to verify and potentially repair file system elements.

GOALS

▶ Recognize the various file systems supported by macOS

▶ Manage disks, partitions, and volumes

▶ Troubleshoot and repair partition and volume issues

Reference 9.1
About File Systems

Before you begin managing storage in macOS, it is important to understand the distinction between storage, partitions, and volumes. Traditionally, computer storage has been defined by spinning disk hardware. However, alternative formats have become extremely popular as they have increased in capacity and performance.

These formats primarily include internal solid-state disks or flash storage, and removable storage like USB flash disks (also called key or thumb disks) and compact flash cards. All are equally viable storage destinations for macOS.

TIP ► Mac computers can start up from USB, FireWire, and Thunderbolt external disks.

Storage Concepts

Without proper formatting, though, any storage technology is nothing more than a big empty bucket of ones and zeros, and consequently not very useful to the Mac. Formatting is the process of applying logic to storage in the form of partitions and volumes. Partitions are used to define boundaries on a storage device. You can define multiple partitions if you want the physical storage to appear as multiple separate storage destinations. Even if you want to use the entire space available on a device as a single contiguous storage location, the area must still be defined by a partition.

Once partitions have been established, the system can create usable volumes inside the partition areas. Volumes define how the files and folders are actually stored on the hardware. In fact, it's the volume that you see represented as a usable storage icon in the Finder. Obviously, a storage device with several partitions, each containing a separate volume, appears as several storage location icons in the Finder.

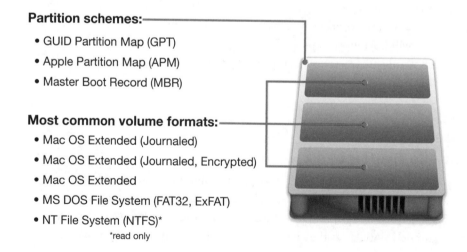

Partition schemes:
- GUID Partition Map (GPT)
- Apple Partition Map (APM)
- Master Boot Record (MBR)

Most common volume formats:
- Mac OS Extended (Journaled)
- Mac OS Extended (Journaled, Encrypted)
- Mac OS Extended
- MS DOS File System (FAT32, ExFAT)
- NT File System (NTFS)*
  *read only

MORE INFO ► macOS Sierra includes support for an entirely new file system known as Apple File System (APFS). Although you can use Terminal commands to create APFS volumes, at this point they are considered experimental and should only be used for testing. However, Apple has announced that future versions of macOS will default to this new file system. You can find out more about APFS at the Apple Developer site, https://developer.apple.com/library/content/documentation/FileManagement/Conceptual/APFS_Guide/Introduction/Introduction.html.

About Partition Schemes

As mentioned earlier, disks must be partitioned to define and possibly segregate the disk's usable space. Every disk requires at least one partition, but macOS can support up to 16 partitions per disk. You learned the advantages and disadvantages of using single and multiple partitions in Lesson 1, "Install macOS Sierra."

As of this writing, macOS supports three types of partition schemes. This may seem excessive, but it's necessary that Mac computers support multiple partition schemes in order to start up computers using modern Intel processors, support older Mac disks, and use standard PC-compatible volumes.

The three partition schemes supported by macOS are:

► GUID Partition Map (GPT)—This is the default partition scheme used by Intel-based Mac computers. It is also the only partition scheme supported for Intel-based Mac computers to start up using disk-based storage. PowerPC-based Mac computers running Mac OS X Tiger 10.4 or later can also access this type of partitioning, but they cannot start up from it. Windows Vista or later and Windows Server 2003 SP1 or later also support disks using GPT.

► Apple Partition Map (APM)—This is the default partition scheme used by previous PowerPC-based Mac computers. It is also the only partition scheme that PowerPC-based Mac computers can start up from. However, all Intel-based Mac computers can also access this type of partitioning. No version of Windows includes built-in support for disks using APM.

► Master Boot Record (MBR)—This is the default partition scheme used by most non-Mac computers, including Windows-compatible PCs. Consequently, this is the default partition scheme you find on most new preformatted storage disks. This partition scheme is also commonly used by peripherals that store to flash memory, such as digital cameras or smartphones. Even though no Mac can start up from this type of partitioning, all Mac computers can fully use MBR partitioned disks.

Obviously, if you have any additional disks formatted with APM or MBR, you have to repartition those disks for them to act as a startup disk for an Intel-based Mac. But if you don't plan on ever using any of these additional disks as a system disk, there is no advantage to repartitioning. Also, you should keep MBR disks unmodified if you want them to be backward compatible with generic PCs or peripherals.

About Volume Formats

The volume format defines how the files and folders are saved to the disk. To maintain compatibility with other operating systems and provide advanced features for later Mac computers, macOS supports a variety of storage volume formats.

Volume formats supported as read/write in macOS are:

▶ Mac OS Standard—This is the legacy volume format used by the classic Mac OS. This format, though a precursor to Mac OS Extended, is not supported as a startup volume for macOS.

▶ Mac OS Extended—This volume format, previously known as OS X Extended, is the legacy format designed and supported by Apple for Mac computers. This format is itself an update from the earlier Mac OS Standard format. Mac OS Extended supports all the advanced features required by macOS, including Unicode filenames, rich metadata, POSIX (Portable Operating System Interface) permissions, access control lists, UNIX-style links, and aliases.

▶ Mac OS Extended (Case-Sensitive)—This Mac OS Extended format adds case sensitivity to the file system. Normally, Mac OS Extended is case-preserving but case-insensitive, which means that a normally formatted Mac volume remembers what case you chose for the characters of a file's name but cannot differentiate between similar filenames where the only difference is the case. In other words, it would not recognize "MYfile" and "myfile" as different filenames. By adding support for case sensitivity, Apple resolved this issue. However, case sensitivity is generally an issue only for volumes that need to support traditional UNIX clients, like those shared from Mac computers running macOS Server. Further, many third-party applications exhibit significant issues when running from a case-sensitive file system. Thus, the case-sensitive option is not supported as a default for macOS client systems.

▶ Mac OS Extended (Journaled) or Mac OS Extended (Case-Sensitive, Journaled)—This feature is an option for the Mac OS Extended format that adds advanced file-system journaling to help preserve volume structure integrity. The journal records what file operations (creation, expansion, deletion, and so on) are in progress at any given moment. If the system crashes or loses power, the journal can be "replayed" to make sure operations that were previously in process are completed rather than left in a half-completed, inconsistent state. This helps avoid the possibility of file corruption and greatly reduces the amount of time it takes to complete the check-and-repair process on the volume after a crash. Because of these enhancements, the required format for a macOS system volume is Mac OS Extended (Journaled).

NOTE ▶ While journaling protects the file structure, it cannot protect the contents of files themselves against corruption. If a large file was half-written when the system crashed, the journal makes sure that the half-file is consistently entered in the volume's file-tracking databases, but it's still only half a file.

▶ Mac OS Extended (Journaled, Encrypted) or Mac OS Extended (Case-Sensitive, Journaled, Encrypted)—This feature is an option to the Mac OS Extended format that adds full disk, XTS-AES 128 encryption. This is the technology behind FileVault system volume encryption. Lesson 10, "Manage FileVault," covers this topic in greater detail.

NOTE ▶ Encrypted Mac OS Extended volumes are not compatible with Mac systems prior to OS X Lion 10.7.

NOTE ▶ No version of Windows includes built-in support for any form of Mac OS volume formats. Thus, if you require a disk that's compatible across both of these common platforms, you should choose a volume format supported by Windows.

▶ File Allocation Table (FAT)—FAT is the legacy volume format used by Windows PCs and by many peripherals. This format has evolved over the years, with each progressive version supporting larger volumes: FAT12, FAT16, and FAT32. Apple Boot Camp supports running Windows XP from a FAT32 volume, but macOS itself cannot start up from such a volume.

▶ Extended File Allocation Table (ExFAT)—Created specifically for large flash storage disks, ExFAT basically extends the legacy FAT architecture to support disks larger than 32 GB. Many flash-based digital camcorders use ExFAT to support the large storage volumes required for high-definition video.

▶ UNIX File System (UFS)—UFS is the legacy native volume format supported by UNIX systems. UFS served as the default UNIX file system for decades. UFS volumes are not supported as startup volumes for macOS. Further, Disk Utility does not support the creation of UFS volumes.

Volume formats supported as read-only in macOS are:

▶ New Technology File System (NTFS)—Windows 7, Windows Vista, Windows XP, and Windows Server all use this as their default native volume format. Once again, Boot Camp supports running Windows from an NTFS volume, but macOS itself cannot write to or start up from such a volume. Further, Disk Utility does not support the creation of NTFS volumes.

> **TIP** ▶ You can add NTFS volume write support to macOS by installing the free, open source NTFS-3G + Ntfsprogs software, available at www.tuxera.com/community/open-source-ntfs-3g/.

▶ ISO 9660 or Compact Disc File System (CDFS)—This is a common standard for read-only CD media. Note, however, that "Mac formatted" CD media can also contain Mac OS Standard formatted volumes.

▶ Universal Disk Format (UDF)—This is a common standard for read-only DVD media. Again, note that "Mac formatted" DVD media can also contain Mac OS Standard volumes.

> **MORE INFO** ▶ Wikipedia has a great comparison of the wide variety of file systems: http://en.wikipedia.org/wiki/Comparison_of_file_systems.

About Core Storage

Core Storage is an additional management layer between the traditional partition scheme and volume formats of a disk. Although this adds complexity to the file system, it also adds significant flexibility. For example, Core Storage allows macOS Sierra to encrypt (or decrypt) a volume without interrupting use of the volume, as used by FileVault system volume encryption. Core Storage also allows for more complex arrangements of multiple disks, as used by Fusion Drive. Further, Core Storage offers increased file system crash protection and more reliable methods for storing file system metadata and catalog data.

In previous Mac operating systems, Core Storage was enabled only if the system used either FileVault system volume encryption or Fusion Drive. With OS X El Capitan 10.11 and later, Core Storage is enabled by default for late-model Mac portable computers even if they aren't using FileVault or a Fusion Drive. Specifically, during an upgrade to OS X El Capitan or later, the installer will automatically enable Core Storage on any Mac portable that supports accelerated disk encryption. Further, on these systems, the Setup Assistant will encourage the user to enable FileVault, as covered in Lesson 2, "Set Up and Configure macOS."

The following graphic represents a typical macOS Sierra system disk. As you can see, the disk uses GPT to define two partitions. The first partition, occupying the majority of the disk, contains the system volume. This partition is managed by Core Storage and is formatted as either a Mac OS Extended (Journaled) volume or a Mac OS Extended (Journaled, Encrypted) volume if FileVault system volume encryption is enabled.

The second partition, occupying the final ~650 MB of the disk, is an "Apple_Boot" formatted volume that contains the Recovery HD system. Aside from providing macOS Recovery functionality, this second partition is intentionally not managed by Core Storage, since it provides the software necessary for a Mac computer's (relatively simple) firmware to understand Core Storage volumes. Thus, the initial startup of macOS is facilitated by the Recovery HD volume.

Partition scheme:
- GUID Partition Map (GPT)
- Core Storage logical volume

Macintosh HD volume:
- Mac OS Extended (Journaled)
- Mac OS Extended (Journaled, Encrypted)

Recovery HD volume:
- Hidden Apple_Boot format volume
- ~650 MB

About Fusion Drive

Mac computers featuring Fusion Drive break from the traditional disk, partition, and volume paradigm. Courtesy of Core Storage, a Mac with Fusion Drive uses two separate physical disks to form one logical storage device. This provides a hybrid storage solution that has both the speed of flash storage and the size of traditional spinning disk media.

The following graphic represents a typical macOS Sierra system disk on a Mac with Fusion Drive. As you can see, each separate physical disk uses GPT to define two partitions. The first partitions of each disk, occupying the majority of each disk, are combined into a single system volume. These two partitions, again from two separate disks, are managed by Core Storage, which has the ability to merge the two separate physical volumes into a single logical volume. The resulting combined volume is formatted as either a Mac OS Extended (Journaled) volume or a Mac OS Extended (Journaled, Encrypted) volume if FileVault system volume encryption is enabled.

The second partition on each disk is intentionally not managed by Core Storage, as it provides the software necessary for the Mac computer's (relatively simple) firmware to understand Core Storage volumes. In the case of Fusion Drive, the smaller flash storage disk contains a ~185 MB "Boot OS X" volume, and the larger spinning disk contains the ~650 MB Recovery HD system. As you can tell from the name, the Boot OS X volume is used to facilitate the initial macOS system startup.

Physical disks:
- Smaller flash storage
- Larger spinning disk

Partition scheme:
- GUID Partition Map (GPT)
- Core Storage logical volume

Macintosh HD volume

Boot OS X volume

Recovery HD volume

MORE INFO ▶ Additional partitions on a Fusion Drive disk can be added only to the larger spinning disk. Thus, additional partitions are not able to take advantage of the flash storage performance increase normally seen with Fusion Drive. For more information, see Apple Support article HT202574, "Mac mini (Late 2012 and later), iMac (Late 2012 and later): About Fusion Drive."

Reference 9.2
Mount, Unmount, and Eject Disks

Mounting a volume is the process by which the system establishes a logical connection to a storage volume. This is not something users normally concern themselves with on the Mac, because the system automatically mounts any volume connected to the Mac. Simply plug a disk in, and the disk's volumes automatically appear in the Finder and Disk Utility.

The only exception to this rule is for Mac OS Extended (Journaled, Encrypted) volumes, which require that you enter a password to unlock the disk's contents.

Ensuring that users properly unmount and eject volumes is critical to maintaining data integrity. Unmounting is the process of having the Mac cleanly disconnect from a disk's volumes, whereas ejecting is the process of having the Mac additionally disconnect electronically from the actual hardware disk or media. When you choose to eject a disk from the Finder, the computer actually unmounts the volumes first and then ejects the disk.

Ejecting Disks

There are five ways to unmount and eject a disk from the Finder:

▶ In the Finder, drag the disk icon to the Trash icon in the Dock. You'll note that the Trash icon changes to an Eject icon, indicating the appropriate action.

▶ In the Finder sidebar, click the small Eject button next to the volume you want to unmount and eject.

▶ In the Finder, select the volume you want to unmount and eject, and then choose File > Eject.

▶ In the Finder, select the volume you want to unmount and eject, and then use the Command-E keyboard shortcut.

▶ In the Finder, select the volume you want to unmount and eject, and then secondary-click (or Control-click) to reveal a pop-up menu allowing you to select Eject.

NOTE ▶ Pressing and holding the Eject key (the farthest top-right key on some Mac keyboards) for a few moments unmounts and ejects only optical media, like CDs or DVDs. If you have more than one optical disc drive, press Option-Eject to eject the second optical disc.

When you use the Finder to unmount and eject a single volume that is part of a disk with several mounted volumes, you see a warning dialog giving you the choice to unmount and eject all the volumes on the disk or just the one you originally selected. You shouldn't experience any problems with a disk if some volumes are mounted and others remain unmounted. Just remember to properly unmount the remaining volumes before you physically disconnect the disk.

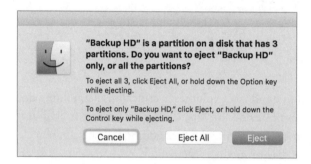

TIP ▶ In the Finder, you can eject all the volumes of a disk without additional confirmation by holding down the Option key while you click the Eject button.

Disk Utility Mount Management

If you're using the Finder, remounting volumes on a connected disk is a bit of a hassle. You must first unmount and eject any remaining volumes and then physically disconnect and reconnect the disk. Alternatively, open /Applications/Utilities/Disk Utility to manually mount and unmount volumes without physically disconnecting and reconnecting the disk.

In the following screenshot of Disk Utility, a variety of volumes are shown. Notice that the volume names from the second disk appear in dimmed text; those volumes are physically connected to the Mac but are not mounted.

To mount an unmounted volume on a connected disk, select the volume's dimmed name and then click the Mount button in the toolbar. The volume immediately mounts and appears in the Finder and as normal text in Disk Utility.

As covered previously, if you try to mount a Mac OS Extended (Journaled, Encrypted) volume, unless the password was previously saved to an open keychain, a dialog will appear where you can enter a password to unlock the disk's contents. Once authenticated, the volume immediately mounts.

> **TIP** ▶ If you often use an encrypted disk, you can save time by saving the disk's password to your keychain. Using Keychain is covered in Lesson 7, "Manage Security and Privacy."

If you have selected a volume to unmount, simply click the Unmount button in the toolbar. If you have selected an entire disk, to unmount all its volumes and eject it, click the Eject button in the toolbar. All the disk's volumes unmount, and then the disk disconnects from the system, disappearing from the Finder and from Disk Utility. In this case, you have to physically disconnect and reconnect the disk for its volumes to be remounted.

Ejecting In-Use Volumes

Any volume that contains files currently in use by an application or system process cannot be unmounted or ejected. The obvious reason for this is to avoid data corruption when a process attempts to write to files on that volume. If you try to eject a volume with in-use files, the Finder does not allow you to do so, but, depending on the situation, it may try to help you eject the volume. If the application or process using the volume belongs to your account, the Finder lets you know via the following dialog. In this case, the resolution is as simple as quitting the suspect application and attempting to eject the volume again.

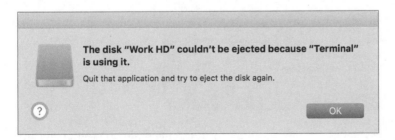

The disk "Work HD" couldn't be ejected because "Terminal" is using it.

Quit that application and try to eject the disk again.

OK

> **NOTE** ▶ As the screenshot shows, using Terminal can prevent you from ejecting a volume. Even if no process is active, just having Terminal open, with the volume as the current working directory, prevents unmounting.

If you don't own the application or process using the volume, the Finder asks if you want to attempt to forcibly eject the volume. To do that, you have to click the Force Eject button twice; the Finder then tries to quit the offending application or process to release the volume you're attempting to eject. If the volume is successfully ejected, you are notified by the dialog.

If this doesn't work or the Finder doesn't tell you which application is the problem, you can always log out the current user to quit all of his or her processes and then log in again, or fully restart the Mac to clear the issue. Although this may seem excessive, it is not advisable to physically disconnect a volume without first unmounting it, as covered in the next section.

Improperly Unmounting or Ejecting

Disconnecting a volume from a Mac that you did not first unmount can lead to data corruption. If you forcibly eject a disk by physically disconnecting it before you unmount it, or if the system loses contact with the disk due to power failure, the Mac warns you with a device removal dialog. You should immediately reconnect the device so the Mac can attempt to verify or repair its contents.

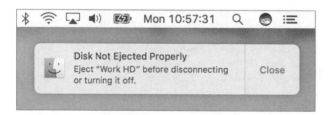

Anytime you reconnect a disk that was improperly unmounted, the Mac automatically runs a file system diagnostic on the disk before it remounts any volumes. Depending on the format and size of the disk, it may take anywhere from a few seconds to several hours for the system to verify the contents of the disk. Again, journaled volumes, like Mac OS Extended (Journaled), verify quite quickly.

If you connect a disk and notice a fair amount of disk activity but the volumes have not mounted yet, the system is probably running a diagnostic on the disk. You can verify that the system is diagnosing a volume by opening the /Applications/Utilities/Activity Monitor application and looking for a background process with "fsck" in its name. Monitoring processes is covered in **Lesson 18, "Manage and Troubleshoot Applications."**

Reference 9.3
Inspect File System Components

If you plan to manage or troubleshoot the computer's file system, you should become fully familiar with the current configuration you're dealing with. You can quickly access a graphical overview of the Mac computer's storage from the Stage pane of the About This Mac dialog, which can be opened from the Apple menu.

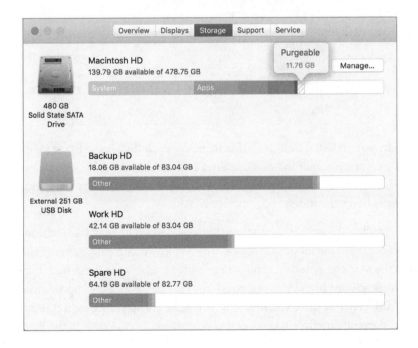

MORE INFO ▸ You can find out more about Purgeable items and the new macOS Sierra storage optimization features (accessed via the Manage button in the About This Mac dialog) in **Lesson 17, "Manage Documents."**

For a more detailed examination of the storage systems, you'll need to use the Disk Utility and System Information applications. These tools allow you to inspect the availability and status of storage hardware currently available to the system.

Examine Storage via Disk Utility

The primary storage management tool included in macOS is /Applications/Utilities /Disk Utility. When you open Disk Utility, it scans the file system for all attached devices and volumes.

The disk storage hardware is listed first, and directly below each disk is the list of volumes. The disk's name is a combination of the manufacturer and model name. Volume names are first set when the volume is formatted but can be changed at any time by the user. Thus, volume names often vary widely.

For example, the preceding screenshot shows three physical disks. The first disk is the internal system disk and contains one mounted volume. This volume is currently selected and also happens to be the Mac computer's current system volume. The second external disk also contains one mounted volume, but as you can guess from the name it's a backup volume. The third external disk contains three volumes, but their light gray coloring indicates that the volumes are not currently mounted. Unmounted volumes will not appear in the Finder.

Also, as you can see in the previous screenshot, selecting any item in Disk Utility will reveal information about the item, including utilization, formatting, and connection information. To gather detailed information about a specific disk or volume in Disk Utility, select the item from the column on the left and then click the Info button in the toolbar.

Envoy Pro Media	
Volume type	Physical Device
BSD device node	disk2
File system	Unknown
Connection	USB
Device tree path	IODeviceTree:/PCI0@0/XHC1@14
Writable	No
Is case-sensitive	No
Volume capacity	251,000,193,024
Available space	0
Free space	0
Used space	251,000,193,024
Owners enabled	No
Is encrypted	No
Can be verified	No
Can be repaired	No
Bootable	No
Journaled	No
Disk number	2
Media name	Envoy Pro Media
Media type	Generic
Ejectable	Yes
Solid state	No
S.M.A.R.T. status	Not Supported

The information gathered from this dialog reveals a great deal about the status of a disk or volume. A particularly helpful piece of information for identifying hardware failure is a disk's S.M.A.R.T. (self-monitoring, analysis, and reporting technology) status. S.M.A.R.T. can automatically determine whether a disk is suffering from some sort of internal hardware failure. Unfortunately, as you can see from the preceding screenshot, many external disks don't support S.M.A.R.T.

Examine Storage via System Information

There are several instances where you may want to double-check the disk's status using /Applications/Utilities/System Information. For example, it's possible that a disk has suffered such catastrophic failure that it doesn't even appear in the Disk Utility list. Another example is that Disk Utility doesn't show hidden volumes such as the Recovery HD volume that is often adjacent to the macOS system volume.

When you open System Information, your first step should be to examine the physical storage devices by selecting one of the storage interfaces. If a physical device does not appear in System Information, it is not available to the Mac in its current state. At that point, you should focus your efforts on troubleshooting the disk hardware. This includes simple fixes, such as looking for loose connections or replacing bad cables, as well as more complex fixes, such as replacing bad hardware like the disk enclosure.

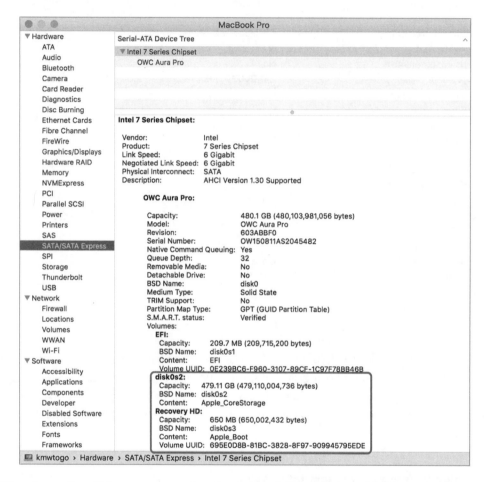

When inspecting disks, you may notice that internal disks are named by the manufacturer, which in many cases is not Apple. Only recent flash-based Mac computers will show the name APPLE SSD. In the previous example screenshot, the system uses a replacement disk, an OWC Aura Pro, connected via SATA, so selecting the SATA/SATA Express section in System Information reveals more information about the hardware.

A bit of confusion when inspecting physical storage in System Information is that Core Storage volumes don't appear with their appropriate volume name. As you can see in the previous screenshot, the OWC Aura Pro disk contains a Core Storage volume, but we can't see its name. One clue, however, is the existence of a Recovery HD volume that's often adjacent to a macOS system volume.

To solve this mystery, you can further inspect the contents of the Storage section in System Information. The Storage section will show you all currently mounted volumes, regardless of origin. The following screenshot was taken on the same system but shows the Storage section in System Information. Note that in the Storage section you can easily identify the physical storage device used for the encrypted Macintosh HD volume, OWC Aura Pro Media, and that the device's S.M.A.R.T. status is Verified.

Yet, every good mystery ends with a twist; in the same screenshot note the name used to describe the File System type. The System Information application uses the term "Journaled HFS+" to describe the file system instead of "Mac OS Extended (Journaled)," as you would see in Disk Utility. The acronym "HFS+" stands for Hierarchical File System Plus, which was the original name for what is now known as Mac OS Extended.

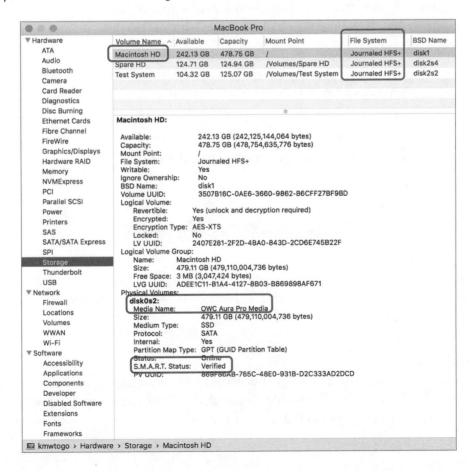

Reference 9.4
Manage File Systems

Again, the primary storage management tool included in macOS Sierra is /Applications/ Utilities/Disk Utility. In this section you will explore how you can use Disk Utility to modify disks and volumes.

TIP ▶ In the Finder, you can rename any volume without having to reformat or erase its content. Simply edit the volume name as you would any other item in the Finder, or, from the Finder sidebar, secondary-click (or Control-click) to rename it.

Format Unreadable Disks

Most new storage devices are either completely blank or formatted for Windows. For the most part, you can use Windows-formatted disks on the Mac without reformatting. However, if you want to install the Mac operating system on a disk, or you have a new disk that is completely blank, you have to erase and format (or initialize) the disk.

If you attach an unformatted disk, the Mac automatically prompts you to open Disk Utility. Once in Disk Utility you can click the Erase button to quickly erase and format the selected disk. Specific instructions for erasing in Disk Utility are covered later in this lesson.

NOTE ▶ If you attach a disk that should work but you get this message, the disk likely has serious problems. See Reference 9.5, "Troubleshoot File Systems," later in this lesson for troubleshooting suggestions.

Partition a Disk

Disk Utility allows you to dynamically partition a disk without destroying any data currently stored on the disk. This functionality is also used to facilitate the Boot Camp setup process and the creation of the hidden Recovery HD during a macOS upgrade installation.

The only downside to dynamic partitioning is that some disks may not support the partition changes you want to make. For instance, some disks may be too full for you to repartition. Also, Disk Utility is less flexible in its ability to modify disks containing encrypted volumes or Fusion Drive disks, and it does not support dynamically partitioning disks formatted with the MBR partition scheme. If you come across any of these issues, you will have to erase the disk, as covered later in this lesson.

NOTE ▶ Always back up important data before making changes to a disk's file system.

NOTE ▶ Modifying a macOS system disk often requires relocating the hidden macOS Recovery HD. Fortunately, Disk Utility handles this automatically for you.

Again, opening Disk Utility reveals a list of connected disks and volumes. Physical disks are identified by the manufacturer and model name of the device. Select the disk (not the volume) that you want to modify, and then click the Partition button in the toolbar.

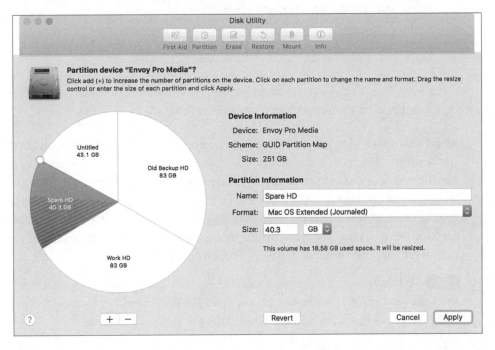

The disk will be represented by a pie chart graphic. Each slice of the pie represents a separate partition and its volume on the disk. The "beginning" of the disk's storage is at the 12:00 position; moving clockwise indicates progression through the available storage, returning to the "end" of the disk at 12:00 again. Thus, the pie chart in the previous screenshot illustrates a disk that would eventually have four partitions. The two partitions of the disk are larger, followed by two smaller partitions, and the second-to-last partition is selected for editing.

The partition interface in Disk Utility allows you to:

▸ Erase and reformat a partition—Selecting a partition slice will reveal the partition's name, format, size, and used space. Selecting a different format from the Format pop-up menu will indicate that you want to erase and reformat the selected partition. The act of erasing and reformatting won't be applied to the disk until you click the Apply button.

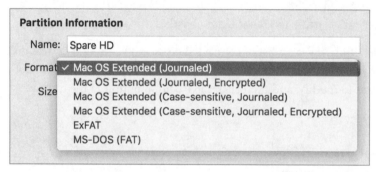

NOTE ▸ In Disk Utility, you can change the partition scheme of a disk only by erasing the entire disk, as covered later in this lesson.

▸ Resize a partition—Drag the small circle indicators at the edge of the pie chart until you reach the desired new size of a partition slice. Alternatively, you can enter a specific partition size in the Size field. As easy as this interface appears, there are a few rules that are automatically enforced. First, you cannot shrink a partition smaller than the current volume's content, as indicated by diagonal hash marks in the selected partition. Also, you cannot move the beginning of an existing partition. Finally, you cannot rearrange the order of existing partitions on the disk.

TIP While viewing the Partition interface in Disk Utility, hold the Shift key to show the used space on all partitions, and hold the Command key to show the small circle indicators that allow you to click and drag to resize a partition.

▸ Add a new partition—Click the Add (+) button below the pie chart to add a new partition. The default behavior will halve the currently selected partition slice.

Remember that you can have as many as 16 partitions per disk, each containing a unique volume. Be sure to choose an appropriate name and volume format from the pop-up menu for each new volume.

▶ Delete a partition—Select the partition slice and click the Delete (–) button below the pie chart. Obviously, indicating that you want a partition deleted will effectively erase that partition's content. The deleted partition's space will be allocated to the previous partition, but you can continue to make adjustments until you click the Apply button. Disk Utility will not actually perform the delete action until you click the Apply button.

Erase a Disk or Volume

In Disk Utility, the act of erasing a disk or volume will automatically format (or initialize) the storage. Again, opening Disk Utility reveals a list of connected disks and volumes. Physical disks are identified by the manufacturer and model name of the device. Volume names vary, but they always appear indented below the disk identifier. Select the disk or volume you want to erase, and then click the Erase button in the toolbar.

When you erase a disk (as opposed to a volume), Disk Utility automatically creates a new volume format and partition scheme. Disk Utility defaults to the Mac OS Extended (Journaled) format and the GUID Partition Map scheme. To select a different format or scheme, select it from the appropriate pop-up menu. Differences between specific volume formats and partition schemes are detailed earlier in this lesson.

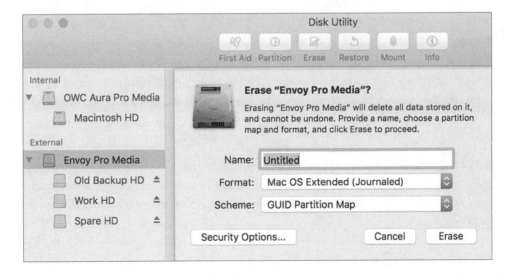

When you erase a volume (as opposed to a disk), Disk Utility automatically creates a new volume format, again defaulting to Mac OS Extended (Journaled). Importantly, when you erase a selected volume, none of the other volumes on the disk are affected. Further, you cannot change the disk's partition scheme—that would affect all volumes on the disk.

NOTE ▶ If you have selected an encrypted volume format, a dialog appears, allowing you to set the encrypted volume's password. Note that, as the dialog states, you are not able to recover data from the encrypted volume if you lose the password. Choose the password wisely.

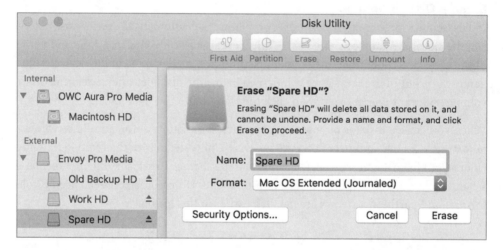

Erasing and reformatting storage destroys any existing volume formatting; a reformatted disk is effectively losing its contents. Yet the default Disk Utility erase process does not actually erase any files from the disk; Disk Utility creates new "empty" volumes by simply replacing the file and folder structures. The old data files still remain on the disk and can be recovered using the appropriate third-party tools.

In fact, there is no such thing as erasing data from a disk—all you can do is write new data on top of the old data. Therefore, if you want to truly "erase" a disk or volume, you must somehow write new nonsensitive data on top of it. When erasing a selected partition or volume in Disk Utility, you also have the option of securely erasing the selected item's content.

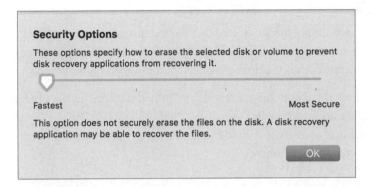

If you require a secure erase, click Security Options to display a dialog with four options along a slider:

▶ Fastest: don't erase data—This is the default action that occurs when you erase or reformat a disk or volume. Obviously, this option does not provide any security from disk-recovery utilities. On the other hand, this choice provides a nearly instantaneous erase option.

▶ Second choice: 2-pass erase—This option writes a first pass of random data and then a second pass of zeros. This is the quickest of the secure erase options, and for most users provides an adequate level of security. This is also the best option for flash-based media because additional passes do not provide more security and can lead to degraded disk performance.

▶ Third choice: 3-pass erase—This is a very secure option that writes two passes of random data followed by a single pass of known data to the disk. According to Apple, this option meets U.S. Department of Energy standards for securely erasing data.

▶ Most Secure: 7-pass erase—This is the most secure option, which according to Apple meets U.S. Department of Defense standards for securely erasing magnetic media. The Mac writes seven different passes of random and patterned data to the disk. Obviously, this method takes the longest to complete.

NOTE ▶ Depending on the size of the selected disk or volume and the secure erase option you choose, this process can take anywhere from seconds to days.

Deleted Files Security

The default macOS behavior simply marks deleted files as free space, leaving the files intact until written on top of by another action. Thus, all files previously "erased" by the system could potentially still be accessible on the disk given the appropriate third-party tools.

macOS Sierra does not have the ability to securely delete individual items in the Finder or the remaining free space on a volume in Disk Utility. You can still use Disk Utility to securely erase a volume, but if security is truly a concern, a better solution would be to store all of your data on encrypted volumes.

This is because all of the data (current or "erased") on an encrypted volume is always scrambled to those who don't have authorization to access its contents. After all, the items you haven't erased are probably more important than the items you have erased. Thus, concerning yourself with securely erasing deleted items is a waste of time when you have the ability to encrypt the entire volume in the first place.

Encrypt an External Disk

Disk Utility cannot convert an existing Mac OS Extended volume to an encrypted volume. Instead, as covered earlier, it can only erase and reformat the volume as encrypted. This is obviously inconvenient if you want to encrypt the contents of an existing disk. Fortunately, in macOS you can easily convert an existing disk to an encrypted disk using the Finder.

There are, however, a few caveats when encrypting an existing disk. First, encrypted Mac OS Extended volumes are only compatible with Mac computers running OS X Lion 10.7 or later. Further, due to the complex nature of solid-state and flash disk controllers, encrypting a disk may still leave some parts of the original data in a recover-able form. To minimize the security risk, it's ideal to encrypt a flash-based disk before saving any sensitive data to it. Finally, the Finder can convert volumes only on disks formatted with the GPT partition scheme.

> **TIP** To encrypt the macOS system volume, you need to enable FileVault. Lesson 10, "Manage FileVault," covers this topic in greater detail.

To encrypt a disk in the Finder, secondary-click (or Control-click) the disk you want to encrypt, and from the shortcut menu choose Encrypt *<diskname>*, where *<diskname>* is the name of the disk you've selected.

The Finder prompts you to set a password and a password hint for the encrypted disk. You must set a password hint, because it's the only thing that will help you recover a lost password. Should you lose the password, there is no way to recover the disk's data. Once you enter these items and then click Encrypt Disk, you may notice that the disk quickly disappears, and then after a few seconds it reappears in the Finder as the system begins encrypting the disk's contents.

Amazingly, you can continue to use the disk as usual while the system encrypts the disk's contents in the background, though you might notice some performance degradation. From this point forward, whenever you attempt to connect the encrypted disk, you are prompted for the disk's password.

> **TIP** Again, you can configure the system to automatically authenticate an encrypted disk by saving the password to your keychain. This can be configured when you reconnect the encrypted disk and are prompted for the disk's password. Using keychains is covered in Lesson 7, "Manage Security and Privacy."

You can see whether the encryption is complete in the Finder by secondary-clicking (or Control-clicking) the disk. In the shortcut menu, a fully encrypted disk shows a Decrypt *<diskname>* option, where *<diskname>* is the name of the disk you've selected.

> **TIP** From the Disk Utility File menu, you can change the password or decrypt an encrypted disk. Obviously, you must know the encrypted disk's current password to perform these operations.

Reference 9.5
Troubleshoot File Systems

Because any operating system requires a functional file system, the software that drives the file system is very reliable. In fact, most file system failures are due to bad hardware or media. No matter how good the software is, though, if the hardware is no longer reading or writing bits, it's pretty much useless to the file system.

File System Troubleshooting First Steps

Your first step is to verify hardware connectivity to the problematic storage device. If the problematic storage is a nonsystem disk, refer to Reference 9.3, "Inspect File System Components," to verify storage hardware functionality.

If the problem appears to involve the system disk, you can attempt to start up from macOS Recovery by holding down Command-R at startup. From macOS Recovery, you can access Disk Utility to inspect and potentially repair the system disk. If the default macOS Recovery system doesn't work, you can use any of the alternative methods detailed in Lesson 3, "Use macOS Recovery."

If, during initial troubleshooting, you determine that catastrophic hardware failure is the problem, there really isn't anything you can do from a software perspective to repair the device. Only a data recovery service, such as DriveSavers, might have a chance of recovering your data.

> **MORE INFO** ▶ DriveSavers is the most popular hard disk recovery service for Mac-formatted volumes. You can find out more at www.drivesaversdatarecovery.com.

Conversely, if you're experiencing file system issues but the storage hardware still appears to function, you may be experiencing partial hardware failure or file system corruption. In these cases, you can try some steps using the built-in utilities in macOS to repair the volumes or at least recover data.

About Disk Utility First Aid

To access data on the disk, the file system must first read the partition scheme and volume directory structure to locate the appropriate bits on the disk that make up the requested items. The partition scheme is used to define the space where volumes exist. The volume directory structure is used by the file system to catalog where files and folders exist on the disk. Obviously, any damage to this information can lead to serious problems, including data loss.

Before any disk is mounted, the Mac automatically performs a quick consistency check to verify the disk's partition scheme and volume directory structure. The system also quickly scans the startup disk during the startup process. However, if the system is unable to mount a disk or its volumes, or you are experiencing problems accessing a disk's content, you can use Disk Utility First Aid to verify and repair the partition scheme or volume directory structures.

To use the First Aid feature in Disk Utility, first double-check that the disk you want to repair is attached to the computer, and then open /Applications/Utilities/Disk Utility. Select the disk or volume you want to verify or repair from the column on the left, and then click the First Aid button in the toolbar.

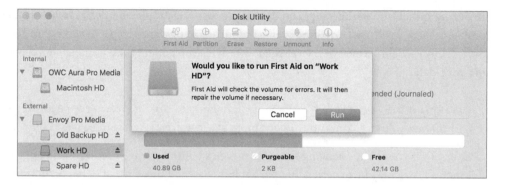

By selecting a disk, you are indicating that you want to repair the selected disk's partition scheme. However, by selecting a volume you are indicating that you want to repair the selected volume's directory structure. As a best practice, you should attempt to repair all components of a problematic disk by starting with the disk's partition scheme, followed by any volumes.

The First Aid verify and repair process may take a few minutes to complete. During this time, Disk Utility shows a progress indicator and log entries in the history area. Click the Show Details disclosure triangle to view more detail in the history log.

If no problems are found, a green checkmark will appear. If problems are uncovered, they appear in bright red text in the log. If the disk has problems, the First Aid process will attempt to repair the issues. The system continues to run the repair process until no more problems are found. This may take a while, because the system may run through the repair process several times.

About Target Disk Mode

Mac hardware has a unique ability to share its internal disks via a feature called target disk mode. Basically, when target disk mode is engaged, instead of starting up normally from the system disk the Mac creates a connection from the internal disks to the FireWire, Thunderbolt, or USB-C ports.

> **MORE INFO ▶** MacBook models that feature only a single USB-C port have limited Time Machine compatibility. These models support Target Disk Mode only via an appropriate USB-C cable. For more information, see Apple Support article HT204360, "Using USB-C and Thunderbolt 3 (USB-C) ports and adapters on your Mac notebook."

Because the target disk mode function is built into the Mac computer's hardware, you can still use this feature even if the installed operating system volume is corrupted. An administrator user can enable target disk mode on a currently running Mac by clicking the Target Disk Mode button in Startup Disk preferences. Alternatively, assuming the system doesn't have a firmware password, any user can engage target disk mode during system startup by holding down the T key while turning on the Mac.

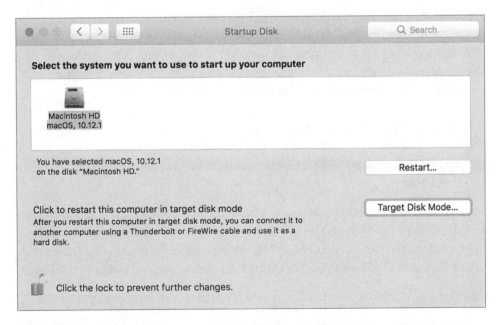

Once target disk mode has been engaged, large FireWire, Thunderbolt, and/or USB symbols appear on the screen, and then you can simply plug the targeted Mac into another fully functioning Mac using a FireWire, Thunderbolt, or USB-C cable.

The targeted Mac's internal volumes mount normally on the other Mac, as if you had plugged in a normal external disk. At this point, you can do anything to the targeted Mac's internal disk that you could do to any local disk, including installations, repairs, and data migration.

As useful as target disk mode is, be aware of a few caveats:

▶ Older USB-A ports on Mac computers do not support target disk mode. However, older Mac computers with USB-A ports can mount disks of newer Mac computers in target disk mode via USB-C with an appropriate USB-C to USB-A adapter.

▶ Target disk mode is not supported on disks that use third-party storage interfaces, like those found on PCI Express expansion cards.

▶ Target disk mode cannot be engaged during system startup when using a Bluetooth wireless keyboard.

▶ Certain forms of hardware failure can prevent a Mac from entering target disk mode. If you suspect this is the case, try using Apple Hardware Test, as covered in **Lesson 26, "Troubleshoot Startup and System Issues."**

Recovering Data from a Nonstarting System

If you are still stuck with a Mac that refuses to fully start up from its internal system disk, you might be able to recover important data off the disk as long as it's functional. You can use the Mac's built-in target disk mode to easily access the internal system disk and transfer important data to another working Mac.

> **NOTE** ▶ If your Mac doesn't support, or is unable to engage, target disk mode, your best bet is to visit an Apple Authorized Service Provider. As an alternative, you could attempt to remove the disk from the troubled computer and attach it to a fully functional Mac.

First, turn on or restart the problematic Mac while holding down the T key to engage target disk mode, and connect the computer to another, fully functioning Mac using an appropriate cable. If the targeted Mac's volume appears in the Finder, first attempt to repair the disk and volumes via Disk Utility First Aid, as detailed earlier in this lesson.

After repairs have been completed, you have a variety of data recovery options:

▶ Use the Finder to manually copy data from the targeted Mac to storage attached to the functioning Mac.

▶ Use Disk Utility on the functioning Mac to create a disk image archive of the targeted Mac's system volume. Creating disk images is covered in Lesson 12, "Use Hidden Items, Shortcuts, and File Archives."

▶ Migrate user data to the other system either manually or using Migration Assistant. Migrating user data is detailed in Lesson 6, "Manage User Home Folders."

▶ After you have migrated the data, use Disk Utility to reformat the targeted Mac's disk, and then attempt to reinstall the operating system. Lesson 1, "Install macOS Sierra," covers this topic in greater detail.

Depending on the amount of corruption to the targeted Mac's system disk, you may not be able to use Disk Utility or Migration Assistant. The disk may simply be too corrupted to recover all that data. In this case, you have to resort to manually copying data.

In general, the items most important to users are stored in their home folder, so you should start there. This can be a time-consuming process, because when the Finder discovers damaged files, you have to manually restart the copy process and omit the damaged files.

> **TIP** ▶ Use the ample spare time between manual file copies to remind the Mac's owner (or yourself) that you wouldn't need to labor over a broken disk if there had been a good backup! **Lesson 15, "Manage Time Machine,"** covers this topic in greater detail.

> **TIP** ▶ Several third-party disk recovery utilities are available for macOS. This guide doesn't recommend one over another; contact an Apple Authorized Service Provider for recommendations.

Exercise 9.1
Repartition a Disk Dynamically

▶ **Prerequisites**

    ▶ You must have created the Local Admin account (Exercise 2.1, "Configure a New macOS System for Exercises," or Exercise 2.2, "Configure an Existing macOS System for Exercises").

    ▶ Your startup volume must be less than half full.

In this exercise, you will partition your computer's internal disk. If you do not want to repartition your internal disk, you can still perform the steps in the "View Disk Information with Disk Utility" section and then skip the rest of this exercise; however, if you choose not to repartition your disk, you will need an external disk to use as a Time Machine backup volume in **Lesson 15, "Manage Time Machine."** You can also partition your disk now and then remove the additional partition after you have finished testing Time Machine.

As always, backing up any important data before partitioning is a good idea.

View Storage Information with About This Mac

Before you repartition your disk, you will gather information about it using About This Mac and Disk Utility.

1   Log in as Local Admin (password: ladminpw, or whatever you chose when you created the account).

2   Choose Apple menu > About This Mac.

3   Click the Storage tab.

This pane shows the volumes mounted on your Mac (usually Macintosh HD will be the only one), and shows how much disk space is in use for several categories of file. You can hover your pointer over the colored sections of the bar to see what category they correspond to.

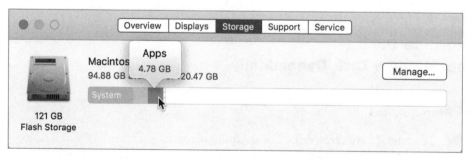

4   Click the Manage button.

System Information opens and shows several options for reducing disk usage on your computer.

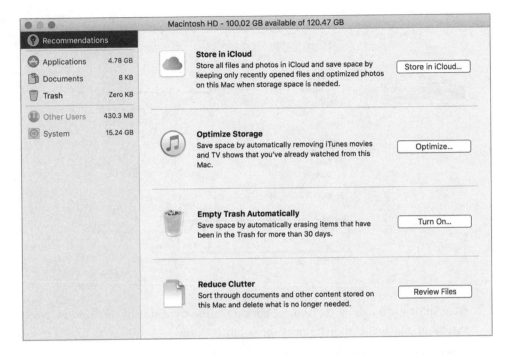

These options are covered in detail in Reference 17.5, "Optimize Local Storage."

5   Click through the other items in the sidebar.

These show details about the different categories of files on your Mac. Note that the Other Users and System categories cannot be viewed in detail.

6   Quit System Information.

View Disk Information with Disk Utility

1   Open Disk Utility from the Utilities folder. Remember that you can reach this folder in the Finder by choosing Go menu > Utilities or by pressing Command-Shift-U.

2   If necessary, select the entry for your startup volume (generally Macintosh HD) in the sidebar.

Basic information about the volume appears in the right side of the window. Note that the volume format is shown under the volume's name.

The volume in the screenshot is listed as a logical volume because it is being managed by Core Storage; if it were not managed by Core Storage, it would be listed as a physical volume instead. Reference 9.1, "About File Systems," describes Core Storage in more detail.

3   Check the amount of used space in the volume. If the volume is more than half full, you will not have enough space to repartition it and should stop this exercise at the end of this section.

4   Click the Info button in the toolbar.

A window opens showing additional details about the volume. You may need to scroll down to see all the window's contents.

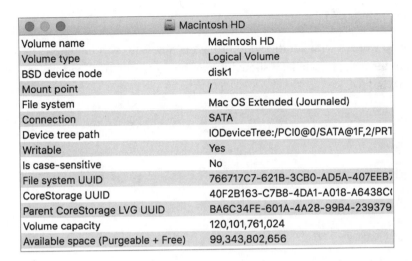

Volume name	Macintosh HD
Volume type	Logical Volume
BSD device node	disk1
Mount point	/
File system	Mac OS Extended (Journaled)
Connection	SATA
Device tree path	IODeviceTree:/PCI0@0/SATA@1F,2/PRT
Writable	Yes
Is case-sensitive	No
File system UUID	766717C7-621B-3CB0-AD5A-407EEB7
CoreStorage UUID	40F2B163-C7B8-4DA1-A018-A6438C(
Parent CoreStorage LVG UUID	BA6C34FE-601A-4A28-99B4-239379
Volume capacity	120,101,761,024
Available space (Purgeable + Free)	99,343,802,656

5   Close the information window.

6   Select the entry for your internal disk (generally the top item) in the sidebar.

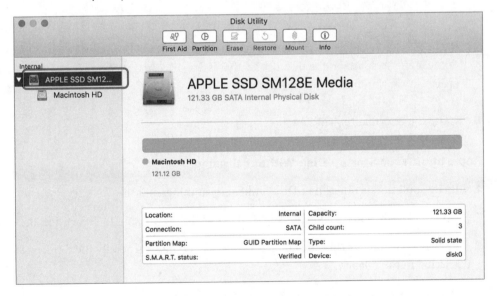

Basic information about the disk (including its total capacity and partition map type) appears near the bottom of the window.

7   Click the Info button in the toolbar.

Again, a window opens with additional information. Since this window shows information about the disk as a whole, it shows different information than you saw in the volume info window.

● ● ● APPLE SSD SM128E Media	
Volume type	Physical Device
BSD device node	disk0
Connection	SATA
Device tree path	IODeviceTree:/PCI0@0/SATA@1F,2/PR1
Writable	No
Is case-sensitive	No
Volume capacity	121,332,826,112
Available space (Purgeable + Free)	0
Purgeable space	0
Free space	0
Used space	121,332,826,112
Owners enabled	No
Is encrypted	No
Can be verified	No

NOTE ▶ The "Available space" and "Free space" entries will normally be zero. These entries refer to space on the disk device that is not allocated to any volume, not to free space within volumes.

8   Close the information window.

Repartition Your Startup Disk Without Erasing

1   If any applications other than Disk Utility are running, quit them.

Do not use any other applications while Disk Utility is working to repartition the disk.

2   In Disk Utility, make sure the entry for your startup disk (generally the top item) is selected in the sidebar.

3   Click the Partition button in the toolbar.

4   Click the Add (+) button below the partition chart.

The disk's layout appears divided into two equally sized partitions.

5   Change the new partition's name to Backup.

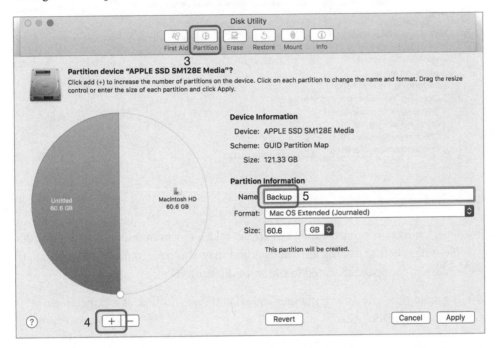

6   Click Apply.

7   In the confirmation dialog, click Partition.

8   If a warning about repartitioning the boot drive appears, click Continue.

9   Click the disclosure triangle labeled Show Details to view the details of the repartitioning process.

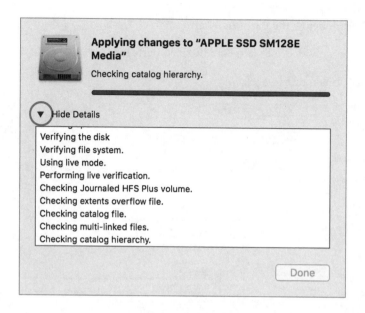

Disk Utility partitions the disk, which can take a few minutes. Disk Utility verifies the file system before making any changes and may also have to move existing data that resides in the space allocated to the second partition.

10 If a dialog appears asking whether you want to use this disk as a Time Machine device, click Don't Use.

11 When the repartitioning is finished, click Done.

Exercise 9.2
Erase a Disk

▶ **Prerequisites**

▶ You must have created the Local Admin account (Exercise 2.1, "Configure a New macOS System for Exercises," or Exercise 2.2, "Configure an Existing macOS System for Exercises").

▶ This exercise requires an erasable external disk, such as a flash drive.

In this exercise, you will use Disk Utility to erase and partition an external disk using a new partition scheme.

Use Disk Utility to Erase and Reformat a Disk

Many external storage systems (USB flash drives, USB and FireWire hard disks, and so on) come preformatted for Windows, using the Master Boot Record (MBR) partition scheme and the FAT32 volume format. For the best compatibility with macOS, you can reformat them to use the GUID partition table (GPT) scheme and Mac OS Extended volume format.

1   If necessary, log in as Local Admin (password: ladminpw, or whatever you chose when you created the account).

2   Plug in the external disk you're using for this exercise.

    WARNING ▶ This exercise erases all information on the external disk. Do not perform this exercise with a disk that contains any files you want to keep.

3   If necessary, open Disk Utility from the Utilities folder.

4   In the sidebar, select the external disk device (or "Apple read/write Media" if you are using the disk image). Be sure to select the device, not the volume or volumes it contains.

5   Click Erase in the toolbar.

6   View the options available in the Format and Scheme pop-up menus, and then choose "Mac OS Extended (Journaled)" and "GUID Partition Map" from them.

7   Name the disk Flash Drive.

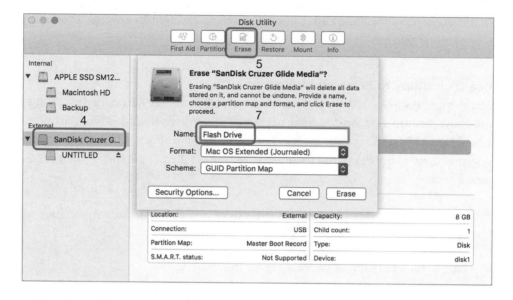

8   Click Erase.

9   Click the disclosure triangle labeled Show Details to view the details of the reformatting process.

10 When the reformatting is finished, click Done.

11 Click the Eject button next to the new volume in the Disk Utility sidebar.

When the volume has finished ejecting, it will vanish from the desktop. It will remain in the Disk Utility sidebar.

12 Unplug the disk from your Mac.

Exercise 9.3
Repair Partitions and Volumes in Target Disk Mode

▶ **Prerequisites**

▶ You must have created the Mayta Mishtuk account (Exercise 6.1, "Restore a Deleted User Account").

▶ You need another computer running macOS Sierra.

▶ Both computers must have FireWire, Thunderbolt, or USB-C interfaces, and you need the appropriate cable to connect them.

In this exercise, you will start your computer in target disk mode and use another computer to check its file structure and to examine its files directly in the Finder. These are techniques that could be used to repair or recover files from a computer that could not start up normally because of file system damage.

NOTE ▶ This exercise and Exercise 9.4, "Repair Partitions and Volumes in Recovery Mode," cover many of the same operations, but they use different modes to run the disk repair tools. You do not need to perform both. Generally, if you have access to another Mac running Sierra and both computers have FireWire, Thunderbolt, or USB-C (and you have the appropriate cable), this is the preferred exercise. If you are participating in a classroom setting, you can perform this exercise with a partner, using one of your computers as the host and the other as the target.

Start Your "Target" Computer in Target Disk Mode

Choose one of your computers to act as a "host" (the computer that will run the disk repair tools) and one to act as a "target" (the computer that will have its disk repaired).

1   Shut down the target computer.

2   Hold down the T key on the target computer while you press the power button. Keep holding the T key until you see a FireWire, Thunderbolt, or USB logo (or some combination) on the screen.

3   When you see the logo on the screen, release the T key.

4   If necessary, log in to the host computer.

5   Connect the two computers with a FireWire, Thunderbolt, or USB-C data cable.

6   If a dialog appears asking whether you want to use this disk as a Time Machine device, click Don't Use.

7   If the target computer's startup disk is encrypted with FileVault, you are prompted for a password to unlock the disk; you can enter the password of any FileVault-enabled account (ladminpw or chris, or whatever password you chose).

Repair the Partition Table and Volume

1   On the host computer, open Disk Utility.

2   In the External section of the Disk Utility sidebar, select the target computer's disk device.

Note that the connection is listed as FireWire, Thunderbolt, or USB-C.

3   Click the First Aid button in the toolbar.

4   In the confirmation dialog, click Run.

5   Click the disclosure triangle labeled Show Details.

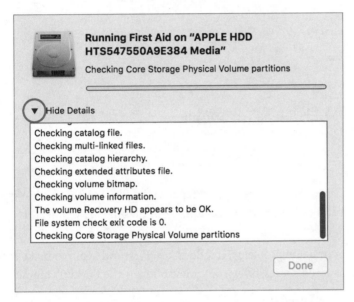

Disk Utility checks (and, if necessary, repairs) the partition table as well as certain hidden disk contents such as the EFI system partition.

Disk Utility shouldn't find any problems; if it does, use First Aid again to make sure that all problems were repaired successfully.

6   When the process finishes, click Done.

7   Select the entry for the target computer's Macintosh HD volume, and then click First Aid again.

8   Click Run, and then click the disclosure triangle labeled Show Details.

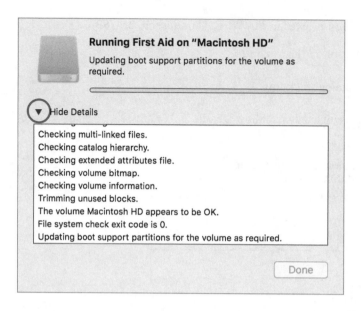

This time, Disk Utility checks (and, if necessary, repairs) the file structure within the Macintosh HD volume. Since there are a large number of files in the volume, this process may take a few minutes.

As before, it should not find any problems; if it does, use First Aid again to make sure that all problems are repaired successfully. You can also repair the Backup volume.

9 When the process finishes, click Done.

10 Quit Disk Utility.

Examine Files Manually in Target Disk Mode

1 In the host computer's Finder, open the Computer view by pressing Command-Shift-C.

Both computers' volumes appear. Generally, you can distinguish them by the target computer's orange volume icons.

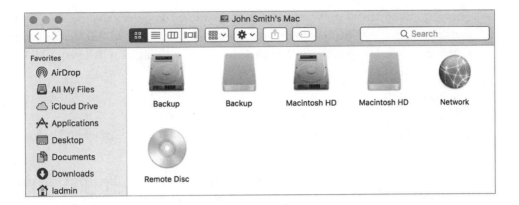

2   Select the target computer's Macintosh HD volume, and choose File menu > Get Info (Command-I).

3   If necessary, expand the Sharing & Permissions section of the Info window.

4   Click the padlock, and authenticate as Local Admin.

5   If necessary, select the "Ignore ownership on this volume" checkbox.

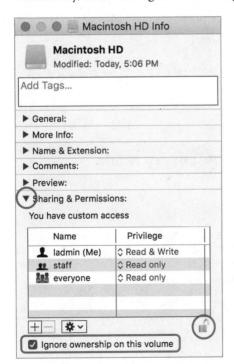

Selecting this option allows you full access to the other computer's volume. This is particularly useful if the other computer has different user accounts so that the file ownership does not match up between the computers. This is discussed in Reference 11.3, "Manage Permissions."

6   Close the Info window.

7   Open the target computer's Macintosh HD volume, and then navigate into Users/ mayta/Desktop.

Because ownership is being ignored, you can access Mayta's files directly. If necessary, you could recover files from a computer this way even if the computer could not start up normally.

8   In the Finder sidebar, Option-click the Eject button next to one of the target computer's volumes.

Holding Option while clicking Eject tells the Finder to eject all volumes on that disk, not just the one you clicked the Eject button for.

9   Wait for the target computer's volumes to vanish from the sidebar and desktop.

10 Press and hold the power button to shut down the target computer, and then unplug the cable after the computer has been turned off.

11 If you are not going to perform the next exercise, restart the target computer normally.

Exercise 9.4
Repair Partitions and Volumes in Recovery Mode

▶ **Prerequisites**

▶   You must have created the Chris Johnson account (Exercise 5.1, "Create a Standard User Account").

▶   Your computer must have a local hidden Recovery HD partition.

In this exercise, you will start your computer in macOS Recovery mode and check its file structure and home folder permissions. These are techniques you can use to repair a computer that will not start up normally because of file system damage.

NOTE ▶ This exercise and Exercise 9.3, "Repair Partitions and Volumes in Target Disk Mode," perform many of the same operations but use different modes to run the disk repair tools. You do not need to perform both.

Repair the Partition Table and Volume

1   Restart your computer, and then hold down Command-R until the gray Apple logo appears on the screen.

2   At the Utilities screen, select Disk Utility and click Continue.

3   If your startup volume is encrypted with FileVault, it appears dimmed in the disks and volumes list; select it, click the Mount button in the toolbar, and then enter the password of any FileVault-enabled account (ladminpw or chris, or whatever password you chose).

4   Select your computer's internal disk device (generally the top entry in the sidebar).

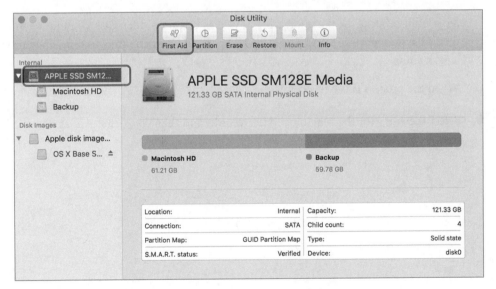

5   Click the First Aid button in the toolbar.

6   In the confirmation dialog, click Run.

7   Click the disclosure triangle labeled Show Details.

Disk Utility checks the partition table as well as certain hidden disk contents such as the EFI system partition and Recovery HD partition and attempts to repair any problems it finds.

8   When the process finishes, click Done.

9   Select the entry for the Macintosh HD volume, and then click First Aid again.

10 Click Run, and then click the disclosure triangle labeled Show Details.

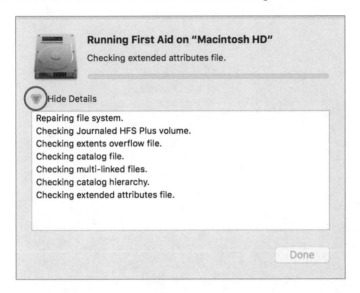

This time, Disk Utility checks the file structure within the Macintosh HD volume and repairs it if necessary.

11 When the process finishes, click Done.

You can also repair the Backup volume if you want.

12 Quit Disk Utility.

Lesson 10

Manage FileVault

Although third-party solutions for full-system volume encryption exist for macOS, these solutions often exhibit issues whenever Apple updates hardware or software. Many third-party full-system volume encryption schemes may stop working during updates, leaving users stranded, with no way to reach their encrypted data.

Apple engineers decided to take this problem into their own hands and introduced a new version of FileVault (sometimes called FileVault 2). In this lesson, you will learn how FileVault protects the system volume and how to enable this protection. You will also learn how to recover a system protected with FileVault when all local users' passwords are lost.

> **NOTE ▸** All instances of "FileVault" in this guide refer to FileVault 2, the newer system volume encryption technology, unless otherwise specified.

GOALS

▸ Describe how FileVault helps protect data

▸ Enable FileVault protection

▸ Regain access to a FileVault-protected Mac when all passwords are lost

Reference 10.1
About FileVault

Although FileVault 2 is often branded as "full disk encryption," it protects the system by encrypting the system volume. Most Mac computers use only one large system volume for all local storage, so this is acceptable in most situations. However, if you make use of more than one volume, consider encrypting the other volumes, as covered in Lesson 9, "Manage File Systems and Storage."

About Full-System Encryption

FileVault 2 protects the system volume by converting it to Mac OS Extended (Journaled, Encrypted) format, which uses XTS-AES-128 encryption with 256-bit keys. This adoption of a full-system volume encryption scheme resolves all the limitations of the older encryption technology used by Mac computers, known as Legacy FileVault. This is because FileVault 2 performs the encryption at the file system driver level of the operating system. Thus, most processes and applications don't even know the system volume is encrypted, so they behave as usual.

> MORE INFO ▸ You can find out more about the specifics of FileVault's encryption from the following Apple Technical White Paper: http://training.apple.com/pdf/ WP_FileVault2.pdf.

The current FileVault solution is more than just a new volume format; it's a system of new technologies that enables your Mac to transition from a standard system volume to a protected system volume. Full details of all the changes required to engineer FileVault are beyond the scope of this guide, but the primary new technologies instrumental in the current version include seamless volume format conversion, user account password synchronization, optional secure key storage on Apple servers for lost password recovery, macOS Recovery for initial system startup, and a new firmware login window.

You can see many of these new pieces at work during startup to an encrypted system volume. What was traditionally a straightforward task—starting up the system—takes on a new level of complexity when you can't read the system volume to start with. Thus, Apple had to devise a method to authenticate and access the protected system volume during startup.

When starting up from an encrypted system, the Mac actually starts from the hidden, unencrypted Recovery HD volume first, to present users with a login window. Users enter their account password, which is then used to access the decryption key that ultimately unlocks the protected system volume. Once the Mac has access to the system volume, startup continues normally, with one exception: users, having already authenticated to unlock encryption, are automatically logged in to their accounts.

> **NOTE** ▸ If the system disk is missing the hidden macOS Recovery HD volume, you cannot enable FileVault. Fortunately, macOS also makes it impossible to accidentally engage it without that volume. Re-creating the Recovery HD volume is covered in Lesson 3, "Use macOS Recovery."

About Legacy FileVault

Prior to OS X Lion 10.7, Legacy FileVault existed as a technology that secured user data by encrypting the user's home folder content. This method, though effective, has a variety of drawbacks. For one, it does not protect data outside the user's home folder. More problematic, though, is that many system management and backup utilities don't work properly with Legacy FileVault home folders. With FileVault 2 system disk encryption, Legacy FileVault home folder encryption is deprecated.

Legacy FileVault is still supported by macOS for existing or migrated user accounts, but you can no longer enable it for new user accounts. If you are currently using a Legacy FileVault account on a Mac computer, the Security & Privacy preferences presents a window prompting you to turn off Legacy FileVault.

> **NOTE** ▸ It is strongly suggested that you turn off Legacy FileVault and switch to the much more robust and secure FileVault 2 system volume encryption. You must completely disable all Legacy FileVault users to enable FileVault 2.

Turning off Legacy FileVault requires a logout and a potentially lengthy copy process as the system migrates the encrypted data back to "regular" data. This also means that turning off Legacy FileVault requires enough free space on the system disk to duplicate an entire decrypted copy of your home folder data. If there is not enough free space, you can't turn off Legacy FileVault. You may want to consider manually migrating a copy of your home folder, as covered in Lesson 6, "Manage User Home Folders."

If you dismiss the first Legacy FileVault dialog, you can always decide later to turn off Legacy FileVault. Return to the Legacy FileVault pane of the Security & Privacy preferences. You can reset the master password from this location as well.

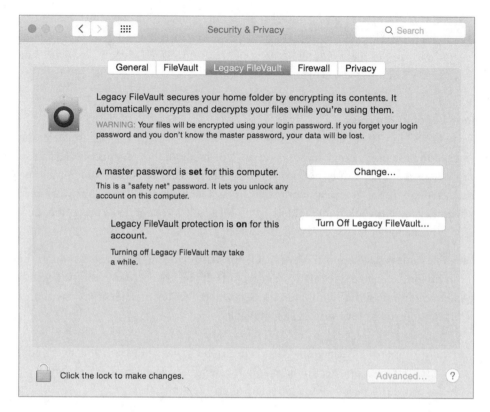

If you decide to stick with Legacy FileVault encrypted home folders, they will behave as they did in Mac OS X Snow Leopard 10.6. Other sections in this lesson cover techniques for managing passwords. Be sure to look for techniques pertaining to Legacy FileVault, because these accounts must be handled differently from standard user accounts.

Reference 10.2
Enable FileVault

In typical Apple style, despite the underlying complexity of transitioning an existing system to a secure encrypted system, turning on FileVault requires only a few simple steps. In fact, as covered in Lesson 2, "Set Up and Configure macOS," late-model Mac portable computers meeting the appropriate criteria will automatically prompt the user to enable FileVault during the Setup Assistant process.

Even if Setup Assistant doesn't prompt you to enable FileVault, an administrator user can enable it at any time from the Security & Privacy preferences. Clicking the Turn On FileVault button initiates the setup process.

Configure FileVault Recovery

During the FileVault setup, a dialog appears that offers two methods for recovering should all FileVault-enabled user passwords be lost. This is a very important decision, because if you do not have authentication or recovery access to the FileVault-protected system volume, then all data will be lost. In this case, the security mechanisms used by FileVault are so strong that not even Apple can help you recover the data.

The first method for recovery is to use an Apple ID (or iCloud) account to unlock the FileVault volume and reset the user's lost password. This new recovery method generates a random FileVault recovery key and then saves it to the user's iCloud account on Apple servers. Although the user cannot see the recovery key, if the need arises the system will be able to retrieve the key from iCloud once the user's Apple ID is authenticated.

NOTE ▶ The macOS interface sometimes uses "iCloud password" instead of "Apple ID password." However, because all Apple services, including iCloud, are accessed via Apple ID authentication, this guide uses the term "Apple ID" when discussing Apple service authentication.

This recovery method obviously requires that the system have Internet access and that the user be signed in using his or her Apple ID to the iCloud service (via the iCloud preferences). However, it does not require that the user's local account password be linked to his or her Apple ID. In other words, the user can continue to use a separate local account password even if the Apple ID account is configured for FileVault recovery.

Finally, it's important to note that only one user's Apple ID account can be configured for FileVault recovery. Other users can be given the ability to log in to the FileVault-protected system, but they do not have access to the recovery key stored in iCloud. Thus, for multiuser systems, it's best that an administrator user enable FileVault and use an appropriate Apple ID account to save the key.

> **NOTE ▶** If you choose to use an Apple ID account for FileVault recovery, it's strongly recommended that you also take advantage of two-step verification or two-factor authentication for the Apple ID. For more information about two-step verification see Apple Support article HT204152, "Two-step verification for Apple ID." For more information about two-factor authentication, see Apple Support article HT204915, "Two-factor authentication for Apple ID," and article HT205075, "Availability of two-factor authentication for Apple ID."

> **NOTE ▶** Previous versions of the Mac operating system allowed you to save a FileVault recovery key with Apple without using an Apple ID. This recovery method is no longer available beginning with OS X Yosemite 10.10.

An alternative method for FileVault recovery that doesn't involve iCloud is the creation of a locally saved recovery key. This randomly generated key can be used later to unlock the FileVault-protected volume and reset the user's lost password. As the dialog states, you will need to manually copy this key and store it somewhere safe other than the computer on which you are currently enabling FileVault. A good choice may be to take a photo with a mobile device, providing it uses strong local security as well.

MORE INFO ▶ For organizations deploying and managing systems en masse, there are more appropriate options for configuring FileVault than the default method covered here. For example, you can use an institutional recovery key for FileVault recovery, as covered in Apple Support article HT202385, "Set a FileVault recovery key for Mac computers in your institution."

Enable Additional Users for FileVault

During the FileVault setup process, if more than one local user exists on the system, a dialog appears where you can enable existing local users to unlock the protected system volume. This grants these other users the ability to start up the system. Click the Enable User button next to each user you want to be able to access the FileVault system volume. These users must then enter their account password to enable this ability. An administrator cannot override this step, because each user must each enter his or her unique password.

Any user not initially enabled to unlock FileVault can be configured for this ability later; just click the Enable User button in the FileVault pane of the Security & Privacy preferences. Only local users or cached mobile network users can be FileVault enabled. New local users or cached mobile network users created after FileVault is turned on are automatically able to unlock FileVault.

Any user password changes that occur will continue to be FileVault enabled as long as those changes occur on the system protected with FileVault. In other words, if you reset the password for a cached mobile user from the network directory server, the account will not be allowed to unlock the local FileVault system volume. To resolve this issue, either you can use a FileVault recovery method or you can log in as another administrator user and then reenable the reset local account by clicking the Enable User button in the FileVault pane of the Security & Privacy preferences.

Restart and Encrypt

Most Mac computers will need to be restarted to begin the system volume encryption. Upon restart of the Mac, notice that the login window appears much more quickly than usual. This is the new FileVault login window, hosted from the hidden Recovery HD volume. You will also notice that only FileVault-enabled users appear here. Authenticate as any FileVault-enabled user, and system startup continues until the user is automatically logged in to his or her account.

From the FileVault pane of the Security & Privacy preferences, you can view the progress of the system volume encryption as well as an estimated completion time. It may take several hours to completely encrypt a system volume. Obviously, the length of time varies greatly, depending on the amount of data that must be encrypted.

NOTE ▶ Due to the complex nature of solid-state and flash disk controllers, encrypting a volume may still leave some parts of the original data in a recoverable form. Thus, to minimize the security risk, enable FileVault before saving any sensitive data to the system volume.

Amazingly, you can close the Security & Privacy preferences and continue to use the Mac as usual, even though the system is slowly encrypting the volume it's running from. No notification appears once encryption is complete, but you can always return to Security & Privacy to check the progress.

NOTE ▶ To conserve battery power, portable Mac computers may pause encryption when they aren't plugged in. The encryption will continue once the Mac portable is connected to a power source.

If for some reason you want to turn off FileVault encryption, you can do so from the same Security & Privacy pane. This requires another system restart and a potentially lengthy decryption process. However, similar to the encryption process to enable FileVault, the decryption process can continue in the background without interrupting the user.

Reference 10.3
Use FileVault Recovery

Although it's highly unlikely on multiuser systems, it's more common than you think for a Mac with a single user to lose the login password. If by some means all FileVault-enabled account passwords are lost on a system protected with FileVault, you may still be able to unlock the system.

The ability to unlock a FileVault-protected system lies with the recovery key. As covered previously, this key can be stored in a user's iCloud service or saved manually by the user. Hopefully, the user either knows his or her Apple ID authentication or has dutifully copied and saved the FileVault recovery key somewhere safe.

About FileVault Recovery

To start the FileVault recovery process, at the FileVault login window select a user and then click the small "?" icon to the right of the password entry field. A message appears suggesting you reset the user's password with a recovery key or an Apple ID. This message will also appear automatically should a user fail to authenticate three times in a row.

NOTE ▶ Only systems that were running OS X Yosemite 10.10 or later during the FileVault-enabling process have the option to use FileVault with Apple ID recovery. Also, on multiuser systems, you will need to select the specific user who enabled FileVault with Apple ID recovery.

The quickest recovery method is to enter the recovery key. Click the arrow next to Recovery Key to enter the key, if you have it. After you successfully enter the key, the system unlocks the system volume and continues the startup process. The traditional Mac login window eventually appears, prompting you to set a new password for the user. Enter a new password twice, then an optional password hint, and then click Reset Password to log in the user.

NOTE ▶ If FileVault was configured using a previous version of macOS and you elected to save the recovery key with Apple, you must contact AppleCare directly to retrieve the key. You can find out how to directly contact AppleCare from Apple Support article HT201232, "Contacting Apple for support and service."

About Apple ID FileVault Recovery

If you select the option to reset the password using an Apple ID, the system will start up into a special Reset Password Assistant that resides only on the hidden Recovery HD volume. This application looks similar to Setup Assistant, but it's specifically designed to provide a way to authenticate the user's Apple ID, retrieve the recovery key from Apple's iCloud servers, and reset the local user's password. Further, the Reset Password Assistant can also help users reset their Apple ID password if it's lost as well.

NOTE ▶ The Reset Password Assistant requires an Internet connection to reach the Apple iCloud servers. The Recovery HD system attempts to automatically connect to the previously used Wi-Fi network, but if this doesn't work you will have to manually configure a network connection. Either connect the Mac to a DHCP-enabled Ethernet network, or move the cursor to the top of the screen and select the Wi-Fi menu to configure a Wi-Fi network.

Once the user authenticates with the Apple ID, the Reset Password Assistant retrieves the recovery key from iCloud and then checks the FileVault-protected Mac for a matching local user account. If the user's local password was linked to his or her Apple ID password, it will be reset to the new password. However, if the user's local password was separate from the Apple ID, the Reset Password Assistant presents a screen where you can enter a new password for the local user account. Once the reset process is complete, restart the system, and then authenticate with the new user account password to gain access to the system.

Lost FileVault Recovery Key

If, in a worst-case scenario, you have lost all FileVault-enabled account passwords and you are unable to access the FileVault recovery key (either by local methods or with Apple), there is no way to recover the data on the system volume. You might as well start up to macOS Recovery (covered in Lesson 3, "Use macOS Recovery") and then erase the system disk (covered in Lesson 9, "Manage File Systems and Storage"). At that point, you could reinstall macOS (covered in Lesson 1, "Install macOS Sierra") or restore from a Time Machine backup (covered in **Lesson 15, "Manage Time Machine"**).

Exercise 10.1
Turn On FileVault

▶ **Prerequisite**

    ▶ You must have created the Local Admin (Exercise 2.1, "Configure a New macOS System for Exercises," or Exercise 2.2, "Configure an Existing macOS System for Exercises") and Chris Johnson (Exercise 5.1, "Create a Standard User Account") accounts.

WARNING ▶ If you lose all the passwords and the recovery key for a FileVault-encrypted volume, you will not be able to regain access to the data stored in it. If you are performing this exercise on your own computer and have any files you do not want to risk losing, you must back up your computer before starting this exercise.

FileVault allows you to encrypt your startup volume and control which users can gain access to the volume. In this exercise, you will turn on FileVault protection for your startup volume. If you do not want to protect your computer with FileVault, you can turn it off in Exercise 10.4, "Turn Off FileVault."

Use System Preferences to Turn On FileVault

1   If necessary, log in as Chris Johnson (password: chris, or whatever you chose when you created the account).

2   Open the Security & Privacy pane in System Preferences.

   If a dialog appears indicating that "You're using an old version of FileVault," it means you have old user accounts set up using Legacy FileVault encryption. You can either click Turn Off Legacy FileVault and follow the prompts to turn it off or click Keep Using Legacy FileVault and skip this lesson's exercises. You cannot use both Legacy FileVault and the current version, FileVault 2, at the same time.

3   Click the FileVault tab.

4   Unlock the preference pane, and authenticate as Local Admin (password: ladminpw).

5   Click Turn On FileVault.

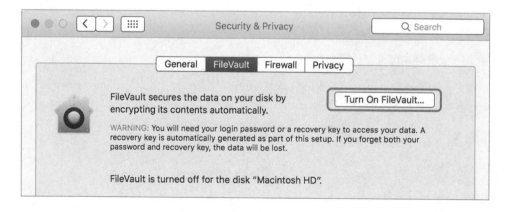

If a dialog appears saying "A recovery key has been set by your company, school, or institution," it means your computer was preloaded with an institutional recovery key (described in Apple Support article HT202385, "Set a FileVault recovery key for Mac computers in your institution"). In this case, click Continue and skip to step 9. You will also not be able to perform Exercise 10.3, "Use a FileVault Recovery Key."

If an institutional key has not been set, a dialog appears giving you the choice of allowing your iCloud account to unlock the disk or creating a recovery key. Note that the dialog will be slightly different if you have not linked the Chris Johnson account to an Apple ID.

6   Select "Create a recovery key and do not use my iCloud account," and click Continue.

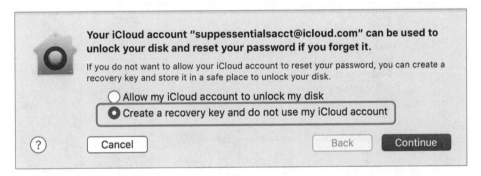

7   Record your recovery key.

The recovery key is a code which can be used to unlock the disk if you forget your password.

Make a copy of this code and store it in a safe place. If you forget your password and lose the recovery key, all the data on your disk will be lost.

W8U6-2KBV-3WG5-L2ZY-HZBQ-662Y

Cancel   Back   Continue

Recovery key: _____

If you are performing these exercises on your own computer and intend to leave FileVault on at the end of these exercises, store the recorded recovery key in a physically secure location.

One convenient option for recording the key is to take a picture of it with a smart-phone (or other camera). However, you should consider the security implications of someone stealing your computer and phone together.

You could also take a screenshot on the computer itself, but then you would need to copy it someplace else to make it available if you get locked out of your computer.

8 Click Continue.

A dialog appears, allowing you to select which users can unlock the disk.

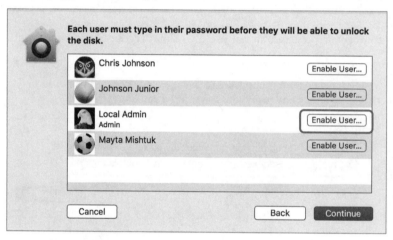

9 Click the Enable User button for Local Admin.

10 Enter the Local Admin password, and then click OK.

11 If the Chris Johnson account is not already enabled (green checkmark to the right of the account), enable it as well.

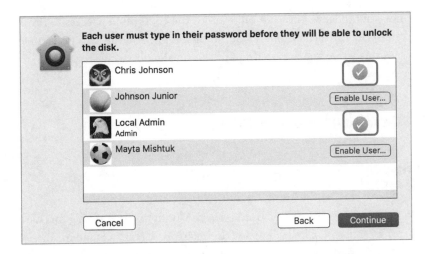

Do not enable any accounts other than Chris Johnson and Local Admin.

12 Click Continue.

13 Click Restart to begin the encryption process.

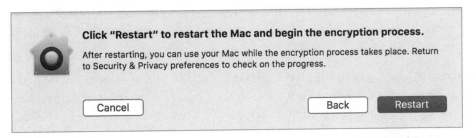

14 If you are prompted to, authenticate as Local Admin.

Your computer restarts, and the FileVault authentication screen appears. This screen is similar to the normal login screen, but only the enabled users, Chris Johnson and Local Admin, are available at this screen. Users who have not been enabled for FileVault cannot start the computer up but can log in after an enabled user has started it.

Encrypting the entire partition takes a while, but you can use the computer normally during the encryption process.

You can now leave your computer at the authentication screen and proceed to Exercise 10.2, "Restart a FileVault-Protected System," or Exercise 10.3, "Use a FileVault Recovery

Key"; if you do not want to leave FileVault on, wait for the encryption process to finish, and then use Exercise 10.4, "Turn Off FileVault," to turn it off. You can also perform exercises from other lessons while you are waiting for it to finish encrypting your disk.

Exercise 10.2
Restart a FileVault-Protected System

▶ **Prerequisites**

▶ You must have created the Local Admin (Exercise 2.1, "Configure a New macOS System for Exercises," or Exercise 2.2, "Configure an Existing macOS System for Exercises"), Chris Johnson (Exercise 5.1, "Create a Standard User Account"), and Mayta Mishtuk (Exercise 6.1, "Restore a Deleted User Account") accounts.

▶ You must have performed Exercise 10.1, "Turn On FileVault."

In this exercise, you'll see how FileVault modifies the macOS startup process by requiring one of the selected user's passwords. Once the computer is fully started, all users may use the computer normally.

Your computer restarts and displays a FileVault access screen. This looks similar to the login screen, but you see only Chris Johnson and Local Admin. The operating system has not started yet because you need to unlock the disk before the system files can be read.

If Find My Mac were turned on, you would also see a Guest account listed here. Selecting Guest starts the computer in a Safari-only mode with no access to the startup volume. This exists primarily to tempt computer thieves into connecting the computer to the Internet, allowing the Find My Mac service to, locate, lock, or wipe the Mac.

Log In to a FileVault-Enabled Account

1   On the FileVault authentication screen, click Chris Johnson.

2   Enter Chris's password, and press Return.

At this point, the normal macOS startup process proceeds, and you are automatically logged in as Chris Johnson. Since you already authenticated as Chris Johnson at the FileVault authentication screen, macOS facilitates an automatic login for you.

3   Select your startup volume from the desktop.

4   In the Finder, choose File menu > Get Info (Command-I).

5   If necessary, click the triangle to expand the General section of the Info window.

The format of the volume is now Mac OS Extended (Journaled, Encrypted).

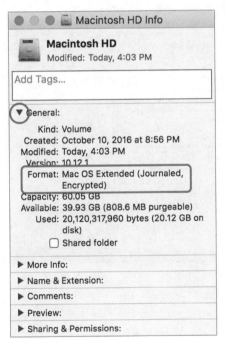

6   Close the Info window.

Enable Another Account for FileVault

1   Open System Preferences, select Security & Privacy, and click the FileVault tab.

A progress indicator shows the encryption status. As you have just seen, FileVault provides some protection immediately, but your data is not fully secured until the encryption process finishes.

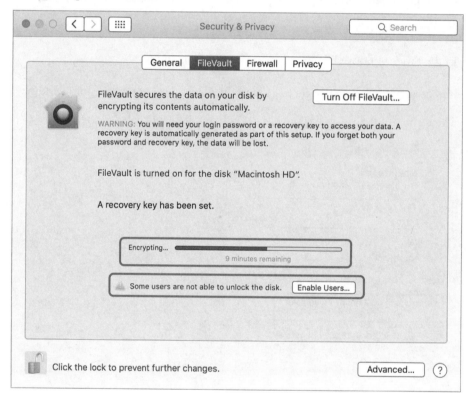

2   Unlock the preference pane, and authenticate as Local Admin.

3   Click Enable Users.

A dialog appears that allows you to enable additional users to start up the computer. You can enable additional users at any time, but you will need to enter each user's password to enable them.

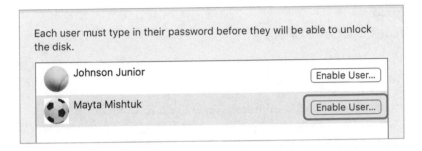

4   Click the Enable User button for Mayta Mishtuk.

5   Enter Mayta's password (mayta, or whatever you chose), and click OK.

Mayta's account now has a green checkmark.

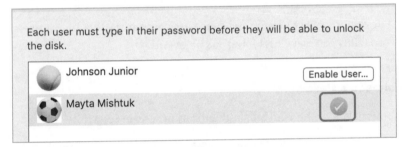

6   Click Done.

7   Quit System Preferences, and log out as Chris Johnson.

The login screen appears. Notice that even though Chris's account was used to gain access to Macintosh HD, all users can now log in normally.

8   If you plan to perform Exercise 10.3, "Use a FileVault Recovery Key," next, click the Restart button at the bottom of the screen.

Exercise 10.3
Use a FileVault Recovery Key

▶ **Prerequisites**

  ▶ You must have created the Local Admin (Exercise 2.1, "Configure a New macOS System for Exercises," or Exercise 2.2, "Configure an Existing macOS System for Exercises") and Chris Johnson (Exercise 5.1, "Create a Standard User Account") accounts.

  ▶ You must have performed Exercise 10.1, "Turn On FileVault," and recorded your recovery key.

You can use the FileVault recovery key to reset user passwords at startup. In this exercise, you will use this capability to reset Chris Johnson's password.

Reset Chris Johnson's Password

1 If your computer is not at the FileVault authentication screen, restart it.

   If you performed Exercise 10.2, the Mayta Mishtuk account now appears on the FileVault authentication screen along with Chris Johnson and Local Admin. If you also see the Johnson Junior account, you may have logged out without restarting the computer, in which case you are seeing the normal login screen, not FileVault.

2 At the FileVault authentication screen, click Chris Johnson.

3 Click the Help (?) button at the right of the Password field or fail to authenticate with the correct password three times.

   You will see an option that lets you reset the password with the recovery key.

4   Click the arrow to start the reset process.

A Recovery Key field replaces the Password field.

5   Enter the recovery key you recorded earlier, and press Return.

If the Recovery Key field shakes and resets, you have not entered the recovery key correctly. If reentering it does not correct the problem, you may have recorded it incorrectly. In this case, you can't perform the password reset portion of this exercise; instead, cancel the password reset by clicking the left-arrow button, log in normally using any of the enabled accounts, and skip the rest of this exercise.

The operating system starts up. Once the startup process finishes, a Reset Password dialog appears under the Chris Johnson account's icon.

6   In the Reset Password dialog, enter vaultpw in the "New password" and "Verify password" fields, and then click Reset Password.

You are now logged in to Chris's account. Since his password has been reset, you receive the warning that the system was unable to unlock his login keychain.

7   Click Continue Log In.

8   If you are prompted, enter the password for Chris's login keychain (chris, or whatever you chose when you created the account).

Restore Chris Johnson's Original Password
To avoid confusion for the rest of the exercises, you will now change the Chris Johnson password back.

1   Open the Users & Groups pane in System Preferences.

2   Click Change Password.

3   Enter vaultpw as the old password, and enter the Chris Johnson account's original
password (chris, or whatever you chose earlier) in the New Password and Verify fields.

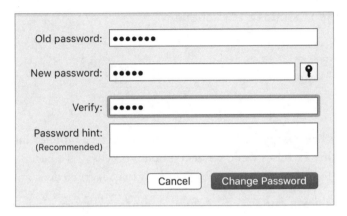

4   Click Change Password.

Note that this also brings Chris's account password back in sync with his keychain
password.

5   Log out as Chris Johnson.

Exercise 10.4
Turn Off FileVault

▶ **Prerequisites**

> ▶ You must have created the Local Admin (Exercise 2.1, "Configure a New
> macOS System for Exercises," or Exercise 2.2, "Configure an Existing macOS
> System for Exercises") and Chris Johnson (Exercise 5.1, "Create a Standard
> User Account") accounts.

> ▶ You must have performed Exercise 10.1, "Turn On FileVault," and the encryp-
> tion process must have finished.

You can turn off FileVault encryption as easily as you turned it on. If you are performing
these exercises on your own and want to leave FileVault protection enabled on your computer, you can skip this exercise.

If you are performing these exercises in a class, you should not skip this exercise.

Turn Off Encryption on the Macintosh HD Volume

1   If necessary, log in as Chris Johnson.

2   Open the Security & Privacy preferences.

3   Click the FileVault tab.

If the encryption process has not finished, you will not be able to turn off FileVault yet. You may perform other exercises while the encryption proceeds in the background and then return to this exercise when the volume is fully encrypted.

4   Click the lock icon, and authenticate as Local Admin. Only administrators can turn FileVault on and off.

5   Click Turn Off FileVault.

You are asked to confirm that you want to turn off FileVault.

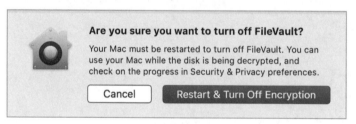

6   Click "Restart & Turn Off Encryption."

7   If you are prompted to do so, reauthenticate as Local Admin.

Your computer restarts, and the decryption process begins. Note that since you authenticated to FileVault when you started up the computer, no special FileVault password is required at this point. As with the encryption process, you can continue to use the computer normally during the decryption process.

Manage Permissions and Sharing

The technologies collectively known as file system permissions are used to control file and folder authorization for macOS. File system permissions work alongside the user account technologies, which control user identification and authentication, to provide the secure multiuser environment of the Mac. File system permissions—just like user accounts—permeate every level of macOS. A thorough investigation of file system ownership and permissions is required to fully understand macOS.

In this lesson, you will learn how file-system ownership and permissions allow for controlled access to protect local files and folders. You will also explore macOS default permission settings that provide secure access to shared files. Finally, you will use the Finder to make ownership and permissions changes.

GOALS

▶ Describe file ownership and permissions

▶ Explore the default shared folders in macOS

▶ Securely manage file and folder access

Reference 11.1
About File System Permissions

Every item on the system volume has permission rules applied to it by macOS. These rules are used to define file and folder access for every standard, administrator, guest, and sharing user. Only users and processes with root account access can ignore file-system permissions rules.

> **NOTE** ▶ The macOS interface sometimes displays the word *privileges* in place of permissions. In general, the meaning of these two terms is similar.

View File System Permissions

Any user can easily identify a file's or folder's permissions via the Info window in the Finder. First, select the file or folder whose permissions you want to identify. You can select multiple items to open multiple Info windows.

There are several ways to access the Finder Info window:

- ▶ Press Command-I.

- ▶ Choose File > Get Info.

- ▶ Use secondary-click or Control-click on the selected item, and then choose Get Info from the shortcut menu (also called a contextual menu).

- ▶ In a Finder window toolbar, click the Action pop-up menu (the gear icon), and then choose Get Info.

Once you open an Info window, click the Sharing & Permissions disclosure triangle to reveal the item's permissions. The permissions list is broken into two columns. To the left is a list of users or groups with access to this item, and to the right is the associated privilege assigned by user or group. Modifying these settings is covered in Reference 11.3, "Manage Permissions."

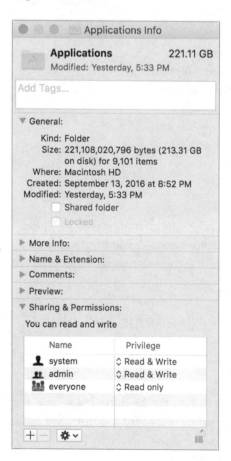

TIP ▶ You can also identify ownership and permissions from the dynamic Inspector window in the Finder. This is a single floating window that automatically refreshes as you select different items in the Finder. To open the Inspector, press Command-Option-I in the Finder.

About Ownership for Permissions

Every file and folder belongs to at least one owner and one group and also has an ownership setting for everyone else. This three-tiered ownership structure provides the basis for file system permissions:

▶ Owner—By default, the owner of an item is the user who created or copied the item to the Mac. For example, users own most of the items in their home folder. The system or root user almost always owns system software items, including system resources and applications. Traditionally, only the owner can change the item's ownership or permissions. Despite this, macOS makes management easier by giving every administrator user the ability to change ownership and permissions regardless of who owns the item.

▶ Group—By default, the group of an item is inherited from the folder it was created in. Thus, most items belong to the staff (the primary group for local users), wheel (the primary group for the root system account), or admin groups. Group ownership is designated to allow users other than the owner access to an item. For instance, even though root owns the /Applications folder, the group is set to admin so administrator users can add and remove applications in this folder.

▶ Everyone—The Everyone setting is used to define access for anyone who isn't the owner and isn't part of the item's group. In other words, this means everyone else. This includes local, sharing, and guest users.

The three-tiered ownership structure presented here has been part of traditional UNIX operating systems for decades. However, with only three levels of permissions to choose from, it is quite difficult to define appropriate access settings for a computer with many user accounts and shared files, as is the case with many servers. Fortunately, as you'll see later, access control lists were developed to allow for nearly limitless ownership and permissions configurations.

About Standard UNIX Permissions

The standard file system permissions structure of macOS is based on standard UNIX-style permissions. This system is also sometimes referred to as POSIX-style permissions. The system may be old, but for most Mac users it is quite adequate, because you can define privilege rules separately at each ownership tier. In other words, the owner, the group, and everyone else have individually specified access to each file or folder. Further, because of the inherent hierarchy built into the file system, where folders can reside inside other folders, you can easily create a complex file structure that allows varying levels of sharing and security.

Apple has streamlined the Finder to allow for the most common permissions options. Alternatively, the full range of UNIX privilege combinations is available from Terminal, but that topic is beyond the scope of this guide.

> **MORE INFO** ▶ Wikipedia has an excellent overview of UNIX-style permissions: http://en.wikipedia.org/wiki/Filesystem_permissions.

File-level permissions options available in the Finder are:

▶   Read & Write—The user or group members can open the file and save changes.

▶   Read Only—The user or group members can open the file but cannot save any changes.

▶   No Access—The user or group members have no access to the file at all.

Folder-level permissions options available in the Finder are:

▶   Read & Write—The user or group members can browse and make changes to the contents of the folder.

▶   Read Only—The user or group members can browse the contents of the folder but cannot make changes to the contents of the folder.

▶   Write Only (Drop Box)—The user or group members cannot browse the Drop Box folder but can copy or move items into it.

▶   No Access—The user or group members have no access to the contents of the folder.

> **NOTE** ▶ Although the Finder doesn't show or allow changes to the UNIX execute permission, it automatically assigns this permission when read access is granted for folders.

About Access Control Lists

Access control lists (ACLs) were developed to expand the standard UNIX permissions architecture to allow more control of file and folder access. macOS adopted a style of ACLs similar to that available on Windows-based NTFS file systems and UNIX systems that support NFSv4. This ACL implementation is extremely flexible but increases complexity by adding more than a dozen unique privilege and inheritance attribute types.

Further, the macOS implementation of ACLs supports an essentially unlimited number of access control entries (ACEs). An ACE is a set of permissions defined for a specific user or group. In other words, ACLs provide a nearly unlimited list of permission rules or ACEs for every file or folder—hence the *list* in *access control list*.

Finally, if an ACL rule applies to a user or group, this rule trumps standard UNIX permissions. However, any users or groups that don't apply to a specific ACL are still bound by the standard permissions currently in place.

Apple does not expect average users to navigate through all the options available using ACLs, so once again the Finder has been streamlined to allow only the most common ACL configurations. In fact, the Finder allows you to assign only ACL attributes that match the most common standard UNIX permissions configurations (previously listed in this lesson). The only feature of ACLs that the Finder actually implements is the ability to have an unlimited number of user or group privilege rules. In other words, the Finder uses the ACL architecture to let you configure unique privileges for an essentially unlimited number of users or groups.

Permissions in a Hierarchical Context

Permissions do not exist in isolation; rather, they are applied in the context of a folder hierarchy. In other words, your access to an item is based on an item's permissions in combination with the permissions of the folder in which it resides. If you're still confused, it's easiest to think of permissions as defining access to an item's content, not to the item itself. Remember the word *content* as you consider the following three simplified examples.

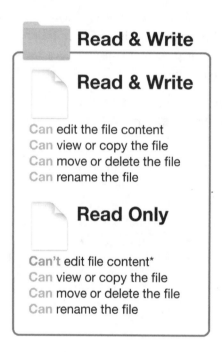

Read & Write

Read & Write

Can edit the file content
Can view or copy the file
Can move or delete the file
Can rename the file

Read Only

Can't edit file content*
Can view or copy the file
Can move or delete the file
Can rename the file

Example 1: You have both read and write permissions to the folder. It's obvious that you should have full access to the first file, as your permissions here are read-and-write as well. You can also view and copy the second file, but you can't make changes to the file's content because your permissions are read-only. Yet you can still move, delete, or rename the second file because you have read-and-write access to the folder's contents. Thus, the second file isn't secure in this example, because you can make a copy of the original file, change the copied file's content, delete the original file, and finally replace it with the modified copy. This is how many applications actually save document changes; thus, the file can in fact be edited.

> **NOTE ▶** The "*" in these examples indicates that actual editing behavior varies based on the application's design. For some applications, you may need read-and-write access to both the file and the folder it's inside to save changes to the file.

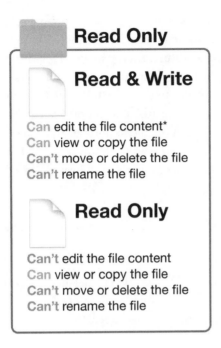

Example 2: You have read-only permission to the folder. You can edit the content of the first file because you have read-and-write access to it, but you can't move, delete, or rename it because you have read-only access to the folder's contents. On the other hand, you can effectively delete the file by erasing its contents. The second file here is the only truly secure file, because you're only allowed to view or copy the file. Granted, you can make changes to the contents of a copied file, but you still can't replace the original.

Example 3: Your permissions are identical to the first document in the first example, with one significant change. The owner of this file has enabled the locked attribute, perhaps through the new macOS version's document control feature. Even though you have read-and-write access to the example folder and file, the locked attribute prevents all users who aren't the file's owner from modifying, moving, deleting, or renaming the file. From most applications, only the owner is allowed to change the file's content or delete it, but the owner can also disable the locked attribute to return the file to normal. You can still make a copy of the locked file, but the copy will be locked as well. However, you will own the copy, so you can disable the locked attribute on the copy, but you still can't delete the original locked file unless you're the owner.

> **MORE INFO** ▸ Managing the locked file attribute is detailed in **Lesson 17, "Manage Documents."**

> **MORE INFO** ▸ With System Integrity Protection (SIP) enabled by default in macOS, no user or process can make any changes to items required by the system. You can find out more about SIP in **Lesson 13, "Manage System Resources."**

Reference 11.2
Examine Permissions for Sharing

Once you have an understanding of the available permissions options in macOS, you should explore how the local file system is set up by default to provide a secure environment that still allows users to share files.

If you don't have fast user switching enabled, as outlined in Lesson 5, "Manage User Accounts," enable it now to make it easy to test file system permissions as different users. Further, to aid in your exploration of the file system, use the Finder Inspector window. This single floating window, which automatically refreshes as you select different items in the Finder, allows you to quickly explore the default permissions settings without having to open multiple Finder Info windows. Open the Inspector from the Finder by pressing Command-Option-I, and then click the disclosure triangle to reveal the Sharing & Permissions section.

NOTE ▶ The Inspector window sports a slightly different title bar than the Info window. Also, the Inspector always floats on top of all other windows in the Finder.

About Home Folder Permissions

The default home folder permissions protect the user's files and also allow them to be shared easily when needed. This starts with the user's home folder. Users are allowed read-and-write access to their home folder, whereas the staff group and everyone else are allowed only read access.

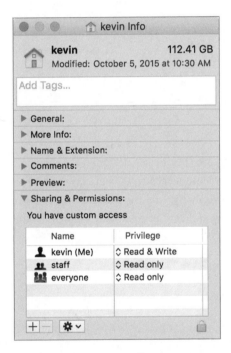

This means that every local user or guest can view the first level of every other user's home folder. (Remember that guests are allowed access to your computer without a password. This is why you can disable guest access in Users & Groups preferences.)

The default home folder permissions may seem insecure until you look at the permissions in context. Most user data is actually stored inside a subfolder in the user's home folder, and if you inspect those subfolders, you'll notice that other users are not allowed to access most of them.

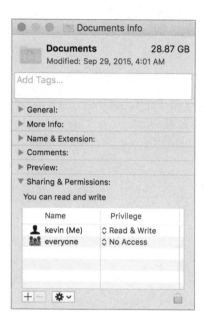

A few subfolders in a user's home folder, however, are specifically designed for sharing. The Public folder and legacy Sites folder remain readable to everyone. A user can easily share files without having to fuss with permissions by simply moving the files into those two folders. Others are able to read those files, but they still cannot make any changes to them.

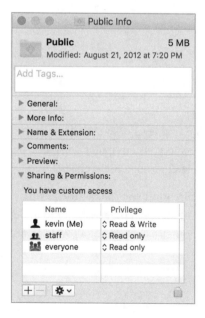

NOTE ▶ By default, user-created files and folders at the root of the home folder have permissions like those of the Public folder. To secure new items at the root of the home folder, change the permissions, as outlined in Reference 11.3, "Manage Permissions."

Looking deeper, you'll notice that one subfolder of the Public folder is Drop Box. This folder's permissions allow all other users to copy files into the folder, even though they cannot see the other files in that folder. This allows other users to discreetly transfer files to a specific user without others knowing.

When items are created or copied, they are owned by the user who performed the create or copy action. This would normally present a problem for a folder like Drop Box, since other users still own the items they have placed in your Drop Box folder. However, there is a custom ACE set for the Drop Box folder that ensures that users are also granted full access to the items in their Drop Box.

About the Shared Folder

An additional folder set aside for local file sharing is the /Users/Shared folder. Notice that this is a general sharing location that allows all local users to read and write items to the folder. Normally this permissions setting would also allow any user to delete another user's item in this folder.

Yet the Inspector window is not showing you the full permissions picture here. A unique permissions setting on the Shared folder prevents other users from being able to delete items they don't own. This permissions setting, known as the "sticky bit," can be viewed and managed only from Terminal.

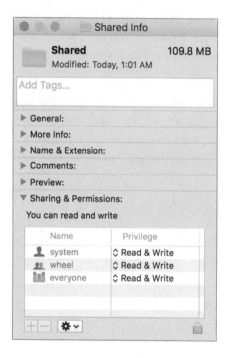

Secure New Items

Once you understand how the macOS file system security architecture works with the folder hierarchy, it's time to consider how this technology is used to secure new items. In this lesson you've already learned that macOS is preconfigured for secure file and folder sharing; however, new items are created with unrestricted read access.

For example, when users create a new file or folder at the root of their home folder, by default, all other users, including guest users, are allowed to view this item's contents. The same is true for new items created by administrators in local areas, such as the root of the system volume and the local Library and Applications folders.

New items are created this way to facilitate sharing so that you do not have to change any permissions to share a new item. All you have to do is place the new item in a folder that other users can access, like the predefined sharing folders covered in the previous section.

It's assumed that if you want to secure a new item, you will place it inside a folder that no one else has access to, such as your home Desktop or Documents folder.

This default behavior is inconvenient if you want to safely store your items in an otherwise public area, like the root of the system volume. To store items in a public area so they are accessible only to the owner requires that you change the item's permissions using either the Finder or Terminal, as outlined later in this lesson.

Specifically, from the Sharing & Permissions section of the Info window, you must remove all other users and all group accounts from the permissions list. You cannot remove the Everyone permission, so you have to set it to No Access. Once you have made these permissions changes, only the owner has access to the item.

NOTE ▶ Despite appearances, in the preceding screenshot Secure Folder does indeed have a group assignment. This is because the Finder hides an item's group permission if no access is granted. Thus, clicking the Delete (–) button to "delete" an item's group permission disables access for the group, but it does not actually remove the group assignment.

Reference 11.3
Manage Permissions

You may find that although the Finder makes permissions management simple, it does so through a form of obfuscation. In other words, the Finder hides the complexity of full UNIX and ACL permissions by showing a simplified view of an item's permissions.

Thus, if you're more comfortable with standard UNIX permissions, or you simply require full access to an item's permissions, you're best served by managing permissions via Terminal. This is, however, beyond the scope of this guide. For the most common permissions settings, the simplified Finder permissions interface is still the quickest and easiest solution.

An example situation you might encounter that requires changing permissions is when you delete a user's account but retain the user's home folder. The system renames that folder "Username (Deleted)," but otherwise leaves it alone. This presents a management problem, as even administrator users won't have full access to the folder's content in the Finder. This section explores the permissions changes an admin would make to get full access to a deleted user's home folder.

Manage Permissions via the Finder

As covered previously in this lesson, you can view and manage permissions in the Sharing & Permissions section of the Info window. To do so, if you aren't the owner of the item, you must click the small lock icon in the lower-right corner of the Info window and authenticate as an administrator user.

Changes made using the Info window are applied immediately. However, as long as you keep the Info window open, the Finder also remembers the original permissions setting for the item. This is useful for testing different permissions configurations, since you can always revert to the original permissions setting. To do that, click the Action pop-up menu (gear icon) at the bottom of the Info window and then choose "Revert changes."

Add a Permissions Entry

To add a new permissions entry for a user or group, click the Add (+) button in the lower-left corner of the Info window. A dialog appears, allowing you to search for and select a user or group. Alternatively, you can create a new Sharing user account by clicking the New Person button or selecting a contact from your Address Book. Creating a new Sharing account requires that you enter a new password for the account.

MORE INFO ▶ Details about creating Sharing user accounts and how to create additional groups are covered in Lesson 5, "Manage User Accounts."

Change Ownership

Even though ACLs allow you to define multiple user permissions for an item, only the user closest to the bottom in the permissions list is the owner of the item. Again, an item's owner who is not an administrator user is allowed to change the privileges of an item. However, only administrator users can change both the ownership and the privileges of an item.

To assign a new owner using the Finder Info window, you must first add that user as an additional permissions entry. Once the user is added, select the user from the permissions list, and then choose "Make *<username>* the owner" from the Action pop-up menu, where *<username>* is the selected user.

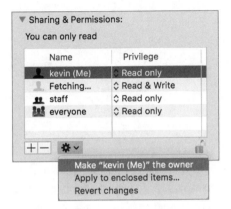

Delete a Permissions Entry

To delete a user or group permissions entry, select the account from the permissions list and click the Delete (–) button in the lower-left corner of the Info window. The Info window doesn't allow you to delete or change the original owner or delete the Everyone privilege of an item. You can use this window to seemingly delete all group privileges, but this isn't truly deleting the group privilege. Instead, it's simply removing all the privileges for the item's original group.

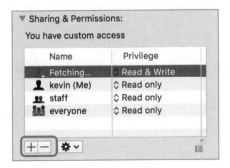

Modify a Permissions Entry

To assign different permissions to an entry, simply click any privilege and then choose another access option for that user or group from the pop-up menu that appears.

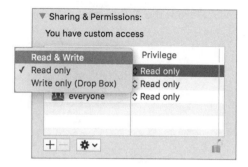

Propagate Folder Permissions

If you are changing a folder's permissions, by default, the Finder does not change the permissions of any items inside the folder. In many cases, you may want to apply the same permissions to the items inside the folder. This task is sometimes known as propagating permissions. You can accomplish this quickly by choosing "Apply to enclosed items" from the Action pop-up menu.

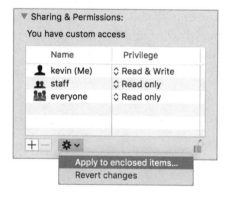

NOTE ▶ Even if you are the owner of a folder, applying permissions to the enclosed folder items may require administrator authentication.

NOTE ▶ Applying permissions to the enclosed folder items applies all permissions settings to all enclosed items, not just the changes you recently made. Further, these changes cannot be easily reverted. The exception to this is that any locked items inside the folder remain in their original state.

About Permissions for Nonsystem Volumes

Portable external disks are useful tools for transferring files and folders from one computer to another. A downside to this technology, though, is that computers can't properly interpret file ownership, because they don't share the same user account database. In other words, most Mac computers don't have the exact same user accounts, so when a disk is moved from one Mac to another, the file ownership from one Mac is meaningless to another.

Unless you plan to implement a centralized network user database so that all your Mac computers *do* share the same user account database, ownership on nonsystem volumes, like those found on external disks, will have to be ignored to prevent access issues. This is the default behavior in macOS for all nonsystem volumes on both internal and external disks. However, this approach introduces the security risk that all local users will have full access to the contents of any nonsystem volumes, including other partitions of a system disk. If you find this an unacceptable risk, you can disable the default behavior and force macOS to honor ownership on nonsystem volumes.

To do this in the Finder, select the nonsystem volume for which you want the system to honor the ownership, and then open the Info window. In the Sharing & Permissions section, click the small lock icon in the lower-right corner, and authenticate as an administrator user to unlock the Sharing & Permissions section. Finally, deselect the "Ignore ownership on this volume" checkbox.

Exercise 11.1
Create Items with Default Permissions

▶ **Prerequisite**

▶ You must have created the Local Admin (Exercise 2.1, "Configure a New macOS System for Exercises," or Exercise 2.2, "Configure an Existing macOS System for Exercises"), Chris Johnson (Exercise 5.1, "Create a Standard User Account"), and Mayta Mishtuk (Exercise 6.1, "Restore a Deleted User Account") accounts.

A thorough understanding of ownership and permissions is essential to supporting and troubleshooting macOS. Permissions control the access to files and folders by users and system services such as the printing system. This exercise introduces permissions in a user's home folder.

Store Files and Folders in Chris Johnson's Home Folder

To see the effects of the macOS default permissions, you will create some items with which to experiment.

1   If necessary, log in as Chris Johnson (password: chris, or whatever you chose when you created the account).

2   Open TextEdit. There should be a shortcut to it in your Dock.

3   If a new "Untitled" document doesn't open, choose File menu > New (or press Command-N).

4   Choose File menu > Save (or press Command-S), name the new file Secret Bonus List, and save it to the desktop. (Note that in a save dialog you can use the shortcut Command-Shift-D to select the desktop.)

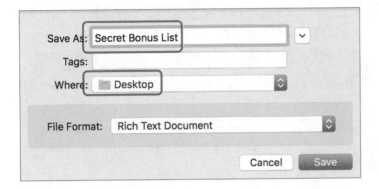

5   Quit TextEdit.

6   In the Finder, navigate to your home folder by choosing Go menu > Home (or pressing Command-Shift-H).

7   Create a new folder by choosing File menu > New Folder (or pressing Command-Shift-N).

8   Name the new folder Payroll Reports, and be sure it is located in your home folder, along with the default user folders.

9   Drag the Secret Bonus List.rtf file from your desktop into the Payroll Reports folder.

    As you will see shortly, this is not a good place to store confidential documents.

Examine Permissions as Another User

Now that Chris Johnson has created a test folder and file, experiment to see what Mayta Mishtuk can do with them.

1   Use the fast user switching menu item (near the right side of the menu bar) to switch to the Mayta Mishtuk account (password: mayta, or whatever you chose when you created the account).

2   In the Finder, navigate to Chris Johnson's home folder.

    Mayta's Finder preferences have not been customized to allow easy access outside her home folder; however, you can reach Chris's home folder by choosing Go menu > Computer (Command-Shift-C) and then opening the Macintosh HD > Users > chris folder.

Note that most of the folders in Chris's home folder have red minus-sign indicators, showing that you are not allowed access to their contents.

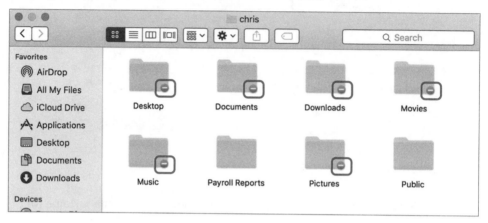

3   Hold the Option key while choosing File menu > Show Inspector (or press Command-Option-I).

The inspector is a variant of the Finder Info window; what makes it different is that it follows your selection in the Finder, allowing you to inspect many items quickly.

4   If necessary, expand the "Sharing & Permissions" section of the inspector window.

5   Select (single-click) the various folders in Chris's home folder, and watch what the inspector shows about their permissions.

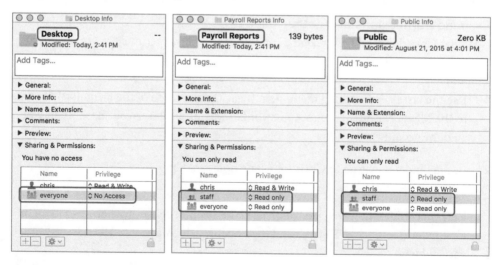

With the exception of Public, the folders that macOS creates by default in the home folder are protected from access by other users (the No Access permission). The Payroll Reports folder, however, was created with staff and everyone allowed read-only access.

6   Click in the background of Chris's home folder.

The inspector shows that staff and everyone are also allowed read-only access to the top level of Chris's home folder.

7   Open the Payroll Reports folder.

The folder opens, and the Secret Bonus List file is visible.

8   Select (single-click) the Secret Bonus List file.

The inspector shows that staff and everyone have read-only access to this as well.

This result may be contrary to what is expected by users. Be sure to guide your users to store their folders in appropriate places, based on the type of access they want to allow for other users. Although others cannot add or remove items stored in the Payroll Reports folder, they can open and read the contents.

9   Open the Secret Bonus List file.

Since the file is readable by everyone but writable only by its owner, Chris Johnson, TextEdit shows that it is locked.

10 Try to enter some text into the file.

TextEdit asks if you would like to create a duplicate so that you can save your changes.

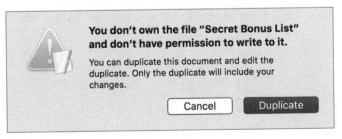

11 Click Duplicate.

A duplicate document named Untitled (Secret Bonus List copy) opens and allows you to enter text.

12 Save the duplicate document to your desktop (leave the name "Secret Bonus List copy").

13 Quit TextEdit.

14 In the Finder, navigate back to Chris's home folder, and open Chris's Public folder.

15 Select the Drop Box folder.

The inspector shows that staff and everyone have write-only access to this folder. Chris has full read and write access, as well as a Custom access control entry (ACE). "Custom" means that the ACE grants something other than normal read and/or write access; in this case, it's an inheritable ACE that will grant Chris additional access to items dropped into this folder.

16 Try to open Chris's Drop Box folder.

The write-only permission does not allow you to open another user's Drop Box folder.

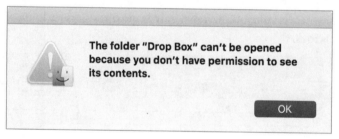

The folder "Drop Box" can't be opened because you don't have permission to see its contents.

OK

17 Try to copy the Secret Bonus List copy from your desktop into Chris Johnson's Drop Box folder.

The Finder warns you that you will not be able to see the items you put into the Drop Box folder.

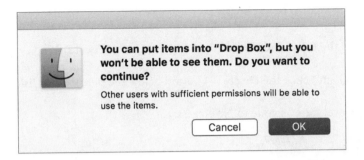

18 Click OK.

Proceed to Exercise 11.2, "Test Permissions Changes," to see how to adjust the permissions on the Payroll Reports folder.

Exercise 11.2
Test Permissions Changes

▶ **Prerequisite**

   ▶   You must have performed Exercise 11.1, "Create Items with Default Permissions."

Chris Johnson will now change the permissions on the Payroll Reports folder and test the results from Mayta Mishtuk's account.

Change Permissions as Chris Johnson

1 Use fast user switching to switch back to Chris Johnson's account.

2 Select the Payroll Reports folder that resides in Chris's home folder, and then choose File menu > Get Info (Command-I).

3   If necessary, expand "Sharing & Permissions."

4   Click the small lock in the Info window, and then authenticate as Local Admin.

5   Select the group (staff), and click the Delete (–) button below the permissions list.

6   Change the privilege level for everyone to No Access.

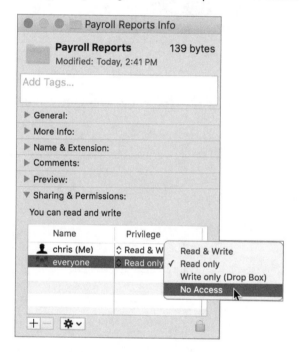

7   Close the Info window.

8   Navigate to Chris's Drop Box folder (inside the Public folder).

9   Select the Secret Bonus List copy that Mayta placed in Chris's Drop Box.

10 Choose File menu > Get Info. If necessary, expand the "Sharing & Permissions" section.

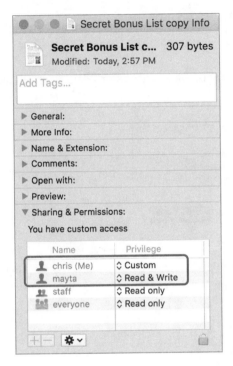

Since Mayta created this file, she is still its owner. However, when she copied it into Chris's Drop Box folder, the inheritable custom access control entry on the Drop Box folder granted Chris full access to it as well.

11 Close the Info window.

12 Open the Secret Bonus List copy, and edit its contents.

The inherited access control allows Chris to edit the file, and the changes will be saved automatically.

13 Quit TextEdit.

Test the New Permissions as Mayta Mishtuk

1   Use fast user switching to switch back to Mayta's account.

2   Try to open the Payroll Reports folder.

    This time you cannot open the folder because the new permissions do not grant you read access.

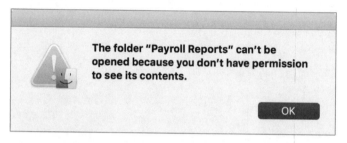

    The default permissions did not protect the Payroll Reports folder as Chris intended, but after changing the permissions, the folder is protected from access by other users.

3   Log out of Mayta's account.

4   At the login window, switch to Chris Johnson.

5   Navigate back to Chris's home folder (Go menu > Home or Command-Shift-H), and drag the Payroll Reports folder to the Trash.

Lesson 12

Use Hidden Items, Shortcuts, and File Archives

macOS includes several technologies for making complex file-system structures appear simple. An excellent example of this is how the Finder displays the macOS file system to the user. By default, the Finder hides much of the complexity of macOS from the user and reveals only four folders at the root (beginning) level of the system volume. Applications also appear to be single icons, despite containing all the resources necessary for modern complex software. Also, many items are shown in intentionally convenient locations but are actually stored elsewhere. Further, archiving technology allows multiple items to be combined into a single compressed file.

In this lesson, you will explore the file-system technologies that assist in hiding, redirecting, and archiving items. This includes an exploration of the hidden items in macOS, including bundles and packages. You will also learn how to manage file-system aliases and links. Finally, you will open and create ZIP archives and disk images.

GOALS

▸ Navigate to hidden files and folders

▸ Examine packages and bundles

▸ Manage aliases and links

▸ Create and open ZIP archives and disk images

Reference 12.1
Examine Hidden Items

Being a fully UNIX-compliant operating system, macOS includes a number of files that the average user never touches. The root level of the Mac system volume contains many resources that UNIX processes require and UNIX administrators expect. Apple made the wise choice of configuring the Finder to hide these items from the average user. On a daily basis, the average user—and even most administrator users—does not need to access any of these items from the graphical interface.

Realistically, the only people who even care about these normally hidden resources are going to be using the command-line interface via Terminal to do their work anyway. In other words, keeping these system items hidden in the Finder not only provides a tidier work environment but also prevents average users from poking around in places they shouldn't go.

As a hybrid of previous UNIX and Mac OS technologies, macOS uses two methods to hide files and folders. The first is a UNIX tradition: using a period at the beginning of the item's name hides the item both in the Finder and while using the default options to list items in Terminal. The second method is a Mac OS tradition: enabling an item's hidden file flag. This method, however, only hides the item in the Finder.

> **NOTE ▶** To prevent user confusion, macOS does not let you hide items using the Finder or any of the default applications. Only from Terminal can a user name items beginning with a period or manage the hidden file flag. Use of Terminal is beyond the scope of this guide.

Reveal Hidden Folders in the Finder

Should you want or need to open normally hidden items in the Finder, you have a choice of several methods. The first two provide access to the most commonly accessed hidden folder: the user's Library folder. The last method involves using the Go menu in the Finder to open any folder, including hidden folders.

The User's Hidden Library Folder

As detailed in **Lesson 13, "Manage System Resources,"** the user's Library folder is full of important resources, but it is hidden in the Finder. Fortunately, the Go menu provides a quick shortcut to this often-visited location. Simply hold down the Option key while clicking the Go menu to reveal the Library menu item.

If you frequently access the user's Library folder, you may want to make it permanently visible. The Finder also has the ability to always show the user's Library folder. Start by making sure the user's home folder appears in the Finder sidebar. You can enable that behavior in the Sidebar settings of the Finder preferences, accessed by choosing Finder > Preferences or pressing Command-Comma. After you have selected the user's home folder in the Finder sidebar, choose View > Show View Options, or press Command-J. From the View Options window, you can select the checkbox to permanently show the user's Library folder.

> **TIP** You can reveal all the hidden items of a folder or volume in the Finder by using the Command-Shift-. (period) keyboard shortcut. The hidden items will remain visible in the current folder or volume until you use the keyboard shortcut again to return the items to their default hidden state.

TIP ▶ If you choose to show the user's Library folder in the Finder, this will also show the user's Library folder in the Go menu, complete with its own keyboard shortcut, Command-Shift-L.

Go to Folder

To reveal any hidden folder in the Finder, choose Go > Go to Folder, or press Command-Shift-G. This opens a dialog that allows you to enter an absolute path to any folder on the Mac. A good starting place is the /private folder, which contains many common UNIX system resources.

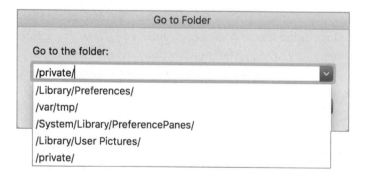

TIP ▶ An incredibly useful shortcut is to use Tab key completion when entering file-system paths. Simply press Tab once you have started a pathname, and the system attempts to automatically fill in the rest of the name. For example, navigating to the /private folder requires only that you enter /**p** and then press Tab. You can also quickly navigate to past destinations from the pop-up menu revealed by clicking the down arrow button to the right of the text field.

Click the Go button after you have entered a path. The Finder reveals the hidden folder in a window. Note the dimmed folder icon representing the normally hidden folder. To save time when you return to the "Go to the folder" dialog, the last path you entered appears there.

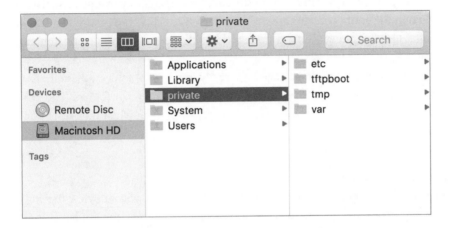

NOTE ▶ Some folders, both visible and hidden, have permissions that do not allow standard or administrator users to view the contents.

Reference 12.2
Examine Bundles and Packages

Sometimes hiding individual items isn't the most efficient solution for hiding data, especially if you need to hide a lot of related files. Conveniently, the file system provides a built-in method for combining files: the common folder. Apple simply modified this existing file-system container by adding the ability to optionally hide a folder's content.

Bundles and packages are folders that contain related executable code and resources used by that code. This allows software developers to easily organize all the resources needed for a complicated product into a single bundle or package while also discouraging normal users from interfering with the resources.

Bundles and packages use the same technique of combining executable code and resources inside folders. The difference is that the Finder treats packages as opaque objects that users, by default, cannot navigate into. For example, where a user sees only a single icon in the Finder representing an application, in reality it is a folder filled with, potentially, thousands of resources.

The word *package* is also used to describe the archive files used by applications to install software—that is, installer packages. This is appropriate, as users cannot, by default, navigate into the contents of an installer package, because the Finder again displays it as a single opaque object. Eventually, Apple introduced the ability to create fully opaque installation packages, wherein the entire contents are inside a single file. This type of installer, known as a flat installer package, prevents users from accidentally revealing installation content.

> **NOTE ▶** Because bundles and packages are really just special folders, these items simply copy over to volumes other than Mac OS Extended as regular folders. The Finder continues to recognize the items as bundles or packages even when they reside on a third-party volume.

Reveal Package Content

Although the Finder default is to hide the contents of a package, you can view the contents of a package from the Finder. To access a package's contents in the Finder, secondary-click (or Control-click) the item you want to explore, and then choose Show Package Contents from the shortcut menu.

Be very careful when exploring this content. Modifying the content of a bundle or package can easily leave the item unstable or unusable. If you can't resist the desire to tinker with a bundle or package, always do so from a copy, and leave the original safely intact.

> **MORE INFO ▶** Tools for creating and modifying bundles and packages are available to those who have Mac Dev Center access. You can find out more about the Apple Developer Program at https://developer.apple.com.

About Package Resources

The anatomy of an installer package is quite simple; it usually contains only a compressed archive of the software to be installed and a few configuration files used by the installer application. Other software bundles and packages are often much more complex, because they contain all the resources necessary for the application or software.

Software bundles or packages often include:

▶ Executable code for multiple platforms

▶ Document description files

▶ Media resources such as images and sounds

▶ User interface description files

▶ Text resources

▶ Resources localized for specific languages

▶ Private software libraries and frameworks

▶ Plug-ins or other software to expand capability

Reference 12.3
Use File-System Shortcuts

Another example of macOS being a hybrid of both UNIX and the classic Mac OS is the provision of multiple methods used for file-system pointers or shortcuts. Generally speaking, file-system shortcuts are files that refer to other files or folders; this allows you to have a single item appear in multiple locations or with multiple names without having to create multiple copies of the item. Both the system and users take advantage of file-system shortcuts to provide access to items from more convenient locations without having to duplicate those items.

> **NOTE ▶** Do not confuse the shortcuts found in the Dock or the Finder sidebar with true file-system shortcuts. Both the Dock and Finder save their references to original items as part of their configuration files, whereas file-system shortcuts appear as individual files that can be located anywhere on a volume.

About File-System Shortcuts

macOS uses three primary file-system shortcut types: aliases, symbolic links, and hard links. To help compare these shortcut types, this section uses a 100 MB disk image file named BigFile.dmg. This file will be referred to using each shortcut type, and you will see the differences illustrated in the Finder Info window.

Aliases

File-system aliases are a holdover from the classic Mac OS but have been updated for macOS duties. Aliases can be created using the Finder but are not recognized by command-line tools in Terminal. Command-line tools think that aliases are nothing more than data files and do not know how to follow their references back to the original items.

Aliases, however, are more resilient than other shortcut types in that, if the original item is replaced or moved, the alias almost never loses the original item. An example of how aliases are used by the operating system is the Finder Burn Folder feature, which allows you to organize files before you burn them to an optical disc. To save space, the Finder populates the burn folder with aliases instead of copies of the original items.

The following screenshot shows the Finder Info window inspecting an alias pointing to BigFile.dmg. Note that the kind is reported as Alias and the file is much smaller than the 100 MB original, weighing in at roughly 760 KB. The extra information in the alias is what allows the system to keep track of the original item should it ever change location.

Symbolic Links

Symbolic link shortcuts are part of the traditional UNIX file system; they are pointers to the file-system path of the original item. Thus, in many cases, if you move the original item, the symbolic link is broken. However, replacing the original item works, because the path remains the same.

In macOS, you can create symbolic links only in Terminal. You cannot create symbolic links from the Finder, but the Finder can follow symbolic links to the original item. An example use of symbolic links in macOS is the way the system layout stores several fundamental UNIX folders in the /private folder but also makes those items available at the root of the file system using symbolic links.

The following screenshot shows the Finder Info window inspecting a symbolic link pointing to BigFile.dmg. Note that the kind is also reported as Alias, but the file itself is tiny, at only 34 bytes. This illustrates that a symbolic link is merely saving a path to the original item. Also note the lack of a Select New Original button, indicating that the Finder cannot repair a symbolic link.

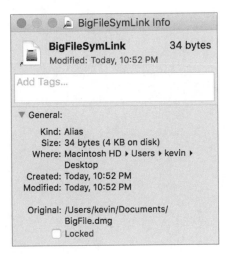

Hard Links

Hard-link shortcuts are also part of the traditional UNIX file system; they are actual additional references to the original item. Think of a normal file as two parts: the bits on the physical disk that make up the file's actual content and a name that points to those bits. Technically, every file always uses at least one hard link. Creating an additional hard link is like creating another name that points to the same bits on the physical disk.

As a result, removing additional hard links does not delete the original item. Furthermore, deleting the "original" item does not delete the actual data or additional hard links. This is because the other hard links still point to the same bits on the disk, which won't be freed until there are no links left to them. With aliases and symbolic links, however, deleting the original item leaves the shortcut pointing at nothing.

You can create hard links only in Terminal. The Finder cannot create hard links, but it can follow them. An example use of hard links in macOS is for Time Machine backups. Time Machine uses hard links to refer to items that have not changed since the previous backup, thus saving a tremendous amount of space. Finally, macOS is unique in its ability to use hard links of both files and folders; again, this is to support Time Machine backups.

The following screenshot shows the Finder Info window inspecting a hard link pointing to BigFile.dmg. Notice that the hard link is reported as Disk Image (as opposed to Alias) and that it has exactly the same file size as the original item, indicating that they share the same bits on the physical disk.

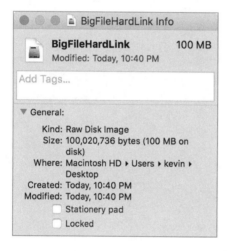

Create Aliases

To create an alias in the Finder, select the item you want to create an alias for and then choose one of the following methods:

▶ Choose File > Make Alias.

▶ Press Command-L.

▶ In a Finder window, choose Make Alias from the Action pop-up menu (small gear icon).

▶ In the Finder, secondary-click (or Control-click) the item, and then choose Make Alias from the shortcut menu.

▶ Drag the original item while holding down the Option and Command keys to drop the alias in another location. This is the only method that doesn't append alias to the new alias filename.

▶ Drag an application to the desktop. This gives users access to the application without the risk of them accidentally removing it from its original installed location.

After you have created the alias, you can rename it or move it anywhere you like. As long as the original item remains somewhere on the original volume—even if it's replaced or its name changes—the Finder can locate the alias. An alias file is easy to recognize by the small curved arrow that appears at the lower-left corner of the icon. From the Finder, you can locate the alias's target by secondary-clicking (or Control-clicking) the alias and then choosing Show Original from the shortcut menu, or by pressing Command-R.

Repair Aliases

In the rare case that an alias is broken—most likely because the original item was copied to another volume and then deleted off the original volume—you can repair the alias in the Finder. One method is to double-click the broken alias; the Finder automatically prompts you to select a new original.

Another option, which can also be used to redirect an existing alias, is to open the Finder Info window and then, in the General area, click the Select New Original button. Both methods open a browser dialog, allowing you to select a new original for the alias.

Reference 12.4
Use File Archives

At its essence, archiving is the practice of saving copies of important information to another location or format better suited for long-term storage or network transfer. Archiving and backup are both synonymous with copying data to another location for safekeeping, but in the context of this guide they are different processes serving different purposes. If you want to know more about backup in macOS, see **Lesson 15, "Manage Time Machine."**

Unlike automated backup solutions, archiving is typically a manual process that involves creating compressed copies of selected data. Archive formats are efficient from a storage and data transfer perspective, but they generally require user interaction. This section focuses on the archive technologies in macOS: ZIP archives and disk images.

About File Archives

macOS includes two archiving technologies: ZIP archives and disk images, both of which allow you to combine multiple files and compress the data into a more efficient file suited for long-term storage or network data transfer.

ZIP archives can be created in the Finder from a selection of files or folders. This is an efficient method for archiving relatively small amounts of data quickly. The ZIP archive format is also widely compatible; many operating systems include software to decompress

ZIP archives back to their original items. However, ZIP archives in macOS do not offer the flexibility provided by disk images.

Disk images, created using Disk Utility, are more widely used in macOS for archiving purposes, because they offer many features not available from ZIP archives. Primarily, disk images allow you to archive the contents of an entire file system, including all files, folders, and their associated metadata, into a single file. The resulting disk image can be compressed, encrypted, made as read-only to prevent modifications, or use any combination of these features. Disk images can also be created as read/write, so you can easily make changes to them over time. Finally, macOS relies on disk images for several core technologies, including software distribution, system imaging, macOS Recovery, NetInstall, Legacy FileVault, and network Time Machine backups.

Disk images are also useful as a personal archive tool. However, disk images created using Disk Utility, as a default, can only be accessed by Mac computers. Other systems require third-party software to access Mac disk image content.

Create ZIP Archives

The Finder allows you to quickly create a compressed ZIP archive from any number of selected items or to expand a ZIP archive to its original number of items. By default, creating a ZIP archive in the Finder doesn't delete the original items, and expanding a ZIP archive doesn't delete the original archive.

To create a ZIP archive in the Finder, select the items you want to archive and compress in the Finder. You can hold down the Shift key to quickly select contiguous lists of items or hold down the Command key to select noncontiguous items. Then simply choose File > Compress <Items>, or secondary-click (or Control-click) the items and choose Compress <Items> from the shortcut menu, where <Items> is the name of a single item or the number of items you have selected.

If the archiving process is going to take more than a few seconds, the Finder shows a progress dialog with the estimated time required to complete the compression task. You can also choose to cancel the archive by clicking the small x button on the far right. When the process finishes, you are left with a ZIP archive named either Archive.zip or <Item>.zip, where <Item> is the name of the single item you chose to archive and compress.

After the archiving process is complete, it's always interesting to compare the size of the original item(s) with the archive's size using the Info or Inspector window in the Finder. In many cases, you can expect at least a 50 percent decrease in file size. On the other hand, many media formats are already quite compressed in their original form, so you may not experience very good results when compressing these types of files.

Expand ZIP Archives

Expanding a ZIP archive in the Finder is as simple as double-clicking the archive file. The Finder, by default, decompresses the entire archive file and places the resulting files and folders in the same folder as the original ZIP archive. The Finder cannot list or extract individual items from a ZIP archive. Also by default, the Finder does not delete the original archive.

If you need more control over how ZIP archives are expanded, open /System/Library/CoreServices/Applications/Archive Utility.app (also searchable via Spotlight), and then choose Archive Utility > Preferences. These preferences allow you to adjust how ZIP archives are both expanded and compressed. Specifically, these preferences include options about how original items are handled after an archive transition.

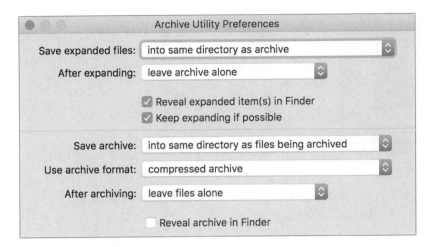

Alternatively, the Archive Utility contains a system preference pane that can be installed if you find you are making frequent changes to these settings. To install this pane, secondary-click (or Control-click) the Archive Utility.app icon and choose Show Package Contents from the shortcut menu. Once you're viewing the package contents in the Finder, navigate to and double-click /Contents/Resources/Archives.prefPane.

Mount Disk Images

If in the past you have manually installed any Apple or third-party software downloaded from the Internet, you have already used a mounted disk image. By default, the Safari web browser automatically mounts any downloaded disk image, but you can also manually mount disk images at any time from the Finder. To access the contents of a disk image, simply double-click the disk image file in the Finder.

This mounts the volume inside the disk image file as if you had just connected a normal storage device. Even if the disk image file is located on a remote file server, you can still mount it as if it were a local disk. You can treat the mounted disk image volume as you would any other storage device by navigating through its hierarchy and selecting files and folders as you need them. Further, if the disk image is read/write, you can add to the contents of the disk image by simply dragging items to the volume.

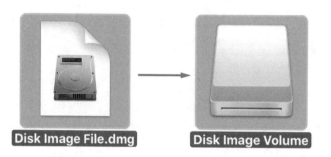

Disk Image File.dmg → **Disk Image Volume**

NOTE ▶ When you are done with a disk image volume, be sure to properly eject it as you would any other removable volume.

Create Empty Disk Images

Using /Applications/Utilities/Disk Utility to make disk images allows you to create blank images, or images containing copies of selected folders or even entire file systems. macOS supports disk images of nearly any size, limited only by local storage capacity.

To create an empty disk image, which you can then fill with content over time, open Disk Utility and then choose File > New Image > Blank Image.

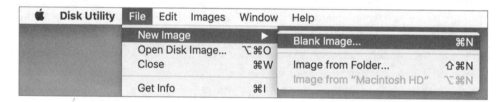

In the New Blank Image dialog, you can define the parameters for the new disk image. At minimum, you need to select a name and destination for the resulting disk image file. You should also enter a name for the volume inside the disk image. The disk image file and volume names do not have to match, but they should be similar so that you can recognize their relationship.

As for disk image size, again you are limited only by the storage destination. However, a very efficient option is to select "sparse disk image" for the image format. With this option selected, the resulting image file will only be as large as it needs to be to store items that are actually in the disk image volume. Any "empty" space inside the disk image volume will occupy zero real storage space. This way, you can define a very large size without having to initially fill the entire storage space.

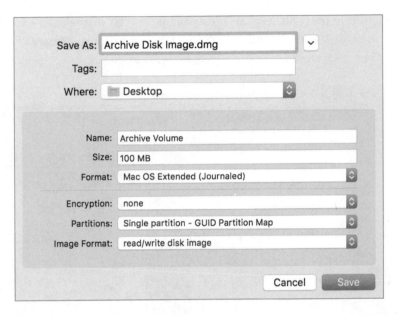

After you have defined your disk image options, click Save to create the disk image. After the system has created the new blank disk image, it automatically mounts it. If you have elected to create a sparse disk image, you can open Info windows in the Finder for both the disk image file and the disk image volume to verify that the volume size is much larger than the image size. As you copy files to the volume, the disk image file automatically grows accordingly.

TIP You can change the format of a disk image at any time in Disk Utility by choosing Images > Convert. This opens a dialog where you can select the image you want to change and save a copy of the image with new options.

Create Disk Image Archives

To create a disk image that contains copies of specific items, open Disk Utility and choose File > New Image > Image from Folder. This opens a file browser window in which you can select the folder you want to copy into a new disk image.

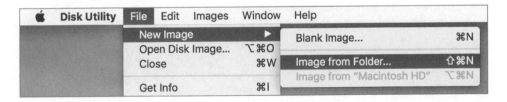

To create a disk image from the contents of an entire volume or disk, first select the source from the Disk Utility window disks list and then choose File > New Image > Image from *<Source>*—where *<Source>* is the name of the selected volume or disk.

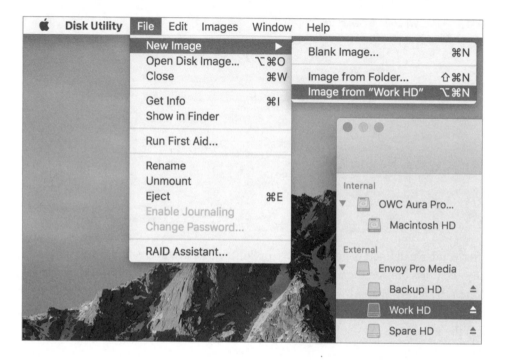

NOTE ▶ Disk Utility can only make disk images of volumes that it can temporarily unmount. Thus, you cannot make a disk image of the currently running system volume.

Once you've selected the disk image source, a Save dialog appears. At minimum, you need to select a name and destination for the resulting disk image file. The name of the volume inside the disk image is automatically set to the name of the selected source. Your options include the ability to compress the disk image contents, which is recommended to save storage space. Also, if the contents of the archive are sensitive, you have the option to enable encryption for the disk image. Selecting that option requires setting a password and hint for the resulting secure disk image. As with many secrets, this password can be saved to a keychain for easy, secure access.

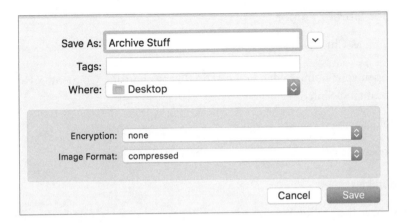

NOTE ▶ Be sure you have enough free space on the destination volume where you plan to save your disk image file.

After you have defined your disk image options, click Save to create the disk image. Depending on the amount of data to be copied and the image format you choose, it can take anywhere from minutes to hours for the disk image copy process to complete. Disk Utility opens a small progress dialog that also allows you to cancel the copying process.

NOTE ▶ To create an image containing items for which you don't have read permissions, you must authenticate as an administrator.

Exercise 12.1
Navigate Hidden Items

▶ **Prerequisite**

▶ You must have created the Chris Johnson account (Exercise 5.1, "Create a Standard User Account").

macOS hides certain portions of its folder structure, both to simplify the user experience and to prevent users from accidentally damaging the workings of the operating system. As an administrator, however, it is sometimes useful to know what these hidden folders are and how to reach them. In this exercise, you will explore some of the hidden folders in macOS.

Examine Your User Library Folder

1   If necessary, log in as Chris Johnson.

2   In the Finder, open your home folder. You can do this by choosing Go menu > Home (or pressing Command-Shift-H).

Note that no folder named Library is visible.

3   In the Finder, open the Go menu, but don't choose anything yet.

4   Press the Option key.

As long as you have the Option key held down, a Library choice appears in the menu.

5   With the Option key held down, choose Library.

This opens the hidden Library folder in Chris's home folder.

6   If necessary, change to column view by choosing View menu > as Columns or by clicking the Column View button in the Finder toolbar.

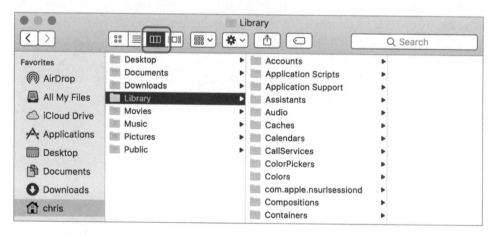

Chris's user Library folder is now shown in Chris's home folder but is dimmed to indicate that it's normally invisible.

7   Explore some of the subfolders in Chris's user Library folder. Note that you can navigate into them normally.

8   Close the Finder window showing Chris's user Library.

9   Press Command-Shift-H to open Chris's home folder in a new Finder window.

The Library folder is not shown.

10 Choose Go menu > Go to Folder (Command-Shift-G).

11 In the "Go to the folder" dialog, enter ~/Li, and press Tab.

The field automatically completes the path to ~/Library/.

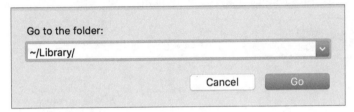

This is an example of specifying a folder by the path to reach it. In this case, the tilde (~) means "start at my home folder," and "/Library" means "then go into the Library folder." This is another way to reach your user Library folder.

12 Click Go.

As before, Chris's user Library folder appears in the Finder.

Note that you could also have reached this folder by entering the full path, "/Users/chris/Library," but the tilde (~) shorthand is an easier way to specify locations in your home folder.

Examine Hidden System Folders

1 Press Command-Shift-G to reopen the "Go to the folder" dialog.

2 This time, enter /L, and press Tab.

The field automatically completes the path to /Library/. This path looks similar to the previous one, but because it does not start with a tilde (~), it specifies a completely different folder. When a path starts with a slash (/), it starts at the top level of the startup volume (sometimes called the *root* of the file system).

3 Click Go.

This time, the Finder opens the Library folder at the top of the startup volume. The next lesson discusses the various Library folders.

This Library folder is not hidden, but you can use the same technique to reach any folder you know the path to, whether or not it is hidden.

4 Use the "Go to the folder" dialog to reach the /private/var/log/ folder (remember, you can type part of a name and then press Tab to complete it).

The /private folder holds some of the macOS "private" system files. The /private/var/log folder holds some of the system log files (there are more in /Library/Logs and ~/Library/Logs). Normally, you do not need to access these in the Finder, so they are hidden from view unless you specifically navigate to them.

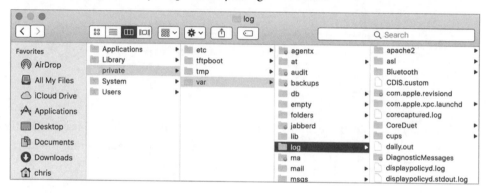

5 Use the "Go to the folder" dialog to reach the /var/log/ folder.

This also takes you to /private/var/log because /var is a symbolic link to /private/var.

Lesson 13

Manage System Resources

It is not unusual for a macOS system volume to contain well over 100,000 folders and 500,000 files just to support the operating system and its applications. As you can imagine, the number of items in a user's home folder varies widely, depending on the user, but even the most frugal of users has thousands of items in the home folder. With this many files on hand, attempting to explore and fully comprehend the macOS file layout may seem like a monumental task. The contrary is true, however: the macOS system files are streamlined and organized in an easy-to-understand layout that is easy to manage and provides strong security.

GOALS

▶ Explore and understand the macOS file layout

▶ Discover common system files, their location, and their purpose

▶ Manage font resources

This lesson focuses on the composition and organization of the files and folders that make up macOS. In this lesson, you, acting as an administrator, will use the file layout to strategically allocate resources. The exercises in this lesson specifically discuss management of font resources, because they are one of those most commonly modified by users. However, many of the same management techniques can be used for other system resources.

Reference 13.1
About macOS File Resources

The macOS system layout is designed to strike a balance between ease of use and advanced functionality. For the basic user, looking at the root (beginning) of the file system from the Finder reveals only four default folders: Applications, Library, Users, and System.

The contents of these four folders represent all that most users, and many administrators, ever need to access. Yet when advanced users look at the system root from

Terminal, they see many more items that the Finder would normally hide. Thus, the complexity and flexibility of a UNIX operating system remains accessible to those users who require it.

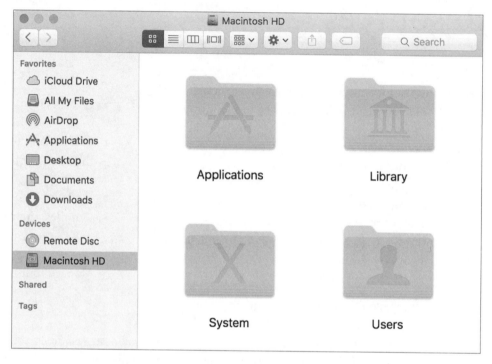

Here are descriptions of the default system root folders you see from the Finder:

▶ Applications—Often called the local Applications folder, this is the default location for applications available to all local users. Only administrator users can make changes to the contents of this folder.

▶ Library—Often called the local Library folder, this is the default location for ancillary system and application resources available to all users of the system. Once again, only administrator users can make changes to the contents of this folder.

▶ System—This folder contains resources required by the operating system for primary functionality. With System Integrity Protection (SIP) enabled by default in macOS, no user or process can make any changes to most of the content of the System folder. Although you can disable SIP, giving administrator users write access to the System folder, this is strongly discouraged because it introduces an unnecessary security risk. All properly created third-party macOS software, including hardware drivers, can function outside of the System folder. Details regarding SIP are covered later in this lesson.

▶ Users—This is the default location for local user home folders. Lesson 6, "Manage User Home Folders," covers this topic in greater detail.

About Library Resources

All macOS-specific system resources can be found in the various Library folders throughout the system volume. A system resource can be generally categorized as any resource that is not a general-use application or user file. That's not to say that applications and user data can't be found in the Library folders. On the contrary, the Library folder is designed to keep both user and system resources organized and separated from the items you use every day. This keeps the /Applications folder and user home folders free from system resource clutter.

Opening any of the Library folders reveals several dozen categories of items. It is not necessary to explore every possible Library item, but you should be familiar with several system resources:

▶ Application Support—This folder can be found in both the user and local Library folders. Any ancillary data needed by an application may end up in this folder. For example, it often contains help files or templates for an application. Once again, application resources are placed here to keep the /Applications folders tidy.

▶ Extensions—Also called kernel extensions, these items are found only in the system and local Library folders. Extensions are low-level drivers that attach themselves to the kernel, or core, of the operating system. Extensions provide driver support for hardware, networking, and peripherals. Extensions load and unload automatically, so there is little need to manage them, as is common in other operating systems. Extensions are covered in greater detail in **Lesson 24, "Troubleshoot Peripherals."**

▶ Fonts—Found in every Library folder, fonts are files that describe typefaces used for both screen display and printing. Font management is covered later in this lesson.

▶ Frameworks—Found in every Library folder, frameworks are repositories of shared code used among different parts of the operating system or applications. Frameworks are similar to extensions in that they load and unload automatically, so again, there is little need to manage these shared code resources. You can view your Mac computer's currently loaded frameworks from the /Applications/Utilities/System Information application.

▶ Keychains—Found in every Library folder, keychains are used to securely store sensitive information, including passwords, certificates, keys, Safari AutoFill information, and notes. Keychain technology is covered in Lesson 7, "Manage Security and Privacy."

▶ LaunchDaemons and LaunchAgents—Both items can be found in the local and system Library folders, and LaunchAgents can also be found in users' Library folders. These launch items are used to define processes that start automatically via the launchd process. macOS uses many background processes, which are all started by launchd. Further, every single process is a child of the launchd process. LaunchAgents are for processes that need to start up only when a user is logged in, whereas LaunchDaemons are used to start processes that always run in the background, even when no users are logged in. More about launchd can be found in **Lesson 26, "Troubleshoot Startup and System Issues."**

▶ Logs—Many system processes and applications archive progress or error messages to log files. Log files can be found in every local Library folder and also the /var/log folder. Technically, an application or process can save log files to any writable location, but the previously mentioned folders are the defaults. You can view log files using the /Applications/Utilities/Console application.

▶ PreferencePanes—PreferencePanes can be found in any Library folder. These items are used by the System Preferences application to provide interfaces for system configuration. Using System Preferences is covered in Lesson 2, "Set Up and Configure macOS."

▶ Preferences—Preferences, found in both local and user libraries, are used to store system and application configuration settings. In other words, every time you configure a setting for any application or system function, it is saved to a preference file. Because preferences play such a critical role in system functionality, they are often the cause of software problems. Troubleshooting preference files is covered in **Lesson 18, "Manage and Troubleshoot Applications."**

▶ Startup Items—Found in only the local and system Library folders, these are precursors to LaunchAgents and LaunchDaemons. macOS no longer supports these legacy Startup Items. In fact, you will have Startup Items only if you've installed third-party software that has not been updated to work with macOS Sierra.

About Resource Hierarchy

Library folders, and thus system resources, are located in each of the four domain areas: user, local, network, and system. Segregating resources into four domains provides increased administrative flexibility, resource security, and system reliability. Resource domains allow for administrative flexibility, because you can choose to allocate certain resources to all users or just specific users. Using resource domains is also more secure, because standard users can add resources only to their own home folder and cannot access other users' resources. In addition, resource domains are more reliable, because in most cases you don't have to make changes to the core system functionality to provide more services.

> **TIP** ► The quickest way to reveal a user's Library folder is to manually go to the folder in the Finder. While holding down the Option key, choose Go > Library to reveal the hidden folder. You can learn more about hidden items in Lesson 12, "Use Hidden Items, Shortcuts, and File Archives."

The four system resource domains are, in order:

► User—Each user has his or her own Library folder in the home folder for resources. When resources are placed here, only the user has access to them. The user's Library folder is hidden by default to prevent users from accidentally making changes that could be detrimental. However, you can still find many thousands of items in this folder, because many applications and processes continue to rely on this location for resources. Also, users can have their own Applications folder within their home folder, provided they create the folder and name it, precisely, Applications.

► Local—Both the root Applications and root Library folders are part of the local resource domain. This is why they are known as the local Applications and local Library folders. Any resources placed in these two folders are available to all local user accounts. By default, only administrator users can make changes to local resources.

► Network—macOS can access system resources in a Library folder and applications in an Applications folder residing on a network file share. Administrators must configure an automounted share to enable the Network resource domain. Configuring automounted shares is beyond the scope of this guide.

► System—Finally, the system domain encompasses all the items necessary to provide core system functionality. This includes an application folder located at /System /Library/CoreServices. Many hidden items at the root of the system volume also make up the system resource domain, but the only one you see in the Finder is the /System /Library folder. Again, with SIP in Sierra, no user or process can modify most of the System folder, with the exception of /System/Library/User Template.

With four different domains containing resources, a strong likelihood exists for overlap in resources, meaning there may be multiple copies of similar resources available to the system and user at any given time. The system is designed to handle this by searching for resources from the most specific (those in the user domain) to the least specific (those in the system domain). The following graphic represents the order in which resource contention is resolved from the user's home folder (1) to the System folder (4).

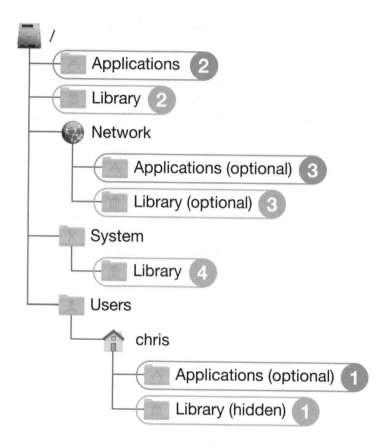

If multiple similar resources are discovered, the system uses the resource most specific to the user. For example, if multiple versions of the font Times New Roman are found—one in the local Library and one in the user's Library—the system uses the copy of the font in the user's Library. In other words, resources in the user's home folder take first priority, thus trumping all other resource locations.

About Application Sandbox Containers

Application sandbox containers add a bit more complexity to file-system organization but greatly enhance the security of running applications. Sandboxed applications are designed in such a way that they are allowed access only to the specific items they need to function.

Because application sandboxing is a recent addition to macOS, many legacy applications do not take advantage of this technology. However, most applications built into macOS and all applications from the Mac App Store are created as sandboxed applications.

As the term *sandbox* implies, these applications are allowed to "play" only in their specific area. These areas are special folders that are referred to as containers. The system manages the content of these containers to ensure that an application is not allowed access to any other items in the file system. In other words, sandboxed applications are more secure because they are allowed access only to the items in their own containers.

Users can also allow a sandboxed application access to other files outside the container, but they must do so by opening the item in the application. In other words, the specific action of a user opening a document outside of an application's container is the only way a sandboxed application is allowed access outside of its container.

Application containers can be found in the user's Library folder. Specifically, the ~/Library/Containers folder contains individual application containers. When a sandboxed application starts up the first time, the system automatically creates a container folder for the application, named with its bundle identifier. The bundle identifier is used for development purposes to identify an application by its creator and application title. For example, the container folder for Notes is ~/Library/Containers/com.apple.Notes.

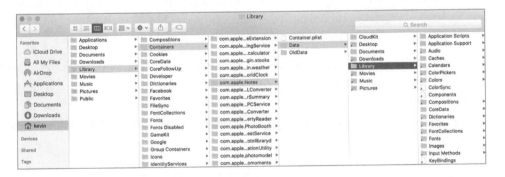

The root content of an application container is a property list file containing application information, a Data folder, and possibly an OldData folder. The Data folder is the application's current active container. Any OldData folder you might find contains previously used application items. The content of the Data folder mostly mimics the user's home folder, but with one key distinction: it contains only the items that the application is allowed to access. Thus, in the Data folder you will find only items specific to the application's function or items the user has explicitly opened in the application.

Items created and managed by the sandboxed application are the only original items in the container Data folder. As covered previously in this lesson, common resource folders used by an application include Application Support and Preferences. If the user has enabled iCloud Drive, you may also find a CloudKit folder for maintaining items stored in iCloud.

Items that originated from other applications or a user's file-opening action are represented as symbolic links that point to the original item outside of the container. The system automatically creates these symbolic links when the user opens an item in the sandboxed application. By representing external items this way, an original item can stay where the user wants it while also being accessible to a sandboxed application that can see only its own container.

About Application Group Containers

Although a user can explicitly allow sandboxed applications to access specific files beyond the application's container, the secure design of sandboxing prevents applications from doing this automatically for themselves. As you can imagine, this keeps applications from automatically taking advantage of each other's resources. Thus, in order to facilitate sharing application resources automatically, developers of sandboxed applications can request that the system create a shared application group container.

Application group containers can also be found in the user's Library folder. Specifically, the ~/Library/Group Containers folder contains shared application containers. When a sandboxed application starts up the first time and requests access to share application resources, the system automatically creates a group container folder for the application, named with its bundle identifier.

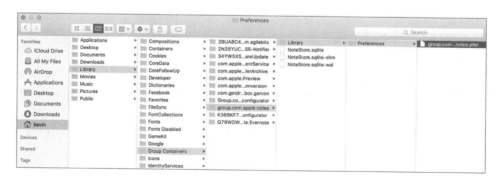

Unlike application sandbox containers that simulate an entire user's home folder, application group containers hold only items to be shared between applications. Again using the Notes application as an example, in the previous screenshot you can see the NoteStore database and notes property list file. In this specific instance, the Notes data is shared so that other applications can access user note entries. The system controls access to this via a security mechanism to ensure that only Apple-verified processes can access the user's Notes database.

Troubleshoot System Resources

System resource issues are rare, and they are generally easy to identify. You may occasionally see an error message calling out an issue with a specific item, but you may also experience a situation where the item appears to be missing. In some cases, the system resource in question may actually be missing, but many times the system ignores a system resource if it determines that the resource is in some way corrupted. The solution for both of these situations is to replace the missing or suspect item with a known working copy.

When troubleshooting system resources, remember to heed the resource domain hierarchy. Using fonts as an example, you may have loaded a specific version of a font in the local Library, as required by your workflow to operate properly. In spite of this, a user may have loaded another version of the same font in his or her home folder. In this case, the system loads the user's font and ignores the font you installed. Therefore, this user may experience workflow problems even though it appears that he or she is using the correct font.

> **TIP** If fonts are missing from within applications but appear to be properly installed, remember to check Font Book—the font may be temporarily disabled. Font Book is covered later in this lesson.

Logging in with another account on the Mac is always a quick way to determine whether the problem is in the user's home folder. You can also use /Applications/Utilities /System Information to list active system resources. System Information always shows the file path of the loaded system resources, so it's easy to spot resources that are loading from the user's Library.

Font File		Kind	Valid	Enabled
Harrington		TrueType	Yes	Yes
HeadlineA.ttf		TrueType	Yes	Yes
Helvetica.dfont		TrueType	Yes	Yes
HelveticaNeue.dfont		TrueType	Yes	Yes
HelveticaNeueDeskInterface.ttc		TrueType	Yes	Yes

Helvetica.dfont:

```
Kind:          TrueType
Valid:         Yes
Enabled:       Yes
Location:      /System/Library/Fonts/Helvetica.dfont
Typefaces:
   Helvetica-LightOblique:
      Full Name:    Helvetica Light Oblique
      Family:       Helvetica
      Style:        Light Oblique
      Version:      10.0d4e1
      Unique Name:  Helvetica Light Oblique; 10.0d4e1; 2015-04-16
      Copyright:    © 1990-2006 Apple Computer Inc. © 1981 Linotype AG
                    © 1990-91 Type Solutions Inc.
      Trademark:    Helvetica is a registered trademark of Linotype AG
      Outline:      Yes
      Valid:        Yes
      Enabled:      Yes
      Duplicate:    No
      Copy Protected:  No
      Embeddable:   Yes
```

kmwtogo › Software › Fonts › Helvetica.dfont

Reference 13.2
About System Integrity Protection

OS X El Capitan 10.11 and later releases include System Integrity Protection (SIP) to further enhance the security of Mac computers. In a nutshell, SIP prevents improper modification of core macOS system items and processes. SIP does this by acting as a meta-permission that prevents write access to system items and processes.

Historically, UNIX systems like macOS have allowed users and processes with root (or System Administrator) access to bypass system permissions. Thus, as covered in Lesson 11, "Manage Permissions and Sharing," any user or process with root access could essentially modify any item on the system volume. Further, processes running as root are normally allowed to modify the memory stores of any running process.

As a default on macOS, any administrator can install software that can potentially request root access. Because many users don't think twice before authenticating an installer or update, an administrator user could easily install malware that could take advantage of root access. This is why, from a security perspective, root access is a significant risk factor.

However, with SIP enabled by default on macOS, users and processes with root are not allowed to modify core system items and processes. Therefore, with SIP enabled, macOS itself is secured from malicious or malformed software that may attempt to breach security mechanisms by modifying system items.

System items protected by SIP include the following folders: /System, /bin, /sbin, and /usr. Almost everything inside these folders is protected, with a few exceptions. The two most prominent exceptions are two folders that are occasionally used by administrators for local customization: /System/Library/User Template and /usr/local. Core applications included with macOS, like System Preferences, are also protected by SIP. This is why repairing system permissions is not necessary with OS X El Capitan or later.

> **MORE INFO ▸** The full list of items protected by SIP can be found in the following text configuration file: /System/Library/Sandbox/rootless.conf. The file itself is obviously protected by SIP as well.

Verify System Integrity Protection

You can test SIP yourself by attempting to modify the permissions of one of these protected folders. For example, the following screenshot shows an administrator attempting to modify the permissions of the /System folder. Note in the screenshot that the security lock icon is open, indicating that this administrator user should have rights to modify the item's permissions, but SIP intervenes.

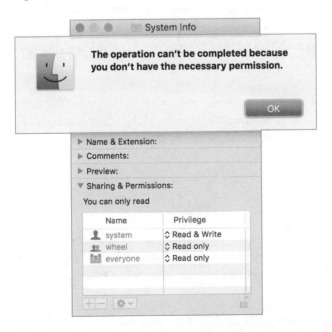

Bypass System Integrity Protection

Because SIP introduces significant new system behavior, older third-party software may not be compatible with this change. Specifically, any software that relies on non-Apple items installed or stored in any of the SIP-protected locations will likely be nonfunctional in macOS Sierra. In fact, during the upgrade to El Capitan or macOS Sierra, the installer will remove any non-Apple items from the SIP-protected locations. Specifically, the items are moved to /Library/SystemMigration/History/Migration-UUID/QuarantineRoot/, where "UUID" is a unique identifier number.

Older peripheral and printer driver software is the most likely to be impacted by SIP. If you discover that a third-party product is impeded by SIP, the best solution is to contact the developer to provide a version compatible with macOS Sierra. If the developer can't get his or her act together in a timely fashion, then you can bypass SIP, but this approach is not recommended or trivial.

SIP can be temporarily bypassed by starting from another, non-SIP-protected system; this includes macOS Recovery systems and systems prior to OS X El Capitan 10.11. You could also place a macOS Sierra system in target disk mode and then connect to another Mac running a previous version of OS X. These methods all allow you to modify a non-SIP-protected system volume. After you've made your changes, restart the Mac back to the macOS Sierra system and your changes should remain.

You can also permanently disable SIP by using the csrutil command when started from macOS Recovery. When SIP is disabled via this command, the setting is saved to the Mac's firmware. Thus, any SIP-compatible system running on this modified Mac will have SIP disabled. Obviously, returning to macOS Recovery to reenable SIP should be attempted as soon as possible.

> **NOTE ▶** Setting a computer firmware password, as detailed in Lesson 8, "Manage Password Changes," can prevent unauthorized bypassing of the Mac computer's system volume, thus ensuring an SIP-protected-system remains protected by the SIP rules.

Reference 13.3
Manage Font Resources

An excellent way to experience the system resource domain hierarchy is by managing fonts. macOS has advanced font-management technology that enables an unlimited number of fonts using nearly any font type, including bitmap, TrueType, OpenType, and all PostScript fonts.

As mentioned, fonts are installed in the various Font folders located in the Library folders throughout the system. A user can manually install fonts by dragging them into the ~/Library/Fonts folder. Further, administrators can install fonts for all users by dragging them into the /Library/Fonts folder. This flexible font system allows administrators to better control font usage. For example, a font vendor's licensing model may only grant specific access for an individual user.

> **MORE INFO** ▸ Every Mac system includes a wealth of high-quality fonts for many different languages. For the most recent list of fonts included with macOS, see Apple Support article HT206872, "Fonts included with macOS Sierra."

Install Fonts via Font Book

macOS does include a rather nice font-management tool, /Applications/Font Book, which automatically installs fonts for you. Font Book can also be used to organize fonts into more manageable collections, enable or disable fonts to simplify font lists, and resolve duplicate fonts.

> **NOTE** ▸ Third-party font-management tools, such as Extensis Suitcase Fusion or Universal Type Server, interrupt Font Book and take over font management for the system.

By default, when a user double-clicks a font in the Finder, Font Book opens and displays a preview of the font. When the user clicks the Install Font button, Font Book automatically copies the font into the Fonts folder in the user's Library folder.

> **NOTE ▶** Font Book, by default, automatically validates a font before installing and enabling it. This helps prevent font problems by making sure the font file isn't compromised. Thus, installing fonts via Font Book is favored over manual installation via the Finder.

When a new font is installed, the Font Book main window appears with the font preview at right. Manually opening Font Book also opens the main window. To preview any currently installed font, click it in the list of fonts. If you want to install additional fonts without leaving the Font Book application, you can do so by clicking the Add (+) button in the Font Book toolbar.

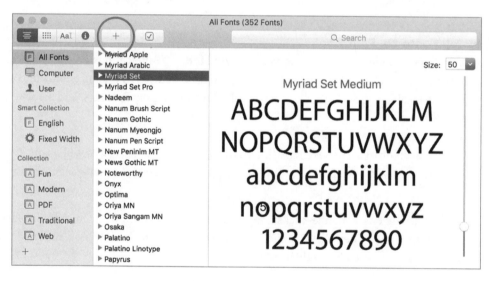

The previous screenshot shows a computer with additional nonsystem fonts installed. As you can see at the top of the first column in Font Book, you can sort by All Fonts, Computer, or User fonts. With Font Book open, you can adjust the default install location for fonts by choosing Font Book > Preferences. If you are an administrator user, you can choose to install fonts to the local Library folder by choosing Computer from the pop-up menu. Close the Font Book Preferences dialog after you have made your selections.

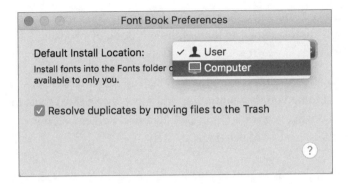

NOTE ► You may need to restart some applications to take advantage of recently added fonts.

NOTE ► You will be prompted to authenticate as an administrator in order to install fonts for all users on the computer.

Disable Fonts via Font Book

If you, or the application you're using, have difficulties choosing fonts from a large list, you can temporarily disable fonts within Font Book by selecting a font and then clicking the Enable/Disable button (it appears as a selected or deselected checkbox) in the toolbar. Disabled fonts appear dimmed in the font list, with "Off" shown next to their name. To enable the font, select it again and click the same checkbox button at the bottom of the font list.

TIP ► In Font Book you can also enable, disable, or remove fonts by selecting them from the list and then using secondary-click (Control-click) to reveal a pop-up menu, allowing you to manage the selected font(s).

Fonts that have multiple copies on your Mac show a small dot next to their name in the font list. You can automatically disable duplicate fonts with Font Book by choosing Edit > Look for Enabled Duplicates.

If you feel the need to remove a font, select it from the font list and then press Delete. A summary dialog appears, reminding you that continuing will move the selected fonts to the Trash. If you are sure this is what you want to do, click Remove. Remember, however, that you can always disable a font instead of deleting it entirely.

NOTE ► With SIP enabled, you can't remove system fonts required by macOS.

Resolve Font Issues via Font Book

If you're having font issues, you can identify problem fonts by forcing Font Book to revalidate all the fonts on your Mac. To do this, select a single font in the Font list, and then press Command-A to select all the fonts. Choose File > Validate Fonts to start the validation process.

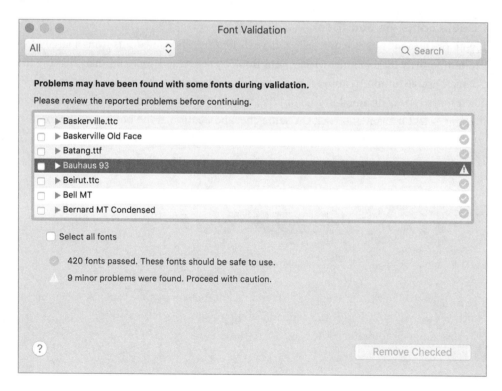

The Font Validation window opens and scans all the selected fonts. This window shows any problem font with a status indicator (exclamation mark icon) to the right of the font's name. To view details about a font issue, click the disclosure triangle to the left of the font name. To remove a problem font, select the checkbox next to its name and then click the Remove Checked button.

If you're still having problems with fonts, a final option in Font Book is to restore all the system fonts to the defaults for macOS. To do this, choose File > Restore Standard Fonts. A dialog appears, verifying your choice. Click Proceed to remove third-party fonts from macOS.

Exercise 13.1
Manage Font Resources

> ### Prerequisite
>
> ▸ You must have created the Local Admin (Exercise 2.1, "Configure a New macOS System for Exercises," or Exercise 2.2, "Configure an Existing macOS System for Exercises") and Chris Johnson (Exercise 5.1, "Create a Standard User Account") accounts.

In this exercise, you will remove a font from /Library/Fonts, where it is available to all users, and install it in a single user's Fonts folder.

Remove a Font
You can use Font Book to watch what happens when you move a font to the Trash.

1 Verify that no users have fast user switching sessions active. If any users other than Chris are logged in, log them out.

2 If necessary, log in as Chris Johnson.

3 Open the Font Book application, which is located in the /Applications folder.

4 Locate Andale Mono in the Font column.

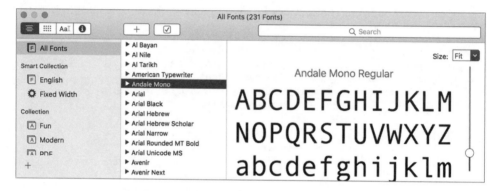

5 In the Finder, navigate to the folder /Library/Fonts. If Macintosh HD is not displayed on Chris's desktop, you can find it in the Computer view, available by choosing Go menu > Computer (or pressing Command-Shift-C and then opening Macintosh HD > Library > Fonts).

6 To verify your location, choose View menu > Show Path Bar.

Make sure the path bar at the bottom of the window matches the following screenshot (although the rest may not match unless you are in column view):

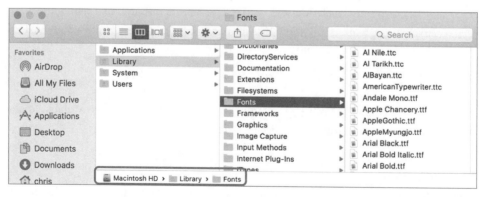

The path bar includes the volume name in the path, so the unix path /Library/Fonts is displayed as "Macintosh HD > Library > Fonts." The fonts in this folder are available to all users on the system.

7   Locate the file Andale Mono.ttf.

8   Drag Andale Mono.ttf to the desktop. As you drag, a cursor with a green badge with a plus sign on it appears attached to the pointer. This indicates that the file will be copied rather than moved.

This will be your backup copy of the Andale Mono font.

9   Move the original Andale Mono.ttf file from /Library/Fonts to the Trash. To do so, you have to authenticate as Local Admin (password: ladmin, or whatever you chose when you created the account).

10   Click the Font Book window to make it the active application.

The Andale Mono font is no longer listed in the Font Book window. Font Book shows a real-time display of all the fonts in the system search path.

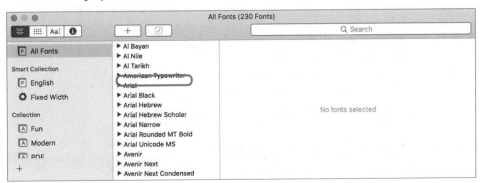

Add a Font for Only One User

You can use Font Book to install a font that only one user of the computer can use.

1   In the Font Book application, choose Font Book menu > Preferences (Command-Comma).

2   Ensure that Default Install Location is set to User.

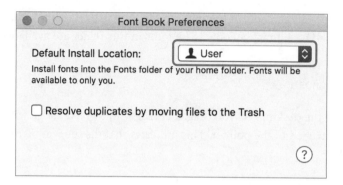

3   Close Font Book Preferences.

4   Switch to the Finder, and double-click Andale Mono.ttf on the desktop.

This opens Andale Mono.ttf in Font Book, which shows a preview of the font and gives you the option to install it.

5   Click Install Font.

6   If necessary, select User from the sidebar.

Andale Mono is the only font installed in Chris's user account.

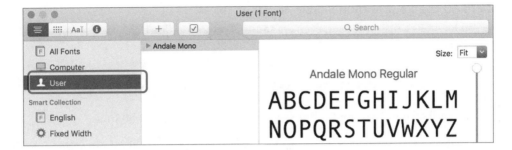

7   Select All Fonts from the sidebar.

Since this shows all available fonts, including those installed just for the current user as well as those installed computerwide, Andale Mono is back in the list.

8   Control-click on Andale Mono, and choose "Show in Finder" from the shortcut menu.

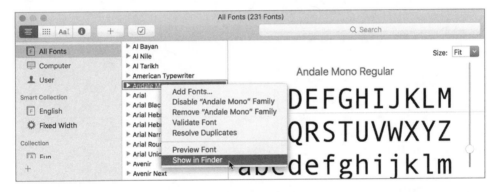

The Finder opens a window displaying the font file. Its path bar shows that it is located in the Fonts folder in Chris's user library, variously referred to as ~/Library/Fonts, /Users/chris/Library/Fonts, and Macintosh HD > Users > chris > Library > Fonts. It is the only font installed there.

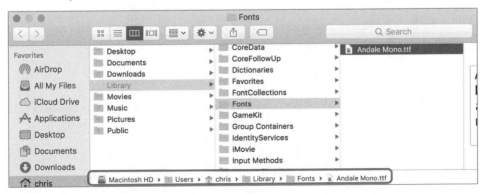

Confirm the Font Is Unavailable to Other Users

If you log in as a different user, even an administrator, you don't have access to the fonts in Chris's Fonts folder.

1   Use fast user switching to switch to the Local Admin account.

2   Open the Font Book application, and look for the Andale Mono font.

Notice that Andale Mono is not visible in Font Book for the Local Admin account. At this time, you could add Andale Mono to this account, just as you added it to Chris's account earlier. You would have to copy the font file to a location that Local Admin can access.

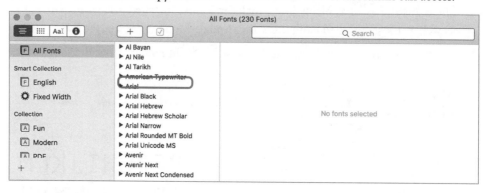

3   Quit Font Book.

Validate Fonts

Since you have changed your font configuration, you will use Font Book to check your new setup.

1   Use fast user switching to switch back in to the Chris Johnson account.

2   In the Font Book window, select All Fonts in the sidebar, click any font in the Font column, and then press Command-A to select all the fonts.

3   Choose File menu > Validate Fonts.

Font Book reads and validates all the font files, checking for any corruption.

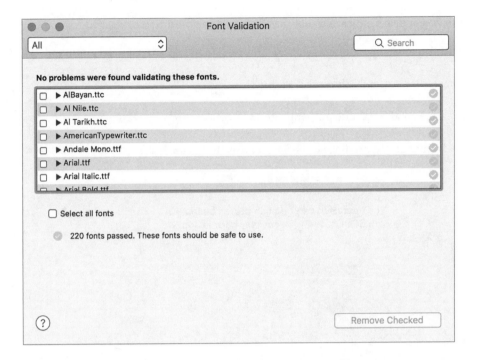

4   When the validation scan finishes, quit Font Book.

5   Log out as Chris Johnson.

Test System Integrity Protection

Unlike the user and local libraries, the system library cannot be modified, even by using administrator rights.

1   Log back in as Local Admin.

2   In the Finder, navigate to /System/Library/Fonts.

3   Find the file Apple Color Emoji.ttc, and drag it to the Trash.

If you can't find this file, make sure you're in the correct Library/Fonts folder. You need to be in the one in the System folder for this part of the exercise.

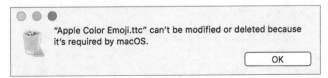

A dialog appears indicating that the file cannot be modified or deleted.

4 With Apple Color Emoji.ttf selected, choose File menu > Get Info (Command-I).

5 If necessary, expand "Sharing & Permissions."

6 Click the small lock, and authenticate as Local Admin.

7 Try to change the privilege level for everyone to "Read & Write."

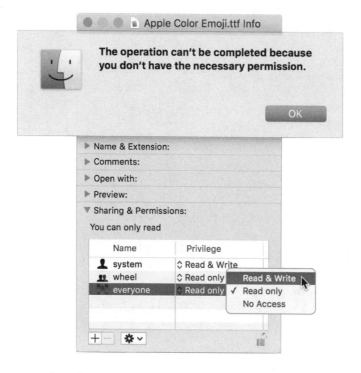

Even though you have authenticated as an administrator, a dialog appears indicating that you don't have the necessary permission.

8 Dismiss the dialog, and close the Info window.

9 If you want, you can try other methods to make modifications in the /System folder, but System Integrity Protection will block all of your attempts.

10 Log out as Local Admin.

Lesson 14

Use Metadata, Spotlight, and Siri

Metadata is data about data. More specifically, metadata is information used to describe content. The most basic forms of file and folder metadata employed by nearly every operating system are names, paths, modification dates, and permissions. These metadata objects are not part of the item's content, yet they are necessary to describe the item in the file system. Mac systems use several types of additional file system metadata for a variety of technologies that ultimately lead to a richer user experience. Apple has expanded on this already rich base by offering a new metadata mechanism—tags—that can be found throughout the system.

This lesson details how macOS makes use of file metadata and how this metadata is stored on various file systems. It also demonstrates how to take advantage of all this metadata by using the file system tags feature, as well as the macOS advanced Spotlight and Siri search technologies.

Reference 14.1
About File System Metadata

Resource forks, dating back to the original Mac OS, are the legacy metadata technology in the Mac operating system. To simplify the user experience, Apple created a forked file system to make complex items, such as applications, appear as a single icon. Forked file systems, such as Mac OS Extended, enable multiple pieces of data to appear as a single item in the file system. In this case, a file appears as a single item but is actually composed of two separate pieces: a data fork and a resource fork. This technology also enables Mac computers to support file type identification in the data fork, whereas the extra information specific to Mac resides in the resource fork. For many years, Mac computers have relied on forked files for storing both data and associated metadata.

macOS Sierra continues and expands metadata use, even helping developers to take advantage of additional metadata items. This enables Apple and other developers to implement unique file-system solutions without having to modify the existing file system. For instance, OS X Snow Leopard 10.6 introduced compressed application code, wherein the executable program files are compressed to save space and then, when needed, automatically decompressed on the fly. To prevent previous Mac operating system versions or older applications from improperly handling these compressed executables, macOS hides the compressed bits in additional metadata locations.

The downside to legacy resource forks, and other types of additional file system metadata, is that some third-party file systems, like FAT, do not know how to properly store this additional data. The solution to this issue is addressed with the AppleDouble file format, covered later in this lesson.

About File Flags and Extended Attributes

macOS also uses metadata in the form of file system flags and extended attributes to implement a variety of system features. In general, file system flags are holdovers from the original Mac operating system and are primarily used to control user access. Examples of file system flags include the hidden flag, covered in Lesson 12, "Use Hidden Items, Short-cuts, and File Archives," and the locked flag, covered in **Lesson 17, "Manage Documents."**

With macOS, Apple needed to expand the range of possible attributes associated with any file or folder, which is where so-called extended attributes come into play. Any process or application can add an arbitrary number of custom attributes to a file or folder. Again, this enables developers to create new forms of metadata without having to modify the existing file system.

For example, file system tags are stored as extended attributes. macOS also uses extended attributes for several general file features, including the stationery pad option, hide extension option, and comments. You can access these items from the Info window in the Finder. The following Info window screenshot shows a document featuring Red and Work file system tags and a searchable text comment.

About File System Tags

File system tags are an upgrade to an older Mac file system metadata technology: Finder labels. Prior to OS X Mavericks 10.9, you could set a single color label for any item in the Finder. File system tags expand on this feature by enabling you to assign multiple tags with custom user-defined tag colors and tag names.

NOTE ▶ Similar to how developers must update their applications to support iCloud, an application must be updated to support file system tags. Thus, some applications may not recognize file-system tags.

You can modify file system tags for documents within any application that presents a Save dialog. You can define tags for documents saved locally and in iCloud. The default file system tags match the Finder labels found in previous Mac computers. However, when selecting tags for a document, you can create a new tag by typing a new name in the Tags field.

You can further customize tags in the Tags pane of the Finder preferences (choose Finder > Preferences). From this pane, you can create additional tags by clicking the Add (+) button, and you can delete existing tags by clicking the Delete (–) button. To rename a tag, click the tag's name, and to change the color, click the tag's color. You can also define which tags are shown in the Finder sidebar by selecting the tag's checkbox, and you can set the tag order by dragging tag entries in the list. Finally, below the tags sidebar list, you can define favorite tags so that they will appear in Finder menus.

NOTE ▶ Items from previous Mac operating systems with Finder labels appear as file-system tags in OS X Mavericks 10.9 and later. Mac operating systems prior to Mavericks are not fully compatible with items using custom tags or with items that use more than one tag. These older Mac operating systems display only the last saved tag of an item, and even then will only display it as a standard Finder label color.

Most importantly, though, macOS includes interfaces that enable you to quickly search for your items or organize your items by file-system tag. In the Finder, you can find tags in the Spotlight search field or the sidebar. In updated applications, you can access tags from a similar Spotlight search and sidebar as well. Using Spotlight for searching is detailed later in this lesson.

MORE INFO ▶ You can find out more about file-system tags in Apple Support article HT202754, "OS X: Tags help you organize your files."

About AppleDouble File Format

Although file-system metadata helps enrich your experience in macOS, compatibility with third-party file systems can be an issue. Only volumes formatted with the Mac OS Extended file system fully support resource forks, data forks, file flags, and extended attributes. Third-party software exists for Windows-based operating systems to enable them to access the extended metadata features of Mac OS Extended. More often, though, users take advantage of the compatibility software built into macOS to help other file systems work with these metadata items.

For most anything other than Mac OS Extended volumes, including FAT volumes, older Xsan volumes, and older NFS shares, macOS stores metadata from the file system in a separate hidden data file. This technique is called AppleDouble.

For example, if you copy a file that contains metadata and is named My Document.docx to a FAT32 volume, macOS automatically splits the file and writes it as two discrete pieces on the FAT32 volume. The file's internal data is written with the same name as the original, but the metadata is written to a file named ._My Document.docx, which remains hidden from the Finder. This works out well for most files, because Windows applications only care about the contents of the data fork. But some files do not take well to being split up, and all the extra dot-underscore files may confuse users of computer systems that rely on other file systems.

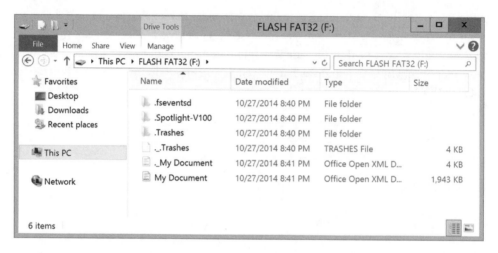

Recent Windows systems default to automatically hiding dot-underscore files. In fact, to acquire the Windows screenshot shown here, showing hidden files had to be manually enabled. Further, macOS includes a method for handling metadata on SMB network shares from NTFS volumes that doesn't require the AppleDouble format. The native file system for current Windows-based computers, NTFS, supports something similar to file forking, known as alternative data streams. The file system writes the metadata to the alternative data stream, so the file appears as a single item on both Windows and macOS.

NOTE ▶ Hidden files named ".DS_Store" are not technically metadata files. Instead, these files are used by the Finder to store folder window view information. Similar to AppleDouble files, .DS-Store files are benign and you shouldn't edit them.

Reference 14.2
Search with Spotlight and Siri

With Spotlight and Siri on macOS Sierra, you can perform nearly instantaneous searches that go wider and deeper than any other portable or desktop computer search technology. For any query, Spotlight and Siri can go beyond simple file-system searches and find relevant information from inside local documents, application function results, and Internet sources. As a default in macOS Sierra, you'll find both the Spotlight and Siri icons in the upper-right corner of the screen between the time and the Notification Center icon at the far right.

Search with Spotlight

Spotlight combines the search results list and search results preview into a Spotlight window that appears on top of your other open windows. You can initiate a Spotlight search by clicking the Spotlight (magnifying glass) icon at the upper-right corner of the screen or by using the default Spotlight keyboard shortcut: Command-Space bar.

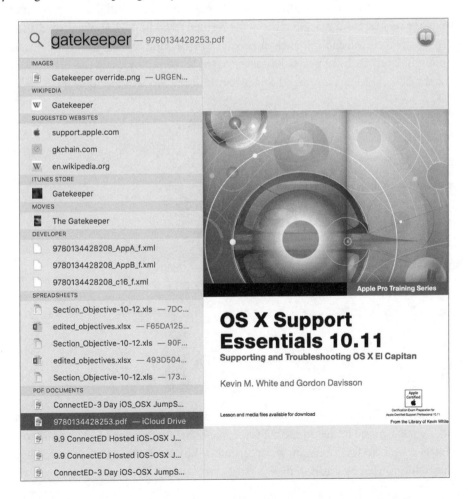

> **TIP** You can also move and resize the Spotlight search results window. Drag in the Spotlight search field to move the window. Drag the bottom edge to change the window's size.

Spotlight search is so fast that the results change in real time as you type in your search query. The left side of the Spotlight window is a list of the search results; the right side is a preview area. Use the arrow keys to navigate the results list, or select an item (by clicking once) to show a preview. Both the results list and preview area are scrollable to reveal more content. Double-clicking an item or pressing Return will open the selected item immediately.

Search with Siri

Siri is new to Mac, available for the first time with macOS Sierra. With Siri you can speak plain-language requests and macOS returns the results, often both in spoken word and a visual representation. You can initiate a Siri request by clicking the Siri icon (to the right of the Spotlight icon) at the upper-right corner of the screen or by using the default Siri keyboard shortcut: holding Command-Space bar until the Siri window appears.

> **TIP** You can change the default keyboard shortcut for Siri from the Siri preferences, as detailed later in this lesson.

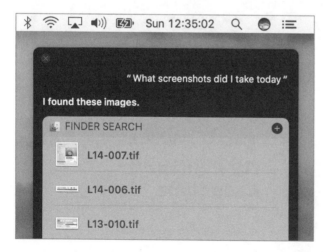

As you speak, Siri will translate your words to text, and more importantly interpret your meaning. As you can see in the preceding screenshot, Siri interpreted "screenshots" to mean "images" and "today" to mean "most recent"—thus returning a Finder search with a list of image files sorted by creation date.

TIP ▶ If Siri misunderstands your spoken words, you can double-click the requested text at the top of the Siri window and type in corrections.

Siri also returns results nearly instantly, but there could be a bit of delay because your Mac must send the translated text to Apple servers to interpret the meaning of your words. In a local file search, Siri leverages Spotlight to provide the file list results.

Double-clicking any item in the Siri search results will open that item in an appropriate application. You can also save the results of a Siri search by clicking the Add (plus icon) button at the top right of the Siri search results. This will create a Notification Center widget that can be accessed by clicking the Notification Center icon, which is always the furthest-right icon in the menu bar.

MORE INFO ▶ This guide primarily focuses on using Siri to search for local items, but Siri is capable of much more. You can find out what else you can ask by initiating a Siri request and then pressing the Esc (Escape) key. You can also check out Apple Support article HT206993, "Use Siri on your Mac."

About Search Results

The preceding Spotlight screenshot shows the results of a Spotlight search for the query "gatekeeper." As you can see, the results list contains documents, mail messages, and even results from Internet sources.

Spotlight can also search inside application data sources. Again, in the preceding Spotlight search result, the selected item being previewed is a PDF of the previous version of this guide stored inside the iBooks library. Note the iBooks application icon in the upper-right corner of the Spotlight search window. As you can see, neither the document's name nor the previewed cover page contains the word "gatekeeper." Instead, Spotlight actually searched inside the text of that rather lengthy PDF file for the word "gatekeeper." Nevertheless, Spotlight can return search results from this long PDF along with results from other sources nearly instantly.

Spotlight and Siri can also take advantage of an application's functions. For example, Spotlight and Siri can perform mathematical calculations and unit conversions (including market-based currency conversion) via integration with the Calculator application.

Again, for local file searches, the metadata technologies covered previously in this lesson are also searchable via Spotlight and Siri, including filenames, file flags, modification dates, and file-system tags. Additionally, many files contain internal metadata used to describe the file's content. For example, many digital camera image files contain additional camera setting information embedded as metadata inside the file. Spotlight and Siri can search through this document-specific metadata information as well.

> **TIP** ▶ The quickest way to open any application on macOS is to search for it using Spotlight. For example, you can quickly find and open Disk Utility using the keyboard. Press Command-Space bar, enter disk, and press Return. You can also use Siri to open applications, but the language interpretation usually takes a little more time.

In addition to local files, Spotlight (and by proxy Siri) can search through the contents of shared files from other Mac clients, servers, AirDisk volumes (disks shared via AirPort Wi-Fi access points), Time Machine backups, and iCloud Drive.

Extending beyond local network services, Spotlight and Siri can search a variety of Internet sources through Apple services known as Spotlight Suggestions and Siri Suggestions. These Apple-hosted services use a combination of search history, location information, and user information to generate relevant search results from a wide variety of Internet sources. Obviously, an Internet connection is required to take advantage of Spotlight Suggestions and Siri Suggestions.

About Spotlight Indexing

Spotlight (and by proxy Siri) is able to perform wide and deep searches of local items and shared files quickly because it works in the background to maintain highly optimized databases of indexed metadata for each attached local volume. When you first set up macOS, it creates these databases by indexing all the available local volumes. The system also indexes new volumes when they are first attached.

On macOS, a background process automatically updates the index databases on the fly as changes are made throughout the file system. Because these indexes are kept current, Spotlight only needs to search the databases to return thorough results. Essentially, Spotlight preemptively searches everything for you in the background, so you don't have to wait for the results when you need them.

> **NOTE** ▶ Spotlight does not create index databases on read-only volumes or write-once media such as optical discs.

> **NOTE** ▶ Spotlight directly indexes Time Machine and AirDisk volumes (drives shared via AirPort Extreme), but it does not index shared volumes from other computers. Spotlight can connect to indexes on shares hosted from other Mac operating systems.

You can find the Spotlight general index databases at the root level of every volume in a folder named .Spotlight-V100. A few applications maintain their own databases separate from these general index databases. One example is the built-in email application Mail, which maintains its own optimized email database in each user's folder at ~/Library/Mail /V2/MailData/Envelope Index.

If you are experiencing problems with local file searching, you can force Spotlight to rebuild the index databases by deleting them and restarting your Mac or by managing the Spotlight preferences, as covered later in this lesson.

About Spotlight Plug-ins

Spotlight can create indexes, and thus search—from an ever-growing variety of local metadata—using plug-in technologies. Each Spotlight plug-in examines specific types of files or databases. Many Spotlight plug-ins are included by default, but Apple and third-party developers can create additional plug-ins to expand Spotlight search capabilities.

Included Spotlight plug-ins enable you to:

▶ Search via basic file metadata, including name, file size, creation date, and modification date

▶ Search via media-specific metadata from picture, music, and video files, including timecode, creator information, and hardware capture information

▶ Search through the contents of a variety of file types, including text files; application databases; audio and video files; Photoshop files; PDF files; Pages, Numbers, and Keynote files; and Microsoft Office files

▶ Search through personal information like the contents in Contacts and Calendar

▶ Search for correspondence information like the contents of Mail emails and Messages chat transcripts

▶ Search for highly relevant information like your favorites or web browser bookmarks and history

▶ Perform Internet searches using Microsoft Bing or Apple Spotlight Suggestions

Spotlight plug-ins, like any other macOS resource, are stored in various Library folders. The Apple built-in Spotlight plug-ins can be found in both the /System/Library/Spotlight folder and the /Library/Spotlight folder. Third-party plug-ins should always be installed in either the /Library/Spotlight folder or the ~/Library/Spotlight folder, depending on who needs access to them.

TIP ▶ You can create custom metadata for Spotlight by entering Spotlight comments in the Info and Inspector windows from the Finder.

About Search Security

To provide security on par with the rest of the file system, Spotlight indexes every item's permissions. Even though Spotlight indexes every item on a volume, it automatically filters search results to show only items that the current user has permissions to access. For example, you can't search the content of another user's Documents folder. Also, the Spotlight index database for a Legacy FileVault user is stored at the root level, inside the user's encrypted home folder, so it's not searchable when the user is logged out.

Be aware, though, when users search through locally attached nonsystem volumes, because they can choose to ignore ownership on these volumes. In other words, all users can search through locally attached nonsystem volumes, including mounted disk images, even if another user attached the device.

Spotlight Suggestions and Siri take advantage of a variety of Apple services and Internet sources, but they always adhere to the Apple Privacy Policy. Apple takes user privacy very seriously and always attempts to keep the user's information as safe as possible while still providing advanced services. Further, you can disable searches that require Internet services in the Spotlight preferences and Siri preferences, as covered later in this lesson.

MORE INFO ▶ Apple's Privacy Policy is clearly outlined and constantly updated at www.apple.com/privacy/.

Perform an Advanced Spotlight Search

The default Spotlight search provides quick and easy search results, but as you've learned in this lesson, Spotlight has a powerful range of search features. You can perform advanced file-system searches by opening a new Finder window and entering your search in the search field, by choosing File > Find, or by pressing Command-F. Selecting an item from the search results shows you the path to the selected item at the bottom of the Finder window. Selecting an item and then pressing the Space bar opens a preview of the selected item.

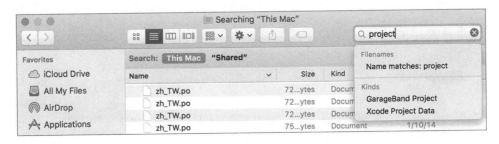

TIP ▶ You can change the default Finder search location by going to Finder preferences, clicking the Advanced tab, and choosing a setting from the "When performing a search" pop-up menu.

You can refine your Spotlight search from the results in a Finder window by clicking the small Add (+) buttons below the search field; this allows you to add as many specific search attributes as you need. After you add a new search attribute, click the first word in the search attribute to choose another type from the pop-up menu.

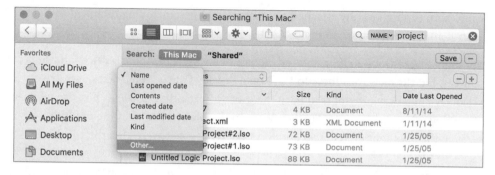

If you don't see the search attribute you're looking for, you can add literally dozens of other attributes that aren't enabled by default. To add search attributes, select any attribute and choose Other from the pop-up menu. In the dialog that appears, you can add search attributes to the pop-up menu. Two especially useful search attributes for administrators are "File visibility" and "System files," neither of which is shown by default in any Spotlight search.

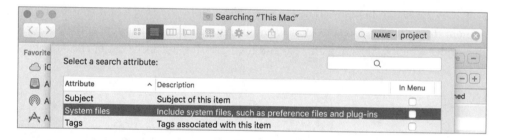

TIP ▶ Take some time to explore the additional search attributes; you may be surprised at the depth of the Spotlight search capabilities. Search attributes include specifying audio file tags, digital camera metadata, authorship information, contact information, and many other metadata types.

Clicking the Save button on the right saves these search criteria as a Smart Folder. Smart Folders are like normal folders in that they can be given a unique name and placed anywhere you like, including the Finder sidebar. Smart Folders are special because their contents always match your search criteria no matter how the file system changes. In fact, the All My Files and Tags items in the Finder sidebar are predefined Smart Folders.

Manage Spotlight Preferences

From Spotlight preferences, any user can choose to disable specific categories so that they do not appear in Spotlight searches. For example, users can choose to disable Spotlight Suggestions if they don't want any search information sent over the Internet. You can also prevent some volumes from being indexed by specifying those volumes in the privacy list. However, by default, all new volumes are automatically indexed, so the user must manually configure Spotlight to ignore a volume.

The Spotlight privacy list is a computer-level setting that remains the same across all user accounts, but it's not protected by administrator access, which means any user can change the privacy list. In this case, the Spotlight privacy list isn't any less secure than the rest of the file system—any user can still have full access to locally connected nonsystem volumes, because the system defaults to ignoring ownership on those volumes.

Opening Spotlight preferences defaults to the Search Results tab, where you can disable specific categories from the search results. Deselect the checkboxes next to the categories you want to ignore. You can also drag categories to change their order in the search results. Each user has his or her own separate Search Results settings.

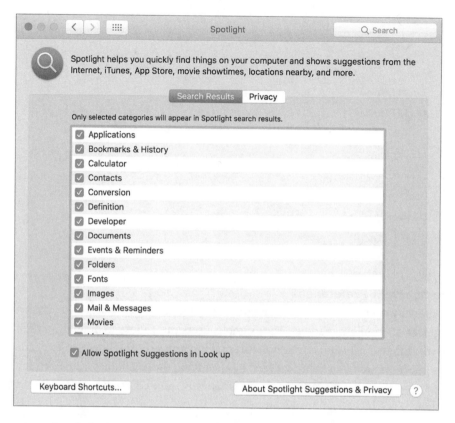

To prevent Spotlight from indexing specific local items, click the Privacy tab to reveal the list of items for Spotlight to ignore. To add new items, click the Add (+) button at the bottom of the privacy list and choose the items from a browser dialog, or drag items into the privacy list. You can delete an item from the privacy list by selecting it and then clicking the Delete (–) button at the bottom of the list.

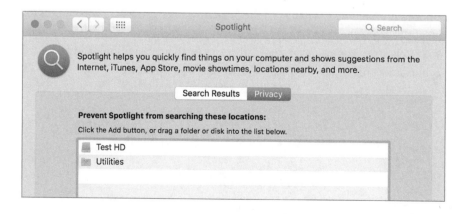

All Spotlight settings are applied immediately. If you add an entire volume to the privacy list, the system deletes the Spotlight index database from that volume. In turn, removing a volume from the privacy list rebuilds the Spotlight index database on that volume. This technique—rebuilding the Spotlight index databases by adding and then removing a volume from the privacy list—is the most common method for resolving problematic Spotlight performance.

Manage Siri Preferences

When you use Siri, the things you say will be recorded and sent to Apple to process your requests. Your device will also send Apple other information, such as your name and nickname; the names, nicknames, and relationships (e.g., "my dad") found in your contacts; song names in your collection; the names of your photo albums; and the names of apps installed on your device (collectively, your "User Data"). All of this data is used to help Siri understand you better and recognize what you say. It is not linked to other data that Apple may have from your use of other Apple services. When you use Siri to search for your documents, the Siri request is sent to Apple, but the names and the content of your documents are not sent to Apple. The search is performed locally on the Mac.

If you have Location Services turned on, the location of your device at the time you make a request will also be sent to Apple to help Siri improve the accuracy of its response to your requests. You may choose to turn off Location Services for Siri. To do so, open System Preferences on your Mac, click Security & Privacy, click Location Services, and deselect the checkbox for Siri.

Siri requires an Internet connection to query Apple services to interpret the meaning of your requests. Siri is enabled by default, and you may not want to have an Internet connection by default.

You may choose to turn off Siri at any time. You can disable Siri with Setup Assistant during a macOS setup or upgrade, or from System Preferences > Siri preferences.

Please visit www.apple.com/privacy for more information.

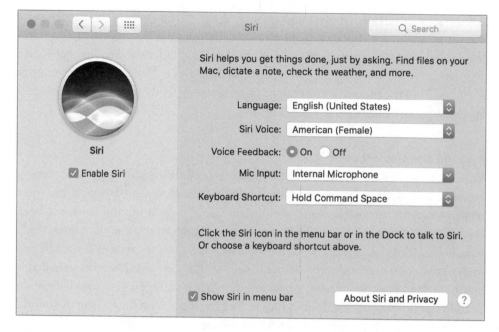

In addition to enabling or disabling Siri, you can adjust several features from Siri preferences, including:

▶ You can select the language that Siri will be expected to translate from. Siri supports over 30 languages and dialects.

▶ You can select the voice that Siri will use to speak responses. The choices in this pop-up menu are based on the selected language. Note that you can also disable the voice feedback entirely.

▶ You can select the microphone input that Siri will use to listen for your requests. The internal microphone on Apple portable computers is optimized for Siri input and often includes noise-cancelation technology. However, for desktop Mac computers lacking a microphone or if you are in a particularly noisy environment, you will be best served by a dedicated headset-style microphone.

▶ You can select the keyboard shortcut used to start a Siri request. Note that you can also disable the Siri menu bar icon if you only want to initiate Siri via the keyboard shortcut.

Exercise 14.1
Examine File Metadata

▶ **Prerequisite**

▶ You must have created the Chris Johnson account (Exercise 5.1, "Create a Standard User Account").

In this exercise, you will examine some file metadata in the Info window in the Finder and add custom metadata.

Use Tag and Comment Metadata

1   If necessary, log in as Chris Johnson.

2   Open Safari, and navigate to www.apple.com.

3   Choose File menu > Save As (or press Command-S).

If File > Save As is not available, the page may not have fully loaded. Click the "X" in the right side of the URL/search field, and the Save As option should become available.

4   In the Tags field, enter Apple Info. The tag may complete automatically if a previous student has performed this exercise using the same iCloud account.

5   In the pop-up menu that appears, click "Create new tag 'Apple Info'" or "Apple Info."

6   If necessary, click elsewhere in the dialog to dismiss the Tags pop-up.

7   Ensure that the location (the Where option) is set to Documents and that Format is set to Web Archive, and then click Save.

8   Quit Safari.

9   In the Finder, navigate to your Documents folder (choose Go menu > Documents, or press Command-Shift-O).

10   Select the web archive file, probably called "Apple," and get info about it (choose File menu > Get Info, or press Command-I).

11   If necessary, expand the General, More Info, and Comments sections of the Info window.

The Info window in the Finder displays a variety of information about the file, from basic metadata such as its size to information about where on the web it came from, as well as the tag you added when you saved it. It also lets you edit some types of metadata.

12   In the Comments section, type The Apple Orchard.

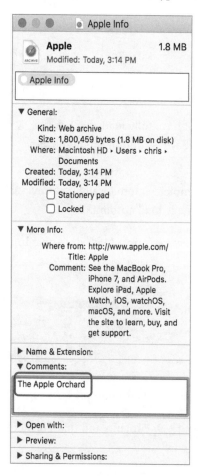

This field adds custom metadata to the file, allowing you to attach searchable comments and keywords. You will see how to use this comment later in this exercise.

13 Close the Info window.

14 If necessary, change the Finder view of the Documents folder to list view (click the List View button in the toolbar, choose View menu > "as List," or press Command-2).

15 Choose View menu > Show View Options (or press Command-J).

16 In the Show Columns section, select Comments and Tags.

Note that this setting applies only to this specific folder. Clicking "Use as Defaults" would make it the default for all folders.

17 Close the View Options window, and, if necessary, widen the Documents window until you can see the Tags and Comments fields.

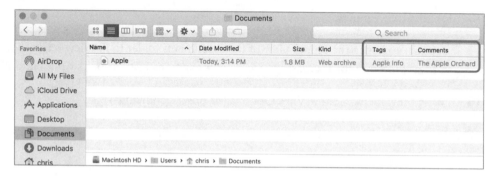

18 Close the Documents window.

Use Spotlight to Search for Documents

1 In the Finder, choose File menu > Find (Command-F).

2 In the search field of the window that opens, type orchard.

The search finds the web archive you saved earlier because the word *orchard* appears in its Spotlight comment. Note that you can also restrict the search to files with *orchard* in the name.

Spotlight can search a wide variety of file metadata as well as the contents of files. It generally displays all possible matches and then suggests ways to narrow the search (for example, only filename matches or "downloaded from" matches).

3   Change the search to apple info.

This time it finds the archive file by its tag and gives you options to restrict the search to name or tag matches only. Since it is searching all file attributes, it may find a number of other matching files.

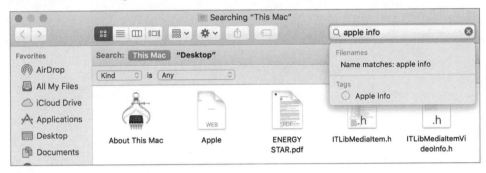

4   Change the search to www.apple.com.

Again, the web archive is found, this time because your search matches the site it was downloaded from. It also finds the Energy_Saver.mobileconfig file in the StudentMa-terials/Lesson2 folder, because it contains a document type descriptor that says it con-forms to a format defined at www.apple.com/DTDs/PropertyList-1.0.dtd. If you had any text files or PDFs that mentioned www.apple.com, they would be listed as well.

Manage Time Machine

Several mature and relatively easy-to-use backup solutions are available for macOS, so you may be wondering why Apple chose to invent its own backup solution. A little research revealed that, before the introduction of Time Machine, only a small percentage of Mac users were backing up their data regularly. So Apple decided that the only way to convince users to back up their systems was to create a backup process that would be as easy to use as possible. The Apple solution was Time Machine.

In this lesson, you will learn how Time Machine enables users to easily browse the backup history of their entire file system. You will become familiar with the configuration of Time Machine. Finally, you will explore multiple methods for recovering data from Time Machine backups.

GOALS

▶ Describe Time Machine technology

▶ Configure Time Machine to back up important data

▶ Restore data or an entire Mac operating system from a Time Machine backup

Reference 15.1
About Time Machine

Aside from being built into macOS, Time Machine has two features that make it fundamentally different from any other solution currently out there. First, configuring Time Machine is so easy it's nearly automatic. The system practically begs you to set up Time Machine if you haven't done so already, and with as little as one click, it's configured.

The second, more significant feature is that Time Machine is so tightly integrated with macOS that users don't even have to exit the application they are currently using to recover data. Applications, both built-in and third-party, can tie directly into Time Machine.

If your application supports Time Machine, you can open Time Machine to view saved versions of files and application data. If your application doesn't support Time Machine, you can open Time Machine and use the Finder to browse the entire file system.

About Backup Disks

Time Machine can save backups to any locally connected Mac OS Extended volume that is not the startup volume. You are allowed to select a backup disk that resides as another partition on the system disk—but this is an incredibly bad idea: if the system disk dies, so does your backup. Consequently, many choose an external USB, FireWire, or Thunderbolt disk as their Time Machine backup disk.

However, external disks have the potential to be lost or stolen. Thus, macOS includes support for an encrypted local backup disk. This option automatically reformats the backup disk as Mac OS Extended (Journaled, Encrypted). Using this option requires setting a password, which is used to access the encrypted Time Machine backup disk.

> **NOTE ▸** Remember that a Time Machine backup can contain a full copy of all your important files. Thus, it's recommended that you choose the encrypted backup disk option, in case your backup disk is ever lost or stolen.

When configured, the encrypted Time Machine disk password is not initially saved. The next time the encrypted backup disk is connected, you will be prompted to enter the password and optionally save it to the secure keychain system for automatic retrieval. If the encrypted disk is connected to another system, you must enter the password to access the backup items. Further, if the original system is lost, you will need to manually enter the disk password to access the backup disk contents. In other words, it is critical that you store the backup disk password using a secure mechanism outside of the Mac.

> **NOTE ▸** If you lose the password used to unlock an encrypted Time Machine backup disk, its contents are lost forever. Not even Apple can recover the data.

If you don't have a local volume suitable for backup, you can select a shared network volume as your backup disk. Time Machine supports network shares by creating a disk image on the share to store the backups. Time Machine in macOS Sierra supports backing up to AFP or SMB network shares. Apple guarantees Time Machine compatibility with shares hosted from macOS Server and Time Capsule. However, support for Time Machine varies for third-party file sharing services. Before relying on a third-party file sharing solution as a Time Machine destination, you should verify support for this feature from the manufacturer.

MORE INFO ► You can find out more about configuring macOS Server as a Time Machine destination from the latest macOS Server help documentation, https://help.apple.com/serverapp/mac.

MORE INFO ► You can find out more about the Airport Time Capsule wireless base station at www.apple.com/airport-time-capsule/.

The storage on network shares used for Time Machine may not be encrypted, but access to a network share is probably configured to require authentication. Although an authentication requirement prevents unauthorized access over a network, it doesn't offer security if the device providing the share is physically located in an insecure environment. Consider the physical aspects of security when placing a Time Machine server or Time Capsule.

For even greater backup protection, you can select more than one Time Machine backup disk. This is especially useful for those who are away from their primary Time Machine backup disk for extended periods. For example, you can choose to back up to a Time Capsule wireless base station at home and also use a portable external disk when traveling.

About Backup Schedule

Logistically, Time Machine uses a sophisticated background process, named backupd, to automatically create new backups of the entire file system every hour. This only works, though, if the backup disk is readily available. As more users go for portable Mac computers, it's becoming increasingly possible that users may be away from their backup disks for quite a while.

Time Machine can also take local snapshots if the backup disk is unavailable. The idea is that even when away from the backup disk, the user at least has access to restore from the local snapshots. This feature is enabled only on Mac portables with Time Machine left in the On state. Once the Mac can locate the backup disk again, the local snapshots are converted to traditional backups and saved to the disk. Time Machine attempts to keep a history of local snapshots available as well, in case you need to restore when the backup disk is offline. To save space, though, this local snapshot history is not as deep as the full backup.

While the Time Machine local snapshots are a convenient new feature, they certainly aren't true backups, because they are located on the same disk they are backing up. If the system disk fails, the local snapshots are lost as well. This is why, when a Mac is not backed up to the backup disk for ten consecutive days, the system warns the user on a regular basis to reconnect that disk. Train your users to ensure their Mac computers are connected to their Time Machine disks on a regular basis. Again, as long as the Mac can connect to the disk, Time Machine automatically handles the backup maintenance.

Another issue that may prevent Time Machine backups is system sleep. If the computer is asleep, it may not run the backup job. To rectify this situation, Time Machine can perform backups while the system is in Power Nap mode. For Mac systems that support Power Nap, even while the system is "sleeping" it still attempts to perform Time Machine backups or local snapshots every hour. Obviously, even with Power Nap enabled, the availability of the backup disk likewise affects the ability of a sleeping system to back up.

> **MORE INFO** ▶ Power Nap details are covered in **Lesson 26, "Troubleshoot Startup and System Issues."**

About Time Machine Backups

Time Machine uses several tricks to keep backups as small as possible so that you can maintain a deep history, but the backup starts out big. The initial Time Machine backup copies almost the entire contents of your file system to the specified backup volume.

To provide fast backups and convenient restores, Time Machine does not use a compressed archive format like many other backup systems. Instead, it copies the items as is to the backup disk. As you'll see later, this permits easy access to those items.

The space-saving comes into play with each subsequent backup. Between backups, a background process similar to the one used by the Spotlight search service automatically tracks any changes to the original file system. When the next scheduled backup occurs, only the items that have changed are copied to the backup volume. Time Machine then combines this new content with hard-link file-system pointers (which occupy nearly zero disk space) to the previous backup content, and creates a simulated view of the entire file system at that point in time.

Time Machine also saves space by ignoring files that do not need to be backed up—ones that can be re-created after a restoration. Generally speaking, Time Machine ignores temporary files, Spotlight indexes, items in the Trash, and anything that can be considered a cache. Of particular note, Time Machine doesn't back up system log files, which you could need for later troubleshooting. Software developers can also instruct Time Machine to ignore specific application data that does not need to be backed up. For example, Internet file storage providers, like Dropbox or OneDrive, can instruct Time Machine to ignore files saved to a cloud service.

MORE INFO ▶ Specifically, Time Machine always ignores files as defined by a configuration file that lives at /System/Library/CoreServices/backupd.bundle/Contents /Resources/StdExclusions.plist. Note that you will not see this list in the exclusions found in the Time Machine preferences.

Eventually, so as not to waste space on your backup volume with historical data that has outlived its usefulness, Time Machine starts "aging out" backups: it keeps hourly backups for only a day, daily backups for a week, and weekly backups until your backup volume is full. After your backup volume is full, Time Machine starts deleting the oldest items first. However, it always keeps at least one copy of every item that is still on your current file system.

NOTE ▶ Do not confuse Time Machine with snapshot technology common on other operating systems. Although snapshots do create multiple instances of a file system through time, they do not provide you with a backup, because they don't actually copy data to another storage device. In other words, if a disk containing file-system snapshots dies, those snapshots are just as lost as the current data on the dead disk.

About Time Machine Limitations

Although Apple has put a lot of work into Time Machine, it is not entirely without issues. The Time Machine backup architecture does not lend itself to handling large files that change often. For example, many database files appear as large, single files to the file system. The database application may be able to change just a few bytes of the large file as a user edits the database, but Time Machine doesn't recognize this, so it creates another copy of the entire database file during the next backup. Obviously, this fills your backup volume much more quickly than if the database had been stored as many smaller files.

This leads to the next Time Machine issue: running out of backup space. Once Time Machine fills up the backup volume, it begins deleting older items to make room for newer ones. Therefore, the depth of your backup history varies based not only on the size of your backup volume but also on how often you change your files and how Time Machine recognizes those changes. Because you cannot change how Time Machine chooses to delete older items, you may discover that items you thought would still be on the backup volume have already been deleted.

TIP ▶ By default, Time Machine lets you know if it needs to delete older items to make space for new backups.

One final issue is that Time Machine can only back up Legacy FileVault accounts when the user is logged out of the system. The solution to this problem is to stop using Legacy FileVault in favor of FileVault 2 system volume encryption, as covered in Lesson 10, "Manage FileVault."

Reference 15.2
Configure Time Machine

Despite the rather complex process going on behind the scenes to make Time Machine possible, configuration couldn't be easier. In fact, Time Machine is enabled by default and waiting for you to pick a backup disk. If you haven't configured a Time Machine backup disk, the system automatically scans the network for a Time Machine network share or waits for you to attach an external disk. If the system locates either, you are prompted to select it as your backup disk. If you select your backup disk with this method, after you click the Use as Backup Disk button, Time Machine is fully configured. It's just that easy.

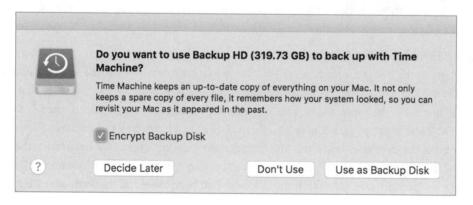

If you make the wise choice to encrypt backups, you need to specify a password to protect the encryption, along with a password hint. Again, initially the system will not automatically remember the encrypted disk's password, but after reconnecting the disk, the user has the option to save the password in a local keychain to perform automated backups. However, also covered previously, if you ever need to access this encrypted disk from another computer, or even on the same Mac using a different system, you must enter the password to gain access to the disk's contents.

> **NOTE ▶** Again, if you lose the password used to unlock an encrypted Time Machine backup disk, its contents are lost forever. Not even Apple can recover the data.

NOTE ► Selecting the option to encrypt the Time Machine backup disk erases the disk's current contents and will reformat the disk as Mac OS Extended (Journaled, Encrypted).

Depending on the amount of data that needs to be backed up and your choice of encryption format, it can take from minutes to hours for the initial backup to complete. The system can encrypt the disk and back up at the same time. Consequently, even if it takes only a few minutes to create the initial backup, the system may have to continue the disk encryption process, which could take several hours, depending on the size and speed of the disk.

Time Machine lets you know when backup operations are complete. Subsequent backups occur automatically in the background. You can verify the last backup, or force an immediate backup, from the Time Machine menu near the clock in the menu bar. You can also open Time Machine preferences from this menu.

NOTE ► If you do not see the Time Machine menu bar item, you can enable it from the Time Machine preferences.

You can also check the progress of any backup task from Time Machine preferences. From this interface, you can cancel the backup by clicking the small x button to the right of the progress bar.

TIP ▶ If you need to eject the Time Machine disk during a backup, you can stop the backup and eject the disk from the Finder sidebar.

Manage Time Machine Preferences

If you need to select a network backup disk, verify the backup status, or manually configure backup settings to better suit your needs, you can do so in Time Machine preferences. You can open Time Machine preferences from System Preferences, from the Time Machine menu, or by secondary-clicking (Control-clicking) the Time Machine icon if it's in the Dock.

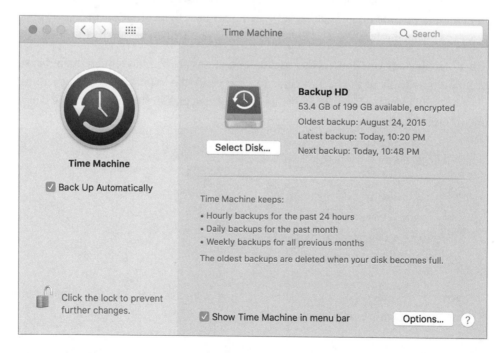

TIP If you want Time Machine to back up only when you say so, deselect the Back Up Automatically checkbox in the Time Machine preferences, and then initiate manual backups from the Time Machine menu. You can also postpone backups by disconnecting from the backup disk, though this works only with locally attached backup disks.

Configure Backup Disks

Again, macOS can select multiple Time Machine backup disks. Depending on the number of backup disks currently configured, the Time Machine preferences will look a bit different.

To add the first backup disk, click the Select Backup Disk button. If you want to modify the configuration of a single backup disk, click the Select Disk button. Finally, if you want to modify the configuration of multiple backup disks, click the text that reads "Add or Remove Backup Disk." Any of these methods reveals the Time Machine backup disk management dialog, which allows you to both add and remove backup disks.

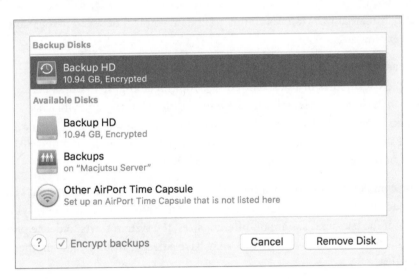

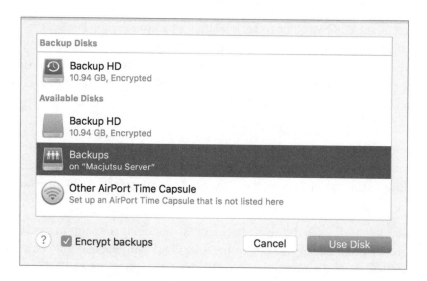

NOTE ▶ If you reselect a disk with a previous backup of this computer, you will be asked if you want to use the existing backup. Alternatively, if you reselect a disk with a previous backup that was restored to this computer, you will be asked if you want to inherit the existing backup.

If you select an additional backup disk, you are prompted to choose whether to replace the originally selected backup disk or to use both disks. You can configure multiple backup disks; however, the system completes backups for each disk separately and will cycle through the disks attempting to back up at least once an hour. For example, if you have two backup disks configured, Time Machine will complete the backup for the first disk, and then in the next hour it will back up to the second disk.

Backups can be completed out of order if one of the disks is missing, but the system still runs only one backup at a time. The system tries to keep a complete backup on every backup disk, but if the backup disks are of different sizes, the system starts to delete older items from the backup. Thus, one backup disk may have a deeper history than another, smaller backup disk.

As covered previously, if you selected a locally connected external disk and the encryption option, you need to specify a password and password hint. If you selected a network share or Time Capsule as the disk, you need to specify an authentication that allows you to access the share. Further, if you elect to encrypt the backup on a network share or Time Capsule, you also need to specify a password and password hint for the encrypted backup. Note that the password used to access the shared storage doesn't, and ideally shouldn't, match the password you specify for the encrypted backup.

Again, all Time Machine authentication information is saved to the keychain system, so backups can occur unattended. Once again, though, it's extremely important that you securely save any authentication information needed for Time Machine somewhere outside the system(s) you're backing up.

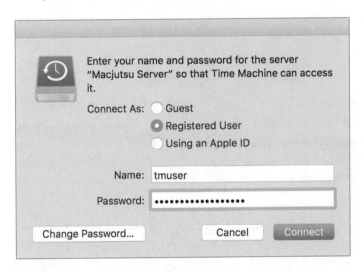

If you configure a new backup disk, Time Machine waits two minutes, allowing you to make further configuration changes before it starts the backup. Again, you can always return to the Time Machine backup disk management dialog to add or remove backup disks.

NOTE ▶ If your portable Mac supports local backup snapshots, this feature is enabled automatically. More information about using local snapshots is covered later in this lesson.

Manage Time Machine Options

Clicking the Options button at the bottom of the Time Machine preferences reveals a dialog where you can adjust backup settings.

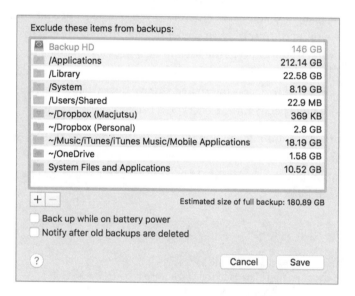

The most important configuration choice you can make with Time Machine is to exclude items from the backup. Obviously, excluding items reduces the amount of space needed for your backups. Note that the system automatically excludes any backup disk; this is to prevent multiple backup disks from backing up each other. It's not uncommon to leave only the /Users folder as the single item to back up—after all, that's where the important user items reside.

You can drag items into the list field, or you can click the Add (+) button at the bottom of the list to reveal a file browser, allowing you to select specific folders or volumes to exclude. Be sure to click Save to close this dialog, because backups will not be made until you have set the options here.

NOTE ▶ If you want to save space by excluding system items, add the /System folder to the exclude list; you will be prompted to exclude all system files or just the /System folder. When presented with this choice, it's best to exclude all system files.

NOTE ▶ If you do not perform a full backup of your system volume, you won't be able to perform a full restoration of it. Instead, you will have to install macOS first, and then you restore the remainder using Migration Assistant, as covered later in this lesson.

Reference 15.3
Restore from Time Machine

Ultimately, a backup solution is only as good as its ability to restore the user's lost data. Time Machine delivers this ability in several different ways. First, you can easily restore individual items by entering the Time Machine interface. Second, you can restore user accounts and entire home folders with Migration Assistant. Third, you can restore an entire macOS system with macOS Recovery. Finally, advanced users can directly navigate through the Time Machine backup via the Finder and manually restore items.

NOTE ▶ Legacy FileVault users cannot access their home folder backup via the standard Time Machine interface. They can, however, use any of the other methods to restore their home folder from a Time Machine backup.

Restore via Time Machine

The restore process for many backup solutions is geared for trained administrators, making user-initiated restoration a difficult proposition. macOS avoids this problem by providing an easy-to-use restore interface. The restore interface is considered by many to be Time Machine's best feature, because of the dynamic interface Apple has created to "look through time." This interface is available by opening the Time Machine application or using the Time Machine menu, which can be turned on via a check box at the bottom of the Time Machine preferences.

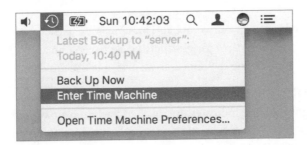

TIP ▶ For quick access to Time Machine, you can also drag its icon to the Dock. From the Time Machine icon, you can secondary-click (or Control-click) to reveal a shortcut menu featuring additional Time Machine commands.

Few applications currently support the Time Machine restore interface, so in most cases you are presented with a historical view in the Finder. The Finder windows let you browse as usual, with one significant addition: you can use the navigation arrows to the right of the window, or the navigation timeline on the far right, to view Finder contents as they have changed over time.

NOTE ▶ If you use an encrypted disk or network share for your backup disk and you are trying to restore from a different system, you will have to enter a password to access the backup data.

NOTE ▶ It may take several moments for your complete Time Machine backup history to appear. You may notice the timeline to the far right "pulsing" between dim and bright coloring. This indicates the system is trying to connect to all available backup disks.

You may notice in the timeline to the right of the screen that the tick mark coloration varies between light and dark. Light coloring indicates the selected backup is unavailable until the backup disk is connected. If you don't have the backup disk handy, you can still restore from local snapshots, as indicated by bright tick marks in the timeline. Obviously, if macOS is able to connect to all backup disks, all tick marks will display brightly, indicating that you can restore from any time.

To aid in your search through time, the Spotlight search field remains active, and you can quickly preview any item by selecting it and then pressing the Space bar. Once you have found the item you are looking for, select it, and then click the Restore button. The Finder returns to "the present" with your recovered file intact where it once was.

Restore via Migration Assistant

You can restore a complete user home folder or other nonsystem data from a Time Machine backup using Migration Assistant. You cannot, however, restore an entire system with Migration Assistant. Restoring an entire system is covered in the next section of this lesson.

When Migration Assistant opens, either during new system setup or when opened from /Applications/Utilities, choose to restore from a Time Machine backup. Once you have selected the backup disk and authenticated to access its content, the remainder of the Migration Assistant process is similar to the standard migration process covered in Lesson 2, "Set Up and Configure macOS," for applications and settings, or in Lesson 6, "Manage User Home Folders," for user-specific items.

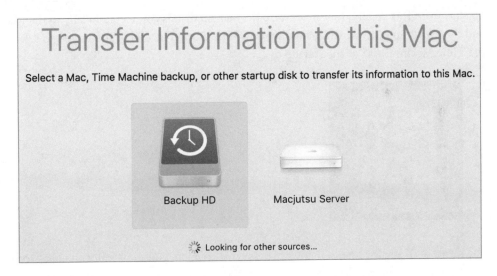

NOTE ▶ After completing the macOS Setup Assistant, only a user with administrator rights can initiate the Migration Assistant process. Starting the Migration Assistant process quits all running applications and logs out all user accounts.

NOTE ▶ Legacy FileVault user accounts can be fully restored only by running Migration Assistant during the initial macOS system setup.

Restore an Entire System

You can restore an entire system volume when the Mac is started up from macOS Recovery. However, this technique assumes you did not exclude any items from your system volume; that is, you left the Time Machine defaults and backed up the entire system volume.

Also, restoring an entire system will erase the destination disk and replace all of its contents with that of the backup. This may be a problem if the backup disk has not been maintained and contains files older than the current system disk. In other words, if you have an older backup you should restore the entire system only as a last resort.

To restore an entire system, you will have to start up from macOS Recovery. You can start up the Mac using the normal macOS Recovery techniques, as covered in Lesson 3, "Use macOS Recovery," or you can actually start up from the macOS Recovery system hidden on a local Time Machine backup disk. When a local Time Machine backup disk is configured, the system automatically copies a disk image of the hidden Recovery HD volume from the system disk to the backup disk. This hidden recovery system can be a lifesaver if the original system disk suffers a catastrophic failure.

To start from this system, first make sure the backup disk is connected locally to the Mac, and then start up the Mac while holding down the Option key. This allows you to select the Time Machine disk as the startup disk.

NOTE ▶ If the Mac has a firmware password enabled, you must enter the password to start up from another system volume. You can find out more about firmware passwords in Lesson 8, "Manage Password Changes."

NOTE ▶ If the Time Machine backup disk is encrypted, you must enter the password to access its contents. This includes starting up from the backup disk's macOS Recovery system.

Once the system has started from macOS Recovery, select Restore From Time Machine Backup in the macOS Utilities window to open the Restore Your System assistant. The assistant first scans for local and network Time Machine backup volumes. Once you have selected the Time Machine volume, you can restore the entire system from any backup instance on that volume to your new system disk.

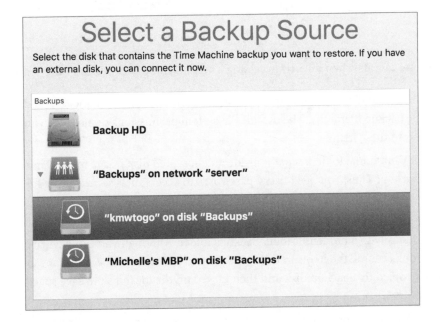

Manually Restore via the Finder

If you are experiencing problems using one of the other Time Machine restoration interfaces, you can always browse the backup from the Finder. The Time Machine backup technology uses file system features that are part of standard Mac OS Extended volumes, so no special software is needed to browse through backup contents.

If you're accessing a locally attached Time Machine backup disk, the backup files are located on the root of the backup disk in a folder named Backups.backupdb. Inside the backup database folder are folders with the name of each computer backed up to that disk. Inside each computer folder are folders named using the date and time of each backup. Finally, inside each dated folder are folders representing each backed-up volume.

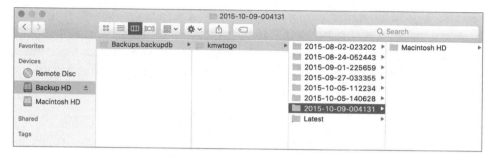

There are several caveats when directly accessing Time Machine backups from the Finder:

▶   Do not directly modify the contents of a Time Machine backup, as doing so could damage the backup hierarchy. The default file system permissions do not give you write access to these items.

▶   Legacy FileVault home folders remain inside an encrypted disk image in the Time Machine backup. Thus, you need users' passwords to access their secure home folder contents.

▶   If your Time Machine configuration supports local snapshots, those snapshots are cached locally to a hidden /.MobileBackups folder. Although you can navigate here and look around, the items in this location aren't permanent, because they are eventually copied to a backup disk and then erased on the local disk to save space.

▶   If you do not have file system permissions to the backup folders, you will have to change the ownership or permissions to open the folders in the Finder. You can find out more about changing permissions in Lesson 11, "Manage Permissions and Sharing."

If you're accessing Time Machine over a network, you need to manually connect to the Time Machine share first. (Connecting to shares is covered in **Lesson 22, "Manage Network Services."**) Once connected, you need to locate the Time Machine backup disk images. They are at the root of the Time Machine share, most commonly named Backups. Each Mac computer's backup is saved as a separate sparse disk image file named with the computer's sharing name.

Double-click to mount the Time Machine backup disk image volume, which is named "Backup of" followed by the computer's name. Remember that if the backup is encrypted, you will have to authenticate again to mount the backup disk image. Inside this volume is the same Backups.backupdb folder and contents you would find on a directly connected Time Machine backup.

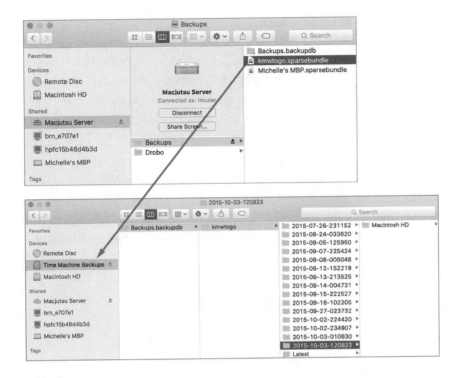

Exercise 15.1
Configure Time Machine

> **Prerequisites**
>
> ► You must have created the Local Admin (Exercise 2.1, "Configure a New macOS System for Exercises," or Exercise 2.2, "Configure an Existing macOS System for Exercises") and Chris Johnson (Exercise 5.1, "Create a Standard User Account") accounts.
>
> ► You must have partitioned your internal disk to create a Backup partition (Exercise 9.1, "Repartition a Disk Dynamically"), have an external disk in Mac OS Extended format, or have a Time Capsule appliance to use for backups.

In this exercise, you will configure Time Machine to back up your user home folders to your internal disk's Backup partition, an external disk drive, or a Time Capsule appliance.

NOTE ► Backing up to a second partition on your computer's internal disk is not a recommended backup strategy because it provides no protection against disk failure or loss of the computer. It is presented in this exercise for demonstration purposes only. If you are performing these exercises on a computer you use for tasks other than exercises, configure it to back up to an external disk, Time Capsule, or macOS Server with the Time Machine service turned on instead.

Configure Exclusions for Time Machine

By default, Time Machine backs up the entire startup volume (excluding some types of files), but for this exercise you will configure it to back up only user files. In most situations, this is sufficient since the system and applications can always be reinstalled; if you want to be able to do a full system restore, do not exclude anything from the backup.

1   If necessary, log in as Chris Johnson.

2   Open System Preferences, and select the Time Machine pane.

3   If necessary, click the lock icon, and authenticate as Local Admin.

4   Select the "Show Time Machine in menu bar" checkbox if it is not already selected.

5   Click the Options button to reveal a dialog allowing you to exclude folders from backups.

    There may already be an entry for /Users/Shared/adi in the exclude list; this is used internally by iBooks, and you can ignore it.

6   Click the Add (+) button at the bottom of the list.

7   Navigate to your startup volume (generally Macintosh HD), and select the Applications, Library, and System folders.

    Note that you can Command-click folders to add them to the selection.

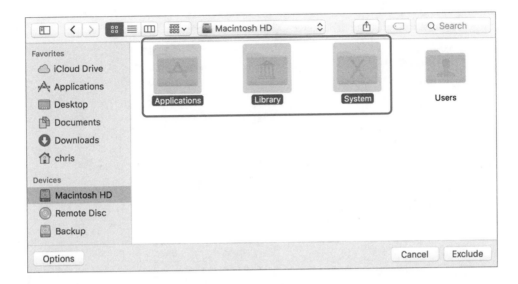

8   Click Exclude.

9   When you see the message "You've chosen to exclude the System folder," click Exclude All System Files.

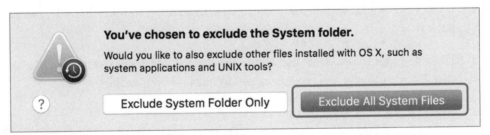

Your exclusion list now looks like the following figure (although the sizes may be different, /Users/Shared/adi may be listed, and the option to back up while on battery power appears only on laptop computers).

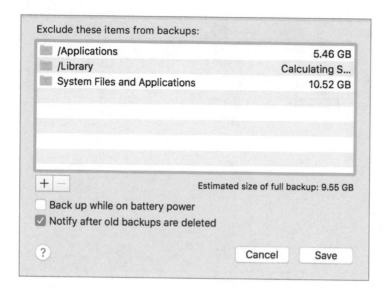

10 Click Save.

Select a Backup Volume

1   If you want to back up this computer to an external disk, connect the disk to the computer now.

2   If a dialog appears asking if you want to use the disk to back up with Time Machine, click Decide Later so that you can configure the backup manually.

3   Select the Back Up Automatically checkbox.

    A dialog appears with a choice of backup targets.

4   Select the volume or Time Capsule you want to back up to. If you do not have an external disk or Time Capsule, use the Backup volume for demonstration purposes.

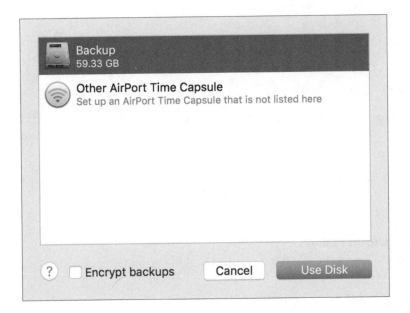

Storing the backup on the same disk as your original data does not protect you in the event of a hard disk failure. It will, however, be sufficient for the purposes of these exercises.

Note the checkbox that allows you to encrypt the backups. This encrypts the backup volume the same way as encrypting it in the Finder.

If you are performing these exercises in a class, do not encrypt the volume since doing so delays the initial backup. If you are performing them on your own, you can encrypt the backup volume if you want; however, you have to wait for the conversion to encrypted format before you can start Exercise 15.2, "Restore Using Time Machine."

5   Click Use Disk.

6   If a dialog appears asking if you are sure you want to back up to the same device your original data is on, click Use Selected Volume.

Time Machine will start backing up in two minutes. You do not have to wait for it before proceeding.

7   Quit System Preferences.

You should now perform Exercise 15.2, "Restore Using Time Machine," to test the backup.

Exercise 15.2
Restore Using Time Machine

▶ **Prerequisite**

▶ You must have performed Exercise 15.1, "Configure Time Machine."

In this exercise, you will learn how to use the Time Machine interface to recover lost files from the backup.

Wait for the Backup to Finish

Before testing the backup, make sure it has finished backing up and is up to date.

1   If necessary, log in as Chris Johnson.

2   Click the Time Machine menu bar item. If the menu indicates that it is still backing up, wait for it to finish.

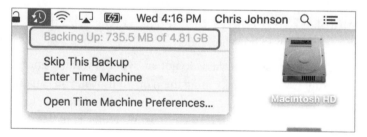

3   If you are notified that the backup is not encrypted, click Close.

4   If you are notified that the backup is complete, click Close.

Delete Some Files

Here you will delete several files and folders from the student materials.

1   In the Finder, open /Users/Shared/StudentMaterials/Lesson15.

2   Move the "Archived announcements" folder to the Trash.

This folder contains the Pretendco company's old media information.

3   If you are prompted to, authenticate as Local Admin.

4   Choose Finder menu > Empty Trash. In the confirmation dialog, click Empty Trash.

Restore a File Using Time Machine

Time Machine allows you to search through your backup to find deleted files, even if you don't remember exactly where they were. You will test this capability by searching for an announcement about Pretendco's plans for solid-state encabulation device (SSED) development.

1   From the Time Machine menu, choose Enter Time Machine.

Time Machine opens and shows snapshots of your files fading into the past.

2   Enter SSED in the search field at the upper right of the window.

No matching files are found, since the only match was in the folder you deleted, and you are viewing files as they exist now.

3   Use the up and down arrows to navigate through time until the file SSED plans.rtf appears.

You can also navigate through time using the timeline along the right side of the screen.

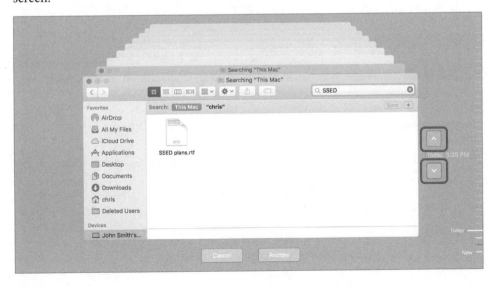

4 Select SSED plans.rtf, and press Command-Y.

A Quick Look preview opens. Quick Look is available in Time Machine so you can verify that you have the right file before restoring it.

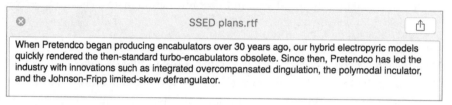

5 Press Command-Y again to close Quick Look.

6 With the file still selected, click Restore.

Since the folder the file was in has also been deleted, Time Machine gives you the option of re-creating the original enclosing folder or choosing a new location for the restore.

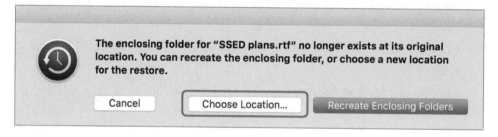

7 Click Choose Location.

8 If necessary, navigate to your Documents folder by selecting it in the sidebar, and then click Choose.

9 If you are prompted, authenticate as Local Admin.

10 In the Finder, navigate to your Documents folder (choose Go menu > Documents, or press Command-Shift-O).

The restored SSED plans.rtf file is visible here.

Restore Directly from Time Machine

When backing up to a local volume, Time Machine stores its backups in the file system. This means you can restore files by directly inspecting the backup and copying files out of it. If you are backing up to a Time Capsule, directly accessing backups is more complex; in that case, you should skip this section of the exercise.

1   In the Finder, open the volume you have chosen to back up to.

2   Open the Backups.backupdb folder. In this folder is a folder for your client. Open it.

This folder contains one or more snapshot folders, named with the date and time they were taken. There is also an alias named Latest that always points to the latest backup.

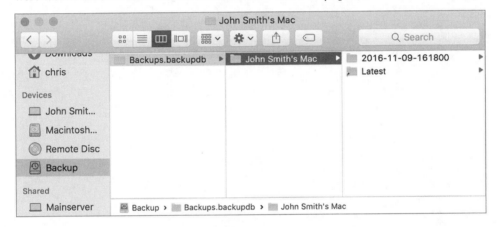

3   Browse through these folders: Latest/Macintosh HD/Users/Shared/StudentMaterials /Lesson15/Archived announcements/2010/04-April.

4   Drag a copy of SSED plans.rtf to your desktop.

5   If prompted, authenticate as Local Admin.

Applications and Processes

Lesson 16
Install Applications

People use computers because they want to run applications, not operating systems. Most users don't care about the technologies underneath as long as the applications they want run smoothly. This is why, despite the growing popularity of Mac computers, users of other platforms are apprehensive about switching. It cannot be ignored that many applications run only on Windows-based computers.

Yet many applications that work only on Mac computers tempt other users because they represent the best solutions available. For several years now, Apple has been responsible for some of the most popular media creation applications with the iLife and Pro production suites. Third-party developers have stepped up their game in the last few years as well, as macOS provides a robust development platform with many unique features. For hundreds of examples, you need look no further than the Mac App Store.

In this lesson you will install applications using both the Mac App Store and traditional installation methods. You will also explore the various application environments and application security measures used in macOS.

GOALS

▶ Install applications from the Mac App Store

▶ Understand application support and security issues

▶ Use traditional installation methods

Reference 16.1
Use the Mac App Store

With traditional installation methods, acquiring the software is often more difficult than actually installing it. Purchasing software in the traditional way means having to search through a variety of distribution channels with different delivery methods and possibly different pricing and versions.

Apple has taken a page from the iOS playbook and simplified software acquisition with the Mac App Store included in macOS. It gives users a single, easy-to-use interface for locating, downloading, and installing software via the Internet. Further, applications from the Mac App Store do not require complex serial numbers or activation codes. Instead, all purchases are associated with an Apple ID and can be installed on any number of computers you own or control.

> **MORE INFO** ▸ If you support Mac computers for a large organization, Apple offers the Volume Purchase Program to acquire multiple licenses for Mac App Store items. You can find out more about Apple management technologies like VPP at https://support.apple.com/business-education/.

Chances are you are already familiar with the Mac App Store, the primary distribution method for all Apple software updates. However, if you have a new Mac with macOS preinstalled, you may not have used the Mac App Store yet. Even if you have used it, you may not be familiar with all its features. This section provides an introduction to the Mac App Store from a support perspective.

> **MORE INFO** ▸ The Mac App Store has its own support site with more details available. You can find the site at www.apple.com/support/mac/app-store/.

About Mac App Store Requirements

Introduced in Mac OS X Snow Leopard 10.6.6, the Mac App Store is the premier location for Mac-compatible software, and it's increasingly the only location where you can get new Apple software. The Mac App Store combines all the steps of acquiring new software into a single interface. These steps, covered in greater detail in the next section, include browsing and searching for new software, downloading and installing software, managing an account for purchasing software, updating installed software, and managing purchased software.

Aside from having Mac OS X Snow Leopard 10.6.6 or later, you must meet two additional requirements to install software from the Mac App Store: an Internet connection and an Apple ID. Obviously you must have an Internet connection to access content from the Mac App Store. A high-speed broadband connection is recommended, but slower connections are adequate, as long as you have the time to wait for the download.

An Apple ID with a verified email address is required to install anything from the Mac App Store, free or otherwise. If you intend to buy non-free items, you must also associate a valid credit card with your Apple ID. However, free items can be downloaded without a credit card. All Apple ID account management can be handled via the Mac App Store, as covered later in this lesson.

NOTE ▶ Local administrator authentication is not required to install items when using the Mac App Store on OS X Mavericks 10.9 or later. As covered later in this lesson, an administrator user can disable the Mac App Store for standard account users from the Parental Controls preferences.

Browse the Mac App Store

Even if you don't have an Apple ID, you can easily browse and search the Mac App Store. To get started, open the App Store in the Dock, or choose App Store from the Apple menu. When the Mac App Store opens, you are greeted with the Featured view.

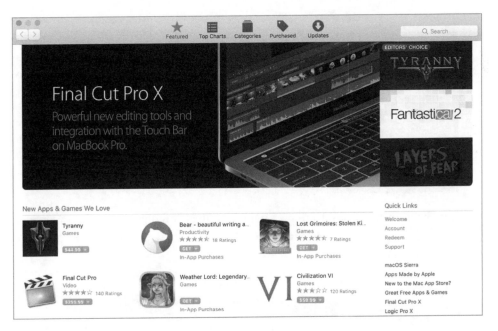

The main area of the Featured view allows you to browse new, popular, and staff favorite items. To the right of the Featured view you'll find Quick Links, which link to specific categories and Mac App Store management features. Across the top of the Mac App Store window is a toolbar. Note the arrow buttons in the upper-left corner that allow you to navigate backward and forward much like a web browser's history. If you're still browsing for new applications, you can click Top Charts to see the most popular items, or click Categories to browse for a specific type of application.

TIP ▸ The buttons in the Mac App Store toolbar correspond to keyboard shortcuts Command-1 through Command-5. For example, use the Command-2 keyboard shortcut to quickly navigate to the Top Charts page.

Search in the Mac App Store

The most direct route for finding a particular application is the search field in the top right of the window. Simply start typing part of the name, and the search immediately returns a list of matching items.

Pressing the Return key or selecting an item from the list returns a search results page, giving you a more detailed view of the matching items. Click an application's icon or name to view the details page.

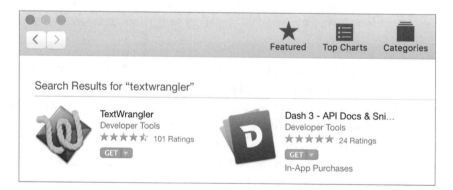

Once you're at an application's details page, you can read more about the application, view application screenshots, and, at the bottom, browse (or write your own) customer ratings and reviews. To the far right you'll also see developer and application information, including version, download size, and system requirements.

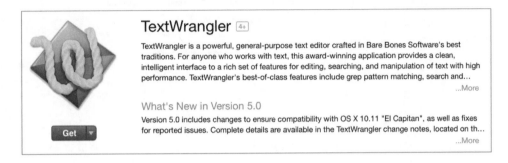

Install from the Mac App Store

Directly under the application's icon, you'll see the application's price. Some applications in the Mac App Store are free and can be purchased without entering any payment information. Paid items require that a valid credit card or PayPal account be associated with the Apple ID that will be used to purchase items. To download and install an item, click the purchase button. The purchase button will either say "Get" for a free application or display the purchase price for a paid application. Click either to start the installation process.

TIP ▶ Clicking the small arrow to the right of the Install button reveals a pop-up menu that allows you to copy or share a link to the selected Mac App Store item.

If you have yet to sign in to the Mac App Store with an Apple ID, or you did not enter an Apple ID during system setup, you are prompted to do so now. If you don't have an Apple ID yet, you can create one in the Mac App Store. Details of the creation and management of accounts are covered in the next section. If, however, you already have an Apple ID that has been previously used to purchase items from any Apple online store, enter it to continue the installation process.

NOTE ▶ On Mac computers with Touch ID you can make purchases in the Mac App Store by authenticating your Apple ID via Touch ID instead of your Apple ID password.

NOTE ▶ You will receive a warning if you try to install an application from the Mac App Store that replaces an earlier version of the same application that was purchased outside the Mac App Store.

Once your Apple ID is validated, the selected application downloads and installs directly to what appears to be Launchpad. In reality, the application is being installed to the /Applications folder. Thus, if you prefer to use the Finder, you can also open the application from this folder. While the application is downloading, a progress bar is shown in the Purchases view of the Mac App Store, in Launchpad, in the Dock icon of Launchpad, and in the Finder. Once the application has been installed, you may notice Launchpad's icon bounce in the Dock. Also, any new or recently updated applications will appear with a blue dot next to their name in Launchpad.

Any item your Apple ID has been used to purchase is always available to update or reinstall from the Mac App Store. You can find out more about this in the "Manage Purchased Applications" section later in this lesson.

Manage Your Store Account

Again, an Apple ID is required to purchase anything from the Mac App Store. If you have purchased items from Apple previously using the Apple Web Store, iTunes Store, or iOS

App Store, you can use the same Apple ID you used for those previous purchases. If you have not purchased anything from Apple via an online store, you can add purchasing information to an existing Apple ID or create a new Apple ID.

The only requirement for creating a new Apple ID is a unique email address, which is used for contact and verification. If your primary email address is from a non-Apple source, you can use that email to define an Apple ID. Alternatively, you can use a free iCloud account, which also provides a free email address, acts as an Apple ID, and can be used to make purchases from any of Apple's online stores. The Mac App Store also supports Family Sharing, which allows one user to organize a group of up to six Apple IDs that can share downloaded Apple items. The Family Sharing organizer is even allowed to create new Apple IDs for children that give them limited access to online purchases from Apple.

You can begin the account management process by clicking the Sign In link, found on the right side of the Mac App Store in the Quick Links list, or by choosing Store > Sign In.

The Mac App Store authentication dialog appears. If you already have an Apple ID, enter it now. If you don't have an Apple ID, or if you want to create a new one just for purchases, click Create Apple ID. What happens next depends on the state of your Apple ID: you can proceed to install items, you need to verify or update your Apple ID information, or you must enter some information to create a new Apple ID.

Your Apple ID Is Ready for Use in the Mac App Store

If your Apple ID has been used to purchase items from Apple previously, it may be ready to go for the Mac App Store. If this is the case, you won't see any other screens. When you are signed in, the first Quick Links item is Welcome followed by your first name. Further, any balance you have on your account will show. You can also verify the signed-in Apple ID by clicking the Store menu. Note that you can sign out from the Store menu as well.

Your Apple ID Needs Updating

If your Apple ID information needs to be verified or updated, you're prompted to review your account. You first need to agree to the Mac App Store terms and conditions, and then you have to verify your Apple ID security details. If you have used this Apple ID with an Apple online store previously, this may be all the verification that's required.

However, if you have never used this Apple ID with an Apple online store, or if your existing billing information is incomplete or out of date, you will have to verify or update your billing information to continue with purchases.

As of this writing, when using the Mac App Store to update or verify the purchasing information of an existing Apple ID, you must enter credit card information.

If you plan to make only free purchases, you have the option to remove your credit card information after your billing information has been verified. In the Mac App Store, you can remove payment information and set the account to None by editing the account payment options.

You're Creating a New Apple ID

If you don't have an Apple ID, or you want to create a new one just for making purchases, you can do so almost entirely from the Mac App Store. After agreeing to the terms and conditions, you are prompted to enter details for a new Apple ID. Whenever you create a new Apple ID, you must first provide account details that include a verifiable email address, three security answers, and your birthday.

As of this writing, if you want to create a new Apple ID for purchases without entering a credit card, you must do so from the iTunes store. If you choose to create a new Apple ID via the Mac App Store, you will have to enter credit card information.

> **MORE INFO ▶** For more information about creating a new Apple ID that can purchase free items without a credit card, see Apple Support article HT204034, "Create or use your Apple ID without a payment method."

Create an Apple ID

Name:	first last
Email address:	name@example.com
	This will be your new Apple ID.
Password:	required
	verify
	Your Apple ID password must be at least 8 characters and include a number, an uppercase letter and a lowercase letter.

After entering your details, you're prompted to provide a payment method. Finally, when creating a new Apple ID, you have to verify the email address specified. The Mac App Store system sends an email verification; click the link inside the email to open a webpage where you can authenticate and verify the account. Once you've done so, you have to sign in to the Mac App Store again to purchase or install any items.

> **NOTE ▶** An individual must be over the age of 13 to create an Apple ID. However, a Family Sharing organizer can create Apple IDs for children that can be granted limited online purchasing ability. Education institutions can create Apple IDs for minors by taking advantage of the Apple School Manager program at http://school.apple.com.

> **NOTE ▶** Purchases made from different Apple IDs cannot be merged. However, a Family Sharing organizer can invite existing Apple IDs into a group so that purchases can be shared.

Verifying and Managing Your Apple ID

Whenever you want to make changes to your Apple ID, you can do so from within the Mac App Store by clicking the Account link in the Quick Links section or by choosing Store > View My Account. From the Account Information page, you can change your Apple ID, payment information, and country or region setting.

> **NOTE ▶** Significant changes made to your Apple ID will generate an automated email letting you know changes have been made. This is a protective measure should someone else attempt to make changes to your Apple ID.

Also, the Apple ID verification screen is the only location where you can create a nickname or change an existing one. Your Apple nickname is used to hide your personal identification in any reviews you post in any of Apple's various online stores.

Manage iCloud Family Sharing

Apple devices with OS X Yosemite 10.10 and later or iOS 8 and later support iCloud Family Sharing, allowing families of up to six people to share each other's iTunes, iBooks, and Mac App Store purchases without sharing account information. In other words, family members can sign in to the Mac App Store with their own personal Apple ID and share purchases with up to five other people in the Family Sharing group.

Although the effects of iCloud Family Sharing can be seen in the Purchases view of the Mac App Store, all management of the Family Sharing group is via the iCloud preferences.

An adult user who is signed in to iCloud on macOS can start, or organize, a Family Sharing group by clicking the Manage Family button in the iCloud preferences.

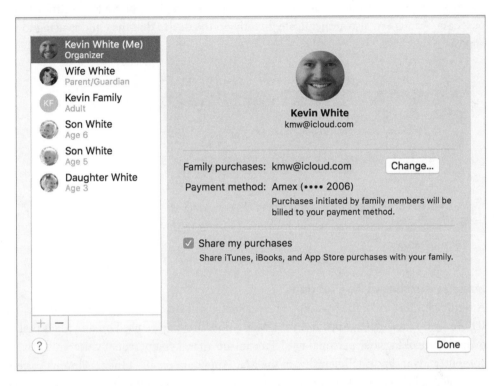

This first Apple ID is designated the "organizer" of the Family Sharing group. The organizer account must be set up with credit card payment information, as all other family members can be allowed to purchase using this payment information. The organizer can invite other adults via their Apple ID to the Family Sharing group and also create new iCloud accounts for children under 13 years of age. Child accounts are given full iCloud service access, including an email address using the @icloud.com domain.

Each member who joins the Family Sharing group is allowed to share existing Apple online purchases with the other group members. However, new purchases for any member of the Family Sharing group are all made via the organizer's payment method. The exception to this rule is that all Family Sharing members can make their own purchases using redemption codes—this includes both monetary and item-specific redemption codes.

Family Sharing users who are children can be required to ask for approval for any purchase, including free items. By default, the organizer is the only person who can approve such requests. Other adult members of the Family Sharing group can also approve purchases if the organizer specifies the adult as a parent or guardian. Adults who can approve purchases will receive a notification on their Apple devices to approve (or decline) each purchase. Adults can also authenticate directly on the device that the child is using to approve a purchase.

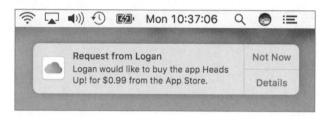

MORE INFO ▶ iCloud Family Sharing also includes the ability to share other services between family members. You can find out more at www.apple.com/icloud /family-sharing/.

Manage Purchased Applications

A significant feature of the Mac App Store is that applications are associated with an Apple ID. According to Apple, "Apps from the Mac App Store may be used on any Macs that you own or control for your personal use." This means that if you personally use multiple Mac computers, you can install items from the Mac App Store on all of them. This is possible because Apple keeps track of the items purchased or installed by your Apple ID. Further, as covered previously, iCloud Family Sharing allows you to easily share Mac App Store purchases.

NOTE ▶ Family Sharing is specifically designed for personal family use. Use of Family Sharing by an organization or institution specifically violates the Apple Store terms and conditions. You can read more at www.apple.com/legal.

To install an application on a Mac that has already been purchased by you or another member of your Family Sharing group, open the Mac App Store, sign in with your Apple ID, and then click the Purchases icon in the toolbar. The Purchases page defaults to showing all the items owned by the signed-in Apple ID, both installed and not installed on the Mac.

If the currently signed-in Apple ID is part of a Family Sharing group, you can also view another family member's purchases by selecting the person's name from the Purchased pop-up menu just above the purchases list. Note that some Mac App Store items cannot be shared. The option to allow purchases to be shared is at the discretion of the application's developer.

Once you have located an already purchased item, simply click the Install button to download and install the latest version of the application to the local Mac. If the button next to a purchased item reads "Open," then the item is already installed on the Mac.

> **TIP** New Mac computers have additional Apple software preinstalled at the factory. Thus, the first time you view purchases in the Mac App Store, you may note these items listed at the top. You can associate these items with your Apple ID by clicking the Accept button.

> **TIP** If you use more than one Mac, you may want to enable automatic downloading of purchased applications. This option can be set from the Mac App Store preferences pane in the System Preferences for every Mac that has been configured with your Apple ID.

> **TIP** Mac App Storage purchases can be hidden by secondary-clicking (or Control-clicking) the purchase. To reveal hidden items you will need to navigate to your account settings. Again, you'll find the Account settings link under the Quick Links on the Featured Mac App Storage page.

Update Mac App Store Applications
Updating applications you originally installed from the Mac App Store is also extremely easy. As covered in Lesson 4, "Update macOS," macOS includes an automatic software update mechanism that is built into the Mac App Store. Automatic updates are enabled by default, and the system reminds you via notification when they are available for

installation. Further, you can enable updates to install automatically without the need for user interaction.

However, you can also manually check for updates by opening the Mac App Store. Every time you open the Mac App Store, it scans your local Mac for any Apple-installed items and compares the results to what's current on the Apple servers.

TIP ▶ If the proper updates don't seem to be appearing for your system, you can force the Mac App Store to reevaluate your installed software by holding down the Option key while opening the Mac App Store. Continue to hold the Option key while you click the Updates button as well.

If updates are available, you may notice in the toolbar that the Updates button has a small number by it. This represents applications that have updates available. Click the Updates button to reveal the list of available updates. You can choose to install individual updates by clicking specific Update buttons, or you can click the Update All button to install all updates.

Limit Access to the Mac App Store

Some items in the Mac App Store, specifically games, may contain content not suitable for children. Because software in the Mac App Store is rated with a system similar to that for motion pictures, you can limit a user's access to specific ratings. Further, if your organization prevents users from installing their own applications, then you may want to disable access to the Mac App Store altogether. If you want to limit access or completely disable the Mac App Store for a user, you can do so via the parental controls.

NOTE ▶ The system will not allow you to delete the Mac App Store, because it is needed to perform system updates.

In Parental Controls preferences, you have several ways to limit applications from the Mac App Store. The easiest method is to simply choose an age requirement from the "Apps to:" pop-up menu in the Stores pane of Parental Controls. Selecting a minimum age here limits the user's ability to both purchase new applications and open any applications already installed from the Mac App Store.

Alternatively, in the Apps pane of Parental Controls you can individually deselect the applications you want to disallow. Scrolling down through the allowed applications list also reveals an option, under the Other Apps disclosure triangle, to disallow the Mac App Store itself. This obviously prevents the restricted user account from installing or updating any item available from the Mac App Store.

MORE INFO ▶ Managing users using the parental controls is further covered in Lesson 5, "Manage User Accounts."

Reference 16.2
About Process Environments

Obviously, applications from the Mac App Store are made specifically to work on macOS. Once you venture beyond the Mac App Store, though, you'll find that there are thousands of other applications that also work on macOS. Aside from the Mac App Store, software can be delivered through a variety of mechanisms.

macOS supports several application environments. Application developers create their products based on support for these environments. Several are specific to macOS, whereas others add support for popular UNIX-based tools. Most importantly, though, average users do not need to concern themselves about which environment their application is using—the system will provide the appropriate resources automatically. The four primary application environments in macOS are native macOS applications, UNIX commands, Java applications, and UNIX applications that use the X Window System.

About Native macOS Applications

Most native macOS applications are created using a development environment known as Xcode. Unsurprisingly, applications designed using Xcode run only on Apple devices. Xcode leverages a variety of programming languages, but the two most often used are Objective-C and Swift.

> **MORE INFO** ▶ To learn more about developing native applications for macOS, see the Apple development resources at https://developer.apple.com/macos/.

macOS Sierra continues to support earlier Mac applications created using a development environment known as Carbon. The Carbon application environment is a streamlined and significantly updated version of the previous Mac OS 9 environment.

However, Apple has made it clear that going forward, new development for macOS applications should not use Carbon. Often, developers must use Objective-C or Swift in Xcode if they want to take advantage of the latest macOS or iOS features. As an example, older Carbon-based applications cannot take advantage of Auto Save and iCloud services.

For this reason, nearly all Apple software and most third-party software available from the Mac App Store is developed using Objective-C or Swift in Xcode. Further, although macOS Sierra still supports Carbon applications, the technology has officially been deprecated, indicating that future releases of macOS may not support Carbon-based applications.

About Legacy Mac Applications

Previous Mac systems supported applications created for Mac OS 9 and for PowerPC processors. The Classic compatibility environment, which enables users to run software created for Mac OS 9, ceased to be supported as of Mac OS X Leopard 10.5. The Rosetta compatibility environment, which enables users to run software created for PowerPC processors, is not supported as of OS X Lion 10.7.

About UNIX Commands

Mac systems have long been both POSIX- and UNIX 03–compliant. Thus, macOS is compatible with most UNIX software. The macOS system foundation, named Darwin, is based on the open source Free Berkeley Software Distribution (FreeBSD) UNIX command-line interface. The command line is most often accessed via the /Applications /Utilities/Terminal application.

> **MORE INFO ▸** To learn more about Darwin, see the Apple open source development resources at https://developer.apple.com/opensource.

About Java Applications

Java is an application environment originally developed by Sun Microsystems but now owned and primarily maintained by Oracle Corporation. The goal of developing software in Java is to create cross-platform applications. This means a developer can write software code that can run on many environments. Although there is Java application runtime support for macOS, it is not included with the default macOS system installation.

> **NOTE ▸** JavaScript, another technology, is used almost exclusively by web browsers and is fundamentally quite different from the Java application runtime. Safari, the web browser included in macOS, provides robust support for JavaScript.

To acquire the latest versions of Java for macOS, you can download and install the Java runtime from Oracle directly at http://java.com/. In fact , the first time you attempt to run a standard Java applet or application on a new Mac system, you are prompted to navigate to the download page for the latest version of Oracle's Java Developer Kit (JDK). The Oracle JDK includes the latest Java runtime environment along with Java developer tools.

NOTE ▶ Although the Java 6 runtime is still available directly from Apple, this legacy Java version is not supported by macOS Sierra. Also, the macOS technology that detects known malware may disable outdated versions of Java with known security issues.

The Java website provides the Java runtime in the form of an installer package that requires administrator authentication. If you know that your users require access to Java applications, you may want to manually download and install the Java runtime as part of your standard macOS configuration.

After installation you can verify the specific Java version supplied by Oracle and adjust other Java settings by opening the Java preferences pane, which appears in the bottom section of System Preferences. Oracle's implementation of the Java runtime features its own proprietary updater mechanism, which can also be managed from the Java preferences.

About X Window System Applications

The X Window System is an extension of the UNIX environment that provides a common graphical applications platform for UNIX workstations. Previous Mac systems included the Apple version of a popular implementation of the X Window System, known as X11. Open /Applications/Utilities/X11 to access X Window System applications.

However, opening this application in OS X El Capitan 10.11 or later redirects you to Apple Support article HT201341, "About X11 for Mac." From that article you are redirected to an open source implementation known as XQuartz, available at http://xquartz.macosforge.org. This is the Apple-supported implementation of the X Windowing System on macOS. Upon installation, the /Applications/Utilities/X11 application is replaced with /Applications /Utilities/XQuartz.

About Open Source Software

By now you may have noticed that quite a bit of macOS is based on something called open source software. Generally speaking, open source is a method of software creation based on the free distribution and contribution of software source code. In other words, it's software whose code is available at no cost to anyone for general use or further modification. Interested individuals are expected and usually encouraged to provide improvements to open source software by adding to the software's code. It's expected that over time this community involvement will yield software products of exceptional quality, often free of cost.

Apple is deeply involved with many open source projects, including not just building on open source but also contributing to existing projects and creating entirely new open source projects. In fact, the core of macOS, Darwin, is an entirely open source operating system that includes more than 200 individual open source projects. Keep in mind, though, that Apple maintains proprietary closed software solutions as part of macOS as well.

> **MORE INFO ▸** To learn more about how Apple is involved in open source development, visit https://developer.apple.com/opensource.

The astounding growth of open source software in the last decade has not only produced some great software but also led to the rise of an entirely new operating system, Linux. With the growing popularity of Linux, high-quality open source applications have taken off as well. Because of the open source and UNIX heritage of macOS, you can also take advantage of many of these open source applications on your Mac. Some open source applications run in the command line, others run through XQuartz, and some have even been converted to full-fledged Mac applications. Take some time to explore these free open source solutions for your Mac—they may be suitable replacements for commercially purchased software.

> **MORE INFO ▸** The MacPorts project hosts over 24,000 open source software titles for macOS at www.macports.org.

Reference 16.3
About Application Security

One of the primary benefits of acquiring applications from the Mac App Store is knowing that Apple has processes for ensuring that the applications are free of malicious software, also known as malware. No system is perfect, but even if a bad application slips by the Apple procedures, the application can be pulled quickly from the store.

Despite the popularity of the Mac App Store, thousands of Mac applications are available only outside of the store. There are many reasons a developer might need to distribute software outside of the Mac App Store, including both technical and licensing issues. Apple recognizes the need for software developers to distribute their wares outside of the Mac App Store. At the same time, though, there is the need to ensure that Mac users are protected from bad software. To this end, macOS includes several application security technologies that help protect users when they install third-party applications.

About Process Security

Again, macOS inherits relatively robust process security due to its UNIX foundation. At both the command line and graphical interface, applications and processes are not allowed to access resources unless they are authorized. Access restrictions in the form of file system permissions are responsible for much of the security here. Simply, a running process is owned by a user and is therefore granted file-system access similar to that of the user.

OS X El Capitan 10.11 and later improve on this security with System Integrity Protection (SIP). SIP prevents processes running as root (or System Administrator) from being able to modify protected core system files and processes. Details regarding SIP are covered in Lesson 13, "Manage System Resources."

Despite these security mechanisms, systemwide privileges are allowed when needed. The most obvious example of this is the Installer application, which requires administrator authorization to install software that affects more than one user. The moral of this story is to beware of applications that require administrator authorization, as you are granting that application system-level access. Of note, the only applications in the Mac App Store that may ask for administrator authorization are those developed by Apple. For example, setup of the macOS Server application requires administrator authorization because it installs additional system services.

About Application Sandboxing

Even with the default process security mechanism in place, an application could still access all the files owned by a user. This gives an application the potential to read all your files and potentially gain unauthorized access to personal information.

A significant security feature in macOS is support for full application and process sandboxing. As the name implies, applications and processes in macOS can "play" inside a restricted environment that has little or no access to other parts of the system. With application sandboxing, applications are granted access only to the items they need through a sophisticated arrangement of rules. This is implemented in macOS via application sandbox containers, as covered in Lesson 13, "Manage System Resources."

It's important to note that application sandboxing is an optional feature that developers must implement in their own time. Apple has already sandboxed any application or process built into macOS that could benefit from this feature. Further, as of June 2012 all applications available from the Mac App Store must use application sandboxing.

About Code Signing

Code-signed applications and processes include a digital signature, which is used by the system to verify the authenticity and integrity of the software code and resources. Code is verified not only on disk but also as it is running. Therefore, even if some part of the application's or process's code is inappropriately changed while it's active, the system can automatically quit it.

In addition to identifying changes to applications, code signing provides guaranteed application identification for other parts of the system, including the keychain, the personal application firewall, Parental Controls preferences, application sandboxing, and Managed Client settings.

Finally, in macOS, code signing is used as the basis of identification for trusting newly installed items. Though code signing is optional, applications that have it are automatically trusted by the system. All Apple software and applications from the Mac App Store are always code signed, and thus trusted by macOS upon installation.

Software developers that choose not to use the Mac App Store can still take advantage of this system. A developer can code sign its installers and applications using an Apple-granted Developer ID. In this way, code-signed applications installed from any origin can be trusted by macOS.

About File Quarantine

macOS includes a file quarantine service that displays a warning when you attempt to open an item downloaded from an external source such as the Internet. Quarantined items include many file types, such as documents, scripts, and disk images. This lesson focuses primarily on quarantine as it relates to downloaded applications.

File quarantine goes into effect only when an item is marked for quarantine by the application that downloaded it. This is true for all applications built into macOS, but it may not be true for third-party applications that can download files. Also, files copied to the Mac using any other method are not marked for quarantine. For example, using the Finder to copy an application from a USB disk does not engage the quarantine system.

When a file is marked, the system requires you to verify your intent to open the item or cancel if you have any suspicions about the safety of an item. Any administrator user can permanently clear the quarantine by clicking Open. After an administrator clears the quarantine, the system will no longer show the quarantine warning. On the other hand, when a standard user clicks Open on a quarantined item, the item opens but the quarantine remains. Thus, subsequent users who try to open the item still get the quarantine warning.

NOTE ▶ The version of TextWrangler that was used to generate the previous screen-shot was downloaded from the developer's website. TextWrangler is also available from the Mac App Store; however, the Mac App Store version is not quarantined because it's from a trusted source: Apple.

File quarantine can also be removed using the **xattr** command-line tool. This is useful for removing quarantine on multiple files at once, or in cases where the Finder can't properly remove the quarantine. To use this tool in the Terminal application, enter xattr –dr com.apple.quarantine, followed by the path of the item.

About Malware Detection

Apple further secures macOS by maintaining a list of known malicious software. If you attempt to open any software on this list, the system presents a warning dialog suggesting that you move the item to the Trash. The list of malicious software is automatically updated via the macOS software update mechanism and is located on your Mac in the file /System/Library/CoreServices/CoreTypes.bundle/Contents/Resources/XProtect.plist.

MORE INFO ▶ To find out more about file quarantine, see Apple Support article HT201940, "About the 'Are you sure you want to open it?' alert (File Quarantine / Known Malware Detection) in OS X."

About Gatekeeper

Gatekeeper is a technology that leverages both code signing and file quarantine to further protect your Mac from malicious applications. Because Gatekeeper relies on the file quarantine system, it restricts only applications downloaded by applications that properly set file quarantine. It does this by giving you the choice to allow downloaded applications from only trusted application sources.

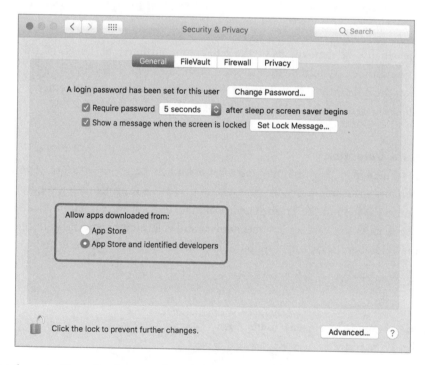

Gatekeeper allows for three modes of application restriction:

▶   App Store—This is the top option in the General pane of the Security & Privacy preferences. This is the most limited option, since it allows only applications from the Mac App Store to open. Even when a version of the application is available from the Mac App Store, if you download the application from somewhere else, it will still be blocked.

▶ App Store and identified developers—This is the second option in the General pane of the Security & Privacy preferences, and is the default option for macOS. As covered previously, developers can use an Apple-verified code-signing certificate to identify their application. If a developer has done this, the application is allowed to open, but the system still presents the file quarantine dialog for downloaded items. If an application isn't properly signed, it will be blocked.

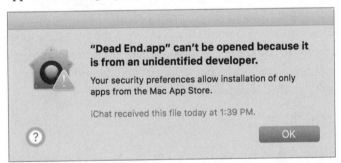

▶ Anywhere—Because this option makes your Mac less safe, it's no longer available as a default in the Security & Privacy preferences. However, you can still enable this option via the following Terminal command: `sudo spctl --master-disable`. This option is similar to the behavior of previous Mac systems that did not include Gatekeeper. All applications are allowed regardless of source, but again the system presents the file quarantine dialog for downloaded items. Selecting this option will present a dialog reminding you that this will make your Mac less safe. Also, as the dialog states, Gatekeeper will reset if no unsigned software is installed in 30 days.

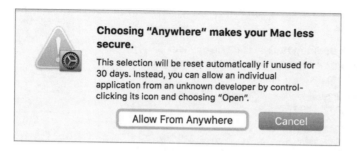

Gatekeeper also identifies modified or damaged applications regardless of your security settings. In this case you are seeing code signing at work, since the system has identified changes to an application from its original state. Thus, the application is either damaged due to file corruption or someone other than the original developer has modified it. In either case you will not be allowed to open the application, because it may cause harm.

MORE INFO ▶ To find out more about Gatekeeper, see Apple Support article HT202491, "OS X: About Gatekeeper."

Temporarily Bypass Gatekeeper

Even with Gatekeeper in place, an administrator user can override the system's settings and allow untrusted applications. In the Finder, an administrator user can secondary-click (or Control-click) the application file and then choose Open from the shortcut menu. The Gatekeeper warning appears to verify the administrator's intent.

TIP ▶ An administrator user can also override the previous item blocked by Gatekeeper in the General tab of the Security & Privacy preferences.

Clicking Open opens the application and clears the file quarantine. However, this may not be enough for all unsigned applications, because some applications may automatically open other background or child applications. Examples include applications that also provide background software to facilitate hardware functionality.

These secondary applications also trigger Gatekeeper. Unfortunately, you will not be able to override the appropriate files from the Finder. In these cases, your first move should be to contact the software developer to ensure you have the latest macOS Sierra–compatible version of the software.

If you absolutely must install untrusted software, you can temporarily allow software by entering the following command in the Terminal: sudo spctl --master-disable. Once you have authenticated this command as an administrator, the Anywhere option becomes available in the General tab of the Security & Privacy preferences. Once you have launched the application and verified its full functionality, the quarantine is cleared, and you can then return the Gatekeeper settings to something more secure.

Reference 16.4
Use Traditional Installation Methods

Traditional installation methods fall into one of two categories: drag-and-drop installations or installation packages. Application developers can choose any method they want to deploy their wares. Often the distinction between the two traditional methods is the complexity of the software being deployed.

If a software developer creates a product that requires only a folder of a few items or even a single item, it's often deployed as a drag-and-drop installation. However, if a software developer creates a product that requires a set of items that must be installed in multiple specific locations throughout the system, it's often deployed as an installation package.

> **NOTE ▶** As covered previously in this lesson, applications downloaded from any source outside of the Mac App Store are subject to file quarantine and Gatekeeper rules.

Install via Drag-and-Drop

Apple pioneered the era of drag-and-drop in computing, so it should come as no surprise that many traditional software installations in macOS are of the simple drag-and-drop variety. In general, macOS doesn't care where an application or process resides. So long as the application itself doesn't have a specific location requirement, applications can run from any location on the Mac. That said, as covered in previous lessons, some locations are more appropriate and secure than others.

Specifically, the /Applications folder is the default location for applications available to all users. Only administrator users can manually make changes to the /Applications folder. If users want to install their own drag-and-drop applications, they can create their own Applications folder in their home folder. However, users can place applications anywhere they please inside their own home folders. Again, many drag-and-drop applications work from any location on the system.

About Drag-and-Drop Application Security

Also, it's important to recognize that because of the default security and permissions model in macOS, no application a standard user is allowed to install and open can interfere with other users on the system. Poorly written or malicious software could potentially harm items in the user's home folder, but as long as the user is not allowed to authenticate as an administrator, it is extremely difficult for the software to cause damage to the system or other users.

Keep in mind, a user could deliberately cause damage to their own items. In short, allowing nonadministrator users the ability to install software is no more dangerous than allowing them to use the computer in the first place.

Install Drag-and-Drop Items

Drag-and-drop software deployed via optical disc, or any other physical medium, is often ready to copy to wherever the user wants to install it. On the other hand, software downloaded from the Internet is almost always deployed in some kind of archive format. As covered in Lesson 12, "Use Hidden Items, Shortcuts, and File Archives," ZIP files and disk images are the most common archive formats for macOS.

In macOS, the Safari browser automatically unarchives ZIP files, by default, to the ~/Downloads folder. Users could technically leave the application in the ~/Downloads folder and continue to open it from there, but they should be trained to move the new application to a more appropriate location in their home folder.

In macOS the Safari browser does not, however, automatically mount a downloaded disk image. A user must double-click a disk image to make its contents available to the Finder. Once the disk image volume is mounted, again the user could technically leave the application inside the disk image and open it from there, but users should be trained to move the new application to another location. This is especially true of disk images, because if the user logs out or restarts the computer, the disk image unmounts.

For many novice users, this would result in their "losing" the application. Fortunately, many developers use a helpful Finder window background graphic that should encourage the user to copy the software to a more appropriate location. An example of this type of installation is found later in the exercise section of this lesson.

About Installation Packages

Installation packages are the default deployment mechanism for most Apple software updates and third-party software that requires the installation of items in multiple locations. Installation packages are deployed via user interaction with the Installer application. When a user opens an installation package, the Installer application opens automatically. This application has the user walk through a few simple screens to configure and initiate the installation process.

Most significantly, installation packages often require administrator user authentication, since they are frequently used to install items that can affect other users and the operating system. Lesson 4, "Update macOS," details using and troubleshooting installation packages for Apple software updates. The same techniques apply to third-party installation packages deployed via the Installer application.

That said, on occasion you will find third-party installers that do not use the Apple Installer application. These installations are easily identified because the installation assets are themselves an application using the .app filename extension. The Apple native installation assets come only in the form of installation packages using the .pkg or .mpkg filename extension. If you have problems with a third-party installer, you must contact the developer for any issues regarding installation, since it has elected to use a proprietary installation mechanism.

Update Installed Software

Similar to installation, there are a variety of methods for keeping installed software up to date:

▶ Apple software and Mac App Store software—Any software acquired via the Mac App Store, including both Apple and third-party software, is also updated via the Mac App Store software update mechanism, as covered previously in this lesson and in Lesson 4, "Update macOS."

▶ Automatically updating third-party software—Automatic update mechanisms for third-party software vary widely. Prior to the Mac App Store, no unified method for providing third-party software updates existed. Thus, software developers often implemented their own automatic update methods. Unfortunately, this means there is no standard method to determine if an application has automatic update capability. You can start by looking in common locations, including the application menu (the menu that appears with the application's name), the application's preferences window, or the application's Help menu. If the third-party item installed a preference pane, it's highly likely any automatic update mechanism will be found within. Finally, it's important to note that nearly all automatic update mechanisms require administrator user authentication.

▶ Manually update third-party software—In some cases the only update mechanism for third-party software is to simply install a newer version. Keep in mind that only administrator users can replace or update software in the /Applications folder. Further, many package installations require administrator user authentication.

Reference 16.5
Remove Installed Software

In many cases, removing installed software is much easier than installing it in the first place. One thing that often surprises veteran Windows support specialists who are new to the Mac is that there's no default Apple software removal mechanism. This is because the vast majority of Mac software can simply be moved to the Trash.

NOTE ▶ System Integrity Protection in macOS Sierra prevents any user from removing core system software and applications.

Software removal methods include:

▶ Mac App Store software—Although it's true that applications installed from the Mac App Store can be dragged to the Trash, you can also remove these applications from Launchpad. To engage Launchpad, double-click its icon in the /Applications folder, or from a Multi-Touch trackpad use the "pinch with thumb and three fingers" gesture. In Launchpad, hold down the Option key, and a small x button appears next to applications installed from the Mac App Store. Click one of the buttons, and the system will remove that application.

▶ Drag to the Trash—Yes, it's true that most applications are "removed enough" if you simply move the primary application icon into the Trash. If the software item is a type of resource, like a preference pane or a font, just locate the item in one of the Library folders and drag it to the Trash. This method may leave some residual support files, but by removing the primary application or resource file you have rendered the software inoperable. This method works for applications installed using a traditional method and via the Mac App Store. Just don't forget to empty the Trash before continuing with your work—a user logout wouldn't hurt either.

▶ Application uninstaller—Only in very rare occasions will third-party software require an uninstaller. The only times you will find an uninstaller are in situations where the software's developer has deemed the removal process complicated enough to warrant an uninstaller. If this is the case, the software developer must provide the uninstaller; it often comes along with the original software installer.

Exercise 16.1
Use the Mac App Store

▶ **Prerequisite**

> ▶ You must have created the Local Admin (Exercise 2.1, "Configure a New macOS System for Exercises," or Exercise 2.2, "Configure an Existing macOS System for Exercises") and Chris Johnson (Exercise 5.1, "Create a Standard User Account") accounts.

In this exercise, you will use the Mac App Store to purchase, download, and install a free application on your computer.

Select an Apple ID to Use with the App Store

NOTE ▶ The exact process of configuring Chris Johnson's account with an Apple ID for the App Store will depend on whether you want to use the same Apple ID for iCloud and App Store purchases and what the Apple ID has been used for in the past. The instructions in this exercise attempt to cover most of the possibilities, but if you find that your experience does not match these instructions, the App Store will be able to guide you through the process.

1   If necessary, log in as Chris Johnson.

2   Open System Preferences, and select the App Store preference pane.

The settings in this preference pane allow you to automate updating and downloading App Store purchases, as well as system software. By default, the App Store automatically checks for all updates and downloads system updates in the background. It also automatically installs new security updates. In addition, you will find an option to automatically update purchased applications, as well as an option to automatically download applications, purchased on other Mac computers using the same Apple ID.

3   If "Automatically download apps purchased on other Macs" is selected, click the lock, authenticate as Local Admin, and deselect the checkbox.

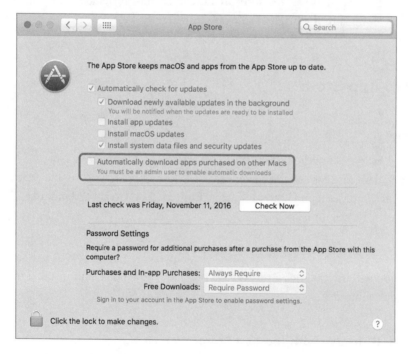

NOTE ▸ Although administrator access is required to change the update settings, you will not need administrator access to install an application from the App Store.

4   Quit System Preferences.

5   From the Apple menu, choose App Store.

6   In the App Store, pull down the Store menu, and see whether it shows you are signed in (it will list "View My Account") or not ("Create Account").

You may have been automatically signed in to the Apple ID you used for iCloud. Apple recommends using the same account for both (see Apple Support article HT204053, "Sign in with your Apple ID on a new device"), but it is also possible to use different Apple IDs for these different functions.

7   If you are signed in but want to use a different Apple ID for App Store purchases, choose Store menu > Sign Out.

You have several choices for an account to use:

▶   You can use the same Apple ID that you are using for iCloud services. If you are performing these exercises as part of a class, you should use this option.

▶   If you have another existing Apple ID, you can choose to use that for the App Store instead.

▶   If you want to create a new Apple ID for use with the App Store, have access to an existing email account that is not already in use as an Apple ID, and want to use it to download free applications from the App Store without supplying a credit card, follow the instructions in Apple Support article HT204034, "Create or use your Apple ID without a payment method." Once the account has been created, you can proceed with this exercise.

▶   If you want to create a new Apple ID for use with the App Store, have access to an existing email account that is not already in use as an Apple ID, and want to supply a credit card for future purchases, click the Create Apple ID button and follow the prompts. The details of this process are not covered here.

8   If the Store menu shows that you are already signed in to the Apple ID you want to use for App Store purchases, skip ahead to the "Select an App to Purchase" section.

9   If you are not already signed in, choose Store menu > Sign In.

10   Enter the Apple ID and password, and click "Sign In."

11   If you used an Apple ID with two-step verification or two-factor authentication enabled, you may be prompted to provide additional verification of your identity. If you cannot do this, click Cancel, choose Store menu > Sign Out, and then either start over using an instructor-provided Apple ID instead of your own or use one of the other options for an Apple ID.

12   If you receive a message that this Apple ID has not yet been used with the iTunes Store, you can do any of the following:

▶   Enable this Apple ID for use with the App Store by clicking Review and following the prompts (the process is not covered in detail here). Note that this may require you to supply a credit card or other payment source.

▶   Switch to a different Apple ID by clicking Cancel, and start over using an Apple ID that has been used with the App Store.

▶   Click Cancel, quit the App Store, and skip this exercise.

Select an App to Purchase

1   Enter the unarchiver in the search field (at the top right of the App Store window), and press Return.

NOTE ▶ If you are performing these exercises in a class, the instructor may recommend a different application for this exercise; in that case, substitute that recommendation for The Unarchiver throughout this exercise.

The App Store may find more than one relevant application. Find a free application named The Unarchiver (or the application your instructor recommended). Note that free applications have a Get button instead of a price (although if the application has already been purchased under this Apple ID, you will see an Install button).

2   Click the free application's name.

The App Store displays more details about this application. Again, there will be a Get button or an Install button.

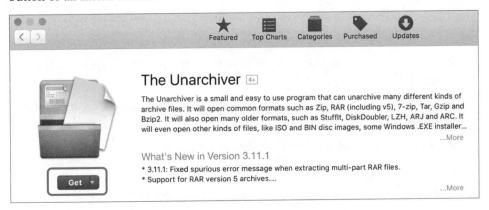

3   Click the Get button or Install button.

4   If the application begins downloading immediately, skip ahead to "Test the App."

5 If it changes to an Install App button, click that to confirm the download.

If additional confirmation or configuration is required, a dialog appears asking you to sign in to download the application. Note that depending on your App Store preference settings, the Apple ID password may be required, even though this is a free application.

6 If you are prompted to, enter the Apple ID password, and click Buy.

7 If you are prompted to ask permission for the purchase, you are using an iCloud child account. In this case, you can do any of the following:

▶ Click Ask, and then continue the exercise after a parent has approved the purchase.

▶ Switch to a different Apple ID by clicking Cancel, choosing Store menu > Sign Out, and then starting over using a different Apple ID.

▶ Click Cancel, quit the App Store, and skip this exercise.

8 If you are prompted for whether to always require a password when making a purchase, choose which policy you prefer and click the appropriate button.

9 If you used an Apple ID with two-step verification or two-factor authentication enabled, you may be prompted to provide additional verification of your identity. If you cannot do this, click Cancel, choose Store menu > Sign Out, and then either start over using an instructor-provided Apple ID instead of your own or use one of the other options for an Apple ID.

10 If you are asked to verify billing information for your Apple ID, click Billing Info, and enter it as requested. If the requested information is not available, click Cancel, choose Store menu > Sign Out, and then either start over using an instructor-provided Apple ID instead of your own or use one of the other options for an Apple ID.

11 If you receive a warning that the terms and conditions have changed, click OK and read the new terms. If you are using your own Apple ID and do not want to agree to them, click Cancel, choose Store menu > Sign Out, and then either use an instructor-provided Apple ID instead of your own or skip this exercise.

After agreeing to the new terms and conditions, you may need to reselect The Unarchiver.

When the application starts downloading, its progress is shown both in the App Store and under the Launchpad icon in the Dock.

Test the App

1 In the Dock, click the Launchpad icon.

If the application has not finished downloading, Launchpad displays its progress. When it finishes, you will see the application's regular icon. A blue dot appears next to its name, indicating that it is new.

2 Click The Unarchiver's icon.

The application launches.

3   If The Unarchiver asks where to extract archives, click "Extract to the same folder."

The Unarchiver Preferences window may open. You do not need to set anything here.

4   Quit the application.

Examine the App Store

1   In the App Store toolbar, click the Purchased icon.

2   Choose Store menu > Reload Page (Command-R) to make sure the list is up to date.

The App Store lists all the applications purchased with this Apple ID. If you are using your own Apple ID, you see your previous purchases; if you are using an instructor-supplied Apple ID, you may see applications that previous students purchased.

If you are using Family Sharing, a pop-up menu will allow you to switch from My Purchases to other family members' purchases. If you have not set up Family Sharing, this menu does not appear.

Note that if you had enabled the "Automatically download applications purchased on other Macs" option in Software Update preferences, any additional applications would be automatically downloaded and installed. Since this option is disabled, you see Install buttons that allow you to download and install them manually.

NOTE ▶ The App Store terms and conditions limit the situations in which an application may be installed on several computers. See www.apple.com/legal/itunes/us/terms.html for the current terms and conditions.

If any other applications are listed, do not install them at this time.

3   In the App Store toolbar, click the Updates button. If you are prompted, authenticate as Local Admin.

This displays updates available for both system software and App Store purchases installed on this computer.

4   Quit the App Store.

Exercise 16.2
Use an Installer Package

▶ **Prerequisite**

▶ You must have created the Local Admin (Exercise 2.1, "Configure a New macOS System for Exercises," or Exercise 2.2, "Configure an Existing macOS System for Exercises") and Chris Johnson (Exercise 5.1, "Create a Standard User Account") accounts.

Traditionally, one common way of distributing software is in the form of an installer package. Although this installation process involves more steps than the App Store method, it also offers some additional capabilities, such as allowing the developer to install files outside of /Applications, allowing the user to choose which optional components to install, and so on. For these reasons, package-based installation is likely to continue to be used for complex applications and other software. In this exercise, you will use it to install a simple application.

Install an App with an Installer Package

1   If necessary, log in as Chris Johnson.

2   Open the StudentMaterials/Lesson16 folder.

3   Open Hello World.dmg.

The image mounts, with the Hello World package inside it.

4   Open Hello World.pkg.

The Installer opens and prepares to install the Hello World application.

5   Click the lock icon at the upper right of the Installer window.

The lock icon indicates that this is a signed package; clicking it displays information about the certificate it was signed with. In this case, it was signed with Gordon Davisson's Developer ID Installer certificate, which was signed by the Developer ID Certification Authority, which in turn was signed by the Apple Root CA. Essentially, this means that the Apple Root CA vouches for the authenticity of the Developer ID Certification Authority, which vouches for the authenticity of Gordon Davisson's certificate, which vouches for the authenticity of the installer package.

This is the standard format of an Apple-issued Developer ID certificate.

6 Click OK to dismiss the certificate dialog.

7 Choose File menu > Show Files.

8 In the window that appears, click the disclosure triangle next to Hello World.

This shows what files the installer package contains. In this case, it is a folder named Hello World containing Hello World.app, Uninstall.app, and some metadata files.

9 Close the "Files from Hello World" window.

10 In the main Installer window, click Continue.

Some packages include additional steps, such as readme information, license agreements, choices of components to install, and so forth. This is a simple package, so it proceeds straight to the install pane.

11 In the Standard Install pane, click Install.

12 Authenticate as Local Admin when prompted.

The installation completes quickly, and the Installer informs you that it was successful.

13 Click Close, and the Installer exits.

14 Eject the disk image.

15 In the Finder, navigate to the Applications folder (you can choose Go menu > Applications or press Command-Shift-A).

Note that a Hello World subfolder has been installed. Inside is the Hello World application and an Uninstall script.

16 Open Launchpad.

Even though it was installed in a subfolder, the new application is displayed along with your other applications.

17 Open Hello World.

Because this application was installed with a package (and the package was properly signed), Gatekeeper does not activate, and no warning is displayed. You will see what happens with an untrusted application in the next exercise.

18 Quit Hello World.

Note that unlike the App Store, there is no standard update process for package-installed applications. Some applications manage their own updates, whereas others require you to manually download and install updates.

Exercise 16.3
Use a Drag-and-Drop Install

▶ **Prerequisite**

- ▶ You must have created the Local Admin (Exercise 2.1, "Configure a New macOS System for Exercises," or Exercise 2.2, "Configure an Existing macOS System for Exercises") and Chris Johnson (Exercise 5.1, "Create a Standard User Account") accounts.

In this exercise, you will examine the process of installing a downloaded application via the drag-and-drop method. The way you will get this application depends on whether you have a server available to support these exercises (either one provided by the classroom or one you set up yourself). If you have a "Mainserver" available, follow option 1; otherwise, follow option 2.

Option 1: Download an Application from Mainserver
Follow these steps if you have a macOS server configured to support these exercises.

1   If necessary, log in as Chris Johnson.

2   Open Safari.

3   Enter mainserver.local.

4   If you receive a warning that Safari can't verify the identity of the website, click Continue.

   Note that continuing after this warning is not generally safe, since the web server might be a fake or impostor, but in this particular case, it should not be a problem.

5   Near the bottom of the page, click the link to download Dead End. When the download is complete, quit Safari.

6   Open Dead-End.dmg from your Downloads folder. Note that there is a shortcut to Downloads in your Dock.

Option 2: Use an Application from StudentMaterials

Follow these steps if you do not have a macOS server configured to support these exercises.

1   If necessary, log in as Chris Johnson.

2   Open the StudentMaterials/Lesson16 folder.

3   Open Dead-End.dmg.

    Note that this disk image contains an application that was previously downloaded from a website and is still in quarantine, so macOS treats it as coming from an untrusted source.

Copy the Application to /Applications

Some applications distributed for drag-and-drop installations come with instructions or hints about how to install them, whereas others simply assume the user will know what to do. The Dead End application comes as a disk image with instructions in the background image.

1   Drag the Dead End icon onto the Applications icon (which is a symbolic link to /Applications).

A dialog appears telling you that modifying Applications requires an administrator name and password.

2   Click the Authenticate button, authenticate as Local Admin, and click OK.

The Finder now copies Dead End into /Applications.

macOS is tolerant, and it allows you to run applications no matter where they're stored, even if they are not in /Applications. Running the copy in the disk image you downloaded would work, but it may cause confusion or slightly odd application behavior, so you should avoid doing this.

Do not launch the Dead End application yet.

3   Eject the disk image.

Test the Gatekeeper Security Settings

1   Open System Preferences, and select the Security & Privacy pane.

2   Click the General tab.

3   If necessary, authenticate and set the "Allow apps downloaded from" option to "App Store and identified developers."

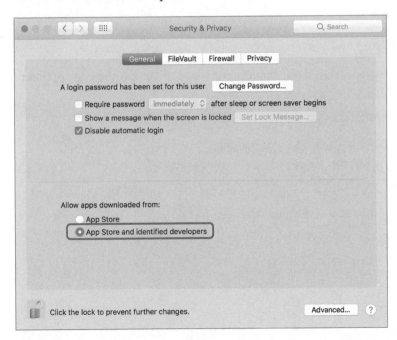

4   Quit System Preferences.

5   In the Finder, navigate to the Applications folder (you can use the shortcut Command-Shift-A).

6   Double-click Dead End.

The file is labeled with some additional metadata to indicate that it is in quarantine because it was downloaded from the Internet. The first time you open it, Gatekeeper checks it against your allowed applications policy. Since the application is not signed with a Developer ID, Gatekeeper does not allow it to open.

7   Click OK.

8   Control-click Dead End, and choose Open from the shortcut menu.

This time, Gatekeeper warns you about the application but gives you the option to bypass its normal policy and open the application.

9 Click Open.

10 When you are prompted, authenticate as Local Admin.

11 If necessary, click the Dead End icon in the Dock to bring it to the foreground.

Do not click "Download the Internet" at this time. If you do, see Exercise 18.1, "Force Applications to Quit," for information on forcing applications to quit. Although this application is not particularly malicious, it doesn't do anything useful either.

12 Quit Dead End (File menu > Quit or Command-Q).

13 Double-click Dead End to reopen it.

This time it opens without the warning. Since you opened it once, your Gatekeeper policy has been modified to allow it to run normally.

14 Quit Dead End again.

Exercise 16.4
Remove Applications

▶ **Prerequisite**

▶ You must have performed Exercise 16.1, "Use the Mac App Store," and Exercise 16.2, "Use an Installer Package."

Because macOS applications are usually just packages (or even single files), all that's necessary to remove them is to drag them to the Trash. A few more complex programs consist of more than just an application, and these will generally include their own uninstaller.

View Installed Applications

1   Open System Information by holding the Option key and choosing Apple menu > System Information.

System Information opens and displays the system report.

2   From the Software section of the sidebar, select Installations.

This part of the report shows software that has been installed on the computer both by the App Store and by package, so it shows both The Unarchiver (or whatever application you installed in Exercise 16.1, "Use the Mac App Store") and Hello World. It does not show software installed by other methods, so even if you installed Dead End (by the drag-and-drop method), it does not appear here.

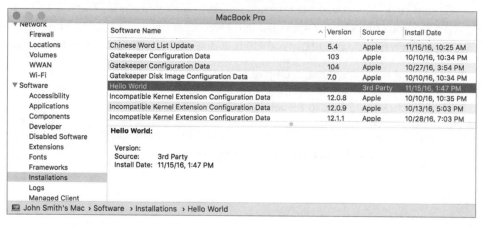

3   Quit System Information.

Remove an Application in Launchpad

1   Open Launchpad.

2   Click The Unarchiver (or whichever application you installed from the App Store), and hold down the mouse until an "X" appears at its top left and the other icons begin to wobble.

In this mode, Launchpad lets you drag application icons around to rearrange them and also use the "X" button to delete applications purchased from the App Store. Since The Unarchiver is the only one you purchased from the App Store, it is the only one that has an "X" by its icon.

3   Click The Unarchiver's "X" button.

4   In the confirmation dialog that appears, click Delete.

5   If you are prompted, authenticate as Local Admin.

The Unarchiver is now uninstalled from your computer. Note that your preference file or files and user data still exist, so if you ever decide to reinstall the program, all of your settings are kept.

6   Click twice in the background to exit Launchpad.

Reinstall an Application in the App Store

1   Open the App Store.

2   In the toolbar, click the Purchased icon.

Since you purchased The Unarchiver, it is listed here and available to reinstall. Depending on the history of the Apple ID you are using, other applications may be listed as well.

3   Click the Install button for The Unarchiver.

4   If you are prompted, enter your Apple ID's password to authenticate to the App Store.

The application is downloaded and reinstalled.

5   Wait for the download to finish, and then quit the App Store.

Remove an Application in the Finder

1   In the Finder, navigate to the Applications folder.

2   Select The Unarchiver, and drag it to the Trash icon in your Dock.

3   When you are prompted, authenticate as Local Admin.

4   Choose Finder menu > Empty Trash, and then click Empty Trash in the confirmation dialog.

The Unarchiver is now uninstalled from your computer.

Remove an Application with an Uninstaller

Since most applications can be uninstalled with the Finder, they don't provide any special uninstaller. Applications that do will vary as to how they provide the uninstaller and exactly how it works. This exercise presents a simple example.

1   In the Finder, navigate to the Applications folder.

2   Open the Hello World folder.

3   Open the Uninstall script in the Hello World folder.

Are you sure you want uninstall Hello World?

Cancel   OK

4   At the confirmation dialog, click OK.

5   When you are prompted, authenticate as Local Admin.

6   Reopen the Applications folder.

The entire Hello World folder has been removed from your computer.

Lesson 17
Manage Documents

For most users, document management is a primary day-to-day computing task. For many years, the act of opening and saving documents on a Mac has remained the same. Yet with the introduction and ultimate success of iOS, Apple has been seriously rethinking how Mac users interact with documents by slowly introducing new technologies into macOS.

OS X Lion 10.7 included significant changes to how documents are saved, with Auto Save and Versions. OS X Mountain Lion 10.8 featured integration that allowed you to save documents from applications to iCloud. OS X Yosemite 10.10 introduced iCloud Drive, which made iCloud on par with local storage. Items saved in iCloud Drive appear just like any other local storage and are fully manageable via the Finder. Finally, macOS Sierra can store Desktop and Documents folders in iCloud automatically.

In this lesson you will manage documents in macOS by starting with Launch Services, which is the mechanism that determines an action when the user double-clicks a document. You will also learn to use Quick Look for previewing most common document types. Then a significant portion of this lesson is dedicated to document management via Auto Save, Versions, and documents in iCloud. You will also see how macOS attempts to automatically resume documents and applications on the user's behalf. Finally, you will learn how macOS Sierra can help you optimize local storage to reclaim space on the system volume.

GOALS

▶ Use Launch Services and Quick Look to open documents

▶ Work with applications that support Auto Save and Versions

▶ Save and open documents saved to iCloud

▶ Optimize local storage to reclaim space on the system volume

Reference 17.1
Open Documents

Aside from a file's name, the most important piece of information about a file is its type. A file's type identification allows macOS to almost always choose the correct application to open when you double-click a file. Launch Services is the technology responsible for helping macOS make the connection between a file's type and the appropriate application. When you double-click a file from the Finder, it asks Launch Services to open the file with the appropriate application. Launch Services identifies the file based on its type and then references an application registration database to determine which application should open the file.

About File Type Identification

Adding a file type identifier to the end of a filename is standard computing practice. This practice complicates naming files because a user must identify and maintain appropriate filename extensions, such as .mp3 for compressed audio files, .jpg for compressed picture files, or .docx for Microsoft Word files.

Current operating systems work around the practice by hiding the filename extension from the user. For the sake of compatibility, Apple adopted this method of file type identification as the default for all versions of the Mac operating system (for example, OS X and macOS).

The Finder hides many filename extensions by default. You can select file type extension visibility from the Finder preferences by choosing Finder > Preferences, clicking the Advanced button, and selecting or deselecting the checkbox next to "Show all filename extensions." The following screenshot shows another Finder option (also enabled by default) that helps to prevent you from accidentally changing a file type identifier. It gives a warning before you attempt to make an extension change.

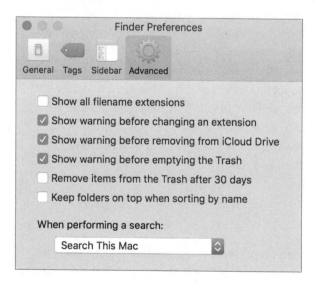

NOTE ▸ Choosing to show all file extensions in the Finder overrides the individual file attribute for hiding an extension, as configured from the Info and Inspector windows in the Finder.

About Application Registration

When you attempt to open a certain file type, Launch Services reads from a database of applications (and the file types each can open) to determine a match. Successful file and application match information is cached so that future attempts to open an application are resolved as quickly as possible. However, after every startup or login, a background process automatically scans for new applications and updates this database. Further, both the Finder and the Installer application keep track of new applications as they arrive on your Mac and add their supported file types to the database.

The application registration system is pretty good at finding matches, so odds are if the system gives you an error message, then you probably don't have the correct application for the file. In macOS, Launch Services maps many common file types to Preview and TextEdit if the primary application is missing. For example, Numbers or Microsoft Excel spreadsheets open in Preview; Pages and Microsoft Word documents open in TextEdit.

TIP ▸ With Quick Look you can preview many common file types, even without having the applications installed. This includes iWork and Microsoft Office documents. Quick Look details are covered later in this lesson.

If Preview, or any other application, can't properly open a specific file type, you can change Launch Services settings to force those files to open in a more appropriate application, as outlined in the following section. Other times, though, Launch Services may not have any idea which application to use for the file type. If you attempt to open a file type that isn't stored in the Launch Services database, macOS prompts you to find an application that supports the file. Alternatively, you can use a new feature in macOS that searches the Mac App Store for a compatible application.

There is no application set to open the document "Notes.vsdx".

Search the App Store for an application that can open this document, or choose an existing application on your computer.

?   Choose Application...   Cancel   Search App Store

Manage Launch Services

From the Info or Inspector windows in the Finder, you can override the Launch Services default application settings for any specific file type.

> **MORE INFO** ▸ Using the Info window to inspect files and folders is detailed in Lesson 11, "Manage Permissions and Sharing."

Once you select the files you want to change Launch Services settings for and have opened an Info window, click the "Open with" disclosure triangle to reveal the default application selected by Launch Services. To change just the selected files' default application, select another application from the pop-up menu. This information is saved to the files' metadata and defines Launch Services settings only for the selected items.

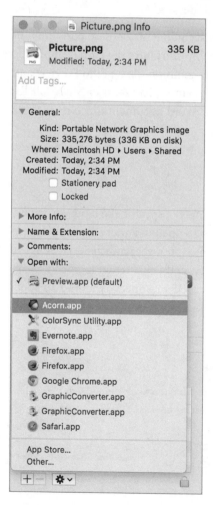

To change the default application for all files of this type, select the application you want to define as the default, and then click the Change All button. This setting is saved per user, so one user's application preferences do not override another's. A user's custom Launch Services settings are saved to the com.apple.LaunchServices.plist preference file in each user's ~/Library/Preferences folder.

You can also modify Launch Services settings in the Finder by secondary-clicking (or Control-clicking) the selected files and then choosing Open With from the shortcut menu. Additionally, holding down the Option key changes the menu command to Always Open With.

Preview Documents via Quick Look

Quick Look enables you to preview nearly any file type without having to open any additional applications, or without having those applications installed. This makes Quick Look the most convenient way to view the contents of any file.

You can open and close Quick Look previews by pressing the Space bar or Command-Y from any Finder view, the Time Machine restore interface, most Open and Save browser dialogs, the Mail application, active printer queues, or any other application that supports Quick Look. Later versions of macOS keep the Quick Look preview window open in the Finder until it's closed. Selecting another item in the Finder changes the Quick Look preview to the newly selected item.

The Quick Look close button is in the upper-left corner, just as in a traditional window. You can also quickly dismiss the Quick Look preview by pressing the Space bar or Command-Y again. With the Quick Look preview window open, you can resize the window by dragging any edge of the window, or you can go to full-screen view by clicking the twin arrow button at the top left of the preview window.

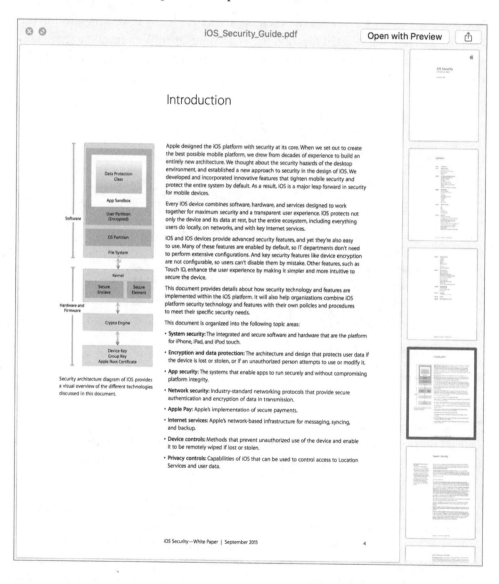

Quick Look technology is also used to provide the Finder with previews for files in icon view, previews in column view, and the preview section of the Info and Inspector windows. Finally, Quick Look also provides previews for the Cover Flow view. This view allows you to browse folder content in a similar way to browsing on Apple iOS mobile devices or in iTunes. You can open Cover Flow view from any Finder window by clicking its icon in the toolbar, which you can find two icons to the left of the action (gear icon) menu, also in the toolbar.

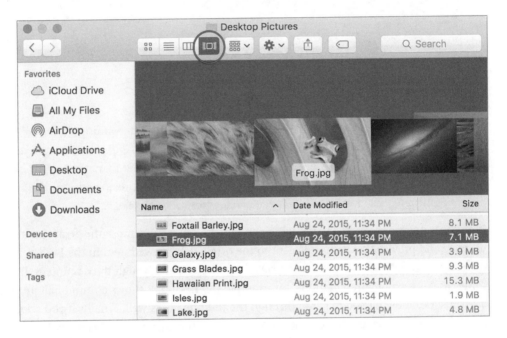

About the Quick Look Window

In the title bar of the Quick Look window, you'll find other useful options for previewing a selected item. For example, you can open a selected item in an application by clicking the "Open with <*Application*>" button, where <*Application*> is the name of the default application for the selected file. The Share button (box with the upward arrow) allows you to quickly share the document.

MORE INFO ▶ The list of options in the Share menu varies depending on the file type of the item being previewed, installed application extensions, and services configured in Internet Accounts preferences. You can find out more about managing application extensions in Lesson 18, "Manage and Troubleshoot Applications," and about configuring Internet services in **Lesson 22, "Manage Network Services."**

If multiple items are selected when you open Quick Look, you can use the arrow keys to navigate and preview the items adjacent to the original previewed item in the Finder. If the previewed file has multiple pages, you'll be able to scroll through the document. In some cases—Keynote presentations, for example—Quick Look shows a thumbnail preview of each slide, allowing you to scroll through the thumbnails as well. Finally, if you select multiple items to preview, the Quick Look window allows some basic slideshow features via buttons at the top left of the window.

About Quick Look Plug-ins

Quick Look is able to preview an ever-growing variety of file types using a plug-in technology. Each Quick Look plug-in is designed to preview specific types of files. Many Quick Look plug-ins are included by default, but Apple and third-party developers can create additional plug-ins to expand the Quick Look preview capabilities.

Included Quick Look plug-ins enable you to:

▶ Preview any audio or video file that can be decoded by QuickTime

▶ Preview a variety of graphics files, including many digital camera files, PDF files, EPS files, and any standard graphics file

▶ Preview a variety of productivity files, including standard text files, script files, and files created by the Pages, Numbers, Keynote, and Microsoft Office suites

▶ Preview a variety of Internet-centric files, including mailboxes, iChat transcripts, and web archives

Quick Look plug-ins, like any other system resource, are stored inside the various Library folders. The built-in Apple Quick Look plug-ins are always found in the /System/Library /QuickLook folder and sometimes appear in the /Library/QuickLook folder. Third-party plug-ins should always be installed in either /Library/QuickLook or the ~/Library /QuickLook folder, depending on who needs access to them.

Reference 17.2
Save Documents

Applications in macOS can take advantage of the built-in automatic document management framework. Applications using this system automatically save for the user, and they can also automatically maintain a history of versions of the user's documents.

In this section, you will learn how Auto Save and Versions work together. These two features work hand in hand with Locked and Resume to maintain the current state of users' work environment even if they log out or restart the Mac.

About Auto Save and Versions

For applications that support Auto Save, once the user saves the first time, no further dialogs appear asking if the application should save changes. In addition, if users want to use the document in another application or share it with other users, they don't have to remember to save the latest version of the document. From the user's point of view, the document seen in the Finder is always the same as the document seen in the application—the location where the document was first saved will always be the latest version.

In addition, applications that support Auto Save also support document versions. This provides an environment where the system automatically maintains a history of changes for any document. Users can easily return a document to a previous state with just a few clicks, or they can navigate to an earlier version of a document and quickly copy specific elements to the latest version of the document.

Users can access a document's version history using an interface very similar to the Time Machine Restore interface. However, from a technical perspective, the document version histories are saved in a hidden folder named .DocumentRevisions-V100 at the root of the disk containing the original document. Again, the most recent version of a document is always automatically saved to its original location and can be copied or shared with other applications or users immediately after a change is made.

Applications that support macOS Auto Save and Versions are easily identified by the content of the File menu in the application. Applications that support Auto Save can be most easily identified by their File > Duplicate menu option (instead of the traditional Save As menu option). Applications compatible with Auto Save also include File > Rename and File > Move To menu options. Updated applications still feature File > Save for saving a document the first time, but upon subsequent usage, the behavior of this menu option changes to saving a version of the document. Most Apple-designed applications, including TextEdit, Preview, Pages, Numbers, and Keynote, already support Auto Save and Versions.

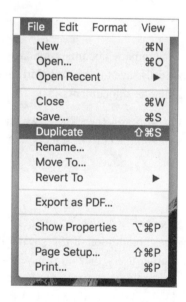

Automatically Save Document Changes

When you open an application that supports Auto Save for the first time, one of two things happens. If you are not signed in to iCloud, or the application does not support saving to iCloud, the application automatically opens a new document. If you are signed in to iCloud and the application supports saving documents to iCloud, you are prompted with an Open dialog. Saving documents to iCloud is covered in the next section of this lesson.

When you start a new document in an application that supports Auto Save, it's actually already saved even though you haven't yet set a location for it. In other words, changes you make to the new document are automatically saved, even if you have yet to explicitly save the document. This is because the document is saved to the Versions history database on the system volume.

TIP ▶ The Auto Save behavior can be disabled from General preferences, as covered later in this lesson.

By default, if you choose to close the document window or application, macOS prompts you to save the document. You can also manually choose File > Save or press the Command-S keyboard shortcut. The resulting Save dialog is similar to that in earlier versions of macOS, allowing you to choose a name and location for the document.

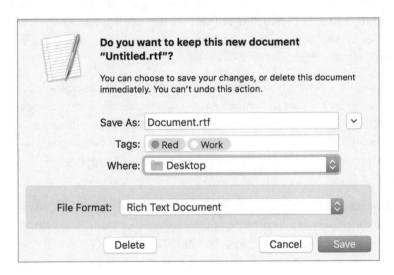

TIP ▶ You can expand a minimized Save dialog to show a full file-system browser by clicking the small arrow to the right of the filename.

Alternatively, you can save a document by clicking its name in the title bar. This reveals a popover dialog similar to the traditional Save dialog. One significant exception is the lack of Cancel and Save buttons. Again taking cues from iOS, entering a change here immediately saves once you click somewhere outside of the dialog. As you'll see throughout the remainder of this lesson, you can return to this popover dialog to save changes to the document as well. For example, renaming the document is as simple as entering a new name and then clicking elsewhere to dismiss the popover dialog.

TIP ▶ Holding the Command key and clicking the document's name in the title bar reveals its path in the file system.

After you have picked a location for the document, you'll never have to save it again. There are many instances that will trigger an auto save, including making a significant change to the document, closing the document window, closing the application, selecting the Finder, or attempting to access the document from another application. Applications also save during pauses in your work, and, if you work continuously, they will at the very least save your work every five minutes.

As you make changes to the document, you may see "Edited" in the document title bar. This is also a visual cue to let the user know the system is automatically saving changes. You can test this by making some changes to the document and then immediately using Quick Look to preview the document by selecting it in the Finder and pressing the Space bar. The Quick Look preview is identical to the open document in the application.

Save Duplicate Documents

If you need to save another copy of a document, you do so by using Duplicate. With the document open, choose File > Duplicate or press the Shift-Command-S keyboard combination. A new window appears with a copy of the document. The filename in the title bar is highlighted, indicating that you can change the name of the duplicate document.

TIP ▶ The Move To command in the File menu moves the original document to a new location without creating a new copy. Even though the document is moved, in most cases the version history is preserved.

The document itself is saved in the same folder as the original document. Again, because Auto Save is at work, you never have to manually save this document again. macOS always saves the changes for you.

If you or your users are more comfortable with the traditional Save As process, this is available as well. If you hold down the Option key, the File > Duplicate menu option changes to File > Save As. Alternatively, you can press the Option-Shift-Command-S keyboard shortcut.

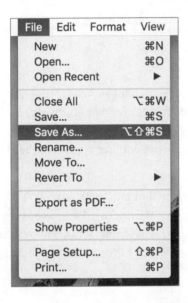

Selecting Save As will reveal a slightly modified Save dialog that gives you the option to also save the changes to the original document. This option is enabled by default, meaning that any changes made up to this point will also be saved to the original document. Disabling this option will cause Save As behavior similar to that in a legacy application that does not support Auto Save. In other words, disabling this feature will revert the original document to its previous state, before the user made any recent changes, and then save a new document with the latest changes.

Selecting the Save As command is effectively the same process as Duplicate, only it also presents the full Save dialog again, allowing you to choose a different filename and location, and then closes the original document. However, this close action is quite subtle—the new document replaces the original document in the active window without any obvious animation.

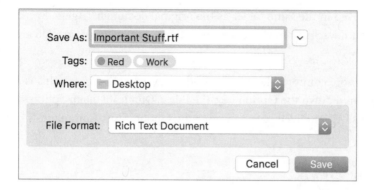

Explore Document Versions

With Versions, applications always maintain a history of your changes. Whenever an application is saved, automatically or manually, a new document version is also saved. If users, perhaps out of habit, attempt to manually save by choosing File > Save or by pressing Command-S, they are essentially telling the system to save another version of the document in the version history.

If you're editing a document and have yet to trigger a manual or automatic save, you can easily revert to the previously saved state by choosing File > Revert To > Last Saved or File > Revert To > Last Opened. If a deeper version history is available, macOS allows you to browse the entire history of a document. To open the version history browser, choose File > Revert To > Browse All Versions.

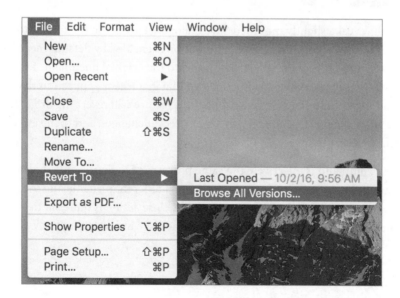

It's important to remember that a document's version history is not saved within the document itself. Instead, document current history is stored only on the volume where the original document is saved—specifically, in the .DocumentRevisions-V100 folder at the root of the volume. Thus, if you share the document by creating or sending a copy of the document, other users will not have access to the document's version history.

> **NOTE ▶** Version history is not always maintained on files being edited from a shared network volume. If you want to ensure that a version history is maintained, you must copy the shared file to a local disk.

If you've ever used Time Machine, the Versions browser interface will look pretty familiar. In fact, if you have Time Machine enabled, as covered in Lesson 15, "Manage Time Machine," an application's version history can go much deeper by showing you versions also saved in the Time Machine backup.

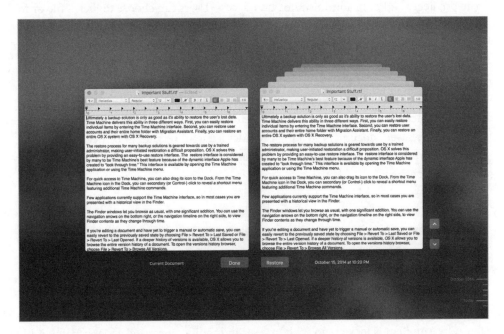

To the left you'll see the current version of the document, and to the right you can see previous versions. Navigate by either clicking a previous version's title bar or using the timeline to the right.

If you want to restore a previous version in its entirety, click Restore. However, if you just want a specific section of a previous version copied to the latest version, simply make a selection inside the previous document and then copy and paste to the current document.

When you are done making targeted edits, click Done to return to the standard application interface.

> **TIP** ▶ In the Versions browser, you can copy and paste using the Command-C and Command-V keyboard shortcuts or by secondary-clicking (or Control-clicking) to reveal a shortcut menu.

> **TIP** ▶ To delete a previous document version, in the Versions browser select the document name in the title bar to reveal a pop-up menu allowing you to choose Delete This Version.

About Locked Files

The Mac OS Extended file system includes a special file and folder attribute that trumps all write privileges and even administrator user access. Users can choose to lock a file or folder that they own from the Finder Info window or any application that supports Auto Save.

Locking an item renders it completely unchangeable by any user except the item's owner. Even administrator users are prevented from making changes to another user's locked file in the graphical interface.

Document locking may seem like an inconvenience, but in a system where changes are automatically saved, document locking provides a useful service. Specifically, locking a document prevents users—or, more appropriately, their applications—from accidentally auto-saving changes.

> **NOTE** ▶ Previous Mac systems automatically locked documents if they had not been edited after a certain amount of time. This feature confused a lot of users, and as a result it is no longer available in macOS.

Manage File Locking via Finder

The Finder and the Info or Inspector windows can be used to view and change a file's lock state. Once an item is locked, no other users can modify, move, delete, or rename it in the Finder.

> **MORE INFO** ▶ Using the Info window to inspect files and folders is detailed in Lesson 11, "Manage Permissions and Sharing."

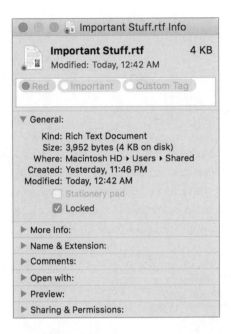

Once the file is locked, the Finder also prevents the owner from moving, renaming, or changing ownership and permissions for the locked item. In fact, if you as the owner try to move a locked item, the Finder defaults to making a copy. However, unlike other users, the owner can return the file to the normal state by disabling the locked attribute from the Info or Inspector window.

> **NOTE ▶** Duplicating a locked document in the Finder simply results in another locked copy of the document. In macOS, only applications that support Auto Save can create an unlocked duplicate of a locked file.

Manage File Locking via an Application

Applications that support Auto Save also provide easy access to document locking. As long as you are the owner of a document, which is often the case if you created the document or are editing a copy of the document, you can manually lock it to prevent further changes. To manually lock a document in an application that supports Auto Save, select the document's filename in the title bar to reveal a popover dialog allowing you to select the Locked checkbox.

Locked documents are clearly marked in the title bar with "Locked" and a small lock icon. As long as you are the owner of a document, you can deselect the Locked checkbox to enable changes. Alternatively, you can start modifying a locked document that you own. A dialog appears, allowing you to verify your intent to unlock and edit the document. Note the Duplicate button, a choice that encourages the user to make a copy for editing.

If you aren't the owner of a locked document, you aren't allowed to unlock it; thus, you aren't allowed to edit it. Also, as covered in Lesson 11, "Manage Permissions and Sharing," if you don't have write file permissions, you are not allowed to edit a document. In both cases the document's title bar displays "Locked."

However, you can treat a locked document as a template by duplicating the document and then editing the copy. Attempting to edit a locked, or otherwise unwritable, document reveals a prompt that allows the user only to duplicate the document.

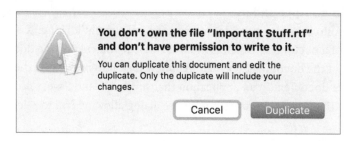

As covered previously, you can also manually duplicate a locked document by choosing File > Duplicate or File > Revert To > Browse All Versions. Again, once the application has duplicated a copy, you can then save the copy as you would a new document.

Reference 17.3
Manage Automatic Resume

A macOS feature ancillary to Auto Save is automatic application resumption. This feature allows supported applications to maintain their current state even if the user logs out or the application is quit. When an application quits, not only are any open documents automatically saved, but the state of the application is saved as well.

Upon application restart, everything returns to how it was when the user quit the application. This includes automatically saving and restoring documents and windows open in the application, the view and scrolling position of each window, and even the user's last selection.

NOTE ▶ Applications that support Resume can also be automatically quit by the system when it's determined that the system resources, specifically memory, are running low. The system quits only applications that are idle (not in active use).

Manage Resuming After Logout

Automatic resumption of applications and windows after logout is, by default, enabled in macOS. A user can, however, permanently prevent this behavior by deselecting the option when prompted to verify logout. This selection remains persistent through multiple user sessions and will change only when the user clicks the checkbox.

TIP ▶ If the resume after logout feature is turned off, you can temporarily enable it by holding down the Option key when you log out.

Manage Resuming After Quit

In the General preferences you'll find other options for automatic resumption. The default behavior for macOS is to close open documents and windows when quitting an application. An alternate option allows for the iOS-like behavior of automatically resuming documents and windows when opening an application. Deselect the "Close windows when quitting an app" checkbox to effectively enable automatic resume of an application's state when you quit it.

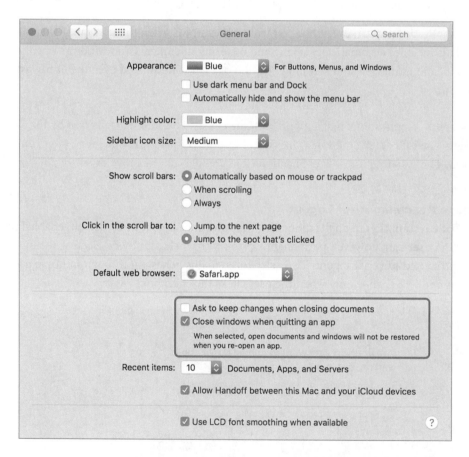

Disable Auto Save

Another option in the General preferences allows you to bring back the legacy macOS behavior of asking the user to save changes upon closing a document. For users who are more comfortable with how the legacy macOS save system behaved, selecting the "Ask to keep changes when closing documents" checkbox will disable the Auto Save feature for any application that supports it.

Many would argue that selecting this option defeats one of the primary advantages of Auto Save: less bother for the user. Further, this may also cause an inconvenient delay or cancellation of the logout process, since the system will have to wait for applications to quit.

> **NOTE ▶** Even if you disable the Auto Save feature, applications that support Auto Save will still retain the rest of their current document management behavior. For example, these applications will still offer a Duplicate menu option and will automatically maintain a version history whenever documents are manually saved.

Reference 17.4
Store Documents in iCloud

Auto Save and Versions were precursors to what was eventually to come: saving documents to iCloud. By allowing macOS applications to automatically open and save documents to iCloud, Apple has added the last fundamental bit of feature parity between iOS and macOS. Quite simply, saving your documents to iCloud is the easiest way to manage documents between multiple Apple devices. OS X Yosemite 10.10 and later include support for the iCloud Drive service, which gives you even greater flexibility when saving documents to iCloud. macOS Sierra takes iCloud integration even further by providing the option to automatically save the entire contents of your Desktop and Documents folders to iCloud Drive.

> **MORE INFO ▶** Although iCloud Drive is covered here in some detail, you can find out more about iCloud Drive from Apple Support article HT201104, "iCloud Drive FAQ."

Turn On iCloud Drive

To store files in iCloud on OS X Yosemite 10.10 and later, a user must be signed in to iCloud and have the iCloud Drive service enabled. Users who have created a new iCloud account with iOS 8 or OS X Yosemite or later will automatically have iCloud Drive enabled when they sign in to iCloud. However, existing iCloud accounts need to be upgraded to support iCloud Drive. When an existing iCloud account signs in to an iOS 8 or OS X Yosemite or later device, the user is asked to upgrade to iCloud Drive. This most often happens during the Setup Assistant process.

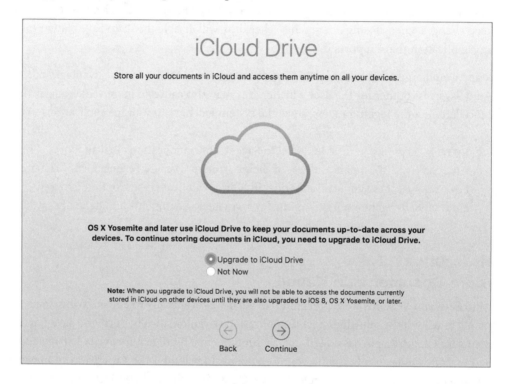

NOTE ▶ During the Setup Assistant process you may also be prompted to store your Desktop and Documents to iCloud Drive. This optional configuration is detailed later in this lesson.

In many ways, iCloud Drive is a better service than the previous iCloud document storage mechanism, so most users will want to upgrade their service. However, a user may want to delay this upgrade, because iCloud Drive is only compatible with iOS 8 or OS X Yosemite 10.10 or later, and the upgrade process to iCloud Drive is one-way. Unfortunately, iCloud document storage features will not be available to users on these systems until they choose to upgrade their iCloud account to include the iCloud Drive service.

TIP ▶ When working on Apple systems that haven't been upgraded (or on systems from other vendors), you can access iCloud Drive documents via most web browsers by signing in to www.icloud.com.

Users who have delayed the upgrade to iCloud Drive can initiate the upgrade in the iCloud preferences by selecting the iCloud Drive checkbox. This will prompt the user to verify the upgrade process. You can also verify that iCloud Drive was enabled from the iCloud preferences.

If iCloud Drive is turned on, clicking the Options button reveals an interface allowing you to configure application-specific iCloud Drive settings. Details regarding specific iCloud Drive options are covered later in this lesson.

Use iCloud Drive

Previous incarnations of iCloud document storage allowed the user to access items stored in iCloud only via specific compatible applications. Although this type of document management is ideal for the app-specific nature of iOS, it was often confusing and limiting on macOS. Not only does macOS have a long history of flexible document management via the Finder, but it's also an operating system designed for multitasking.

iCloud Drive brings iCloud document management in line with traditional macOS behavior. The "Drive" in iCloud Drive is not a misnomer, since iCloud storage will appear as if it were a normally connected disk. All Finder document management features work as expected on iCloud Drive content: move, copy, rename, folder creation, and so forth.

> **NOTE ▶** iCloud Drive copy status is indicated by a "pie chart" indicator immediately to the right of iCloud Drive in the Finder's sidebar. If there is no pie chart icon, all items are fully stored in iCloud.

TIP ▶ By default, iCloud Drive appears in the Finder's sidebar, but it can also be accessed from the Finder's Go menu or by using the Command-Shift-I keyboard shortcut.

iCloud Drive also appears in Open and Save dialogs for any application. In other words, with iCloud Drive, applications do not have to be specifically designed to support iCloud document storage.

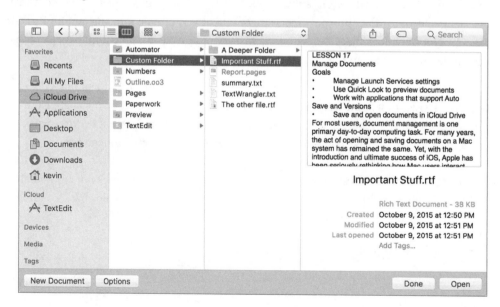

Again, just as with a normal disk, with iCloud Drive you can create custom folder hierarchies and save documents inside any folder you choose. You may notice that iCloud Drive is automatically populated with application-specific folders. These folders are created by the applications to facilitate iOS-style document management.

TIP ▶ In the previous screenshot you'll notice "TextEdit" in the sidebar just below "iCloud" and also a TextEdit folder in iCloud Drive. These two locations are the same; the sidebar location is simply a shortcut to the TextEdit-specific folder in iCloud Drive.

It's important to remember that even though you are allowed to create custom folders for documents, not all iOS apps will recognize documents located outside their specific folders. In other words, custom folders at the root of iCloud Drive cannot be seen by some iOS apps. However, most updated iOS apps that are iCloud Drive compatible can open documents from anywhere within your iCloud Drive. Also, you can create custom folders inside each application-specific folder to organize your documents.

TIP ▶ Custom folders and documents saved to iCloud Drive can be accessed via the iCloud website, www.icloud.com, and on iOS via the iCloud Drive app. Further, items in iCloud Drive can be easily shared with others, which allows for collaborative document editing.

Store Desktop and Documents in iCloud Drive

macOS Sierra introduces the ability to automatically save all the content in your Desktop and Documents folders to iCloud Drive. Similar to enabling iCloud Drive for the first time, the macOS Sierra Setup Assistant will ask if you would like to store files from Documents and Desktop in iCloud Drive. However, unlike upgrading to iCloud Drive, choosing to save your Desktop and Documents folders to iCloud is reversible should you decide to turn off this feature, as covered later in this lesson.

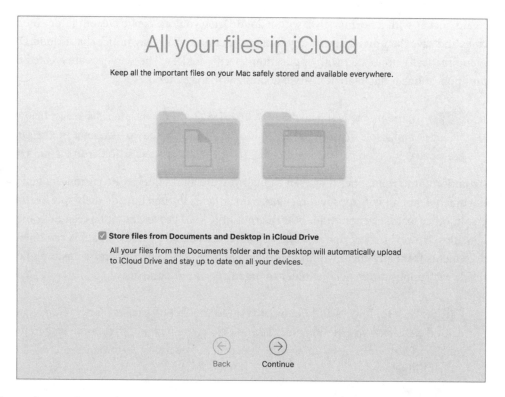

If you choose, during the Setup Assistant process, not to store Desktop and Documents in iCloud Drive, you can enable this feature at any time from the iCloud Drive options in iCloud preferences.

When you turn on Desktop & Documents Folders in the iCloud preferences for the first time per iCloud account, the Desktop and Documents folders from your home folder on that Mac will be moved in their entirety to iCloud Drive.

Even after the move to iCloud, the Finder experience will mostly remain the same as before: items in your Desktop folder will appear both in the Finder and on the desktop background. Accessing your Desktop and Documents folders from the Finder's Go menu and keyboard shortcuts, Command-Shift-D and Command-Shift O, work as before. In fact, the only difference is that Desktop and Documents now appear in the Finder's sidebar under iCloud.

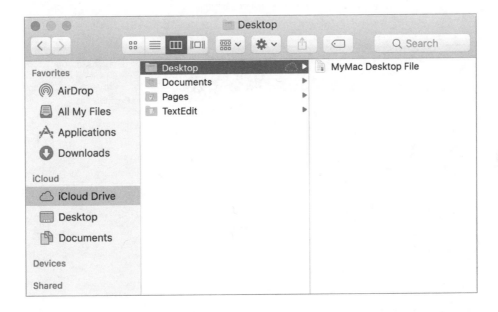

NOTE ▶ With Desktop and Documents folders in iCloud Drive, the Finder will not show these items in your home folder. Interestingly, when using the command line via Terminal the Desktop and Documents folders appear in their normal path location at the root of your home folder.

You'll notice in the previous screenshot that your Desktop and Documents folders appear both in the Finder's sidebar and inside iCloud Drive. You'll also notice that any previous folders and files in iCloud Drive remain in their normal locations.

An iCloud account can have only one set of Desktop and Documents folders in iCloud Drive. Thus, the first Mac where you enable Desktop & Documents Folders in iCloud preferences will define the base contents in iCloud Drive, and content from additional Mac computers will be represented by newly created subfolders. For example, if you enable Desktop & Documents Folders in iCloud preferences on a second Mac, the items inside Desktop and Documents from that Mac will be moved into a subfolder bearing the computer's name.

NOTE ▶ Make sure the initial upload to iCloud Drive of the items from the previous Mac is fully complete before you enable Desktop & Documents Folders in iCloud Drive on another Mac (as indicated by the lack of the pie chart status icon to the right of iCloud Drive in the Finder's sidebar). This will ensure that all the items are available to all the Mac computers with iCloud Drive.

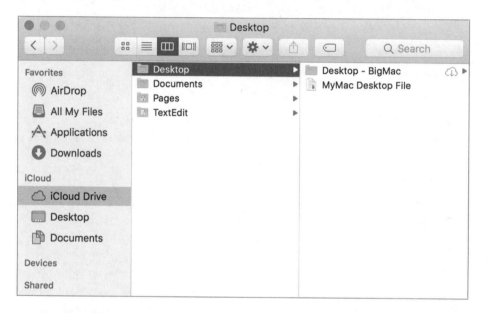

As you can see in the previous screenshot, another Mac named "BigMac" was added as a second computer with Desktop & Documents Folders in iCloud preferences enabled for the account. This move was necessary so that the items already in the Desktop and Documents folders in iCloud Drive could replace the local Desktop and Documents folders on BigMac. Now the content from the Desktop and Documents folders on the original Mac and on BigMac are available on both computers.

After setting up additional Mac computers, if you desire to have a "singular" Desktop and Documents folder experience, you must move the items out of the computer-named subfolders to the base folders. Remember that with iCloud Drive, changes made on one Mac will automatically apply to other Mac computers with the same iCloud account. Thus, reorganization of your Desktop and Documents folders on one Mac will automatically apply to your configured Mac computers. Eventually, if you move all items out of the computer-named subfolders, these folders can be deleted, leaving you with all the content in one set of Desktop and Documents folders available to all your Mac computers via iCloud Drive.

Remove Items from iCloud Drive

To remove something from iCloud Drive, move it out of an iCloud Drive folder to either the Trash or any other local file on your Mac. Importantly, this act will also remove the item from all other devices using iCloud Drive. In other words, moving something from iCloud Drive to a local folder on your Mac will remove the item from both iCloud and any other Apple device configured for iCloud Drive.

Because iCloud Drive items appear right alongside locally stored items on your Mac, it can be easy for you to accidentally remove an item from iCloud Drive. As such, a default behavior of macOS is to warn you any time you are moving something out of iCloud Drive.

This dialog can be disabled from the Advanced tab of the Finder preferences, but it's probably not a good idea for most users. After all, dismissing an occasional reminder is much better than finding out the hard way that you accidentally removed an important document from all your Apple devices.

About iCloud Drive Local Storage

With the exception of the Desktop and Documents folders, all items saved in iCloud Drive are maintained locally in each user's ~/Library/Mobile Documents/ folder. If Desktop and Documents storage in iCloud Drive is enabled, those items are maintained locally in their normal locations, ~/Desktop and ~/Documents. Although you can see the Mobile Documents folder in the Finder, double-clicking this folder will automatically redirect you to the root iCloud Drive view in the Finder.

However, if you were to navigate to the Mobile Documents folder via Terminal, you would indeed be able to view and manipulate the folder's contents. If Desktop & Documents Folders in iCloud preferences is enabled, you'll also find symbolic links for these folders in the ~/Library/Mobile Documents/com~apple~CloudDocs folder that point back to the normal location for these items inside your home folder.

Avoid modifying content with unclear names in the Mobile Documents folder. Application-specific folders, custom user folders, and all documents are clearly visible via Terminal navigation. Also, any changes to the contents of the Mobile Documents folder are automatically saved to iCloud Drive as you make them.

Speaking of making changes to iCloud Drive, the transfer process is highly sophisticated and efficient. In the worst case, a user should notice only a few moments' delay before the changes are reflected to all devices configured for iCloud Drive. This is because, if multiple devices on the same network share an iCloud account, they transfer the data locally to improve performance. Also, if you make changes to iCloud Drive while offline, macOS caches the changes and then silently pushes them the very next moment an Internet connection to the iCloud servers becomes available.

About iCloud Drive Optimized Storage

In an effort to optimize local storage, iCloud Drive in macOS Sierra keeps older files and infrequently used files only in iCloud Drive. Items in iCloud Drive that have not yet been downloaded locally to a Mac will appear with an iCloud download icon.

Attempting to access items that have not yet downloaded will automatically download the items to the local Mac. This may take a few moments if the items are large or your Internet access is slower. If you want to prevent iCloud Drive from trying to optimize storage, you can force it to always save items locally as well. This can be configured by deselecting the Optimize Mac Storage checkbox at the bottom of the iCloud Drive options dialog found in the iCloud preferences.

MORE INFO ► The last part of this lesson has more information regarding all the new storage optimization features of macOS Sierra.

Turn Off iCloud Drive Features

The default behavior when iCloud Drive is enabled for macOS Sierra is that compatible applications are allowed to save to iCloud. From the iCloud Drive options dialog of the iCloud preferences, you can selectively hide iCloud Drive from individual applications.

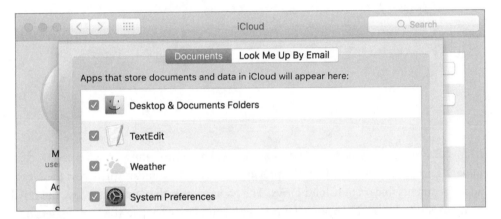

In this dialog, deselecting a checkbox next to an application will hide documents and data from that application. Hiding doesn't delete any existing data in iCloud; it prevents the application from accessing iCloud Drive and hides the associated folder from the Finder.

TIP ► In the Look Me Up By Email tab of the iCloud Drive options, you can also prevent applications from allowing other users to find your information for iCloud document sharing.

Also in the iCloud Drive options dialog, you can choose to turn off Desktop & Documents Folders by deselecting the adjacent checkbox. Doing so will not remove any items from iCloud Drive or from any other Apple devices. Instead, doing so will revert the iCloud Drive configuration for the Mac back to using local-only Desktop and Documents folders.

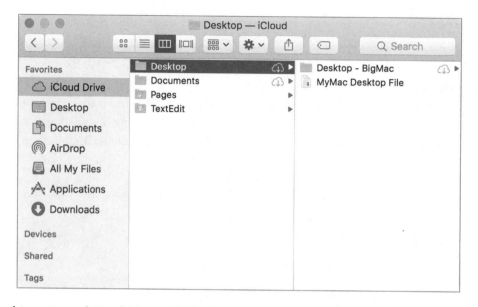

In this case your home folder on the local Mac will have new empty Desktop and Documents folders. Further, as you can see in the previous screenshot, you can still access the Desktop and Documents folders in iCloud Drive. The good news is that nothing is lost, but it will be up to you to move or copy any items from iCloud Drive back to the local folders on your Mac. Just remember, moving something from iCloud Drive to another folder on your local Mac will remove that item from iCloud Drive and all configured Apple devices.

Finally, if you decide to completely turn off all iCloud Drive features you can do so by deselecting the iCloud Drive checkbox in the iCloud preferences. Turning off iCloud Drive completely will present you with two options.

Again, neither option here will remove any items from iCloud Drive or remove any items other Apple devices configured for it. Instead, selecting the Remove From Mac button will remove all iCloud Drive items from the local Mac. On the other hand, selecting the "Keep a Copy" button will create an iCloud Drive (Archive) folder in your home folder on the local Mac. This local archive folder will contain copies of all the items currently in your iCloud Drive.

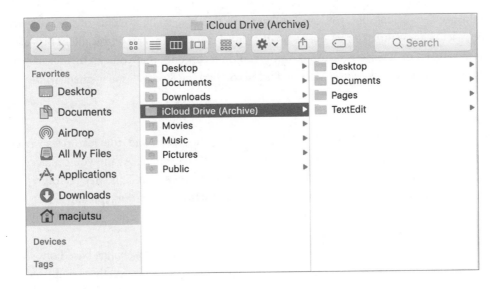

Reference 17.5
Optimize Local Storage

The previous section showed how you can store your documents in iCloud Drive and, as a default in macOS Sierra, perhaps even save storage space on your Mac by only keeping the most used files on local storage. This is one of many storage optimization features new in macOS Sierra that can help you regain local storage space on your Mac.

Inspect Local Storage

You can get an idea of how storage is currently being used on your Mac from the Storage pane of the About This Mac dialog. Again, you can access About This Mac from the Apple menu.

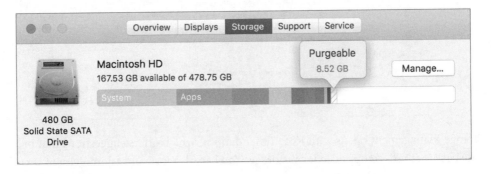

In the previous screenshot, you can see that while this Mac still has plenty of storage space left, macOS has estimated that over 8.5 GB of local storage items are Purgeable. This calculation is based on a variety of storage optimization techniques that you can further inspect and implement by clicking the Manage button to open the Storage Management window.

About Storage Management

In macOS Sierra, System Information is significantly upgraded and now features a variety of storage optimization features available in Storage Management. Again, you can access this window by clicking Manage in the Storage pane of the About This Mac dialog. Alternatively, you can open /Application/Utilities/System Information.app and select Window > Storage Management from the menus.

> NOTE ▸ The Storage Management interface will dynamically change based on what features you have enabled in macOS. As such, it may not look exactly as it appears in this guide.

Storage Management opens with Recommendations, which offers suggestions that provide easy methods to optimize local storage. You can also inspect and implement specific space-saving optimizations by selecting items from the list on the right of the Storage Management pane.

From Recommendations you can optimize storage by:

▶ Clicking "Store in iCloud" brings up a dialog allowing you to turn on iCloud Desktop and Documents in iCloud Drive and iCloud Photo Library. Both of these selections can save considerable local space by relegating infrequently used items to iCloud storage only. Initially this may not save much space locally, but over time it could save a considerable amount of space. These settings can also be reached from iCloud and Photos preferences.

▶ Clicking Optimize Storage reveals a dialog allowing you to turn on the automatic removal of watched movies and TV shows in iTunes and minimize the number of downloaded email attachments. These settings can also be reached from iTunes and Mail preferences.

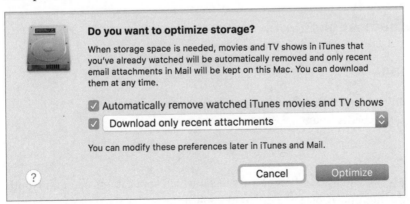

▶ Clicking the Turn On button will enable the option for the Finder to automatically empty local items from the Trash if they have been there for more than 30 days.

▶ Clicking Review Files brings you to the Documents view of the Storage Management window. From here you can easily view your largest and least used documents on the local Mac. You can easily delete items you no longer need by clicking the small "x" button that's revealed when you hover the mouse over an item in the Documents list.

TIP ▶ The Documents list in Storage Manager features similar organizational features as the Finder. Specifically, you can change the sort by clicking the column titles and you can select multiple items by using Command-click or Shift-click.

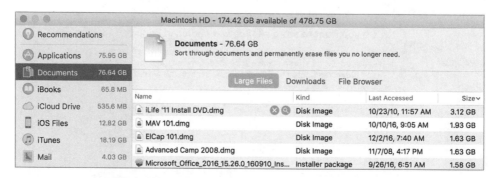

▶ Selecting a storage category in the far-left column of Storage Manager enables you to inspect, and potentially remove, large files that you may not need. For example, every iOS device you sync to your Mac using iTunes creates backup and app update files that can consume a significant portion of the system volume.

Exercise 17.1
Use Alternate Applications

▶ **Prerequisite**

  ▶ You must have created the Chris Johnson account (Exercise 5.1, "Create a Standard User Account").

In this exercise, you will learn different ways to set which applications open files, both when making a one-time choice of a different application and when permanently changing the default application for a particular file type. You will also use the macOS Quick

Look feature, which lets you see the contents of common file types without opening an application.

View a File with Quick Look

1   If necessary, log in as Chris Johnson.

2   In the Finder, open the StudentMaterials/Lesson17 folder.

3   Copy the file Pet Sitter Notes to your desktop.

    The file has no visible extension, although the icon may indicate its file type.

4   Select (single-click) the Pet Sitter Notes document on your desktop.

5   Choose File menu > Quick Look "Pet Sitter Notes" (or press Command-Y).

    Quick Look displays a preview of the document. Note that you could click the button near the top right to open the document in TextEdit (currently the default application for this type of document).

    TIP You can also use Quick Look to view a document by selecting it in the Finder and pressing the Space bar. However, if you have the filename selected rather than the file itself, pressing the Space bar will begin to edit the filename. If you do this by mistake, you can delete the filename and press Return; since the filename cannot be blank, the Finder displays an error and restores the original filename. Alternatively, you can use the Finder's undo capability to restore the file's name.

    TIP Yet another way to use Quick Look is to Control-click the document and choose Quick Look "filename" from the shortcut menu.

6   Press Command-Y to close the Quick Look window.

Choose an Application to Open a File Once

1   Double-click Pet Sitter Notes on your desktop.

    The file opens in TextEdit. Note that TextEdit does not display the document's headings or background image.

2   On your desktop, Control-click the file.

3   In the shortcut menu, mouse over the Open With choice.

A submenu opens showing the applications available that can open this type of document.

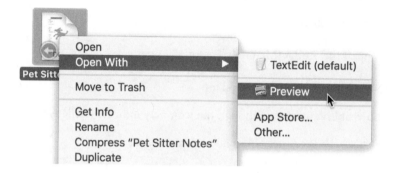

4   In the Open With submenu, choose Preview.

The file opens in Preview.

Note that editing the same file in two different applications at the same time can lead to unpredictable results. In this case you are only viewing the file, so it is not a problem.

5   Compare how the file is displayed in TextEdit and in Preview.

Preview gives a richer view of the file, showing a background image and headings that TextEdit does not show. On the other hand, TextEdit lets you edit its content, whereas Preview does not. Depending on what you want to do with the document, you might prefer either one.

6   Close the document in both applications.

7   Double-click the document again.

It opens in TextEdit because the Open With choice you made earlier was not a permanent setting.

8   Close the document.

Permanently Change the Default Application for a File Type

1   In the Finder, select the Pet Sitter Notes document.

2   Choose File menu > Get Info (Command-I).

3   If necessary, expand the General and Name & Extension sections of the Info window.

This is a Word 97 document, and it has a file extension of .doc, which is hidden.

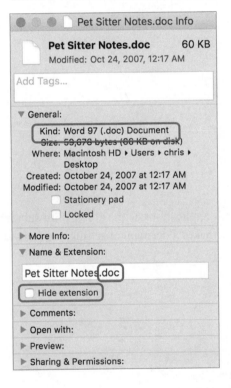

4   Deselect "Hide extension." The extension will now be visible in the view of your desktop in the Finder.

5   Expand the "Open with" section of the Info window, and then choose Preview from its pop-up menu.

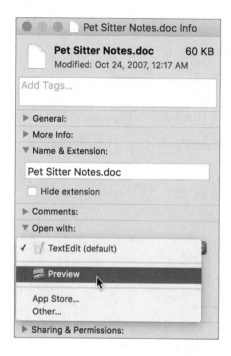

Note that this menu shows the same possible applications as the Open With submenu in the Finder. Choosing an application here makes a permanent setting, but only for this specific file.

6   Click Change All.

7   In the confirmation dialog, click Continue.

You have now changed the default application for opening documents with the extension .doc in Chris Johnson's account. This setting is permanent (until you change it to something else).

8 Close the Info window.

9 Double-click the document on your desktop.

It opens in Preview.

10 Quit Preview.

11 Move Pet Sitter Notes.doc from your desktop to the Trash.

12 In the Finder, reopen the StudentMaterials/Lesson17 folder, and examine the original Pet Sitter Notes document there.

Note that its filename extension is not shown. When you used Get Info to show the extension of the copy on your desktop, it affected only that specific file.

13 Double-click the original Pet Sitter Notes.

It opens in Preview because you used Change All in the Info window to apply the setting to all Word 97 documents.

14 Quit Preview.

Exercise 17.2
Use Auto Save and Versions

▶ **Prerequisite**

▶ You must have created the Chris Johnson account (Exercise 5.1, "Create a Standard User Account").

Many support issues derive from users losing work either because they did not save changes to a document or because they did save after making unfortunate changes. In applications that support it, macOS provides the capability to periodically save changes automatically and to keep multiple previous versions of a document. This means users don't have to worry about whether they should—or shouldn't—save the documents they're working on.

In this exercise, you will edit a file in TextEdit, save several versions, and roll back to an earlier version.

Experiment with Auto Save

1   If necessary, log in as Chris Johnson.

2   Open System Preferences, and select the General pane.

3   Ensure that "Ask to keep changes when closing documents" is not selected and that "Close windows when quitting an app" is selected.

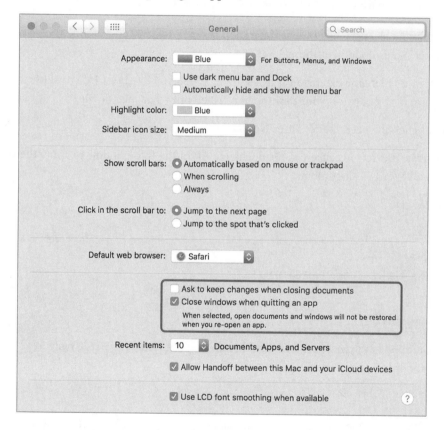

These are the default settings in macOS Sierra. Selecting "Ask to keep changes when closing documents" would turn off the Auto Save feature you are about to test. Deselecting "Close windows when quitting an app" would make apps remember open documents and windows when you quit and reopen the application.

4   Quit System Preferences.

5   If necessary, navigate to StudentMaterials/Lesson17.

6   Copy Pretendco Report.rtfd to your desktop, and open the copy.

7   Add some text to the file.

Notice that the window's title bar now indicates its status as Edited.

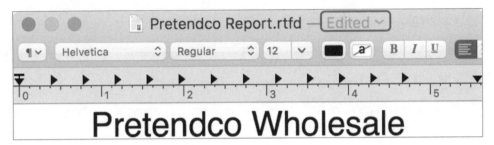

8   Switch to the Finder, select your copy of the Pretendco Report file, and choose File menu > Get Info (Command-I).

Notice that it has been modified within the last minute or so (your edits were saved automatically).

9   Close the Info window.

10 Switch to TextEdit, and add some more text to the file.

11 Select the file in the Finder, and choose File menu > Quick Look "Pretendco Report.rtfd" (Command-Y).

The Quick Look view shows all the text you added to the file.

12 Close the Quick Look window.

Work with Multiple Versions

1   Switch to TextEdit, and choose File menu > Save (or press Command-S).

This looks like a "normal" save command, but what it actually does is save a restorable version of the file.

Although TextEdit saves changes to the live document frequently, it saves a restorable version only when explicitly told to.

2   Delete the graphic from the document.

3   Quit TextEdit.

Notice that you are not prompted to save changes; they were saved automatically.

4   Reopen the Pretendco Report file.

5   Choose File menu > Revert To > Previous Save.

The graphic is restored.

6   Add more text to the document, and choose File menu > Save (Command-S) again.

7   Add still more text, and examine the File > Revert To submenu.

It now lists options to restore to the last-saved version, to restore to the last-opened version, or to browse all versions.

8   Choose File menu > Revert To > Browse All Versions.

TextEdit displays a full-screen version browser, showing the current document state on the left and saved versions on the right. This view is similar to the Time Machine restore interface and actually shows versions from the Time Machine backups as well as restorable versions created by the application.

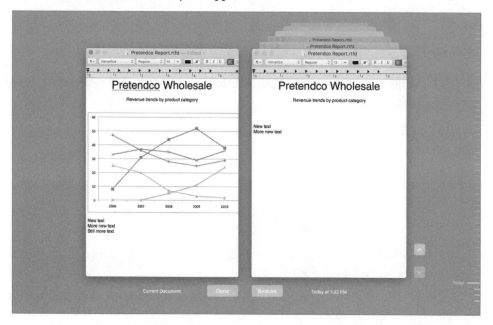

9   Experiment with the two windows. Note that you can switch between saved versions by clicking their title bars in the stack, by clicking the arrows to the right of the stack, or by using the timeline on the right side of the screen. You can also use editing controls, including copying and pasting content from old versions into the current document.

10   Click Done to exit the history browser.

11   Quit TextEdit.

Exercise 17.3
Manage Document Locking

▶ **Prerequisite**

   ▶   You must have created the Local Admin (Exercise 2.1, "Configure a New macOS System for Exercises," or Exercise 2.2, "Configure an Existing macOS System for Exercises") and Chris Johnson (Exercise 5.1, "Create a Standard User Account") accounts.

In this exercise, you will explore options for locking documents to prevent accidental changes.

Lock and Unlock a Document

1   If necessary, log in as Chris Johnson.

2   If you have not performed Exercise 17.2, "Use Auto Save and Versions," copy StudentMaterials/Lesson17/Pretendco Report.rtfd to your desktop.

3   Select your copy of the Pretendco Report document, and choose File menu > Get Info (Command-I).

4   In the General section of the Info window, select the Locked checkbox.

Notice that the document's icon now has a small padlock in its corner.

5 Close the Info window.

6 Open the document.

Notice that the window's title bar now indicates its status as Locked.

7 Attempt to add some text to the document.

A dialog appears telling you the file is locked and gives options for how to deal with the locked file.

8 Click Unlock.

The padlock vanishes from the document's icon on your desktop.

9 Add some text to the document.

10 Click the document name in the title bar, and then select the Locked checkbox.

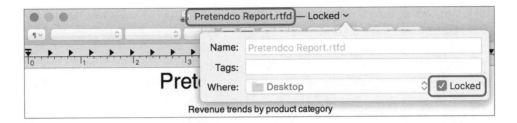

The padlock reappears on the document's icon on your desktop.

Since you are the owner of the document, you can lock and unlock it freely, in either the Finder or an editor that supports Auto Save.

11 Quit TextEdit.

Exercise 17.4
Store Documents in iCloud

> **Prerequisites**
>
> ► You must have created the Chris Johnson (Exercise 5.1, "Create a Standard User Account") and Mayta Mishtuk (Exercise 6.1, "Restore a Deleted User Account") accounts.

macOS allows applications to save documents to the Internet by way of iCloud Drive and then access them from any computer tied to the same iCloud account.

Enable iCloud Features

1 If necessary, log in as Chris Johnson.

2 Open System Preferences, and select the iCloud pane.

If you are already signed in to iCloud, skip to the next section, "Configure iCloud Drive."

3   If you are not already signed in to use iCloud, enter your iCloud Apple ID and password, and then click Sign In.

Note that if you do not already have an Apple ID, you can create one here; however, the ID creation process is not covered in this exercise.

4   If you are prompted to accept the iCloud terms and conditions, read through the new terms. If they are acceptable to you, agree to the terms and click Continue; otherwise, click Cancel and skip this exercise.

5   If the Apple ID is protected by two-step verification or two-factor authentication, follow the prompts to complete the authentication process.

6   If you are prompted to set up two-factor authentication, click Not Now, and then click Don't Upgrade in the confirmation dialog.

7   When you are prompted for which features to set up, leave "Use iCloud for Mail, Contacts, Calendars, Reminders, Notes, and Safari" selected, deselect Use Find My Mac, and then click Next.

If a dialog appears asking if you want to upgrade to iCloud Drive, this indicates that your iCloud account is being used to store documents in an older format and must be upgraded to use iCloud Drive.

WARNING ▶ If you still use this iCloud account from a Mac running OS X Mavericks 10.9 or earlier or an iPhone or iPad running iOS 7 or earlier, upgrading to iCloud Drive will make the documents currently stored in iCloud inaccessible to those devices until they are upgraded to at least OS X Yosemite 10.10/iOS 8. See **Reference 17.4, "Store Documents in iCloud,"** for details.

NOTE ▶ If you do not want to upgrade at this time, click Cancel, quit System Preferences, and skip the rest of this exercise.

8   If you are sure you want to upgrade the iCloud account to iCloud Drive, click Continue in the confirmation dialog.

9   If a dialog appears recommending requiring a password to unlock your screen, click Not Now.

10   If a dialog appears asking for your Apple ID password to set up iCloud Keychain, click Cancel.

Enter your Apple ID password to set up iCloud Keychain.
Enter the Apple ID password for "suppessentialsacct@me.com".

Password: `Required`   Forgot Password?

Cancel   OK

11   Skip to step 6 of the next section.

Configure iCloud Drive

1   If iCloud preferences requires you to enter your password, click Enter Password and authenticate to iCloud.

2   If necessary, select Contacts.

3   Verify that iCloud Drive is selected. If it is, skip to step 6.

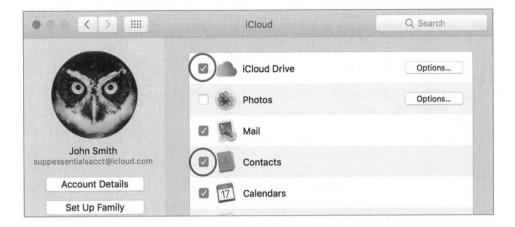

If iCloud Drive is not selected, this normally indicates you are using an iCloud account that was set up by an older version of macOS or iOS and does not yet support iCloud Drive.

4   If you want to upgrade to iCloud Drive, select the checkbox iCloud Drive.

WARNING ▸ If you still use this iCloud account from a Mac running OS X Mavericks 10.9 or earlier or an iPhone or iPad running iOS 7 or earlier, upgrading to iCloud Drive will make the documents currently stored in iCloud inaccessible to those devices until they are upgraded to at least OS X Yosemite 10.10/iOS 8. See **Reference 17.4, "Store Documents in iCloud,"** for details.

NOTE ▸ If you do not want to upgrade at this time, click Cancel, quit System Preferences, and skip the rest of this exercise.

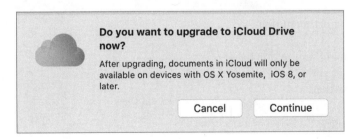

5   If you are sure you want to upgrade the iCloud account to iCloud Drive, click Continue in the confirmation dialog.

6   Click the Options button to the right of iCloud Drive.

The iCloud Drive options dialog lets you control which applications have access to your iCloud documents and your email address.

7   In the Documents tab, make sure TextEdit is selected.

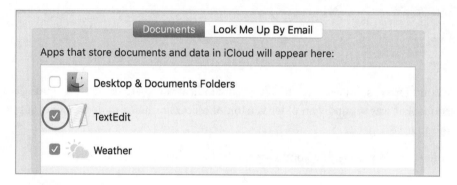

8   Click Done.

9   Quit System Preferences.

Save a Document to iCloud

1   If you have not performed Exercise 17.2, "Use Auto Save and Versions," copy StudentMaterials/Lesson17/Pretendco Report.rtfd to your desktop.

2   Open the Pretendco Report document.

3   Click the document's name in the title bar.

4   If necessary, deselect Locked.

5   From the Where pop-up menu, choose iCloud Drive.

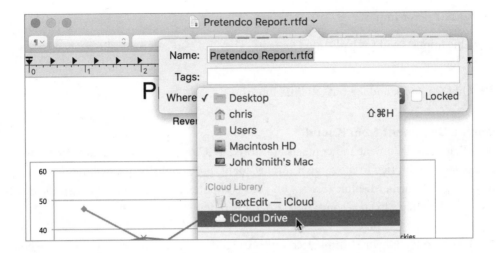

6   If a dialog appears indicating that an item with the same name (Pretendco Report.rtf) already exists in the same folder, a previous student may have left this item in the iCloud account. Click Replace to replace the old copy with yours.

The document's icon vanishes from your desktop.

7   Quit TextEdit.

8   In the Finder, navigate to StudentMaterials/Lesson17.

9   Open the file vCards.vcf.

The Contacts application opens, and a dialog appears to confirm that you want to add the contacts.

If the dialog indicates that some cards are duplicates, this may be because a previous student left them in the iCloud account you are using.

10 Click Add or Import.

This imports eight vCards into Contacts. They are also automatically pushed to the iCloud servers.

11 Quit Contacts, and log out as Chris Johnson.

Open a Document from iCloud

Now that your document and contacts are stored in iCloud, they are available from any computer account tied to the same iCloud account. For simplicity, you will demonstrate this using the Mayta Mishtuk account on your computer, but iCloud could push the documents and contacts to an account on a different computer just as well.

1 Log in to the Mayta Mishtuk account (password: mayta, or whatever you chose when you created the account).

2 Open System Preferences, and select the iCloud pane.

3 If iCloud is not set up in Mayta's account, enter the iCloud Apple ID and password you used with the Chris Johnson account, and click Sign In.

4 If the Apple ID is protected by two-step verification or two-factor authentication, follow the prompts to complete the authentication process.

5 If you are prompted to set up two-factor authentication, click Not Now, and then click Don't Upgrade in the confirmation dialog.

6   When you are prompted for which features to set up, leave "Use iCloud for Mail, Contacts, Calendars, Reminders, Notes, and Safari" selected, deselect Use Find My Mac, and then click Next.

7   If a dialog appears recommending requiring a password to unlock your screen, click Not Now.

8   If a dialog appears asking for your Apple ID password to set up iCloud Keychain, click Cancel.

9   Make sure that iCloud Drive and Contacts are selected.

10 Quit System Preferences.

11 In the Finder, choose Go menu > iCloud Drive (Command-Shift-I).

If Pretendco Report has not downloaded to Mayta's account yet, it will have a cloud icon indicating that it is available from iCloud.

Pretendco
Report.rtfd

12 Double-click Pretendco Report.

The document downloads (if necessary), and opens in TextEdit.

13 Add some text to the document.

Your edits are automatically saved to the iCloud servers and are available to any other computers using this iCloud account.

14 Quit TextEdit.

15 In the Finder, choose Go menu > All My Files (Command-Shift-F).

Pretendco Report is listed; the All My Files view shows both local documents and those in iCloud Drive.

16 In the search field, enter pretendco.

Pretendco Report is shown in the results, even though it is stored in iCloud Drive.

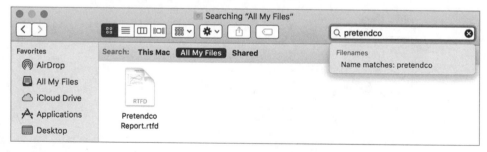

Use Contacts from iCloud

1   Open the Contacts application.

    The contacts from the Chris Johnson account appear.

2   Quit Contacts, and log out as Mayta Mishtuk.

Verify Your Changes as Chris Johnson

1   Log back in as Chris Johnson.

2   In the Finder, choose Go menu > iCloud Drive (Command-Shift-I).

3   Open Pretendco Report.

4   Verify that the edit you made as Mayta appears. Note that you may have to wait a few moments for the document to update.

5   Quit TextEdit.

Lesson 18

Manage and Troubleshoot Applications

For many macOS support professionals, their most common day-to-day task is troubleshooting application issues. The successful resolution of an application issue most often depends on previous experience with the application. Specific application issues, however, are beyond the scope of this guide.

At the same time, support professionals dealing with new applications or new issues must rely on their ability to effectively gather relevant information and their knowledge of general system technologies. This lesson primarily addresses these two application troubleshooting aspects. So that you have a better understanding of the pieces in play, this lesson first defines key elements of the macOS process architecture. You will then learn to gather information about applications and processes. The remainder of this lesson covers a variety of general troubleshooting techniques that can be used for any type of application.

GOALS

▶ Understand and support the various application types

▶ Manage application extensions and widgets in Notification Center

▶ Monitor and control processes and applications

▶ Explore various application troubleshooting techniques

Reference 18.1
About Applications and Processes

A process is any instance of executable code that is currently activated and addressed in system memory. In other words, a process is anything that is currently "running" or "open." macOS handles processes very efficiently, so even when a process is idle, and probably consuming no processor resources, it's still considered active, because it has dedicated address space in system memory. The four general process types are applications, commands, daemons, and agents.

About macOS Process Types

Applications are a specific category of process that is generally identified as something the user opened in the graphical interface. Commands are also normally opened by the user but are only available at the command-line interface. The key similarity between most applications and commands is that they are running in the user's space. In other words, most applications and commands are started, stopped, and limited to accessing resources available only to the user.

Processes that run on behalf of the system fall into another category, daemons, also referred to as background processes because they rarely have any user interface. Daemons usually launch during system startup and remain active the entire time the Mac is up and running; consequently, most daemons run with root or systemwide access to all resources. These background daemons are responsible for most of the automatic system features, such as detecting network changes and maintaining the Spotlight search metadata index.

Agents are technically also daemons, or background processes. The primary difference is that agents run only when a user is logged in to the system. Agents are always started automatically for the user by the system. Although applications and commands can also be opened automatically, they are not controlled by the system the way agents are. Most important, all of these process types are considered part of the user's space because they are executed with the same access privileges the user has.

About macOS Memory Management

macOS is a desirable platform for running applications and other processes because it combines a rock-solid UNIX foundation with an advanced graphical user interface. Users will most likely recognize the interface elements right away, but it's the underlying foundation that keeps things running so smoothly.

The primary feature in macOS that keeps processes secure is protected memory. Similarly to how the file system prevents users from meddling with items they shouldn't, processes are also kept separate and secure in system memory. The system manages all memory allocation so that processes are not allowed to interfere with each other's system memory space. In other words, an ill-behaved or crashed application does not normally affect any other process on the system.

macOS also automatically manages system memory for processes at their request. Although real system memory is clearly limited by hardware, the system dynamically allocates both real and virtual memory when needed. Thus, the only memory limitations in macOS are the size of installed RAM and the amount of free space you have available on your system volume.

Further, macOS includes software-based memory compression that both increases performance and reduces energy usage. Instead of the wasteful practice of swapping memory out to disk when too many processes are active, the system first compresses the content used by less active processes to free up space for more active processes. This greatly reduces traffic between active memory and the virtual memory swap files on the system disk.

64-Bit versus 32-Bit Mode

macOS supports both 32-bit and 64-bit modes simultaneously. A process running in 64-bit mode has the ability to individually access more than 4 GB of system memory, can perform higher-precision computational functions much faster, and can take advantage of Intel's updated x86-64 architecture for improved performance and security. All Mac computers compatible with macOS Sierra feature 64-bit-capable processors and can take advantage of 64-bit system features.

In Sierra, nearly the entire operating system and almost all included applications run in 64-bit mode. In fact, only one of the main built-in applications is still limited to 32-bit mode: DVD Player.

Although moving most of the applications to support 64-bit mode generally improves performance, this advancement is not without drawbacks. Namely, applications that run in 64-bit mode can't take advantage of any 32-bit code. This means any application that uses plug-in technology may suffer from compatibility issues with third-party plug-ins that have not been updated to support 64-bit mode.

Examples of plug-in software affected by this issue include:

▶ Printer drivers that add interfaces for the printer dialog

▶ Screen savers

▶ Audio device drivers known as audio units

▶ Spotlight metadata import plug-ins

▶ Quick Look preview plug-ins

▶ Dashboard widgets that require plug-in code (though most widgets don't use extra code, so they should work without issues)

▶ Safari plug-ins

In short, applications running in 64-bit mode do not load 32-bit plug-ins. If you need to use a third-party 32-bit plug-in with a 64-bit-capable application, you have to force the application to run in 32-bit mode on most Mac systems. This can be accomplished from the Finder Info or Inspector window by simply selecting the "Open in 32-bit mode" checkbox. Obviously, forcing 32-bit mode may make the application run more slowly, but this is required to use nonupdated plug-ins.

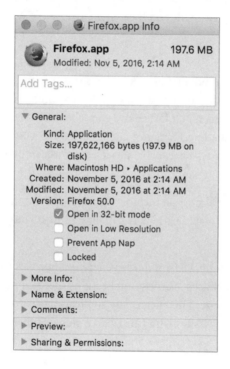

NOTE ▶ The "Open in Low Resolution" checkbox appears only on new Mac computers featuring Retina displays. This option prevents the use of high-resolution application assets, which also may not be compatible with older application plug-ins.

One system application automatically switches modes for you: System Preferences. When a user tries to open a third-party 32-bit System Preferences plug-in, often called a System Preferences pane, a prompt to restart System Preferences appears. If the user clicks OK (the default), System Preferences restarts in 32-bit mode and loads the selected pane.

NOTE ▶ With the exception of Dashboard and System Preferences, third-party plug-ins that tie into a system resource or background process must support 64-bit mode to work with macOS.

Reference 18.2
Manage Application Extensions

Application extensions allow applications to take advantage of functionality and content from other applications. In this section you will explore how application extensions blur the line between separate applications in macOS.

> **NOTE ▶** Don't confuse application extensions with kernel extensions. Application extensions add functionality to applications, whereas kernel extensions primarily add hardware compatibility to the system. You can find out more about kernel extensions in **Lesson 24, "Troubleshoot Peripherals."**

About Application Extensions

macOS has long included cross-application integration through methods like copy and paste, the Services menu, and AppleScript. Although these older methods are still viable, application extensions provide a standard framework that allows applications from completely different developers to directly interact with each other—so much so that with application extensions one application's features can appear as if they are built in to another application.

Examples of application extensions possible for macOS include:

▶ Action menu—Application extensions can add more options to the Action menu. The Action menu is an interface that allows a user to manipulate a document. With application extensions, the features from one application can be used in another application to manipulate the document.

▶ Finder—Application extensions can add file-system functionality exposed in the Finder. As an example, the popular third-party cloud storage solution Dropbox includes an application extension that adds a pop-up menu to the Finder toolbar where you can manage Dropbox settings for specific files.

▶ Photos—Application extensions can add photo manipulation tools to the built-in macOS Photos application.

▶ Share menu—Application extensions can add more options to the Share menu, allowing users to directly share content from one application with other applications or Internet services.

▶ Today view—Application extensions can add functionality in the form of widgets that appear in the Today view of Notification Center. In OS X Yosemite 10.10 and later, this ability largely replaces the need for Dashboard widgets.

As an example of application extensions in macOS, the Preview application includes markup features that allow you to manipulate pictures or PDF documents. This includes the ability to add custom shapes, text, or even your digital signature to existing documents. You can access these features in Preview by clicking the Markup button (toolbox icon) in the toolbar.

The markup features of Preview are also available as an application extension that can be used by any other application. In macOS, the Mail application can take advantage of markup features within an email that contains a picture or PDF document. When replying to a message in Mail, click the Include Attachments button in the toolbar and then the Action button (downward arrow icon) at the top right of the document to reveal the markup features. Again, other application extensions can add their custom actions here as well.

Manage Application Extensions

Several application extensions are included with macOS, and additional application extensions are "installed" automatically with the application that is providing the additional functionality. In other words, applications that integrate via application extensions include the application extension resources inside the application bundle. Thus, the user will never have to see or install specific application extensions.

A user can inspect the installed application extensions and enable or disable their functionality from the Extensions preferences. The following screenshot shows the markup action included with macOS via the Preview application. For example, deselecting the checkbox next to the Markup item would prevent that application extension from appearing in other applications. Also note the OneDrive and Dropbox application extensions listed under Finder. This application extension is installed automatically with the Dropbox application.

Items in the Share menu can also be enabled or disabled from the Extensions preferences. However, keep in mind that the user will need to be signed in to an Internet-based sharing service to activate its associated application extension. Users can sign in to most Internet services via the Internet Accounts preferences, as covered in **Lesson 22, "Manage Network Services."**

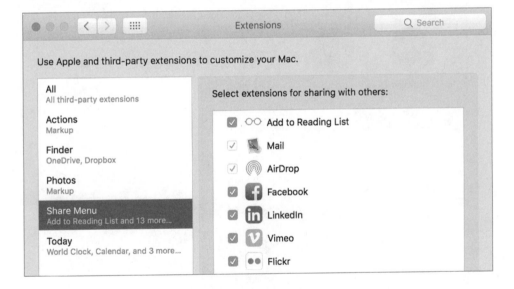

Use Notification Center Today View

The Today view in Notification Center offers a range of information and functionality that can be customized to the user's preference. Notification Center is accessed by clicking the farthest-right button in the menu bar, and the default view is Today.

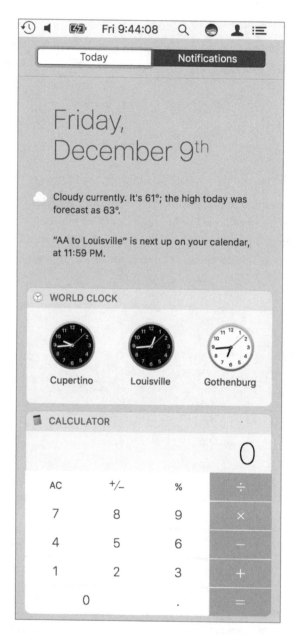

The Today view largely replaces functionality found in an older macOS technology, Dashboard widgets. In fact, application extensions that can be used in the Today view are referred to as widgets. However, from a technology standpoint, legacy Dashboard widgets are not the same. Widgets in the Today view of Notification Center are implemented through application extensions, whereas older Dashboard widgets were installed in their own Widgets folder within a Library folder.

> **TIP** macOS Sierra still includes the ability to use legacy Dashboard widgets, although it's hidden by default. Access to the Dashboard can be managed via the Mission Control preferences.

Like other application extensions, widgets in the Today view are included with the application that is providing the functionality or service. For example, the Calculator application extension is built in to the Calculator application included with macOS. Also, as with other application extensions, you can disable or enable widgets in the Today view from the Extensions preferences.

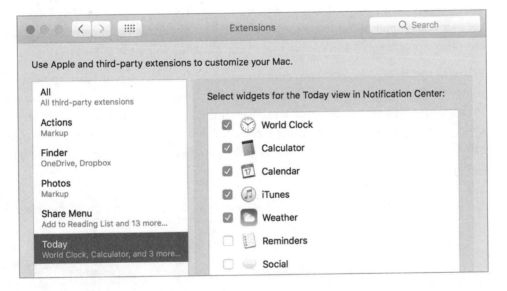

> **TIP** Widgets in the Today view can also be managed by clicking the button at the bottom center of Notification Center. This button most often says Edit, but it can also display as <#> New, where <#> is the number of newly added application extensions that can present widgets in the Today view.

> **TIP** You can install more widgets from the Mac App Store. On the Featured page of the Mac App Store, in the Quick Links section at the bottom right, you'll find a link to popular Notification Center widgets.

Reference 18.3
Monitor Applications and Processes

macOS provides several methods for identifying and managing applications and processes. As covered previously, you can still use the Finder Info window to inspect basic application information, but you can find out a lot more about an application from System Information. If you need to inspect an application or process as it's running on the Mac, use the Activity Monitor application.

Monitor Applications via System Information

If you want to quickly gather information about all the applications on your Mac, use the /Applications/Utilities/System Information application. When you select the Applications category in System Information, the content of all available Application folders is scanned. This includes /Applications, /Applications/Utilities, ~/Applications, /System/Library/, and any other Applications folders at the root of any mounted volumes.

From the applications list, select an entry to reveal its name, version number, application source modification date, and application type. The application's source, in the "Obtained from" column, is based on the code-signing certificate used to create the application. Unidentified applications do not contain this code signature. Also note that applications installed as part of macOS do not show as being purchased from the Mac App Store but instead show just "Apple."

Application Name	Version	Obtained from	Last Modified	64-Bit (Intel)
Blackmagic Disk Speed Test	3.0	Mac App Store	9/9/16, 1:07 AM	Yes
Blizzard Error	2.2.6.0	Identified Developer	10/18/15, 10:53 PM	No
Blizzard Error	1.5.5.0	Identified Developer	11/8/15, 2:07 PM	No
Bluetooth File Exchange	5.0.1	Apple	11/1/16, 2:44 PM	Yes
Bluetooth Setup Assistant	5.0.1	Apple	11/1/16, 2:44 PM	Yes
BluetoothUIServer	5.0.1	Apple	11/1/16, 2:44 PM	Yes
Bonjour Browser	1.5.6	Unknown	7/18/06, 2:00 AM	No
Boot Camp Assistant	6.1.0	Apple	11/1/16, 2:44 PM	Yes
BrokenAge	2.0.0	Unknown	2/26/14, 12:54 PM	No
Brother MFC-8860DN	12	Unknown	7/30/16, 11:17 PM	Yes
Brother Scanner	2.6.0	Identified Developer	10/25/15, 5:25 PM	Yes
Brother Status Monitor	3.19.0	Identified Developer	10/25/15, 5:25 PM	Yes
Build Web Page	10.1	Apple	11/1/16, 2:44 PM	Yes
Calculator	10.8	Apple	11/1/16, 2:44 PM	Yes
Calendar	9.0	Apple	11/1/16, 2:44 PM	Yes

Calculator:

Version: 10.8
Obtained from: Apple
Last Modified: 11/1/16, 2:44 PM
Kind: Intel
64-Bit (Intel): Yes
Signed by: Software Signing, Apple Code Signing Certification Authority, Apple Root CA
Location: /Applications/Calculator.app
Get Info String: 10.8, Copyright © 2001-2013, Apple Inc.

MyMac › Software › Applications › Calculator

Monitor Processes via Activity Monitor

The primary application in macOS for monitoring processes as they are running is /Applications/Utilities/Activity Monitor. This extremely useful tool shows you the vital signs of any currently running process and of the system as a whole. If an application has stopped responding or has become noticeably slow, check Activity Monitor. Also, check here if the overall system is running noticeably slower. Activity Monitor helps you identify an application or background process that is using a significant percentage of system resources.

The main window of Activity Monitor presents a list of running processes and applications that belong to the current user. Below the process list you'll see overall system statistics. The default columns in Activity Monitor allow you to examine various process statistics:

▶ Process Name—This is the name of the running process chosen by the developer who created it.

▶ % CPU—This number is the percentage of total CPU usage the process is consuming. Note that the maximum percentage possible is 100 percent times the number of processor cores. For example, a Mac featuring an Intel Core i7 presents a total of eight processor cores to the system.

▶ CPU Time—This is the amount of time a process has been active on the system since the last startup.

▶ Threads—Each process is further broken down into the number of thread operations. Multithreading helps increase a process's responsiveness by enabling it to perform multiple simultaneous tasks. Multithreading also increases performance, as each thread of a single process can run on a separate processor core.

▶ Idle Wake Ups—This is the number of times a process has been woken up from a paused "sleep" state since the process was last started.

▶ Process Identification (PID)—Each process has a unique identifier number. The numbers are assigned in sequence as processes are opened after system startup. Note that the PIDs are "recycled" after 65,535 has been reached.

▶ User—Per the UNIX application security model, each process is opened on behalf of a particular user. Thus, each application has file-system access corresponding to the assigned user account.

By default, Activity Monitor shows only processes running for the currently logged-in user. To increase your view of all active processes, choose View > All Processes. You can also adjust the number of statistics shown in the columns and the update frequency from the View menu.

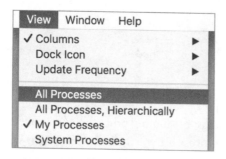

TIP ▶ To narrow down your view, use the Spotlight search filter in the upper-right corner of the Activity Monitor window.

To sort the process list by column, simply click any column title. Click the column title again to toggle between ascending and descending sorts. By viewing all processes and then re-sorting the list by % CPU, you can determine whether any process is using excessive resources.

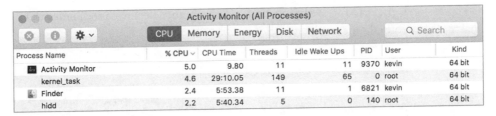

To further inspect an individual process, double-click its name in the Activity Monitor list. This reveals a window showing detailed process information.

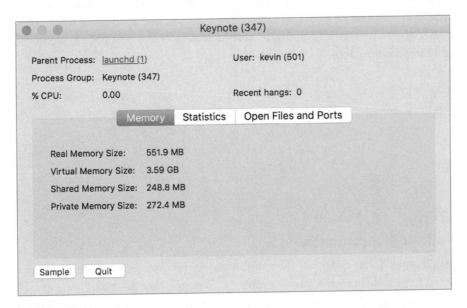

Although CPU utilization is generally the most important statistic for monitoring process activity, the Activity Monitor application can also monitor memory, energy, disk, and network utilization. Click through the tabs at the top of the Activity Monitor window to view the different categories. These monitoring features are invaluable for troubleshooting because they show you real-time system statistics.

TIP Hover your mouse over any statistic at the bottom of the Activity Monitor window to view a description of the statistic.

Of particular note are the Swap Used and Compressed statistics under the Memory tab. These numbers are a historical account, since the last system startup, of how much active process data has been swapped out to local storage or compressed to save space.

Compression is preferred to swapping, because it's a higher-performance approach to making more room in memory.

MEMORY PRESSURE	Physical Memory:	16.00 GB	App Memory:	7.60 GB
	Memory Used:	9.31 GB	Wired Memory:	1.70 GB
	Cached Files:	5.61 GB	Compressed:	0 bytes
	Swap Used:	0 bytes		

A low number of swap usage is acceptable, but a high number of swap usage indicates that the system does not have enough real memory to meet the user's application demands. In other words, the system only "swaps out" when it does not have enough real memory, thus slowing system performance.

> **MORE INFO** ▶ Take time to explore all the features available from the Activity Monitor menu options. For an even more detailed process inspector, check out the Instruments application installed as part of the optional Xcode Developer Tools found on the Mac App Store. For more information about using Activity Monitor see Apple Support article HT201464, "Use Activity Monitor on your Mac."

Reference 18.4
Troubleshoot Applications

Application issues are as diverse as the applications themselves. Just as each application is designed to provide unique features, problems often manifest in unique ways as well. Fortunately, you can take a variety of general troubleshooting steps when diagnosing and resolving an application issue.

> **MORE INFO** ▶ Apple maintains a list of software known to be incompatible. You can find out more about how macOS handles incompatible software in Apple Support article HT201861, "About incompatible software on your Mac."

General Application Troubleshooting

The actions in the following list are in order from the least to the most invasive and time-consuming. Actions are also generally presented according to the likelihood of their success in resolving the issue, from most to least likely. Generally, when troubleshooting applications, start with one of these actions:

▶ Restart the application—Often, restarting an application resolves the issue, or at least resolves application responsiveness. In some cases, the application may become unresponsive and you may have to force quit it to restart it, as detailed later in this lesson.

▶ Try another known working document—This is an excellent method to determine whether a document has become corrupted and is the cause of the problem. If you discover that the problem's source is a corrupted document file, usually the best solution is to restore the document from an earlier backup. As covered in Lesson 15, "Manage Time Machine," macOS includes a sophisticated and easy-to-use backup system.

▶ Try another application—Many common document types can be opened by multiple Mac applications. Try opening the troublesome document in another application. If this works, save a new "clean" version of the document from the other application.

▶ Try another user account—Use this method to determine whether a user-specific resource file is the cause of the problem. If the application problem doesn't occur when using another account, search for corrupted application caches, preferences, and resource files in the suspect user's Library folder. Creating a temporary account to test—and then deleting it—is quite easy, as covered in Lesson 5, "Manage User Accounts."

▶ Check diagnostic reports and log files—This is the last information-gathering step to take before you start replacing items. Few applications keep detailed log files; however, every time an application crashes, the macOS diagnostic reporting feature saves a diagnostic report of the crash information. Using the Console application to view diagnostic reports is detailed later in this lesson.

▶ Delete cache files—To increase performance, many applications create cache folders in the /Library/Caches, ~/Library/Caches, and ~/Library/Saved Application State folders. A specific application's cache folder almost always matches the application's name. Although not the most likely application resource to cause problems, cache folders can be easily deleted without affecting the user's information. Once you delete an application's cache folder, the application creates a new one the next time you open it. One cache type that can't be removed easily from the Finder are the various font caches. However, the system font caches are cleared during a safe boot, as covered in **Lesson 26, "Troubleshoot Startup and System Issues."**

TIP The ~/Library folder is hidden by default in macOS. The easiest way to reveal this folder in the Finder is to hold down the Option key and choose Go > Library.

▶ Replace preference files—Corrupted preference files are one of the most likely of all application resources to cause problems, because they change often and are required for the application to function properly. Application preference troubleshooting is detailed later in this lesson.

▶ Replace application resources—Although corrupted application resources can certainly cause problems, they are the least likely source of problems, since application resources are rarely changed. Application resource troubleshooting is also detailed later in this lesson.

Force Quit Applications

It's pretty easy to tell when an application becomes unresponsive—it stops reacting to your mouse clicks, and the pointer often changes to a wait cursor (spinning pinwheel) and stays that way for more than a minute. Hence, the terms *spinning-wheel* and *beach-balling* have become slang for a frozen Mac application.

Because the forward-most application controls the menu bar, it may seem as if the application has locked you out of the Mac entirely. But moving the cursor from the frozen application window to another application window or the desktop usually returns the pointer to normal—and you can then click another application or the desktop to regain control of your Mac.

macOS provides no less than three methods to force quit applications from the graphical interface:

▶ From the Force Quit Applications dialog—Choose Apple menu > Force Quit, or press Command-Option-Escape, to open the Force Quit Applications dialog. A frozen application appears with "(not responding)" next to its name. To force quit, select any application and click Force Quit. Note that you only have the ability to restart the Finder—the system automatically restarts the Finder if it's quit.

▶ From the Dock—Use secondary-click (or Control-click), or hold down the application's icon in the Dock, to display the application shortcut menu. If the Dock has recognized that the application is frozen, simply choose Force Quit from this menu. Otherwise, hold down the Option key to change the Quit menu command to Force Quit.

▶ From Activity Monitor—Open /Applications/Utilities/Activity Monitor, and then select the application you want to quit from the process list. Next, click the "X in an "octagon" button on the far-left edge of the Activity Monitor toolbar, and then click the Force Quit button. Activity Monitor is the only built-in graphical application that also allows administrator users to quit or force quit any other user process or background system process.

NOTE ▶ In Activity Monitor, individual webpages in Safari are shown as separate processes. This gives you the ability to force quit individual pages that may have crashed in Safari.

About Diagnostic Reports

To help diagnose persistent issues, the macOS diagnostic reporting feature springs into action whenever an application quits unexpectedly (commonly known as a crash) or stops functioning (commonly known as a hang) and you have to force quit it. This process displays a warning dialog that lets the user know a problem has occurred.

More importantly, this process records log files that detail the circumstances surrounding the application's crash or hang. If you click the Report button when the warning dialog appears, you can see the diagnostic report and, optionally, add comments to send to Apple.

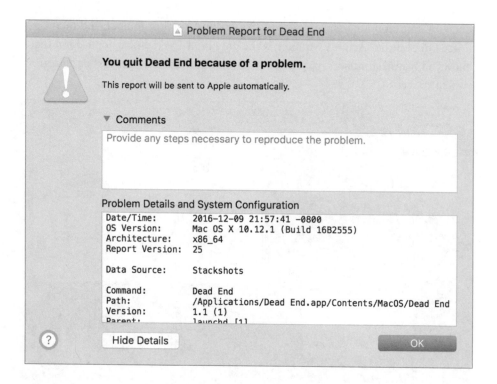

TIP You can turn off the automatic sending of diagnostic reports to Apple from the Security & Privacy preferences.

View Diagnostics via Console

Even if you don't send the report to Apple, you can revisit diagnostic messages and reports later; they are always saved to the system volume. macOS Sierra keeps a variety of log files that range from short usage messages to detailed problem reports. The easiest way to view these logs is to open the /Applications/Utilities/Console application and then to make sure all the logs are showing by clicking Diagnostics and Usage Data in the sidebar.

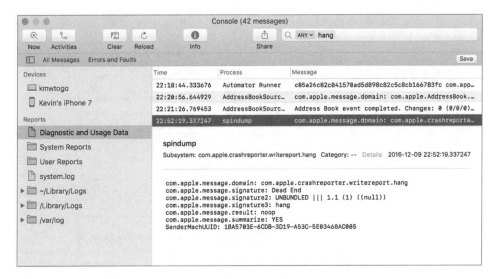

Short diagnostic messages that show both general usage and problems are saved to /private/var/log/DiagnosticMessages. These messages can be viewed in Console by selecting Diagnostics and Usage Data in the log list. Processes in macOS Sierra can generate hundreds of diagnostic messages a day, so most of them are benign. However, as you can see in the previous screenshot, the Dead End application has experienced a "hang."

More detailed diagnostic messages are created in cases where processes have hung or crashed. If the problem report was generated by something running for the user, the log is saved to the user's ~/Library/Logs/DiagnosticReports folder. These reports can be seen in Console by selecting User Reports in the log list. However, if the problem report was generated by something running as the system, the log is saved in the local /Library/Logs /DiagnosticReports folder. These reports can be seen in Console by selecting System Reports in the log list.

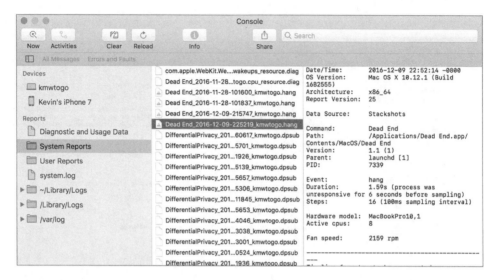

The diagnostic reports are chronologically listed, and each report entry is named by the application followed by the date and time in 24-hour notation. These diagnostic report logs include highly technical information that many won't understand, but they also include key pieces of information that may help the average troubleshooter diagnose the issue. For example, diagnostic reports often indicate which files were being used by the application at the time. One of the reported files could be the source of the problem due to corruption.

Troubleshoot Preferences

Applications primarily access two types of often-changing files when they are in use: the documents for which the application handles viewing or editing, and the preference files that contain all the application's settings. From an administration perspective, preference files are often more important, because they may contain settings that are required for an application to work properly. For instance, an application's serial number or registration information is often stored in a preference file.

Preference files can be found in any Library folder, but most application preferences end up in the user's Library. Application preferences are kept in user home folders because the local Library should be used only for system preferences. More important, this enables each user to have his or her own application settings that do not interfere with other users' settings. By this logic, it's clear that if you're troubleshooting a system process, you should look for its preferences in the /Library folder.

TIP ▶ The ~/Library folder is hidden by default in macOS. The easiest way to reveal this folder in the Finder is to hold the Option key and choose Go > Library.

Most application and system preference files are saved as property list files. The naming scheme for a property list file usually has the unique bundle identifier for the application first, followed by the file type .plist. For example, the Finder preference file is named com.apple.finder.plist. This naming scheme may seem strange at first, but it helps avoid confusion by identifying the software's developer along with the application itself.

Many applications are still not sandboxed, so they use the default preference folder for standard applications: the ~/Library/Preferences folder. The full path to the Finder preference file is /Users/<*username*>/Library/Preferences/com.apple.finder.plist, where <*username*> is the account name of the user.

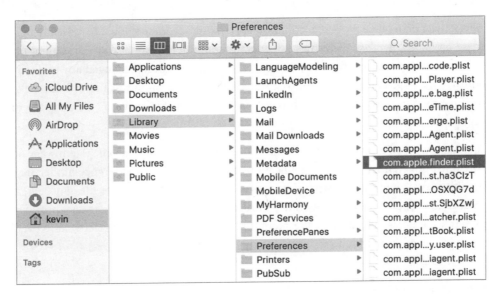

NOTE ▶ Any lock files associated with a preference file can be largely ignored, since they don't contain any data and are simply the result of a legacy OS X Lion 10.7 behavior.

For sandboxed applications, the preference will be located in either the Containers or Group Containers folder. Specifically, these folders are ~/Library/Containers/<*BundleID*>/Data/Library/Preferences and ~/Library/Group Containers/<*BundleID*>/Library/Preferences, where <*BundleID*> is the unique bundle identifier for the application.

For example, the identifier for the Mail application is com.apple.mail. Therefore, for a user with the account name "kevin," the full path to the Mail application's preference file is /Users/kevin/Library/Containers/com.apple.mail/Data/Library/Preferences /com.apple.mail.plist.

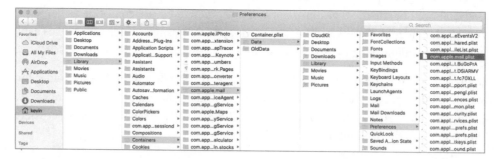

Application preference files are a common application resource known historically to cause problems. Because these files can contain both internal application configuration information and user-configured preferences, even if you haven't changed any preferences, odds are the application is constantly storing new information in this file. It is the only file required by most applications that is regularly being rewritten, so it has the potential to become corrupted.

Apple has worked to make its own applications and the user preference system wary of corrupted preference files. Many applications that use the Apple preference model, including third-party applications, simply recognize the corrupted preference file, ignore it, and create a new one. However, many other third-party applications use their own proprietary preference models that are not as resilient. In these cases, corrupted preferences typically result in an application that crashes frequently or during startup.

Resolve Corrupted Preferences

The most convenient method of isolating a corrupted preference in the latter case is to rename the suspect preference file. If any part of the preference filename is different than expected, the application ignores it and creates a new preference file. So, in the Finder, add an identifier to the end of the suspect preference filename—something like ".bad." Alternatively, to make the preference file easier to find later, you could simply put a tilde (~) at the beginning of the file's name, which causes the Finder to put it at the beginning of the file listing when sorted alphabetically.

The preference architecture in macOS is maintained by a background server process known as cfprefsd. To improve performance, this process uses memory caching to store preference information. After you remove a potentially corrupted preference, you should restart this process to clear its cache. As covered previously, you can force any process to quit from Activity Monitor. Because cfprefsd should always be running, the system automatically restarts it when you force it to quit. Also, be sure to force quit only the cfprefsd process owned by the appropriate user.

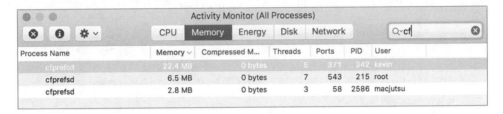

After you have removed the preference file and restarted the cfprefsd process, opening the application or process creates a new preference file based on the code's defaults. If this resolves the issue and doesn't remove any irreplaceable settings, go ahead and trash the old preference file; if not, move on to resource troubleshooting.

If you eventually resolve the problem elsewhere, you can then restore the previous settings by deleting the newer preference file and then removing the filename identifier you added to the original preference file. Again, don't forget to restart the cfprefsd process. The benefit of replacing the previous preference file is that you don't lose any of the settings or custom configuration saved in the file.

View and Edit Preference Files

One of the primary advantages of using the property list file format is that it can generally be understood by humans. During your troubleshooting, you may find it advantageous to verify settings by directly viewing the contents of the configuration property list file. Many applications and processes keep additional settings items in these files and may not have a graphical interface for configuration.

> **NOTE ▶** Some third-party applications do not store their preference files as property lists. Thus, they will likely use a different naming convention, and you will probably not be able to view or edit the file's contents.

The content of a property list file is formatted as either plain-text Extensible Markup Language (XML) or binary. The XML format is relatively human-readable, with normal text interspersed with special text tags that define the data structure for the information. Thus, you can view and attempt to decipher the XML code of plain-text-formatted property list files using any text-reading application.

Binary-encoded files are only readable using special tools designed to convert the binary code into human-readable format. Fortunately, macOS includes a Quick Look plug-in that allows you to easily view the contents of either type of property list file by simply pressing the Space bar while you have the file selected in the Finder.

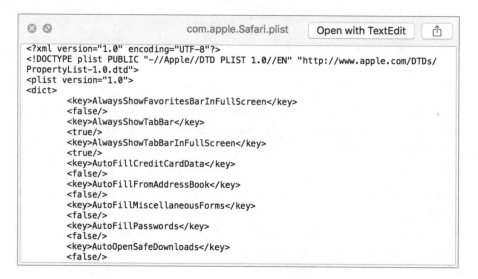

If you need to edit a property list file, avoid using TextEdit, since it will improperly format any property list file that is saved as a binary. The most complete graphical application from Apple for editing property list files is Xcode. The Xcode application can decode binary property list files, and it enables you to view and edit any property list in an easy-to-read hierarchical format. Again, Xcode is an optional install that can be found in the Mac App Store.

Key	Type	Value
▼ Root	Dictionary	(160 items)
DidMigrateWebKit1Preferences	Boolean	YES
NSWindow Frame WBBlockedPlugins	String	907 582 752 522 0 0 2560 1417
UserStyleSheetEnabled	Boolean	NO
__WebInspectorPageGroup__.WebKit2l...	Boolean	NO
SkipLoadingExtensionsAtLaunch	Boolean	NO
AlwaysShowFavoritesBarInFullScreen	Boolean	NO
NSNavPanelExpandedSizeForOpenMode	String	{705, 437}
▶ NSToolbar Configuration BrowserWind...	Dictionary	(6 items)
NSWindow Frame HTMLSource	String	457 429 738 584 0 0 1920 1178
▶ RecentWebSearches	Array	(10 items)
WebKitShouldPrintBackgroundsPrefer...	Boolean	NO
AutoShowToolbarInFullScreen	Boolean	NO
HomePage	String	
DidMigrateNewBookmarkSheetToRea...	Boolean	YES
ClearBrowsingDataLastIntervalUsed	String	all history
DidMigrateExtensionSettingsToExtensi...	Boolean	YES

NOTE ▶ Avoid editing property list files that are currently in use by a running application or process. However, if you need to edit a property list that may be in use, make sure to restart the cfprefsd process, as covered earlier in this lesson.

Troubleshoot Application Resources

Although it's rare, corrupted application software and associated nonpreference resources can be a source of application problems. These types of files rarely, if ever, change after the initial application installation, so the likelihood that such a resource is the cause of a problem is low.

However, keep in mind that many applications use other resources, such as fonts, plug-ins, and keychains, from the local and user Library folders as well as items in the Application Support folder. The hard part is locating the suspect resource; once you have, the fix is to simply remove or replace the corrupted resource and restart the application.

NOTE ▶ Applications running in 64-bit mode do not load plug-in resources that support only 32-bit mode. This compatibility issue is covered earlier in this lesson.

Remember that corrupted resources in the user's home folder Library affect only that user, whereas corrupted resources in the local Library affect all users. Use this fact to narrow your search when looking for a corrupted resource. Further, application and diagnostic report logs, covered earlier in this lesson, may tell you which resources the application was attempting to access when it crashed. Obviously, those resources should be your primary suspects.

If the application exhibits problems with only one user, attempt to locate the specific resource at the root of the problem in the user's Library folder. Start with the usual suspects; if you find a resource that you think could be causing the problem, move that resource out of the user's Library folder and restart the application.

> **NOTE ▸** Some applications have a habit of storing their resources in the user's Documents folder, so you may want to check there as well.

If you've determined that the application issue is persistent across all user accounts, start by reinstalling or upgrading to the latest version of the application. You will probably find that a newer version of the application is available—one that likely includes bug fixes. At the very least, by reinstalling you replace any potentially corrupted files that are part of the standard application. If you continue to experience problems after reinstalling the application, search through the local Library resources to find and remove or replace the corrupted resource.

> **NOTE ▸** If you are discovering a large number of corrupted files, this probably indicates a much more serious file system or storage hardware issue. Troubleshooting these items is covered in Lesson 9, "Manage File Systems and Storage."

Exercise 18.1
Force Applications to Quit

▶ **Prerequisites**

> ▸ You must have created the Chris Johnson account (Exercise 5.1, "Create a Standard User Account").

> ▸ You must have installed the Dead End application (Exercise 16.3, "Use a Drag-and-Drop Install").

In this exercise, you will learn how to determine when an application has become unresponsive. You will see various ways to force unresponsive applications to quit: from the Dock, using the Force Quit window, and using Activity Monitor. Even background processes without a user interface can have issues and stop running, so you'll learn how to manage these processes as well. You will also see how to open an application in 32-bit mode.

Force an Application to Quit via the Dock

1 If necessary, log in as Chris Johnson.

2 Open the Dead End application you installed in Exercise 16.3, "Use a Drag-and-Drop Install."

The primary purpose of Dead End is to become unresponsive, giving you an opportunity to practice different ways to force an application to quit.

Dead End opens a window with a "Download the Internet" button.

3 Click "Download the Internet."

Dead End becomes unresponsive. After a few seconds you may see the wait cursor (a colored pinwheel). Note that the wait cursor appears only when you mouse over the Dead End window or (if Dead End is in the foreground) the menu bar.

4 Control-click the Dead End icon in the Dock, and then choose Force Quit from the shortcut menu. Alternatively, you could click and hold the Dead End icon in the Dock and then choose Force Quit from the pop-up menu.

If Force Quit does not appear in the menu, repeat step 3 or hold down the Option key. When you hold down the Option key, Quit changes to Force Quit, and you can then choose it to force Dead End to quit.

Use the Force Quit Window

1   Open the Dead End application again so you can try another method of forcing an application to quit.

One way to open applications you've used recently is by going to the Apple menu and choosing Recent Items. By default, the system remembers the last ten applications you've opened.

2   Click "Download the Internet."

3   Press Command-Option-Escape to open the Force Quit Applications window.

Note that it will take about 15 seconds before Dead End is shown as "not responding."

4   Select Dead End, and click Force Quit.

5   In the confirmation dialog, click Force Quit.

6   If you are given the opportunity to send a report to Apple, click Ignore.

7   Close the Force Quit Applications window.

Use Activity Monitor

There may be times when you need another method to force an application to quit. Activity Monitor not only forces applications to quit but also allows you to review all processes running on the computer, gather information, and quit them when necessary.

1   Open Dead End.

2   Click "Download the Internet."

3   Open Activity Monitor (from the Utilities folder).

Even though the wait cursor appears in Dead End, you can still click the desktop to make the Finder active or click in the Dock to use Launchpad. A single unresponsive application should not affect the rest of the system.

Activity Monitor displays a list of all running processes. When you open this window, it shows some processes that you will recognize as applications. It also shows other processes running in the background that do not have a graphical user interface.

4   If necessary, click the CPU tab above the process list.

5   If the "% CPU" in the table header is not already selected, click it twice to get a top-down (most to least) list of processes in terms of their CPU usage. The arrowhead that appears next to "% CPU" should point downward.

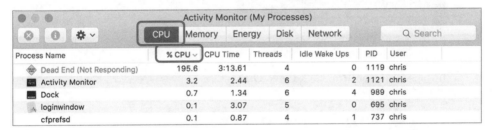

6   Look for the Dead End process by name. It should be at the top.

The name of an unresponsive application appears in red with a note declaring the application is "Not Responding." As you look at the Dead End process, notice how the CPU usage is close to 200 percent. You can see how an application can hijack your CPU, even though the application is not responding and appears to be doing nothing.

Note that the % CPU statistic refers to the percentage of a CPU core being used. Current Mac computers have multiple cores and hyperthreading, so even "200%" CPU utilization is not fully using the computer's CPU power.

7   Choose Window menu > CPU Usage. This opens a window that displays how many processor cores your computer has and how busy each one is.

This example screenshot was taken on a computer with two physical cores, but hyperthreading allows each of those to do two things at once, giving it four virtual cores. As you can see, 200 percent is only half what it is capable of.

8   Select Dead End in the process list, and then click the quit process button (its icon is an "X" in an octagon) on the toolbar.

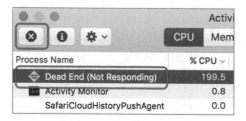

9   When asked to confirm, click Force Quit.

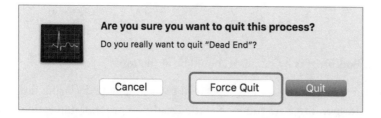

Note that Quit is the default option in the dialog that appears. However, since Dead End is not responding, it will not respond to a normal Quit command either. Therefore, you need to use Force Quit to stop this process from running.

Dead End disappears from the process list in the Activity Monitor window and from the Dock. After a few seconds, the CPU Usage window updates to show that utilization has decreased.

Unlike the Dock and Force Quit Applications window, Activity Monitor is capable of forcing background processes to quit. Background processes are generally programs that are launched automatically to provide some part of the system's functionality. Normally, you will not have to manage them explicitly, but in a few cases forcing them to quit is useful.

10 Select SystemUIServer in the process list. It may help to use the Search field in the upper right of the window. Remember its process ID (PID) number, shown in a column to the right.

SystemUIServer manages the menu bar items on the right side of the menu bar. Each menu bar item runs as a plug-in inside of the SystemUIServer, and if one of them locks up, it might be necessary to force SystemUIServer to quit.

11 With SystemUIServer selected, click the quit process ("X") button, and then watch the right side of the menu bar as you click Force Quit.

The right side of the menu bar goes blank, and then the menu bar items reappear. Examine your process list, and notice that SystemUIServer is running but with a different process ID than it had before.

What has happened is that the launchd process (another background process) has detected that SystemUIServer exited and has automatically relaunched it. launchd is responsible for starting and monitoring many of the system's background processes and restarts them if necessary.

Not all processes can be safely forced to quit this way. For example, forcing WindowServer (a system process) to quit would immediately end your login session. **Lesson 26, "Troubleshoot Startup and System Issues,"** discusses launchd in more detail.

12 Leave Activity Monitor open for the next section.

Open an Application in 32-Bit Mode

Most applications that come with macOS Sierra can run only in 64-bit mode; however, some can run in either 32- or 64-bit mode but normally run in 64-bit mode. If you need to, you can run these applications in 32-bit mode (for example, in case they need to load a plug-in that runs only in 32-bit mode).

1   In Activity Monitor, choose View menu > Columns > Kind.

This adds a Kind column to the display, showing what mode each process is running in. Normally, all the processes run in 64-bit mode.

2   Open Dead End.

3   In Activity Monitor, find the Dead End process, and note that its Kind is also listed as 64 bit.

4   Quit Dead End.

5   In the Finder, select the Dead End application, and choose File menu > Get Info (Command-I).

6   In the General section of the Info window, select "Open in 32-bit mode."

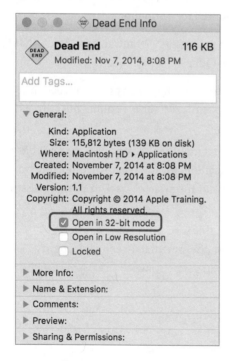

You will also see several other options; exactly which are available depends on the application, as well as whether you are using a Retina display.

7   Close the Info window, and reopen the Dead End application.

8   In Activity Monitor, find the new Dead End process.

Its Kind is now listed as 32 bit.

9   Quit Dead End.

View System Processes and Usage

1   In Activity Monitor, choose View menu > All Processes.

You see many more processes appear in the process list. In addition to the background processes within your user session (sometimes called *agents*), macOS has many background processes (sometimes called *daemons*) running outside of your login session.

2   At the top of the Activity Monitor window, switch through the CPU, Memory, Energy, Disk, and Network tabs, and examine the information they display for each process, as well as the overall statistics at the bottom of the window.

3   If you are continuing to Exercise 18.2, leave Activity Monitor running because you will use it again.

Exercise 18.2
Troubleshoot Preferences

▶ **Prerequisite**

▶   You must have created the Chris Johnson account (Exercise 5.1, "Create a Standard User Account").

Most application preferences are created and stored for individual users in their personal Library folder. This compartmental approach can help when you are troubleshooting application issues. You'll learn how to set and restore a preference and see the effect of moving a preference file out of the ~/Library folder.

Create and Locate Preview Preferences

1   If necessary, log in as Chris Johnson.

2   Open Preview from the Applications folder.

3   Open Preview preferences by choosing Preview menu > Preferences (Command-Comma).

    Note that the default setting for "When opening files" is "Open groups of files in the same window."

4   Select "Open all files in one window."

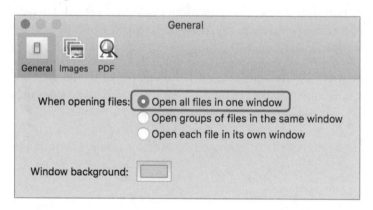

5   Close the Preferences window, and quit Preview.

6   In the Finder, open ~/Library.

    Remember that since the user Library folder is invisible, the easiest way to navigate to this folder is to hold down the Option key and choose Go menu > Library.

    Preview is a sandboxed application, so its real preference file is not in the ~/Library /Preferences folder but in a sandbox container. See Reference 13.1, "About macOS File Resources," for more details about sandbox containers.

7   In the ~/Library folder, open the Containers folder and then the com.apple.Preview folder under that.

It contains a Data subfolder, with a structure that mirrors your home folder. Most of its contents are aliases, pointing to their "real" counterparts.

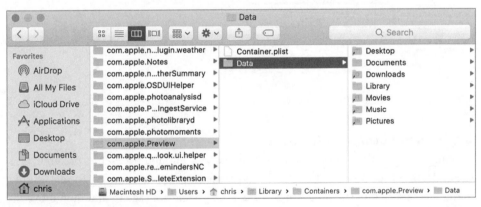

8   Navigate down to Data/Library/Preferences, and select the com.apple.Preview.plist file.

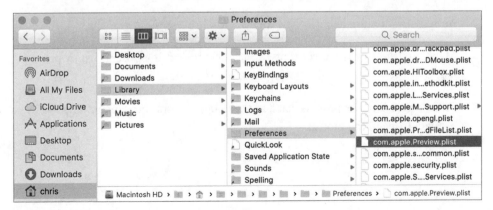

9   Use Quick Look to view the preference file's contents (Command-Y).

The preferences setting you made is listed here, although in somewhat cryptic form.

```
⊗ ⊘                    com.apple.Preview.plist    Open with TextEdit    ⬆

<?xml version="1.0" encoding="UTF-8"?>
<!DOCTYPE plist PUBLIC "-//Apple//DTD PLIST 1.0//EN" "http://www.apple.com/DTDs/
PropertyList-1.0.dtd">
<plist version="1.0">
<dict>
        <key>NSToolbar Configuration com.apple.NSColorPanel</key>
        <dict>
                <key>TB Is Shown</key>
                <integer>1</integer>
        </dict>
        <key>NSWindow Frame NSNavPanelAutosaveName</key>
        <string>284 262 712 448 0 0 1280 777 </string>
        <key>NSWindow Frame PVPreferences</key>
        <string>390 389 446 172 0 0 1280 777 </string>
        <key>PVGeneralSelectedPane</key>
        <integer>0</integer>
        <key>PVImageOpeningMode</key>
        <integer>0</integer>
</dict>
</plist>
```

10 Close the Quick Look window.

Disable and Restore Preferences

Moving an application's preferences file is not always enough to reset its preferences, since the preferences agent (named cfprefsd) may remember its old settings. To make sure the preferences reset, quit the program and then the preferences agent, and then move the file.

1   If the Activity Monitor utility is not running, open it.

2   In Activity Monitor, choose View menu > My Processes.

3   Make sure Preview is not running (it may help to sort the process list by process name, or use the Search field). If it is running, quit it.

4   Select cfprefsd in the process list, and then click the quit process button (the "X" in an octagon icon) in the toolbar.

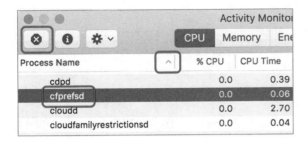

5 In the confirmation dialog, click Quit. Since the process is responding normally, it is not necessary to use Force Quit.

A new cfprefsd process will start automatically when it is needed. This sometimes happens so quickly that you may not see it vanish from the Activity Monitor list.

6 Switch to the Finder, and drag the com.apple.Preview.plist file to your desktop. Leave the Preferences folder open for later.

7 Open Preview again, and open its preferences (choose Preview menu > Preferences, or press Command-Comma).

The setting for "When opening files" has reset to its default of "Open groups of files in the same window."

8 Quit Preview.

9 Switch back to Activity Monitor, and quit cfprefsd again.

10 In the Finder, move the com.apple.Preview.plist file from your desktop back into the Preferences folder.

11 If you are notified that a newer item named com.apple.Preview.plist already exists, click Replace.

12 Open Preview again, and open its preferences.

This time your custom preference setting ("Open all files in one window") has been restored.

13 Quit Preview.

Manage Corrupted Preferences

macOS has some built-in features for dealing with corrupted preference files. You will explore what happens when a preference file becomes corrupted.

1 Use Activity Monitor to quit cfprefsd again.

2 In the Finder, Control-click the com.apple.Preview.plist file, and choose Open With > TextEdit from the shortcut menu.

Some PLIST files are stored in an XML/text format, which TextEdit can edit like any other text document. This PLIST file, however, is stored in a binary format TextEdit cannot fully display or edit. As a result, you see only part of the file's contents.

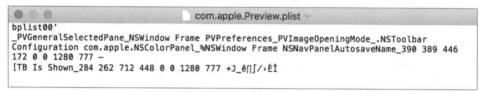

3 Add some new text anywhere in the document.

4 Quit TextEdit. Note that the changes are saved automatically.

5 Try to view the file using Quick Look (select it and press Command-Y).

By editing the file as if it were plain text, you have damaged its binary structure. As a result, Quick Look cannot display its contents and shows a generic view.

6   Close the Quick Look window.

7   Reopen Preview, and open its preferences.

Since the preferences file was damaged, the system has reset it, and the setting for "When opening files" has reset to its default of "Open groups of files in the same window."

8   Quit Preview, Activity Monitor, and any other apps that are still open.

9   Log out as Chris Johnson.

Exercise 18.3
Examine Application Diagnostics

▶ **Prerequisites**

▶ You must have created the Local Admin (Exercise 2.1, "Configure a New macOS System for Exercises," or Exercise 2.2, "Configure an Existing macOS System for Exercises") and Chris Johnson (Exercise 5.1, "Create a Standard User Account") accounts.

▶ You must have installed and forced the Dead End application to quit (Exercise 16.3, "Use a Drag-and-Drop Install," and Exercise 18.1, "Force Applications to Quit").

The Console utility is the primary tool in macOS for viewing system activity and event logs. In this exercise, you will use it to view diagnostic logs and to search the system log for application events.

View System Activity

1   If necessary, log out as Chris Johnson.

2   Log in as Local Admin.

The log files you'll examine in this exercise are readable only by administrators.

3   Open the Console utility.

Console is the primary tool in macOS for viewing logs. Its sidebar lets you view the computer's general log, as well as specific log files.

4   If necessary, select your computer in the Devices section of the sidebar.

5   In the toolbar, make sure that Now is selected, and Activities is not selected.

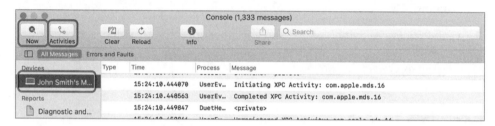

This view shows a wide variety of background events in macOS as they happen.

6   Select one of the events.

7   If necessary, select Info in the toolbar.

Details about the event are shown in the pane below the event list.

Gather Information About the Dead End Application

1   In the Reports section of the sidebar, select "Diagnostic and Usage Data" (the full name will not be visible).

2   In the Search field, enter dead end (the application you used in Exercise 18.1).

3   Scroll to the top of the message list.

If you performed Exercise 16.3 within the last few days, the first few messages relate to the first time you ran the Dead End application. The application was initially denied by the Gatekeeper policy, but then when you overrode that a rule was added allowing it to run.

4   If there are any "assessment denied" messages, select one.

Among other things, the message details will include the application's bundle ID (com.apple.training.Dead-End) and the reason access was denied ("no usable signature," because the application is not code-signed).

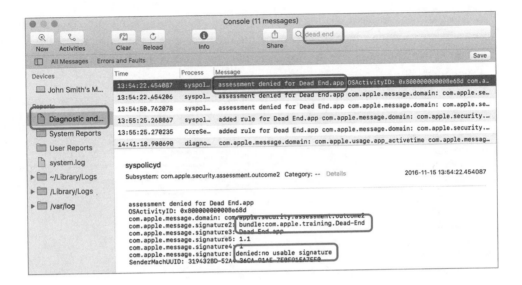

5   Click the Now button in the toolbar to show the latest messages.

The more recent messages relate to Dead End hanging or using excessive CPU time.

6   Select some of the recent messages and examine their details. Some of the messages from the spindump process will list the domain "com.apple.crashreporter.writereport .hang," which means that spindump wrote out a report with details of Dead End's status because it was not responding. You will view these reports shortly.

Note that although you see messages relating to Dead End hanging, you do not see anything about it being force-quit. To see that, you must look in a different place.

7   In the Console sidebar, select "system.log."

8   In the Search field, enter dead end.

Here you also see messages relating to spindump saving reports about Dead End, but nothing about Dead End being force-quit. There are messages in this log about it being force-quit, but they identify the application by its bundle ID (com.apple.training.Dead-End) rather than its name.

It is normal to have to look through multiple logs and do multiple searches for relevant messages, in order to piece together the full story of a particular problem or event.

9   Change the Search field to dead-end.

Now you see messages relating to the Dead End application being force-quit, and in each case showing which other process did the force-quit. In addition to the Dock and Activity Monitor, you see "loginwindow," the process that handles the Force Quit window.

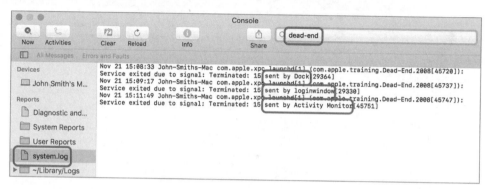

10 In the sidebar, select System Reports.

A second column opens, listing log files in this category. Unlike the other logs you've viewed so far, which list sequences of events, each of these files contains a detailed report about a single event.

11 In the second column, select one of the log files that starts "Dead End."

12 Erase the Search field to show the file's full contents.

Each file here shows that the system detected a problem with Dead End—hanging, using excessive CPU resources, or both. They give details about what was happening inside the Dead End application, and also list other related processes and what they were doing.

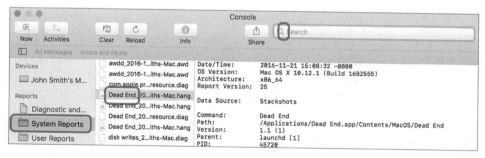

13 Quit Console and log out as Local Admin.

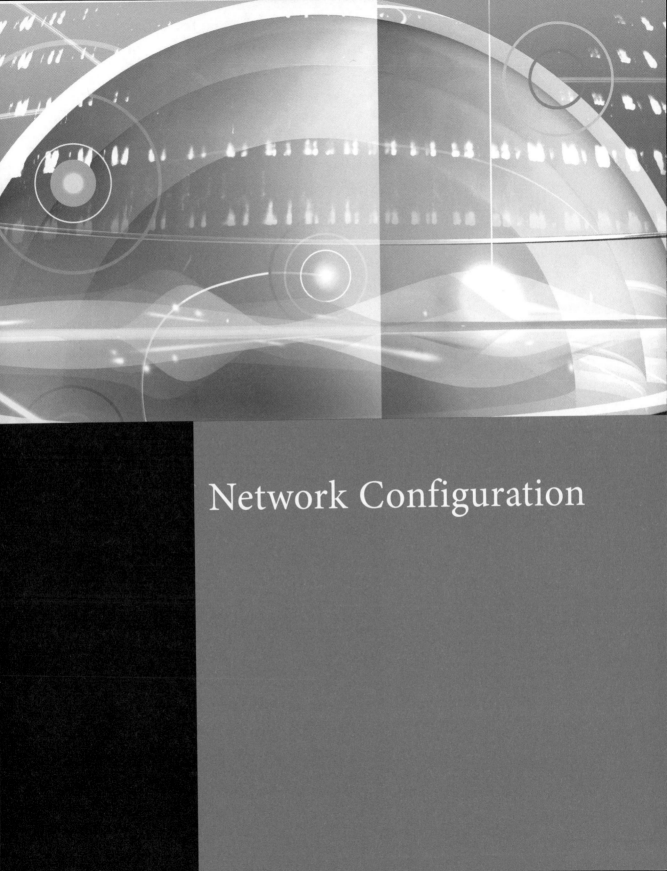

Network Configuration

Lesson 19

Manage Basic Network Settings

The ability to share information between computers across a network has always been important. During the early years of personal computer development, vendors designed their own proprietary local network systems. Yet although these vendor-specific technologies were suitable for private networks, they didn't allow for direct communication between dissimilar networks. Special hardware or software had to be put in place to translate from one vendor's network to another.

Around the same time, researchers were working at the behest of various U.S. organizations to create a wide area network (WAN) standard for military and governmental use. From this research was born the Internet protocol suite known as TCP/IP. The marriage of the Transmission Control Protocol (TCP) and the Internet Protocol (IP) became the universal language that allows computers to communicate on the Internet. This standard became so pervasive that nearly every network today, from small local networks all the way up to the largest long-distance network on Earth, the Internet, is based on the TCP/IP suite.

It should come as no surprise, then, that macOS includes a robust TCP/IP implementation. In fact, the first computer systems to popularize the use of TCP/IP were UNIX systems. Thus, much of the TCP/IP software built into every version of macOS is based on open source UNIX software that was established long before macOS ever existed as a product from Apple.

In this lesson, you will configure basic settings for both Ethernet and Wi-Fi networks. Before that, though, you must have a fundamental understanding of core network concepts, to which the first part of this lesson is devoted.

GOALS

▶ Describe fundamental TCP/IP network concepts

▶ Configure and monitor basic network settings

▶ Connect to a Wi-Fi network

Reference 19.1
About Network Terminology

Properly configuring and troubleshooting networking on any operating system requires a basic understanding of fundamental network concepts. Due to the widespread adoption of standardized network technology, the following network overview applies to nearly any operating system, macOS included. Basic network terminology is covered first, followed by an overview of the processes involved in actual data delivery across a network.

It's best to explore networking from a layered perspective. In fact, an established seven-layer model is used to describe network technologies: the Open Systems Interconnection reference model (known as the OSI model). Exploring networking using the OSI model goes beyond the scope of this guide.

> **MORE INFO** ▶ For more details on the OSI model for describing computer networks, refer to the Wikipedia entry http://en.wikipedia.org/wiki/OSI_model.

Consequently, networking concepts will be presented in a more simplistic abstraction of three basic elements:

▶ Network interface—The network interface is the medium through which network data flows. Network interfaces can be physical or virtual. The most common physical network interfaces for computers are Ethernet and 802.11 wireless networking, which is most commonly known as Wi-Fi. Virtual network interfaces are also available that can be used to increase the functionality of the physical interface: for example, a virtual private network (VPN) that uses the existing physical network interface to provide a secure connection without the need for a dedicated physical interface.

▶ Network protocol—A protocol defines a set of standard rules used for data representation, signaling, authentication, or error detection across network interfaces. Primarily, protocols are designed to ensure that all data is communicated properly and completely. Specific protocols have a narrow focus, so often multiple protocols are combined or layered to provide a complete network solution. For example, the combined TCP/IP protocol suite provides only for the addressing and end-to-end transport of data across the Internet; dozens of other protocols are required for something as simple as checking your email or browsing a website.

▶ Network service—In the context of network preferences, the term network service describes a configuration assigned to a network interface. For example, in the Network preferences, you will see the Wi-Fi service listed; this represents the connection settings for the Wi-Fi network interface. A fundamental feature of macOS is the ability to support multiple network services, or connections, for each individual network interface, be it physical or virtual.

NOTE ▶ A different definition of network service is used in **Lesson 22, "Manage Network Services," and Lesson 23, "Manage Host Sharing and Personal Firewall."** There, a network service is information provided on the network by a server for use by clients. Common examples in these lessons include file-sharing services, messaging services, and collaboration services. Often, a specific set of protocols is used to define how the particular service works.

Simplifying computer network technology to only three distinct elements does not provide a detailed abstraction, but it still shows clearly how each is related to the others. When a network interface, service, or protocol is created, it is often put through a review process before it's deemed a network standard. Standards committees are formed with members from multiple network organizations and vendors to ensure that new network standards remain interoperable with existing network standards. Most networking technologies in use today have been ratified by a standards body, so you may often come across an interface, protocol, or service labeled as a "standard."

About MAC Addresses

The Media Access Control (MAC) address is used to uniquely identify a physical network interface on a local network. Each physical network interface has at least one MAC address associated with it.

Because the most common network interface is Ethernet, people often refer to MAC addresses as Ethernet addresses. Still, nearly every other network interface type also uses some type of MAC address for unique identification. This includes, but isn't limited to, Wi-Fi, Bluetooth, and FireWire.

A MAC address is usually a 48-bit number represented by six groups of two-digit hexadecimal numbers separated by colons. For example, a typical MAC address would look something like this: 00:1C:B3:D7:2F:99. The first three number groups make up the organizationally unique identifier (OUI), and the last three number groups identify the network device itself. In other words, you can use the first three number groups of a MAC address to identify who made the network device.

MORE INFO ▶ The Institute of Electrical and Electronics Engineers (IEEE) maintains a searchable database of publicly listed OUIs on its website: http://standards.ieee.org/ develop/regauth/oui/public.html.

About IP Addresses

Communicating with computers on both local and remote networks requires an IP address. IP addresses, unlike MAC addresses, are not permanently tied to a network interface. Instead, they are assigned to the network interface based on the local network to which it's connected. This means that if you have a portable computer, every new network you connect to will probably require a new IP address. If necessary, you can assign multiple IP addresses to each network interface, but this approach is often only used for computers that are providing network services.

Currently two standards exist for IP addresses: IPv4 and IPv6. IPv4 was the first widely used IP addressing scheme and is the most common today. An IPv4 address is a 32-bit number represented by four groups of three-digit numbers, also known as octets, separated by periods. Each octet has a value between 0 and 255. For example, a typical IPv4 address would look something like this: 10.1.45.186.

With IPv4, a little over 4 billon unique addresses exist. This may seem like a lot, but considering how many new network-ready devices come out, and the number of people who want to own multiple network-ready gadgets, this number isn't really big enough. For the time being, the available IPv4 addresses are extended by using network routers that can share a single routable, or "real-world," IPv4 address across a range of reusable private network addresses. This is how most home networks are configured, but it is only a temporary solution for what's to come next.

The successor to IPv4 is IPv6, but because IPv4 is so much a part of the backbone of the Internet, the transition to IPv6 has been slow. The main advantage to IPv6 is a much larger address space—so large, in fact, that every person on Earth could have roughly 1.2 x 1019 copies of the entire IPv4 address range. This may appear to be a ridiculous number of IP addresses, but the design goal of IPv6 was to eliminate the need for private addressing and allow for easier address reassignment and changing to a new network.

An IPv6 address is a 128-bit number that is presented in eight groups of four-digit hexadecimal numbers separated by colons. Hexadecimal numbers use a base-16 digit system, so after the number 9 you use the letters A through F. For example, a typical IPv6 address would look something like this: 2C01:0EF9:0000:0000:0000:0000:142D:57AB. Long strings of zeros in an IPv6 address can be abbreviated using a double colon, resulting in an address more like this: 2C01:0EF9::142D:57AB.

About Subnet Masks

The computer uses the subnet mask to determine the IPv4 address range of the local network. Networks based on the IPv6 protocol do not require subnet masks. A subnet mask is similar to an IPv4 address in that it's a 32-bit number arranged in four groups of octets. The computer applies the subnet mask to its own IP address to determine the local network's address range. The nonzero bits in a subnet mask (typically 255) correspond to the portion of the IP address that determines which network the address is on. The zero bits correspond to the portion of the IP address that differs between hosts on the same network.

For example, assuming your computer has an IP address of 10.1.5.3 and a commonly used subnet mask of 255.255.255.0, the local network is defined as hosts that have IP addresses ranging from 10.1.5.1 to 10.1.5.254.

> **MORE INFO** ▶ Another way of writing the subnet mask is known as Classless Inter-Domain Routing (CIDR) notation. This is written as the IP address, a slash, and then the number of 1 bits in the subnet mask. The previous subnet example would be 10.1.5.3/24. You can find out more about CIDR notation from Wikipedia: http://en.wikipedia.org/wiki/Classless_Inter-Domain_Routing.

Whenever the computer attempts to communicate with another network device, it applies the subnet mask to the destination IP address of the other device to determine whether it's on the local network as well. If so, the computer attempts to directly access the other network device. If not, the other device is clearly on another network, and the computer sends all communications bound for that other device to the router address.

About Router Addresses

Routers are network devices that manage connections between separate networks; as their name implies, they route network traffic between the networks they bridge. Routing tables are maintained by routers to determine where network traffic goes. Even if a router is presented with traffic destined for a network that the router is unaware of, it still routes the traffic to another router that it thinks is closer to the final destination. Thus, routers literally are the brains of the Internet.

To reach computers beyond the local network, your computer needs to be configured with the IP address of the router that connects the local network with another network or, more commonly in residential situations, an Internet service provider. Typically, the router's address is at the beginning of the local address range, and it's always in the same subnet. Using the previous example, assuming your computer has an IP address of 10.1.5.3 and a commonly used subnet mask of 255.255.255.0, the local network IP address range would be 10.1.5.0 to 10.1.5.255, and the router address would most likely be 10.1.5.1.

About TCP

Transmission Control Protocol (TCP) is the primary protocol used to facilitate end-to-end data connectivity between two IP devices. TCP is the preferred transport mechanism for many Internet services because it guarantees reliable and in-order delivery of data. In other words, IP provides network addressing and data routing, and TCP ensures that the data arrives at its destination complete. The combination of these two protocols encompasses the TCP/IP suite, commonly known as the Internet protocol suite.

The TCP/IP protocol suite chops continuous data streams into many individual packets of information before they are sent across the network. This is because IP networks use packet-switching technology to route and transmit data. Almost all digital networking technologies are packet based, because this provides efficient transport for network connections that aren't always reliable. Remember that the TCP/IP protocol was originally designed with the military in mind, so packet-based network technology is ideal because it's designed to work around communications link failures. This is why sophisticated routing hardware was originally developed for TCP/IP networks—so that data could be literally rerouted and re-sent should a network link go down.

A lesser-used protocol known as User Datagram Protocol (UDP) is also attached to the TCP/IP suite. UDP is a simpler protocol that does not guarantee the reliability or ordering of data sent across networks. This may seem like a poor choice for networking, but in some cases UDP is preferred because it provides better performance than TCP. Examples of network services that use UDP include Domain Name System (DNS), media streaming, voice over IP (VoIP), and online gaming. These services have been designed to tolerate lost or out-of-order data so that they can benefit from UDP's increased performance.

MORE INFO ▸ For more information on the Internet protocol suite, refer to this Wikipedia entry: http://en.wikipedia.org/wiki/internet_protocol_suite.

Reference 19.2
About Network Activity

Manually assigning an IP address, a subnet mask, and a router address is technically all that is needed to configure a computer to use TCP/IP-based networking on both local area networks (LANs) and WANs. Yet two other network services are almost always involved in basic network functionality: Dynamic Host Configuration Protocol (DHCP) and DNS. These two services, combined with TCP/IP, characterize core network functionality that provides the foundation for nearly any network service.

About LAN Traffic

Most LANs use some form of wired or wireless connection. Once the network interface has been established, TCP/IP networking must be configured, either manually or via DHCP. Once both these steps are complete, network communication can begin.

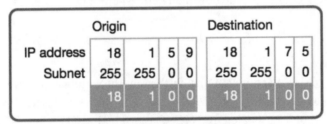

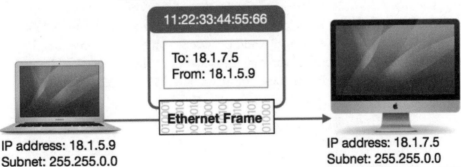

TCP/IP packets are encased inside Ethernet frames to travel across the local network. The TCP/IP packet includes the originating IP and destination IP addresses along with the data to be sent. The network device applies the subnet mask setting to determine whether the destination IP address is on the local network. If so, it consults its Address Resolution Protocol (ARP) table to see whether it knows the MAC address corresponding to the destination IP address. Each network host maintains and continuously updates an ARP table of known MAC addresses that correspond to IP addresses on the local network. If the MAC address is not listed yet, it broadcasts an ARP request to the local network asking the destination device to reply with its MAC address, and adds the reply to its ARP table for next time. Once the MAC address is determined, an outgoing Ethernet frame, encasing the TCP/IP packet, is sent using the destination MAC address.

The other network device likely returns some information as well, using the same technique of transferring TCP/IP packets inside MAC-addressed Ethernet frames. This goes on and on for thousands of packets every second to complete a data stream. For standard Ethernet the maximum frame size is only 1500 bytes (that's roughly 1.5 kilobytes, or 0.0015 megabytes), so you can imagine how many Ethernet frames are necessary to transmit even a small file.

About WAN Traffic

Sending data over a WAN differs only in that data is sent through one or more network routers to reach its intended destination. WANs exist in all shapes and sizes, from a small WAN perhaps used to connect separate LANs in a large building all the way up to the biggest and most popular WAN, the Internet.

NOTE ▶ This WAN example is simplified for the purposes of easy explanation. It's now very common to use a router with Network Address Translation (NAT). This allows you to use use one real-world IP address as the external interface for your router and then internally you can use as many private internal IP addresses as you want. Private IP address ranges are 10.0.0.0–10.255.255.255, 172.16.0.0–172.31.255.255, and 192.168.0.0–192.168.255.255.

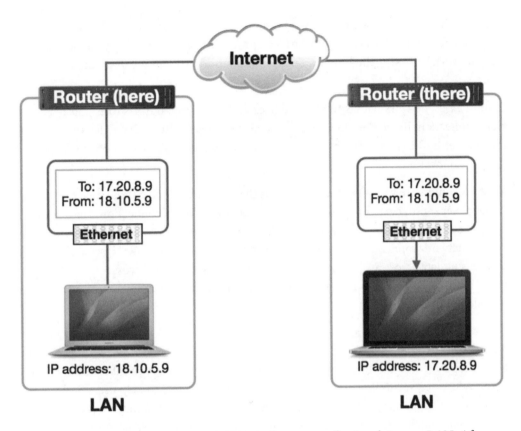

Initially, transferring data across a WAN is similar to transferring data on a LAN. After all, the first stop for the data destined for the WAN is at the network router on the local network. The network device prepares the packets as before by encasing the TCP/IP packets inside Ethernet frames. Once again, the subnet mask is applied to the destination IP address to determine whether the address is on the local network. In this case, the network device determines that the destination is not on the local network, so it sends the data to the router. Because the router is on the local network, the transmission between the local network client and the router is identical to standard LAN traffic.

Once the router receives the Ethernet-encased TCP/IP packets, it examines the destination IP address and uses a routing table to determine the next closest destination for this packet. This almost always involves sending the packet to another router closer to the destination. In fact, only the last router in the path sends the data to the destination network device.

Network routers also often perform some sort of hardware interface conversion, as WAN network links are rarely standard copper Ethernet connections. The router strips the Ethernet container away from the original TCP/IP packet and then rewraps it in another container that is appropriate for the WAN connection. Obviously, the final router has to prepare the TCP/IP packet for the last leg of the journey on the destination device's local network by rewrapping it in an Ethernet frame addressed to the destination's MAC address.

In most cases, network data is transferred back and forth several times to establish a complete connection. Remember that these packet sizes are very small. The default packet size for Internet traffic is also 1500 bytes, with a maximum packet size of 65,535 bytes for most TCP/IP connections.

Network routers are highly optimized devices that can easily handle thousands of data packets every second, so for small amounts of data many WAN connections "feel" as fast as LAN connections. Conversely, a lot of latency is introduced from all the different routers and network connections involved in transferring data across a WAN, so sending large amounts of data across a WAN is often much slower than sending across a LAN. Thus, many users' favorite time-wasting computer practice was born: waiting for an Internet download or upload.

About DNS

Most people are bad at remembering strings of seemingly arbitrary numbers used to define addresses, so additional technology is often implemented to help users find addresses. Even the simplest mobile phones feature a contact list so that users don't have to remember phone numbers. For TCP/IP networks, the Domain Name System (DNS) makes network addressing much more approachable to normal humans.

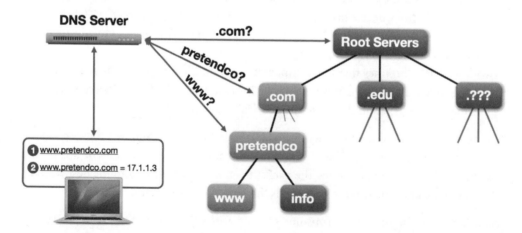

In essence, DNS is a worldwide network of domain servers with the task of maintaining human-friendly host names used to easily locate specific network IP addresses. If you've spent any time at all on the Internet, you're already familiar with the DNS naming convention. For example, the Apple website is located at www.apple.com. Any network device can have a host name, but only those network devices providing a service that needs to be easily located need to have host name entries on a DNS server. Devices providing shared services, such as printers and server computers, are the most common devices to have DNS entries.

The hierarchical DNS naming convention relates directly to the hierarchical structure of the DNS domain architecture. As you know, DNS names are broken into labels separated by periods. Each label represents a different level, or domain, of the DNS hierarchy.

The top of the DNS hierarchy is the root or "." domain. The names that are part of the root domain are the familiar abbreviations at the end of nearly every Internet resource. Common examples are .com, .edu, and .gov, among others, including various country codes. These top-level domains (TLDs) are hosted by a consortium of commercial and governmental organizations.

Below the TLDs, individual organizations or users host or rent their own DNS domains. For example, Apple hosts several DNS servers that are known by the TLD servers to maintain the apple.com domain. Apple can host an unlimited number of host names inside the apple.com domain. Apple can also create unlimited names in the domain by preceding "apple.com" with any text. Examples include www.apple.com, training.apple.com, and developer.apple.com.

When a local network device needs to resolve a DNS name into the corresponding IP address, it sends the name query to the IP address of a DNS server. The IP address for a DNS server is usually configured along with the other TCP/IP address information for the network device. The DNS server searches its local and cached name records first. If the requested name isn't found locally, the server queries other domain servers in the DNS hierarchy.

This process may take a while, so DNS servers temporarily cache any names they have recently resolved to provide a quicker response for future requests. Querying a DNS server to resolve an IP address given a known host name is called a forward lookup, whereas querying a DNS server to resolve a host name from a known IP address is called a reverse lookup. When initially configured, network clients query the DNS server with a reverse lookup of its own IP address to determine whether the network client has its own DNS name.

MORE INFO ▶ For more information on DNS, refer to this Wikipedia entry: http://en.wikipedia.org/wiki/Domain_Name_System.

MORE INFO ▶ Bonjour is a name discovery service that uses a name space similar to DNS. Bonjour is covered in **Lesson 22, "Manage Network Services."**

About DHCP

Although not required to provide network functionality, Dynamic Host Configuration Protocol (DHCP) is used by nearly all network clients to automatically acquire preliminary TCP/IP configuration. In some situations, an administrator user may still choose to manually enter TCP/IP networking configuration information. This is often the case with network devices that are providing network services. However, manually configuring multitudes of network clients is tedious work subject to human error. Thus, even on rigorously managed networks, DHCP is still widely used to configure network clients.

NOTE ▶ DHCP is specifically designed to assign IPv4 addressing; IPv6 addressing is handled automatically via other mechanisms.

NOTE ▶ A precursor to DHCP is Bootstrap Protocol (BOOTP). DHCP is backward compatible with BOOTP but provides greater functionality and reliability.

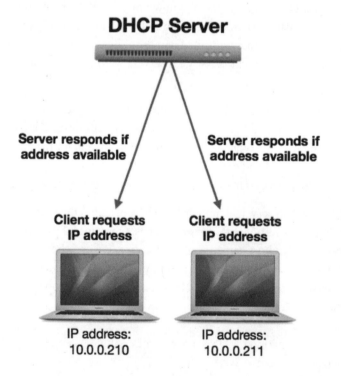

A DHCP server is required to provide the service. On many networks, the network routers provide the DHCP service, but in some cases a dedicated server or network appliance can be used for this purpose. When a network device becomes active on the network, it first negotiates a link with the hardware interface, and then sends out a broadcast to the local network requesting DHCP information. Because the new network client doesn't yet have an IP address, it uses the network interface's MAC address for identification.

If a DHCP server that is listening has available addresses, it sends back a reply to the client with TCP/IP configuration information. At a minimum, this information includes an IP address, a subnet mask, a router, and a DHCP lease time that defines how long the client can retain the address before it's given away. Ancillary DHCP information often also includes DNS configuration.

> **MORE INFO** ▶ For more information on DHCP, refer to this Wikipedia entry: http://en.wikipedia.org/wiki/Dhcp.

Reference 19.3
Configure Basic Network Settings

Initial networking configuration is handled by Setup Assistant, which runs the first time you start up a new Mac or a fresh macOS system installation. Setup Assistant makes it easy for even a novice user to configure network settings. Yet even if you choose not to set up networking during the initial system setup process, the Mac automatically enables any active network interface, including connecting to unrestricted wireless networks, and attempts to configure TCP/IP via DHCP. Consequently, for many users macOS does not require any initial network configuration at all.

> **MORE INFO** ▶ Advanced network configuration techniques are covered in Lesson 20, "Manage Advanced Network Settings."

About Network Preferences

If network changes are required after initial setup, you can still use Network Setup Assistant to help guide you through the network configuration process. You can access Network Setup Assistant by first clicking the "Assist me" button at the bottom of Network preferences, and then click the Assistant button.

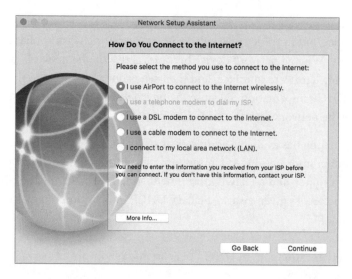

Although this tool is helpful for novice users, get familiar with all network configuration options so you're prepared for any potential network situation or troubleshooting issue. All network preferences and configuration windows are consolidated into a unified interface. Thus, all network settings can be found in Network preferences. Note that Network preferences are available only to administrator users. A standard user attempting to open Network preferences will notice a lock in the lower-right corner. However, because DHCP is enabled by default for Ethernet and Wi-Fi interfaces, for most situations network configuration is automatic.

NOTE ► In the preceding screenshot, note that DHCP is also providing configuration for the DNS server. Recognize that if no DNS server IP address is configured, your Mac cannot resolve DNS host names. Thus, in most cases Internet connections will fail.

Select Wi-Fi Networks

Wireless networking, also known by the technical specification 802.11 or the more common "Wi-Fi," has become the dominant local network connectivity standard. Ethernet is certainly still popular, but Wi-Fi has cut the cord by allowing easy network access for an ever-increasing number of portable devices. Apple made basic Wi-Fi network management a breeze with automatic Wi-Fi network discovery and the Wi-Fi status menu. These Wi-Fi setup mechanisms give nonadministrator users access to the most commonly needed Wi-Fi network settings.

macOS always remembers Wi-Fi networks that were previously connected, by default. Thus, if you start up or wake a portable Mac, it will attempt to locate and reconnect to any previously connected Wi-Fi networks. If an appropriate Wi-Fi network isn't found, you will need to manually select a new one from the Wi-Fi status menu near the upper-right corner of the display. When you select this menu, the Wi-Fi background process automatically scans for any advertised networks that are within range so you can choose among them.

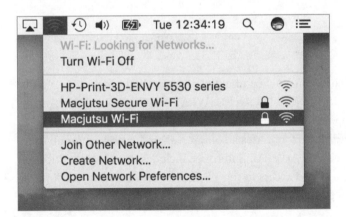

A service set identifier (SSID) identifies a Wi-Fi network's name and associated configuration information. An administrator of the devices providing Wi-Fi services sets the network's name and configuration settings. macOS uses the information in the SSID configuration to automatically establish Wi-Fi network communications.

Aside from Wi-Fi network names, the most important indicator this menu shows is the relative strength of any Wi-Fi network, as indicated by the number of black bars compared to gray bars. The more black bars displayed, the greater the strength of the Wi-Fi signal.

Authenticate to Wi-Fi Networks

If you select an open wireless network, the Mac immediately connects, but if you select a secure wireless network, as indicated by the small lock icon, you have to enter the network password. When you select a secure network, in most cases the system automatically negotiates the authentication type, and for many networks you need only enter a common shared Wi-Fi password.

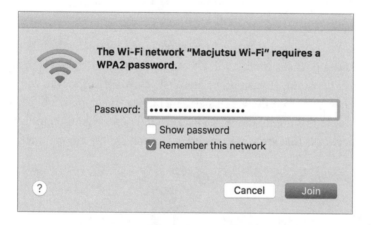

macOS supports the most common Wi-Fi authentication standards, including Wired Equivalent Privacy (WEP), Wi-Fi Protected Access (WPA), and Wi-Fi Protected Access II (WPA2). This includes support for WPA/WPA2 in both their personal and enterprise forms. Essentially, WPA/WPA2 Personal uses a common shared password for all users of the Wi-Fi network, whereas WPA/WPA2 Enterprise includes 802.1X authentication, which allows for per-user password access to the Wi-Fi network. WPA/WPA2 Enterprise authentication is covered in the next section of this lesson.

> **NOTE ▶** It is well known that WEP is an easily compromised security protocol and should be avoided. Thus, WPA/WPA2 are preferred protocols.

If you join a WEP or WPA/WPA2 Personal Wi-Fi network, the system automatically saves the passwords to the System keychain. This is what allows the Mac to automatically reconnect to the Wi-Fi network immediately after startup or waking up. Also, because the password is saved to the System keychain, all users can access the wireless network without needing to reenter the password.

> **MORE INFO** ▶ Details of the Keychain system are covered in Lesson 7, "Manage Security and Privacy."

Authenticate to Automatic WPA Enterprise Networks

If you join and authenticate to a wireless network that uses WPA or WPA2 Enterprise, it's implied that the authentication is handled via 802.1X. Thus, joining this type of network automatically creates an 802.1X service configuration.

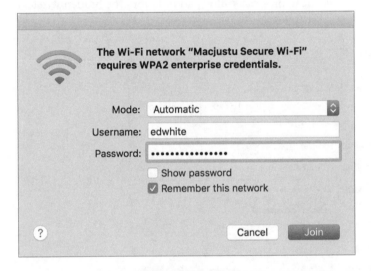

As you can see in this screenshot, when 802.1X is used, you must enter both a username and password to authenticate the connection. You may also be prompted with a server certificate verification dialog. You must accept this certificate to continue, but completing the configuration requires administrator authentication.

A user with administrator rights is required because this will add the wireless authentication server certificate to the System keychain. Assuming the server configuration doesn't change, you will only have to accept this certificate once per system. Future connections to this wireless network will require only that users enter their normal authentication credentials.

Join Hidden Wi-Fi Networks

In some cases, wireless networks may not advertise their availability. You can connect to these hidden wireless networks (also called closed networks) as long as you know their network name (or SSID) by choosing Join Other Network from the Wi-Fi status menu. In the dialog, you can enter all the appropriate information to join the hidden wireless network.

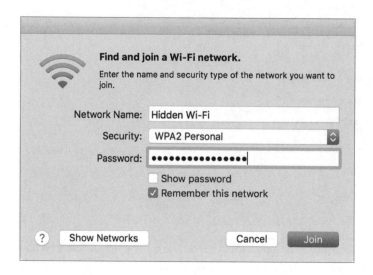

Create an Ad Hoc Wi-Fi Network

If you are unable to connect to a standard wireless network, you can create an ad hoc wireless network using your Mac computer's Wi-Fi connection to share files wirelessly with other computers. Choose Create Network from the Wi-Fi status menu and then enter the wireless network name that will be used to connect to your ad hoc network. Other devices will select this name to join your Mac computer's Wi-Fi network.

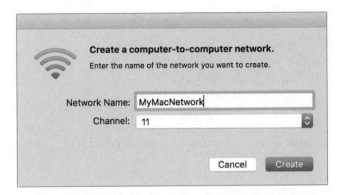

Leaving an ad hoc network enabled on your Mac is a potential security risk. Thus, you should only leave it enabled when you need to use it. To prevent other computers from connecting to the ad hoc network, turn off the Wi-Fi hardware or choose another wireless network from the Wi-Fi status menu.

> **MORE INFO** ▶ Do not confuse the creation of an ad hoc Wi-Fi network with the macOS AirDrop Wi-Fi sharing feature. Creating a Wi-Fi network has permanence, and it can be used by other non–macOS systems. AirDrop allows for only temporary connections Mac computers. You can find out more about AirDrop in **Lesson 23, "Manage Host Sharing and Personal Firewall."**

Exercise 19.1
Connect to a Wi-Fi Network

▶ **Prerequisites**

- ▶ You must have created the Local Admin (Exercise 2.1, "Configure a New macOS System for Exercises," or Exercise 2.2, "Configure an Existing macOS System for Exercises") and Chris Johnson (Exercise 5.1, "Create a Standard User Account") accounts.

- ▶ Your computer must have a Wi-Fi interface, and you must have access to an available Wi-Fi network that you are not already connected to.

macOS makes joining a wireless network simple. In this exercise, you will examine the process of finding and joining a wireless network.

Verify Your Network Settings

1   If necessary, log in as Chris Johnson.

2   Open System Preferences, and select the Network pane.

3   Click the padlock, and authenticate as Local Admin.

4   Select the Wi-Fi service from the sidebar. If you do not have Wi-Fi service, you cannot perform this exercise.

5   If necessary, click the Turn Wi-Fi On button.

6   If necessary, select "Show Wi-Fi status in menu bar."

7   Click Advanced.

8   Examine the options available on the Wi-Fi tab.

The Preferred Networks list allows you to control which networks this computer joins automatically and includes an option to add networks to this list as your computer joins them. You can also control whether administrator authorization is required for certain operations.

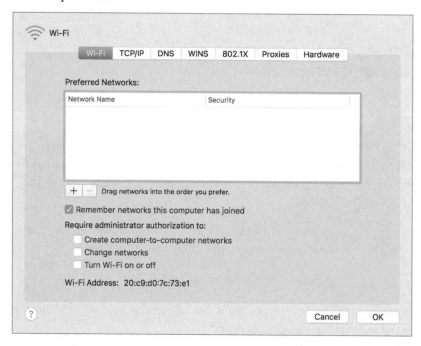

9 Click OK.

10 If you made any changes, click Apply.

11 Click the Wi-Fi status menu.

A list of visible networks in your area is shown. Note that it may take a few seconds for your computer to discover all the local networks.

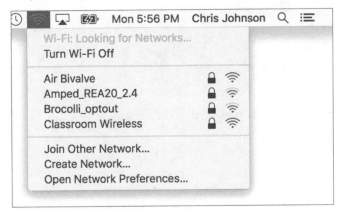

Note that this list is also available in Network preferences, in the Network Name pop-up menu.

If you are performing these exercises in a class, the instructor provides you with the name of the network to join (and, if necessary, security information for it).

If the network you want to join is shown in the list, follow the steps in the section "Option 1: Join a Visible Network." If it is not shown, the network may be configured as invisible (or "SSID broadcast disabled"), in which case you need to follow the steps in the section "Option 2: Join an Invisible Network."

Option 1: Join a Visible Network

1 Choose the network you want to join from the Wi-Fi status menu.

If the wireless network is encrypted, you are prompted for the network password. Selecting the "Remember this network" option allows your computer to automatically reconnect to this network whenever it is available.

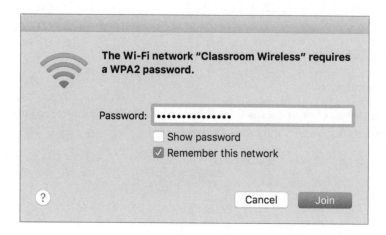

2 If you are prompted, enter the network password, and click Join.

Skip ahead to the "Verify Your Connection" section.

Option 2: Join an Invisible Network

1 Choose Join Other Network from the Wi-Fi status menu.

2 Enter the network's name (SSID).

3 If the network is encrypted, you need to know its encryption type as well as the password. Choose the encryption type from the Security pop-up menu, and then enter the network password. Selecting the "Remember this network" option allows your computer to automatically reconnect to this network whenever it is available.

4   Enter the security information, and click Join.

Verify Your Connection

If macOS detects that the wireless network you have joined is connected to a captive portal, it opens a window showing the portal's sign-in page.

1   If a captive portal window appears, follow its instructions to get full network access. A captive portal might require you to agree to its terms of service, authenticate, watch an advertisement, or meet other requirements before it allows you full network access.

2   In Network preferences, look at the status indicator next to the Wi-Fi service.

The status indicator will be green if the computer is connected to a network and has address information configured. If the indicator is not green, you did not successfully join the network and may have to troubleshoot the connection.

3   Click the Wi-Fi status menu.

It shows a number of arcs to indicate the signal strength of the wireless network. If all the arcs are light gray, you are not joined to a wireless network or are receiving only a weak signal.

4   Option-click the Wi-Fi status menu.

The menu opens and displays additional information about your connection, including the current wireless speed ("Transmit rate") and signal strength (RSSI; note that –50 is a strong signal, and –100 is a weak one).

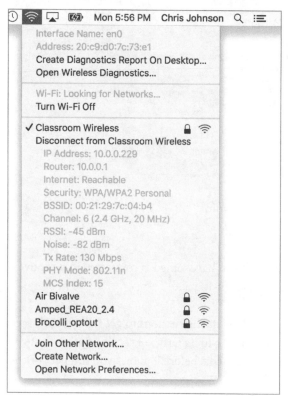

Exercise 19.2
Monitor Network Connectivity

▶ **Prerequisite**

▶ You must have created the Chris Johnson account (Exercise 5.1, "Create a Standard User Account").

In this exercise, you will break your primary network connection and observe how that change is reflected in the Network pane of System Preferences. The Network pane dynamically updates as network connectivity changes, so it is a valuable tool for troubleshooting connectivity issues.

Monitor Connectivity via Network Preferences

The Network Status view of Network preferences shows the status of all active configured network interfaces. User-initiated connections such as PPP and VPN are also listed. Users can view the Network Status pane to verify their active connections in order of priority.

1   If necessary, log in as Chris Johnson.

2   If necessary, open System Preferences, and select the Network pane.

Notice the status of your network connections on the left side of the window. The green status indicators show which network services are active, and their order shows their priority. Whichever service is at the top of the list is your current "primary" service, and it is used for all Internet connectivity. Make a note of which service is currently the primary service.

If you do not have any services with green status indicators, you do not have a network connection and cannot perform this exercise.

3   Select the current primary service.

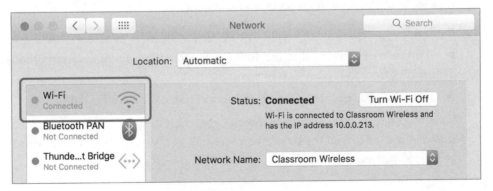

4   Watch the status indicators and service order as you disable the connection for your primary network service. How to do this depends on what type of service it is:

▶   If it is an Ethernet service, unplug the Ethernet cable from your computer.

▶   If it is a Wi-Fi service, click the Turn Wi-Fi Off button.

▶   If it is a dial-in or mobile broadband service, click the Disconnect button.

When the service is disabled, its status indicator turns red or yellow, and it drops down in the service order. If you have another active service, it becomes the new primary service.

The detailed view on the right also changes to indicate why the service is disabled.

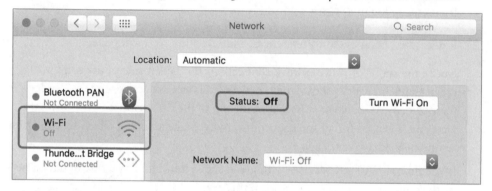

5   Again, watch the status indicators and service order as you reenable the connection. How to do this depends on what type of service it is:

▶   If it is an Ethernet service, plug the Ethernet cable back into your computer.

▶   If it is a Wi-Fi service, click the Turn Wi-Fi On button, and if necessary, choose the network from the Network Name pop-up menu.

▶   If it is a dial-in or mobile broadband service, click the Connect button.

It may take a few seconds for the network connection to appear and the service to reconfigure itself. When the service becomes fully active, its status indicator turns green, and it rises to the top of the service list.

Lesson 20

Manage Advanced Network Settings

A strong understanding of network fundamentals is required to properly configure advanced network settings without error. Consequently, this lesson builds on the network essentials topics covered in the previous lesson. This lesson focuses squarely on the unique and powerful macOS user interface for managing network configuration, Network preferences. First, this lesson presents an overview of the macOS network configuration architecture and supported network interfaces and protocols. You will then dive deeper into the more advanced network configuration options.

GOALS

▸ Understand the macOS network configuration architecture

▸ Manage multiple network locations and service interfaces

▸ Configure advanced network settings

Reference 20.1
Manage Network Locations

Similarly to how applications are designed to save information to any number of individual documents, macOS enables you to save network settings to any number of individual network configurations, known as network locations. A network location contains all network interface, service, and protocol settings, allowing you to configure as many unique network locations as you need for different situations. For example, you could create one network location for home and a different one for work. Each location would contain all the appropriate settings for that location's network state.

A network location can contain numerous active network service interfaces. This allows you to define a single location with multiple network connections. The system automatically prioritizes multiple service interfaces based on a service order that you set. Details about using multiple network service interfaces are covered throughout this lesson.

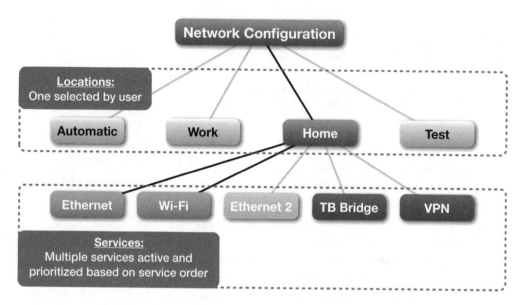

It is not necessary to add new network locations to change network settings, but it is more convenient, because you can easily switch back to the previous network location if you make a mistake. Thus, creating additional network locations is an essential network troubleshooting technique. Also, because macOS always requires one active network location, if you ever want to temporarily turn off networking you have to create a new location with all the network service interfaces disabled.

Configure Network Locations

The default network location on macOS is called Automatic. Despite this, this first location is no more automatic than any other network location you create. The initial location is called Automatic to indicate that it attempts to automatically initialize any network service interface to establish a TCP/IP connection via DHCP—but all network locations, regardless of their name, attempt this as well.

To configure network locations, open Network preferences by choosing Apple menu > System Preferences and then clicking the Network icon. You may have to click the lock icon in the lower-left corner and authenticate as an administrator user to unlock Network preferences. Choose Edit Locations from the Location pop-up menu to reveal the interface for editing network locations.

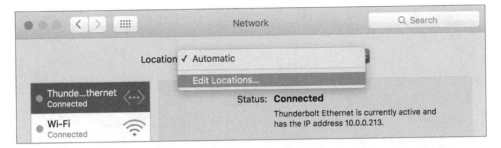

To add a new location with default settings, click the Add (+) button and then enter a new name for the location. Or you can duplicate an existing location by selecting its name from the Locations list, clicking the Action button (gear icon), and then choosing Duplicate Location from the pop-up menu. Finally, double-clicking a location name allows you to rename it.

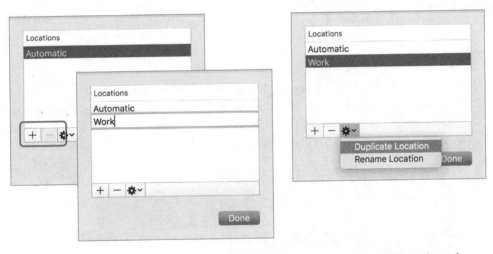

When you are finished making location changes, click Done to return to Network preferences. Network preferences automatically loads the newly created location but won't apply the location settings to the system. If you want to work with another location, choose it from the Location pop-up menu, and Network preferences loads it but won't apply it to the system.

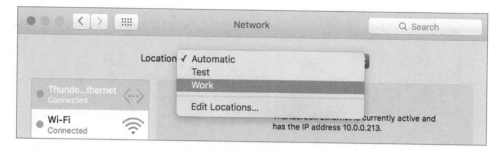

You may have noticed that the network settings are different from all the other system preferences in that you must click Apply to activate the new settings. This allows you to easily prepare new network locations and services without disrupting the current network configuration.

TIP ▶ If you make a mistake at any time using Network preferences, click Revert to return to the current active network configuration.

Select a Network Location

Though you can certainly choose and apply a different network location from Network preferences, only administrator users have this ability, since normal users do not have access to Network preferences. Conversely, all users (including standard users) can quickly and easily change the network location by choosing Apple menu > Location > <location name>.

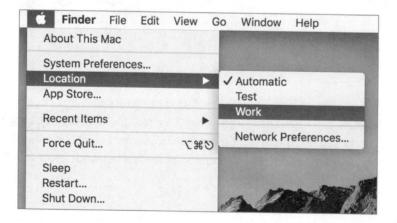

This applies the selected network location. Keep in mind that changing locations may interrupt network connections. Once a network location is selected, it remains active until another location is selected. Even if other users log in to the Mac or the Mac is restarted, the selected network location remains active.

NOTE ▶ The Location menu option does not appear in the Apple menu if only one network location exists. Thus, from an administrative perspective, if you want to configure the system so that standard users cannot change network locations, do not configure additional network locations.

Reference 20.2
About Network Interfaces and Protocols

Mac hardware has a long history of providing built-in network connectivity. Apple started including Ethernet on Mac computers as early as 1991, and it was the first manufacturer to have wireless as a built-in option when it introduced the iBook in 1999. Mac models have varied over the years as network technologies have grown increasingly faster and more affordable.

About Network Hardware Interfaces

You can identify the hardware network service interfaces available to your Mac from the /Applications/Utilities/System Information or /System/Library/CoreServices/Applications /Network Utility applications. Many of these interfaces automatically appear as a network service in Network preferences.

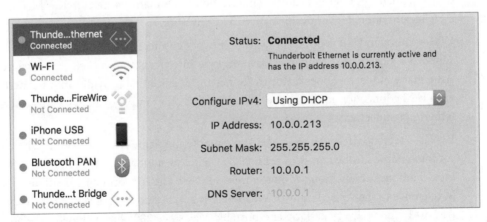

The newest hardware interface on Mac computers is Thunderbolt 3, a very high-speed connection technology. Thunderbolt, in all its versions, is also extremely flexible, allowing for a wide variety of adapters. For example, Apple offers a Thunderbolt-to–Gigabit Ethernet Adapter and a Thunderbolt-to-FireWire adapter. In the previous screenshot, note the awkward name truncation for the attached Thunderbolt adapters.

macOS includes built-in support for the following hardware network interfaces:

▶ Bluetooth—This relatively low-speed wireless interface has become popular as a short-range connectivity standard. Every recent Mac that includes Wi-Fi support also includes Bluetooth. macOS supports Bluetooth as a network bridge to some mobile phones and hotspots, like iPhones, that can provide Internet connectivity via a cellular network.

▶ Ethernet—Ethernet is the family of IEEE 802.3 standards that define most modern wired LANs. Every Mac desktop since 1997 has included standard built-in Ethernet connectivity, with some models even featuring multiple Ethernet interfaces. Until recently most Mac portables also included standard built-in Ethernet connectivity. However, with the prevalence of Wi-Fi networks and the popularity of smaller portable devices, recent Mac portables are dropping standard Ethernet connectivity. For these systems Apple offers optional USB Ethernet (100baseT) and Thunderbolt-to–Gigabit Ethernet adapters.

▶ FireWire—FireWire is the Apple marketing name for the IEEE 1394 connection standard. Though not a common network standard, macOS includes software that allows you to create small ad hoc networks using daisy-chained FireWire cables. FireWire is standard on many older Mac models.

▶ Thunderbolt Bridge—As with FireWire, you can create small ad hoc networks using daisy-chained Thunderbolt cables. Thunderbolt is standard on most newer Mac systems and offers higher performance than FireWire.

▶ USB—Although USB is not technically a network connectivity standard, macOS supports a variety of USB adapters that provide Internet access via cellular networks. Also, many modern phones feature a "tethering" service that provides Internet access via a USB connection to the phone. The iPhone is an example of a device that offers tethering connectivity.

▶ Wi-Fi—Previously referred to by the Apple marketing name AirPort, Wi-Fi is the more common name for the family of IEEE 802.11 wireless standards, which have become the default implementation for most wireless LANs. The AirPort name is still used in reference to the Apple family of Wi-Fi network base stations: AirPort Express and AirPort Extreme. Every desktop and portable Mac since 2006 has included standard built-in Wi-Fi connectivity. Wi-Fi was an option for older Mac Pro computers, but starting with the new smaller Mac Pro design in 2013, Wi-Fi is standard.

About Cellular Internet Connections

Internet access via cellular networks is nothing new, but in the last few years this type of connectivity has seen a huge growth in popularity. With most major carriers offering ever-faster near-broadband speeds and expanded geographical coverage, many people are relying on cellular networks as their primary Internet access. As a result, a variety of devices and methods are available for providing cellular Internet access for your Mac.

NOTE ▶ The capabilities and configuration of cellular devices vary greatly. Check with your cellular device vendor about how to enable Internet access for your specific device.

macOS supports use of cellular Internet connections via:

▶ Bluetooth personal area network (PAN)—Many current cellular devices allow for Internet connectivity by acting as a small router providing a PAN available via Bluetooth wireless. For example, an iPhone can provide Internet access via Bluetooth PAN. As with any Bluetooth device, you must first pair your Mac with the mobile device, as covered in Lesson 24, "Troubleshoot Peripherals." Once the two are paired, configuration should be automatic—the Mac should configure TCP/IP using DHCP hosted from the cellular device. You have to initiate the connection by clicking the Connect button in Network preferences or by choosing the device and clicking "Connect to Network" in the Bluetooth status menu.

▶ USB cellular network adapters—Again, USB is not technically a network connectivity standard, but macOS supports a variety of USB adapters and tethered phones that provide cellular Internet access. The iPhone is an example of such a device, and in typical Apple fashion all configuration on the Mac is automatic. If tethering is available on your mobile phone data plan, plug an iPhone in via the USB adapter cable, and then on the iPhone turn on the Personal Hotspot feature. Conversely, third-party cellular Internet devices vary, and many require the installation and configuration of third-party drivers.

▶ Wi-Fi PAN—As with Bluetooth, many cellular devices can act as a small Wi-Fi access point. Thus, any device that supports Wi-Fi can connect to the cellular device without any special software. On any iOS device that supports cellular connections, you can enable Personal Hotspot for Wi-Fi. Select the Wi-Fi network the iOS device is hosting and provide authentication, if necessary. iOS devices running iOS 8 or later and Mac computers running OS X Yosemite 10.10 or later can take advantage of Handoff to automatically authenticate to another iOS device acting as a personal hotspot. This automatic authentication requires that Handoff is enabled and that you are signed in to iCloud on both devices. Once you're connected, inspecting the Wi-Fi connection in Network preferences reveals that the iOS device appears identical to a traditional Wi-Fi router.

About Virtual Network Services

A virtual network service is a logical network within a hardware network interface. Think of a virtual network service as providing another unique network interface by carving out a section of an established network connection.

Some virtual network services are used to increase security by encrypting data before it travels across an IP network, and others are used to segregate or aggregate network traffic across LAN connections. macOS includes client software that enables you to connect to many common virtual network services and establish a virtual network service interface.

If necessary, you can define multiple separate virtual network service interfaces for each network location. Virtual network service interfaces are not always tied to a specific physical network interface; the system attempts to seek out the most appropriate route when multiple active connections are available. Likewise, any virtual network service interface that is not destined for a LAN connection is always routed to the primary active network service interface.

> **NOTE ▶** Third-party virtualization tools, like Parallels Desktop and VMware Fusion, also use virtual network interfaces to provide networking for multiple simultaneous operating systems.

macOS includes built-in support for the following virtual network services:

▶ Point-to-Point Protocol over Ethernet (PPPoE)—This protocol is used by some service providers to directly connect your Mac to a modem providing a high-speed digital subscriber line (DSL) Internet connection.

▶ Virtual private network (VPN)—By far the most commonly used virtual network service, VPNs are primarily used to create secure virtual connections to private LANs over the Internet. Configuring VPN connections is detailed later in this lesson.

▶ Virtual local area network (VLAN)—The macOS VLAN implementation allows you to define separate independent LAN services on a single physical network interface.

▶ Link aggregate—This service allows you to define a single virtual LAN service using multiple physical network interfaces. macOS uses the standard Link Aggregation Control Protocol (LACP), also known as IEEE 802.3ad.

▶ 6to4—This service creates a VPN, of sorts, to transfer IPv6 packets across an IPv4 network. There is no enhanced security when using a 6to4 connection, but your Mac will appear to be directly connected to a remote IPv6 LAN. The differences between IPv4 and IPv6 were covered in the previous lesson.

About Network Protocols

Each network service interface provides connectivity for a number of standard networking protocols. Network preferences show primary protocol settings whenever you select a service from the services list, but many protocol configuration options are available only by clicking the Advanced button.

macOS includes built-in support for the following network protocols:

▶ TCP/IP configured via DHCP—As explained in Lesson 19, "Manage Basic Network Settings," TCP/IP is the primary network protocol for LANs and WANs, and DHCP is a popular network service that automatically configures TCP/IP clients.

▶ TCP/IP configured manually—If you do not have DHCP service on your local network, or if you want to ensure that the TCP/IP settings never change, you can manually configure TCP/IP settings.

▶ DNS—As covered in the previous lesson, DNS provides host names for IP network devices. DNS settings are often configured alongside TCP/IP settings either by DHCP or manual configuration. macOS supports multiple DNS servers and search domains.

▶ Wireless Ethernet (Wi-Fi) protocol options—The wireless nature of Wi-Fi often requires additional configuration to facilitate network selection and authentication.

► Authenticated Ethernet via 802.1X—The 802.1X protocol is used to secure Ethernet networks (both wired and Wi-Fi) by allowing only properly authenticated network clients to join the LAN.

► Network Basic Input/Output System (NetBIOS) and Windows Internet Naming Service (WINS)—NetBIOS and WINS are protocols most often used by older Windows-based computers to provide network identification and service discovery.

► IP proxies—Proxy servers act as intermediaries between a network client and a requested service and are used to enhance performance or provide an additional layer of security and content filtering.

► Ethernet hardware options—macOS supports both automatic and manual Ethernet hardware configuration, as covered later in this lesson.

► External (analog) modem with PPP—For many years this was the only method for accomplishing any sort of digital computer-based communication. macOS still supports this method, but since it is so rarely used in this age of broadband Internet, analog modem configuration is not covered in this guide.

► Point-to-Point Protocol (PPP)—PPP is an older protocol originally intended for use with analog modems. Again, macOS still supports PPP for analog modems, but it also supports PPP for Bluetooth dial-up networking and PPPoE connectivity. Again, the rarity of this protocol's use today means that PPP configuration is not covered in this guide.

Reference 20.3
Manage Network Service Interfaces

Typically, having multiple active network service interfaces means you also have multiple active IP addresses. To handle multiple IP addresses, macOS also features IP network multihoming. In fact, macOS supports multiple IP addresses for each physical network interface. Thus, the network service list can contain multiple instances of the same physical network interface. Again, a network service in this context is a single configuration of a physical network interface.

About Using Multiple Simultaneous Interfaces

macOS supports multiple simultaneous network service interfaces. For example, you can have both an active wired Ethernet connection and an active Wi-Fi, or wireless Ethernet, connection at the same time. In other words, you can configure as many separate network service interfaces with as many unique IP addresses as you need. This may seem like overkill for most Mac clients, but remember that macOS acts as the foundation for macOS Server as well.

For some servers, multilink multihoming networking is a requirement, but Mac clients can also benefit from this technology. You may have a work environment where you have one insecure network for general Internet traffic and another network for secure internal transactions. With macOS, you can be on both of these networks at the same time. However, the first fully configured active service in the list is the primary network service interface.

In most cases the primary network service interface is used for all WAN connectivity, Internet connectivity, and DNS host name resolution. The exception to this is when the primary network interface is lacking a router configuration. In this case, the system treats the next fully configured active service as the primary network service interface.

When multiple IP addresses are available, the system can communicate via any of those network service interfaces, but it will attempt to pick the most appropriate route for every network connection. As described in the previous lesson, a network client uses the subnet mask to determine whether an outgoing transmission is on the LAN. macOS takes this a step further by examining all active LANs when determining a destination for outgoing transmission. Because a LAN connection is always faster than a WAN connection, macOS always routes outgoing transmissions to the most appropriate LAN.

Any network connections that are not destined for a LAN that your Mac is connected to are sent to the router address of the primary active network service interface, which should be the topmost service listed in Network preferences. Again, in most cases this means the primary active network service interface is responsible for all WAN connections, Internet connections, and DNS host name resolution. Any active network service interface with a valid TCP/IP setting is considered, but the primary active network service interface is automatically selected based on the network service order. You can manually configure the network service order, as outlined later in this lesson.

Using the previous example, in which you have a Mac active on both wired Ethernet and Wi-Fi, the default network service order prioritizes wired Ethernet over Wi-Fi because wired is almost always faster. Thus, in this example, even though you have two active valid network service interfaces, the primary active network service interface is the wired Ethernet connection.

NOTE ▶ macOS features automatic source routing. This means that incoming connections to your Mac over a specific network service interface are always responded to on the same interface, regardless of the service order.

View the Network Services List

Every time you open Network preferences, the system identifies all available network service interfaces. Even if a physical network interface is not connected or properly configured, it creates a configuration for that interface, which shows up in the network services list. In Network preferences, each network interface is tied to one or more network services.

A quick glance at the network services list clearly shows the status of all network interfaces and their configured services. Network services with a red indicator are not connected, a yellow indicator shows services that are connected but not properly configured, and a green indicator shows connected and configured network services.

The active service at the top of this list is the primary network service interface, as defined by the network service order. This list updates dynamically as new services become active or as active services become disconnected, so it's always the first place to check when attempting to troubleshoot a network issue.

Manage Network Services

To manage network interfaces and their configured services, open and (if necessary) unlock Network preferences. First, make sure the network location you want to edit is selected in the Location pop-up menu, or configure a new network location, as detailed earlier in this lesson.

To configure a specific network service, select it from the network services list. Remember that each network service has its own settings separate from the other services. The configuration area to the right of the list changes to reflect primary options available to the selected service. Clicking Advanced reveals all the advanced network protocol options available to the selected network service.

To create another configurable instance of a network interface, click the Add (+) button at the bottom of the network services list. This reveals a dialog that allows you to choose a new interface instance from the pop-up menu and then assign it a unique service name to identify it in the services list. Creating additional instances of a network service enables you to assign multiple IP addresses to a single network interface.

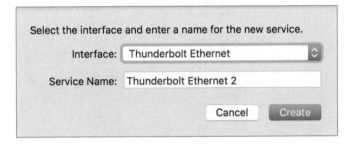

To make a service inactive, select it from the services list, click the Action button (gear icon), and then choose Make Service Inactive from the pop-up menu. An inactive service never activates, even if connected and properly configured. You can also delete an existing network service by selecting its name from the services list and then clicking the Delete (–) button at the bottom of the list. Deactivating or deleting a network service from this list is the only way to disable a hardware network interface in macOS.

NOTE ▸ You are not allowed to delete network service interfaces configured as part of a configuration profile. To delete these network services, you must delete their associated configuration profile from the Profiles system preferences.

Clicking the Action button (gear icon) at the bottom of the network services list reveals a pop-up menu with several management options. For example, you can duplicate an existing network service by selecting its name from the services list and then choosing Duplicate Service from the pop-up menu. Using this menu, you can also rename an existing network service. Finally, you can modify the active network service interface order by choosing Set Service Order from the pop-up menu.

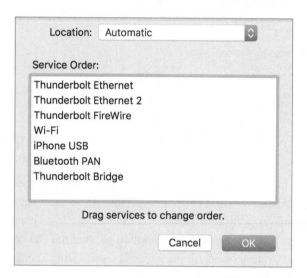

The Service Order dialog allows you to drag network services into your preferred order for selection as the primary network interface. Click OK when you have finished reordering, and the system automatically reevaluates the active network service interfaces based on the new order. Also, don't forget that you must also click Apply in Network preferences to activate and save all the changes to the currently selected network location.

TIP ▸ If you make a mistake at any time using Network preferences, click Revert to return to the currently active network configuration.

Reference 20.4
Configure VPN Settings

A VPN is an encrypted tunnel from your client to the network routing device providing the VPN service. Once it is established, your Mac will appear to have a direct connection to the LAN that the VPN device is sharing. So even if you're on a wireless Internet connection thousands of miles away from your LAN, a VPN connection provides a virtual network interface as if your computer were directly attached to that LAN. macOS supports three common VPN protocols: the Layer 2 Tunneling Protocol over Internet Protocol Security (L2TP over IPSec), Cisco's IPSec, and Internet Key Exchange version 2 (IKEv2).

> **NOTE** ▶ macOS Sierra doesn't support the Point-to-Point Tunneling Protocol (PPTP) VPN standard. This older VPN protocol has long been considered an insecure option. For more information see Apple Support article HT206844, "Prepare for removal of PPTP VPN before you upgrade to iOS 10 and macOS Sierra."

> **NOTE** ▶ Some VPN services require a third-party VPN client. Third-party VPN clients usually include a custom interface for managing the connection. Although you may see the virtual network interface provided by the third-party VPN client in Network preferences, it's usually not configurable from there.

Use a VPN Configuration Profile

By far the easiest method for managing VPN configuration is to do so via a configuration profile. As detailed in Lesson 2, "Set Up and Configure macOS," a configuration profile is a file that contains instructions for specific settings. The administrator of a VPN system can provide a VPN profile whose relevant settings can easily be configured by opening the profile on a Mac.

Installed configuration profiles can be verified from Profiles preferences. Once a configuration profile is installed, all the appropriate VPN settings should be configured for you. To establish the VPN tunnel, a user needs only to initiate the VPN connection, as covered later in this lesson.

Manually Configure VPN Settings

Even with a VPN configuration profile, you may find it necessary to verify or further manage VPN connections from Network preferences. Or if the administrator of the VPN service is unable to provide a configuration profile, you need to manually configure VPN services. To add a VPN interface, click the Add (+) button at the bottom of the network services list in Network preferences. This reveals a dialog where you can add a new network service interface.

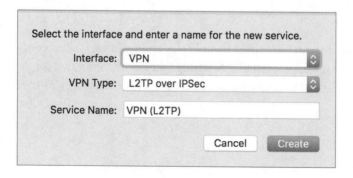

From the new network service interface dialog, you must choose the appropriate VPN protocol from the VPN Type pop-up menu. Again, macOS supports the L2TP over IPSec, Cisco IPSec VPN, and IKEv2 protocols. All three have similar configuration options, but for the purposes of this lesson L2TP is used because it has a few more authentication and advanced options. If you're going to have more than one type of VPN protocol, you may want to enter a descriptive name for the service.

Once you create the new VPN interface, select it from the network services list, and basic VPN configuration settings appear to the right. To configure VPN settings, first enter the VPN server address and, if you use user-based authentication, an account name.

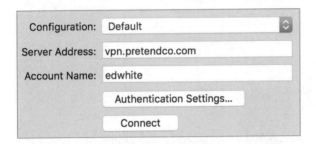

TIP If you do want to set multiple VPN configurations, choose Add Configuration from the Configuration pop-up menu. In the dialog, provide a name for the new VPN configuration and click Create. You can also delete and rename your configuration from this pop-up menu.

You must also define authentication methods by clicking the Authentication Settings button and then specifying user and computer authentication settings. The VPN administrator can provide you with the appropriate authentication settings. Supplying a password here adds it to the system keychain. If the field is left blank, the user is prompted for the password when connecting.

User Authentication:

○ Password: [   ]

● RSA SecurID

○ Certificate [Select...]

○ Kerberos

○ CryptoCard

Machine Authentication:

● Shared Secret: [··············]

○ Certificate [Select...]

Group Name: [   ]

(Optional)

[Cancel] [OK]

To configure advanced VPN settings, click the Advanced button in Network preferences. In the Advanced Settings dialog, click the Options tab to view general VPN options. The most important optional setting is to send all traffic over the VPN connection. By default, active VPN connections do not move to the top of the network services list. Thus, the system routes traffic to the VPN service only if the destination IP address is part of the LAN that the VPN service is providing or if the VPN server supplies special routing information.

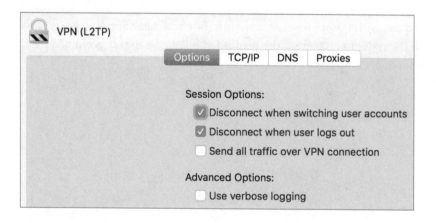

VPN (L2TP)

[Options] [TCP/IP] [DNS] [Proxies]

Session Options:

☑ Disconnect when switching user accounts

☑ Disconnect when user logs out

☐ Send all traffic over VPN connection

Advanced Options:

☐ Use verbose logging

NOTE ▶ macOS supports automatic VPN connections via certificate-based authentication and the VPN on Demand service. However, these VPN connections can be configured only through the use of configuration profiles.

Connect to a VPN

VPN connections are not typically always-on connections. macOS supports automatic VPN connections with the VPN on Demand feature, but many users may still manually enable VPN connections when necessary. You can make accessing VPN connectivity options much easier by selecting the "Show VPN status in menu bar" checkbox in Network preferences. The VPN menu bar item allows you to easily select VPN configurations and connect, disconnect, and monitor VPN connections. You can also manually connect and disconnect the VPN link from Network preferences.

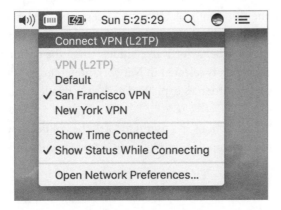

VPNs are usually implemented in situations where user authentication is required, so for many, initiating a VPN connection prompts an authentication dialog. Note that the VPN connection dialog does not offer to save the user's authentication information to the keychain. This is an intentional design decision, as some VPN protocols require manual authentication every time a connection is established.

Once the connection is authenticated and established, the VPN process automatically configures TCP/IP and DNS settings using the PPP protocol. VPN interfaces are, by default, set at the bottom of the network service order, so they do not automatically become the primary network interface when activated. This behavior is overridden when the optional "Send all traffic over VPN connection" checkbox is selected in Network preferences. You can also manually reorder the network service order, as explained earlier in this lesson.

TIP When troubleshooting VPN connections, it's useful to view the connection log info in /var/log/system.log. From the /Application/Utilities/Console application, you can view the system log.

Reference 20.5
Configure Advanced Network Settings

The advanced network configuration techniques covered in this section are largely optional for many configurations. However, for those who are tasked with supporting macOS systems, it's important to have a full understanding of all the configuration choices available in Network preferences.

Manually Configure TCP/IP

Many network situations do not require any manual intervention to configure TCP/IP and DNS, as the DHCP or PPP services automatically acquire these settings. The default configuration for all Ethernet and Wi-Fi services is to automatically engage the DHCP process as soon as the interface becomes active. To verify TCP/IP and DNS settings for hardware or virtual Ethernet services when using the DHCP service, select the service from Network preferences.

> **NOTE** ▶ IPv6 addressing information is automatically detected as well, if available. However, automatic IPv6 configuration is not provided by standard DHCP or PPP services.

> **NOTE** ▶ Automatically configured DNS settings show as gray text, which indicates that you can override these settings by manually entering DNS information, as covered later in this section.

Network service interfaces that may require a manual connection process, like Wi-Fi, VPN, and PPPoE interfaces, automatically engage the DHCP or PPP process to acquire TCP/IP and DNS settings. To verify TCP/IP and DNS settings when using these interfaces, select the service from the services list and then click Advanced in Network preferences. In the Advanced Settings dialog, you can click the TCP/IP or DNS tabs to view their respective settings. You can also verify network settings of any other interface this way.

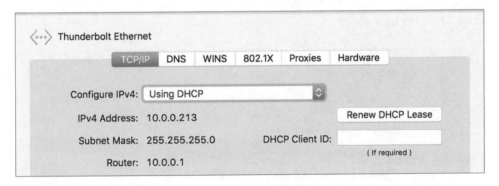

Despite the convenience of automatic TCP/IP and DNS configuration, there may be times when manual configuration is required. For example, the network server providing the DHCP service requires a manual configuration. In fact, most network devices that provide services, like servers or printers, use manually entered network configuration information so that they don't run the risk of changing to a different TCP/IP address should DHCP reset.

> **NOTE** ▶ In some DHCP configurations, a DHCP client ID must be set. You can access this setting by clicking Advanced and then selecting the TCP/IP tab.

If you want to keep using DHCP but manually assign just the IP address, choose "Using DHCP with manual address" from the Configure IPv4 menu. You only have to manually enter an IPv4 address for the Mac, as the rest of the TCP/IP settings remain as populated by DHCP.

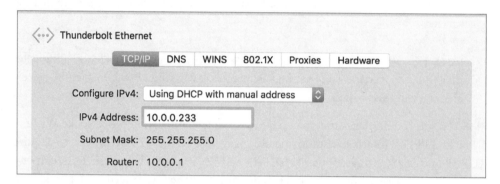

However, if you want to manually enter all TCP/IP settings, choose Manually from the Configure IPv4 menu. At a minimum you have to manually enter the IP address, the subnet mask (for this you can also use CIDR notation), and the router address. The user interface caches the TCP/IP settings from the DHCP service, so you may only have to enter a new IPv4 address.

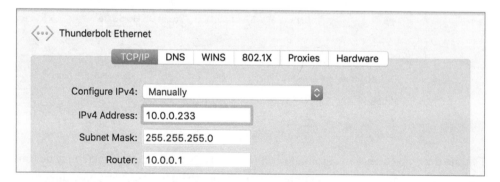

If you have to manually set up IPv6 settings as well, choose Manually from the Configure IPv6 menu. At a minimum you have to manually enter the IPv6 address, router address, and prefix length. The user interface caches any automatic IPv6 settings, so you may only have to enter a new IPv6 address.

Whenever you choose to manually configure IPv4, you should also verify DNS server settings. To configure DNS, click the DNS tab to view the DNS settings. Again, the user interface caches the DNS settings from the DHCP service, so you may not have to enter any DNS settings at all.

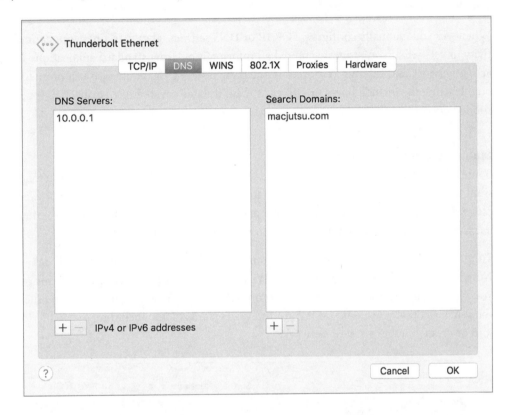

NOTE ▶ If the IP address of a DNS server is not specified, the Mac will not be able to resolve DNS host names.

If you are configuring manually, configure at least one DNS server. Click the Add (+) button at the bottom of the DNS server list to add a new server, and then enter the server's IP address. Entering a search domain is optional. Click the Add button (+) at the bottom of the Search Domains list, and then enter the domain name.

If you configure multiple DNS servers or search domains, the system attempts to access those resources in the order in which they appear in the list. To edit an address, double-click its entry in the list. You can delete an entry by selecting it and clicking the Delete (–) button at the bottom of the list.

When you have entered all the appropriate IP and DNS settings, click OK to dismiss the Advanced Settings dialog, and then click Apply in Network preferences to save and activate the changes.

Whenever you manually configure TCP/IP or DNS settings, always test network connectivity to verify that you properly entered all information. Using standard applications to access network and Internet resources is one basic test, but you could also test more thoroughly using the included network diagnostic utilities, as covered in Lesson 21, "Troubleshoot Network Issues."

Manually Configure Wi-Fi

Some administrators may find a need to restrict some of the wireless features. You may want to require that the Mac connect only to specific secure wireless networks, for example, or that the Mac always connect to one particular network. In these situations, you can use the advanced Wi-Fi configuration options in Network preferences.

To manage advanced Wi-Fi options and connections, open and (if necessary) unlock Network preferences, and then select the Wi-Fi service from the services list. At this point you can configure basic Wi-Fi settings from the Network Name pop-up menu, in much the same way that you would do it from the Wi-Fi status menu, including the ability to join or create another wireless network.

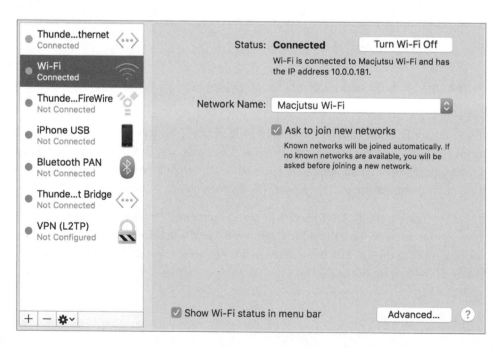

At this point you can also manage the ability for nonadministrator users to select Wi-Fi networks:

▶   When optionally enabled, the "Ask to join new networks" checkbox will have the system prompt the user to select another Wi-Fi network in the area when the Mac can't find a preconfigured wireless network.

▶   Enabled as a default, the "Show Wi-Fi status in menu bar" checkbox will allow any user to select a wireless network from the Wi-Fi status menu. However, disabling this doesn't prevent a user from choosing a wireless network if the Mac presents a wireless discovery dialog.

Clicking the Advanced button reveals the Advanced Settings dialog. If the Wi-Fi tab at the top is not selected, click it to view the advanced Wi-Fi settings.

From the top half of the advanced Wi-Fi settings pane, you can manage a list of preferred wireless networks. By default, wireless networks that were added previously appear here as well. If you disable user access to Wi-Fi settings as just described, the system connects only to the preferred wireless networks in this list.

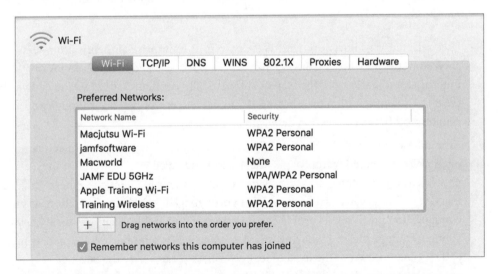

To add a new wireless network, click the Add (+) button at the bottom of the Preferred Networks list and then either join a wireless network in range or manually enter the information for a hidden or not-currently-in-range network. To edit a network, double-click its entry in the list, or you can delete a network by selecting it and clicking the Delete (–) button at the bottom of the list.

At the bottom of the advanced Wi-Fi settings pane, you have several settings that allow for more specific Wi-Fi administration options. Thus, if you choose to leave the Wi-Fi status menu available to regular users, you can restrict certain settings to only administrator users. Remember to close the Advanced dialog and then click Apply in Network preferences to save and activate the changes.

Require administrator authorization to:
- [ ] Create computer-to-computer networks
- [ ] Change networks
- [ ] Turn Wi-Fi on or off

About 802.1X Configuration

The 802.1X protocol is used to secure both wired and wireless (Wi-Fi) Ethernet networks by allowing only properly authenticated network clients to join the LAN. Networks using 802.1X do not allow any traffic until the network client properly authenticates to the network.

To facilitate 802.1X authentication, macOS provides two methods for automatic configuration:

▶ User-selected Wi-Fi network with WPA or WPA2 Enterprise authentication—As covered in the previous lesson, if a Wi-Fi network is selected that uses WPA or WPA2 Enterprise authentication, the system automatically configures 802.1X. You can verify the 802.1X configuration by selecting Wi-Fi in Network preferences, though you cannot modify the connection details in any way.

▶ Administrator-provided 802.1X configuration profile—The 802.1X architecture often relies on shared secrets or certificates to validate client connections; thus, a network administrator must securely deploy these items to client computers. In macOS, the only way to set up non–Wi-Fi or managed 802.1X configurations is via a configuration profile. This profile can be deployed by double-clicking a local copy of a configuration profile or by having the Mac managed by a mobile device management (MDM) solution. From the local Mac, however, you can verify the 802.1X configuration by selecting the 802.1X tab from among the Advanced Configuration panes of Network preferences.

MORE INFO ▶ macOS Server can provide MDM services through Profile Manager. You can find out more about Profile Manager in macOS Server at www.apple.com/macos/server/.

Configure NetBIOS and WINS

NetBIOS and WINS run on top of TCP/IP to provide network identification and service discovery. NetBIOS and WINS are used primarily by legacy Windows-based systems to provide identification and service discovery on LANs, whereas WINS is used to identify and locate NetBIOS network devices on WANs. You can think of WINS as a form of DNS for NetBIOS network clients.

Current Windows networks now use Dynamic DNS as a solution for network client discovery, but macOS still supports NetBIOS and WINS to support legacy network configurations. Further, these discovery protocols are mainly used to provide naming for the Server Message Block (SMB) protocol commonly used to share files and printers. In other words, the NetBIOS name is there to provide support for SMB sharing services hosted from your Mac, as covered in Lesson 23, "Manage Host Sharing and Personal Firewall."

NOTE ▶ macOS supports NetBIOS and WINS on any active network interface except for VPN connections.

macOS automatically configures your computer's NetBIOS name based on your Mac computer's sharing name, and for many networks this should be sufficient. If your Mac is on a larger legacy Windows network and you want to share resources from your Mac with other network clients, you may want to manually select the NetBIOS workgroup. NetBIOS workgroups are used to make navigation easier on large networks by grouping devices into smaller collections. You may have to manually configure the WINS service to provide faster NetBIOS resolution.

NOTE ▶ It's not required that you configure NetBIOS and WINS to connect to Windows resources. For certain legacy Windows clients, however, it may help.

To manually configure NetBIOS and WINS settings, open and (if necessary) unlock Network preferences, select the network service you want to configure from the network services list, and then click Advanced. In the Advanced Settings dialog, click the WINS tab to view the NetBIOS and WINS settings.

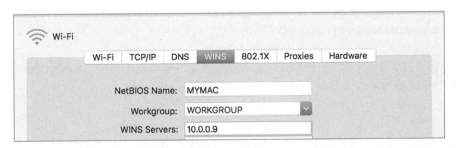

To manually configure NetBIOS, start by entering a unique name, and then choose a workgroup from the pop-up menu. It may take a while for the NetBIOS workgroup list to refresh, thus preventing you from selecting it from the pop-up menu. If you already know the name of the workgroup you want the Mac to be in, you can manually enter the workgroup name.

> **NOTE ▶** NetBIOS names and workgroup names are in all capital letters and cannot contain any special characters or spaces.

To enable WINS, enter at least one WINS server IP address. Click the Add (+) button at the bottom of the WINS server list to add a new server, and then enter the server's IP address. If you configure multiple WINS servers, the system attempts to access those resources in the order in which they appear in the list. To edit a server address, double-click its entry in the list; or you can delete a server by selecting it and clicking the Delete (–) button at the bottom of the list.

When you have entered all the appropriate NetBIOS and WINS settings, remember to close the Advanced dialog and then click Apply in Network preferences to save and activate the changes.

Configure Network Proxies

Proxy servers act as intermediaries between a network client and a requested service. Proxy servers are often used to enhance the performance of slow WAN or Internet connections by caching recently requested data so that future connections appear faster to local network clients. Primarily, though, proxy servers are implemented so that network administrators can limit network connections to unauthorized servers or resources. Administrators can manage lists of approved resources, having the proxy servers allow access to those resources only.

macOS supports proxy services for File Transfer Protocol (FTP), web protocols (HTTP and HTTPS), streaming (RTSP), SOCKS, and Gopher. For proxy configuration, macOS supports manual configurations, automatic proxy configuration using local or network-hosted proxy autoconfiguration (PAC) files, and fully automatic proxy discovery via the Web Proxy Autodiscovery Protocol (WPAD).

> **NOTE ▶** It's highly likely that you will have to acquire specific proxy configuration instructions from a network administrator.

To enable and configure proxy settings, open and (if necessary) unlock Network preferences, select the network service you want to configure from the network services list, and then click Advanced. Click the Proxies tab at the top to view the proxy settings.

At this point you will perform one of three routines, depending on your network's proxy implementation:

▶ If your proxy service supports WPAD, enable the Auto Proxy Discovery checkbox.

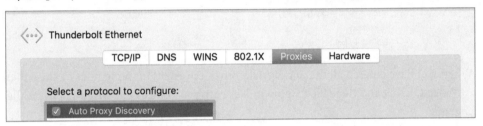

▶ If you have access to a PAC file, select the Automatic Proxy Configuration checkbox at the bottom of the proxy protocols list. You must then specify a network-hosted PAC file by entering the full network path to the file in the URL field.

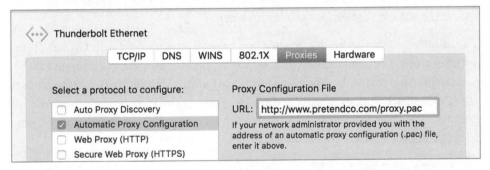

▶ To manually configure proxy settings, select the checkboxes next to each protocol you want to send through the proxy servers. Select each protocol individually to enter the proxy connection information provided by the network administrator. At the bottom you can also elect to bypass the proxy for specific additional hosts and domains.

When you have entered all the appropriate proxy information, remember to close the Advanced dialog and then click Apply in Network preferences to save and activate the changes.

Manually Configure Ethernet

Ethernet connections are designed to establish connection settings automatically. Yet macOS allows you to manually configure Ethernet options from Network preferences should the automatic selections prove problematic.

The most common case for this is when you have an environment with Gigabit Ethernet switches and old or substandard wired infrastructure. In this case it's common for the Mac to attempt to automatically establish a gigabit connection but ultimately fail because the wired infrastructure doesn't support the high speeds. The most common symptom is that even with the Ethernet switch showing that the Mac has an active connection, Network preferences on the Mac shows Ethernet as disconnected.

To manually configure Ethernet settings, open and (if necessary) unlock Network preferences, select the Ethernet service you want to configure from the network services list, and then click Advanced. Click the Hardware tab at the top to view the current automatically configured Ethernet hardware settings.

To manually configure Ethernet options, choose Manually from the Configure menu. The system caches the current automatically configured Ethernet settings, so you do not have to change all the settings. The system also populates the Speed, Duplex, and MTU options based on your Mac computer's network hardware. Make your custom selections from these pop-up menus.

When you have selected all the appropriate Ethernet hardware settings, remember to close the Advanced dialog and then click Apply in Network preferences to save and activate the changes.

Exercise 20.1
Configure Network Locations

▶ **Prerequisites**

- ▶ You must have created the Local Admin (Exercise 2.1, "Configure a New macOS System for Exercises," or Exercise 2.2, "Configure an Existing macOS System for Exercises") and Chris Johnson (Exercise 5.1, "Create a Standard User Account") accounts.

- ▶ This exercise requires a specific network configuration; it can be performed only in a classroom with the proper network setup or after you have configured your network according to the Optional Network Setup Instructions (available after you register your copy of this guide at www.peachpit.com/register).

Some network configurations do not have a Dynamic Host Configuration Protocol (DHCP) server, or there may be times when the DHCP server fails. In these instances, to establish and maintain network access, a macOS computer configured to obtain an IP address via DHCP self-assigns an IP address.

Turn Off the DHCP Service

If you are performing these exercises in a class, the instructor will turn off the classroom DHCP service.

If you are performing these exercises on your own, follow the instructions in the "Turn Off DHCP for Exercise 20.1" section of the Optional Network Setup Instructions.

Examine Your DHCP-Supplied Configuration

1   If necessary, log in as Chris Johnson.

2   If necessary, open System Preferences, and select the Network pane.

3   If necessary, click the padlock, and authenticate as Local Admin.

4   Select the primary network service.

    Even though the DHCP service has been turned off, the service still indicates that it is configured using DHCP and has valid network settings. This is because the DHCP service gave it the configuration information before it shut down, and the information is still valid.

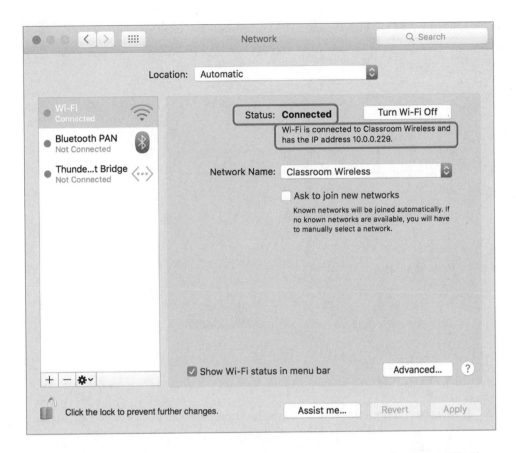

Note that your display probably appears different from this screenshot, especially if you have different network services connected.

Create a DHCP-Based Network Location

1   From the Location pop-up menu, choose Edit Locations.

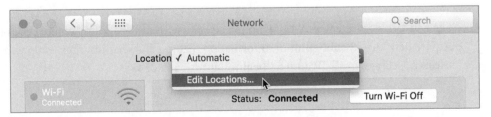

2   Click the Add (+) button under the Locations list to create a new location.

3   Enter Dynamic as the name of the new location.

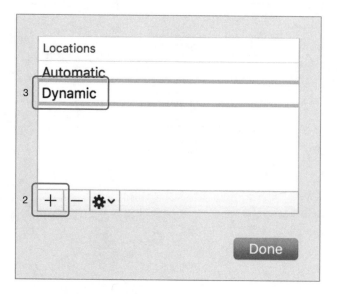

4   Click Done.

5   If necessary, choose the new Dynamic location from the Location pop-up menu.

6   Click Apply.

Network preferences is one of a few places in macOS where you must click Apply before your settings take effect.

7   If necessary, select the network service that is set up for these exercises (that is, the one that DHCP was just turned off for). If it is a wireless network, you may need to rejoin it.

The network service enters a Not Connected state with no IP address while it tries to acquire new DHCP configuration information. After a few seconds, it gives up and selects a "self-assigned" IP address beginning with 169.254.

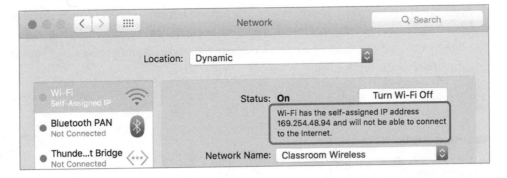

The status indicator for the service will be yellow, indicating that it is connected but not properly configured.

Note that with this "self-assigned" configuration, there is no router or DNS server for that service. Therefore, this network service cannot be used to reach the Internet over IP version 4.

8   Open Safari, and try to browse the web.

If you have another active network service with a valid Internet connection, you can still reach the Internet. macOS uses the router and DNS from lower-priority network services if the primary service does not have a router configured. It will also use IPv6 (version 6 of the internet protocol) if that is available and the web servers you are connecting to support it.

If you do not have another active network service, you cannot reach the Internet. Internet connectivity is available on the network you are connected to, but you cannot use it without proper IP settings.

9   If you have a server set up to support these exercises (either in a classroom or because you set one up according to the Mainserver Setup Instructions), try to browse to mainserver.local.

As long as you are on the same network as Mainserver, this works. Even though you have a self-assigned IP address, you can still communicate with other computers on your network. Bonjour allows you to look up .local names using multicast DNS (mDNS), giving you an easy way of connecting to local resources.

10   Quit Safari.

11 In Network preferences, check for any other active network services (other than the network set up for these exercises). If there are any, disable them by selecting them one by one and choosing Make Service Inactive from the Action (gear icon) pop-up menu below the service list.

12 If necessary, click Apply.

Create a Static Network Location

You will configure a new location called Static with a static IP address. The IP address you will use for your computer will be in the form 10.0.0.*n*2.

If you are performing these exercises in a class, your instructor will provide you with a student number you should use as *n*. For example, student #3 would use 10.0.0.32, and student #17 would use 10.0.0.172.

If you are performing these exercises on your own, use the address 10.0.0.12.

1   From the Location pop-up menu, choose Edit Locations.

2   From the Action (gear icon) pop-up menu, choose Duplicate Location.

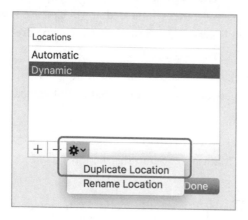

3   Name the new location Static, and click Done.

4   Use the Location pop-up menu to switch to the new Static location, if it is not already selected.

5   Click Apply.

6   Select the network service that is set up for these exercises from the service list on the left. It will most likely be either Ethernet or Wi-Fi.

7   Click Advanced.

8   If necessary, click the TCP/IP tab.

9   From the Configure IPv4 pop-up menu, choose Manually.

10   In the IPv4 Address field, enter 10.0.0.n2/24 (where n is either your student number if you are in class or 1 if you are on your own).

In other words, if you are on your own, you enter 10.0.0.12/24; if you are student #17 in a class, you enter 10.0.0.172/24.

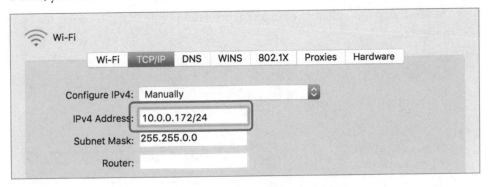

11   Press Tab.

The "/24" is a shorthand (called CIDR notation) corresponding to the subnet mask 255.255.255.0, so that field will be automatically filled in as soon as you press Tab. macOS will also guess that the router is at 10.0.0.1 (which is correct for this network). See https://en.wikipedia.org/wiki/Classless_Inter-Domain_Routing for more information.

12   Click DNS.

13   Click the Add (+) button under the DNS Servers list, and enter the appropriate address:

▶   If you are performing these exercises in a classroom or have a macOS server configured to support the exercises, enter 10.0.0.2.

▶   If you are performing these exercises without a macOS server, enter 10.0.0.1.

14 Click the Add (+) button under the Search Domains list, and enter pretendco.com.

15 Click OK to dismiss the advanced settings dialog.

16 Click Apply.

The service's status indicator changes to green to indicate that it is connected and fully configured.

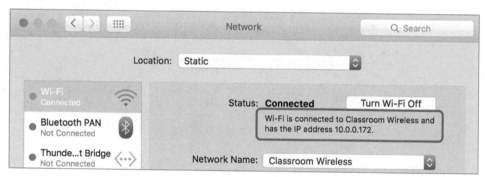

17 Quit System Preferences.

Test Web Access

At this point you have correctly configured your computer to work on the network. Now, use Safari to verify that you can access the Apple website.

1 Open Safari.

You will use Safari to test network access throughout this exercise. But to make sure you are testing actual network connections rather than just loading pages from Safari's caches, you will need to empty its caches first.

2   Choose Safari menu > Preferences (Command-Comma).

3   Click the Advanced tab in the preferences toolbar.

4   Select "Show Develop menu in menu bar," and then close the preferences window.

5   Choose Develop menu > Empty Caches (Command-Option-E).

6   In the address bar, type www.apple.com, and press Return.

If Safari is already trying to load a page from the Internet, you don't need to wait for it to finish or time out. If everything is working, the Apple website appears.

If the Apple website does not load, there is something wrong with your network settings or connection, and you should troubleshoot it before proceeding. First, verify your network settings match the previous instructions. If they are correct, consult **Lesson 21, "Troubleshoot Network Issues."**

7   Quit Safari.

Exercise 20.2
Configure Network Service Order

▶ **Prerequisites**

- ▶ You must have created the Local Admin (Exercise 2.1, "Configure a New macOS System for Exercises," or Exercise 2.2, "Configure an Existing macOS System for Exercises") and Chris Johnson (Exercise 5.1, "Create a Standard User Account") accounts.

- ▶ You must have performed Exercise 20.1, "Configure Network Locations."

The network service order determines which service is used to reach the Internet. Because of this, it is important to understand how network service order is determined and what its effects are.

Create a Multihomed Location

1   If necessary, open the Network pane in System Preferences, and authenticate as Local Admin.

2   From the Location pop-up menu, choose Edit Locations.

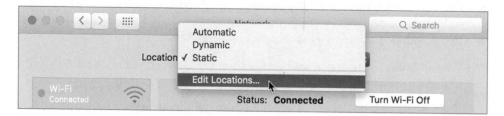

3   Select the Static location, and then choose Duplicate Location from the Action (gear icon) pop-menu below the locations list.

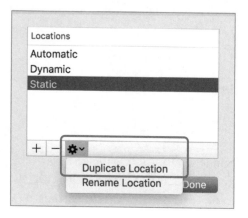

4   Name the new location Multihomed, and click Done.

5   Switch to the Multihomed location, if necessary.

6   Click Apply.

7   Select the primary network service (the one at the top of the list on the left).

8 From the Action (gear icon) pop-up menu below the service list, choose Rename Service.

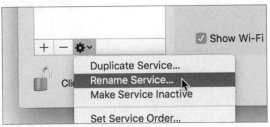

9 Enter With DNS in the New Name field, and click Rename.

10 Click Apply.

11 From the Action (gear icon) pop-up menu, choose Duplicate Service.

12 Enter Without DNS in the Name field, and click Duplicate.

You now have two network services using the same interface. Essentially, this means you have two sets of network configurations (IP address, subnet mask, and so on) running through the same connector (or wireless network).

13 Select the Without DNS service, and click Advanced.

14 Click TCP/IP.

15 Increase the last number of the IPv4 address by 1 (for example, if it was 10.0.0.172, change it to 10.0.0.173).

16 Click DNS.

17 Select the entry in the DNS Servers list, and click the Delete (–) button below the list to remove it.

The DNS Servers list is now empty.

18 Click OK to dismiss the advanced settings.

19 Click Apply.

At this point, both the With DNS and Without DNS services have a green status indicator, and the With DNS service is at the top of the list.

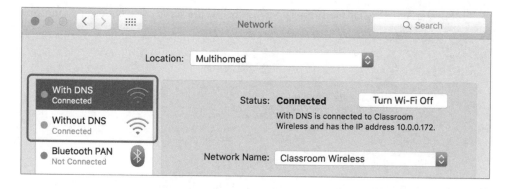

20 Open Safari, and attempt to browse the web.

You can now browse the web normally. If it does not work, check the setup you have done.

Change the Service Order

1 Switch to Network preferences.

2 From the Action (gear icon) pop-up menu, choose Set Service Order.

This list controls the normal order of the services. The system always reprioritizes the services based on their status (active services always bubble up to the top), but among the active services, this controls which is the primary.

3 Drag the Without DNS service to the top of the list, and then click OK.

The Without DNS service now moves to the top of the service list, but it is not actually used as the primary service until you apply the change.

4   Click Apply.

5   Quit and reopen Safari.

6   Choose Develop menu > Empty Caches (Command-Option-E).

7   Again, try to browse the web.

You are presented with a page that tells you that "Safari Can't Find the Server" or "You Are Not Connected to the Internet." Specifically, what this means is that it cannot find a name server to resolve the name.

The Without DNS service now has priority over the With DNS service (it is higher on the list). Because Without DNS is not configured with any name servers, it cannot look up any websites by name and so fails with this message.

8   From the Apple menu, choose Location > Static.

This submenu allows you to switch locations without having to open Network preferences.

9   Reload the page in Safari (note that it may reload automatically after a short delay). This time it works because the Static location has DNS settings associated with its highest-priority (and only) service.

10   If you are not going on to the next exercise, quit Safari and System Preferences.

Exercise 20.3
Configure VPN Settings

▶ **Prerequisites**

▶   You must have created the Local Admin (Exercise 2.1, "Configure a New macOS System for Exercises," or Exercise 2.2, "Configure an Existing macOS System for Exercises") and Chris Johnson (Exercise 5.1, "Create a Standard User Account") accounts.

▶   You must be performing these exercises in a class or have set up your own server configured as described in the Mainserver Setup Instructions.

Virtual private networks (VPNs) are commonly used to securely access a remote network. With a VPN connection you establish an encrypted tunnel over the public Internet to the remote network. The encryption protects your data while it is transmitted. macOS supports three types of VPNs: Layer 2 Tunneling Protocol over IPSec (L2TP), Cisco IPSec, and Internet Key Exchange version 2 (IKEv2). You can configure a VPN service manually in macOS, but the preferred way to set one up is with a configuration profile.

In this exercise, you will use a configuration profile to set up a VPN connection from your computer to Mainserver's private network.

Try to Connect to a Private Service

1   If necessary, log in as Chris Johnson.

2   If necessary, open Safari.

3   Use the address bar to access internal.pretendco.com.

Safari may try to reach the site for a while, but it will eventually fail to connect. The site internal.pretendco.com is accessible only from the private network, and you have not yet joined that.

4   Leave Safari open in the background.

Configure a VPN Service

1   Open the file StudentMaterials/Lesson20/VPN.mobileconfig.

The profile opens in the Profiles pane of System Preferences.

2   Click Show Profile.

The profile contains the settings to connect to mainserver.local using the L2TP protocol. You can scroll down to see more details.

3   Click Continue, and then click Continue again to install the profile.

The profile does not specify a username to authenticate to the VPN server, so you need to enter one.

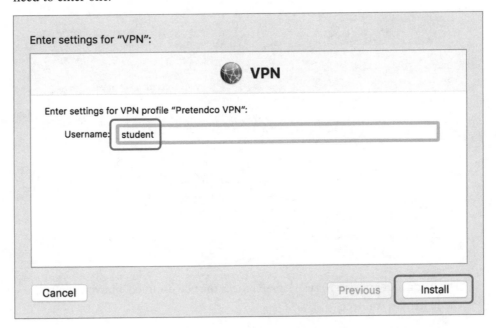

4   Enter the username student, and click Install.

5   When you are prompted, authenticate as Local Admin.

Profile preferences now lists the VPN profile as installed on this computer.

6   Switch to Network preferences.

7   Select the VPN service that has been added to your current location.

All the settings in the profile have been applied, along with the username you entered.

8   Select "Show VPN status in menu bar."

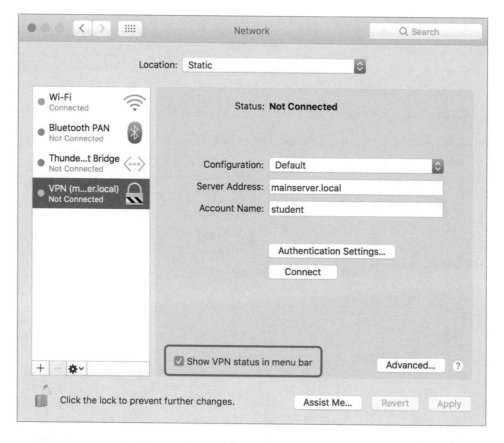

The Connect button in Network preferences may be dimmed, but you can still use the menu item to connect.

9   From the VPN menu item, choose "Connect VPN (mainserver.local)."

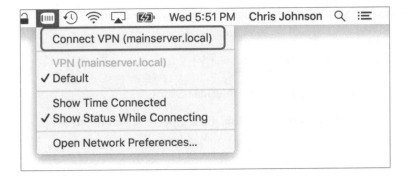

10 When you are prompted to authenticate to the VPN server, enter the password student (the user name is already filled in), and click OK.

It may take a few seconds to connect. When it does, the VPN service's status changes.

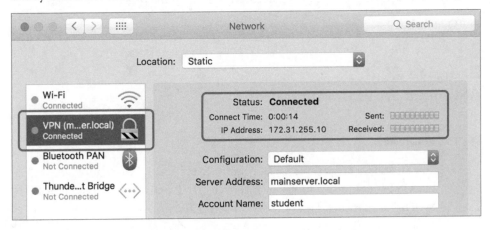

Check Your VPN Connectivity

Now that you are connected to the classroom network via VPN, you will access a network resource that was previously unreachable.

1   Switch to Safari.

2   If the internal website didn't load automatically, use the address bar to access internal.pretendco.com.

3   If you receive a warning that Safari can't verify the identity of the website, click Continue.

The page loads successfully this time. Since you are now connected to the private network, you have access to internal services and resources.

4 From the VPN menu item, choose "Disconnect VPN (mainserver.local)."

5 In Safari, press Command-R to reload the internal website.

Safari may continue to display the page while it attempts to reload it, but the progress bar under the address bar shows that it does not get far.

After a delay, you are informed that Safari can't open the page.

6 Quit Safari.

Exercise 20.4
Advanced Wi-Fi Configuration

> **Prerequisites**

> ▶ You must have created the Local Admin (Exercise 2.1, "Configure a New macOS System for Exercises," or Exercise 2.2, "Configure an Existing macOS System for Exercises") and Chris Johnson (Exercise 5.1, "Create a Standard User Account") accounts.

> ▶ Your computer must have a Wi-Fi interface, and you must have access to at least two Wi-Fi networks (at least one of which is visible).

In this exercise, you will learn to use the Preferred Networks list to control how your computer joins Wi-Fi networks.

Create a Wi-Fi-Only Location

1 If necessary, log in as Chris Johnson, open Network preferences, and authenticate as Local Admin.

2   Make a mental note of the currently selected location so that you can return to it at the end of the exercise.

3   From the Location pop-up menu, choose Edit Locations.

4   Click the Add (+) button under the Locations list to create a new location.

5   Enter Wi-Fi Only as the name of the new location.

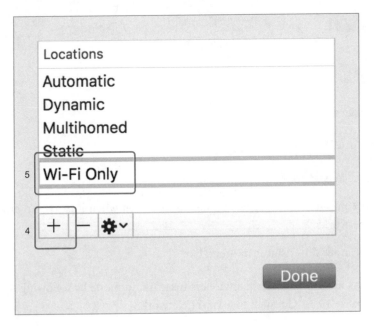

6   Click Done.

7   If necessary, choose the new Wi-Fi location from the Location pop-up menu.

8   Click Apply.

9   In the network service list, make the services other than Wi-Fi inactive. Do this one by one by selecting a service and then, from the Action (gear icon) pop-up menu below the service list, choosing Make Service Inactive.

When you are done, all services except Wi-Fi are listed as Inactive.

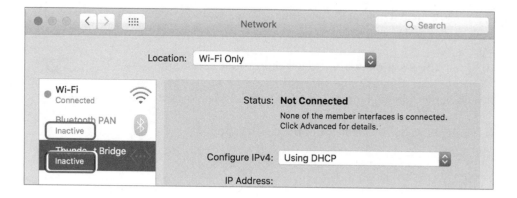

10 Click Apply.

11 Select the Wi-Fi service.

12 If necessary, click Turn Wi-Fi On.

13 If necessary, deselect "Ask to join new networks."

This prevents your computer from suggesting networks to you when it can't find any of your preferred networks.

14 If necessary, select "Show Wi-Fi status in menu bar."

15 If your computer has not already joined a wireless network, join one by following the instructions in Exercise 19.1, "Connect to a Wi-Fi Network."

Clear the Preferred Networks List

1 Click Advanced.

2 Examine the Preferred Networks list.

This is the list of wireless networks that your computer will join automatically any time it is in range of them. If there is more than one in range, it joins the one that is highest on the list.

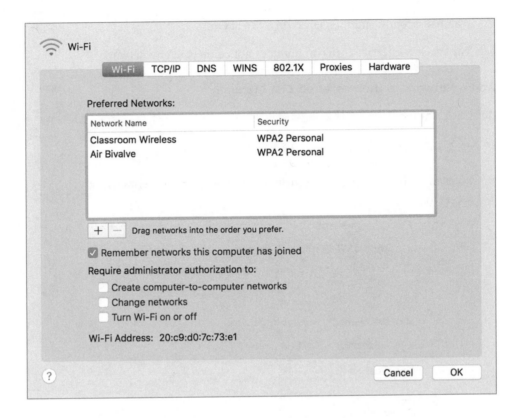

WARNING ▶ Removing wireless networks from this list will remove their passwords from your keychain, so you will need to reenter their passwords the next time you join them. If there are any remembered networks that you do not know the passwords for, you can use Keychain Access to view their passwords and record them before removing them from this list. See Reference 7.2, "Manage Secrets in Keychain," for the details of this process.

3 Clear the list by selecting each entry and clicking the Delete (–) button at the bottom of the list.

4 Make sure "Remember networks this computer has joined" is selected.

5 When the list is empty, click OK and then click Apply. If prompted, authenticate as Local Admin.

6 Click Turn Wi-Fi Off.

7   Wait ten seconds, and then click Turn Wi-Fi On.

The wireless interface turns on but does not connect to any network.

Add a Network to the Preferred List Manually

1   Click Advanced.

2   Click the Add (+) button under the Preferred Networks list.

3   Enter the network name and security information for another network you have access to.

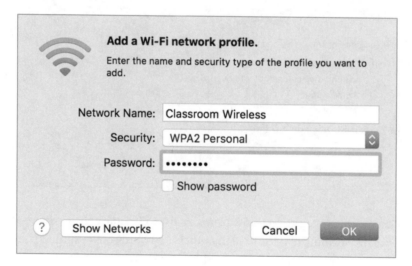

Add a Wi-Fi network profile.

Enter the name and security type of the profile you want to add.

Network Name: Classroom Wireless

Security: WPA2 Personal

Password: ••••••••

☐ Show password

?   Show Networks   Cancel   OK

4   Click OK to add the entry.

5   Click OK to dismiss the advanced settings, and then click Apply. If prompted, authenticate as Local Admin.

Your computer should automatically join the wireless network. If it does not, there may be a problem with the manual entry, such as a typo in the name or password or an incorrect security mode. In this case, you could remove it from the list and then try adding it back in.

NOTE ▶ If you performed Exercise 20.1, "Configure Network Locations," using this wireless network, you will need to turn the DHCP service back on by reversing the process described in the "Turn Off DHCP for Exercise 20.1" section of the Optional Network Setup Instructions.

Add a Network to the Preferred List by Joining It

1   From the Network Name pop-up menu, choose another of the wireless networks you have access to.

2   If necessary, enter the network password to join it.

3   Click Advanced.

The network you joined has been added to the bottom of the preferred list. This is because the "Remember networks this computer has joined" option is selected.

4   Click OK to dismiss the advanced settings dialog.

Test the Preferred Network Order

1   Click Turn Wi-Fi Off. Wait ten seconds, and then click Turn Wi-Fi On.

After a short delay, your computer rejoins the network you added manually.

2   Click Advanced.

3   Change the Preferred Networks order by dragging the current wireless network to the bottom of the list.

4   Click OK, and then click Apply.

5   Click Turn Wi-Fi Off. Wait ten seconds, and then click Turn Wi-Fi On.

This time, your computer joins the network you added by joining because it is now first in the Preferred Networks list.

6   Switch back to the network location you were in at the beginning of the exercise (generally the Static location, if you have one), and click Apply.

7   Quit System Preferences.

Lesson 21

Troubleshoot Network Issues

This lesson builds on the network topics covered in Lesson 19, "Manage Basic Network Settings," and Lesson 20, "Manage Advanced Network Settings." A solid understanding of general network technologies and the macOS network configuration architecture is necessary to effectively troubleshoot network issues from a Mac. This lesson first covers general network troubleshooting and common network issues. Then, digging deeper, you will learn how to use the built-in macOS network troubleshooting tools, including the Network Diagnostics and Network Utility applications.

GOALS

▶ Identify and resolve network configuration issues

▶ Verify network configuration via Network preferences

▶ Describe how to use Network Utility to aid in troubleshooting

Reference 21.1
Troubleshoot General Network Issues

The most important thing to remember about troubleshooting network issues is that it is often not the computer's fault. You should consider many other points of failure when dealing with LAN and Internet connection issues. So the second most important thing to remember about troubleshooting network issues is that you need to isolate the cause of the problem before attempting generic resolutions.

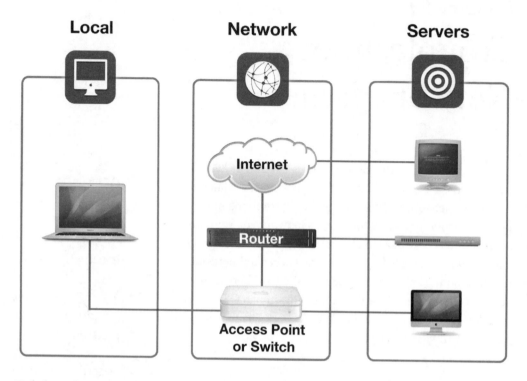

To help isolate network issues, you can categorize them into three general areas:

▶ Local issues—These are usually related to either improperly configured network settings or disconnected network connections.

▶ Network issues—These are by far the hardest to pinpoint—literally hundreds of points of failure could be involved. It always helps to be familiar with the physical topology of your network. Start by checking the devices that provide network access closest to your Mac. Something as simple as a bad Ethernet port on a network switch can cause problems. As you move on to investigating devices farther away from your Mac, you will find that it's often easiest to start your investigation using the network diagnostic utilities included with macOS.

▶ Service issues—These issues are related to the actual network device or service you are trying to access. For example, the devices providing DHCP or DNS services could be temporarily down or improperly configured. It's often easy to determine whether the problem is with the service alone by testing other network services. If the other network services work, you're probably not dealing with network or local issues. Again, macOS provides some useful diagnostic tools for testing service availability.

Troubleshooting network services is also covered in Lesson 22, "Manage Network Services."

You will be using three main tools for diagnosing network issues in macOS: Network preferences, Network Diagnostics, and Network Utility.

Verify Network Preferences Status

One of the diagnostic tools you should always check first is Network preferences. Network preferences features a dynamically updating list that shows you the current status of any network interface. If a network connection is not working, you will find out about it here first.

Network status indicators are as follows:

▶ Green—The connection is active and configured with TCP/IP settings. This, however, does not guarantee that the service is using the proper TCP/IP settings.

▶ Yellow—The connection is active but the TCP/IP settings are not properly configured. If you are still experiencing problems with this service, double-check the network settings. If the settings appear sound, move on to the other diagnostic utilities.

▶ Red—This status usually indicates either improperly configured network settings or disconnected network interfaces. If this is an always-on interface, check for proper physical connectivity. If this is a virtual or Point-to-Point Protocol connection, double-check the settings and attempt to reconnect.

About Common Network Issues

A good starting point for resolving network issues is to quickly verify some of the most common causes. You can think of this list as items you should check every time you're having an issue. To put it another way, verify common issues before hunting down exotic ones. This includes verifying Ethernet connectivity, Wi-Fi connectivity, DHCP services, and DNS services.

Ethernet Connectivity Issues

For well over a century, those supporting any electronic device have heeded these words: "Check the cable first!" If you're using an Ethernet connection, always verify the physical connection to the Mac, and if possible verify the entire Ethernet run back to the switch. If that's not possible, try swapping your local Ethernet cable or use a different Ethernet port.

You should also verify the Ethernet status from Network preferences, as detailed in the next section. Also, keep an eye out for substandard Ethernet cabling or problematic switching hardware. A symptom of these issues would be a large number of packet errors, which you can verify with Network Utility, as covered later in this lesson.

You may also find that while the Ethernet switch registers a link, Network preferences still shows the link as down. This issue may be resolved by manually setting a slower speed in the advanced hardware settings of Network preferences, as covered in Lesson 20, "Manage Advanced Network Settings."

> **MORE INFO** ▶ Built-in network hardware can sometimes become unresponsive and may benefit from resetting the Mac's NVRAM or SMC. You can find out more about resetting these items from Apple Support articles HT204063, "How to Reset NVRAM on your Mac," and HT201295, "Reset the System Management Controller (SMC) on your Mac."

Wi-Fi Connectivity Issues

A modern version of "Check the cable first!" would certainly be "Check the Wi-Fi first!" After all, when you're using Wi-Fi networking, the wireless signal represents the "physical" network connection. Start by verifying that you are connected to the correct SSID from the Wi-Fi status menu or Network preferences. Often, if the Mac detects a problem the Wi-Fi status menu shows an exclamation point (!), indicating that there is a problem with the wireless network.

The Wi-Fi status menu can also serve as a diagnostic tool if you hold down the Option key when choosing this menu item. This view shows connection statistics for the currently selected Wi-Fi network. Of particular note is the Tx Rate entry, which shows (in megabits per second) the current data rate for the selected Wi-Fi network. The Wi-Fi status menu is capable of other diagnostic tricks, including helping you quickly identify network issues and opening the Wireless Diagnostics application.

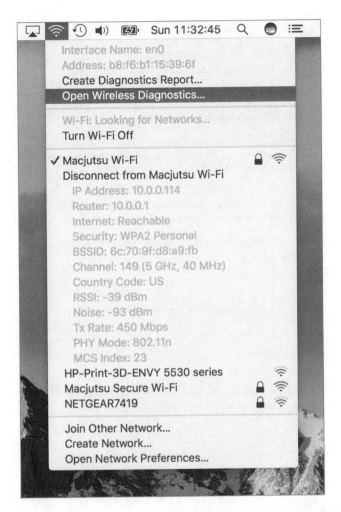

Opening the Wireless Diagnostics application reveals an assistant interface. The first feature of the Wireless Diagnostics application is to create and save a diagnostic report archive. The creation of the diagnostic report requires administrator authentication, but it will collect a huge amount of information about the Mac computer's wireless and network configuration. The resulting compressed archive will automatically appear only in the /var/tmp folder.

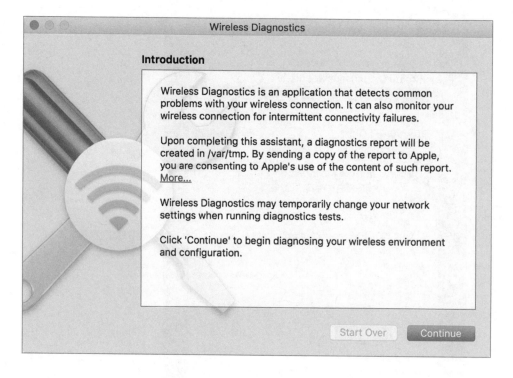

NOTE ▶ When you select the option Create Diagnostics Report from the Wi-Fi menu, it will send the diagnostic report directly to Apple, bypassing your ability to inspect the report's content.

The wireless diagnostics archive contains relevant files that would help experienced technical support staff diagnose a tricky connection issue. Of course, you can certainly expand the archive generated by the Wireless Diagnostics application and explore the contents on your own. However, the details of the collected items are beyond the scope of this guide.

Despite the potential complexity of the diagnostic reports, in the Wireless Diagnostics application you'll also find a variety of additional advanced wireless network utilities. Whenever you have the application open, you can reveal these additional utilities from the Window menu.

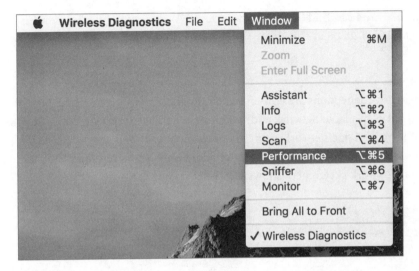

Again, descriptions of detailed use of these advanced wireless tools are beyond the scope of this guide. However, when working with wireless vendors or support specialists in trying to resolve tricky wireless issues, you will find that these wireless utilities are extremely valuable. For example, the Performance window provides a real-time view of the radio signal quality. With the wireless performance utility open, you can physically move a Mac portable device around an area to identify wireless "dead zones."

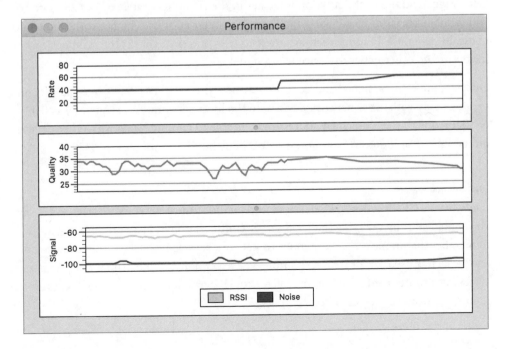

> **MORE INFO ▶** You can find out more about Apple Wireless Diagnostics from Apple Support article HT202663, "Check for Wi-Fi issues using your Mac."

DHCP Service Issues

Most client network connections are configured automatically via DHCP. If the DHCP server has run out of available network addresses—or if no DHCP service is available, as is the case with small ad hoc networks—the client automatically generates a self-assigned address. Sometimes this automatic assignment of addressing is referred to as "link-local addressing," but Network preferences shows it as Self-Assigned.

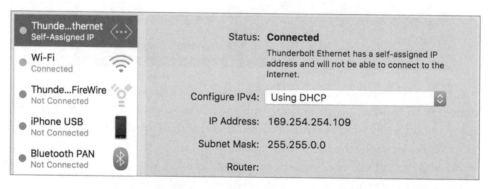

Self-assigned address configuration is always in the IP address range of 169.254.xxx.xxx, with a subnet mask of 255.255.0.0 and lacking a router address. The network client automatically generates a random self-assigned address and then checks the local network to make sure no other network device is using that address.

Once a unique self-assigned address is established, the network client can establish connections only with other network devices on the local network. Consequently, a client configured with a self-assigned address may be able to communicate with other devices on the LAN, but it doesn't have access to WAN or Internet resources.

DNS Service Issues

Aside from TCP/IP settings, DNS is a requirement for most network services. As always, you should start by verifying the DNS server configuration in Network preferences. Remember that in most cases the topmost network service interface is the primary one, and as such is used for all DNS resolution. The exception is if the primary network service is lacking a router configuration, in which case DNS resolution falls to the next fully configured network service interface.

Though it's rare, the macOS DNS resolution services can sometimes cache out-of-date DNS information and return inaccurate results. If you suspect your DNS issues are due to old information, you can either restart the Mac or flush the DNS service caches. You can find out more about this process from Apple Support article HT202516, "Reset the DNS cache in OS X."

Use Network Diagnostics

macOS includes Network Diagnostics Assistant to help you troubleshoot common network issues. Some networking applications automatically open this assistant when they encounter a network issue. You can also open it manually by clicking Assist Me at the bottom of Network preferences and then clicking the Diagnostics button.

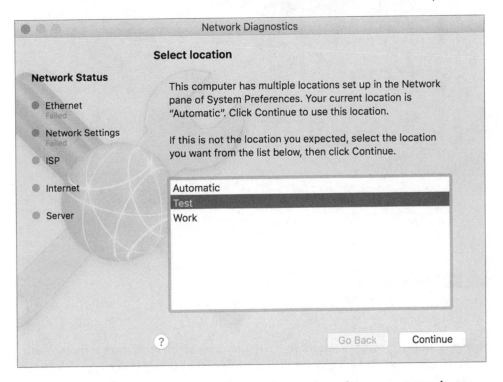

Network Diagnostics Assistant asks you a few simple questions about your network setup, and then, based on your answers, it runs a battery of tests to determine where the problem might be occurring. Test results are displayed using colored indicators on the left side of the window. If there are problems, the assistant makes suggestions for resolution.

Reference 21.2
Troubleshoot Using Network Utility

Network preferences and Network Diagnostics Assistant are good places to start trouble-shooting network issues, but the most powerful application in macOS for diagnosing network issues is Network Utility. In macOS, this application is buried in the /System/Library/CoreServices/Applications folder. The quickest way to find it, or really anything on the Mac, is to use Spotlight.

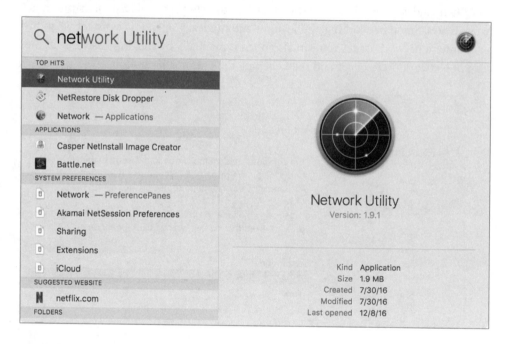

TIP ▸ You can also use Spotlight to search for and open the Wireless Diagnostics application, or any other useful application found in /System/Library/CoreServices/Applications.

Network Utility provides a selection of popular network identification and diagnostic tools. In fact, most of the tools in Network Utility are based on UNIX command-line network utilities that have been used by network administrators for years.

Network Utility is broken up into the following sections:

▶ Info—Allows you to inspect details regarding hardware network interfaces

▶ Netstat—Shows routing information and network statistics

▶ Ping—A fundamental network troubleshooting tool that lets you test network connectivity and latency

▶ Lookup—Lets you test DNS resolution

▶ Traceroute—Helps you analyze how your network connections are routed to their destination

▶ Whois—Lets you query whois database servers and find the owner of a DNS domain name or IP address of registered hosts

▶ Finger—Enables you to gather information based on a user account name from a network service

▶ Port Scan—A handy tool for determining whether a network device has services available

Network Utility can also be opened when your Mac is started from macOS Recovery, as covered in Lesson 3, "Use macOS Recovery." Whenever the Mac is started from macOS Recovery, you can open Network Utility by choosing it from the Utilities menu. However, when running from a macOS Recovery system, you do not have access to Network preferences. This means the Mac does not automatically activate built-in wired Ethernet connections and attempt to acquire configuration via DHCP. Alternatively, the Wi-Fi status menu is available, allowing you to temporarily connect to wireless networks.

Network Utility: Interface Information

When you open Network Utility, you first see the Info section. This section lets you view the detailed status of any hardware network interface. Even if you've opened Network Utility to use another section, always take a few moments to verify that the network interface is properly activated.

Start by selecting the specific interface you're having issues with from the pop-up menu. You'll notice that the selections here do not necessarily match the service names given in Network preferences. Instead, this menu shows the interfaces using their interface type and UNIX-given names.

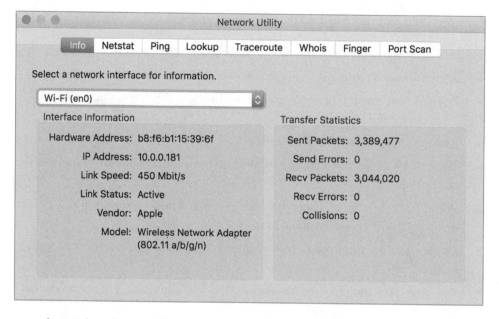

Once you have selected an interface, you can view general interface information to the left and transfer statistics to the right. The primary pieces of information you're looking for here are link status, link speed, and IP address(es). Only active hardware network interfaces show as such, and the link speed indicates whether the interface is establishing a proper connection. Obviously, a proper IP address is required to establish a TCP/IP connection. You can also identify the selected interface's MAC address, which is used to identify this particular interface on the LAN.

As a final validation of the selected network interface, you can view recent transfer statistics. If you open other network applications to stir up some network traffic, you can verify that packets are being sent and received from this interface. If you are seeing activity here but still experiencing problems, the issue is most likely due to a network or service problem and not the actual network interface. Or, if this interface is experiencing transfer errors, a local network hardware connectivity issue may be the root of your problem.

To resolve hardware network interface issues, always start by checking the physical connection. With wired networks, try different network ports or cabling to rule out physical connection issues. With wireless networks, double-check the Wi-Fi settings and the configuration of any wireless base stations. On rare occasions, you may find that the Mac computer's network hardware is somehow no longer working properly, in which case you should take your Mac to an Apple Authorized Service Provider.

Network Utility: Ping

If you have determined that your network settings are properly configured and the hardware network interface appears to be working correctly but you are still experiencing network issues, your next step is to test network connectivity using the ping tool. The ping tool is the most fundamental network test to determine whether your Mac can successfully send and receive data to another network device. Your Mac sends a ping data packet to the destination IP address, and the other device returns the ping packet to indicate connectivity.

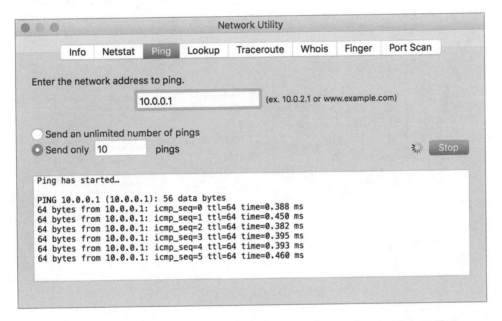

To use ping, open Network Utility and then click the Ping tab. Start by entering an IP address to a device on the LAN that should always be accessible, like the network router. Remember that using a domain name assumes that your Mac is properly communicating with a DNS server, which might not be the case if you're troubleshooting connectivity issues.

Click the Ping button to initiate the ping process. If the ping is successful, it returns the amount of time it took for the ping to travel to the network device and back. This is typically within milliseconds; experiencing ping times any longer than a full second is unusual.

> **NOTE** ▶ Some network administrators view excessive pinging as a threat, so many configure their firewalls to block pings or set up their network devices not to respond to any network pings.

Once you have established successful pings to local devices, you can branch out to WAN or Internet addresses. Using the ping tool, you may find that everything works except for the one service you were looking for that prompted you to start troubleshooting the network.

Network Utility: Lookup

If you are able to successfully ping other network devices by their IP address but attempting to connect to another device by its host name doesn't work, you are experiencing issues related to DNS. The network lookup process allows you to test name resolution against your DNS server.

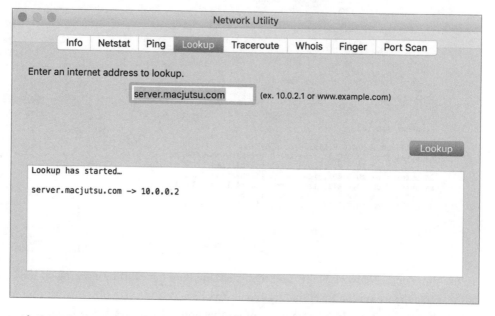

To verify DNS lookup, open Network Utility and then click the Lookup tab. Start by entering the host name of a device or service in your local domain. If you can resolve local host names but not Internet host names, this indicates that your local DNS server is resolving local names but is not properly connecting to the worldwide DNS network. If you don't have a local domain, you can use any Internet host name.

> **NOTE** ▶ The DNS results in the Lookup feature of Network Utility are considerably briefer than in previous versions of macOS. This simplified output shows only those IP addresses the Mac will attempt to connect with given the host name specified.

Click the Lookup button to initiate the network lookup process. A successful forward lookup returns the IP address of the host name you entered. A successful reverse lookup returns the host name of the IP address you entered. If you are unable to successfully return any lookups, your Mac is not connecting to the DNS server. You can verify this by pinging the DNS server IP address to test for basic connectivity.

Network Utility: Traceroute

If you are able to connect to some network resources but not others, use the network traceroute utility to determine where the connection is breaking down. Remember that WAN and Internet connections require the data to travel through many network routers to find their destination. The traceroute tool examines every network hop between routers using the ping tool to determine where connections fail or slow down.

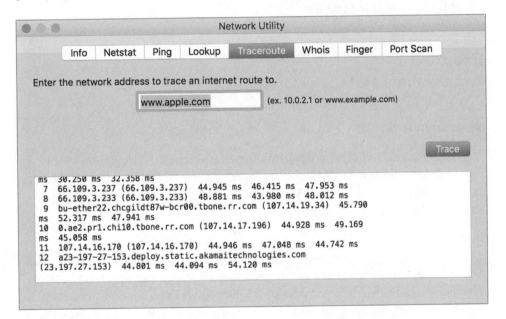

To verify a network TCP/IP route, open Network Utility and then click the Traceroute tab. Start by entering an IP address to a device on the LAN that should always be accessible, like the network router. Remember that using a domain name assumes that your Mac is properly communicating with a DNS server, which might not be the case if you're trouble-shooting connectivity issues.

Click the Trace button to initiate the traceroute process. If traceroute is successful, it returns with the list of routers required to complete the connection and the amount of time it took for the ping to travel to each network router. It sends three probes at each distance, so three times are listed for each hop. Again, the delay is typically measured in milliseconds; experiencing delay times of any longer than a full second is unusual.

> **NOTE ▶** If traceroute doesn't get a reply from any router along the way, it shows an asterisk instead of listing the router address.

> **NOTE ▶** Again, some network administrators view excessive pinging as a threat, so many configure their firewalls to block pings or set up network devices not to respond to any network pings.

Once you have established successful routes to local devices, you can branch out to WAN or Internet addresses. Using the traceroute tool, you may find that a specific network router is the cause of the problem.

Exercise 21.1
Troubleshoot Network Connectivity

> ▶ **Prerequisite**
>
> > ▶ You must have created the Local Admin (Exercise 2.1, "Configure a New macOS System for Exercises," or Exercise 2.2, "Configure an Existing macOS System for Exercises") and Chris Johnson (Exercise 5.1, "Create a Standard User Account") accounts.

Network connectivity issues can be complex, but familiarity with the arsenal of tools included in macOS will help you develop a solid plan of attack for their resolution. In this exercise, you will misconfigure your network settings and then use the built-in troubleshooting tools in macOS to see how they show the symptoms of the problem and allow you to isolate the problem.

Break Your Network Settings

1   If necessary, log in as Chris Johnson.

2   If necessary, open the Network pane in System Preferences, and authenticate as Local Admin.

3   Note the currently selected location so that you can return to it at the end of the exercise.

4   From the Location pop-up menu, choose Edit Locations.

5   Select the current location, and then choose Duplicate Location from the Action (gear icon) pop-up menu below the location list.

6   Name the new location Broken DNS, and then click Done.

7   Switch to the Broken DNS location, if necessary.

8   Click Apply.

9   Select the primary network service (the one at the top of the list on the left), and click Advanced.

10   Click DNS.

11   Click the Add (+) button under the DNS Servers list, and add the server address 127.0.0.55.

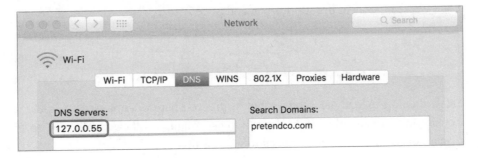

No DNS server is available at this address. The 127.0.0 prefix is reserved for computers to talk to themselves (known as *local loopback* addresses), but macOS uses only 127.0.0.1 for this. As a result, this is effectively an invalid address.

12   If there are any other entries in the DNS Servers list, make a note of them so you can add them back later, and then use the Delete (–) button to remove them.

13 Click TCP/IP.

14 From the Configure IPv6 pop-up menu, choose "Link-local only."

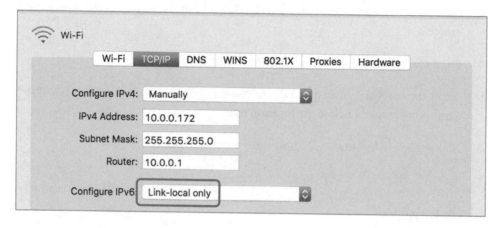

This will prevent IPv6 from acting as an alternate Internet connection.

15 Click OK, and then click Apply.

Observe the Problem

1 Open Safari.

2 Enter www.apple.com in the address bar, and press Return.

Safari attempts to load the webpage, but its progress bar does not get far because it is not able to reach anything. If you leave it long enough, it will eventually give up and display an error, but you do not need to wait for this.

3 Quit Safari.

Check the Network Status in Network Preferences

When you are experiencing a network problem, one of the first things to check is the network service status in Network preferences. This allows you to spot simple problems without having to go into more detailed diagnostics.

1   If necessary, open System Preferences, and select the Network pane.

2   Examine the status indicators next to the network services, as well as the order in which they appear in the list.

If the network service you expected to be active were not showing a green status indicator, it would immediately tell you that something was wrong with the connection (loose cable, not joined to wireless network, and so on) or that critical settings were missing (no IP address, and so on).

If the wrong service were at the top of the list, it would indicate either that the service order was set incorrectly or that unexpected services were active.

In this case, the expected service is green and at the top of the list, so more detailed troubleshooting is necessary.

Use Network Diagnostics

Network Diagnostics helps users diagnose and fix basic network problems. You will use it to gather more information about the problem.

1   In Network preferences, click Assist Me near the bottom of the window.

A dialog asks if you want assistance setting up a new network configuration or solving a network problem.

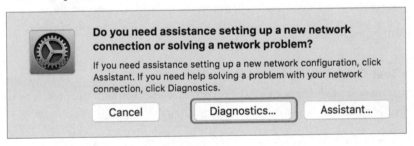

2   Click Diagnostics.

Network Diagnostics opens and automatically runs a series of automated tests. Several status indicators show the results.

In the following example, the Wi-Fi, Wi-Fi Settings, Network Settings, and ISP tests passed (that is, there is a live Wi-Fi connection, it has network settings associated with it, and it can reach as far as your Internet provider), but the Internet and Server tests failed. Your results may differ depending on what type of connection you have.

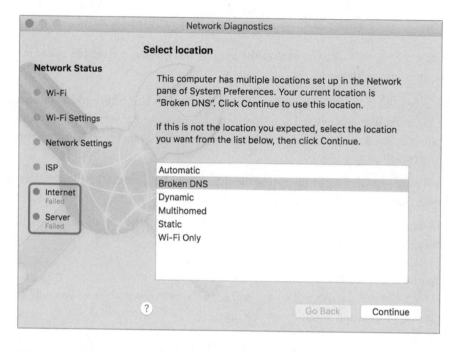

The Network Diagnostics tool gives a little more information about what parts of your network connection are working and which aren't, and may even identify the cause of the problem. You could use Network Diagnostics to troubleshoot and repair this, but instead you will take this opportunity to see what Network Utility can show.

3   Quit Network Diagnostics.

Use Ping to Test Connectivity

In this section, you will use Network Utility's ping tool. Ping's primary purpose is to test network connectivity, but as you will see it can also test DNS resolution.

Network Utility is in /System/Library/CoreServices/Applications, but you can launch it easily with Spotlight.

1   Press Command-Space bar to activate Spotlight.

2   Enter network, and then click Network Utility in the search results. Note that it may not be the first result.

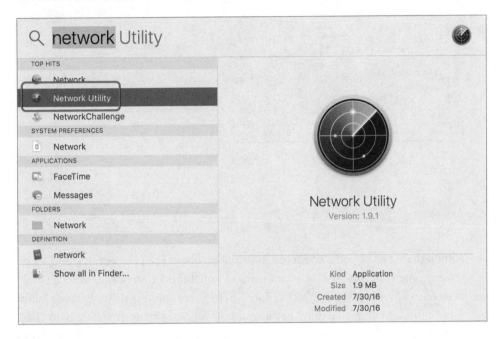

3   In Network Utility, click the Ping tab.

4   In the "Enter the network address to ping" field, type the domain name of the server you are trying to reach (www.apple.com).

5   Enter 5 in the "Send only" field, and make sure it is selected.

6   Click the Ping button.

After about 30 seconds, you receive a message telling you that it could not resolve www.apple.com. This message indicates that the ping tool was not able to use DNS to look up, or *resolve*, the name www.apple.com and match it to an IP address to send the ping to. In this case, you know that the name www.apple.com is valid because you have used it before, so this indicates that something is wrong with DNS.

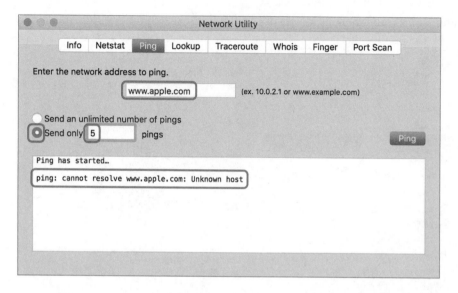

Although this gives you some more information about the problem, it still does not tell you where the problem is. It can be hard to tell the difference between a DNS problem and a complete network failure. If DNS resolution is the only thing failing, it can mimic a complete failure because almost all network access starts with (and depends on) a DNS lookup. On the other hand, if the network is completely disconnected, most attempts to use the network fail at the DNS step, so the only visible symptoms will be DNS errors.

One good way to distinguish between a DNS-only problem and a complete network failure is to try to reach a server by its numeric IP address. This bypasses the usual DNS lookup and hence works even if DNS is broken.

7   In the "Enter the network address to ping" field, enter the numeric IP address 8.8.8.8. This is an easy-to-remember address of a public server maintained by Google.

8   Click Ping.

This time, ping reaches the remote computer successfully and shows statistics for its five test pings.

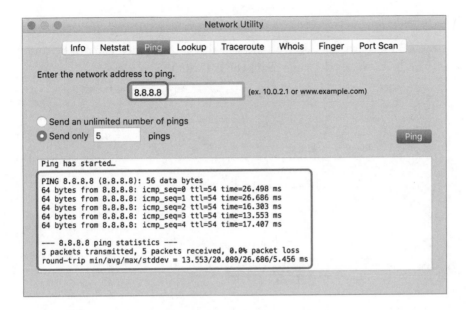

This tells you that your basic network connectivity is OK; it is likely just DNS that is not working.

NOTE ▸ If ping is unable to reach the server at 8.8.8.8, it may indicate that your computer is behind a tightly locked-down firewall. Ping probes are sometimes used in network attacks, and as a result some firewalls are configured to block them. Firewalls increase network security, but they can also complicate troubleshooting considerably.

TIP ▸ If ping was unable to reach the remote server, you could use the traceroute tool to test connectivity in more detail. Traceroute attempts to find out what network routers your packets go through on their way to the remote computer. If your packets are not making it all the way to the remote computer, traceroute can often tell you how far they are getting, which tells you more about where the problem is.

Use Lookup to Test DNS

Although the ping tool's error ("cannot resolve") already indicates a DNS problem, it is worth trying the lookup tool to see if it gives a more specific error.

1   In Network Utility, click the Lookup tab.

2   In the "Enter an internet address to lookup" field, enter the address www.apple.com.

3   Click Lookup.

After about 30 seconds, you receive a message that the operation couldn't be completed. This is essentially the same result you got with the ping tool.

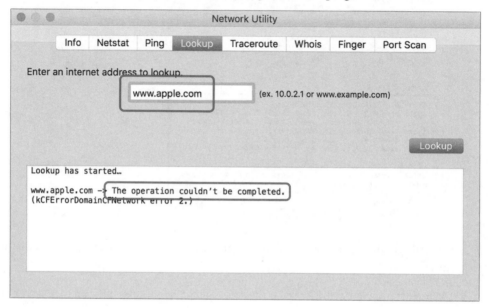

Switch to Working Network Settings

1   From Apple menu > Locations submenu, choose the location you were using at the beginning of this exercise.

Unlike the Broken DNS location, this one has valid settings, so your Internet connectivity should be back to normal.

2   In the Network Utility, click Lookup again.

This time the lookup tool reaches a DNS server and finds the IP address corresponding to the domain name www.apple.com.

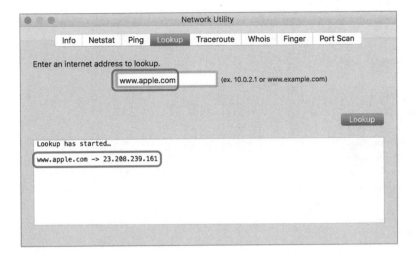

Note that the address you see may be different from the one shown here because the Apple website is served by a number of servers scattered around the Internet and uses DNS to direct you to a server near your network location for faster access.

If you knew what specific address the name should resolve to, you could verify that, but the fact that it resolved to an IP address at all is a good indication that DNS is working.

3   Open Safari, and try browsing a website.

This time, Safari is able to successfully load webpages from the Internet.

Monitor Network Traffic

You can use the Network Utility Info pane to view low-level network interface settings and to monitor network throughput on a per-interface basis.

1   Switch to Network Utility, and click the Info tab.

2   Select your computer's primary network interface from the pop-up menu.

The left side of the pane shows information about the active network connection, and the right side shows statistics about the network packets sent and received through this interface.

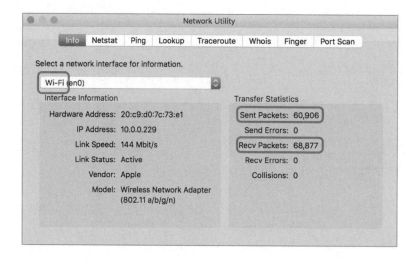

3   Arrange the Safari and Network Utility windows so that Safari is in front but not blocking the Transfer Statistics section of the Network Utility window.

4   In Safari, press Command-R to reload the current page.

     The Sent Packets and Recv Packets entries increase while Safari reloads the current page.

5   In Network Utility, select another network interface from the pop-up menu.

6   Switch to Safari, and reload the current page.

     The packet counts for this interface might increase slightly because of miscellaneous network chatter but should not respond specifically to refreshing in Safari.

     You can use this feature of Network Utility to see which network interface your connections are actually running through.

7   Quit Safari, Network Utility, and System Preferences.

Network Services

Lesson 22

Manage Network Services

Current operating systems provide a wide range of network and Internet service options, but all of them share the basic network architecture of client software, which accesses network services, and server software, which provides network services. macOS includes support for many popular network protocols, allowing you to connect and access a wide variety of shared network services.

This lesson first discusses the architecture of network services, in a general sense. Then you will be introduced to the key network service applications built into macOS. You will then learn how macOS can access popular file-sharing services. Finally, this lesson covers techniques for troubleshooting network services when problems arise.

Reference 22.1
About Network Services

From an architectural standpoint, shared network services are defined by client software (designed to access the service) and server software (designed to provide the service). The network service communication between the client and server software is facilitated by commonly known network protocols and standards.

By adhering to such standards, software developers can create unique yet compatible network client and server software. This allows you to choose the software tool that best fits your needs. For instance, you can use the built-in macOS Mail client created by Apple to access mail services provided by Apple, Google, Yahoo, or Microsoft.

GOALS

▸ Describe how macOS accesses shared network services

▸ Configure built-in macOS network applications

▸ Browse and access network file services using the Finder

▸ Troubleshoot network shared service issues

About Network Services Software

Some client software takes the form of dedicated applications, as is the case with many Internet services, like email and web browsing. Other client software is integrated into the operating system—file and print services, for example. In either case, when you establish a network service connection, settings for that service are saved on the local computer to preference files. These client preferences often include resource locations and authentication information.

On the other side of this relationship is the server software, which is responsible for providing access to the shared resource. Properly setting up server software is usually a much more complicated affair. Server administrators may spend weeks designing, configuring, and administering the software that provides network services. Server-side settings include configuration options, protocol settings, and account information.

About Network Services Communication

Network clients and servers, sometimes of different makes, communicate using commonly known network protocols or network standards. A protocol becomes a standard once it is widely adopted and ratified by a standards committee. Part of what defines a specific network protocol is which TCP or UDP (User Datagram Protocol) ports are used for communications.

A primary feature of both the TCP and UDP transport mechanisms is the ability to handle multiple simultaneous connections and service protocols. This is accomplished by assigning each communication service to a specific port number or port range. Both TCP and UDP connection ports are defined between 0 and 65,535.

For instance, the standard TCP port for web traffic is port 80. When troubleshooting a network service, you must know the port numbers or ranges for that service. Apple maintains a list of commonly used network services and their associated TCP or UDP ports at Apple Support article HT202944, "TCP and UDP ports used by Apple software products."

> **NOTE ▶** This guide assumes the default port numbers and port ranges for each network service. Network administrators may choose to use a different port number than the default for testing, to "hide" a service, or to bypass router restrictions.

About Network Service Identification

At a minimum, accessing a network service requires knowledge of the service's local network or Internet location. Some network services feature dynamic service discovery, which allows you to easily locate a network service by simply browsing a list of available services. In other cases, you must manually identify the service's location with a specific network host address or name. Examples of both methods are detailed later in this lesson.

Finally, some network services are so popular that macOS includes built-in mechanisms for automatically locating the appropriate network service resources. Services in this last category are mainly configured via the Internet Accounts preferences, also covered later in this lesson.

Once you have located and connected to a network service, you often need to prove your identity to that service provider. This process is called authentication. Successful authentication to a network service is usually the last step in establishing a connection to that service. Once a connection is established, security technologies are normally in place to ensure that you're allowed to access only certain resources. This process is called authorization. Both of these fundamental network service concepts, authentication and authorization, will be covered throughout this lesson and the next, Lesson 23, "Manage Host Sharing and Personal Firewall."

About Dynamic Service Discovery

Requiring users to manually enter network addresses to access a network service isn't very user friendly. What if you join a new network without knowing the exact names of all its available resources? Or what if the shared resource you need is hosted from another client computer that doesn't have a DNS host name or the same IP address every time? To address these issues, macOS supports dynamic network service discovery protocols.

Dynamic network service discovery protocols allow you to browse local area and wide area network resources without knowing specific service addresses. In a nutshell, network devices providing services advertise the availability of their services on the network. As available network resources change, or as you move your client to different networks, the service discovery protocols dynamically update the list of available services.

macOS makes ample use of dynamic network service discovery throughout. For example, dynamic network service discovery allows you to browse for available network file shares with the Finder or to locate new network printers from the Printers & Scanners preferences. Other network applications built into macOS use service discovery to locate a variety of shared resources, including Messages, Image Capture, Photos, iTunes, Safari, and the macOS Server application. Third-party network applications also take advantage of dynamic network service discovery.

It is important to remember that the discovery protocol is used only to help you and the system locate available services. Once the discovery protocol provides your computer with a list of available services, its job is done. When you connect to a discovered service, the Mac establishes a connection to the service using the service's protocol. For example, the Bonjour service discovery protocol can provide the Mac with a list of available screen-sharing systems, but when you select a Mac server from this list, the Mac establishes a screen-sharing connection to the server using the Virtual Network Computing (VNC) protocol.

> NOTE ► Mac OS X Snow Leopard 10.6 and later are no longer compatible with the AppleTalk network browsing or service connections.

Bonjour

Bonjour is the Apple implementation of Zero Configuration Networking, or Zeroconf, a collection of standards drafts that provide automatic local network configuration, naming, and service discovery. Bonjour uses a broadcast discovery protocol known as multicast DNS (mDNS) on UDP port 5353.

> MORE INFO ► You can find out more about Bonjour at www.apple.com/support/bonjour/.

Bonjour is the primary set of dynamic network service discovery protocols used by macOS native services and applications. Bonjour is preferred because it is based on TCP/IP standards, so it integrates well with other TCP/IP-based network services. macOS also includes support for Wide-Area Bonjour, allowing you to browse WAN resources as well as LAN resources.

Whereas local Bonjour requires no configuration, Wide-Area Bonjour requires that your Mac be configured to use a DNS server and search domain that supports the protocol. Configuring DNS is covered in Lesson 19, "Manage Basic Network Settings," and Lesson 20, "Manage Advanced Network Settings."

> MORE INFO ► macOS also supports network identification via the Back to My Mac feature in iCloud. However, a Back to My Mac system can be located only by the iCloud user who set it up. In other words, it doesn't help other users locate your system. You can find out more about Back to My Mac from Apple Support article HT204618, "Set up and use Back to My Mac."

Server Message Block

Originally designed by Microsoft, Server Message Block (SMB) has become the most common network service for sharing files and printers. SMB also includes a network discovery service that runs on UDP ports 137 and 138. Most current operating systems that provide support for SMB sharing also support dynamic discovery via SMB.

Despite the preferred status of SMB as the default file-sharing protocol in OS X Yosemite 10.10 and later, the network discovery portion of SMB is still not preferred over Bonjour. However, macOS does support browsing through the legacy NetBIOS and WINS protocols. Details on configuration of NetBIOS and WINS are covered in Lesson 20, "Manage Advanced Network Settings."

About Network Host Addressing

At a minimum, all network hosts can be reached by their IP address. For most people, though, IP addresses are hard to remember, so other technologies have been created to give network hosts human-friendly network names.

Network host identification methods include:

▶ IP address(es)—The primary network identifier for your Mac, an IP address, can always be used to establish a network connection.

▶ DNS host name—All Mac computers have a host name configured via one of two methods. Traditionally, these names are hosted on a DNS server configured by administration at the DNS server. The Mac attempts to resolve its host name by performing a DNS reverse lookup on its primary IP address. However, many network clients don't have properly configured DNS host names because of the administrative overhead required to create and update client DNS entries. So if the Mac can't resolve a host name from the DNS server, it uses the Bonjour name instead.

▶ Computer name—This name is used by other Apple systems to identify your Mac. The computer name is part of the Apple Bonjour implementation and is set in the Sharing preferences. The computer name is also used by AirDrop peer-to-peer file sharing.

▶ Bonjour name—As covered previously, Bonjour is the macOS primary dynamic network discovery protocol; in addition, Bonjour provides a convenient naming system for use on a local network. The Bonjour name is usually similar to the computer name, but it differs in that it conforms to DNS naming standards and ends with .local. This allows the Bonjour name to be supported by more network devices than the standard computer name, which is generally recognized only by Apple systems. This name is also set in the Sharing preferences.

▶ NetBIOS/WINS name—This name is used for the legacy Windows dynamic network discovery protocols as part of the SMB service. This name is set in either the Sharing or Network preferences.

Identifier	Example	Set by	Used by
IP address	10.1.17.2	Network preferences	Any network host
DNS hostname	client17.pretendco.com	Defined by DNS server	Any network host
Computer name	Client 17	Sharing preferences	Mac systems (Bonjour or AirDrop)
Bonjour name	Client-17.local	Sharing preferences	Bonjour hosts
SMB (NetBIOS) name	CLIENT17	Network preferences	SMB hosts

Reference 22.2
Configure Network Service Applications

Because of the widespread adoption of TCP/IP for nearly all LAN, WAN, and Internet communications, there really isn't any difference between how you access a "standard network service" and an "Internet service." With few exceptions, nearly all network services work the same way across a LAN as they do across the Internet. The primary difference between the two is the scope of service. Services like email and instant messaging can certainly work on a local level, but these services are also designed to communicate across separate networks and between servers. macOS includes a range of client applications designed to access different network services.

> **TIP** ▶ Although this guide focuses on the network client software built into macOS, many excellent third-party network clients are available for the Mac. In fact, when troubleshooting a network access problem, using an alternative network client is an excellent way to determine whether the issue is specific to your primary client software.

Use Safari Web Browser

macOS Sierra includes the updated Safari web browser. Safari is an efficient and robust browser that supports most websites. By far the most popular and ubiquitous network service, the Hypertext Transfer Protocol (HTTP) handles web communication using TCP port 80. Secure web communication, known by the acronym HTTPS, encrypts HTTP over a Secure Sockets Layer (SSL) or, more recently, over a Transport Layer Security (TLS) connection that by default uses TCP port 443.

Generally, little additional network configuration is required to use web services. You only need to provide the web browser with the Uniform Resource Locator (URL) or web address of the resource to which you want to connect. In macOS Sierra, Safari defaults to the most secure TLS communication even if you don't specify HTTPS in the URL. The only exception is if you have to configure web proxies, as described in Lesson 20, "Manage Advanced Network Settings."

> **MORE INFO** ▶ You can find out more about Safari from the Apple website at www.apple.com/safari.

About Internet Accounts Preferences

A feature clearly influenced by iOS, the Internet Accounts preferences provides a single unified interface for configuring network service accounts. Formerly known as Mail, Contacts & Calendars preferences, the Internet Accounts preferences is used to configure a variety of macOS applications and services. In other words, entering a single network service account in the Internet Accounts preferences configures all appropriate network service applications built into macOS.

Through the Internet Accounts preferences, macOS can be configured to use network service accounts for Apple iCloud, Microsoft Exchange, Google, Twitter, Facebook, LinkedIn, Yahoo, AOL, Vimeo, Flickr, and other common network service protocols, including those hosted from a system running macOS Server.

NOTE ▶ macOS requires Microsoft Exchange Server 2007 Service Pack 1 Update Rollup 4 or later, with Exchange Web Services enabled. The Mail application also supports the various Microsoft-hosted Exchange services.

NOTE ▶ The Internet Accounts preferences also includes support for services popular in non-English-speaking countries. These services appear automatically when the appropriate region is selected in the Language & Region preferences.

Each different service type includes varying levels of support for built-in macOS applications and services. For example, signing in with a Twitter account configures the system so that you can tweet from Notification Center or any supported application—whereas signing in to a service that provides multiple features, like Google or Yahoo, in turn configures multiple applications, including Mail, Notes, Calendar, Reminders, Contacts, and Messages. Apple iCloud includes support for even more features, including iCloud Drive, Photos, Safari, iCloud Keychain, Back to My Mac, Find My Mac, and FaceTime.

Configure Network Service Accounts

The best method for configuring network service accounts in macOS is by using the Internet Accounts preferences. Simply click an included service provider to get the sign-up process started. This reveals a service sign-in dialog, wherein each service will likely provide its own unique authentication dialog.

TIP If you don't see the Internet Accounts list of services, simply click the small Add (+) button at the lower-right corner of the preferences pane.

If you are signing in to a service with multiple features, after you successfully authenticate, you will be allowed to enable any available options for the service. You can also return to the Internet Accounts preferences at any point to enable or disable a service feature. Additionally, from there you can verify or reenter account information by clicking the Details button.

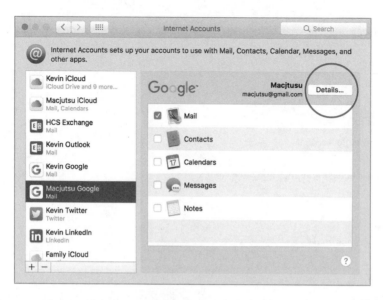

If you need to configure an Internet service that's not listed in the Internet Accounts preferences, or you need to configure a local service provided by your organization, click Add Other Account at the bottom of the services list. This reveals a dialog allowing you to manually configure services for Mail, Notes, Calendar, Reminders, Contacts, and Messages. In many cases, if you add a service this way you will likely have to define additional configuration information. This information should be provided to you by an administrator of the service.

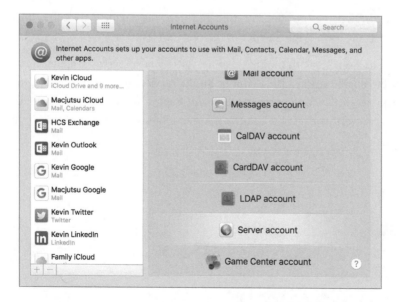

If you choose "Server account," the following dialog searches the local network for an OS X Server 10.7 or later system that provides compatible services.

You can select your server from the list or enter the host name of a server that's not on your local network. Because macOS can automatically detect macOS Server services, you'll only need to enter network account authentication to complete the setup.

macOS can also accept a configuration profile for automatic configuration of network service accounts settings. A network administrator would provide a configuration profile containing all the necessary settings to properly configure the macOS network applications for a specific network service account. These settings can be deployed by simply double-clicking a local copy of a configuration profile or by having the Mac managed by a mobile device management (MDM) solution.

> **MORE INFO ▶** macOS Server can provide MDM services through Profile Manager. You can find out more about Profile Manager in macOS Server at www.apple.com/macos/server/.

Configure Mail

macOS includes the Mail application for handling email communications. Mail supports all standard email protocols and their encrypted counterparts, along with a variety of authentication standards. Mail also includes support for Exchange-based services.

With this many service options, properly configuring mail service settings can be quite daunting. Ideally, Mail is configured automatically via the Internet Accounts preferences or via a configuration profile. In fact, in the Mail application, selecting the menu option Mail > Accounts will redirect you to the Internet Accounts preferences.

Mail also includes its own account setup assistant that will walk you through the process of configuring mail account settings. This assistant starts automatically if no account has been set when Mail is opened, but you can start it at any time by selecting Mail > Add Account. The assistant first presents an interface similar to that found in the Internet Accounts preferences.

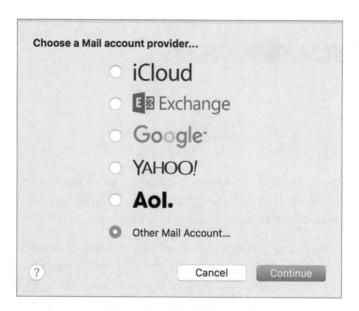

When you select one of these default mail account types, the assistant attempts to automatically determine the appropriate mail protocol, security, and authentication settings. This includes support for the Autodiscovery feature of Microsoft Exchange Server. Further, when you set up a mail account here, the system will automatically attempt to configure Notes, Calendar, Reminders, and Contacts as well.

If you need to configure Mail for an account type not listed in the defaults, select the Other Mail Account option. After entering basic mail account information, the assistant attempts to automatically determine the appropriate mail settings. If your mail service uses a nonstandard configuration or is unreachable, you may have to manually enter the mail service settings here. This means you may need to work with the service administrator to obtain the appropriate configuration settings.

NOTE ► If you need to further tweak mail service settings, you'll find advanced options in the Mail Accounts preferences, accessed by selecting Mail > Preferences. When the Mail preferences window opens, click the Accounts button in the toolbar to view and manage all Mail accounts.

In summary, macOS Mail support the following email services:

► Standard mailbox access protocols—The standard protocol used between mail clients and mail servers for receiving mail is either Post Office Protocol (POP) on TCP port 110 or Internet Message Access Protocol (IMAP) on TCP port 143. Both protocols can also be encrypted with an SSL connection. By default, encrypted POP uses TCP port 995 and encrypted IMAP uses TCP port 993. Finally, iCloud defaults to secure IMAP.

► Standard mail-sending protocols—The standard protocol used for sending mail from clients to servers and from server to server is Simple Mail Transfer Protocol (SMTP) on TCP port 25. Again, SMTP can be encrypted with an SSL connection on port 25, 465, or 587. The port used for secure SMTP varies by mail server function and administrator preference. Finally, iCloud defaults to secure SMTP.

► Exchange-based mail service—Although popular, these services do not use mail standards for client communication. Instead, Mail communicates using the EWS protocol. EWS uses the standard ports for web traffic: TCP port 80 for standard transport and TCP port 443 for secure transport.

Configure Notes

Notes in OS X El Capitan 10.11 or later goes well beyond simple text notes by allowing you to include nearly any media in a note, including photos, video, map coordinates, and freehand drawn scribbles. As a default, Notes will save to the local system, but you can also have all your notes available on multiple devices when the Notes application is configured with a compatible service account.

The ability for Notes to contain media beyond simple text also required a significant change to how notes are saved via a network service. Notes in macOS Sierra defaults to saving via iCloud. This change was necessary to support the rich media that the new Notes application allows.

The legacy network service method for Notes is still available but only supports simple text notes. This legacy method utilizes EWS (Exchange Web Services) or IMAP mail services as the mechanism for saving the notes. In this case, the Notes application creates a special Notes mailbox on your mail service and automatically manages this mailbox; thus, the Mail application ignores this mailbox. However, you may notice this mailbox when using older versions of Mail or third-party mail clients.

> **TIP** ▸ You can also share individual notes to others via alternative network services, like iMessage or Facebook, by clicking the Share button (up-pointing arrow inside a box) in the Notes toolbar.

Upgrade a Legacy Notes Account

Users with a Notes account that have upgraded from OS X Yosemite 10.10 or earlier will be automatically prompted to upgrade to the new Notes sharing service.

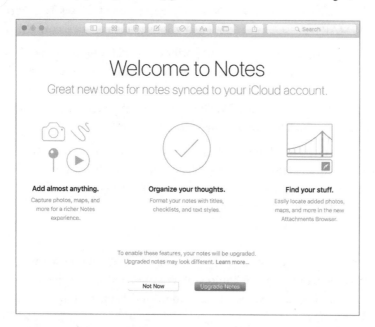

Accepting this one-way upgrade will move your existing notes to iCloud, which allows for all the features in Notes for OS X El Capitan 10.11 or later. Obviously, this upgrade requires that the user be signed in to iCloud. This also means that your upgraded notes are compatible only with the Notes application on iOS 9 or later. For this reason, if you still use Notes on devices with previous systems, you may not wish to upgrade immediately. If you plan to wait initially, at any point later you can upgrade by clicking the Upgrade button at the top of the notes listing.

TIP ▶ Apple devices running previous systems, or any non-Apple devices, can also access upgraded notes from the iCloud website.

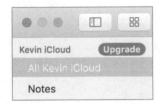

MORE INFO ▶ You can find out more about the Notes upgrade process from Apple Support article HT204987, "Upgrade your Notes app."

Configure a New Notes Account

Ideally, Notes will have been configured automatically along with other services via the iCloud or Internet Accounts preferences. In fact, in the Notes application, selecting the menu option Notes > Accounts will redirect you to the Internet Accounts preferences. As an option, the Internet Accounts preferences allow you to configure Notes without also configuring iCloud or the Mail application. However, without access to an iCloud account, Notes will use the legacy network service method that requires use of an EWS or IMAP mail service from a network service provider.

Configure Calendar and Reminders

macOS includes a scheduling application, Calendar, previously known as iCal. Although Calendar can certainly work on its own for managing your calendar information on your local Mac, it also integrates with a variety of network calendar services based on the EWS or CalDAV protocols. CalDAV, or Calendaring Extensions to WebDAV, as its name states, extends WebDAV (Web Distributed Authoring and Versioning), which is itself an extension of HTTP.

Ideally, Calendar will already have been configured automatically along with Mail via the Internet Accounts preferences or a configuration profile. In fact, in the Calendar application, selecting the menu option Calendar > Accounts redirects you to the Internet Accounts preferences.

Calendar also includes its own account setup assistant, which will walk you through the process of configuring mail account settings. This assistant doesn't start automatically when the Calendar application is opened, but you can start it at any time by selecting Calendar > Add Account.

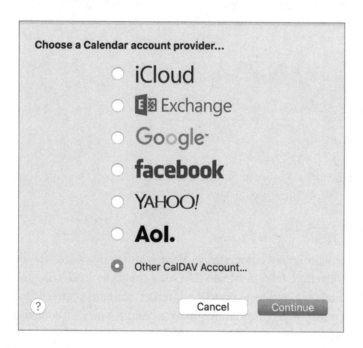

When you select one of these default calendar account types, the assistant attempts to automatically determine the appropriate calendar service security and authentication settings. This includes support for the Autodiscovery feature of Microsoft Exchange Server. Further, when you set up a calendar account here, the system will automatically attempt to configure Mail, Notes, Reminders, and Contacts as well.

If you need to configure Calendar for an account type not listed in the defaults, select the option Other CalDAV Account. After entering the user mail address and account password, the assistant attempts to automatically determine the appropriate CalDAV settings. If your mail service uses a nonstandard configuration or is unreachable, you may have to manually enter the CalDAV service settings here. This means you may need to work with the service administrator to obtain the appropriate configuration settings.

NOTE ► If you need to further tweak calendar service settings, you'll find advanced options in the Calendar Accounts preferences, accessed by selecting Calendar > Preferences. When the Calendar preferences window opens, select the Accounts button in the toolbar to view and manage all calendar service accounts.

Closely related to Calendar is the Reminders application, which allows you to maintain a personal to-do list. Reminders enables to-do lists to be saved on the local system, but you can also have to-do lists available on multiple devices when the Reminders application is configured for access to calendar services. This is because Reminders utilizes EWS or CalDAV network calendar services as the mechanism for saving the notes. Reminders creates to-do calendar events and automatically manages these events. Thus, the Calendar application ignores to-do events. However, many third-party calendar applications support to-do events within their interface; this includes previous versions of OS X iCal.

Ideally, Reminders will have been configured automatically along with other services via the Internet Accounts preferences or via a configuration profile. In fact, in the Reminders application, selecting the menu option Reminders > Accounts redirects you to the Internet Accounts preferences. As an option, the Internet Accounts preferences allow you to configure Reminders without also configuring Calendar. However, the Reminders application still requires use of an EWS or CalDAV calendar service from a network service provider.

Also like the Calendar application, Reminders includes its own account setup assistant, which will walk you through the process of configuring mail account settings. This assistant doesn't start automatically when the Reminders application is opened, but you can start it at any time by selecting Reminders > Add Account. The assistant presents an interface similar to the Calendar Setup Assistant because again, Reminders only connects to EWS or CalDAV services. As of this writing, Reminders doesn't support Facebook or Google calendar services.

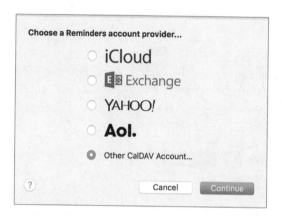

In summary, Calendar and Reminders support the following network calendar services:

▶ CalDAV collaborative calendaring—Calendar supports a network calendar standard known as CalDAV. This standard uses WebDAV as a transport mechanism on TCP port 8008 or 8443 for encrypted communication, but CalDAV adds the administrative processes required to facilitate calendar and scheduling collaboration. The macOS Server Calendar service is based on CalDAV. Furthermore, CalDAV is being developed as an open standard, so any vendor can create software that provides or connects to CalDAV services.

▶ Internet-based calendar services—Calendar and Reminders can use a variety of Internet-based calendar services, including iCloud, Yahoo, and Google calendar services. All three of these services are based on CalDAV and use the encrypted HTTPS protocol over TCP port 443.

▶ Exchange-based calendaring service—Calendar includes support for this popular calendar service. Again, the macOS Exchange integration relies on EWS, which uses TCP port 80 for standard transport and TCP port 443 for secure transport.

▶ Calendar web publishing and subscription—Calendar allows you to share your calendar information by publishing iCalendar files to WebDAV-enabled web servers. Because, as mentioned, WebDAV is an extension to the HTTP protocol, it runs over TCP port 80, or TCP port 443 if encrypted. You can also subscribe to iCalendar files, identified by the filename extension .ics, hosted on WebDAV servers. Configuration is fairly easy—accessing a shared calendar is identical to accessing a webpage. Simply provide the Calendar application with the URL of the iCalendar file. Although calendar publishing enables you to easily share calendars one way over the web, it doesn't provide a true collaborative calendaring environment.

MORE INFO ▶ Apple hosts dozens of compatible calendars at www.apple.com/ downloads/macosx/calendars.

▶ Calendar email invitation—Calendar, again using iCalendar files, is integrated with Mail to automatically send and receive calendar invitations as email attachments. In this case the transport mechanism is whatever your primary mail account is configured to use. Although this method isn't a calendaring standard, most popular mail and calendar clients can use this method.

Configure Contacts

macOS includes a contact management application, Contacts, previously known as Address Book. Similarly to other macOS network applications, Contacts, although it can certainly work on its own for managing nonshared contact information on your Mac, also integrates with a variety of network contact services based on EWS, CardDAV (Card Distributed Authoring and Versioning), or LDAP (Lightweight Directory Access Protocol).

Again, ideally Contacts is configured automatically via Internet Accounts preferences or a configuration profile. However, Contacts also features an easy-to-use setup assistant for configuring specific contact or directory network service accounts. You can start it at any time by selecting Contacts > Add Account. The assistant first presents an interface similar to that found in the Internet Accounts preferences.

When you select one of these default contacts account types, the assistant attempts to automatically determine the appropriate account settings. This includes support for the Autodiscovery feature of Microsoft Exchange Server. Further, when you set up a contacts account here, the system will automatically attempt to configure Mail, Notes, Calendar, and Reminders as well.

If you need to configure Contacts for an account type not listed in the defaults, select the last option, Other Contacts Account. The only two other account types supported by the Contacts application are CardDAV and LDAP. Select the account type from the pop-up menu, and then provide the server and authentication information. You may need to work with the service administrator to obtain the appropriate configuration settings.

NOTE ▶ If you need to further tweak contact service settings, you'll find advanced options in the Contacts Accounts preferences, accessed by selecting Contacts > Preferences. When the Contacts preferences window opens, click the Accounts button in the toolbar to view and manage all contact service accounts.

In summary, Contacts supports the following network contact services:

▶ CardDAV contacts service—Contacts supports a network contacts service standard known as CardDAV. Here again, as the name implies, this standard uses WebDAV as a transport mechanism on TCP port 8800 or 8843 for encrypted communication. The macOS Server Contacts service is based on CardDAV. Furthermore, CardDAV is being developed as an open standard, so any vendor can create software that provides or connects to CardDAV services.

NOTE ▶ The Apple selection of TCP ports 8800 and 8843 for CardDAV is not based on any assigned standard. Some implementations of CardDAV may use the standard ports for HTTP(S) and TCP, ports 80 and 443, for encrypted communication.

▶ Internet-based contact services—Contacts can use a variety of Internet-based contact services, including iCloud, Google, Facebook, LinkedIn, and Yahoo contact services. All of these services are based on CardDAV and use the encrypted HTTPS protocol over TCP port 443.

▶ Exchange-based contact service—Contacts includes support for this popular contact sharing service. Again, the macOS Exchange integration relies on EWS, which uses TCP port 80 for standard transport and TCP port 443 for secure transport.

▶ Directory service contacts—Contacts can search contact databases via LDAP, the standard for network directory services, which uses TCP port 389 for standard transport and TCP port 636 for secure transport. Contacts can be configured for LDAP services either directly from its account setup assistant or via integration with the macOS systemwide directory service, as configured in the Users & Groups preferences.

Configure Messages

Instant messaging has grown well beyond text chatting with Messages, the application formerly known as iChat, included with macOS. Messages supports peer-to-peer file sharing, remote screen sharing, and high-resolution Messages Theater for sharing video from supported applications. Finally, Messages also includes support for the push-based messaging service iMessage, which allows you to communicate with iOS devices as well.

NOTE ▶ Messages in macOS Sierra supports audio and video communications through FaceTime. Configuring FaceTime is detailed later in this lesson.

Again, ideally Messages will have been configured automatically when you signed in to iCloud or via a configuration profile. However, Messages also includes its own account setup assistant that will walk you through the process of configuring messaging account settings. This assistant starts automatically if no account has been set when Messages is opened, but you can start it at any time by selecting Messages > Add Account.

You can enter any valid Apple ID to configure iMessage. After authentication, you may be prompted to choose additional iMessage identifiers that can be used to reach you, like other email accounts or mobile numbers. If you choose to skip configuration of iMessage, the Messages Setup Assistant then presents an interface similar to that found in the Internet Accounts preferences. You can also start this assistant at any time by selecting the menu option Messages > Add Account.

When you select one of these default messaging account types, the assistant attempts to automatically determine the appropriate account settings. If you need to configure Messages for an account type not listed in the defaults, select the last option, Other Messages Account. The only other account type supported by Messages is a manually configured Jabber service. Curiously, you can also choose to configure the three account types seen from the default list.

Select the account type from the pop-up menu and then provide the server and authentication information. You may need to work with the service administrator to obtain the appropriate configuration settings.

NOTE ▶ If you need to further tweak message service settings, you'll find advanced options in the Messages Accounts preferences, accessed by selecting Messages > Preferences. When the Messages preferences window opens, click the Accounts button in the toolbar to view and manage all message service accounts.

In summary, Messages supports the following categories of chat services:

▶ Internet messaging services—Messages supports AOL Instant Messenger (AIM), Google Talk, and Yahoo chat accounts. Assuming you have already registered for an account through one of these service providers, configuring Messages simply entails entering your account name and password.

▶ iMessage—The iMessage service is unique to Apple and can also be configured via Internet Accounts preferences or iCloud preferences. The iMessage protocol is facilitated via the Apple Push Notification service (APNs), which uses TCP port 5223, and fallback on Wi-Fi only to port 443. APNs is highly efficient for devices that rely on battery power and may occasionally lose network connectivity. This makes the iMessage service ideal for messaging with mobile Mac computers and iOS devices. However, Messages is limited to a single iMessage account per computer user account.

▶ Short Message Service (SMS)—If you are signed in to the iMessage service using the same Apple ID on both your Mac and an iPhone running iOS 8 or later, you can send and receive SMS messages via the iMessage protocol through an iPhone cellular connection. You must manually enable this feature on your iPhone in Settings > Messages before SMS messaging will be available to your Mac. For more information, see Apple Support article HT204681, "Use Continuity to connect your Mac, iPhone, iPad, iPod touch, and Apple Watch."

▶ Privately hosted messaging services—Messages works with open source Jabber servers, including the OS X Server Messages service. Jabber servers are based on the Extensible Messaging and Presence Protocol (XMPP), which uses TCP port 5222 or 5223 for encrypted communication.

▶ Ad hoc messaging—Messages can use the Bonjour network discovery protocol to automatically find other Messages or iChat users. No configuration is necessary to access Bonjour messaging. Bonjour details are covered in Lesson 23, "Manage Host Sharing and Personal Firewall."

Messages is compatible with a wide variety of messaging features and instant messaging protocols—which means it uses far too many TCP and UDP ports to list here. However, if you are having trouble with the iMessages service specifically, you should verify availability of APNs via Apple Support article HT202078, "If you use FaceTime and iMessage behind a firewall."

Configure FaceTime

FaceTime provides macOS Sierra with audio and video conferencing abilities, including the ability to answer or call standard phone numbers via a compatible iPhone. Similar to the iMessages service, FaceTime is unique to Apple and leverages APNs to initiate audio or video communications.

To use FaceTime your Mac must also be connected to a compatible camera and micro-phone. All macOS Sierra–compatible iMac and MacBook computers feature built-in cam-eras and microphones that are FaceTime compatible.

Again, ideally FaceTime will have been configured automatically when you signed in to iCloud. However, Messages also includes its own account setup assistant that will walk you through the process of configuring messaging account settings. This assistant starts auto-matically if no account has been set when Messages is opened.

You can enter any valid Apple ID to configure FaceTime. After authentication, you may be prompted to choose additional FaceTime identifiers that can be used to reach you, like other email accounts or, if you have FaceTime on your iPhone, other mobile numbers. Unlike other network service client applications, you must sign in to use FaceTime and you can only sign in to one account per local user account.

To handle phone calls on your Mac via FaceTime, you will need to be signed in to FaceTime on both your Mac and iPhone with iOS 8 or later. You will have to sign in to FaceTime on your iPhone first to enable FaceTime cellular phone calls. You should also check to ensure your iPhone cellular number is enabled in the FaceTime preferences on your Mac, which you can access by selecting the menu option FaceTime > Preferences.

Once signed in to FaceTime, the service is always ready to send and receive FaceTime calls, even when you quit the FaceTime application. If you wish to turn off FaceTime calls, you can do so from within the FaceTime application by selecting the menu option FaceTime > Turn FaceTime Off or by using the Command-K keyboard shortcut. To start receiving FaceTime calls again, use the same keyboard shortcut or choose Turn FaceTime On from the same menu. Finally, you can permanently halt all calls to your Mac by signing out of your account from the FaceTime preferences.

FaceTime uses a variety of standard and non-reserved TCP and UDP ports to facilitate calls. Specifically, you should verify availability of the ports in Apple Support article HT202078, "If you use FaceTime and iMessage behind a firewall."

Reference 22.3
Connect to File-Sharing Services

The Finder provides two methods for connecting to a network file system: automatically discovering shared resources by browsing them in the Finder Network folder or manually connecting by entering the address of the server providing the file service.

About File-Sharing Services

Many protocols exist for transferring files across networks and the Internet, but the most efficient are those designed specifically to share file systems. Network file servers can make entire file systems available to your client computer across the network.

Client software built into the macOS Finder can mount a network file service much as it would mount a locally connected storage volume. Once a network file service is mounted to the Mac, you can read, write, and manipulate files and folders as if you were accessing a local file system.

Additionally, access privileges to network file services are defined by the same ownership and permissions architecture used by local file systems. Details on file systems, ownership, and permissions are covered in Lesson 11, "Manage Permissions and Sharing."

macOS provides built-in support for these network file service protocols:

▶ Server Message Block version 3 (SMB 3) on TCP ports 139 and 445—This is the default (and preferred) file-sharing protocol for OS X Yosemite 10.10 and later. Historically, the SMB protocol was mainly used by Windows systems, but many other platforms have adopted support for some version of this protocol. The SMB 3 implementation in macOS works with advanced SMB features such as end-to-end encryption (if enabled on the server), per-packet signatures and validation, Distributed File Service (DFS) architecture, resource compounding, large maximum transmission unit (MTU) support, and aggressive performance caching. Finally, macOS maintains backward compatibility with older SMB standards.

▶ Apple Filing Protocol (AFP) version 3 on TCP port 548 or encrypted over Secure Shell (SSH) on TCP port 22—This is the traditional Apple native network file service. The current version of AFP is compatible with all the features of the Apple native file system, Mac OS Extended. Further, AFP is still the default for backup systems that are based on Time Machine.

▶ Network File System (NFS) version 4, which may use a variety of TCP or UDP ports—Used primarily by UNIX systems, NFS supports many advanced file-system features used by macOS.

▶ WebDAV on TCP port 80 (HTTP) or encrypted on TCP port 443 (HTTPS)—As mentioned earlier, this protocol is an extension to the common HTTP service and provides basic read/write file services.

▶ File Transfer Protocol (FTP) on TCP ports 20 and 21 or encrypted on TCP port 989 and 990 (FTPS)—This protocol is in many ways the lowest common denominator of file systems. FTP is supported by nearly every computing platform, but it provides only the most basic file-system functionality. Further, the Finder supports only read capability for FTP or FTPS shares.

NOTE ▶ Don't confuse FTPS (FTP-SSL) with another, similar protocol, SFTP (SSH File Transfer Protocol). The distinction is that FTPS uses SSL encryption on TCP port 990, and SFTP uses SSH encryption on TCP port 22. The Finder does not support FTPS. However, both are supported in Terminal.

Browse File-Sharing Services

You can browse for dynamically discovered file services from two locations in the Finder. The first location is the Shared list located in the Finder sidebar or within the Open dialog of any application. If it's enabled in Finder preferences, the Shared list is ideal for quickly discovering computers providing file services on a small network. The Shared list shows only the first eight discovered computers providing services. If additional servers are discovered, the last item in the Shared list, All, is a link to the Finder Network folder.

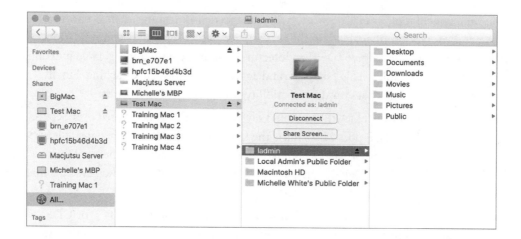

TIP ▶ The Finder Shared list shows servers that you are currently connected to, even if they didn't originally appear in the Shared list.

The Finder Network folder is a special place in macOS. The Network folder is not a standard folder at all; it's an amalgamation of all dynamically discovered network file services and all currently mounted file systems, including manually mounted ones. Obviously, the Network folder is constantly changing based on information gathered from the two dynamic network service discovery protocols compatible with macOS—Bonjour and SMB/NetBIOS/WINS—so you can browse only SMB or AFP file services from the Network folder.

TIP ▶ The Finder also lets you browse to screen-sharing (VNC) hosts via Bonjour, as covered in Lesson 23, "Manage Host Sharing and Personal Firewall."

Smaller networks may have only one level of network services. Conversely, if you have a larger network that features multiple service discovery domains, they appear as subfolders inside the Network folder. Each subfolder is named by the domain it represents. Items inside the domain subfolders represent shared resources configured for that specific network area.

To browse and connect to an SMB or AFP file service from the Finder sidebar, select the computer you want to connect to from the Shared list, or select a computer from the Finder Network folder. In the Finder, the quickest route to the Network folder is either to choose Go > Network from the menu bar or to press Shift-Command-K. Selecting a computer from either the Shared list or the Network folder yields similar results.

NOTE ▶ When browsing in the Finder, if you select a server that supports both SMB and AFP, OS X Yosemite 10.10 and later default to using the SMB protocol. Further, it will always use the most secure version of the SMB protocol supported by the sharing service.

About Automatic File-Sharing Service Authentication

The moment you select a computer providing services, the Mac attempts to automatically authenticate using one of three methods:

▶ If you are using Kerberos single sign-on authentication, the Mac attempts to authenticate to the selected computer using your Kerberos credentials.

▶ If you are using non-Kerberos authentication but you have connected to the selected computer before and chosen to save the authentication information to your keychain, the Mac attempts to use the saved information.

▶ The Mac attempts to authenticate as a guest user. Keep in mind that guest access is a file service option that many administrators disable.

If the Mac succeeds in authenticating to the selected computer, the Finder shows you the account name it connected with and also lists the shared volumes available to this account. Selecting a shared volume connects and mounts its file system.

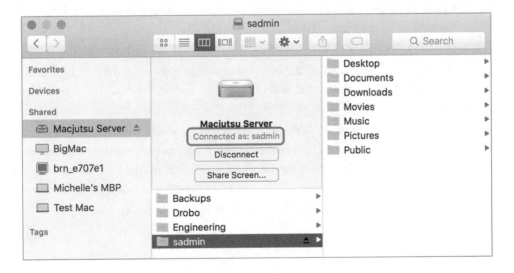

About Manual File-Sharing Service Authentication

If the Mac was unable to automatically connect to the selected computer, or if you need to authenticate with a different account, click the Connect As button to open an authentication dialog.

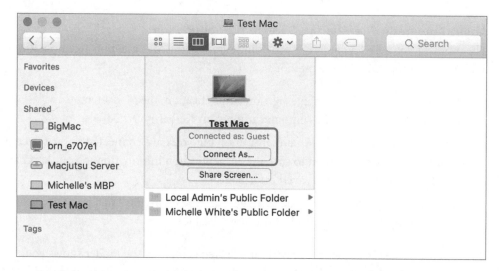

You can authenticate to a sharing service using one of three methods:

▶ Selecting the Guest radio button, if available, indicates that you wish to connect anonymously to the file service.

▶ Selecting the Registered User radio button enables you to authenticate using a local or network account known by the computer providing the shared items. Optionally, you can select the checkbox that saves this authentication information to your login keychain.

▶ Selecting the "Using an Apple ID" radio button enables you to authenticate to an SMB or AFP share using an Apple ID. For this option to appear, both the local Mac and the computer hosting the share must be running macOS. Further, the local accounts on both systems must be tied to an Apple ID, as covered in Lesson 5, "Manage User Accounts."

Click the Connect button, and the Mac authenticates and shows you a new list of shared volumes available to the account. Each available share appears as a folder. Click once on a shared item to connect and mount its file system.

Manually Connect to File-Sharing Services

To manually connect to a file service, you must specify a network identifier (URL) for the file server providing the service. You may also have to enter authentication information and choose or enter the name of a specific shared resource path. When connecting to an SMB or AFP service, you can authenticate first and then choose a shared item, or optionally provide a path. Conversely, when connecting to an NFS, WebDAV (HTTP), or FTP service, you may have to specify the shared items or full path as part of the server address and then authenticate if required.

Manually Connect to SMB or AFP

To manually connect to an SMB or AFP file service from the Finder, choose Go > Connect to Server, or press Command-K, to open the Finder "Connect to Server" dialog. In the Server Address field, enter smb:// or afp://, followed by the server's IP address, DNS host name, computer name, or Bonjour name.

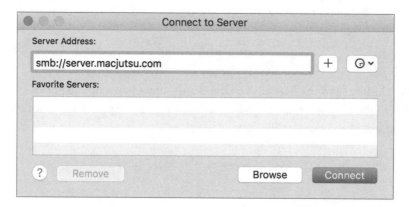

If you don't specify a protocol prefix, the "Connect to Server" dialog will attempt to pick the appropriate file-sharing protocol. Again, the preferred default file-sharing protocol for OS X Yosemite 10.10 and later is SMB 3. Optionally, after the server address, you can enter another slash and then the name of a specific shared item. This bypasses the dialog for selecting a specific file share.

> **TIP** Clicking Browse in the "Connect to Server" dialog brings you to the Finder Network folder, allowing you to browse for a server, as covered previously in this lesson.

If automatic file service authentication is available, as covered earlier in this lesson, you do not have to enter authentication information. If it isn't available, a dialog appears requiring you to enter authentication information. Likewise, this authentication dialog is identical to the one covered earlier in this lesson.

Once you have authenticated to the file service, you are presented with the list of shared volumes that your account is allowed to access. Select the shared item you want to mount. Optionally, you can hold down the Command key to select multiple shared items from the list.

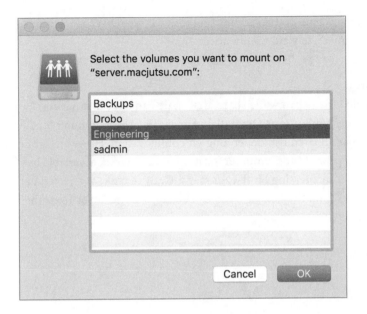

Manually Connect to NFS, WebDAV, or FTP

To manually connect to an NFS, WebDAV, or FTP file service from the Finder, choose Go > Connect to Server, or press Command-K, to open the Finder "Connect to Server" dialog.

In the Server Address field, enter one of the following:

▶   nfs://, followed by the server address, another slash, and then the absolute file path of the shared items.

▶   http:// for WebDAV (or https:// for WebDAV encrypted via SSL), followed by the server address. Each WebDAV site has only one mountable share, but you can optionally enter another slash and then specify a folder inside the WebDAV share.

▶   ftp:// (or ftps:// for FTP encrypted via SSL), followed by the server address. FTP servers also have only one mountable root share, but you can optionally enter another slash and then specify a folder inside the FTP share.

Depending on the protocol settings, you may be presented with an authentication dialog. Specifically, NFS connections never display an authentication dialog. The NFS protocol uses the local user that you're already logged in as for authorization purposes or Kerberos single sign-on authentication.

If you are presented with an authentication dialog, enter the appropriate authentication information there. Optionally, you can select the checkbox that saves this authentication information to your login keychain. When connecting to NFS, WebDAV, or FTP file services, the share mounts immediately after authentication.

About Mounted Shares

Once the Mac has mounted the network file share, that share can appear in several locations from the Finder or any application's Open dialog, including the Computer location, the desktop, and the sidebar's Shared list, depending on configuration. However, mounted network volumes always appear at the Computer location in the Finder, accessible by choosing Go > Computer or by pressing Shift-Command-C. By default, connected network volumes do not show up on the desktop. You can change this behavior from the General tab of the Finder Preferences dialog.

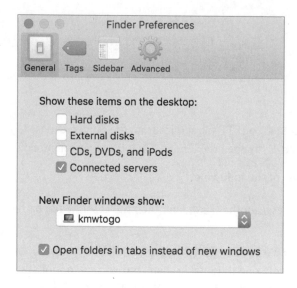

TIP ▶ Remember that the sidebar also appears in any application's Open dialog with exactly the same items that are available from the Finder.

Manually entering server information every time you connect to a server is a hassle. Two features in the "Connect to Server" dialog make this process efficient for your users. The dialog maintains a history of your past server connections. You can access this history by clicking the small clock icon to the right of the Server Address field. Also, you can create a list of favorite servers by clicking the Add (+) button to the right of the Server Address field.

Disconnect Mounted Shares

It is important to recognize that the Mac treats mounted network volumes similarly to locally attached volumes, so you must remember to always properly unmount and eject network volumes when you're done with them. Mounted network volumes are unmounted and ejected from the Finder using the same techniques you would use on a locally connected volume. Unmounting and ejecting volumes is covered in Lesson 9, "Manage File Systems and Storage." One difference in working with mounted volumes is that the Eject button appears multiple times in the Finder, wherever the server name or the shared items appear.

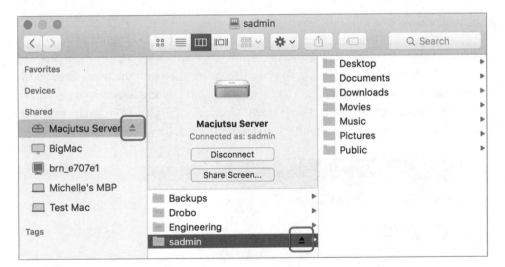

In practice, though, it's difficult for users to remember they have network shares mounted, since there is no locally attached hardware device to remind them. Further, laptop users often roam out of wireless network range without even thinking about what network shares they may have mounted.

If a network change or problem disconnects the Mac from a mounted network share, the Mac spends several minutes attempting to reconnect to the server hosting the shared items. If after several minutes the Mac cannot reconnect to the server, the system will fully disconnect from the share.

Automatically Connect to File Shares

On a positive note, because the Finder treats mounted network shares as similar to other file-system items, you can save time and make life easier for youself and your users by creating automatic connections to network shared items. One method is to have a network share mount automatically when a user logs in by adding the network share to the user's login items. Managing login items is covered in Lesson 5, "Manage User Accounts."

Alternatively, you can create easy-to-use shortcuts to often-used network shares. One method involves creating Dock shortcuts by dragging network shares or their enclosed items to the right side of the Dock. You can also create aliases on the user's desktop that link to often-used network shares or even specific items inside a network share. (Creating aliases is covered in Lesson 12, "Use Hidden Items, Shortcuts, and File Archives.") Either method you use automatically connects to the network share when the item is selected.

TIP ▸ You cannot drag items from the Finder sidebar or the Network browser to the login items on the Dock. Instead, select the network share from the desktop or the Computer location in the Finder. You can access the Computer location in the Finder by choosing Go > Computer.

TIP ▸ Remember that by using Kerberos single sign-on authentication or by saving authentication information to the keychain, you can bypass authentication dialogs as well.

Reference 22.4
Troubleshoot Network Services

To effectively troubleshoot a network issue, you must isolate the issue into one of three categories: local, network, or service. Most issues involving failure to access network services probably fall under the service category. This means that you should probably focus most of your efforts on troubleshooting the specific service you're having issues with.

However, before digging too deep into troubleshooting the specific network service, quickly check for general network issues. First, check to see whether other network services are working. Opening a web browser and navigating to a few different local and Internet websites is always a good general network connectivity test.

To be thorough, also test other network services, or test from other computers on the same network. If you're experiencing problems connecting to a file server but you can connect to web servers, chances are your TCP/IP configuration is fine, and you should concentrate on the specifics of the file server. If you're only experiencing problems with one particular service, you probably don't have local or network issues, and you should focus your efforts on troubleshooting just that service.

If other network clients or services aren't working either, your issue is likely related to local or network issues. Double-check local network settings to ensure proper configuration from both the Network preferences and Network Utility. If you find that other computers aren't working, you might have a widespread network issue that goes beyond troubleshooting the client computers. For more information on general network troubleshooting, see Lesson 21, "Troubleshoot Network Issues."

TIP ▸ If you're experiencing problems with a service provided by Apple, you can check real-time Apple service status at this website: www.apple.com/support/systemstatus/.

Use Network Utility: Port Scan

Once you decide to focus on troubleshooting a problematic network service, one of your most important diagnostic tools is the network Port Scan utility. Part of the Network Utility application, Port Scan scans for any open network service ports on the specified network address.

> **TIP** ▶ The quickest way to open Network Utility is via the Spotlight search menu. Usually searching simply for "net" will list Network Utility in the search results.

As covered earlier in this lesson, network service protocols are tied to specific TCP and UDP network ports. Network devices providing a service must leave the appropriate network ports open to accept incoming connections from other network clients. Port Scan reveals whether the required ports are indeed open. If the ports aren't open, that device either is not providing the expected service or is configured to provide the service in a nonstandard method. Either way, this indicates that the issue lies with the device providing the service, not with your Mac.

To verify network service availability, start by opening Network Utility and clicking the Ping tab at the top. Before scanning the ports, check for basic network connectivity by attempting to ping the device that is supposed to be providing the service. Enter the device's network address or host name and click the Ping button.

If the ping is successful, it returns with the amount of time it took for the ping to travel to the network device and then return. Assuming you have network connectivity to the other device, continue with the port scan.

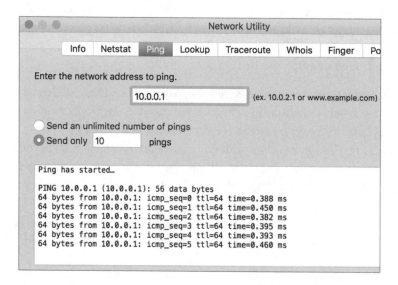

To scan for a network service, start by clicking the Port Scan tab. Again, enter the network address or host name of the device that is supposed to be providing the service. If you're only troubleshooting a specific service, limit the scan to just that service's default ports by selecting the appropriate checkbox and entering a beginning and ending port range.

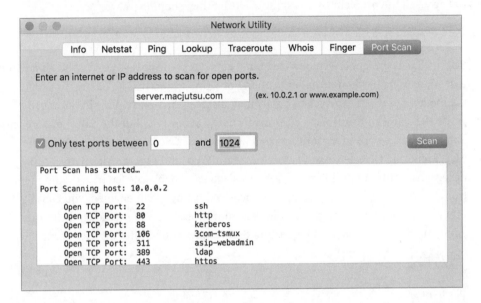

There are 65,535 available TCP and UDP network ports, so scanning all of them is unnecessary and overly time intensive. Even if you don't know the specific port, most common ports are between 0 and 1024. Further, network administrators view repeated network pings and broad port scans as a threat. Thus, some network devices are configured not to respond even when working properly. In general, you should avoid excessive network pinging and scanning an unnecessarily broad range of ports when testing others' servers.

Once you have defined the port range, you're ready to click the Scan button to initiate the scan process. Depending on the scan range you choose, it may take several minutes to complete the scan. Any open ports discovered are listed along with the associated network protocol, if known.

> **NOTE ▶** There are some inaccuracies with the protocol reporting of the Port Scan feature. For example, port 106 (listed as 3com-tsmux) is actually the macOS Server password service, and port 625 (listed as dec_dlm) is actually the directory service proxy. This is because these ports are registered by the Internet Assigned Numbers Authority (www.iana.org) for the reported protocols. However, Apple is using these numbers for its own purposes.

Troubleshoot Network Applications

Aside from general network service troubleshooting, you can try a few application-specific troubleshooting techniques. First, double-check any application-specific configuration and preference settings. It takes only a few moments, and you may find that users have inadvertently caused the problem by changing a setting they shouldn't have.

Be aware of these specifics when troubleshooting network applications:

▶ Safari—Safari is a good web browser, but webpages aren't always perfect. You may find that some websites do not render properly or work correctly with Safari. To provide the most secure web experience, Safari may disable third-party plug-ins. You can verify the status of third-party plug-ins from the Security tab of the Safari preferences. You might also want to try a third-party web browser. Several are available for the Mac, including Google Chrome, Firefox, OmniWeb, and Opera. Alternatively, for deeper inspection of problematic webpages you can enable the Safari Develop menu from the Advanced tab of Safari preferences. With this menu enabled, you can dig into the details of a webpage or try advanced troubleshooting methods, including emptying Safari's caches and requesting the website with a different user agent.

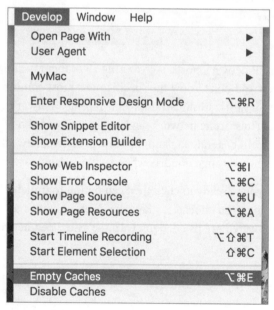

▶ Mail—Improper mail account configuration settings are the most common cause of Mail application issues. Fortunately, the Mail application includes a built-in account diagnostic tool, Mail Connection Doctor, that attempts to establish a connection with all configured incoming and outgoing mail servers. To open Mail Connection Doctor, choose Window > Connection Doctor within the Mail application. If a problem is found, a suggested resolution is offered, but for a more detailed diagnostic view, click the Show Detail button to reveal the progress log, and then click the Check Again button to rerun the tests.

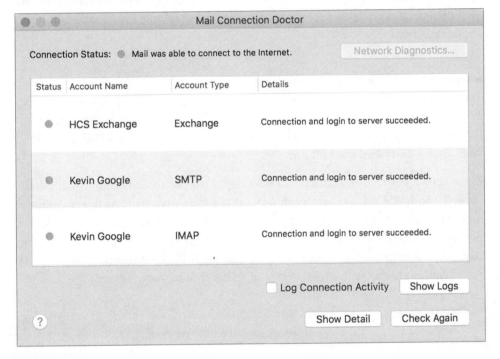

TIP ▶ Apple also provides an online Mail Setup Assistant database that may help you identify mail client configuration issues: www.apple.com/support/mail-settings-lookup/.

Troubleshoot File-Sharing Services

There are a few known macOS file-service issues you should be aware of. They aren't software bugs in the sense that something is broken and requires a fix. Rather, these issues represent compatibility and design choices that are intentional but may still cause you problems.

AppleDouble Issues

As covered in Lesson 14, "Use Metadata, Spotlight, and Siri," macOS uses separate metadata stores. The NFS and WebDAV file-sharing protocols do not support metadata of this type. Thus, when files are written to a mounted NFS or WebDAV volume, macOS automatically splits these files into two separate files.

With this practice, commonly known as AppleDouble, the data retains the original name, but the metadata is saved with a period and underscore before the original name. The Finder recognizes these split files and shows only a single file to the user. However, users on other operating systems see two separate files and may have trouble accessing the appropriate one.

Microsoft's Services for Macintosh Issues

You may encounter another issue when trying to access an AFP network volume from a Windows file server. Windows servers prior to 2008 include Services for Macintosh (SFM), which provides only the legacy AFP 2 file service. macOS is still compatible with AFP 2 but is optimized for AFP 3.1.

Many known performance issues exist with AFP 2, so you should avoid it at all costs. Ideally, you should use a system running macOS Server to provide AFP services for your network. However, if you must keep the Windows file server, you can add AFP 3.1 support by installing Acronis Access Connect (formerly ExtremeZ-IP) (www.acronis.com). Also remember that macOS clients include a robust SMB client that natively connects to your Windows server with a high degree of reliability and performance.

> **MORE INFO** ▸ macOS works with legacy AFP only if you follow the steps in Apple Support article HT200160, "Connecting to legacy AFP services." If you have problems with some SMB services you may also want to try the steps in Apple Support article HT204021, "If you can use AFP but not SMB to mount a file server."

Exercise 22.1
Configure a Network Service Account

▶ **Prerequisites**

   ▸ You must have created the Chris Johnson account (Exercise 5.1, "Create a Standard User Account").

   ▸ You must be performing these exercises in a class or have set up your own server configured as in the Mainserver Setup Instructions.

The client applications built into macOS can use a wide variety of network services, and the Internet Accounts pane in System Preferences makes setting up suites of services easy. You have already set up iCloud-based services on your computer. In this exercise, you will also configure your computer to use services provided by a macOS server.

View Your Existing Network Accounts

1   If necessary, log in as Chris Johnson.

2   Open the Contacts application.

3   Open Contacts preferences by choosing Contacts menu > Preferences (Command-Comma).

4   Click the Accounts button to see the accounts your Contacts application is configured to use.

   If you have configured iCloud services for the Chris Johnson account, you will see the iCloud account listed here.

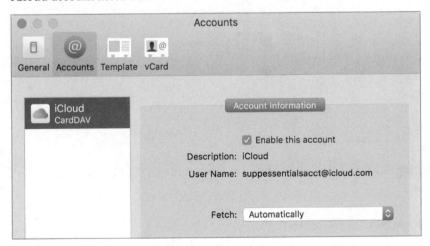

You could use this pane of Contacts preferences to view and add network accounts for Contacts, but often you have accounts that are used for groups of related services.

5   Close the Contacts preferences window, and quit Contacts.

6   Open System Preferences, and select the Internet Accounts pane.

If you are signed in to iCloud, your iCloud account information is listed on the left side of the window. You can manage iCloud settings here, as well as in iCloud preferences. You may also see a Game Center account listed.

7   If your iCloud account is listed on the left, select it, and then deselect the Mail service on the right.

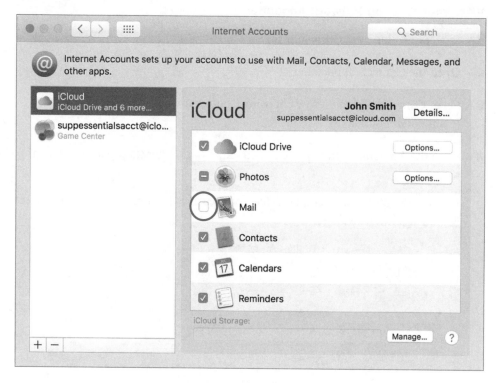

Not having iCloud mail mixed with the new account will simplify testing later in the exercise.

Set Up a New Network Account

1   If a list of account types is not shown on the right, click the Add (+) button under the account list.

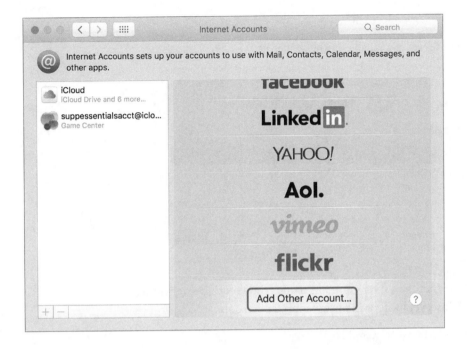

2   Scroll to the bottom of the list, and click Add Other Account.

More account types appear at the bottom of the list.

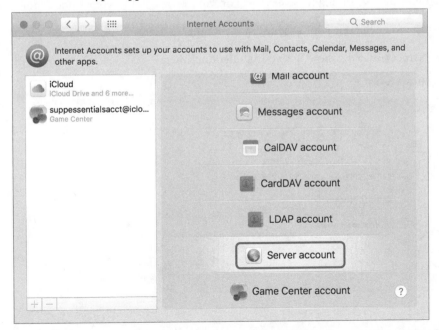

3   Click "Server account."

Mainserver is available in the server list.

Note that the server's domain name (shown on the right) might be either Mainserver.local or mainserver.pretendco.com.

4   Select Mainserver, and click Next.

You are prompted for the server account you want to use. If you are performing these exercises in a class, your account name will include your student number or seat number. If you are performing these exercises on your own, use 1 as your student number.

5   Enter the following for your account information:

User Name: studentn (where *n* is your student number)

Password: student

6   Click "Sign in." If you receive an error message, check the settings and try again.

A dialog may appear indicating that Internet Accounts can't verify the identity of the server; if it does not, you have already configured your computer to trust the server, and you can skip to step 10.

Again, the server's domain name may be listed as either "mainserver.local" or "mainserver.pretendco.com."

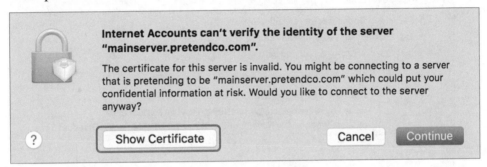

This appears because Internet Accounts is attempting to make a secure connection using SSL but the SSL certificate the server presents has not been signed by a trusted certificate authority (CA). The host name listed in the certificate may also not match the host name Internet Accounts is using to connect to the server. Thus, Internet Accounts cannot tell whether the server is the one you intend to connect to or an impostor.

This problem can occur because the server is not properly configured but also might indicate that you have reached a malicious fake. Unfortunately, there is often no reliable way to tell whether or not there is a real problem. In this case, it is occurring because Mainserver is not run by the legitimate owner of pretendco.com; it is a fake, but it is a harmless fake.

7   Click Show Certificate.

The dialog expands and displays more details about the server's SSL certificate.

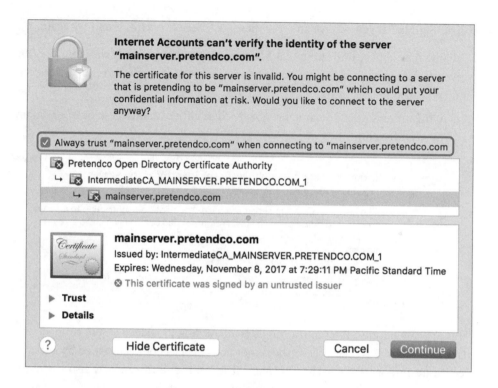

8   Select "Always trust," and then click Continue.

This adds the certificate to your keychain and creates a trust policy so that this server certificate will automatically be trusted in the future. Note that if you had been connected to an external server on the Internet (especially one that handles sensitive information, such as your bank's web server), it would have been safer to cancel the connection.

9   Authenticate as Chris Johnson to confirm the new trust policy.

10 In the "Select the apps..." dialog, deselect VPN, and click Done.

Setting up the VPN service would make changes to the Mac computer's network configuration, which would require administrator authentication. Also, you may have already configured the VPN service using a configuration profile in Exercise 20.3, "Configure VPN Settings."

11 When the account setup finishes, quit System Preferences.

Test Your New Account

1 Open the Contacts application.

2 Open Contacts preferences (choose Contacts menu > Preferences, or press Command-Comma).

3 Click the Accounts button, and select the Server account.

Since this account is being managed by Internet Accounts preferences, not many configuration options appear here.

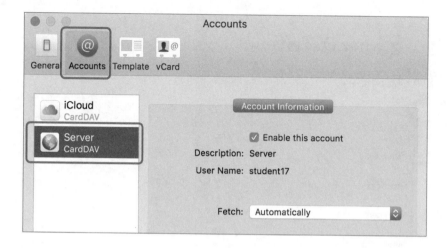

4   Close the Contacts preferences window, and quit Contacts.

5   Open the Mail application.

6   If a warning appears indicating that Mail can't verify the identity of the server, repeat the process of showing the certificate and marking it as always trusted.

Mail checks for new messages in your macOS Server account. You should have a welcome message from the server team.

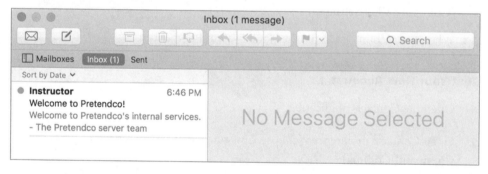

If you also had iCloud messages, you may have missed the step to turn off iCloud mail; return to Internet Accounts preferences, select your iCloud account, and turn off its mail service.

7   Open Mail preferences (choose Mail menu > Preferences, or press Command-Comma).

8   Click the Accounts button.

9   Select the macOS Server account.

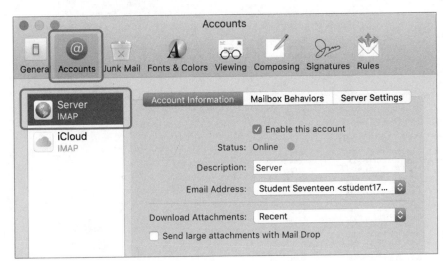

10 Close the Mail preferences window, and quit Mail.

Scan the Server

To prepare for Exercise 22.3, "Troubleshoot Network Services," you will record a baseline of what services Mainserver provides when everything is working normally.

1   Open Network Utility (remember that you can press Command–Space bar and use Spotlight to find it).

2   Click the Port Scan tab.

The port scan tool scans a server or other IP address to see what network ports are accepting connections. This is explored in more detail in Exercise 22.3, "Troubleshoot Network Services."

3   Enter the server address mainserver.local in the IP address field.

4   Select the "Only test ports between" option, and set the range to 1 through 1024.

5   Click Scan.

6   Wait for it to finish scanning, and then expand the Network Utility window until all the results are visible.

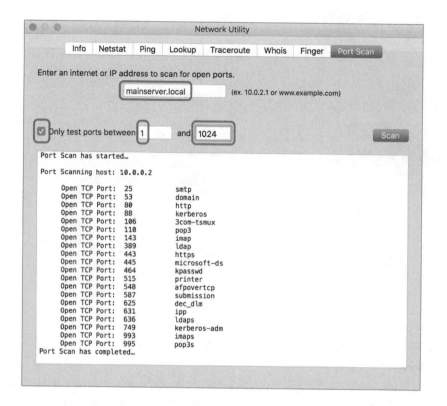

Your results may not exactly match those shown here. To record your results, you will take a screenshot of the Network Utility window. For more about taking screenshots in macOS, see Exercise 6.1, "Restore a Deleted User Account."

7   Press Command-Shift-4; then release those keys, and press the Space bar.

The cursor changes to a camera icon, and the region of the screen it is over is highlighted in blue.

8   Move the pointer over the Network Utility window, and then click to record its contents.

The image is saved to your desktop with the name "Screen Shot" followed by the date and time it was taken.

9   Quit Network Utility.

Exercise 22.2
Use File-Sharing Services

Many protocols can be used to transfer files across networks and over the Internet, but some of the most efficient are designed specifically to share file systems, such as AFP and SMB. In this exercise, you will use a Finder window and the "Connect to Server" command from the Finder Go menu to connect to shared AFP and SMB volumes on another computer, copy a file from the server to your desktop, and copy the file back to the server.

Browse to an SMB Share

These steps will lead you through the process of using the sidebar to mount an SMB volume on the desktop.

1   If necessary, log in as Chris Johnson.

2   In the Finder window, select Mainserver in the Shared section of the sidebar.

   If Mainserver is not shown, click All in the sidebar, and then double-click Mainserver in the network view.

   Your Mac contacts Mainserver and logs in automatically as a guest.

3   Click the Connect As button.

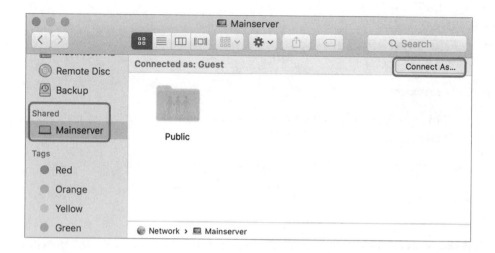

4   When prompted to authenticate, select Registered User, enter the name student and the password student, select "Remember this password in my keychain," and click Connect.

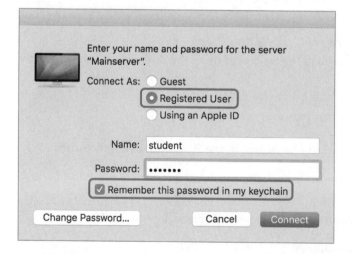

You are now connected to Mainserver with the "student" account. The Finder window shows that you now have access to more shared folders than you did as a guest. The SMB Shared folder is available only over the SMB protocol, so its appearance here indicates that this is the protocol being used to connect to Mainserver.

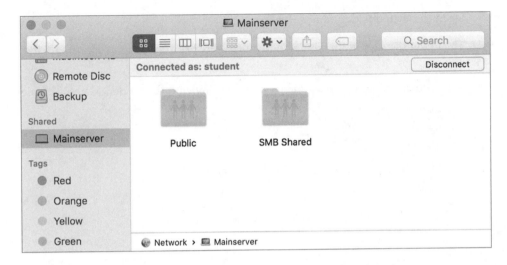

Now you will take a look at what you can see in the Public folder on the server.

5   Open Finder preferences (choose Finder menu > Preferences, or press Command-comma), click General, and select "Connected servers," if it is not already selected.

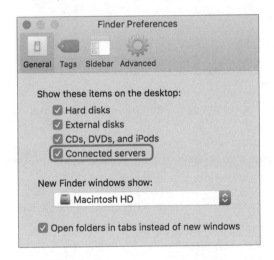

This shows mounted server volumes on the desktop. Since you have not mounted any shared folders yet, nothing new appears on the desktop at this point.

6   Close the Finder Preferences window.

7 Open the shared folder named Public.

The folder displays in the Finder, and a new network volume icon appears on the desktop.

In the Public folder you see a file (copy.rtf), along with the StudentMaterials folder.

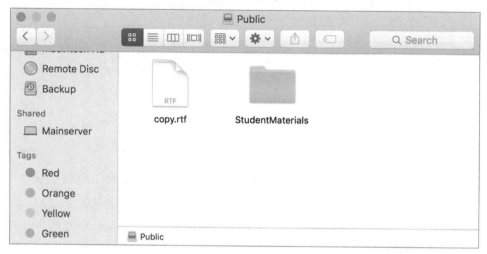

Copy Files to a Network Share

You will use the Finder to copy files to a shared folder mounted over SMB.

1 Drag copy.rtf to your desktop. Since you are dragging from one volume to another, this copies the file rather than moving it.

2 Rename your copy of copy.rtf to Student *n*.rtf (where *n* is your student number if you are in a class or 1 if you are performing these exercises on your own).

You can rename a file by selecting it and pressing Return or by clicking the filename and waiting a moment.

3 Select Mainserver in the Finder sidebar. This returns you to the view of available shared folders.

4 Open the SMB Shared folder. Its icon will appear on your desktop.

5 Drag the renamed file from your desktop onto the SMB Shared folder.

Automatically Mount a Network Share

macOS provides several ways to memorize a share point to allow easy access to it. In this section, you will configure your user preferences to automatically mount a share point whenever you log in.

1 Open System Preferences, and select the Users & Groups preferences.

2 With Chris Johnson selected in the user list, click the Login Items tab.

Note that you do not need to authenticate as an administrator to access your login items; they are a personal preference, so standard users can manage their own login items.

3 Drag the SMB Shared icon from your desktop to the login items list.

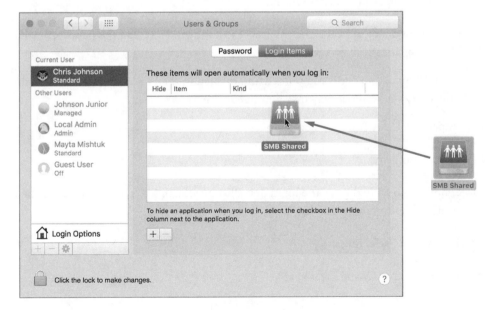

Anything in your login items list will be automatically opened every time you log in. It can include applications, documents, folders, and so on. By adding a shared folder, you have configured it to mount every time you log in. Since you also memorized the server account name and password when you connected, the connection should be fully automatic.

4   Quit System Preferences.

5   Disconnect from Mainserver by clicking the Eject button next to Mainserver in the Finder sidebar.

Disconnecting from the server automatically unmounts both the Public and SMB Shared folders. You can also unmount them individually if you prefer.

6   Log out and back in as Chris Johnson.

7   If a connect dialog appears, click Connect to confirm. Note that the password will be filled automatically from your keychain.

The SMB Shared folder is remounted and opened in the Finder. Note that if you are connecting via Wi-Fi, it may take a minute or so to reconnect.

8   Reopen the Users & Groups preferences.

9   Click Login Items.

10 Remove SMB Shared from the login items list by selecting it and then clicking the Delete (−) button under the list.

11 Quit System Preferences.

12 Disconnect from Mainserver again.

Manually Connect to an AFP Share

These steps will lead you through the process of using "Connect to Server" (in the Finder) to mount an AFP volume on the desktop.

1   In the Finder, choose Go menu > Connect to Server (Command-K).

2   In the Server Address field, enter afp://mainserver.local to connect using the AFP protocol.

3   Before you click Connect, click the Add (+) button to the right of the Server Address field.

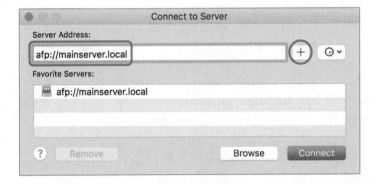

This adds the server URL to your Favorite Servers list. This is another way to allow easy access to a shared folder.

4   Click Connect.

5   Use the same credentials you used when connecting over SMB, and select "Remember this password in my keychain." Click Connect.

Note that although you have already memorized the SMB password for the server, this is a different file service, and you must also memorize its password.

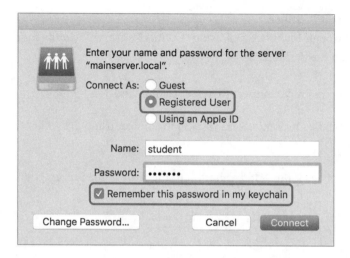

Since you entered a connection URL that did not specify a shared folder to mount, you will be asked which folders you want to mount. Note that this time you do not see the SMB Shared folder, but you do see the AFP Shared folder.

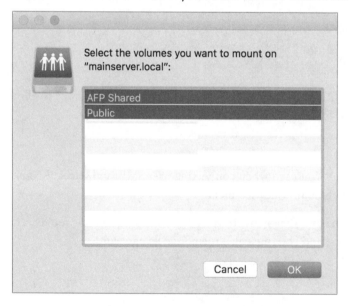

6   Select the Public and AFP Shared folders, and click OK.

The volumes mount, and you see the same files in Public that you saw when connecting using SMB. You have connected to the same folder on the server, so this is not surprising.

7   Drag the Student *n*.rtf file from your desktop to the AFP Shared folder.

8   Disconnect from the server, either by dragging the volume icons to the Trash or by clicking the Eject button in the Finder sidebar.

Exercise 22.3
Troubleshoot Network Services

▶ **Prerequisites**

- ▶ You must have created the Chris Johnson account (Exercise 5.1, "Create a Standard User Account").

- ▶ You must be performing these exercises in a class or have set up your own server configured as in the Mainserver Setup Instructions.

- ▶ You must have performed Exercise 22.1, "Configure a Network Service Account."

In this exercise, the mail service will fail, and you will use several network service troubleshooting tools to investigate the problem.

Turn Off the Mail Service or Wait for the Instructor to Do So

If you are performing these exercises in class, notify the instructor that you are ready for the mail service to be turned off, and wait for the instructor to tell you to proceed; then skip to "Troubleshoot with the Mail.app Connection Doctor."

If you are performing these exercises on your own, follow these steps on your server computer to turn off the mail service:

1   On your server computer, log in as Local Admin.

2   Open the Server application.

3   Select Mail from the sidebar.

4   Turn the service off.

5 Quit the Server application, and return to your regular exercise computer.

Troubleshoot with the Mail.app Connection Doctor

1 If necessary, log in as Chris Johnson.

2 Open the Mail application.

Mail displays an Account Error alert.

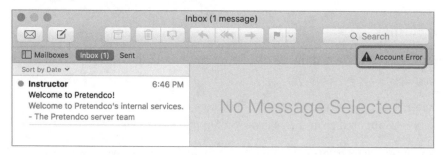

3 Click the Account Error alert.

A dialog appears with more information about the problem.

Note that depending on your network setup, the error you see may refer to "mainserver.local" instead of "mainserver.pretendco.com."

The Mail application has a built-in Connection Doctor that can do basic service diagnostics.

4 Click Open Connection Doctor in the dialog.

The Connection Doctor opens and runs a series of tests to see which parts of your mail service are working. In this case, it detects that your Internet connection is working (the green Connection Status indicator at the top) but that neither the mail sending service (SMTP) nor the receiving service (IMAP) is working because it cannot connect to either service.

Note that an iCloud IMAP service may be listed. The Connection Doctor may test it even though the service is turned off.

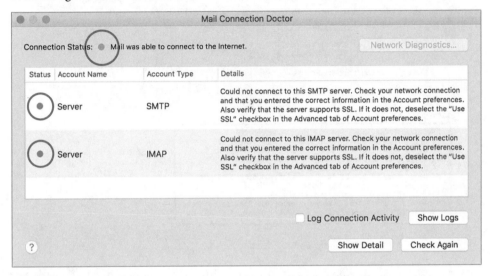

If this were a minor glitch, the Mail Connection Doctor might be able to point you to a solution. In this case, it indicates that it "Could not connect…" to the macOS Server over either the SMTP or the IMAP protocol. Because the server appears to be completely unreachable, you will now turn to Network Utility for further troubleshooting.

5   Close the Mail Connection Doctor window.

6   Quit Mail.

Troubleshoot with Network Utility

1   Open Network Utility. Remember that you can use Spotlight to find it.

Since Mail is unable to reach the server, you should first test to make sure the network connections between your computer and the server are working.

2   Click the Ping tab.

3   In the "Enter the network address to ping" field, enter mainserver.local.

4   Click Ping.

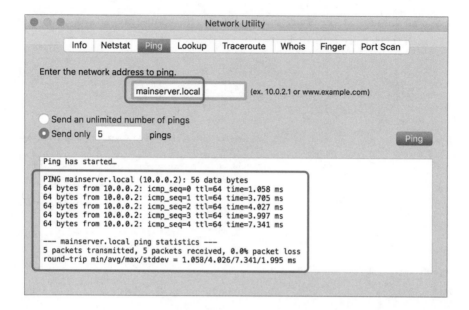

The ping probes are able to reach the server. This tells you that the network connection between your computer and the server is working, so you need to move on to the services you are trying to use.

5   Click the Port Scan tab.

The port scan tool can scan a server to see what TCP port numbers it has services running on; usually, you can tell what services are available based on the port numbers.

NOTE ▶ Many malicious network attacks start with or employ port scans, so this type of troubleshooting might be interpreted as an attack. Before you scan ports on a target computer, request permission from its owner or a network or server administrator, if possible. As a general rule, only scan ports on computers you have responsibility for. Many environments employ automatic countermeasures. Simply scanning a server may get your computer or IP address blacklisted, preventing you from knowing whether you have resolved the problem you are troubleshooting.

6   If necessary, enter the server address mainserver.local in the IP address field.

7   If necessary, select the "Only test ports between" option, and set the range to 1 through 1024.

8 Click Scan.

9 Watch the scan as it identifies the open ports.

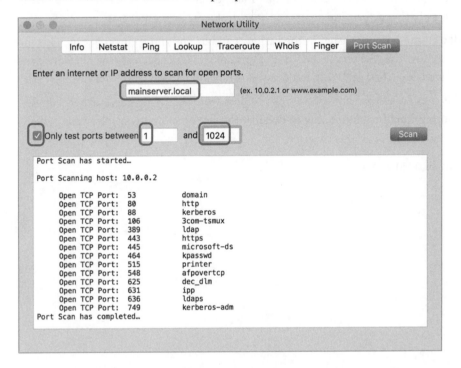

The port scan lists the open ports it finds, along with the names of the services usually associated with them. For example, port 80 is the standard (or "well-known") port
for web services (the HTTP protocol), and port 548 is the standard port for the Apple
Filing Protocol ("afpovertcp"). These well-known ports are commonly used in the
industry and facilitate interoperability across different vendors' implementations of
the same protocols. To test whether a computer has an HTTP (web) server, you would
run a port scan on it and test whether TCP port 80 is open. HTTPS (an SSL-secured
web service) normally uses TCP port 443, so if HTTPS requests are not working, port
443 might be blocked or inactive.

For a listing of many ports used by Apple products, see Apple Support article
HT202944, "TCP and UDP ports used by Apple software products."

10 Open the screenshot you took in Exercise 22.1, "Configure a Network Service
Account," showing which ports were open when the services were working, and compare it with the current scan.

In this case, you are trying to troubleshoot the mail service, which normally involves TCP ports 25 (SMTP), 110 (POP3), 143 (IMAP), 587 (message submission), 933 (IMAPS), and 995 (POP3S). Note that mail servers that use proprietary protocols such as Exchange provide access to those protocols over other port numbers.

All of those ports are listed in the earlier scan but not in the current scan. This indicates either that the server does not offer mail service (which is true here since the service is switched off) or that a firewall is blocking access to the service.

This is as far as you can resolve this problem from the client side; further troubleshooting would mean looking in detail at the server and network firewalls, which is beyond the scope of this exercise.

11 Quit all open applications.

Lesson 23

Manage Host Sharing and Personal Firewall

Although macOS Server requires a separate purchase in the Mac App Store, macOS already includes many of the core technologies that make macOS Server possible. Of course, macOS Server supports additional advanced network services and administration tools, but the two share the same software for providing several network services.

In this lesson, you will focus on using macOS as both a network client and a shared resource for a variety of network and Internet services. After an introduction to the general concepts of providing shared services, you will delve into remotely controlling Mac computers via screen-sharing services. Then you will see how to use AirDrop—the easiest way to share files between Apple devices. You will also learn how to secure access to shared resources from macOS using the built-in personal firewall. Finally, this lesson covers general troubleshooting methods to resolve issues that may arise when you attempt to share services from your Mac.

GOALS

▶ Examine and enable host-sharing services built into macOS

▶ Use screen-sharing tools to access other network hosts

▶ Use AirDrop to quickly and easily share files

▶ Secure shared services by configuring the personal firewall

▶ Troubleshoot shared service issues

Reference 23.1
Enable Host-Sharing Services

macOS includes an assortment of shared network services, and you'll now see how to manage them. These shared services vary in implementation and purpose, but they all allow users to remotely access resources on the Mac providing the service. They are also all easily enabled and managed from the Sharing preferences.

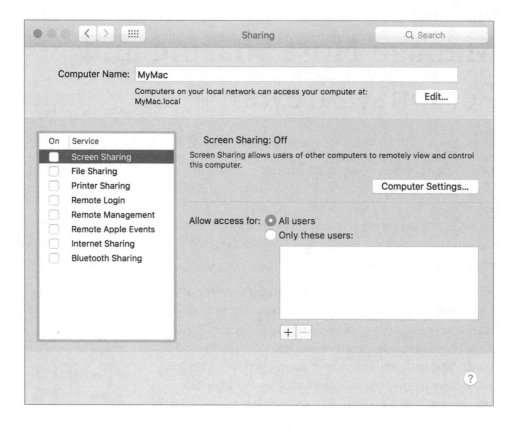

NOTE ▶ Users cannot access services on a Mac in sleep mode. You can turn off your Mac computer's automatic sleep activation or enable automatic waking for network access from the Energy Saver preferences. Automatic wake on both wired and wireless networks works on macOS if your network hardware supports it. You can find out more from Apple Support article HT201960, "About Wake on Demand and Bonjour Sleep Proxy."

It's important to recognize the security risk involved in providing a service that allows other users to control processes on your Mac. Obviously, if you're providing a service that allows remote control and execution of software, it's certainly possible for an attacker to cause trouble. Thus, it's paramount that when you enable these types of services you choose strong security settings. Using strong passwords is a good start, but you can also configure limited access to these services from the Sharing preferences.

Configure Network Identification

You may be unable to control your Mac computer's IP address or DNS host name, because the network administrator usually controls these. But as long as the Mac has properly configured TCP/IP settings, as outlined in Lesson 19, "Manage Basic Network Settings," your configuration is complete for these two identifiers. If your Mac has multiple IP addresses or DNS host names properly configured, it also accepts connections from those.

For dynamic network discovery protocols, though, your Mac uses network identification that can be set locally by an administrator. By default, your Mac automatically chooses a name based either on its DNS name or on the name of the user created with the Setup Assistant. However, at any time an administrator user can change the Mac computer's network identifier from the Sharing preferences. Simply enter a name in the Computer Name field, and the system sets the name for each available discovery protocol.

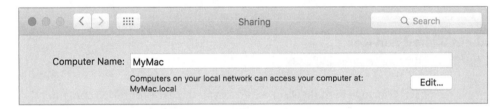

For example, if you enter the computer name MyMac, the Bonjour name is set to MyMac.local and the NetBIOS/WINS name is set to MYMAC. If the name you choose is already taken by another local device, the Mac automatically appends a number to the end of the name. NetBIOS/WINS may require additional configuration if your network uses multiple domains or workgroups, as covered in Lesson 20, "Manage Advanced Network Settings."

The local Bonjour service needs no additional configuration, but if you want to set a custom Bonjour name, click the Edit button below the Computer Name field to reveal the Local Hostname field. From this interface you can also register your Mac computer's identification for Wide-Area Bonjour. Wide-Area Bonjour uses an intermediary service to facilitate Bonjour browsing to networks outside of the computer's current subnet. If this service is available on your network, select the "Use dynamic global hostname" checkbox to reveal the Wide-Area Bonjour settings.

Use this name to reach this computer from machines on your local subnet.

Local Hostname: MyMac.local

☑ Use dynamic global hostname

Hostname:

User:

Password:

☐ Advertise services in this domain using Bonjour

?   Cancel   OK

About Shared Services

The macOS sharing services include:

▶ DVD or CD Sharing (Remote Disc)—Allows you to share your Mac computer's optical disc, if available, via the network. It's primarily designed to let you install software for Mac computers that lack a built-in optical disc. Do not confuse Remote Disc with standard file-sharing services covered later in this lesson. This service differs in several key respects: it shares only what is on the optical disc, you cannot configure user-specific access, and it can only be accessed via Bonjour. By enabling this service, the launchd control process starts the ODSAgent background process, which listens for Remote Disc requests on a very high randomly selected TCP port. This service can be accessed only by other Mac computers from the Finder sidebar or the Migration Assistant application.

MORE INFO ▶ For more information about Remote Disc, see Apple Support article HT203973, "Use the CD or DVD drive from another computer with your Mac."

MORE INFO ▶ Details on the launchd control process are covered in Lesson 26, "Troubleshoot Startup and System Issues."

▶ Screen Sharing—Allows remote control of your Mac. Using this service is detailed later in this lesson.

▶ File Sharing—Allows remote access to your Mac computer's file system via the Server Message Block (SMB) Protocol and Apple Filing Protocol (AFP) network file-sharing services. When you enable the File Sharing service, the launchd control process listens for SMB service requests on TCP port 445 and automatically starts the smbd process as necessary to handle any requests. Further, the launchd control process listens for AFP service requests on TCP port 548 and automatically starts the AppleFileServer process as necessary to handle any requests. By default on macOS, only standard and administrator users have access to file-sharing services, but you can modify access for other users as outlined in Lesson 11, "Manage Permissions and Sharing."

MORE INFO ▶ Connecting to file-sharing services is covered in Lesson 22, "Manage Network Services."

▶ Printer Sharing—Allows network access to printers that are directly attached to your Mac. Using this service is covered in Lesson 25, "Manage Printers and Scanners."

▶ Scanner Sharing—Allows network access to document scanners that are configured for your Mac. This service works only with other Mac computers on a local network (Bonjour) via the Image Capture application. This service also operates only on a per-user basis, and is available only when the user is logged in. When this service is enabled, the launchd control process listens for scanner-sharing requests on a very high randomly selected TCP port and starts the Image Capture Extension background process as needed to handle any requests. The only additional configuration is that you can, from the Sharing preferences, enable specific scanners if you have more than one attached.

▶ Remote Login—Allows remote control of your Mac computer's command line via Secure Shell (SSH). Further, SSH remote login allows you to securely transfer files using Secure File Transfer Protocol (SFTP) or the secure copy command scp. With Remote Login enabled, the launchd control process listens for remote login service requests on TCP 22 and starts the sshd background process as needed to handle any requests. By default, all standard and administrator user accounts are allowed to access the service. Command-line usage is beyond the scope of this guide; thus, using SSH is beyond the scope of this guide.

▶ Remote Management—Augments the Screen Sharing service to allow remote administration of your Mac via the Apple Remote Desktop (ARD) application. This service is covered in greater detail later in this lesson.

▶ Remote Apple Events—Allows applications and AppleScripts on another Mac to communicate with applications and services on your Mac. This service is most often used to facilitate automated AppleScript workflows between applications running on separate Mac computers. When this service is enabled, the launchd control process listens for remote Apple Events requests on TCP and UDP port 3130 and starts the AEServer background process as needed to handle any requests. By default, all nonguest user accounts are allowed to access the service, but you can limit this to specific users from the Sharing preferences.

▶   Internet Sharing—Allows your Mac to "reshare" a single network or Internet connection with any other network interface. For example, if your Mac had Internet access via a cellular network USB adapter, you could enable Internet Sharing for the Mac computer's Wi-Fi and turn it into a wireless access point for the other computers. When you enable the Internet Sharing service, the launchd process starts several background processes. The natd process performs the Network Address Translation (NAT) service that allows multiple network clients to share a single network or Internet connection. The bootpd process provides the DHCP automatic network configuration service for the network devices connected via your Mac. When a network device connects to your Mac computer's shared network connection, it automatically obtains an IP address, usually in the 10.0.2.X range. Finally, the named process provides DNS resolution for network devices connected to the Internet via your Mac.

▶   Bluetooth Sharing—Allows access to your Mac via Bluetooth short-range wireless. Using this service is covered in Lesson 24, "Troubleshoot Peripherals."

Reference 23.2
Control Remote Computers

Providing remote phone support can be arduous. Inexperienced users don't know how to properly communicate the issues they are experiencing and may not be able to describe what they are seeing on the screen. Further, attempting to describe the steps involved in performing troubleshooting or administrative tasks to an inexperienced user over the phone is, at best, time-consuming for both parties.

When it comes to troubleshooting or administration, nothing beats actually seeing the computer's screen and controlling its mouse and keyboard. macOS includes built-in software that allows you to view and control the graphical interface via three methods: system Screen Sharing, Messages screen-sharing, and Remote Management.

About Screen-Sharing Services

Both system Screen Sharing and Messages screen-sharing are included with macOS Sierra, and their use is covered in the following sections of this lesson. A standard installation of macOS includes only the client-side software for Remote Management. The administrative side of Remote Management, Apple Remote Desktop (ARD), used to control other Mac computers, is a separate purchase available from the Mac App Store.

> **NOTE ▶** Mac computers with OS X Lion 10.7 or later can remotely control Mac computers with macOS Sierra via Screen Sharing. Further, macOS Sierra can remotely control Mac operating systems earlier than OS X Lion that have an updated ARD Remote Management agent.

Screen Sharing is a subset of Remote Management, so when you enable Remote Management, you are also enabling Screen Sharing. This may seem a bit confusing if you look at the Sharing preferences interface, which deselects the Screen Sharing checkbox when Remote Management is enabled. Rest assured, though, enabling Remote Management also enables Screen Sharing. Thus, you can save yourself a step by initially configuring Remote Management, which allows for both ARD and Screen Sharing access.

> **MORE INFO ▶** ARD is beyond the scope of this guide. You can find out more about ARD here: http://help.apple.com/remotedesktop/mac/.

All Apple screen-sharing services are based on a modified version of the Virtual Network Computing (VNC) protocol. The primary modification is the use of optional encryption for both viewing and controlling traffic. Another change is the ability to copy files and clipboard content between Mac computers using Screen Sharing.

Further, macOS allows you to access a virtual desktop on another Mac via Screen Sharing. In other words, Screen Sharing allows you to have your own virtual login on another Mac, completely separate from the login currently being used by the local user. This feature is similar to fast user switching (covered in Lesson 5, "Manage User Accounts"), except the second user is entirely remote via Screen Sharing and potentially using the computer at the same time as the local user.

> **MORE INFO ▶** VNC is a cross-platform standard for remote control, so if configured properly, the macOS Screen Sharing service integrates well with other third-party VNC-based systems. Thus, your Mac can control (or be controlled by) any other VNC-based software regardless of operating system or platform. For more details on VNC, refer to its Wikipedia entry, https://en.wikipedia.org/wiki/Virtual_Network_Computing.

Enable System Screen Sharing

Before you can access a Mac remotely via Screen Sharing, the remote Mac must first have the Screen Sharing service enabled. To enable Screen Sharing for your Mac, open the Sharing preferences, click the lock icon in the lower-left corner, and authenticate as an administrator user to unlock the preferences.

> **NOTE ▸** Again, the Screen Sharing service is a subset of the Remote Management service. Thus, if Remote Management is enabled, the Screen Sharing checkbox is unavailable.

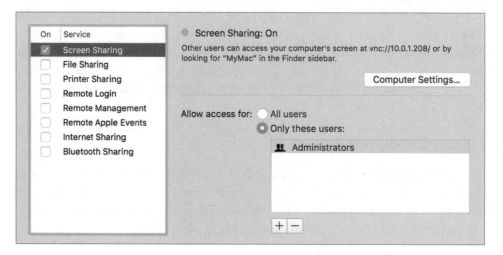

Select the Screen Sharing checkbox in the Service list to turn on Screen Sharing. The launchd control process starts the AppleVNCServer background process, which listens for Screen Sharing service requests on TCP and UDP port 5900. By default, only administrator user accounts are allowed to access the service.

Optionally, you can adjust Screen Sharing access by selecting the "All users" radio button or by using the Add (+) and Delete (–) buttons at the bottom of the users list. When adding accounts, a dialog appears allowing you to select the specific users or groups you want to grant Screen Sharing access. You can select existing users or groups, or you can create a new Sharing user account by clicking the New Person button or selecting a contact from your Contacts.

Also optionally, you can allow a wider range of operating systems to access your Mac computer's Screen Sharing service by clicking the Computer Settings button. This reveals a dialog where you can enable guest and standard VNC screen-sharing access.

☐ Anyone may request permission to control screen

☐ VNC viewers may control screen with password: [　　　　　]

Cancel   OK

When attempting to access your Mac computer's screen, the currently logged-in user must authorize the session. By default, only local authorized users and groups are allowed to use Screen Sharing. Select the "Anyone may request permission to control screen" checkbox to allow anyone (from another Mac) to ask permission to share the screen. For this feature to work, you must remove any access restrictions for Screen Sharing by allowing access to all users.

Standard third-party VNC viewers cannot authenticate using the secure methods employed by the macOS Screen Sharing service. Thus, if you select the "VNC viewers may control screen with password" checkbox, you must also set a specific password for VNC access. Remember that all standard VNC traffic is unencrypted. Further, standard VNC viewers cannot use the Screen Sharing service's clipboard copy, file copy, or virtual desktop features.

Connect via Screen Sharing

The process to connect to and control another computer for Screen Sharing is similar to how you connect to a shared file system. From the Finder, you can connect to another computer that has Screen Sharing, Remote Management, or VNC enabled. You can initiate the connection using one of two methods. The first method works only for Screen Sharing or Remote Management service hosts on the local network. In the Finder, browse to and select the computer from the Finder sidebar Shared list or the Finder Network folder, and then click the Share Screen button.

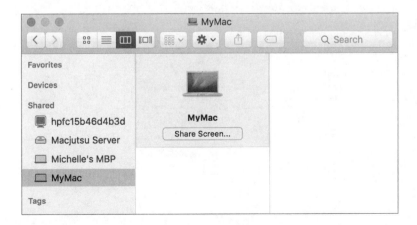

The second method allows you to connect to and control any host providing Screen Sharing, Remote Management, or standard VNC services. In the Finder, choose Go > Connect to Server. In the "Connect to Server" dialog, enter vnc://, followed by the computer's IP address, DNS host name, or Bonjour name, and then click Connect.

Regardless of the connection method, the macOS automatically opens the /System/Library/CoreServices/Applications/Screen Sharing application and initiates a connection to the specified host. You are presented with a dialog that requires you to make an authentication choice.

NOTE ▶ If you are using Kerberos single sign-on or have previously saved your authentication information to a keychain, the Mac automatically authenticates for you and doesn't present the authentication dialog.

The first authentication choice, which appears only if you are connecting to macOS with this option enabled, is to ask the current user for permission. The second authentication choice, the default for any system, is to authenticate with a user account. As a final option, you can select the checkbox that saves this information to your login keychain. Once you have made your authentication selection, click Connect to continue.

Depending on the remote computer's system, one of three situations occurs when Screen Sharing establishes the connection:

▶ If the remote computer is not a Mac running macOS, you will instantly connect to the current screen of the remote computer.

▶ If the remote computer is a Mac running macOS and no one is logged in, or if you authenticated as the currently logged-in user, or if the currently logged-in user is not an administrator, you will instantly connect to the current screen of the remote Mac.

▶ If the remote computer is a Mac running macOS and you authenticated as a different user from the administrator who is currently logged in to the Mac, you are presented with a dialog allowing you to choose between asking permission or logging in as yourself to a virtual desktop.

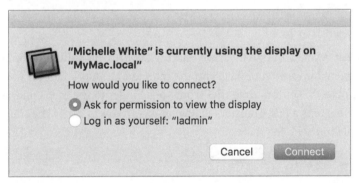

When presented with this Screen Sharing dialog, if you choose the option to ask for permission, the remote administrator user is prompted with a dialog to either allow or deny you access. The remote user's choice dictates whether you can connect. If, however, you choose to log in as yourself, you are instantly connected to a new virtual screen that logs in to your account. In this case, the other user does not directly know that you are remotely using the computer, but the user could verify by examining the Fast User Switching menu or the Users & Groups preferences.

TIP ▶ If you need the ability to control another user's session without asking permission, you should enable the Remote Management service instead of the Screen Sharing service. With Remote Management enabled, when you connect via Screen Sharing the remote user is not asked for permission. The Remote Management service is also designed for use with the Apple Remote Desktop management application, as covered later in this lesson.

Control Another Mac via Screen Sharing

Once you are connected to the remote Mac, a new window opens, titled with the controlled Mac computer's name, showing a live view of the controlled Mac computer's screen(s). Whenever this window is active, all keyboard entries and mouse movements are sent to the controlled Mac. For example, pressing Command-Q quits the active application on the Mac being controlled. Thus, to quit the Screen Sharing application, you have to click the close (X) button in the upper-left corner of the window. More options are available in the Screen Sharing toolbar when you select View > Show Toolbar.

The buttons in the toolbar reveal additional Screen Sharing features, including the option of sharing clipboard content between your Mac and the remote Mac. Optionally, if the remote Mac is running macOS, you can drag files from your Finder to the Mac computer's remote desktop. Doing so opens a File Transfers dialog, allowing you to verify the transfer progress or cancel the file transfer.

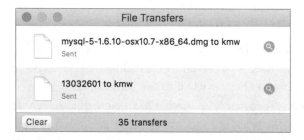

While using the Screen Sharing application, check the preference options by choosing Screen Sharing > Preferences. Use these preferences to adjust screen size and quality settings.

If you are experiencing slow performance, adjust these settings for faster performance. Some network connections, such as crowded wireless or dial-up connections, are so slow that these preferences don't matter much; you have to wait for the screen to redraw.

About Messages Screen-Sharing

The included Messages application, formerly known as iChat, can be used to initiate a screen-sharing session and, as an added bonus, simultaneously provides voice chat services between the administrator Mac and the controlled Mac. Messages screen sharing also makes it much easier to locate other Mac computers to control, because Messages automatically resolves the location of remote computers based on your active chats or available buddies. Further, Messages also supports reverse screen sharing—the administrator Mac can push its screen to display on another Mac for demonstration purposes.

Messages does not require a Mac to have system Screen Sharing enabled in Sharing preferences. This is because Messages includes a quick and easy authorization process for initiating a screen-sharing session via iCloud authentication and the iMessage communication service. Obviously, this requires that users on both Mac computers be signed in to iCloud and iMessage. Details regarding signing in to iMessage and iCloud are covered in Lesson 22, "Manage Network Services."

> **NOTE ▶** With Messages or iChat in OS X Yosemite 10.9 or earlier, you can only initiate a screen-sharing session via AIM- or Jabber-based messaging accounts. With Messages on OS X El Capitan 10.10 or later, you can initiate a screen-sharing session only via iCloud authentication and the iMessage service.

Control Another Mac via Messages

To initiate a Messages screen-sharing session, you must have already started an iMessage chat with the other user. Assuming this is the case, you can select the chat history of the other user in the main Messages window. Once you've selected the user, click the Details text button in the top right of the main Messages window. This opens a pop-up dialog where you can click the Screen Sharing button and then choose either "Invite to share my screen" or "Ask to share screen." As you can tell from these choices, screen sharing in Messages works in both directions.

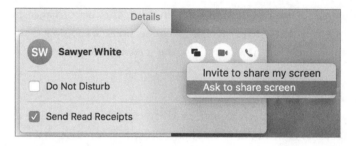

The user on the other Mac will see an authorization dialog offering the choice to accept or decline your request to share screens. With Messages you cannot force other users to share their screens; they have the sole power to allow or deny your request.

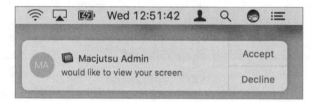

If the other user clicks the Accept button, she will be prompted again to verify the screen-sharing session and select whether you can control or only observe her screen. The idea is that the user may want to think twice about sharing her screen with someone she may not trust. Again, the other user has the sole power to allow you to control or observe her Mac.

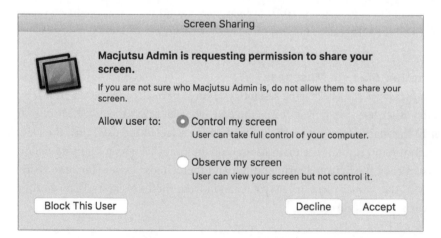

Once the other user has accepted the screen-sharing session, the Screen Sharing application initiates the connection. Further, if both computers support voice chat, Messages automatically starts a voice chat session between the two computers. You may need to configure Audio/Video settings in the Messages preferences for this feature to work properly.

Messages leverages the same Screen Sharing application used by the system Screen Sharing service, as covered previously in this lesson. The only exception is that, by the other user's choice, you may not have control of the remote computer. As you can see in the following screenshot of the Screen Sharing toolbar, the binocular Control button is selected, indicating that you can observe but not control.

In this case, clicking the shared screen will have no direct effect, except that it will show a magnifying glass–style circle on the remote screen. This is to help users identify something you may be trying to assist them with.

You can request remote control access to the user's Mac by selecting the mouse cursor Control button. This will issue another notification prompt to the remote user for her to agree to allow you to control the computer. Alternatively, the other user can select the Screen Sharing menu to allow for remote control.

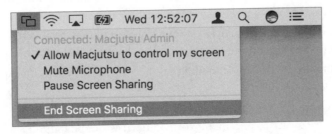

As you can see in the previous screenshot, the user can also manage other features of the Messages screen-sharing session from this menu, including the ability to end the session.

Reference 23.3
Share Files via AirDrop

In addition to traditional file-sharing services, macOS features a peer-to-peer Wi-Fi file-sharing service called AirDrop. Although AirDrop isn't available for all Apple devices, it's the easiest way to share files between Apple devices, both macOS and iOS, that are in close proximity.

About AirDrop

AirDrop uses Wi-Fi networking, but the radio frequencies it uses are outside the Mac computer's normal network connection; thus, it does not travel across your established network. In fact, you don't need a network at all to use AirDrop, because it creates a closed network between local devices.

The most significant feature of AirDrop is that it requires no setup or configuration. Users who want to share items need only navigate to the AirDrop sharing interface, and macOS presents a browser where they can select other users to easily share files with. AirDrop handles all the details of peer-to-peer file sharing, including discovery, easy authentication, and secure file transfer using Transport Layer Security (TLS) encryption.

AirDrop works only between Apple devices within local Wi-Fi and Bluetooth range. This range varies based on several factors, but it's generally limited to 30 feet. Also, AirDrop was specifically designed to provide direct file sharing for selected items, as opposed to traditional file sharing, which allows the user to browse another computer's file system. Finally, AirDrop is supported only on devices with the appropriate system software and wireless hardware.

There are currently two implementations for AirDrop. The most recent implementation for AirDrop uses Bluetooth 4.0 wireless for discovery (due to its low power requirements) and then faster Wi-Fi for the data transfer. The later AirDrop implementation allows for sharing between iOS devices and Mac computers and is available on iOS 7 and later and OS X Yosemite 10.10 and later. The previous AirDrop implementation uses only Wi-Fi and is limited to sharing between Mac computers. It is available on OS X Lion 10.7 and later. AirDrop hardware compatibility varies depending on the Wi-Fi and Bluetooth capabilities built into the Apple devices.

> **MORE INFO** ▶ AirDrop hardware requirements for iOS devices can be found in Apple Support article HT204144, "How to use AirDrop with your iPhone, iPad, or iPod touch," and for Mac models in Apple Support article HT203106, "Use AirDrop to send content from your Mac."

You can also verify whether a Mac supports AirDrop in the Finder by clicking the Go menu. If an AirDrop menu option appears, the Mac supports AirDrop.

Send Items via AirDrop

To quickly share files between Apple devices that support AirDrop, you start by finding other devices in the AirDrop discovery window. On macOS computers, you can open this interface by selecting the AirDrop icon in the Finder sidebar, choosing Go > AirDrop, or pressing Shift-Command-R. Any of these methods opens the AirDrop discovery interface in a Finder window, allowing you to share any item you can drag to this Finder window.

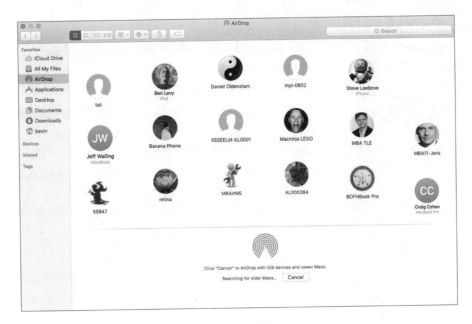

NOTE ▶ If the Mac computer's Wi-Fi or Bluetooth interface is turned off, click the Turn On button to enable AirDrop.

Alternatively, you can engage AirDrop to share a specific open document by clicking the Share button (the box with an up-pointing arrow) at the top of the document window. This will also open the AirDrop discovery interface, but it will share the currently selected document as well. On an iOS device, tapping the Share button is the only way to share an item with another AirDrop device.

Whenever you open the AirDrop discovery interface, the system automatically scans for other AirDrop devices within local wireless range. Other AirDrop devices will appear automatically as long as AirDrop is enabled and using a compatible discovery method. The reasons you might not be able to find a specific AirDrop device are covered in the next section of this lesson.

Once AirDrop has found the other device you want to transfer an item to, sending the item is quite simple. If you are in the Finder, drag a file or folder on top of the icon representing the other device. If you are in a Share window, click the icon representing the other device. In either case, AirDrop will notify the other device that you would like to share something.

On the other device, a notification appears where the user can accept (or decline) the incoming item. On a Mac, the user is given three choices: If the Accept button is clicked, the item is transferred to the user's Downloads folder. Clicking Accept & Open saves to the same location and then automatically opens the item. Clicking Decline cancels the transfer and notifies the other user in the AirDrop interface.

About AirDrop Discovery

There are several reasons your Mac might not be able to discover another AirDrop device. First, start with the basics: is AirDrop enabled on the other devices? On another Mac, open the AirDrop window in the Finder to enable AirDrop. On an iOS device, swipe up from the bottom of the screen to open Control Center, and make sure AirDrop is enabled. If this doesn't solve your AirDrop discovery issues, things get a bit complicated.

As covered previously, there are currently two AirDrop implementations. The more recent implementation works only on newer Apple devices with more recent Apple operating system versions (iOS 7 and OS X Yosemite 10.10 and later). The earlier implementation works only on older Mac computer models or Mac computers with earlier Mac operating systems (OS X Lion 10.7 through OS X Mavericks 10.9). The two AirDrop implementations are not compatible. Thus, it's possible you won't be able to find the other device you're trying to share with in the AirDrop discovery interface.

If you are using an older Mac running OS X Yosemite 10.10 or later, it's possible that your Mac doesn't have Bluetooth 4.0 and therefore defaults to the previous AirDrop discovery method. You can confirm this on your Mac from the AirDrop discovery interface; the text below the AirDrop icon will read, "To share with someone using a Mac..."

In this case, even though your older Mac computer is running OS X Yosemite 10.10 or later, the wireless hardware is compatible only with the previous AirDrop discovery method. As a default you will not be able to discover iOS devices or any newer Mac computers running OS X Yosemite 10.10 or later. This is because iOS devices and newer Mac computers running OS X Yosemite 10.10 or later default to the latest AirDrop implementation, which utilizes Bluetooth 4.0 for discovery.

You can force a newer Mac to use the previous AirDrop discovery method by clicking the words "Don't see who you're looking for?" at the bottom of the AirDrop interface. Clicking the "Search for an Older Mac" button will switch to the previous AirDrop discovery method.

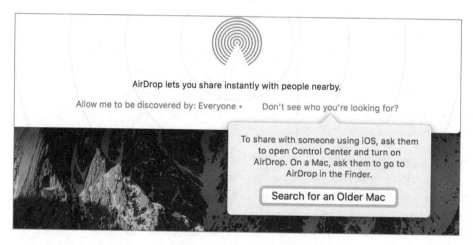

Again, this will allow your newer Mac with OS X Yosemite 10.10 or later to discover older Mac computers and Mac computers with earlier Mac operating systems. In this mode your Mac will temporarily lose iOS devices and other newer Mac computers with OS X Yosemite 10.10 or later. Every time you open the AirDrop interface on a newer Mac computer, it resets to the new AirDrop discovery method.

For devices using the newer AirDrop method, AirDrop defaults to a safer mode that limits discovery to only users with matching information in your Contacts. This may also limit your ability to discover other devices in the AirDrop discovery interface. To resolve this issue, on the other device you can set AirDrop discovery to allow everyone. To change AirDrop discoverability on macOS, click the words "Allow me to be discovered by" at the bottom of the AirDrop interface. To change AirDrop discoverability on iOS, in Control Center tap the AirDrop button.

Reference 23.4
Manage the Personal Firewall

From a network services standpoint, your Mac is already very secure, because, by default, only a few essential services are running that respond to external requests. Even once you start providing individual shared services, your Mac is designed to respond only to those services that are enabled.

Further, services that could cause trouble if compromised, like File Sharing or Screen Sharing, can be configured to have limited access authorization. Still, users can open third-party applications or background services that could leave a Mac vulnerable to a network attack.

> **TIP** To maintain a high level of network security, you should leave sharing services off unless absolutely necessary. If you do enable sharing services, be sure to limit authorization access as much as possible.

About the Personal Firewall

The most common method for securing network services is to configure a firewall, which blocks unauthorized network service access. Most networks use a firewall to limit inbound traffic from an Internet connection.

In fact, most home routers, like AirPort base stations, are by design also network firewalls. While network-level firewalls block unauthorized Internet traffic into your network, they don't block traffic that originated from inside your network to your Mac. Also, if your Mac is mobile and is often joining new networks, odds are that every new network you join will have different firewall rules.

Thus, to prevent unauthorized network services from allowing incoming connections to your specific Mac, you can enable the built-in personal firewall. A personal firewall blocks unauthorized connections to your Mac no matter where they originated. The macOS firewall also features a single-click configuration that provides a high level of network service security, which works for most users.

A standard firewall uses rules based on service port numbers. As you've learned in this lesson, each service defaults to a standard port or set of ports. However, some network services, like Messages, use a wide range of dynamic ports. If you were to manually configure a traditional firewall, you would have to make dozens of rules for every potential port the user may need.

To resolve this issue, the macOS firewall uses an adaptive technology that allows connections based on applications and service needs, without you having to know the specific ports they use. For example, you can authorize Messages to accept any incoming connection without configuring all of the individual TCP and UDP ports used by the Messages application.

The personal firewall also leverages another built-in feature, code signing, to ensure that allowed applications and services aren't changed without your knowledge. Further, code signing allows Apple and third-party developers to provide a guarantee that their software hasn't been tampered with. This level of verifiable trust allows you to configure the firewall in default mode with a single click, automatically allowing signed applications and services to receive incoming connections.

Finally, because the personal firewall is fully dynamic, it opens only the necessary ports when the application or service is running. Again, using Messages as an example, the personal firewall allows only incoming connections to the required ports if Messages is running. If the application quits because the user logs out, the firewall closes the associated ports. Having the required ports open only when an application or service needs them provides an extra layer of security not found with traditional firewalls.

Turn On the Personal Firewall

To enable and configure the macOS personal firewall, open Security & Privacy preferences, click the lock icon in the lower-left corner, and authenticate as an administrator user to unlock Security & Privacy preferences. Select the Firewall tab, and then click the Turn On Firewall button to enable the default firewall rules. Once enabled, this button changes to a Turn Off Firewall button, allowing you to turn off the firewall.

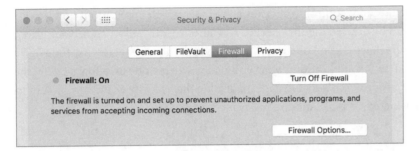

The default firewall configuration is to allow incoming traffic for established connections (connections that were initiated from your Mac and are expecting a return) and for any signed software or enabled service. This level of security is adequate for most users.

Configure the Personal Firewall

If you want to customize the firewall, you can reveal any additional firewall configuration by clicking the Firewall Options button. From the firewall options window, a list of services currently allowed appears. Without any additional configuration, sharing services enabled from the Sharing preferences automatically appear in the list of allowed services. Conversely, deselecting a shared service from the Sharing preferences removes the service from the list of allowed services.

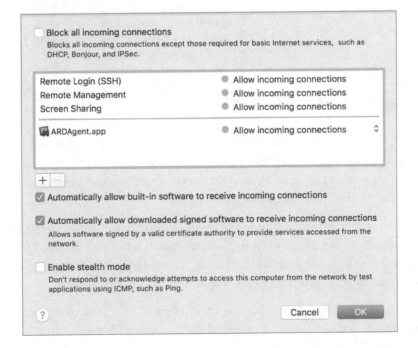

Optionally, for a bit more control, you can manually set which applications and services the firewall allows by deselecting the checkbox to automatically allow signed software. With this firewall choice, as you open new network applications for the first time or update existing network applications, you see a dialog where you can allow or deny the new network application. This dialog appears outside the Security & Privacy preferences whenever a new network application requests incoming access.

If you are manually setting network application and service firewall access, you can always return to the Advanced Firewall dialog to review the list of items and either delete items from the list or specifically disallow certain items.

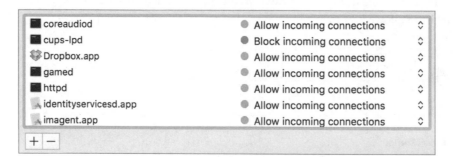

For a bit more security, you can select the "Enable stealth mode" checkbox to prevent response or acknowledgment of a failed attempt to the requesting host. With this enabled, your Mac does not respond to any unauthorized network connections, including network diagnostic protocols like ping, traceroute, and port scan.

In other words, your computer simply ignores the request instead of returning a response of failure to the requesting host. However, your Mac still responds to other allowed services. This includes, by default, Bonjour, which dutifully announces your Mac computer's presence, thus preventing your Mac from being truly hidden on the network.

When the utmost security is needed, you can select the "Block all incoming connections" checkbox. Notice that selecting this option automatically selects stealth mode as well.

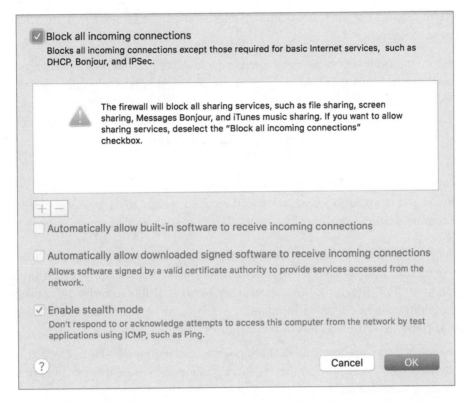

When blocking all incoming connections, your Mac does not respond to any incoming network connections except for those required for basic network services or established connections, such as those needed to browse the web or check email. Obviously, this prevents any shared service or application hosted on your Mac from working remotely.

Reference 23.5
Troubleshoot Shared Services

If you're providing a shared service from your Mac and others are having trouble reaching it, you must first consider how established the service is to determine where to focus your efforts. For example, if your Mac has been reliably providing a shared service for a while but now a single client computer has trouble accessing the service, troubleshoot the client computer before troubleshooting your shared Mac.

Otherwise, if multiple clients cannot access your shared Mac, you may indeed have an issue with the sharing service. After ruling out other potential local client and network issues, you can safely assume that the problem lies with the Mac providing shared services.

If so, shared network service issues fall into two general categories: service communication and service access.

Service communication issues are manifested by an inability to establish a connection to the shared service. If you are presented with an authentication dialog, the client and server are establishing a proper connection, and you should troubleshoot the issue as a service access issue. However, if authentication fails, or you can authenticate but you're not authorized to access the service, then you are experiencing a service access issue.

Troubleshoot Network Service Communication

If you are unable to establish a connection to the shared service, this may signal a network service communication issue. Use these methods to troubleshoot that type of issue:

▶ Double-check the shared Mac network configuration—From Network preferences, make sure the Mac computer's network interfaces are active and configured with the appropriate TCP/IP settings. You can also use Network Utility to verify the network configuration. If a DNS server is providing a host name for your shared Mac, use the Lookup tool in Network Utility to verify the host name.

▶ Double-check the Mac computer's sharing service configuration—From the Sharing preferences, verify the Mac computer's sharing name and ensure that the appropriate services are enabled and configured.

▶ Double-check the Mac computer's firewall configuration—From the Security & Privacy preferences, first temporarily stop the firewall to see whether turning it off makes a difference. If you are able to establish a connection, adjust the list of allowed services and applications before you restart the firewall.

▶ Check for basic network connectivity to the shared Mac—First, turn off the firewall's stealth mode, and then, from another Mac, use the Network Utility ping tool to check for basic connectivity to the shared Mac. If you can't ping the shared Mac, you're probably having a network-level issue that goes beyond service troubleshooting.

▶ Check for network service port connectivity to the shared Mac—First, turn off the firewall's stealth mode, and then, from another Mac, use the Network Utility port scan tool to verify that the expected network service ports are accessible. If the shared Mac is configured properly, the appropriate network service ports should register as open. If there are network routers between the network clients and the shared Mac, consider the possibility that a network administrator has decided to block access to those ports.

Troubleshoot Network Service Access

Failure to authenticate or be granted authorization to a shared service is considered a network service access issue. Use the following to troubleshoot these access issues:

▶ Verify the local user account settings—When using local user accounts, make sure the correct authentication information is being used. You may find that the user is not using the right information, and you may have to reset the account password. (Troubleshooting user account issues is covered in Lesson 5, "Manage User Accounts.") Also, some services do not allow the use of guest and sharing-only user accounts. Further, the standard VNC service uses password information that is not directly linked to a user account.

▶ Double-check directory service settings—If you use a network directory service in your environment, verify that the Mac is properly communicating with the directory service by checking its status in the Directory Utility application. Even if you're only trying to use local accounts, any directory service issues can cause authentication problems. Some services, like Remote Management, do not by default allow you to authenticate with accounts hosted from network directories.

▶ Double-check shared service access settings—Several authenticated sharing services allow you to configure access lists. Use Sharing preferences to verify that the appropriate user accounts are allowed to access the shared service.

Exercise 23.1
Use Host-Sharing Services

▶ **Prerequisites**

    ▶ You must have created the Local Admin (Exercise 2.1, "Configure a New macOS System for Exercises," or Exercise 2.2, "Configure an Existing macOS System for Exercises") and Chris Johnson (Exercise 5.1, "Create a Standard User Account") accounts.

    ▶ You need another Mac running macOS Sierra on the same network as your primary Mac. If you are performing these exercises in a class, you will work with a partner.

In this exercise, you will use the macOS screen-sharing capability to control another computer remotely. You will use both the option to share the current user's session and the option to use a virtual display to log in as a different user.

Turn On Screen Sharing

1   If the Local Admin account is logged in (even as a background session), log it out.

2   If necessary, log in as Chris Johnson.

3   Open System Preferences, and select the Sharing pane.

4   Click the lock icon, and authenticate as Local Admin.

5   Select the checkbox next to Remote Management, if it is not already selected.

Note that although you will be using screen sharing, you are configuring it via the Remote Management service. Remote Management includes screen sharing as an optional capability. If you look at the checkbox for the Screen Sharing service, you'll see that it is dimmed; this does not mean the service is unavailable but rather that it is being controlled by Remote Management.

6   Ensure that "All users" is selected for "Allow access for."

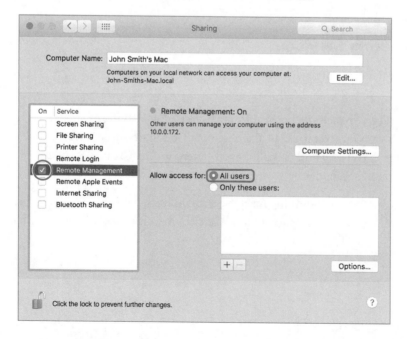

7 Click Options.

8 Ensure that all options are selected. An easy way to do this is to Option-click a check-box until all the checkboxes are selected.

9 Click OK, and then quit System Preferences.

Remotely Control Another Computer's Screen

In this section, you will use screen sharing to control another computer. Which computer you will control depends on whether you are performing these exercises in a class or on your own:

▶ If you are in a class, you will work with a partner and take turns controlling each other's computers.

▶ If you are performing these exercises on your own, you will perform this section from another computer and use it to control your primary exercise computer.

1 If you are working with a partner, wait for her to finish turning on and configuring Remote Management, and then decide who will go first. If your partner goes first, wait for her to finish this section before starting.

2 If you are on your own, log in to the other computer.

3 In the Finder, choose Go menu > Network (or press Command-Shift-K).

The computer you are going to control appears in the display of shared computers on the local network. Note that this shows computers offering file sharing, screen sharing, or both.

The Finder sidebar also displays local computers offering sharing services, but it shows only a limited number. The network view shows all of them.

4 Double-click the computer you will control in the Network window.

Since the other computer does not offer file-sharing service, your computer only has the option to share its screen.

5   Click Share Screen.

6   Authenticate as Chris Johnson. Note that you can use the account's short name (chris) and that if you are working with a partner who used a different password for the Chris Johnson account, you must use her password.

7   Click Connect.

Screen sharing begins, and you see a window with a live, interactive picture of the other computer's desktop.

8   Open System Preferences on the other computer, and select the Desktop & Screen Saver pane.

9   Select a different picture for the other computer's desktop.

10   Press Command-Q.

This quits System Preferences on the other computer. You cannot use standard short-cuts to control the Screen Sharing application itself.

11   Click the green Full Screen button in the title bar of the Screen Sharing window.

The window expands and takes over your entire screen. In full-screen mode, your display is a virtual mirror of the other computer's display.

12 Move your mouse to the top of the screen, and leave it there for a few seconds.

The Screen Sharing menu, window controls, and toolbar appear at the top of the screen. This allows you to exit full-screen mode or access the Screen Sharing controls.

13 Choose Screen Sharing menu > Quit Screen Sharing.

14 If you are working with a partner, switch roles, and have your partner repeat these steps.

Connect to a Virtual Display

By connecting to another Mac as a different user, you can work with a virtual display instead of sharing the local user's display. As in the previous section, you will either work with a partner (although this time you can both work at once, rather than taking turns) or connect to your primary exercise Mac from another Mac.

1 If necessary, wait for your partner to finish the previous section.

2 If necessary, reopen the Network view (press Command-Shift-K), and select the computer you will control.

3 Click Share Screen.

4 This time authenticate as Local Admin (you can use the short name ladmin), and click Connect.

Since you authenticated as a different user than is logged in to the other computer, you are now presented with the choice of sharing the current user's display or logging in as a different user with a virtual display.

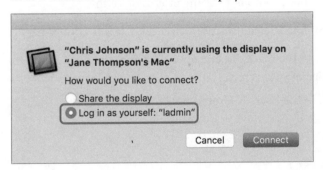

5   Select "Log in as yourself," and click Connect.

A screen-sharing window opens and displays a login screen for your partner's computer. The orange checkmark next to Chris Johnson indicates that Chris is already logged in to the computer.

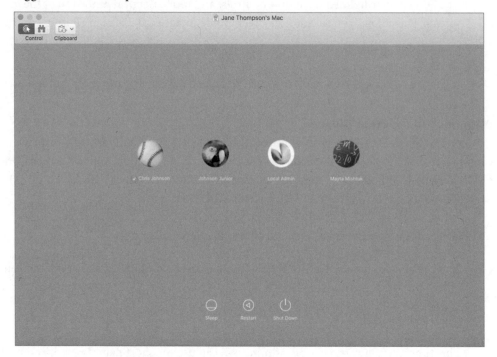

6   Log in to your partner's computer as Local Admin.

This virtual screen capability makes it easy to remotely manage users' Mac computers without disturbing them. Note that if you are in a class, your partner is connecting to your Mac at the same time, but you do not see any indication of this.

7   On the other Mac, open System Preferences, and select the Users & Groups pane.

If you use the Apple menu or the Dock, be sure to use the one contained in the window, not the one at the edge of your screen.

Do not make any changes in the Users & Groups preferences at this time.

8   Quit System Preferences on your partner's computer.

9   Click the fast user switching menu on the other computer.

You see that both Chris Johnson (either your partner or the session you left logged in there) and Local Admin (you) are now logged in to the other computer. Your virtual display is treated as a fast user switching session.

10 From the remote menu bar, choose Apple menu > Log Out Local Admin, and then click the Log Out button.

If you disconnect screen sharing without logging out first, you leave behind an orphaned fast user switching session.

11 From the menu bar at the top of the screen, choose Screen Sharing menu > Quit Screen Sharing.

12 If you are working with a partner, wait for him to finish before starting the next exercise.

13 If you are working on your own, move back to your primary exercise Mac for the first part of the next exercise.

Exercise 23.2
Configure the Personal Firewall

▶ **Prerequisites**

- ▶ You must have created the Local Admin (Exercise 2.1, "Configure a New macOS System for Exercises," or Exercise 2.2, "Configure an Existing macOS System for Exercises") and Chris Johnson (Exercise 5.1, "Create a Standard User Account") accounts.

- ▶ You need another computer running macOS on the same network as your primary computer. If you are performing these exercises in a class, you will work with a partner.

A firewall blocks network traffic based on port numbers and protocols. The macOS firewall allows only ports based on application and service requests. The macOS built-in firewall is simple to configure from the user interface. In this exercise, you will turn on the firewall and start a network-aware application. Then, you will view the firewall log. You will also configure the advanced stealth option and see that it blocks responses to network pings.

Enable the Firewall

1   If necessary, log in as Chris Johnson.

2   Open the Security & Privacy pane in System Preferences.

3   Click the Firewall tab.

4   Click the lock icon, and authenticate as Local Admin.

5   Click Turn On Firewall.

6   Click Firewall Options.

Notice that Remote Management and Screen Sharing are already on the list as "Allow incoming connections." The system assumes that if you turn on a service in the Sharing pane, you must want users to be able to connect to it, so it automatically allows those services through the firewall.

7   Deselect "Automatically allow built-in software to receive incoming connections" and "Automatically allow downloaded signed software to receive incoming connections."

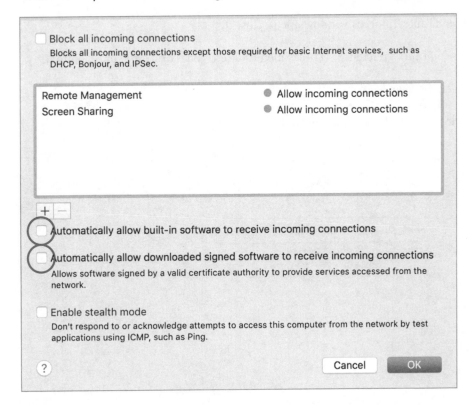

8   Click OK.

9   Quit System Preferences.

> **NOTE ▶** With the firewall in this mode, you may receive alerts about various system components attempting to accept incoming connections. A common example is "ubd" (the ubiquity daemon, part of iCloud). It is generally safe to allow these through the firewall.

Test Firewall Settings

1   Open iTunes, which is in the Applications folder.

2   If you see the iTunes software license agreement, click Agree.

3   If you see a message telling you a new version of iTunes is available, click Don't Download.

4   If an iTunes Tutorials window opens, close it.

5   Open iTunes preferences (iTunes menu > Preferences or Command-Comma).

6   Click the Sharing icon.

7   Select the checkbox "Share my library on my local network."

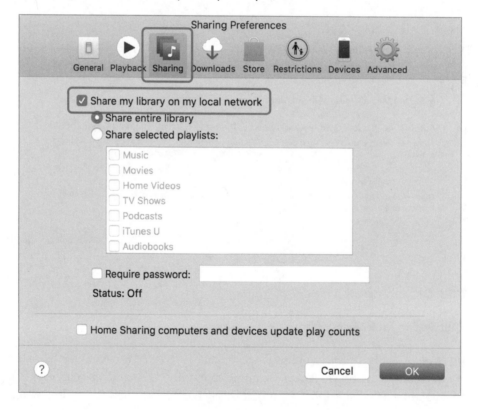

8   Click OK.

9   In the copyright reminder dialog, click OK (you may need to drag an iTunes dialog out of the way to get to it).

10 If a dialog appears asking if you want the application iTunes.app to accept incoming connections, click Deny; you will allow it later in the firewall preferences. Note that clicking Allow would prompt for an administrator password to allow the exception to the firewall rules.

iTunes displays a dialog indicating that the firewall settings prevent you from using some iTunes features.

If you click Ignore here, iTunes music sharing would turn on, but other computers would not be able to connect to it and listen to your songs.

11 Click Open Firewall Preferences.

12 In the Firewall pane of the Security & Privacy pane of System Preferences, authenticate if necessary, and then click Firewall Options.

Notice that iTunes has been added to the list and is set to "Block incoming connections."

13 Click "Block incoming connections," and choose "Allow incoming connections" from the pop-up menu that appears.

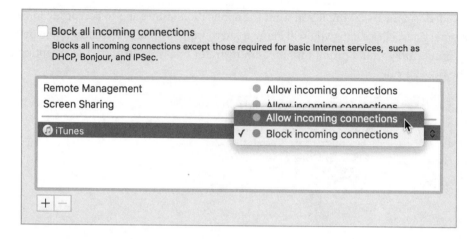

Since you have authenticated as an administrator, you can change the firewall policy for any specific application.

14 Click OK to dismiss the Firewall Options dialog.

15 Quit iTunes, but leave System Preferences open.

Test Stealth Mode

As in the previous exercise, you will either work with a partner or connect to your primary exercise computer from another computer.

1 In System Preferences, switch to the Sharing pane.

Note your computer's Bonjour name, listed beneath its computer name.

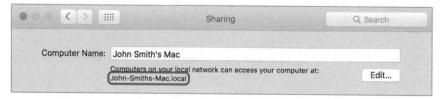

2 If you are working on your own, switch to your other computer.

3 Open Network Utility. Remember that you can find it with Spotlight.

4 Click the Ping tab.

5   If you are working with a partner, ask for her computer's Bonjour name, and enter it as the network address to ping. If you are working on your own, enter the Bonjour name of your primary exercise Mac.

6   If necessary, set it to send only five pings, and click Ping.

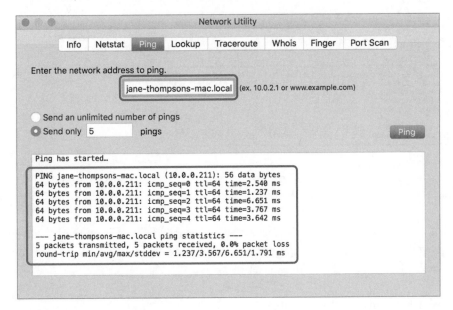

You should see successful pings.

7   If you are working with a partner, wait for her to finish pinging your computer. If you are working on your own, switch to your primary exercise computer.

8   Switch to System Preferences, switch to the Security & Privacy pane, and open Firewall Options.

9   Select "Enable stealth mode," and click OK.

10 If you are working with a partner, wait for her to finish turning on stealth mode. If you are working on your own, switch to your other computer.

11 Switch to Network Utility, and click Ping to rerun the connectivity test.

    After a few seconds, "Request timeout" messages appear in Network Utility.

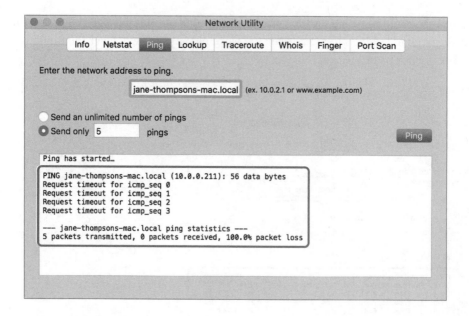

NOTE ▶ Although stealth mode is an excellent security feature, it interferes with network troubleshooting. If a computer does not respond to a ping, in addition to checking cables you should check firewall settings.

12 On your Mac, turn off the firewall.

13 Quit all running programs.

System Management

Troubleshoot Peripherals

Apple pioneered the concept of automatic peripheral support with the original Mac. This feature, commonly known as plug-and-play, is now supported with varying success in all current operating systems. Peripheral hardware has also improved—now the most common connectivity standards support hot-pluggable or even wireless connections. macOS is compatible with all popular peripheral standards, demonstrating continued commitment by Apple to making peripheral use as easy as possible.

At the start of this lesson, you'll learn how macOS supports different peripheral technologies. Then you'll learn how to manage and troubleshoot both wired and wireless (Bluetooth) peripherals connected to macOS systems.

GOALS

▶ Understand and manage macOS peripheral connectivity

▶ Pair Bluetooth devices to your Mac

▶ Troubleshoot peripheral and driver issues

Reference 24.1
About Peripheral Technologies

For the purposes of this lesson, a peripheral is any non-networked device to which your computer system can be directly connected. A peripheral is also controlled by the computer, whereas network devices are shared.

Given the wide range of devices included in this definition, this lesson shows you how to categorize devices by their connectivity type and device class. A good understanding of the available connection methods and device types is necessary for you to manage and troubleshoot peripherals, which is the goal of this lesson.

NOTE ▶ This lesson covers only connection technologies included with Mac systems that support macOS Sierra.

About Peripheral Connectivity

Most peripherals communicate with the Mac system via a connection mechanism commonly known as a bus. Bus connections are the most common peripheral connection types because they allow for a variety of different peripheral devices. Bus connections also allow multiple peripherals to connect to your Mac simultaneously.

Dozens of peripheral connectivity standards have been developed over the years, but in the last decade three have dominated the personal computing market: Universal Serial Bus (USB), FireWire, and Bluetooth. A fourth peripheral bus, Thunderbolt, represents the fastest and most capable personal computing peripheral bus to date. However, this connection type is common only on recent Mac computers.

The status of each of these four peripheral buses (and the items they are attached to) can be examined in macOS via the System Information application. You can access System Information by holding down the Option key and choosing Apple menu > System Information. Once System Information is open, select a hardware interface from the Contents list to view its information.

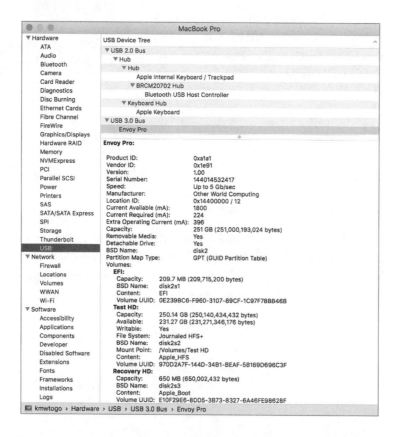

MORE INFO ▶ Using System Information for further troubleshooting peripherals is covered later in this lesson.

About Universal Serial Bus

Standard on every Mac that supports macOS, Universal Serial Bus (USB) is by far the most popular peripheral connection. In fact, every single type of peripheral can be found in USB versions. You're probably already aware of the external USB ports on your Mac, but you may not know that Intel-based Mac computers also use USB for internal connectivity. For example, the MacBook keyboard, trackpad, infrared receiver, iSight camera, and Bluetooth controller are all connected via internal USB connections.

USB was originally designed by Intel and is a hot-pluggable interface that allows users to connect and disconnect devices while they are on, or hot. USB is also a highly expandable connection platform that allows for daisy-chained connections. So you can connect one USB device to your Mac, and then connect another USB device to the first, and so on. The USB specification allows for up to 127 simultaneous devices per host controller. Most Mac computers have at least two externally accessible USB host controllers.

About USB Performance

Four USB versions are currently supported by Apple hardware: USB 1.1, USB 2.0, USB 3.0, and USB-C (USB 3.1). Despite significant upgrades in performance, all USB ports on Mac systems are ultimately backward compatible with USB 1.1 devices. Physically, most Mac computers still feature USB-A ports that support up to the USB 3.0 specification. Only the latest Mac computers that feature the more recent USB-C ports require an adapter to support peripherals made for the more common USB-A ports.

MORE INFO ▶ You can find out more about USB at the official USB Implementers Forum website: www.usb.org.

The various USB versions offer the following performance characteristics:

▶ USB 1.1 supports low-speed connections at 1.5 megabits per second (Mbit/s) and full-speed connections at up to 12 Mbit/s. All Mac systems that support macOS Sierra support USB 1.1.

▶ USB 2.0 supports high-speed connections up to a theoretical maximum of 480 Mbit/s. In practice, though, high-speed USB 2.0 connections fall short of the theoretical maximum due to the compression algorithms in use. All Mac systems that support macOS Sierra also support a minimum of USB 2.0.

▶ USB 3.0 supports superspeed connections up to a theoretical maximum of 5 Gbit/s (5 gigabits per second, or about 5000 Mbit/s). Peripherals and devices that support USB 3.0 are often identified by the use of bright-blue plastic for the interior of the physical connection, although no Apple device uses blue for identification. Mac systems introduced in mid-2012 and later support USB 3.0. You can also verify USB 3.0 support from the USB section of System Information.

MORE INFO ▶ You can find out more about USB 3.0 from Apple Support article HT201163, "Using USB 3 devices on Mac computers."

▶ USB-C (USB 3.1) supports superspeed connections up to a theoretical maximum of 10 Gbit/s. USB-C also introduced a new smaller, reversible connection that was developed by Intel and Apple. Mac computers featuring USB-C also support DisplayPort 1.3 video and internal battery charging via the same connection. Also, as covered later in this lesson, the latest Mac computers support Thunderbolt 3 via the same USB-C port. This allows for radical simplification in ports, with the latest Retina MacBook computers sporting only a single USB-C port for all purposes. A variety of USB-C adapters are available that allow for simultaneous connection to multiple peripherals, a display, and battery charging. Finally, USB-C is the only version of USB that supports target disk mode.

MORE INFO ▶ You can find out more about USB-C from Apple support article HT204360, "Using USB-C and Thunderbolt 3 (USB-C) ports and adapters on your Mac notebook."

About USB Power Delivery

All Mac computers featuring USB-A ports can supply up to 2.5 watts of power (500 mA of current at 5 volts) to the connected devices, which is all that some types of devices need to operate. Unpowered hubs, including those built into many USB keyboards, split the available power among their ports, usually supplying only 0.5 watts (100 mA) to each, enough for only very low-power devices. When the system detects that there is not enough power for a connected device, it displays a low-power notification and disables the device.

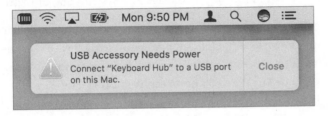

If you see this notification, you can verify the power issue by opening /Applications /Utilities/System Information and selecting USB from the report list. Selecting any USB device displays the electric current available to, and desired by, the device. You can try resolving USB power issues by connecting the peripheral directly to the Mac or through a powered hub, which uses an external power connection to supply full power to the attached device. Peripherals that require even more power to operate, such as printers or large disk drives, generally also include a separate power source.

Mac computers featuring USB-C ports have significantly upgraded power delivery specifications. This new standard allows a Mac to provide up to 15 watts of power (3000 mA of current at 5 volts). Even more convenient, Mac portable computers charge via USB-C at up to 100 watts of power (5000 mA of current at 20 volts)—again, proving USB-C to be the first peripheral connection to fit almost all needs (see "About Thunderbolt" later in this lesson).

About FireWire

Also standard on many Mac systems that support macOS, FireWire is a high-speed, general-purpose peripheral connection originally developed by Apple. FireWire has been ratified by the Institute of Electrical and Electronics Engineers (IEEE) as standard IEEE-1394 and has been adopted as a standard interface for many digital video devices.

Like USB, FireWire supports hot-pluggable and daisy-chained connections. Using hubs, each FireWire host controller can support up to 63 devices simultaneously. FireWire host controllers also allow your Mac to be used in target disk mode without the need for a functional operating system, as covered in Lesson 9, "Manage File Systems and Storage."

All Mac systems with FireWire ports support FireWire 400 with a maximum transfer rate of up to 400 Mbit/s, and most newer Mac computers support FireWire 800 with a maximum transfer rate of up to 800 Mbit/s. These two FireWire standards use different port connections, but Mac computers with FireWire 800 ports can connect to FireWire 400 devices with an appropriate adapter. Newer Mac systems that feature Thunderbolt ports also support FireWire via the Apple Thunderbolt to FireWire Adapter.

Finally, FireWire ports on Mac systems generally supply about 7 watts per port, compared with the 2.5 watts for USB-A. In its heyday, this higher power capacity made FireWire the preferred connection for external bus-powered portable hard drives, because no additional power source was required.

Alas, the FireWire standard's days are numbered. The additional cost and complexity of FireWire host controllers makes the technology impractical for many simple peripherals, such as mice, keyboards, and flash drives, which are well served by USB. And at the high end, the tremendous speed and flexibility of the newer Thunderbolt standard makes FireWire obsolete.

> **MORE INFO** ▶ You can find out more about FireWire at the official 1394 Trade Association website: www.1394ta.org.

About Thunderbolt

Originally designed by Intel, then later in collaboration with Apple, Thunderbolt represents the latest in peripheral connectivity. At a minimum this standard folds PCI Express and DisplayPort data into a single connection and cable. Further, Thunderbolt 3 adds USB compatibility and advanced power management to provide a peripheral connectivity standard that can serve any need.

Thunderbolt provides for unmatched peripheral flexibility due to its mix of PCI Express, DisplayPort, and USB connectivity. With the appropriate adapters, a single Thunderbolt connection can provide access to any other networking, storage, peripheral, video, or audio connection. For example, a Thunderbolt display can provide not only a high-definition digital display but also a built-in camera, a microphone, audio speakers, USB ports, FireWire ports, Gigabit Ethernet ports, additional Thunderbolt ports for another peripheral, and even enough power to charge portable Mac computers—all through a single Thunderbolt cable from the Mac to the display.

One Thunderbolt host computer connection supports a hub or daisy chain of up to six devices, with up to two of these devices high-resolution displays. Further, Mac systems with Thunderbolt can be used in target disk mode without the need for a functional operating system, as covered in Lesson 9, "Manage File Systems and Storage."

Physically, the original Thunderbolt and Thunderbolt 2 connector is identical to Mini DisplayPort. Thus, any Mac computer with Thunderbolt or Thunderbolt 2 can also accept Mini DisplayPort without the need for any adapters. Only copper Thunderbolt cabling can deliver power, but it is limited to a maximum 3-meter length. Optical Thunderbolt cabling is available in lengths of up to 100 meters.

> NOTE ▶ Mini DisplayPort devices and cables don't support the additional PCI Express data used by Thunderbolt. Thus, items that only support Mini DisplayPort should be the last connection in a Thunderbolt daisy chain. You can identify items compatible with Thunderbolt by an icon that looks like a lightning bolt, whereas items compatible with only Mini DisplayPort feature an icon that looks like a flat-panel display.

The latest Thunderbolt 3 standard has adopted the USB-C port. Thus, any Mac computer that features Thunderbolt 3 can also accept USB-C without the need for any adapters. Again, only copper Thunderbolt cabling can deliver power and it is limited to a maximum 3-meter length. As of this writing, optical Thunderbolt 3 cabling is not yet available, but it is part of the specification.

> NOTE ▶ USB-C devices and cables don't support the additional PCI Express data used by Thunderbolt. Thus, items that only support USB-C should be the last connection in a Thunderbolt daisy chain. Again, items compatible with Thunderbolt feature a lightning bolt icon, whereas items compatible with only USB-C feature the USB icon.

All this connectivity through one cable means that Thunderbolt provides significant data rates. In fact, Thunderbolt is the fastest external peripheral bus to date:

▶ Thunderbolt provides two bidirectional 10 Gbit/s (10,000 Mbit/s) channels. This means a total of 20 Gbit/s outbound and 20 Gbit/s inbound. With the first version of Thunderbolt, these channels can't be combined to provide full bandwidth to a single peripheral. Thus, a single Thunderbolt peripheral has a maximum bandwidth of 10 Gbit/s, but the full bandwidth can be used when multiple peripherals are part of a single Thunderbolt chain. Thunderbolt also features DisplayPort 1.1 signaling, which allows for high-definition display resolutions. Copper Thunderbolt cabling also supplies up to 10 watts of power to connected devices, again providing more power than any previous external peripheral bus.

▶ Thunderbolt 2 supports channel aggregation, wherein a single peripheral can take advantage of the full 20 Gbit/s throughput.

▶ Thunderbolt 3 provides two bidirectional 20 Gbit/s (20,000 Mbit/s) channels, providing a total of 40 Gbit/s outbound and 40 Gbit/s inbound. Thunderbolt 3 also features DisplayPort 1.2 signaling, which allows for 4K and 5K display resolutions. Finally, Thunderbolt 3 is fully backward compatible with USB-C (USB 3.1) signaling and power delivery, as covered earlier in this lesson.

MORE INFO ▶ You can find out more about Thunderbolt at Apple's official website, www.apple.com/thunderbolt.

About Bluetooth

Bluetooth is a short-range wireless peripheral connection standard originally developed by Ericsson for mobile phone headsets. Most Bluetooth devices have a range of only 1 to 10 meters, ideal for peripherals but inadequate for wireless networking. Further, Bluetooth is designed for connections not nearly as fast as wireless Ethernet. However, Bluetooth has the advantage of working with low-power devices.

As Bluetooth increased in popularity, computer manufacturers adopted it for wireless peripherals as well. In addition to providing a wireless connection between your Mac and mobile phone, Bluetooth allows your Mac to use wireless headsets, mice, keyboards, and printers. Most Mac computers that support macOS include Bluetooth wireless, and for those that don't, you can easily add it with a USB-to-Bluetooth adapter. Configuring Bluetooth is covered later in this lesson.

All Mac systems compatible with macOS Sierra include built-in support for Bluetooth. Depending on the age of the Mac, one of two Bluetooth variations is included:

▶ Any Mac capable of running macOS Sierra supports Bluetooth 1.2 with a maximum transfer rate of 721 kilobits per second (kbit/s) and Bluetooth 2.1 + Extended Data Rate (EDR) with a maximum transfer speed of up to 3 Mbit/s.

▶ Mac systems dating from 2011 or later support all previous versions of Bluetooth in addition to Bluetooth 3.0 + High Speed (HS) with a maximum transfer speed of up to 24 Mbit/s and Bluetooth 4.0 with low-energy support. Bluetooth low-energy (BLE) mode isn't very fast, at a maximum of 200 kbit/s, but it uses much less energy, is quicker to pair with devices, and sports a larger maximum range. The Continuity features in iOS 7 and OS X Yosemite 10.10 and later (Handoff, Instant Hotspot, Phone Calling, and so on) are made possible due to the efficiencies of Bluetooth 4.0 wireless.

MORE INFO ▶ You can find out more about Bluetooth at the official Bluetooth Technology Information website: www.bluetooth.com.

Reference 24.2
Manage Bluetooth Devices

Because Bluetooth is a wireless technology, some configuration is required to connect your Mac to a Bluetooth device. The process of connecting Bluetooth devices is known as pairing. Once two devices are paired, they act as if they were directly connected to each other. The macOS Bluetooth preferences make the process of configuring Bluetooth devices easy.

NOTE ▶ When desktop Mac computers are purchased with Bluetooth wireless input devices, the Mac and its associated peripherals are factory-paired and require no further pairing.

The quickest way to manage Bluetooth devices is to click the Bluetooth status menu. First, make sure your Mac computer's Bluetooth is turned on.

Pair a Bluetooth Device

Before you begin the pairing process, you will need to enable Discoverable Mode on the Bluetooth device you're going to pair with your Mac. Each device is different, so you may have to consult the device's user guide to enable Discoverable Mode.

> **MORE INFO ▶** The Continuity features in OS X Yosemite 10.10 and later (Handoff, Instant Hotspot, Phone Calling, and so on) utilize Bluetooth 4.0, but traditional Bluetooth pairing isn't required. Instead, the continuity features automatically connect as long as all devices are signed in to the same iCloud account. Find out more about Handoff from Apple Support article HT204681, "Use Continuity to connect your Mac, iPhone, iPad, iPod touch, and Apple Watch."

From the Bluetooth status menu, select Open Bluetooth Preferences. You can also open the Bluetooth preferences using any other technique you prefer to access the System Preferences application. Once open, the Bluetooth preferences will scan for any Bluetooth devices in range that are in Discoverable Mode. In the following screenshot of the Bluetooth preferences you can see two states for a device: a connected device and a device waiting to be paired.

Alternatively, with Bluetooth preferences open, the Mac itself is put in Bluetooth Discoverable Mode. Discoverable Mode advertises your Mac as a Bluetooth resource to any device within range, which could invite unwanted attention to your Mac. So the only time you should be in Discoverable Mode is when you're attempting to pair your Mac with a Bluetooth device. In other words, you shouldn't leave Bluetooth preferences open for too long.

It may take several moments for the device's name to appear. Once it does, select it and click the Pair button. For most Bluetooth devices, a passcode must be used to authorize pairing. Depending on the device, you will perform one of the following:

▶ Complete the pairing with little interaction by using an automatically generated passcode. This is often what will happen with a device that has no method to verify the passcode, such as a Bluetooth mouse.

▶ Enter a predefined passcode on your Mac, as specified in the device's user guide, and click Continue to authorize the pairing.

▶ Allow the Bluetooth Setup Assistant to create a random passcode, which you then enter or verify on the Bluetooth device to authorize the pairing. In this example of pairing to an iPhone, the passcode is generated automatically.

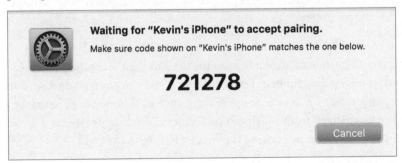

The Bluetooth Setup Assistant automatically detects the capabilities of your Bluetooth device and may present you with additional configuration screens. Continue through these screens until you complete the setup process. When the pairing is complete, you can verify the pairing at any time by reopening Bluetooth preferences. Again, a device doesn't have to be currently connected to maintain pairing status with the Mac.

Remember, however, that opening Bluetooth preferences puts your Mac in Bluetooth Discoverable Mode, so a safer (and probably quicker) method for verifying Bluetooth devices is via the Bluetooth status menu. Notice that this menu indicates a connected device using bold letters.

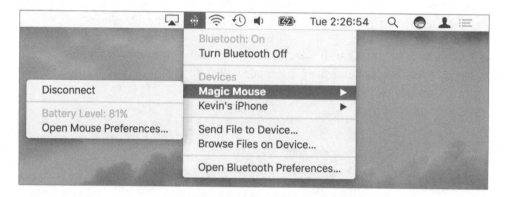

NOTE ▶ The system will also save Bluetooth input device parings, like mice and keyboards, to NVRAM so that they can be used prior to the system fully starting up. This is necessary to support FileVault and startup keyboard shortcuts when using Bluetooth input devices.

Manage Bluetooth Settings

You can adjust settings such as the peripheral's name from the Bluetooth preferences. To access all the Bluetooth management settings, open the Bluetooth preferences from either the Apple menu > System Preferences or the Bluetooth status menu > Open Bluetooth Preferences.

To manage a Bluetooth peripheral, select it from the list and then secondary-click (or Control-click) to reveal a pop-up menu. From this menu you can connect or disconnect a device, and possibly rename a device. Some devices, such as iPhones, are named on the device and cannot be changed from Bluetooth preferences. You can also delete a device pairing from this pop-up menu by clicking the small x button to the right.

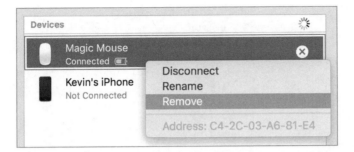

Clicking the Advanced button at the bottom of the Bluetooth preferences reveals a dialog where you can adjust additional Bluetooth settings. The settings here are extremely important for desktop systems that use only wireless keyboards and mice.

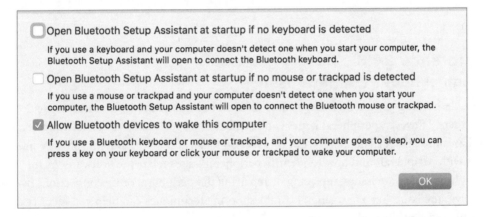

Finally, you'll find Bluetooth sharing settings in the Shared preferences. Like all other sharing services, Bluetooth sharing is off by default. Enabling Bluetooth sharing should only be considered as a last resort when traditional file-sharing methods aren't possible. Lesson 23, "Manage Host Sharing and Personal Firewall," discusses a variety of alternative file-sharing methods, including AirDrop wireless file sharing.

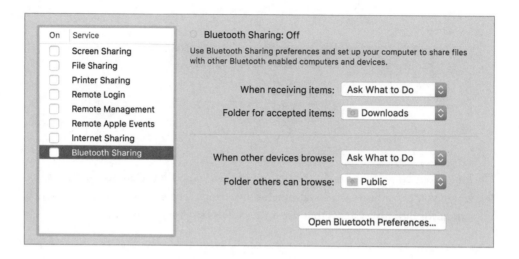

Reference 24.3
Troubleshoot Peripheral Issues

Troubleshooting peripheral issues can be difficult because of the wide variety of devices out there. However, peripheral issues can usually be categorized as either software related or hardware related. The first part of this section looks at how the system software interacts with peripherals and how to identify peripheral issues related to software. As for peripheral hardware issues, replacing or repairing the peripheral or its connections usually resolves the issue. Yet a few general troubleshooting techniques can help you identify and possibly resolve the problem.

About Peripheral Device Classes

Peripherals are divided into device classes based on their primary function. macOS includes built-in software drivers that allow your Mac to interact with peripherals from all device classes. Although these built-in drivers may provide basic support, many third-party devices require device-specific drivers for full functionality. Detailed information about software drivers is covered in the next section.

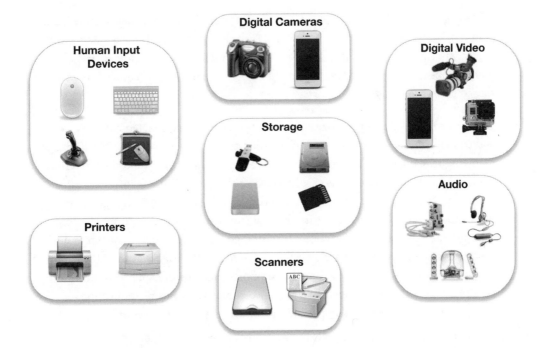

Device classes as defined in macOS include:

▶ Human input devices (HIDs)—Peripherals that allow you to directly enter information or control the Mac interface. Examples are keyboards, mice, trackpads, game controllers, tablets, and even Braille interfaces.

▶ Storage devices—Internal disks, flash disks, optical discs, and iPods. Storage peripherals are covered in Lesson 9, "Manage File Systems and Storage."

▶ Printers—Printers of all types and fax machines. Printing is covered in Lesson 25, "Manage Printers and Scanners."

▶ Scanners—Flatbed, negative, slide, and drum scanners. macOS supports scanners via the Image Capture framework, which allows you to control scanners from /Applications/Image Capture or any other compatible third-party capture application, such as Photoshop. This topic is also covered in Lesson 25, "Manage Printers and Scanners."

TIP ▶ The Image Capture application supports both locally attached scanners and scanners being shared via the network. Further, the Sharing preferences also allow you to share a locally attached scanner to the network. Network scanner discovery is accomplished using Bonjour, so usually no additional setup is required to locate shared scanning resources.

▶ Digital cameras—These peripherals include both directly connected cameras and camera storage cards mounted to the Mac computer's file system. Recall that many digital cameras, when connected to a computer, simply extend their internal storage to the computer. In this case, macOS accesses the camera's internal storage, or any directly attached camera storage cards, as it does any other storage device. Applications like iPhoto or Aperture then take over to copy the picture files from the camera storage to the Mac computer's storage. Some cameras support a tethered capture mode in which they are directly controlled by the Mac and send the captured picture data directly to the Mac. macOS supports this type of camera connection via the Image Capture framework, which also allows you to use /Applications /Image Capture or another compatible third-party capture application.

▶ Video devices—These peripherals include video cameras and video converters connected via USB, FireWire, Thunderbolt, or an expansion bus. macOS supports these video devices via the QuickTime framework, which allows you to use /Applications/QuickTime Player or any other compatible video application, such as iMovie or Final Cut Pro.

▶ Audio devices—These peripherals include external audio interfaces connected via USB, FireWire, Thunderbolt, or an expansion bus. macOS supports these audio devices via the Core Audio framework, so you can use any compatible audio application, such as GarageBand or Logic Pro.

About Peripheral Device Drivers

One of the primary responsibilities of the system software is to act as an intermediary between peripherals and applications. If an application supports a general device class, the operating system handles all the technical details of communicating with each model of peripheral in that class.

Here's an example: For an application to receive user input, it needs to receive information from the keyboard, mouse, trackpad, and the like, but it doesn't need to know any details about how to interpret the electrical signals from that device, because that's handled by the operating system. This separation of peripherals and applications by the operating system allows you to use nearly any combination of the two with few incompatibilities.

macOS supports peripherals using device drivers, specialized pieces of software that allow peripherals to interoperate with the system. Some peripherals are supported via a generic driver, but many require a device driver created specifically for the peripheral. Although macOS includes a decent selection of common device drivers, you may have to install third-party device drivers to support your peripherals. Nearly all device drivers are installed using an installer utility that places the driver software in the correct resource folder on your Mac. Device drivers are implemented in one of three ways: kernel extensions, framework plug-ins, or applications.

macOS uses a driver only if it's already installed. In other words, if you're adding support for a new third-party peripheral that requires custom drivers, install those drivers first before you connect the peripheral to the Mac. Further, it's always best to check the peripheral manufacturer's website to obtain the latest version of the driver software.

Device driver implementations in macOS include:

▶ Kernel extensions (KEXTs)—This is a special type of software created to add peripheral support at the lowest level of macOS: the system kernel. KEXTs load and unload from the system automatically, so there's no need to manage them aside from making sure they are installed in the correct locations. Although some KEXTs are hidden inside application bundles, most are located in the /System/Library/Extensions or /Library/Extensions folders. Remember that in general, nearly all the items in the /System folder are part of the standard macOS install. Examples of peripherals that use KEXTs are human input devices, storage devices, audio and video devices, and other expansion cards.

▶ Framework plug-ins—This type of device driver adds support for a specific peripheral to an existing system framework. For example, support for additional scanners and digital cameras is facilitated via plug-ins to the Image Capture framework.

▶ Applications—In some cases a peripheral is best supported by an application written just for that peripheral. Examples are the iPod, iPhone, and iPad, which are managed by the iTunes application.

Inspect Kernel Extensions

Even though the macOS kernel is designed to manage KEXTs without user interaction, you may still need to verify that a specific KEXT is loaded. You can view the currently installed and loaded KEXTs from the System Information application (while holding down the Option key, choose Apple menu > System Information). Once System Information is open, select the Extensions item in the Contents list; it may take a few moments for the system to scan all currently installed KEXTs. Once the list appears, you can further inspect individual KEXTs by selecting them from this list. Sorting this list by the Loaded column clearly indicates which KEXTs are in use by the system.

A key feature of macOS is support for a 64-bit kernel, thus necessitating 64-bit KEXTs. OS X Mountain Lion 10.8 and later require that the kernel start up in 64-bit mode. From System Information, you can easily verify that all loaded kernel extensions support this mode. However, third-party KEXTs that have not made the transition won't work, because macOS simply ignores any KEXTs that don't support 64-bit mode or are not properly signed by Apple.

Troubleshoot General Peripheral Issues

Use the following techniques for general peripheral troubleshooting:

▶ Always check System Information first. If you remember only one peripheral troubleshooting technique, it should be this. Connected peripherals appear in System Information regardless of whether their software driver is functioning. In other words, if a connected peripheral does not show up in System Information, then you are almost certainly experiencing a hardware failure. If a connected peripheral appears as normal in System Information, you are probably experiencing a software driver issue. In that case, use System Information to validate whether the expected kernel extensions are loaded.

▶ Unplug and then reconnect the peripheral. Doing this reinitializes the peripheral connection and forces macOS to reload any peripheral-specific drivers.

▶ Plug the peripheral into a different port or use a different cable. This helps you rule out any bad hardware, including host ports, cables, and inoperable hubs.

▶ Unplug other devices on the same bus. Another device on the shared bus may be causing an issue.

▶ Resolve potential USB power issues. As covered previously in this lesson, the USB interface can prove problematic if devices are trying to draw too much power. Try plugging the USB device directly into the Mac instead of a USB hub.

▶ Shut down the Mac, fully power down all peripherals, and then restart everything. This tried-and-true troubleshooting technique reinitializes all the peripheral connections and reloads all the software drivers.

▶ Try the peripheral with another Mac. This helps you determine whether the issue is with your Mac or the peripheral. If the device doesn't work with other computers, your Mac is not the source of the issue.

▶ Check for system software and driver software updates. Software bugs are constantly being fixed, so it's always a good time to check for software updates. You can use the macOS built-in software update system, but you should also check the peripheral manufacturer's website for the latest driver updates.

▶ Check for computer and peripheral software updates. Like software updates, firmware updates may also be necessary to resolve your peripheral issue. This possibility is especially likely for more sophisticated devices like the iPod, iPhone, and iPad, which have their own internal software as well.

Exercise 24.1
Examine Peripherals via System Information

▶ **Prerequisite**

  ▶ You must have created the Chris Johnson account (Exercise 5.1, "Manage User
    Accounts").

In an earlier exercise, you used System Information to view information about your hard
disk. Because it is bus oriented, System Information is extremely useful when troubleshooting peripheral issues. In this exercise, you will use System Information to identify
devices on a particular bus. Most Mac computers have several USB ports and use USB
internally for several devices. In a class, your instructor may choose to do this exercise as
a demonstration if the equipment in the room doesn't provide USB devices.

Examine Internal Devices

1   If necessary, log in as Chris Johnson.

2   Click the Apple menu.

3   Hold down the Option key.

     The first item in the Apple menu changes from "About This Mac" to "System
     Information."

4   With the Option key held down, choose System Information from the Apple menu.

     A System Information report opens with the Hardware Overview displayed. The Con-
     tents list on the left displays all the report topics that System Information can gener-
     ate, listed in three main sections: Hardware, Network, and Software.

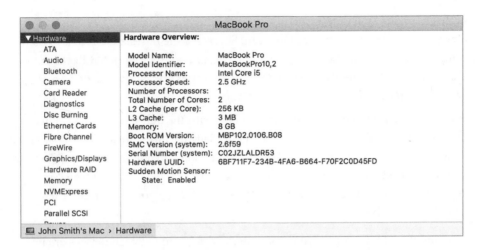

There are several ways of opening System Information. In an earlier exercise, you opened it by choosing Apple menu > About This Mac and then clicking System Report.

5   In the Hardware list on the left, click Graphics/Displays.

This shows information about your Mac computer's graphics adapters and displays.

6   In the Hardware list, click USB to view devices connected to the USB bus.

USB is a common peripheral bus. It is often used for keyboards, mice, trackpads, printers, scanners, storage devices, and digital cameras.

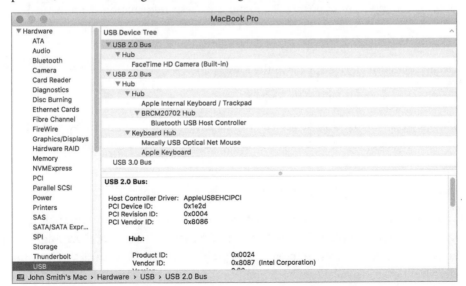

In this example, System Information indicates that there are three USB buses, two of which have devices connected to them. Several of the buses are internal to the computer; in this example, the FaceTime HD Camera, Apple Internal Keyboard / Trackpad, and Bluetooth USB Host Controller entries are all internal devices connected to internal USB buses.

If a device is connected to a hub, it is listed beneath the hub and indented. This example shows a Keyboard Hub entry with a Macally USB Optical Net Mouse and an Apple Keyboard connected. Although the hub and keyboard are separate devices at the USB level, they are both parts of a single physical device: an Apple USB keyboard. Most USB keyboards contain a built-in hub so you can attach other USB devices to them.

7   Examine the USB report for your computer and determine which devices are internal and which are external.

Examine External USB Devices (Optional)

For this section, you will need at least one external USB device connected to your computer. If you are performing these exercises in class, your instructor may be able to provide a device. If no suitable USB device is available, quit System Information and skip the rest of this exercise.

1   If it isn't already connected, plug in the external USB device, and refresh the System Information report by choosing File menu > Refresh Information (Command-R).

2   Select an external USB device in the USB report for your computer.

Details about the device appear in the lower pane.

3   Examine the speed listed for the device.

The speed at which a USB device can run depends not only on its own capability but also on the speeds of the port and any intermediate hubs through which it is connected.

4   Examine the Current Available and Current Required figures.

Your computer can supply only a certain amount of electrical power through each of its USB ports, and if there are too many devices chained off a port, there might not be enough for all the devices. To prevent this problem, macOS keeps track of how much electrical power is available at each point in the USB bus and disables devices if it calculates that not enough power is available for them.

5   While viewing the USB information, unplug the device from your computer (if it is a storage device, eject it first), plug it into a different USB port, and then choose File menu > Refresh Information (Command-R).

System Information does not update its display unless you tell it to do so.

6   Locate the external device in the report to see whether it has changed places or whether any of its statistics have changed.

7   If you have an external hub available, try plugging the device in via that, and then refresh the display in System Information.

Note whether enough power is available from the hub to run the device and whether its speed decreased because of being connected through a hub.

8   Quit System Information.

Manage Printers and Scanners

Apple and Adobe began the desktop publishing revolution by introducing the first high-quality printing solution for personal computers. Although Adobe created the PostScript printing system, Apple was the first to include it in both the Macintosh operating system and the first PostScript printer, the Apple LaserWriter. Apple has continued to pioneer advancements in printing software with macOS by adopting a printing workflow based on the Adobe Portable Document Format (PDF) and the Common UNIX Printing System (CUPS).

In this lesson you'll learn how macOS works with different print and scan technologies and how to manage and troubleshoot printers and multifunction devices connected to your Mac.

Reference 25.1
About Printing in macOS

Robust printing has always been an important part of the Mac operating system because of its popularity with graphic design users. macOS continues this tradition with an updated printing system featuring redesigned and simplified printing interfaces.

About CUPS

macOS uses the open source Common UNIX Printing System 2.2, or CUPS, to manage local printing. Originally an independent product, CUPS was purchased by Apple and remains an open source project. Architecturally, CUPS uses the Internet Printing Protocol (IPP) standard as the basis for managing printing tasks and uses PostScript Printer Description (PPD) files as the basis for printer drivers. Though still used by CUPS, the PPD name is a bit of a misnomer, since non-PostScript printers can also be described by these files.

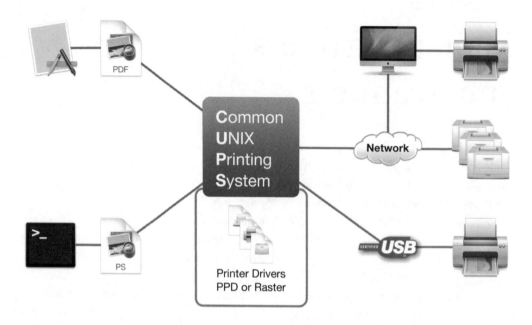

A print job starts when a user prints either from an application in the graphical user interface or by using the print commands in Terminal. When you print from an application, the Quartz graphics system in macOS generates a Portable Document Format (PDF) file. When you print from the command line, a PostScript (PS) file is generated. In either case, the file created is called a spool file and is placed inside the /var/spool/cups folder.

The CUPS background process, cupsd, takes this spool file and passes it through a series of filter processes known as the print chain. These processes convert the spool file to a format that is understood by the destination printer, and then ultimately communicate this information to the printer.

> **MORE INFO ▸** CUPS provides capabilities beyond the scope of this text. To find out more, visit the official CUPS website at www.cups.org.

About CUPS Drivers

Before you can print, you must configure printer settings, which includes associating an appropriate printer driver with the printing device. This association happens automatically as you configure a new printing device; however, the system must have the printer driver installed before it can use the printer. Apple supplies printer drivers for most popular models, including Brother, Canon, Epson, Fuji-Xerox, HP, Lexmark, Ricoh, and Samsung.

MORE INFO ► For a complete list of printer and scanner drivers available from Apple for macOS, refer to Apple Support article HT201465, "Printer and scanner software for macOS Sierra, El Capitan, Yosemite, and Mavericks."

The macOS installer is designed to save space on the system volume and to avoid installation of unnecessary print drivers. New installations of macOS include only Apple and generic print drivers. macOS upgrade installations install only drivers for printers in use by the Mac. It's expected that additional print drivers will be acquired via the Internet.

If you attempt to add a printer the Mac does not have the driver for, and you are connected to the Internet, the system prompts you to automatically download and install the driver using the Apple software update service. You can also manually download and install printer drivers from the Apple support website. These Apple printer driver installers often include multiple printer drivers from the same manufacturer.

NOTE ► You must log in or authenticate as an administrator user to install printer drivers either manually or via software update.

Obviously, if you aren't connected to the Internet, you have to acquire the printer driver manually, though some standard PostScript and Printer Command Language (PCL) printers can use the built-in generic printer drivers. Also, if Apple doesn't provide the printer driver via its software update system, you have to manually acquire the appropriate driver, often directly from the printer's manufacturer.

A few of the built-in Apple printer drivers are installed in /System/Library/Printers/ Libraries, but all the third-party printer drivers are installed to the /Library/Printers folder. The primary folder for drivers is the PPD folder, but you may notice other vendor folders that contain ancillary printer driver resources.

Once you've added a printer configuration, a copy of the PPD with the name of the device is placed in the /etc/cups/ppd folder and two configuration files are modified: /etc/cups/ printers.conf and /Library/Preferences/org.cups.printers.plist. Finally, the first time a user prints or accesses a printer queue, the system creates a printer queue application, again with the name of the device, in the ~/Library/Printers folder in the user's home folder.

Reference 25.2
Configure Printers and Scanners

How you physically connect to a printer determines how you configure macOS to print to the printer. In many cases, printer configuration is extremely easy and mostly automatic. For example, directly attached and local network printers are automatically configured with little user interaction. However, older printers or nonlocal network printers require a bit more manual configuration.

> **TIP** When adding supported multifunction printers, scanning and faxing services are configured along with general printing services.

> **TIP** The entirety of the macOS printing configuration is stored inside the /etc/cups folder. Copying this folder to other macOS systems duplicates the entire print system configuration. Just be sure to verify that the file-system permissions on the copied /etc/cups folder match the original copy.

Configure a Directly Attached Printer

If your Mac already has the correct printer driver for a directly attached USB or FireWire printer, the system automatically detects the appropriate settings and configures the new printer for you as soon as you plug it in. If the printer provides faxing and scan support, the system should automatically configure this as well.

You can verify that the printer was added by opening the Print dialog from any application (File > Print) or from the Printers & Scanners preferences. In the Printers & Scanners preferences, you can tell that printers are locally connected if their location has the same name as the local Mac computer's sharing name.

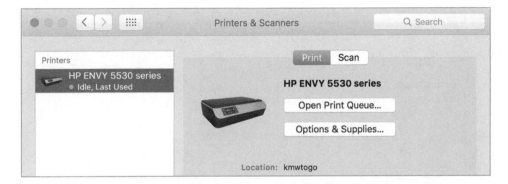

This automatic configuration occurs only if the appropriate printer driver is installed. If the driver isn't installed but is available from Apple, you are prompted with the automatic software update installer when you plug in the printer.

Again, you must be logged in to macOS as an administrator user to install the printer driver and configure the printer. Thus, if a nonadministrator user attaches a new printer for the first time, there is a good chance macOS won't configure the printer because the driver is missing. Also, if a printer driver for a directly attached printer is unavailable from Apple, then nothing happens automatically when you plug it in. An administrator user has to manually acquire and install the printer driver to get it working.

Configure a Local Network Printer

Network printer configurations must be manually added, but Apple makes this process incredibly easy for any printer that supports compatible local network discovery protocols. macOS can automatically discover standalone printers that support Bonjour (or mDNS), standalone printers that support AirPrint, and any printer shared via another Mac or AirPort wireless base station.

> **MORE INFO** ► For more information about the AirPrint protocol, including a list of printers that support this new protocol, refer to Apple Support article HT201311, "About AirPrint."

If the printer you want to add is being advertised via a supported service discovery protocol on the local network, then all you need to do is select it from the Print dialog (File > Print) from any application. Once in the Print dialog, select the Printer pop-up menu, and the system scans the local network for available printers to select.

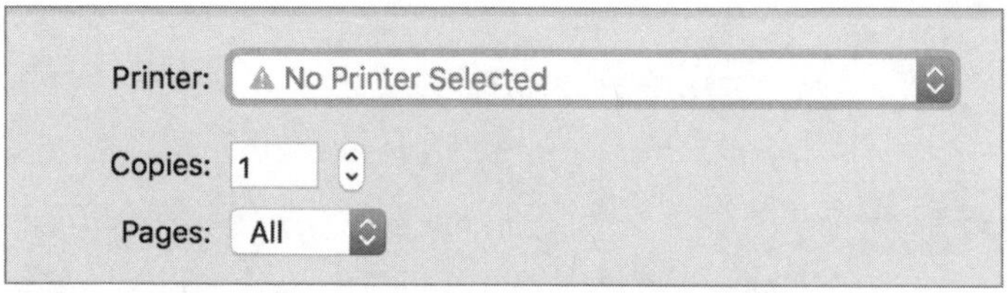

Printer: ⚠ No Printer Selected

Copies: 1

Pages: All

Printer ✓ ⚠ No Printer Selected

Nearby Printers
Brother MFC-8860DN
HP ENVY 5530 series [6D4B3D]

Add Printer...
Printers & Scanners Preferences...

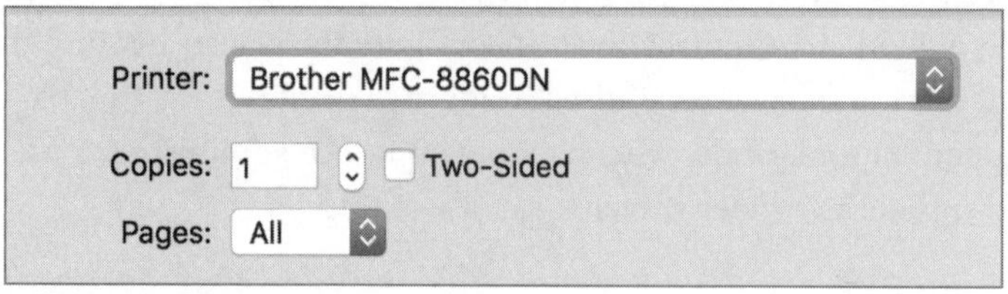

Printer: Brother MFC-8860DN

Copies: 1   ☐ Two-Sided

Pages: All

As covered previously, the Mac either configures the printer with a preinstalled driver or prompts you to download the driver from the Apple software update service. Again, the system should also automatically configure fax and scan support for multifunction devices. If a printer driver must be added, once again only an administrator user can do that.

NOTE ▶ If a network printer requires authentication, you may have to enter the name and password of an administrator before you can print to the shared printer.

Manually Configure a Printer

If the network printer doesn't support automatic network discovery via Bonjour, then you must configure it manually via the Add Printer window. Also, if a directly attached printer does not automatically configure, then you can manually add it. You can open the Add Printer window at any time to manually add new printers or multifunction devices. Again, nonadministrator users have to provide administrator authentication to access the Add Printer window.

NOTE ▶ Mac OS X Snow Leopard 10.6 and later are not compatible with the AppleTalk network protocol, so printing via AppleTalk network printers is unavailable in these versions.

To manually add a new printer or multifunction device, you can open the Add Printer window via one of the following methods:

▶ From any application, open a Print dialog by choosing File > Print. Next, from the Printer pop-up menu, choose Add Printer.

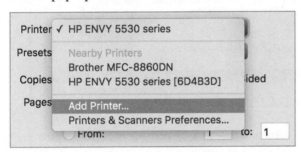

▶ Open the Printers & Scanners preferences by choosing Apple menu > System Preferences and then clicking the Printers & Scanners icon. If necessary, click the lock icon in the lower-left corner and authenticate as an administrator user to unlock the Printers & Scanners preferences. Finally, click the Add (+) button at the bottom of the Printers list. If there are nearby network printers, a pop-up menu appears allowing you to easily select those printers. If the printer you need to configure doesn't appear in the menu, then select the "Add Printer or Scanner" option to manually configure a new printer via the Add Printer window.

▶ From the Finder, open the /System/Library/CoreServices/AddPrinter application. This application's icon can also be placed in the Dock.

The Add Printer window features several panes for selecting a printer or multifunction device. These panes are accessed by clicking the following buttons in the toolbar:

▶ Default—This browser lets you select directly attached USB and FireWire printers and network printers discovered using Bonjour (or mDNS), AirPrint, or network directory services.

▶ IP—This dialog allows you to manually enter the IP address or DNS host name of a Line Printer Daemon (LPD), IPP, or HP JetDirect printer. You must select the appropriate protocol from the pop-up menu and enter the printer's address. Entering a printer queue is usually optional.

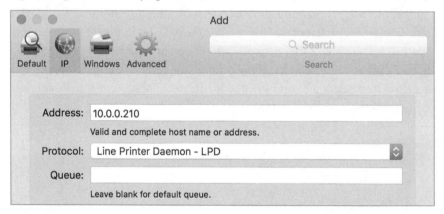

▶ Windows—This browser lets you select printers shared via the Server Message Block (SMB) printer sharing protocol. Double-click an SMB server and authenticate to access the server's shared printers.

► Advanced—This advanced configuration choice lets you manually enter the printer location. This is only necessary in very rare circumstances when the system cannot properly autolocate a printer. The Advanced button is hidden by default. To reveal this button, secondary-click (or Control-click) in the Add Printer toolbar to reveal a pop-up menu. From this menu choose Customize Toolbar and then drag the Advanced button into the toolbar.

After you select a printer or multifunction device from the top half of the new printer configuration dialog, macOS completes the bottom half for you using information it has discovered. This includes automatically selecting the appropriate printer driver if possible. Often this information isn't ideal, and you can easily change it. The Name and Location fields are only there to help you identify the device, so you can set those to anything you like.

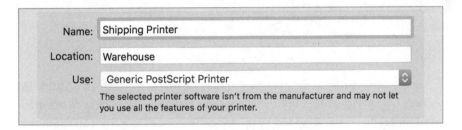

If you're configuring an LPD printer connection, you also have to manually specify the appropriate printer driver. This step can also occur with HP JetDirect and SMB printer connections.

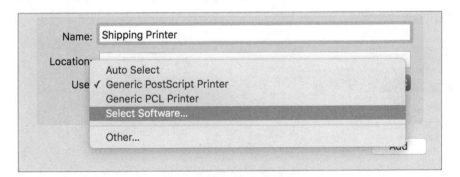

To select a specific printer driver, choose Select Software from the Use pop-up menu. You can manually scroll through the list of installed printer drivers, but using the Spotlight field to narrow the search is much quicker.

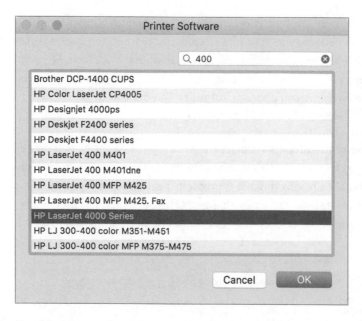

Finally, if you are configuring an IP printer, you may be presented with an additional dialog to select any special printer options. Once you complete the printer configuration, you can verify that the printer is added by opening the Print dialog from any application or the Printers & Scanners preferences. In the Printers & Scanners preferences, you can tell which printers are connected via the network if their location is shown as something different than your local Mac computer's sharing name. Also, as shown in the following screenshot, multifunction devices show a Scan tab, indicating that macOS has configured the scanning driver software.

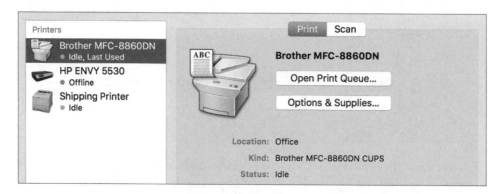

Modify an Existing Printer

You may find it necessary to edit a printer configuration after you set it up. From the Printers & Scanners preferences, you can:

▶ Delete a printer configuration—Select the item you want to delete from the printer list, and then click the Delete (–) button at the bottom of the list.

▶ Set printing defaults—From the two pop-up menus at the bottom of the Printers & Scanners preferences, choose the default printer and paper size. Use caution when setting the default printer for Last Printer Used; you will effectively have no permanent default printer—the default destination for print jobs may constantly change.

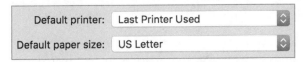

NOTE ▶ Depending on the printer model, you may not be allowed to modify the print driver settings from the Printers & Scanners preferences. To change a printer's selected driver, you must delete the printer and then add it again.

▶ Open a print queue—Select a printer from the list and then click the Open Print Queue button. Details on print queues are covered later in this lesson.

▶ Edit an existing configuration and check supply levels—Select a printer from the list and then click the Options & Supplies button. In the resulting dialog, you can easily edit the printer's configuration—including changing the printer's name—and, if available, check the printer supply levels and open the printer's hardware configuration utility.

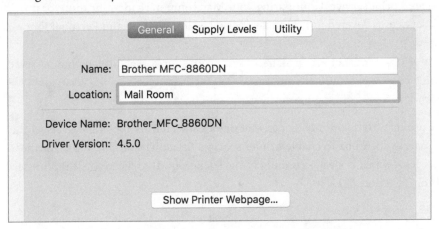

▶ Manage scanning—Select a multifunction device from the list and then select the Scan tab. From this interface, you can open the scanner image capture interface or enable local network scanner sharing.

Share Printers

It's easy to share printer configurations with macOS. Your Mac computer's shared print service is made available via the IPP printer sharing protocols. Although macOS and Windows are both compatible with IPP, different versions of Windows may require additional drivers for IPP. Also, the IPP protocol supports automatic printer driver configuration and installation for macOS, so when another Mac user connects to your Mac computer's shared print service, that user's system automatically selects, and downloads if necessary, the appropriate printer drivers.

The CUPS-shared print service also allows other network clients to easily locate your shared printer configurations with Bonjour. Again, macOS and Windows work with both discovery protocols, but whereas macOS is compatible with Bonjour, different versions of Windows may require additional drivers for Bonjour. Alternatively, network clients can manually enter your Mac computer's IP address or DNS host name to access your computer's shared print service. Configuring your Mac computer's identification for providing network services is covered in Lesson 23, "Manage Host Sharing and Personal Firewall."

> **NOTE** ▶ Users cannot access shared print services on a Mac in sleep mode. You can disable your Mac computer's automatic sleep activation or enable "Wake for Wi-Fi network access" from the Energy Saver preferences.

To share printers from your Mac, open and unlock the Sharing preferences. Select the Printer Sharing checkbox to enable printer sharing. Selecting this checkbox tells the cupsd process (which is always running in the background) to listen for IPP print service requests on TCP port 631.

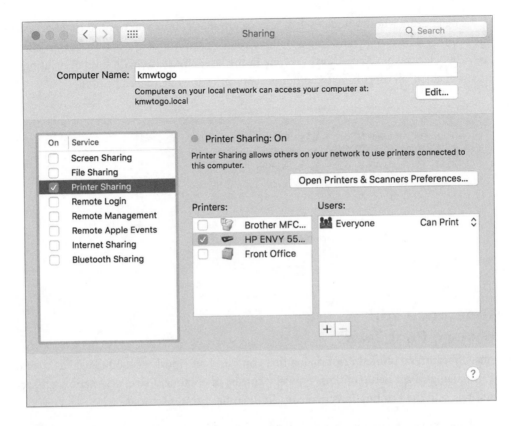

TIP ▶ If your Mac is configured to use a document scanner, you can enable scanner sharing from Sharing preferences as well. This allows you to share the scanner with other Mac systems on the local network.

By default, no printers are shared. To enable sharing for printer configurations, select the checkboxes next to the printers you wish to share. Optionally, you can limit who is allowed to print to your shared printers. By default, all users are allowed access to your shared printing devices. To limit access, select a shared device from the Printers list and then click the Add (+) button at the bottom of the Users list.

NOTE ▶ To avoid confusion, you shouldn't reshare network printers using your Mac computer's shared print services if network printers are already available on your network.

A dialog appears where you can select user or group accounts you want to grant access to the printing device. When adding accounts, you can also choose to deny access to guest users by selecting No Access for Everyone in the Users list. Also, with limited printing access enabled, all users have to authenticate to print to your shared printer.

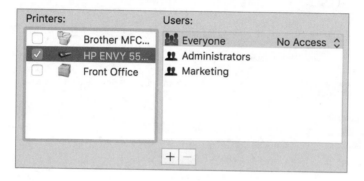

Reference 25.3
Manage Print Jobs

macOS features a unified Print dialog that combines previously separate Page Setup and Print dialogs. Page Setup options typically consist of document size, orientation, and scale settings, and the Print options make up all the other printer settings.

For backward compatibility, macOS allows older applications to continue to use separate Page Setup and Print dialogs, but older applications can also use the new, unified printing interface when you open a Print dialog. In other words, some older applications have document settings in both the Page Setup and Print dialogs.

This unified Print dialog also features two modes. The basic mode allows you to quickly preview and start a print job using default settings, and the details mode allows you to specify any page or print option and manage print setting presets.

> **NOTE** ▶ Some applications, especially graphic design and desktop publishing applications, use custom dialogs for printing that may look different from the standard Print dialog covered in this lesson.

Start a Print Job

To start a print job using default print settings, from an application, choose File > Print or press Command-P.

NOTE ▶ Some applications bypass the Print dialog and send the print job to your default printer when you use Command-P.

When the Print dialog appears, in some cases it slides out of the application's window title bar; in other cases it appears as its own separate dialog. Most applications show a print preview, whereas some may just show the basic print options. The default printer and print preset are selected, but you can choose the number of pages, copies, and duplex (two-sided) options, if available. Customizing printer presets is covered in the next section of this lesson.

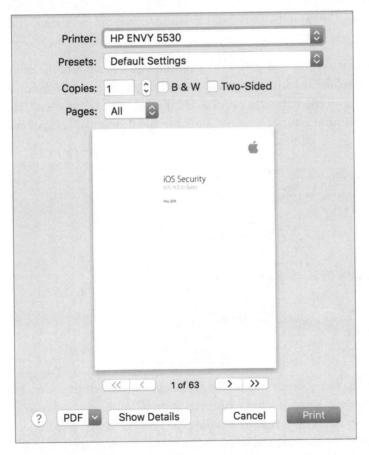

When the print job is started, the system automatically opens the print queue application associated with the destination printer. Although no window opens if the print job is successful, you can click the print queue in the Dock.

Configure Detailed Print Settings and Presets

To start a print job that uses custom print settings, from an application again open the Print dialog. Whenever you open the Print dialog, the default printer and print presets are selected, but you can choose any other configured printer or set of presets from the associated pop-up menu.

Clicking the Show Details button expands the Print dialog to its full details mode. In the full details mode, you can click the Hide Details button to return to the basic Print dialog mode. The Print dialog also remembers which mode you last used for each application. In other words, every application starts with a basic Print dialog the first time you print, but for subsequent print jobs, the Print dialog defaults to whatever you did last time in that application.

On the left side of the details Print dialog, you can page through a preview of the print job, much like the preview in the basic Print dialog. Any changes you make to the page layout settings are instantly reflected in the preview. On the right side of the dialog, you can configure all possible print settings for most applications. The top half features more detailed page setup and print settings.

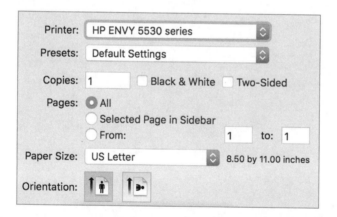

Settings on the bottom half vary depending on the application you're printing from and your selected printer's driver. You can select a category of print settings to modify by choosing it from the pop-up menu that separates the print settings from top to bottom. The settings list and configuration options within will vary for different applications, printers, and printer drivers.

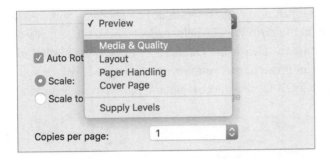

TIP ▶ If the selected printer is a multifunction device that provides fax support, one of the items in the Print Settings pop-up menu is Send Fax. From here, you can define fax settings to be used on the multifunction device to send a fax instead of printing a document.

To save the current print settings as a preset, choose Save Current Settings as Preset from the Presets pop-up menu. Select whether you want this preset to apply to all printers or just the currently selected printer. By saving a preset, you make it accessible from the Presets pop-up menu in the details view of any Print dialog. The print presets are saved to the ~/Library/Preferences/com.apple.print.custompresets.plist file, so each user has his or her own custom print presets.

NOTE ▶ Print presets do not save application-specific settings.

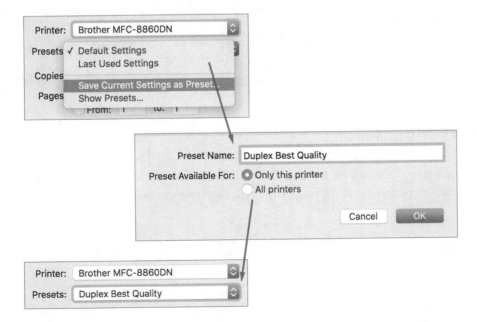

To manage existing print presets, open the print Presets dialog by choosing Show Presets from the Presets pop-up menu. In the print Presets dialog, select a preset to see its settings and values, and optionally use the Delete and Duplicate buttons at the bottom of the presets list. Double-clicking a print preset allows you to rename the preset. When you are done managing print presets, click OK to save the changes and return to the Print dialog.

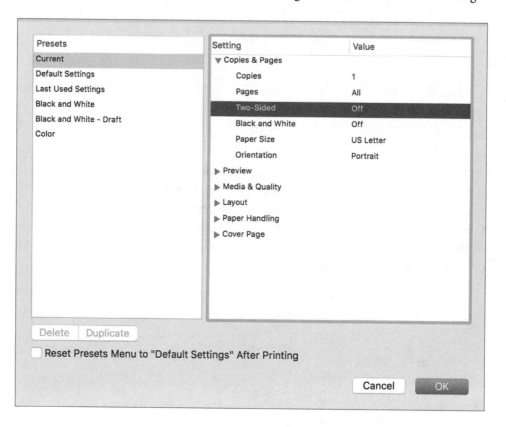

Create PDF Documents

macOS includes a built-in PDF architecture and editing tools. The full Adobe Acrobat suite has more advanced PDF features, but macOS includes all the tools to create PDF documents or perform basic editing. Any application that can print can also use the

Quartz imaging system in macOS to generate high-quality PDF documents. In any Print dialog, click the PDF button. A pop-up menu appears, which you can use to save a PDF to any location.

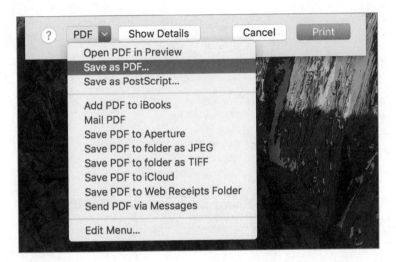

From the PDF pop-up menu, you can also specify a PDF service that is designed to accept and automatically process PDF files. Some preset services are built in, but you can add your own PDF services by choosing Edit Menu from the PDF pop-up menu. Or you can manually add PDF services to the /Library/PDF Services or the ~/Library/PDF Services folders, depending on who needs access to the PDF services. To create custom PDF services, you can use either the /Applications/Utilities/AppleScript Editor application or the /Applications/Automator application.

The macOS /Applications/Preview application also offers comprehensive PDF editing functionality—you can edit and adjust individual elements, reorder pages, crop the document, add annotations, fill out form data, and apply digital signatures using an attached video camera. From Preview, you can also convert PDF files to other formats or resave the PDF file using more appropriate settings.

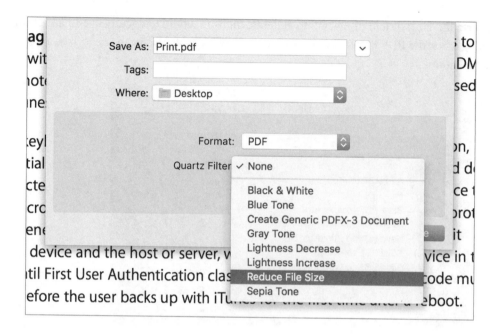

Manage Printer Queues

As stated previously, when a print job is started, the spool file is placed inside the /var/spool/cups folder, and then CUPS takes over to process the file and send it to the printer. When you print from the graphical interface, macOS opens a print queue application to manage the print job. If a job completes quickly, the file is only in the print queue for a few moments, and the print queue application quits when done.

However, printers always seem to be the most problematic of peripherals, so occasionally your Mac will not be able to complete the print job. The printer queue application remains open until the print job finishes or you resolve the print issue. If the system detects an error with the printer, it stops all print jobs to that device. You can still issue print jobs, but they fill up in the device's queue.

To manage print job queues, you can access the printer queue application using one of the following methods:

▶   If a printer queue is already open, click its icon in the Dock. In the following example screenshot, the printer queue's Dock icon shows a "1" in the red badge icon, indicating that there is currently one job in the queue. Also, as you can see by the orange connection badge icon, this printer queue is experiencing network issues that are preventing the print job from completing.

- ► You can manually open a printer queue from the Printers & Scanners preferences by selecting the device from the printer list and then clicking the Open Print Queue button.

- ► You can also manually open a printer queue from the Finder by navigating to the ~/Library/Printers folder.

When the printer queue opens, you immediately see the current status of the printer and any currently queued print jobs. A typical example of something you see when a printer queue is not responding is multiple versions of the same job in queue because the user has incorrectly assumed that sending the print job again would fix the issue. The system automatically detects when the printer becomes available again, assuming the queue isn't paused.

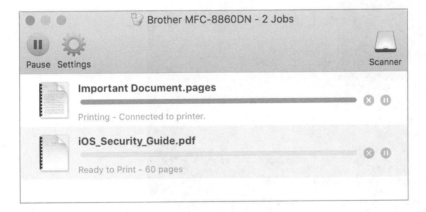

To pause or resume the printer queue, click the Pause or Resume button (the button toggles between the two modes) in the queue application toolbar. To hold or resume a specific print job, select it from the job list and then click the small Pause or Resume button to the right of the print job progress bar (again, the button toggles between the two). You can also delete a job by selecting it from the job list and then clicking the small x button to the right of the print job progress bar.

> **TIP** Selecting a job in the printer queue list and pressing the Space bar opens a Quick Look preview window for the print job.

> **TIP** You can reorder print jobs in the printer queue by dragging the job you want to reorder in the list. You can also drag jobs from one printer's queue window to another's.

Some other features are also available in the printer queue application's toolbar. For instance, you can reconfigure the printer's settings by clicking the Settings button in the toolbar. Also, if the queue is for a supported multifunction printer, you can click the Scanner button in the toolbar to open the Scanner interface. Scanning to multifunction devices both locally and via the network is possible in macOS.

Once you are done managing a printer queue, it's acceptable to leave the application running. You may find it useful to leave often-used printer queues in the Dock for direct access. Secondary-click (or Control-click) the queue application's Dock icon and, from the shortcut menu, choose Options > Keep in Dock.

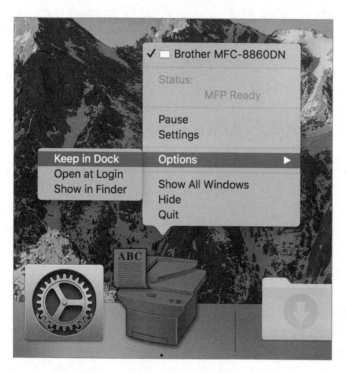

You can also provide quick access to all your printer queues by dragging the ~/Library/ Printers folder from the Finder to your Dock. Clicking this folder in your Dock reveals all configured devices. An added benefit to having your printers in the Dock is that you can drag a document on top of a printer icon to quickly print a single copy of the document.

Reference 25.4
Troubleshoot Printing Issues

You will probably experience more printing issues caused by hardware than by software. However, this being a reference about macOS, the following is a series of mostly software-based general print system troubleshooting techniques.

▶ Always check the printer queue application first. The printer queue application always shows the first symptoms of an issue, and odds are you were made aware of the issue by the queue. The printer queue lets you know if there is a printer connection issue, but you should also check to be sure that the queue is not paused and that none of the jobs is on hold. Sometimes deleting old print jobs from the queue helps clear the problem.

▶ Double-check page and print settings. If the job is printing but doesn't print correctly, double-check page and print settings using the Print dialog details mode.

▶ Review the PDF output of the application. Remember that the CUPS workflow is application > PDF > CUPS > printer. Thus, verifying whether the PDF looks correct lets you know if the source of the problem is with the application or the printing system.

▶ Print from another application. If you suspect the application is at the root of the problem, try printing from another application. You can also print a test page while in the printer queue application by choosing Printer > Print Test Page.

▶ Check the printer hardware. Many recent printers have diagnostic screens or printed reports that can help you identify a hardware issue. Many also have a software utility or a built-in webpage that reports errors. Clicking the Printer Setup button in the printer queue application toolbar accesses these management interfaces. Also, don't forget to double-check cables and connections. Finally, you may be well served by contacting the printer manufacturer to diagnose printer hardware issues.

▶ For faxing issues, check phone line and phone settings. When sending faxes via a multifunction device, you may encounter issues that are outside your control because you are relying on the phone system and another user's fax hardware. As with any faxing issue, you also need to check for fax modem problems.

▶ For directly connected printers, use peripheral troubleshooting techniques. For printers connected via USB or FireWire, use the peripheral troubleshooting techniques outlined in Lesson 24, "Troubleshoot Peripherals."

▶ For network printers, use network troubleshooting techniques. For printers connected via a network connection, use the network troubleshooting techniques described in Lesson 21, "Troubleshoot Network Issues," and Lesson 22, "Manage Network Services."

▶ Delete and then reconfigure printers. From the Printers & Scanners preferences, delete and then reconfigure a troublesome printer using the techniques outlined earlier in this lesson. Doing so resets the device's drivers and queue.

▶ Reset the entire print system. Sometimes it's necessary to reset the entire printing system. From the Printers & Scanners preferences, secondary-click (or Control-click) in the printers list and choose "Reset printing system" from the shortcut menu. Click OK in the verification dialog. Next you'll have to authenticate as an administrator user. This clears all configured devices, shared settings, custom presets, and queued print jobs. Although this may seem drastic, it's likely to clear up any software-related printing issues.

▶ Review CUPS log files. Like other system services, CUPS writes all important activity to log files. You can access these logs while in any printer queue application by choosing Printer > Log & History. This opens the Console utility to the CUPS error_log file. While in the Console, you can also check the CUPS access_log and page_log files located in /private/var/log/cups.

NOTE ▶ The CUPS error_log file may not exist if the CUPS service hasn't yet logged any serious print errors.

▶ Reinstall or update printer drivers. Again, software bugs are always being fixed, so it's good to check for printer driver updates. You can use the macOS built-in software update system to check for system updates and many printer updates. However, be sure to also check the printer manufacturer's website for the latest printer driver updates.

MORE INFO ▶ For advanced print system management and troubleshooting, you can access the Mac CUPS web interface by opening a web browser, entering the URL http://localhost:631, and then following the web interface setup instructions.

Exercise 25.1
Configure Printing

▶ **Prerequisites**

▶ You must have created the Local Admin (Exercise 2.1, "Configure a New macOS System for Exercises," or Exercise 2.2, "Configure an Existing macOS System for Exercises") and Chris Johnson (Exercise 5.1, "Create a Standard User Account") accounts.

▶ You must have a network printer that supports Bonjour or a classroom server with the proper server setup or have configured your own server using the Mainserver Setup Instructions.

Configure a Bonjour Printer

In this exercise, you will discover and configure a network printer via the Bonjour service discovery protocol. If you are performing these exercises in class, you will use a print queue shared from Mainserver.

1   If necessary, log in as Chris Johnson.

2   Open System Preferences, and select the Printers & Scanners pane.

3   If necessary, click the lock icon, and authenticate as Local Admin.

4   Click the Add (+) button under the printer list.

5   If a pop-up menu appears, choose "Add Printer or Scanner."

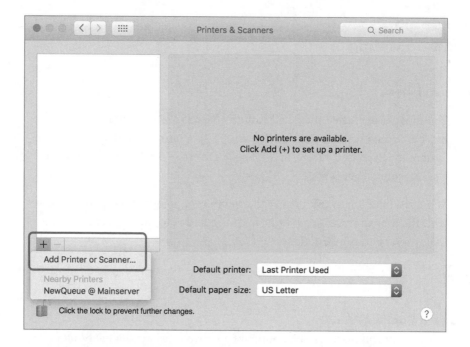

The Add Printer window opens, showing a list of nearby printers.

NOTE ▸ What you see on your computer will vary considerably depending on the model of printer you are using; the screenshots that follow are intended to illustrate the range of possibilities and will not match what you actually see. If your computer did not find any Bonjour printers nearby, see **Reference 25.2, "Configure Printers and Scanners,"** for more options.

6   Select the printer you want to use in the printer list. If you are using the print queue shared from Mainserver, it appears as "NewQueue @ Mainserver."

Depending on the type of printer, one of several things may happen:

▸   If a driver for the printer is installed on your computer, if a driver is available from the computer sharing the printer, or if an AirPrint driver is available from the printer itself, it is selected automatically and shown in the Use pop-up menu.

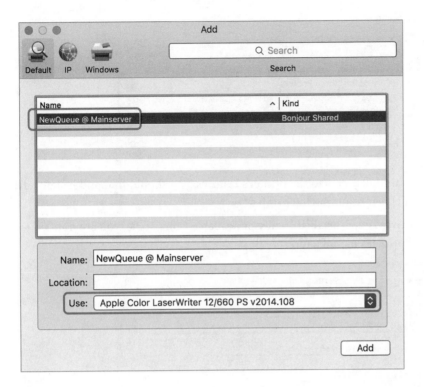

▶ If the driver is not available locally, it may be available from the Apple software update servers.

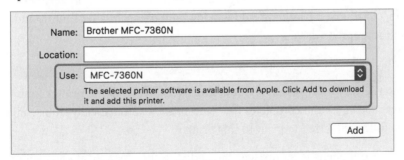

In this case, adding the printer will automatically download and install the appropriate driver package. Depending on the package size and your Internet connection speed, this may take a while.

▶ If the driver is not installed locally or available from Apple, a generic driver may be available to provide basic printing capability.

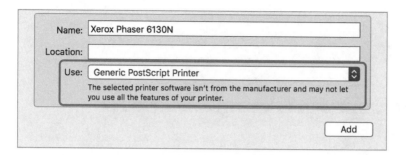

If you want full access to the printer's features, you should find and install a driver for this model before adding the printer.

▶ If the driver is not installed locally or available from Apple, you are notified to contact the printer's manufacturer.

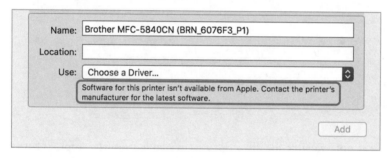

In this case, you need to find and install a driver (probably from the printer's manufacturer) to proceed. Close the Add window, and try again after finding and installing the appropriate driver.

7   With the printer selected, click Add.

Your computer fetches information about optional features from the printer itself (or the computer sharing it) and completes the setup process automatically. Your computer is now fully configured to print to this printer.

8   When the new print queue is set up, select it, and click the Open Print Queue button.

This lets you view and manage print jobs waiting to go to the printer, as well as view and change settings for the print queue. Depending on the printer's capabilities, you may see additional options such as a Scanner button.

9   Click the Settings button.

A dialog opens that allows you to view and change information about the print queue's configuration. These settings are also accessible directly from Printers & Scanners preferences by clicking the Options & Supplies button.

The General pane allows you to configure the name and location displayed for the printer. It is often useful to name printers that would otherwise have only their model name listed.

10   Change the name and location to something more descriptive. If you are using "New-Queue @ Mainserver," use the following:

Name: Pretendco Network Printer

Location: Main server

If you are using an actual printer, enter a real description.

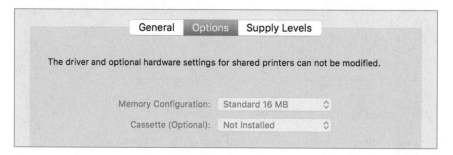

The other tabs in the Settings dialog vary considerably between different printer models; you are unlikely to see all the options shown in the following screenshots.

11 If there is an Options tab, click it.

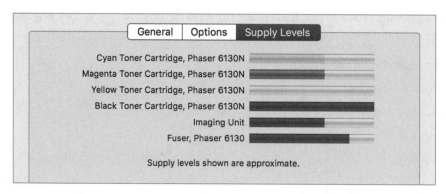

If this printer is shared from a Mac, that Mac controls what options are configured for the printer. If you are connecting to the printer directly, you can change the options if necessary.

12 If there is a Supply Levels tab, click it.

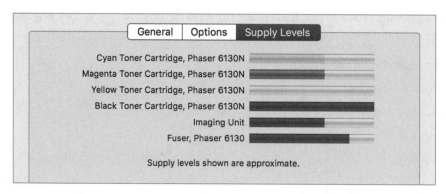

If you are connecting to the printer directly and the printer supports it, you can view the printer's supply levels here.

13 If there is a Utility tab, click it.

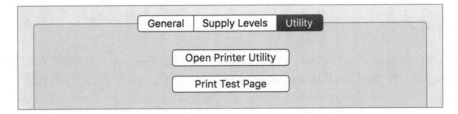

This tab of the printer setup gives you access to any utilities supplied by this printer's driver. The functions available here vary depending on the printer model you are using. Some drivers include a separate utility program, which can be opened from this tab.

14 Click OK to dismiss the Settings dialog.

15 Quit the printer queue. Note that although it is not really an application, it acts like one, including by offering a Quit option under its "application" menu.

Exercise 25.2
Manage Printing

▶ **Prerequisites**

▶ You must have created the Chris Johnson account (Exercise 5.1, "Create a Standard User Account").

▶ You must have at least one print queue set up on your computer. You can use Exercise 25.1, "Configure Printing," to set up a Bonjour-based network printer or set up a different type of printer as described in Reference 25.2, "Configure Printers and Scanners."

This exercise explores both basic and advanced features of the macOS Print dialog, including saving a set of print options as a preset, printing to PDF format, and managing PDF workflows.

Print to a Printer

In this section, you will print to one of the printers you just set up. If you are printing to NewQueue on Mainserver, it does not connect to a physical printer, so no printed output appears.

1 If necessary, log in as Chris Johnson.

2 Open the Student *n*.rtf file from your desktop. If this file does not exist, open TextEdit, type some text into the blank document that opens, and save it to your desktop as Student *n* (where *n* is your student number or 1 if you are working on your own).

3 In TextEdit, choose File menu > Print (Command-P).

4 In the Print dialog, choose a printer from the Printer pop-up menu.

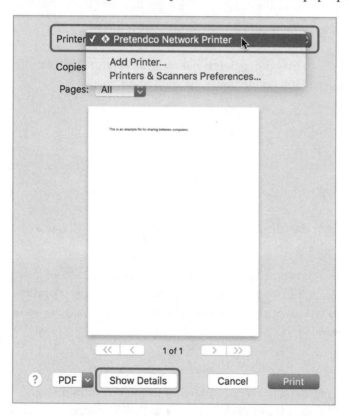

5   Click Show Details.

The Print dialog expands to show additional print settings.

6   Choose Layout from the configuration pop-up menu (initially set to TextEdit).

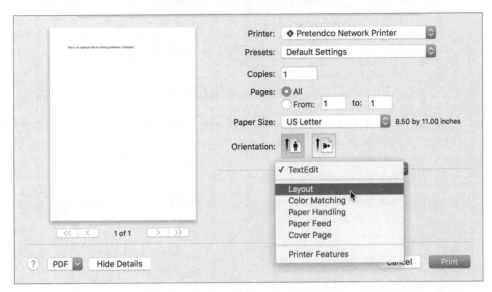

7   From the "Pages per Sheet" pop-up menu, choose 6.

8   From the Border pop-up menu, choose Single Thin Line.

As you change the settings, the preview on the left shows the effects of your changes.

9   From the Presets pop-up menu, choose "Save Current Settings as Preset."

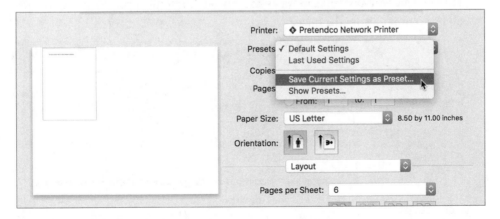

10 Name the preset 6-up with border, make it available for all printers, and click OK.

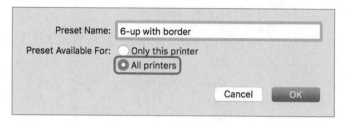

These print settings are now available from the Presets menu whenever you print.

11 Use the Presets pop-up menu to switch between Default Settings and 6-up with border, and watch the effect on the print settings.

12 Click Print.

The print queue icon appears in your Dock, showing the number of jobs in the queue (1).

Manage a Print Queue

1 If you can, click the printer queue in your Dock before it vanishes.

In the queue window, you can watch the job get sent to the printer (or Mainserver) and be removed from the queue.

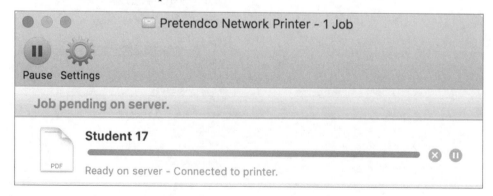

2   If the printer queue icon vanishes from your Dock before you have a chance to click it, open the Printers & Scanners preferences, select the print queue on the left, and click Open Print Queue.

3   In the print queue window, click Pause.

4   Switch to TextEdit, and print the document again.

5   When you are warned that the printer has been paused, click "Add to Printer."

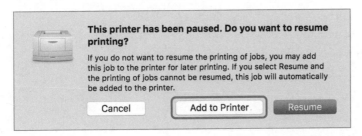

6   Switch to the print queue window. If your document is not shown, quit the print queue, and then reopen it from Printers & Scanners preferences.

Your document is shown as "Ready to Print."

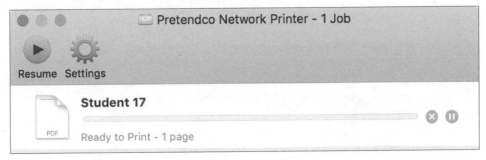

7   Double-click the document in the print queue.

A Quick Look window opens, allowing you to preview the print job.

8   Close the Quick Look window, and click the Jobs menu.

This menu has options to hold, resume, or delete individual print jobs. Most of them are also available within the print queue window.

9 Click the delete ("X") button to the right of the print job.

The job vanishes from the print queue.

10 Quit the print queue.

Print to PDF

The macOS print architecture can do a good deal more than print. In this section, you will use it to produce PDF files.

1 Switch to TextEdit, and press Command-P.

2 Click the PDF button near the bottom left of the Print dialog.

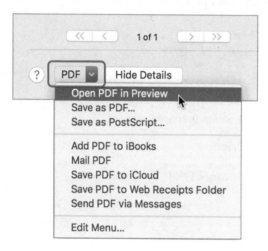

3 Choose "Open PDF in Preview."

CUPS produces a PDF version of your document, and it opens in Preview. This feature provides an easy way to do a full-scale preview of documents before printing them. Note that there are Cancel and Print buttons near the bottom right of the window.

4 Click Cancel. This both closes the document and quits the Preview application.

5 In TextEdit, press Command-P again.

6 From the PDF pop-up menu, choose "Save as PDF."

7 Save the PDF to your desktop.

Install a PDF Service

You can add choices to the PDF menu by placing items in a Library/PDF Services folder. Supported item types include additional applications to open PDFs, folders in which to save PDFs, scripts and workflows to process PDFs, and aliases to any of these.

1   Open the Lesson25 folder in StudentMaterials.

2   Open "Save Encrypted PDF.workflow."

This file is a print plug-in created with Automator, one of the easy-to-use Apple automation tools for macOS. Since it is a print plug-in, Automator offers to install it for you.

3   Click Install.

4   When you are informed that the installation is complete, click Done.

5   Switch to the Finder; then hold the Option key, and choose Go menu > Library.

6   Inside the user Library, open the PDF Services folder.

When you clicked Install, the Save Encrypted PDF workflow was placed here. You can also place items in /Library/PDF Services to make them available to all users on this computer.

7   Close the PDF Services folder.

8   Switch to TextEdit, and press Command-P.

9   From the PDF pop-up menu, choose Save Encrypted PDF.

Save Encrypted PDF is an Automator workflow that takes a PDF (produced by CUPS), encrypts it, and saves it to the desktop.

10 When you are prompted to, enter pdfpw in the Password and Verify fields, and then click Continue.

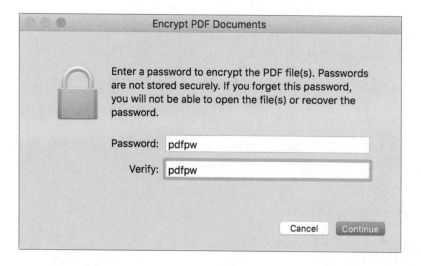

It may take a few seconds for the workflow to do its work. When it is ready, the encrypted PDF appears on your desktop.

Student 17
(Encrypted).pdf

11 Double-click the encrypted file.

The file opens in Preview, which requests the password.

This document is password protected.

Please enter the password below.

12 Reenter the encryption password pdfpw, and then press Return.

Preview decrypts the document and displays it normally.

13 Quit all running applications.

Exercise 25.3
Troubleshoot the Printing System

▶ **Prerequisites**

▶ You must have created the Local Admin (Exercise 2.1, "Configure a New
macOS System for Exercises," or Exercise 2.2, "Configure an Existing macOS
System for Exercises") and Chris Johnson (Exercise 5.1, "Create a Standard
User Account") accounts.

▶ You must have at least one print queue set up on your computer.

Troubleshooting printing involves understanding what goes on during the print process. In this exercise, you will examine the logs that are available from the print system as well as how to completely reset the printing configuration if needed.

Examine the CUPS Logs

macOS tracks many different events, including printing, through logs. You can view logs of both system and user events in the Console application. In this exercise, you will use Console to view the available CUPS logs.

1   If necessary, log in as Chris Johnson.

2   Open Console from the Utilities folder.

3   Click the disclosure triangle next to /var/log to display the list of logs, and then select "cups."

Because the CUPS logs are located in the hidden folder /var/log in the macOS file system, they are displayed under /var/log in the Console window.

4   Click access_log in the second column.

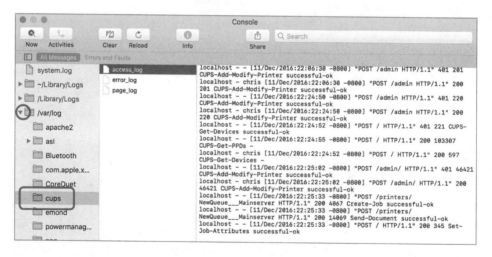

If you have printed, as you did previously, entries appear in the access log. There may also be entries in the page log for each job.

5   If there are page_log and error_log files, select them and examine their contents as well.

6   Quit Console.

Reset the Printing System

If you can't print to your printer and you've tried other solutions, you can restore the printing system to "factory defaults" by resetting it. This process deletes all printers from your printer list, all information about all completed print jobs, and all printer presets. Because this completely resets information, it's likely to be your last option rather than your first.

1   Open System Preferences, and click Printers & Scanners.

2   If necessary, click the lock icon, and authenticate as Local Admin.

3   Hold the Control key, and click in the printer list.

4   Choose "Reset printing system" from the menu that appears.

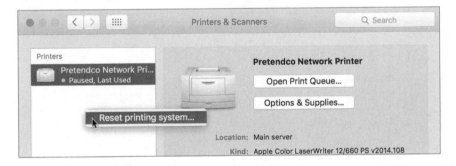

5   Click Reset when asked to confirm.

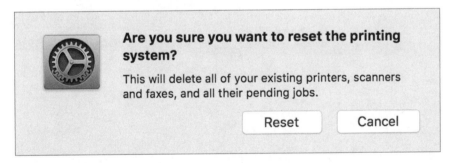

6   If you are prompted to, authenticate as Local Admin.

    You can re-add your printers when the process is complete, if you like.

7   Quit System Preferences.

Troubleshoot Startup and System Issues

Startup certainly isn't the most glamorous part of macOS, but it's clearly important and technically quite impressive. Apple has improved startup and runtime processes with every revision of macOS. When things work correctly, the startup process often takes under 30 seconds. Obviously, users appreciate a quick startup, but most aren't aware of what goes on during system startup, because their Mac computers usually work properly.

However, when things do go wrong during system startup, users often fear the worst. Novice users may assume that if their Mac won't start up they will lose important documents. But the system startup process can fail due to many issues that probably won't result in any user data loss. It's important to properly diagnose startup issues so that you can get the Mac up and running or at least try to recover data.

This lesson focuses on the process that your Mac goes through from the moment you press the power button until you ultimately reach the Finder. You will identify the essential files and processes required to successfully start up macOS. You will also explore macOS sleep modes, logout, and shutdown. You will then learn about the various startup shortcuts and diagnostic modes that work with macOS. Finally, the end of this lesson focuses on methods that will enable you to effectively troubleshoot system initialization and user session issues.

GOALS

▶ Describe the macOS startup process

▶ Examine essential files and processes required to successfully start up

▶ Learn about the various macOS startup modes

▶ Troubleshoot processes used at startup and login

Reference 26.1
Understand System Initialization

This section examines the main stages of the macOS startup procedure. The stages of system startup can be categorized as either initiation (the processes required to start macOS) or user session (the processes required to prepare the user environment). At each stage, the Mac presents an audible or visual cue to help you validate startup progress. The startup cues discussed here are what you'll experience during a typical startup. Any deviation will be covered as you learn more about the startup process.

System Initialization

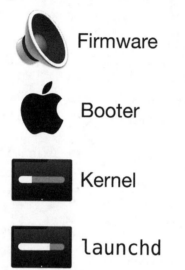

Firmware

Booter

Kernel

launchd

The four main system initialization stages are, in order:

- Firmware—At this stage the Mac computer's hardware is tested and initialized, and then the booter is located and started. Successful completion of this stage can result in an audible startup sound, if audio output is available, and a bright flash from the power-on light, if the Mac has one. Your best clue is that the primary display should power on. Older Mac models will start with a light gray background, but newer Mac models will start with a black background, so it might be difficult to tell whether the display is active.

- Booter—The main job of the booter is to load the macOS kernel and essential hardware drivers, known as kernel extensions (KEXTs), into main memory and then allow the kernel to take over. The booter stage is indicated by the appearance of the Apple logo on the main display.

▶ Kernel—The kernel provides the macOS foundation and loads additional drivers and the core BSD UNIX operating system. In macOS Sierra, loading of the kernel is indicated by the appearance of a progress bar under the Apple logo on the main display.

▶ launchd—Once the core operating system is loaded, it starts the first nonkernel process, launchd, which is responsible for loading the remainder of the system. This stage is indicated by the progress bar under the Apple logo on the main display. Successful completion of this stage results in the appearance of either the login screen or the Finder, depending on whether FileVault is enabled or the user is set to automatically log in.

System Initialization: Firmware

Your Mac computer's firmware, also called BootROM, resides on flash memory chips built into the main computer board. When you start up a Mac, even before it starts macOS, the firmware acts as a mini operating system with just enough software to get things going. Specifically, the firmware tests and initializes the hardware, and then locates and starts the macOS booter.

Intel-based Mac computers feature firmware based on the Intel Extensible Firmware Interface (EFI) technology. Aside from supporting the Intel processor hardware, EFI enables your Mac to start up from macOS, Windows, or any other Intel-compatible operating system.

> **MORE INFO** ▶ EFI is an extremely flexible boot architecture and is now managed by the Unified EFI Forum. In fact, EFI will soon be known as Unified Extensible Firmware Interface (UEFI). You can find out more at www.uefi.org.

Power-On Self-Test

The first thing your Mac firmware does when it powers on is the Power-On Self-Test (POST). The POST tests built-in hardware components such as processors, system memory, network interfaces, and peripheral interfaces. When your Mac passes the POST, you may hear the startup sound and the displays should power on. Your best clue is the display, as the startup sound may not be audible for your Mac. For example, if your Mac is connected to external speakers that are turned off or very low, you will not hear the startup sound. Also, the latest MacBook computers no longer make a sound on startup as a default configuration. After a successful POST, the firmware goes on to locate the booter file.

> **NOTE** ▶ Mac computers perform the POST only during a startup, not during a restart.

If your Mac fails the POST, the display remains blank or off and you may get hardware error codes. Depending on the age and model of your Mac, these error codes may manifest as audible tones, a series of flashes from the external power-on light, or internal diagnostic lights illuminating. You may even see a combination of these things. Regardless of which error code you experience, it indicates that a hardware problem exists that macOS cannot control. You can visit the Apple support website, at www.apple.com/support, to identify your specific Mac error code, or you can take your Mac to an Apple Authorized Service Provider.

Booter Selection

By default, the firmware picks the system booter file that was last specified from Startup Disk preferences in macOS or the Boot Camp control panel in Windows. The booter file's location is saved in your Mac computer's nonvolatile RAM (NVRAM) so that it persists across Mac restarts. If the booter file is found, EFI starts the booter process and the Mac begins to start up. This is indicated by the appearance of the Apple logo in the center of the main display.

If the firmware cannot locate a booter file, a flashing folder icon with a question mark appears. Troubleshooting this issue is covered later in this lesson.

NOTE ▶ During startup, most Mac computers feature a white background with dark gray icons. However, some late-model Mac computers will feature a black background with white icons during startup.

FileVault Unlock

If the system disk is protected with FileVault system volume encryption, the macOS booter cannot be accessed until the system disk is unlocked by a user. With FileVault, the Mac begins initial startup from the macOS Recovery HD, where a special EFI booter resides that presents the user with an authentication screen much like the login window. The FileVault authentication unlock screen appears just a few seconds after POST and looks very similar to the standard macOS login window.

Once the user successfully authenticates and unlocks the encrypted system disk, the EFI firmware is granted access to the system volume containing the macOS booter. Startup then continues as usual, with one exception: because the user has already authenticated to unlock the disk, macOS will automatically log in without the user having to authenticate again at the login window. This automatic login happens only once per startup and only for the user who unlocked the encrypted system disk.

Startup Shortcuts

Your Mac firmware also supports many keyboard shortcuts, which, when pressed and held down during initial power-on, allow you to modify the startup process. Some of these shortcuts alter the booter selection, and others modify how macOS starts up. Startup shortcuts are also detailed later in this lesson.

Firmware Updates

Boot read-only memory, or Boot ROM, refers to older versions of firmware technology that are not upgradable. Your Mac firmware, however, is upgradable, and on Intel-based Mac computers it's even replaceable if it becomes damaged.

The macOS software update service may automatically update some Mac firmware, but you can also check the Apple Support website for the latest list of Mac firmware updates. Apple Support article HT201518, "About EFI and SMC firmware updates for Intel-based Mac computers," maintains a list of Mac firmware updates. You can replace your Intel-based Mac computer's firmware using a firmware restoration CD, as outlined in Apple Support article HT201692, "About the Firmware Restoration CD (Intel-based Macs)."

MORE INFO ▶ You can extend your Intel-based Mac computer's EFI capabilities using the rEFInd boot manager available at www.rodsbooks.com/refind.

System Initialization: Booter

The booter process is launched by your Mac firmware and is responsible for loading the macOS kernel and enough essential KEXTs that the kernel can take over the system and continue the startup process. Your Mac firmware also passes on any special startup mode instructions for the booter to handle, such as entering safe mode when the user is holding down the Shift key. The booter process resides at /System/Library/CoreServices/boot.efi.

To expedite the startup process, the booter loads cached files whenever possible. These files contain an optimized kernel and cached KEXTs that load much more quickly than if the Mac had to load them from scratch. These caches are located in the /System/Library/Caches/com.apple.kext.caches folder. If macOS detects a problem or you start macOS in safe mode, these caches are discarded and the kernel-loading process takes longer.

As covered previously, the booter process is indicated at startup by the Apple icon in the center of the main display. If the booter successfully loads the kernel, this is indicated by a small progress bar below the Apple icon. However, some late-model Mac computers start up so fast you may not see the progress bar before the next stage is indicated.

If your Mac is set to use a network disk and the firmware successfully locates the booter from a NetInstall service, you again see the Apple icon. However, in this case the booter and the cached kernel information must be downloaded from the NetInstall service. This process is indicated by a small, spinning globe icon below the Apple icon. The globe icon is replaced by the standard progress bar once the kernel has been successfully loaded from the NetInstall service.

Finally, if the booter is unable to load the kernel, a prohibitory icon takes the place of the Apple icon. Again, troubleshooting this issue is covered later in this lesson.

System Initialization: Kernel
Once the booter has successfully loaded the kernel and essential KEXTs, the kernel itself takes over the startup process. The kernel has now loaded enough KEXTs to read the entire

file system, allowing it to load any additional KEXTs and start the core BSD UNIX operating system. Again, a progress bar below the Apple icon indicates the kernel startup progress.

Finally, the kernel starts the first normal (nonkernel) process, launchd, which is ultimately the parent process for every other process. During system startup, the progress bar below the Apple logo is an indication that the kernel has fully loaded and the launchd process is starting other items.

Again, in most cases the kernel is loaded by the booter from cached files. However, the kernel is also located on the system volume at /mach_kernel. This file is normally hidden from users in the graphical user interface, because they don't need access to it. Many other hidden files and folders at the root of the system volume are necessary for the BSD UNIX operating system, and again, the average user doesn't need access to these items. As covered in Lesson 24, "Troubleshoot Peripherals," KEXTs reside in the /System/Library/Extensions and /Library/Extensions folders.

System Initialization: launchd

Once the kernel is up and running, the Mac is ready to start running processes at the behest of the system and, eventually, human users. Again, the first nonkernel process started is launchd, located at /sbin/launchd, which runs as root and is given the process identification number of 1. In UNIX terms, launchd is the first parent process that spawns other child processes, and those processes go on to spawn other child processes.

The first task for the launchd process is to complete the system initialization by starting all other system processes. The launchd process is highly optimized, so the system initialization process takes only a few moments and is difficult to visually discern. The best indication that you have reached this point is that the Apple logo is replaced by the login window or the user's desktop background.

If you have a Mac system with multiple displays, you may also notice a brief flash coming from the secondary displays as they power on. This is a result of launchd starting the WindowServer process, which is responsible for drawing the macOS user interface, but it's still a good indication that things are progressing through the system startup process.

The launchd process expedites system initialization by starting multiple system processes simultaneously, whenever possible, and starting only essential system processes at startup. After startup, the launchd process automatically starts and stops additional system processes as needed. By dynamically managing system processes, launchd keeps your Mac responsive and running as efficiently as possible.

> **MORE INFO ►** launchd is an extremely powerful open source system for managing services. Learn more about launchd by reading its manual page in Terminal.

launchd Items

As covered in Lesson 13, "Manage System Resources," launchd manages system processes as described by launchd preference files in the /System/Library/LaunchDaemons folder. Third-party processes can also be managed when described by launchd preference files in the /Library/LaunchDaemons folder.

Apple strongly encourages all developers to adopt the launchd system for all automatically started processes, but the launchd process also supports legacy startup routines. This includes support for running the traditional UNIX /etc/rc.local script during system initialization, if present, though this script is not included on macOS by default.

> **NOTE ►** macOS Sierra does not support legacy startup items. Thus, items from previous systems in /System/Library/StartupItems or /Library/StartupItems are ignored.

Viewing the launchd Hierarchy

You may find it beneficial to open /Applications/Utilities/Activity Monitor and examine the process listing as you learn about how macOS starts up the user environment. The Activity Monitor application lists all processes along with their identification numbers and parent-child relationships. In Activity Monitor, you see this relationship best if you choose View > All Processes, Hierarchically. You can also view a process's parent process by double-clicking its name in the list. Detailed information about using Activity Monitor is covered in Lesson 18, "Manage and Troubleshoot Applications."

Process Name	Memory	Compressed M...	Threads	Ports	PID ∧	User
▼ kernel_task	1.32 GB	0 bytes	146	0	0	root
▼ launchd	24.3 MB	1.6 MB	5	2,245	1	root
syslogd	2.5 MB	168 KB	7	226	89	root
UserEventAgent	11.2 MB	1.3 MB	6	429	90	root

Reference 26.2
About User Sessions

Eventually, after enough system processes have started, macOS begins the processes responsible for managing the user session.

User Session

 `loginwindow`

 `launchd`

 User environment

The three main user session stages are, in order:

► loginwindow—This is the process responsible for presenting the login screen and eventually logging the user in to macOS. Successful completion of this stage results in initialization of the user environment, thus allowing user applications to run.

► launchd—The launchd process works in conjunction with the loginwindow process to initialize the user environment and start any user processes or applications.

► User environment—This is the "space" in which users' processes and applications exist when they are logged in to macOS. Obviously, the user environment is maintained by the loginwindow and launchd processes.

User Session: Login Window

A soon as the system has started enough processes to present the login window, the launchd process starts /System/Library/CoreServices/loginwindow. The loginwindow process has the ability to run as both a background process and a graphical interface application. It coordinates the login screen and, along with the opendirectoryd process, authenticates the user. After authentication, loginwindow, in conjunction with the launchd process, also initializes the graphical user interface environment and continues to run as a background process to maintain the user session.

By default in macOS, the user must authenticate using the login screen, or the loginwindow can be set to automatically authenticate a user at startup. As covered previously, the system also automatically logs in a user who provides authentication to unlock FileVault during startup. The loginwindow settings are stored in the /Library/Preferences /com.apple.login-window.plist preference file. As covered in Lesson 5, "Manage User Accounts," you can configure loginwindow settings from the Users & Groups preferences.

If no users are logged in to the Mac, the loginwindow process is owned by the root user. Once a user successfully authenticates, the loginwindow process switches ownership to this user and then proceeds to set up the graphical user interface environment with help from the launchd process.

User Session: launchd

The moment a user is authenticated, the loginwindow and launchd processes work together to initialize the user's environment. If fast user switching is enabled, the launchd process starts additional processes to initialize and maintain each user's environment.

The loginwindow and launchd processes set up the graphical user interface environment by:

▶ Retrieving the user account information from opendirectoryd and applying any account settings

▶ Configuring the mouse, keyboard, and system sound using the user's preferences

▶ Loading the user's computing environment: preferences, environment variables, devices and file permissions, and keychain access

▶ Opening the Dock (also responsible for Mission Control and Dashboard), Finder, and SystemUIServer (responsible for user interface elements like menu extras on the right side of the menu bar)

▶ Automatically opening the user's login items

▶ Automatically resuming any application that was open before the last logout, by default, in macOS

It's important to understand the differences among the various autostarting mechanisms in macOS: launch daemons, startup items, launch agents, and login items. Launch daemons and startup items are started during system initialization by the launchd process on behalf of the root user. Conversely, launch agents and login items are started only on behalf of a specific user. In other words, launch daemons and startup items affect the system as a whole, whereas launch agents and login items affect individual users.

Specifically, launch agents are started by the launchd process on behalf of the user. Launch agents can be started at any time, as long as the user's account is logged in to macOS. Most launch agents are started during the initialization of the user environment, but they could also be started afterward or on a regular repeating basis, depending on need. Launch agents provided by the system can be found in /System/Library/LaunchAgents, whereas third-party launch agents should be located in either /Library/LaunchAgents or ~/Library/LaunchAgents.

Finally, login items are started only at the very end of the initialization of the user environment. The loginwindow process, again with help from launchd, is responsible for starting a user's login items. The user's login item list is stored in the ~/Library/Preferences/login-window.plist preference file. As covered in Lesson 5, "Manage User Accounts," you can configure a user's login item list from the Users & Groups preferences.

Again, from Activity Monitor you can examine the resulting user processes. It's especially helpful if the process list shows all processes and you click the word User to sort the list of processes by user name.

The User Environment

The loginwindow processes continue to run as long as the user is logged in to the session. The launchd process starts all user processes and applications, and the user's loginwindow process monitors and maintains the user session.

The user's loginwindow process monitors the user session by:

▶ Managing logout, restart, and shutdown procedures

▶ Managing the Force Quit Applications window, which includes monitoring the currently active applications and responding to user requests to forcibly quit applications

▶ Writing any standard-error output to the user's console.log file

While the user is logged in to the session, the launchd process automatically restarts any user application that should remain open, such as the Finder or the Dock. If the user's loginwindow process is ended, whether intentionally or unexpectedly, all the user's applications and processes immediately quit without saving changes. If this happens, the launchd process then automatically restarts the loginwindow process as if the Mac had just started up. In other words, the loginwindow, depending on configuration, either displays the login screen or automatically logs in the specified user.

Reference 26.3
About Sleep Modes, Logout, and Shutdown

At the other end of the spectrum, but still related, are the processes required to pause or end the user session. The main distinction is that your Mac computer's sleep function does not quit any open processes, whereas if you log out or shut down the Mac, macOS will quit open processes. You can manually issue a sleep, logout, or shutdown command from the Apple menu.

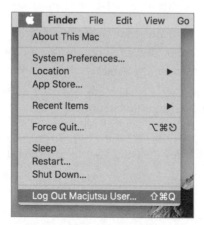

NOTE ▶ Quickly pressing the power button on your Mac immediately puts the computer to sleep. However, holding this button for more than a few seconds will force the Mac to shut down. Although this is useful if the Mac is unresponsive, you don't want to shut your Mac down like this on a regular basis because it may lead to data loss.

However, other processes and applications can also initiate sleep, logout, or shutdown commands. For instance, the Installer and Mac Store applications can request a restart when the installation of new or updated software requires it.

Further, you can configure a Mac to automatically perform certain commands. You can put the Mac to sleep after a period of inactivity with settings in Energy Saver preferences; set a schedule to sleep, shut down, or start up the Mac with settings in the Schedule dialog of the Energy Saver preferences; automatically log out users after a period of inactivity with settings in the Security & Privacy preferences; and automatically log out managed users with settings in the Parental Controls preferences. Many of these settings can be managed remotely from Apple Remote Desktop or from a management server.

The Mac sleep function is convenient because it does not quit any active processes or applications. Instead, the macOS kernel pauses all processes and then essentially shuts down all the hardware. This greatly reduces the amount of power used. As an example, newer portable Mac computers can remain in sleep mode for up to a month on a single battery charge. Waking your Mac from sleep mode restarts the hardware, and the kernel resumes all processes and applications from the point at which you left them.

Safe Sleep and Standby Modes

Mac computers that are compatible with macOS Sierra support either safe sleep or standby modes that use no power. Older Mac computers with mechanical disks support safe sleep, and newer Mac computers with flash storage also support an automatic standby mode. When Mac computers go to sleep, they copy the entire contents of system memory to an image file on the system volume. This way, if a Mac stays in sleep mode long enough to completely drain the battery, no data is lost when the Mac has to fully shut down.

A Mac in safe sleep mode must be restarted just like a Mac that was shut down. In other words, you can restart a Mac in safe sleep mode only by pressing the power button. When you restart a Mac from safe sleep mode, the booter process reloads the saved memory image from the system volume instead of proceeding with the normal startup process.

The booter process indicates that the Mac is restarting from safe sleep mode by showing a light gray version of your Mac screen as it appeared when sleep was initiated and a small white segmented progress bar at the bottom of the main display.

It should take only a few moments to reload system memory, and the kernel resumes all processes and applications. If FileVault system volume encryption is enabled, the safe sleep wake process is preceded by the FileVault authentication unlock screen.

Newer Mac computers with flash storage will enter a power-saving standby mode automatically when they are asleep and completely idle for more than one hour (if manufactured before 2013) or after three hours (if manufactured in 2103 or later). However, "completely idle" means that the system detects zero network or peripheral activity for more than four hours. Unlike Mac computers in safe sleep, Mac computers in standby mode do not need to be restarted and can be woken when you interact with the keyboard, trackpad, or mouse. During wake you may notice a small, white, segmented progress bar at the bottom of the screen, similar to that of safe sleep mode, although in most cases, when a newer Mac wakes from standby it's so fast you may not even notice.

> **MORE INFO** ▶ You can find out more about safe sleep and standby modes, including which Mac models support these modes, from Apple Support articles HT201635, "If you see a progress bar when your Mac wakes from sleep," and HT202124, "About standby on your Mac."

Power Nap

Mac computers introduced after mid-2011 that feature all flash storage, like MacBook Air models, support Power Nap. This feature allows your Mac to occasionally wake from sleep in a low-power mode—known as "dark wake" because the display does not power up—and perform essential background tasks. Many built-in macOS applications and services can work in Power Nap, including Mail, Contacts, Calendar, Reminders, Notes, iCloud Drive, Photo Stream, Mac App Store updates, Time Machine backup, Find My Mac updates, VPN on demand, and MDM configuration profile updates.

> **NOTE** ▶ Power Nap updates only applications that are running when sleep is initiated. Further, if the user logs out of the system before it goes to sleep, the user's items do not update.

For Mac computers that support Power Nap, it is enabled by default and will function whenever your Mac is connected to a power adapter. You can verify or adjust this setting from the Energy Saver settings. You can also optionally enable Power Nap for when your Mac is running from battery power, although this obviously means the charge won't last as long as it would during normal system sleep.

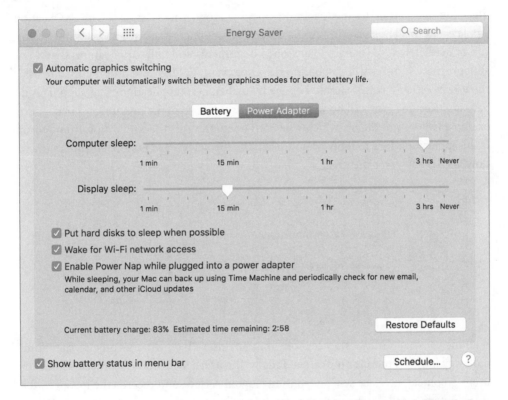

When a Mac is put to sleep with Power Nap enabled, it first waits 30 minutes before dark-waking to check for updates. After that, it dark-wakes every hour to check for updates. You can verify that Power Nap has been active by searching in Console for entries with "wake."

MORE INFO ▶ Some Mac computers require firmware updates to support Power Nap. You can find out more about Power Nap and any required updates from Apple Support article HT204032, "How Power Nap works on your Mac."

Logout

Users can log out anytime they want to end their user session, but they also have to log out to shut down or restart the Mac. When the currently logged-in user chooses to log out, the user's loginwindow process manages all logout functions with help from the launchd process.

Once the user authorizes the logout, the loginwindow process issues a Quit Application Apple event to all applications. Applications that support Auto Save and Resume features can immediately save changes to any open documents and quit. Applications that do not support these features still respond to the Quit event, but they are programmed to ask the user whether changes should be saved. Further, even applications that support Auto Save and Resume may still be waiting for the user if certain dialogs are left open. A great example is the Print dialog, which when left open prevents the application from quitting. If the application fails to reply or quit itself, the logout process is stopped and loginwindow displays an error message.

If all the user's applications successfully quit, the user's loginwindow process then forcibly quits any background user processes. Finally, the user's loginwindow process closes the user's graphical interface session, runs any logout scripts, and records the logout to the main system.log file. If the user chooses only to log out, as opposed to shutting down or restarting, the user's loginwindow quits, the launchd process restarts a new loginwindow process owned by the root user, and the login screen appears.

Shutdown and Restart

When a logged-in user chooses to shut down or restart the Mac, again the user's loginwindow process manages all logout functions with help from the launchd process. First, the user's loginwindow process logs out the current user. If other users are logged in via fast user switching, the loginwindow process asks for administrator user authentication and, if it's granted, forcibly quits all other users' processes and applications, possibly losing user data.

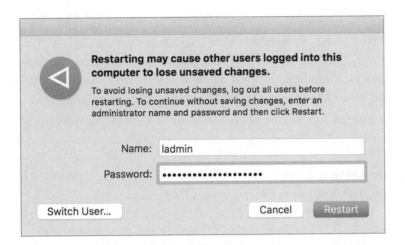

After all user sessions are logged out, the user's loginwindow process tells the kernel to issue the quit command to all remaining system processes. Processes like loginwindow should quit promptly, but the kernel must wait for processes that remain responsive while they are going through the motions of quitting. If system processes don't respond after a few seconds, the kernel forcibly quits those processes. Once all processes are quit, the kernel stops the launchd process and then shuts down the system. If the user chose to restart the Mac, the computer's firmware begins the macOS startup process once again.

Reference 26.4
Use Startup Shortcuts

Your Mac firmware supports many keyboard shortcuts, which, when pressed and held down during initial power-on, allow you to modify the startup process. Some of these shortcuts modify the booter selection, whereas others modify how macOS starts up. These alternative startup and diagnostic modes are often used for troubleshooting system issues.

There are, however, several caveats to using startup shortcuts:

▶ If the Mac has firmware password protection enabled, all startup shortcuts are disabled until the user enters the Mac computer's firmware password. Even after the user authenticates, the only two startup shortcuts that work are access to the Startup Manager and macOS Recovery. Using a firmware password is covered in Lesson 7, "Manage Security and Privacy."

▶ When using startup shortcuts, Mac computers with FileVault enabled must still be authenticated and unlocked to proceed with system startup.

▶ Some hardware does not support startup shortcuts, including some third-party keyboards and keyboards connected via certain USB hubs or a keyboard-video-mouse (KVM) switch. Also, although Bluetooth wireless keyboards should allow for startup shortcuts, they can be problematic. Consequently, a Mac administrator should always have a wired USB keyboard and mouse handy for troubleshooting Mac desktop computers.

▶ Startup volumes selected with a shortcut are not saved in NVRAM, so this setting does not persist between system restarts.

Select an Alternate System

Mac startup shortcuts that allow you to select another system include:

▶ Option—Starts up into the Startup Manager, which allows you to select any volume containing a valid system to start up from. This includes internal volumes, optical disc volumes, some external volumes, and, on later Mac models, Wi-Fi networks and NetBoot images.

▶ D—Starts up to the local Apple Hardware Test or Apple Diagnostics (for Mac computers released after June 2013), if available. If no local resources are available, Mac computers released after July 2011 will start up to Apple Hardware Test or Apple Diagnostics via an Internet connection to Apple servers. Use of these tools is beyond the scope of this guide, but you can find out more from Apple Support articles HT201257, "Using Apple Hardware Test," and HT202731, "Using Apple Diagnostics."

▶ Option-D—This shortcut forces startup to Apple Hardware Test or Apple Diagnostics via an Internet connection to Apple servers. Again, this option is only available to Mac computers released after July 2011.

▶ N—Starts up from the last-used NetBoot server, or the default NetBoot server if none was previously used. The Mac shows a flashing or spinning globe icon in the center of the main display until it locates the NetBoot server, at which point it shows the Apple logo.

▶ Option-N—This shortcut is similar to holding down the N key, but it always starts up from the current default NetBoot server instead of the last-used NetBoot server.

▶ Command-R—Starts up to the local macOS Recovery, if available. If no local macOS Recovery is found, Mac computers released after July 2011 will start up to macOS Internet Recovery via an Internet connection to Apple servers. Lesson 3, "Use macOS Recovery," covers this topic in greater detail.

▶ Command-Option-R—This shortcut forces startup to macOS Internet Recovery via an Internet connection to Apple servers. Again, this option is only available to Mac computers released after July 2011.

Modify macOS Startup

Mac startup shortcuts that modify the macOS default startup include:

▶ Shift—Starts up macOS in safe mode. During safe mode, the system clears specific caches, carefully tests startup procedures, and limits automatically launched processes during each stage. While running in safe mode, many nonessential system and third-party items are ignored. (Details on safe mode are covered throughout the troubleshooting sections later in this lesson.) You can recognize a Mac that is in safe mode if the words "Safe Boot" appear in bright red text in the upper-right corner of the login screen. You can also verify safe mode after login by opening System Information and selecting the software item.

▶ Command-V—Starts up macOS in verbose mode. In verbose mode, the system does not hide the startup progress from you. Instead, you see a black background with white text showing details of the startup process.

▶ Command-S—Starts up macOS in single-user mode. When starting up in single-user mode, the system starts only core kernel and BSD UNIX operating system functionality. You must be familiar with the command-line interface to use single-user mode.

Other Startup Shortcuts

Here are some other useful Mac startup shortcuts:

▶ T—For Mac computers with built-in FireWire, Thunderbolt, or USB-C ports, holding down this key starts up a Mac in target disk mode, allowing other computers to access the Mac computer's internal drives. Target disk mode details are covered in Lesson 9, "Manage File Systems and Storage."

▶ Command-Option-P-R—This shortcut resets NVRAM settings and restarts a Mac.

▶ Eject key, F12 key, mouse, or trackpad button—These shortcuts eject any removable media, including optical discs.

Reference 26.5
Troubleshoot System Initialization

Once you can identify the various stages—and know which processes and files are responsible for each—you are well on your way to diagnosing any startup issue. As an aid, the troubleshooting sections outlined here are organized by each stage of the system initialization process.

Also, you will learn how each of the three primary macOS diagnostic startup modes—verbose mode, safe mode, and single-user mode—help resolve or identify issues. These three modes are initiated at the firmware stage but affect the remaining system initialization process at each stage. The ramifications of each diagnostic startup mode are covered with each stage throughout this section.

Troubleshoot Firmware Issues

Issues at the firmware stage are indicated by the inability of your Mac to reach the point where the Apple logo appears. The key to troubleshooting at this point is to determine whether this issue is related to the Mac computer's hardware or system volume.

> **MORE INFO** ▶ Mac computers experiencing significant hardware issues may benefit from a resetting the Mac computer's NVRAM or SMC. You can find out more about resetting these items from Apple Support articles HT204063, "How to Reset NVRAM on your Mac," and HT201295, "Reset the System Management Controller (SMC) on your Mac."

Serious Hardware Issues

If you don't hear the startup sound, see a power-on light flash, or notice the display powering on, the Mac hardware may not have passed the POST.

> **NOTE** ▶ As covered previously in this lesson, there are a variety of reasons your Mac computer may not make a startup sound. For example, the latest Mac portable computers do not sound during startup as a default configuration.

You may also hear a series of audible diagnostic tones or see a series of power-on flashes. If this is the case, your Mac has a fundamental hardware issue. For more information about these startup sounds, see Apple Support article HT202768, "About Mac computer startup tones."

You can always check for simple things first. Is the Mac plugged into an electrical outlet? Are the keyboard and mouse working properly? Ultimately, a failure to pass the POST is usually indicative of a serious hardware issue. If this is the case, you'll be best served by taking your Mac to an Apple Store or Apple Authorized Service Provider.

System Volume Issues

If your Mac passes the POST but you are left with a flashing question mark folder icon, it means the firmware cannot locate a valid system volume or booter file. The Mac computer's main processor and components are probably working correctly, and you may just have a software issue. Hold down the Option key during startup and use the Startup Manager to locate system volumes.

To troubleshoot system volume issues:

▶ If the original system volume appears, select it to start up from it. If your Mac starts up from the system on the volume, open Startup Disk preferences to reset the volume as the startup disk. You can also attempt to define the startup disk when booted from another system volume, like an external macOS Recovery disk, as covered in Lesson 3, "Use macOS Recovery."

▶ If the original system volume appears but your Mac still cannot find a valid system or booter, you may need to reinstall macOS on that volume. As always, back up any important data from that volume before you make significant changes.

▶ If your original system volume does not appear, the issue lies with that storage device. Start up from another system, like an external macOS Recovery disk, and use the storage troubleshooting techniques outlined in Lesson 9, "Manage File Systems and Storage."

Troubleshoot Booter Issues

Issues at the booter stage are indicated by a flashing prohibitory icon—evidence of a failure to load the kernel.

To troubleshoot the booter:

▶ If you're starting up a Mac from a volume containing an operating system the Mac has never booted from, the prohibitory icon usually indicates that the version of macOS on the volume is not compatible with your Mac computer's hardware. This is an extremely rare case that occurs mainly when a new Mac is restored using an older system image. The solution at this point is to reinstall macOS using macOS Recovery, which should install a version that is known to work with your hardware.

▶ Start up the Mac while holding down the Shift key to initiate safe mode. The booter first attempts to verify and repair the startup volume. If repairs are necessary, the Mac automatically restarts before continuing. If this happens, continue to hold down the Shift key. The booter verifies the startup volume again, and if the volume appears to be working properly, the booter attempts to load the kernel and essential KEXTs once more. The booter uses the most judicial, and slowest, process to load these items and clears both the KEXT and font caches. If successful, the booter passes off the system to the kernel, which continues to safe-boot.

▶ If the booter cannot find or load a valid kernel, you may need to reinstall macOS on that volume.

Troubleshoot Kernel Issues

Issues at the kernel stage are indicated by an inability to reach the login window or automatic login process, as evidence of a failure to load KEXTs, the core UNIX operating system, and ultimately the launchd process. If this is the case, your Mac is stuck at the Apple logo startup screen and the Apple icon or progress bar may stay visible indefinitely, again signaling a failure to complete the startup process.

To troubleshoot the kernel:

▶ Start up the Mac while holding down the Shift key to initiate safe mode. In addition to the safe mode procedures covered later in this lesson, this forces the kernel to ignore all third-party KEXTs. If this strategy is successful, the kernel starts the launchd process, which continues to start up in safe mode. Completing the kernel startup stage via safe mode indicates the issue may be a third-party KEXT, so you should start up in verbose mode to try to identify the problematic KEXT.

▶ Start up the Mac while holding down Command-V to initiate verbose mode. The Mac shows you the startup process details as a continuous string of text. If the text stops, the startup process has probably also stopped, and you should examine the end of the text for troubleshooting clues. When you find a suspicious item, move it to a quarantine folder and then restart the Mac without safe mode, to see if the problem was resolved. This may be easier said than done—accessing the Mac computer's disk to locate and remove the item may not be possible if the Mac is crashing during startup. This is an example in which target disk mode shines. As covered in Lesson 9, "Manage File Systems and Storage," you can easily modify the contents of a problematic Mac system volume using target disk mode and a second Mac.

NOTE ▶ If your troublesome Mac successfully starts up in safe mode and you're trying to find the issue, do not use safe mode and verbose mode at the same time. If the startup process succeeds, verbose mode will eventually be replaced by the standard startup interface, and you will not have time to identify problematic items.

▶ If the kernel cannot completely load during safe mode, or you are unable to locate and repair the problematic items, you may need to reinstall macOS on that volume.

Troubleshoot launchd Issues

Issues at this stage are indicated by an inability to reach the login screen or log in a user (evidence of a failure by the launchd process). If the launchd process is not able to complete the system initialization, the loginwindow process does not start.

To troubleshoot launchd issues:

▶ Start up the Mac while holding down the Shift key to initiate safe mode. In addition to the safe mode procedures covered earlier in this lesson, safe mode forces the launchd process to ignore all third-party fonts, launch daemons, and startup items. If starting up in safe mode is successful, the launchd process starts the loginwindow. At this point the Mac has fully started up and is now running in safe mode. Completing the system initialization process via safe mode indicates the issue may be a third-party system initialization item, and you should start up in verbose mode to try to identify the problematic item.

▶ Start up the Mac while holding down Command-V to initiate verbose mode. Again, if the text stops scrolling down the screen, examine the end of the text for troubleshooting clues; if you find a suspicious item, move it to another folder and then restart the Mac normally.

▶ At this point you may be able to successfully start up in safe mode into the Finder. If so, use the Finder interface to quarantine suspicious items.

▶ While working in safe mode, you may also consider removing or renaming system cache and preference files, since they can be corrupted and cause startup issues. Begin by removing /Library/Caches, because those files contain easily replaced information. As far as system preferences go, you can remove any setting stored in the /Library /Preferences or /Library/Preferences/SystemConfiguration folders you're comfortable with having to reconfigure. A much safer solution is to rename individual system preference files in these folders. Once you have moved or replaced these items, restart the Mac, and macOS will automatically replace these items with clean versions.

▶ If starting up in safe mode continues to fail or you have located a suspicious system item you need to remove, start up the Mac while holding down Command-S to initiate single-user mode. You'll see a minimal command-line interface that enables you to move suspicious files to a quarantine folder. If you want to modify files and folders in single-user mode, you have to prepare the system volume. Start by entering /sbin/fsck -fy to verify and repair the startup volume. Repeat this command until you see a message stating that the disk appears to be OK. Only then should you enter /sbin/mount -uw / to mount the startup volume as a read-and-write file system. Once you have made your changes, you can exit single-user mode and continue to start up the Mac by entering the exit command, or you can shut down the Mac by entering the shutdown -h now command.

▶ If the system initialization process cannot complete during the startup in safe mode or you are unable to locate and repair the problematic items, you may need to reinstall macOS on that volume.

Reference 26.6
Troubleshoot User Sessions

If the loginwindow process is not able to initialize the user environment, the user will never be given control of the graphical interface. You may see the user's desktop background picture, but no applications load, including the Dock and the Finder. Or it may appear that the user session starts, but then the login screen reappears.

Safe Mode Login

At this point you should first attempt a safe mode login, which is initiated by holding down the Shift key while you click the Log In button at the login screen. You can actually perform a safe mode login whenever you want to troubleshoot user issues, even if you did not first start up in safe mode.

With safe mode enabled, the loginwindow process does not automatically open any user-defined login items or applications that are set to resume. Further, the launchd process does not start any user-specific LaunchAgents. Obviously, if a safe mode login resolves your user session issue, you need to adjust the user's Login Items list from the Users & Groups preferences or adjust any items in the /Library/LaunchAgents or ~/Library/LaunchAgents folder.

If a safe mode login doesn't resolve your user session issue, you can refer to other troubleshooting sections in this guide. Primarily, you should follow the troubleshooting steps outlined in Lesson 5, "Manage User Accounts."

Troubleshoot Logout and Shutdown Issues

An inability to log out or shut down is almost always the result of an application or process that refuses to quit. If you're unable to log out, as long as you maintain control of the graphical interface you can attempt to forcibly quit stubborn processes using the techniques outlined in Lesson 18, "Manage and Troubleshoot Applications."

You may find that the loginwindow process has closed your user session but the Mac refuses to shut down. This is indicated by a blank screen after all your applications have quit. You should let macOS attempt to shut down naturally, but if it takes longer than a few minutes, it means a system process is refusing to quit. You can force your Mac to shut down by holding down the power-on button until the Mac powers off.

NOTE ▶ When you restart a Mac, the firmware does not perform a full POST during the subsequent startup process. Thus, if you're troubleshooting hardware issues, you should always shut down and then start up, never restart.

Exercise 26.1
Examine System Startup

▶ **Prerequisite**

▶ You must have created the Chris Johnson account (Exercise 5.1, "Create a Standard User Account").

As macOS starts up, it gives auditory or visual cues as to which step of the startup process is currently being performed. If the startup process fails to complete, identifying the step where it halted can help illuminate the cause of the issue. In this exercise, you will observe the normal startup process of macOS and identify steps in the startup sequence using audible and visible cues.

Identify Steps in the Startup Process

1   If your computer is on, shut it down. You can use the Apple menu or (if you are not logged in) the buttons on the login screen to shut it down.

2   Start up your Mac.

3   As the Mac is starting up, use the following table to note the major steps occurring during the startup process (from turning the Mac on through the user environment appearing). Certain steps may not apply since you are not testing hardware issues or situations in which the startup device cannot be found.

Record the startup process associated with each visible or audible stage of the startup process. Refer to Reference 26.1, "Understand System Initialization." When you reach a login screen (either FileVault or the regular login window), log in as Chris Johnson.

NOTE ▶ If your Mac is encrypted with FileVault, there will be an additional startup step for the FileVault unlock screen; note where it occurs in the startup sequence.

Visual or auditory cue	Startup step or process executing at startup step
Startup chime	
Apple logo	
FileVault authentication (if enabled)	
Progress indicator below Apple logo or FileVault user icon	
Arrow pointer appears	
Login screen (if FileVault is not enabled)	
Desktop and Dock appear	

Exercise 26.2
Use Single-User Mode

▶ **Prerequisite**

> ▶ If your Mac has a Retina display, you may need a magnifying glass to read the text in single-user mode.

In this exercise, you will start up your Mac in verbose mode and then single-user mode; you will then proceed to the user interface and identify various files used during startup.

If your Mac has a Retina display, you may find that the text is too small to read easily in both verbose and single-user modes. In this case, using a magnifying glass is recommended.

Start Up in Verbose Mode

1   Before restarting in verbose mode, review the sequence you observed in Exercise 26.1, "Examine System Startup." In verbose mode, the basic startup sequence is the same, but what you will see on the screen is different.

2   Restart your computer, and immediately hold down Command-V. Continue holding Command-V until you see text or the FileVault authentication screen appear. When you reach a login screen, log in as Chris Johnson.

3   Fill in the following table with the sequence of cues you observe during a verbose startup, and contrast it with what you saw during a normal startup.

Normal startup	Verbose startup
Startup chime	
Apple logo	
FileVault authentication (if enabled)	
Progress indicator below Apple logo or FileVault user icon	
Arrow pointer appears	
Login screen (if FileVault is not enabled)	
Desktop and Dock appear	

During the verbose segment of the startup process, you will see messages from the kernel and launch daemons describing what they are doing and any problems they encounter. The messages can be somewhat cryptic if you are not familiar with the details of the kernel's and launch daemons' operations. Try to discern what is happening "behind the scenes" as your computer starts up.

If you are using FileVault, you will see that verbose mode shows some output from the firmware phase of startup, then switches to the normal FileVault authentication screen, then switches back to verbose display of output from the kernel, launchd, and the launch daemons. This is because the kernel, launchd, and the launch daemons that verbose mode displays are on the encrypted system volume and cannot start until after that volume has been unlocked.

4   Shut down your Mac.

As your Mac shuts down, you may see it reenter verbose mode for a few moments. This occurs after WindowServer shuts down but before the kernel shuts down.

Use Single-User Mode

1   Restart your Mac, and immediately hold down Command-S. Continue holding Command-S until the Mac restarts and you see text or the FileVault authentication screen appear. If your Mac is protected by FileVault, log in as Chris Johnson to allow the Mac to start up.

Single-user mode starts off a lot like verbose mode, displaying information about the startup process. But unlike verbose mode, the startup process halts just after launchd starts. The graphical user interface does not start; instead, it gives you a full-screen command-line interface.

When your Mac finishes starting up into single-user mode, macOS displays instructions on how to remount the startup disk with read/write access and how to continue the startup process to multiuser mode, the usual run mode of macOS or any other UNIX system.

```
*** Single-user boot ***
Root device is mounted read-only
Enabling and disabling services is not supported in single-user mode,
and disabled services will not be respected when loading services
while in single-user mode.
To mount the root device as read-write:
    $ /sbin/fsck -fy
    $ /sbin/mount -uw /
To boot the system:
    $ exit
localhost:/ root#
```

The last line is a prompt that tells you to enter a command. Note that the prompt ends with a # instead of the more usual $. This tells you that you are logged in as the super user (root, or System Administrator). Sometimes, messages from the kernel or launchd may also be printed here; if this happens, you can press Return to get a new prompt.

2   To force a check of the file system's integrity, enter the command "/sbin/fsck -fy", and press Return.

NOTE ▶ Single-user mode always uses the US-English keyboard layout, no matter what your actual keyboard layout is.

The computer runs a file-system consistency check, correcting any errors that it finds and is able to repair. This is essentially the same as using Repair Disk in Disk Utility. On today's large disks, this can take a while, especially if there are many files and folders in the file system. This is one of the advantages of file-system journaling. Most of the time, a complete fsck does not need to occur, so startup is much faster.

If fsck displays something like "The volume Macintosh HD appears to be OK," you may proceed to the next step. If its final message is "The filesystem was modified," it found and fixed at least one issue, and you should rerun it to make sure there are no additional issues.

3   To remount the startup disk with write access enabled, type "/sbin/mount -uw /", and press Return.

You are given a new prompt a few seconds later. With this command you can make changes to the disk.

This command should not generate any output (other than a new prompt) if it runs correctly. If it generates an alert or other output, double-check your typing. The most common errors with this command are leaving off the trailing slash ("/") and not having spaces where they are needed.

4   Get a process listing with the command "ps -ax".

You see a much shorter list than you will ever see in Activity Monitor. At process ID 1, you see the system launchd. Process ID 2 is "-sh" (actually bash), which is the command shell with which you are interacting. The last process is your ps command. The OS is in a minimal state.

5   Examine the system log file with the command "less +G /var/log/system.log". Note that the command line is generally case sensitive, so it is important to capitalize the "+G".

The "+G" option to less tells it to start at the end of the file (that is, show the most recent log events). Usually, when you need to examine logs in single-user mode, it is because you want to find out what happened just before the system crashed, so starting at the end is more convenient than starting at the beginning. You can scan through the log by pressing "b" to move backward in the file and pressing the Space bar to move forward.

Unfortunately, it does not know how large the screen is, so the display can get confused as you move backward and forward. The best way to fix this is to force it to redisplay the part you are interested in by backing up past it with the "b" key and then pressing the Space bar to display forward to the part you want to read.

6   When you are through examining the log, press "q" to exit.

Create a New Administrator Account

If you lose the password to your administrator account, you now know several ways to reset its password, but if the account becomes completely unusable, this will not allow you to regain control of the Mac. In this section, you will see how to use single-user mode to create a new administrator account.

1   Move to the /var/db folder with the command "cd /var/db".

2   Verify that this worked with the command "pwd".

This should print "/var/db", indicating your new location in the file system. If it does not match this, the command did not work right, and you must try again before proceeding. This section of the exercise involves deleting files, and since you are running as the root user, you are capable of deleting almost anything (or everything). It is important to be careful when you are running commands as the root user.

3   Start typing the command "rm .AppleSe" (be sure to capitalize the A and S), but do not press Return yet.

4   Press Tab.

If you typed the command correctly, it autocompletes to "rm .AppleSetupDone". If pressing Tab does not make it autocomplete, you have not typed the command correctly and must correct it and try again. Note that you cannot use the mouse to select text to change, although you can use the Left and Right Arrow keys to move backward and forward on the command line.

If you cannot get the command to autocomplete, something is still wrong, and you should not proceed with the exercise. You can always press Control-C and then use the command "exit" to exit single-user mode.

The /var/db/.AppleSetupDone file is a placeholder file, which indicates that Setup Assistant has run on this Mac; deleting it makes the Mac rerun Setup Assistant the next time it starts up.

5   If the command autocompleted correctly, press Return to run it.

6   If you see a message starting with override, enter "y", and press Return.

7   If you see the message "rm: .AppleSetupDone: Read-only file system", the mount command in step 3 of the previous section did not work; reenter that command, and then try again from step 2 of this section.

8   If the rm command does not display an error, exit single-user mode with the command "exit".

The computer exits single-user mode and continues starting up the operating system. With the .AppleSetupDone file gone, it runs Setup Assistant again just as though this were a new computer.

9   Step through the Setup Assistant screens (see Exercise 2.1, "Configure a New macOS System for Exercises," for detailed instructions). Do not sign in with your Apple ID. When you reach the Create Your Computer Account screen, enter the following information:

Full Name: New Admin

Account Name: newadmin

If you are performing this exercise in a class, enter newadminpw in the Password and Verify fields. If you are performing this exercise on your own, you should select a more secure password for the New Admin account.

After you finish Setup Assistant, you are automatically logged in to the New Admin account.

10   Open System Preferences, and select the Users & Groups pane.

All your old accounts are still there; New Admin has simply been added to them.

11   Quit System Preferences.

Index